Zak Ruvalcaba

Adobe®
Dreamweaver® CS4

UNLEASHED

SAMS | 800 East 96th Street, Indianapolis, Indiana 46240 USA

Adobe® Dreamweaver® CS4 Unleashed

ISBN-13: 978-0-672-33039-1

ISBN-10: 0-672-33039-3

Library of Congress Cataloging-in-Publication Data:

Ruvalcaba, Zak.

　　Adobe Dreamweaver CS4 unleashed / Zak Ruvalcaba.

　　　　p. cm.

　　Includes bibliographical references and index.

　　ISBN-13: 978-0-672-33039-1 (pbk.)

　　ISBN-10: 0-672-33039-3 (pbk.)

　　1. Dreamweaver (Computer file)　2. Web sites–Authoring programs. 3. Web sites–Design.　I. Title.

　　TK5105.8885.D74R8732 2009

　　006.7'8—dc22

　　　　　　　　　　　　　　　　　　　　　　2008047295

Printed in the United States of America

First Printing December 2008

Trademarks

All terms mentioned in this book that are known to be trademarks or service marks have been appropriately capitalized. Sams Publishing cannot attest to the accuracy of this information. Use of a term in this book should not be regarded as affecting the validity of any trademark or service mark.

Warning and Disclaimer

Bulk Sales

Sams Publishing offers excellent discounts on this book when ordered in quantity for bulk purchases or special sales. For more information, please contact

U.S. Corporate and Government Sales
1-800-382-3419
corpsales@pearsontechgroup.com

For sales outside of the U.S., please contact

International Sales
international@pearson.com

Acquisitions Editor
Mark Taber

Development Editor
Michael Thurston

Managing Editor
Kristy Hart

Project Editor
Andy Beaster

Copy Editor
Seth Kerney

Indexer
Rebecca Salerno

Proofreader
San Dee Phillips

Technical Editor
Kevin Ruse

Publishing Coordinator
Vanessa Evans

Book Designer
Gary Adair

Composition
Nonie Ratcliff

Contents at a Glance

NOTE

Register this book at informit.com/register for convenient access to updates, errata, and downloads for the book, including Appendixes A, B, C, and D in PDF format, as well as source code and files from the book's examples.

Table of Contents

> **NOTE**
>
> Register this book at informit.com/register for convenient access to updates, errata, and downloads for the book, including Appendixes A, B, C, and D in PDF format, as well as source code and files from the book's examples.

NOTE

Register this book at informit.com/register for convenient access to updates, errata, and downloads for the book, including Appendixes A, B, C, and D in PDF format, as well as source code and files from the book's examples.

About the Author

Zak Ruvalcaba has been researching, designing, and developing for the Web since 1995. He holds a bachelor's degree from San Diego State University and a master of science degree in instructional technology from National University in San Diego. He served as creative director with EPIC Solutions until 1998. His expertise in developing web applications led him to a position as manager of web development at SkyDesk Inc., where he developed web applications for such companies as Gateway, HP, Toshiba, IBM, Intuit, Peachtree, Dell, and Microsoft. He has worked for such companies as ADCS, Inc., and Wireless Knowledge, and as a wireless software engineer developing .NET solutions for companies such as Mellon Financial, Goldman Saks, TV Guide, Healthbanks, The Gartner Group, Microsoft, Qualcomm, and Commerce One.

His skill set includes technologies and languages from HTML/XHTML, XML/XSLT, JavaScript, CSS, ASP, ASP.NET, Visual Basic .NET, C#, ADO.NET, Web Services, SQL, T-SQL, Flash/ActionScript, and ColdFusion.

Aside from teaching and holding design lectures on various technologies and tools including Dreamweaver, Flash, and ASP.NET for the San Diego Community College District, Mt. San Jacinto Community College, and Palomar Community College, Zak Ruvalcaba is also the author of *10 Minute Guide to Dreamweaver 4* by Que Publishing, *Build Your Own ASP.NET 3.5 Website Using C# and VB* by SitePoint Press, and *Beginning Expression Web* by Wrox Press.

Zak Ruvalcaba is a Microsoft Certified Application Developer for .NET (MCAD) and a Microsoft Certified Solutions Developer for .NET (MCSD).

Dedication

I would like to dedicate this book to my family.

Acknowledgments

Writing a book is a tremendous effort and takes dedication and patience from all who are involved. A sincere thank you to my editors Mark Taber and Michael Thurston, as well as the technical editor Kevin Ruse for being on top of this book.

We Want to Hear from You!

As the reader of this book, *you* are our most important critic and commentator. We value your opinion and want to know what we're doing right, what we could do better, what areas you'd like to see us publish in, and any other words of wisdom you're willing to pass our way.

You can email or write me directly to let me know what you did or didn't like about this book—as well as what we can do to make our books stronger.

Please note that I cannot help you with technical problems related to the topic of this book, and that due to the high volume of mail I receive, I might not be able to reply to every message.

When you write, please be sure to include this book's title and author as well as your name and phone or email address. I will carefully review your comments and share them with the author and editors who worked on the book.

Email: webdev@samspublishing.com

Mail: Mark Taber
      Associate Publisher
      Sams Publishing
      800 East 96th Street
      Indianapolis, IN 46240 USA

Reader Services

Visit our website and register this book at informit.com/register for convenient access to any updates, downloads, or errata that might be available for this book.

Introduction

Over a decade ago—when I used Dreamweaver 1.0 for the first time, I was amazed at how far ahead of its time it was. The capability to incorporate JavaScript Behaviors, styles, and pinpoint accurate designs truly amazed me. I was a skeptic when it came to visual editors and preferred Notepad whenever possible. Dreamweaver changed that for me and made me look at web development in a whole new light.

Dreamweaver has become the industry's leading web development environment, far surpassing any other. Still, many consider Dreamweaver a simple visual editor that accomplishes little more than aiding in the development of static web pages. The mindset is that visual editors lack the true complexity that it takes to create rich and powerful web applications that encompass client-side technologies such as HTML, CSS, and JavaScript while leveraging server-side technologies like ASP, PHP, and ColdFusion. Dreamweaver obliterates the stigma by captivating the developer in a vast, intuitive, and feature-rich environment.

If you've picked up this book, chances are you're interested in the world of web design and development and, more specifically, how Dreamweaver can help you succeed in these endeavors. Whether you're a seasoned developer, a print designer looking to expand your base of knowledge to the Web, or a home user who wants to create a family website, Dreamweaver offers the features and flexibility to get you on your way quickly and effortlessly. This book introduces you to the many features available through Dreamweaver using a fun, yet concise, approach.

What's Inside, Part by Part

Part I, "Getting Up to Speed with Dreamweaver CS4"—Starting off gently, this part introduces you to Dreamweaver CS4. Moving from Chapter 1, "The Dreamweaver CS4 Interface," to Chapter 3, "Dreamweaver Site Management," you'll learn about the many panels, inspectors, and windows that Dreamweaver reveals within its development environment. You'll also learn about defining and managing a site, building a simple web page, and finally, defining Dreamweaver preferences for customizing how you work with Dreamweaver.

Part II, "Static Web Page Development"—Generally considered the heart of the book, this part covers topics related to static web page development. You'll learn about web page structuring using tables, advanced page formatting and structuring using cascading style sheets, designing forms with form elements, and incorporating behaviors into your web pages.

Part III, "Team Collaboration and Task Automation"—Although most consider Dreamweaver a great tool for building web pages, the truth is that Dreamweaver provides many tools for working with web pages within teams. In this part you'll learn about the many aspects in Dreamweaver that facilitate the collaborative process, such as file check in and check out, Design Notes, and integration with Contribute. You'll also learn about the many components, such as templates and library items, built in to Dreamweaver for enhancing the workflow process.

Part IV, "Incorporating Multimedia and Animation"—Developers and designers who are building media-rich sites should concentrate on this part. The chapters in this part of the book cover integration with Flash, Fireworks, and Photoshop, as well as video and audio.

Part V, "Building Dynamic Web Pages"—The chapters in this part prepare you for working with dynamic web pages. As you'll see, the chapters in this part cover an introduction to web applications, server-side technologies, databases, the language used to extract, insert, delete, and update data within databases in SQL, and retrieving data from, inserting data into, deleting data from, and updating data within databases. You'll also learn how to build search functionality, secure your web pages, work with XML web services and ColdFusion components, and even learn to use Adobe's Spry framework for Ajax.

Part VI, "Online Appendixes"—This part consists of various detailed appendixes on accessibility, extensibility, working with frames and framesets, and how to define preferences within Dreamweaver. These items are available free from www.informit.com/title/9780672330391.

What's Inside, Chapter by Chapter

Chapter 1, "The Dreamweaver CS4 Interface," covers the Dreamweaver interface: document views, toolbars, inspectors, panels, and status bars. By the end of the chapter, you should feel fairly comfortable with the Dreamweaver CS4 development environment.

Chapter 2, "Building a Web Page," covers the essentials of building a web page within Dreamweaver. By the end of this chapter, you'll understand how to use page properties, various HTML elements, and graphics to create your first web page in Dreamweaver.

Chapter 3, "Dreamweaver Site Management," covers site management, including defining a site, file check in and check out, working with site maps, and defining local and remote folders.

Chapter 4, "Web Page Structuring Using Tables," covers traditional methods for structuring web pages using tables. In this chapter, you'll learn about tables, rows, columns, nested tables, and more.

Chapter 5, "Page Formatting Using Cascading Style Sheets," covers the types of style sheets, how to apply them, and the various properties for text, backgrounds, borders, lists, positioning, and more.

Chapter 6, "Page Structuring Using Cascading Style Sheets," defines AP `<div>`s, the cornerstones for pinpoint accurate positioning of elements in Dreamweaver. Ever wonder how to make a web page look like a printed brochure? AP `<div>`s are your answer.

Chapter 7, "HTML Forms," covers HTML forms, which are the front-ends to web applications. eBay, E*TRADE, and AutoBytel, among other high visibility sites, use forms in their applications to facilitate data collection from the user. In this chapter, you'll learn how these types of forms are constructed. We'll discuss forms and the various types of form elements used within forms.

Chapter 8, "Using Behaviors," covers Dreamweaver's JavaScript Behaviors. In this chapter, you'll learn the basics of JavaScript, including events, actions, and more.

Chapter 9, "Building Dreamweaver Websites Within Teams," covers features within Dreamweaver that facilitate integration and collaboration within teams. Topics such as file check-in and check-out, file column sharing, and Design Notes are covered in this chapter.

Chapter 10, "Managing Website Content Using Contribute," covers integration with Adobe's content management and sharing program, Contribute. In this chapter, you'll learn about users and roles, applying user settings, and even editing web page content using Contribute.

Chapter 11, "Enhancing Workflow," covers potentially overlooked features within Dreamweaver that might help you do your job faster and more efficiently. Features such as the Results panel, Find and Replace, various commands, and the Assets panel, are covered here.

Chapter 12, "Working with Templates and Library Items," covers Dreamweaver templates in depth. A good understanding of templates and the workflow surrounding them can make you more efficient. This chapter also covers library items that, like templates, provide greater efficiency and global content editing from a centralized location. In this chapter, you'll learn how to convert features (such as navigation menus) of your website to library items, which ultimately makes your navigation menus reusable and global to your website as a whole.

Chapter 13, "Incorporating Video and Audio," covers important features for linking and embedding video and audio files in your web pages.

Chapter 14, "Integrating with Fireworks, Photoshop, and Flash," covers integration with Adobe's popular image-editing programs: Fireworks, Photoshop, and Flash. In this chapter, you'll learn about round-trip graphics editing, creating web-based photo albums, and optimizing images. It also covers Dreamweaver's integration with Flash—round-trip Flash editing, what parameters Flash movies accept, and how to trigger different Flash movie properties using Behaviors.

Chapter 15, "Introduction to Web Applications," effectively makes the transition from static web page development to server-side web page development. You'll learn about web architecture, server-side technologies, and database options.

Chapter 16, "Working with Server-Side Technologies," begins to dig deeper into the world of server-side web development. In this chapter, you'll learn about the various server-side technologies, including ASP, ASP.NET, ColdFusion, and PHP.

Chapter 17, "A Database Primer," covers the basics (tables, rows, columns) and more advanced topics such as stored procedures, triggers, views, keys, and normalization. The chapter concludes with the development of the book's project database.

Chapter 18, "A SQL Primer," covers selecting, inserting, updating, and deleting data. It also breaks down SQL into the different clauses and covers joins and sub queries.

Chapters 19 through 23 contain an in-depth tutorial on building a web store application with ASP, PHP, and ColdFusion. The chapters include real-life detailed code for catalogs, user registration, personalization, search functionality, and security.

Chapter 24, "Working with the Spry Framework for Ajax," discusses Adobe's newest framework for Ajax. You'll learn how to create Spry Datasets for creating performance-minded web pages that are fed in from XML files. Additionally, you'll see how to incorporate Spry widgets and effects for creating engaging and eye-catching web pages.

The free online appendixes cover other important information:

Appendix A, "Accessibility," covers the standards and how to apply them. It also touches on the impact of accessibility on design and development efforts.

Appendix B, "Extending Dreamweaver,"covers extending Dreamweaver with objects and behaviors. It also covers sharing those extensions with others.

Appendix C, "Defining Preferences," covers every customizable feature for improving how you work with Dreamweaver. Everything from customizing code coloring to setting keyboard shortcuts is outlined in this appendix.

Appendix D, "Working with Frames and Framesets," covers frames and framesets, including advantages and disadvantages to using them and why.

As you can see—and as you will read—I've covered just about every aspect of web development using Dreamweaver CS4. While reading, you can follow along with the step-by-step projects by downloading the support files from www.informit.com/register or from this book's companion website located at www.dreamweaverunleashed.com. Thank you for picking up a copy of this book—and enjoy!

—Zak Ruvalcaba

PART I

Getting Up to Speed with Dreamweaver CS4

IN THIS PART

The Dreamweaver CS4 Interface

The good news is Dreamweaver provides numerous windows, panels, inspectors, and toolbars for streamlining the way you build websites. The bad news, unfortunately, is that Dreamweaver provides numerous windows, panels, inspectors, and toolbars for streamlining the way you build websites. Why so many windows, panels, and so on? Dreamweaver is unprecedented in the feature set it provides, allowing developers complete control when building websites and applications. For instance, the Document window allows developers visual editing with unusually precise, pinpoint accuracy; an Insert panel for visually adding HTML elements within the development environment; and numerous panels and inspectors for customizing those elements after they've been inserted. For every benefit Dreamweaver provides to developers in terms of customization, the learning curve goes up. This chapter aims at leveling the learning curve by introducing you, step-by-step, to the myriad of windows, panels, inspectors, toolbars, and menus. We'll start by outlining some of the latest and greatest features added to the newest edition of Dreamweaver. We'll then transition over to the development environment that makes Dreamweaver the industry standard web development tool. Although I won't deconstruct each feature, I will provide a gentle, yet concise, overview of each piece of functionality that Dreamweaver has to offer before unveiling them in greater detail as the book unfolds.

New Dreamweaver CS4 Features

Welcome to the best release of Dreamweaver to date! As you'll see throughout this section, Adobe heeded the call of developers by releasing features that users have been requesting for quite some time—features such as tighter CSS best practices, integration with the OWL interface (Operating system Widget Library), code hinting for Ajax and JavaScript, Adobe AIR authoring support, and more. Although most of the features discussed in this section seem like they would be obvious additions to a program like Dreamweaver (and for the most part are integrated into various other Adobe programs, as well), they do represent the newest and most exciting feature enhancements to a program that is already chock-full of workflow and process improvements. The newest features are outlined briefly in Table 1.1.

TABLE 1.1   New Dreamweaver CS4 Features

Feature	Description
Live View	Built directly on top of the open source rendering engine WebKit, the Live View and Live Code View make it possible for you to display your web pages and applications directly from within Dreamweaver without ever having to leave the development environment. Simply click the Live View button and Dreamweaver instantly renders your page as if you were viewing it in the browser.
Related Files	The new Related Files bar shows filenames that are referenced by a current document. Simply open a document and Dreamweaver instantly displays a Related Files bar that shows referenced/linked CSS, JavaScript, PHP, or XML files on which your document depends. Even better, accessing these files to edit them is simply a matter of clicking the filename within the Related Files bar.
Code Navigator	The new Code Navigator pop-up window shows you code sources that affect the selected element. Simply roll your cursor over an element and Dreamweaver displays the Code Navigator icon. Clicking the icon displays the Code Navigator pop-up window, which allows for the direct editing of the code source, not unlike the Quick Tag Editor currently within the Property inspector.
Revamped Property Inspector	In Adobe's continued effort to support best practices and standards, the Property inspector received a major facelift. For instance, rather than displaying a single view of possible options for text, the new Property inspector is separated into two distinct groups: HTML and CSS. Choose the HTML category to make property modifications that otherwise wouldn't be practical or possible in CSS, such as formats, hyperlinks, bold, italic, lists, and indenting (blockquote). Alternatively, choose the CSS category to make property modifications to elements that otherwise would have been added as non-standards-compliant deprecated code/tags in previous versions of Dreamweaver.

TABLE 1.1   New Dreamweaver CS4 Features

Feature	Description
Code hinting for Ajax and JavaScript	Dreamweaver CS4 now supports inline code hints for core JavaScript objects and primitive data types. Additionally, support for popular JavaScript frameworks such as jQuery, Prototype, and Spry are also supported.
Photoshop Smart Objects	Continuing with the evolution of Dreamweaver and Photoshop integration, Adobe delivers with Smart Objects. In a nutshell, Smart Objects make it possible to drag-and-drop a PSD file directly from the Files panel and into a page. Dreamweaver immediately allows you to optimize the image and then save it as either a JPG or a GIF file. If you ever make changes to the original PSD file in Photoshop, the Smart Object in Dreamweaver is "smart" enough to detect the change and then update the file that relies on the original PSD.
Subversion integration	Although Dreamweaver has always supported versioning in some capacity, versioning has never received the attention that it has in Dreamweaver CS4. In previous versions of Dreamweaver, versioning and source control differed from programs such as Microsoft's Visual SourceSafe or open-source methods such as WebDAV. And while file explorer specific techniques exist, file versioning, rollbacks, and checking in/out have dramatically improved due in large part to their integration with Subversion, an open-source versioning software package that integrates directly with Dreamweaver. No longer is the installation of third-party software or antiquated command-line utilities required!
Adobe AIR authoring support	Dreamweaver now directly integrates support for one of Adobe's newest platforms in Adobe AIR. *AIR*, which stands for *Adobe Integrated Runtime*, makes it possible for developers to use standard web technologies to build rich Internet applications that port directly to the desktop and are platform agnostic and device-independent.
New user interface	Like most versions of Dreamweaver, the user interface was revamped to look more like current Adobe programs. Integration with the OWL (Operating system Widget Library) interface is now present, making the application friendlier and easier to work with for users who are already familiar with other Adobe products.

The Welcome Screen

If you've cheated and opened Dreamweaver for a sneak peak, you've probably noticed the assortment of grayed-out windows or panels spread throughout Dreamweaver's interface. As a matter of fact, opening Dreamweaver for the first time reveals an interface similar to Figure 1.1.

FIGURE 1.1   Dreamweaver introduces an assortment of panels, toolbars, and windows.

As you can see, there are numerous features that we'll dive into throughout this chapter. For now however, let's begin with the most obvious window in front of you, the Welcome screen.

An optional window, the Welcome screen is a centralized window of resources. Through the Welcome screen you can open a recent item, create a new document based on a preconfigured page type, define new sites, visit the Dreamweaver Exchange, or simply learn about the newest features in Dreamweaver by taking a quick tour and watching featured video-based tutorials. There's nothing more to this window; for the most part, it's simply a quick way of opening new or existing documents within Dreamweaver. For the time being, we'll use the Welcome screen to create a new HTML document. To begin, click the HTML link under the Create New category on the Welcome screen. Immediately, the Welcome screen disappears and a new Document window appears similar to Figure 1.2.

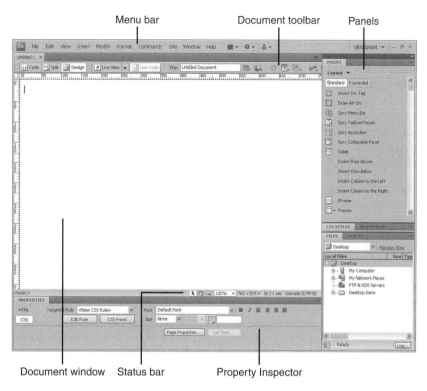

FIGURE 1.2   All your websites and applications will be developed within the Document window.

Don't be concerned when the Start page disappears, it will reappear again when all Document window instances have been closed. Or, if you prefer not to ever see the Welcome screen again, you may also check the box within the Welcome screen that reads Don't Show Again. This will prevent the Welcome screen from appearing whenever you either launch Dreamweaver or close all Document windows. If you do enable this check box and find that you want the Welcome screen to be visible again, you can always enable the preference within the Preferences dialog box by choosing Edit, Preferences. Within the General category, check or uncheck the Show Welcome Screen check box. The Preferences dialog is covered in much more detail in the online Appendix C, "Defining Preferences."

Before we get too far ahead of ourselves, however, let's discuss what just happened to the Dreamweaver environment by diving right into the Document window.

The Document Window

The single most important Dreamweaver window is the Document window. The Document window, simply put, is where all the action happens and where all your creative energy will be focused as you develop websites and applications.

The versatility of the Document window is immediately noticeable when you place your cursor within the window and start typing. Although the Document window's job ranges from simple word processor to basic image editor, as you will see, it combines those roles well to deliver a familiar approach to web development. To aid you in that development, the Document window provides the following functionalities, also visible in Figure 1.2:

▶ **The Tabbed File Chooser and Related Files bar**—Dreamweaver allows you to open and work with multiple files simultaneously. You can navigate between files using the Tabbed File Chooser. Furthermore, the Related Files bar displays filenames that your open file depends on to function correctly.

▶ **The Document toolbar**—Advanced features for working with the documents are located within this toolbar. Features such as customizing how you view and interact with the Document window's Code and Design views, setting the title of the document, accessibility scanning utilities, file management features, and so on are all located here.

▶ **The Standard toolbar**—You'll find basic options for interacting with the current open window here, along with visual icons for opening, saving, copying, pasting, and so on. The Standard toolbar isn't visible by default. To open it (and have it appear just below the Document toolbar), choose View, Toolbars, Standard.

▶ **The Style Rendering toolbar**—The Style Rendering toolbar displays icons that you can select to see how your page will look in various media types. Options exist for print, handheld devices, projectors, teletype machines, televisions, and more. The Style Rendering toolbar is another toolbar that isn't visible by default. To open it (and have it appear just below the Document toolbar), choose View, Toolbars, Style Rendering.

▶ **The status bar**—The status bar, located at the bottom of the Document window, includes functionalities such as the Tag Selector, zoom tools, the Hand tool, the Window Sizer menu, and a window size and download time indicator.

The Tabbed File Chooser and Related Files Bar

When multiple files are open within Dreamweaver, each document is separated by a tab near the top of the Document window. As shown in Figure 1.3, you can easily work with different open documents by choosing the appropriate tab from the tabbed file chooser.

You'll also notice that each tab contains an asterisk next to the filename. Referred to as the "dirty dot," this is provided simply to alert you that either the file has not been previously saved or a change has been made, thus making it "dirty," to the file since the last save. Saving each document with a unique filename removes the asterisk from the tab. OS X users will notice that, just like other OS X apps, the standard Close widget on the Document window will be filled in if the document is "dirty."

Tabbed file chooser   File path

Related files bar

FIGURE 1.3   Swap between open documents by choosing the appropriate open file from the tabbed file chooser.

You can also use the context menu for additional options within the tabs by right-clicking (Control+clicking) a tab. Doing this reveals additional options (located in the context menu) for creating a new document, opening an existing document, closing an existing document, closing all documents, closing other documents except for the visible one, saving the document, saving a document with a specific name, saving all documents, reverting to a previously saved version of the document, or comparing the local document with a remote version.

NOTE

Context menus are covered in more detail later in this chapter. For now, note that the context menu is accessible by right-clicking (Control+clicking) a particular portion of the user interface.

To the far right of the tabbed file chooser, you'll see a new feature for Dreamweaver CS4 in the file path. This simple text label displays the full path to the file that you're currently working with.

Under the Tabbed File Chooser, you'll see another new feature added to Dreamweaver CS4 in the Related Files bar. This handy display shows filenames that are referenced by the current document. As you can see in Figure 1.3, both styles.css and dropdown.css are files that are referenced directly by my open file index.html. I can quickly open each file for editing by clicking the text-based label or right-clicking on the related file to access the context menu and then choosing the Open as Separate File option to have the related file open as a new document and be made available as a new tab within the Tabbed File Chooser.

NOTE

When related files aren't found for a document, the Related Files Bar simply doesn't show up. The Related Files Bar only becomes visible when Dreamweaver detects that a document has direct references to style sheet files (CSS), external JavaScript files, and so on.

The Document Toolbar

The Document toolbar provides you with advanced functionality that would otherwise be available only from various other menus. Highlighted in Figure 1.4, the Document toolbar allows you to quickly control the visual dynamics of the page, check for accessibility and browsers errors, upload documents to a remote server, and more.

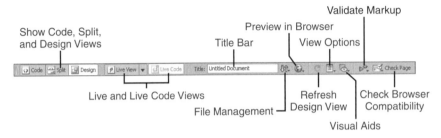

FIGURE 1.4   The Document toolbar allows you to control the visual dynamics of the Document window, among other things.

> **NOTE**
>
> You can hide/display the Document toolbar by choosing View, Toolbars, Document. Additionally, you can right-click on the Document toolbar to access the context menu and then uncheck Document to hide the toolbar.

As you can see from Figure 1.4, the Document toolbar's functionality can be broken into the following categories:

- **Show Code, Split, and Design Views**—With a click of a single icon, Dreamweaver allows you to quickly switch from Design to Code view, or even a split between the two.

- **Live View and Live Code View**—One of the newest additions to Dreamweaver comes by way of the Live View. The Live View button, situated next to the Code, Split, and Design View buttons, makes it possible for developers to see their web pages as they would be rendered within the browser. You can interact with your pages and view JavaScript effects such as rollovers, fly-out menus, and more, all without having to switch to a dedicated web browser. The complementary Live Code View shows the HTML in the web page, which is especially useful when JavaScript code is used to manipulate the appearance, functionality, or content directly on the page. The Live Code View can also be used to work directly with server-side pages that rely on databases to dynamically display data within the browser. Again, rather than switching to a dedicated browser to display your dynamic pages, simply click the Live Code View button to see the dynamic server-side processing in action.

- **Title Bar**—Allows you to add a unique title to your page.

- **File Management**—Allows you to quickly retrieve from and upload to a remote server. Also provides you with the capability to check into or out of source control (covered with more detail in Chapter 3, "Dreamweaver Site Management"), maintain Design Notes, locate a file within a defined site, and more.

- **Preview in Browser**—This feature launches your design within up to 16 predefined browsers, allowing you to preview your work. Furthermore, an option to launch Adobe Device Central is also located within this submenu of items. In a nutshell, Adobe Device Central is a program that allows you to view web pages and applications within a myriad of mobile devices, including cell phones and handheld devices or PDAs.

- **Refresh Design View**—When in Split view, this icon, when clicked, refreshes the Design view to reflect changes and modifications made in Code view. You can also press F5 to refresh the Design view when in Code view.

- **View Options**—Provides numerous additional view options for both the Code and Design views. Options include viewing head content, rulers, and guides. In Code view, these options change to allow word wrapping, line numbers, syntax coloring, and more. Many of the options that you'll find within this menu are also available within the View menu in the Menu bar.

- **Visual Aids**—Options available within this menu enable you to control visibility of visual aids, table borders, frame borders, image maps, table widths, as well as various CSS layout options. Many of the options that you'll find within this menu are also available by choosing View, Visual Aids from the Menu bar.

- **Validate Markup**—Options within this submenu enable you to validate the current document, current site, or selected files within a site against a Document Type Definition (DTD), covered later in the chapter.

- **Check Browser Compatibility**—Displays a warning icon when Dreamweaver detects that the page structure will conflict with preconfigured target browsers. Options within this submenu enable you to run browser compatibility checks, accessibility checks, and more.

Now that you have a basic idea as to what features the Document toolbar provides, let's delve a bit deeper into the functionality that each feature exposes.

Show Code, Split, and Design Views

Whether you're a seasoned HTML developer or a converted print designer who prefers a visual representation of your web page, the Show Code, Split, and Design view options will accommodate your work style. Located in the top-left hand corner of the Document toolbar, the Show Code, Split, and Design view options allow you to work in the following views:

▶ **Code View**—As Figure 1.5 shows, when the Code View button is selected, the Document window converts to an HTML editor.

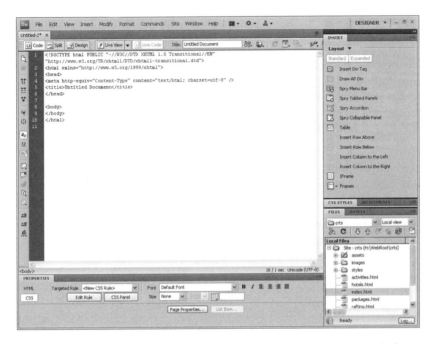

FIGURE 1.5   Switch to Code view when you want to work with the code for your web page.

▶ **Design View**—The Design view, which is the default view in which Dreamweaver opens, lets you visually add and place items within the Document window.

▶ **Split Code/Design View**—As Figure 1.6 shows, the Split Code/Design view gives you the best of both worlds. Not only do you have the option of working with the document's HTML, but you can also work within the visual editing environment at the same time.

Live View and Live Code View

One of the features that received a giant face lift was the set of buttons used for displaying web pages that rely on client-side and server-side code to operate directly within Dreamweaver's built-in browser. These two buttons, Live View and Live Code View, make it possible for developers to see their web pages as they would be rendered within the browser, all without ever having to leave the development confines of Dreamweaver.

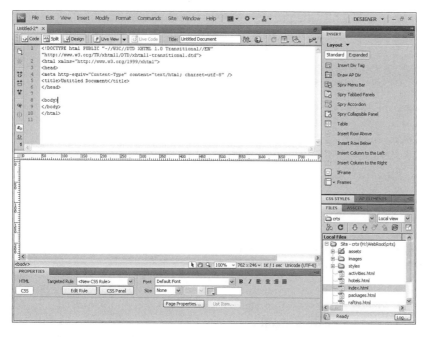

FIGURE 1.6   The Split Code/Design view affords you the best of both the HTML authoring and visual designing worlds.

The buttons make it possible to interact with your pages and view JavaScript effects such as rollovers, fly-out menus, and more. The complementary Live Code view shows the HTML in the web page, which is especially useful when JavaScript code is used to manipulate either the appearance, functionality, or content directly on the page. The Live Code view can also work directly with server-side pages that rely on databases to dynamically display data within the browser. Again, rather than switching to a dedicated browser to display your dynamic pages, simply click the Live Code View button to see the dynamic server-side processing in action.

In general, six features are available from the Live View submenu set of options, each allowing you to customize how you interact with client-side code such as JavaScript within Dreamweaver's built-in browsing interface. These options include the following:

▶ **Freeze JavaScript**—Freezes the processing of JavaScript code. This is useful in multi-level event scenarios in which you might want to examine the inclusion of CSS or additional JavaScript code while a feature is being used. Imagine freezing a fly-out menu to examine the CSS that makes up the "look" of the fly-out menu when it's visible.

▶ **Disable JavaScript**—Disables the processing of JavaScript entirely while the page is being shown in Dreamweaver's built-in web browser. This is especially useful in situations in which you want to test a web page and don't want JavaScript functionality to get in the way. Furthermore, you might want to use this feature to test what your page might look like in browsers that don't support JavaScript.

▶ **Disable Plugins**—Disables plugins from being referenced by the page. This is handy when you don't want content that requires the use of a plugin such as Flash, Director, or audio within a web page to interfere with the rendering/testing of the page within Dreamweaver's built-in browser.

▶ **Use Testing Server for Document Source**—Check this option when you want Dreamweaver to reference files that you have stored on a testing server to be used when viewing the document within Dreamweaver's built-in browser.

▶ **Use Local Files for Document Source**—Check this option (default) when you want Dreamweaver to reference files that you have stored locally to be used when viewing the document within Dreamweaver's built-in browser.

▶ **HTTP Request Settings**—Click this option to launch the View Settings dialog box. You can use this dialog box to configure additional parameters and values that Dreamweaver should automatically append to the URL string when previewed in Dreamweaver's built-in browser. You can also configure the method of execution as either GET or POST for the page.

The Live Code view, on the other hand, doesn't include a submenu of options. It's simply clicked on or off to enable or disable the Live Code view.

The Title Bar

One of the most obvious features of your page is its title. This is the descriptive text that appears at the top of the browser window just to the right of the browser's icon. The title of your page is the first item that appears within search engine results, so it's important that you add a good, descriptive title that contains key phrases about your website. Dreamweaver provides a few methods for adding the title to your page, but none more obvious than the Title: text box within the Document toolbar. By default, Dreamweaver places the text Untitled Document within the text box. To customize the text, place your cursor in the text box, change the text to something that best describes your page, and press Enter (Return) or Tab.

File Management

Covered with more detail in "Part III: Team Collaboration and Task Automation," the File Management option allows you to quickly upload files to and retrieve files from your remote server, check in and check out files from source control, maintain Design Notes, and so on. A quick list of features within this menu is outlined here:

▶ **Turn Off Read Only (Unlock)**—Turns off the read-only attribute for a file.

▶ **Get**—Retrieves the most recent version of a file from the remote server.

▶ **Check Out**—Checks out a file from source control with full permissions.

▶ **Put**—Puts the most recent version of a saved file to the remote server.

▶ **Check In**—Checks a file back into source control.

▶ **Undo Check Out**—When working in a team collaborative environment and source control is enabled, choose this option when changes have been made that you regret. This option will undo the check-out status and revert the file back to its previous state. All changes made while the file was checked out are then lost.

▶ **Show Checked Out By**—Displays the name, hyperlinked with the email address, of the person who has the file checked out.

▶ **Design Notes**—When Design Notes are enabled for a site, this option allows you to maintain Design Notes for the current page.

▶ **Locate in Site**—After a site has been defined (covered in the next chapter), this option allows you to locate the saved version of the open file within the Files panel.

Preview in Browser

Although the Live View and Live Code View options are great ways to quickly view your pages in Dreamweaver's built-in browser, nothing beats the real thing. The Live View and Live Code View options only display your page in Dreamweaver's built-in browser, however. What if you want to preview your web page in Internet Explorer? How about Opera, Flock, or Safari for Windows? This is where the Preview in Browser option comes in handy. The Preview in Browser option makes it possible for you to install the browser of your choice, and then open the page you're working with within Dreamweaver directly in that browser by selecting it from this submenu of browser options. To see this feature in action, select the Preview in Browser icon and choose Preview In *<your browser>*. Immediately your browser of choice will launch and your page will appear within it.

> **NOTE**
>
> We will be using this feature in nearly every example in this book. Because this is the case, it's important to mention that pressing F12 is the shortcut for previewing your page in the primary browser and is the term we will be referring to throughout the book. You may also define a secondary browser within which you can quickly open your page. The shortcut key to open a page within a secondary browser is Ctrl+F12 (Option+F12).

By default, Dreamweaver displays the browsers that it detects upon installation. If you happen to install a new browser after you've installed Dreamweaver, don't worry; you can still add new browsers to the Preview in Browser menu. In Appendix C, we'll do just that.

Refresh Design View

While in Split Code/Design view, you can use this option to quickly refresh the Design view as you make changes to the code. You can also press the F5 key to refresh the Design view.

At first glance, this feature might not make a whole lot of sense. To understand why this feature is necessary, you must first understand how Dreamweaver processes HTML. Because HTML requires opening and closing tags and sometimes even nested tags in between, it's nearly impossible for Dreamweaver to render HTML in Design view before you've actually completed working with the tag's structure. For this reason, Dreamweaver lets you complete your tag and then allows you to refresh Design view to see the results of the changes.

View Options

You can use the View Options menu to configure viewing preferences within your page. Depending on which view you're currently in (Code, Split, or Design), the View Options menu will tailor itself accordingly. If you're in Split Code/Design view for instance, the View Options menu displays similar to Figure 1.7, displaying a complete list of design options on top, followed by code-specific options below.

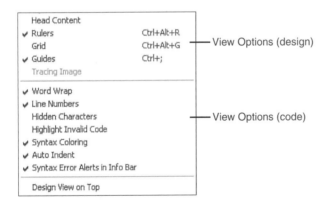

FIGURE 1.7   The View Options menu in Split Code/Design view.

The options within the View Options menu that are specific to the Code view include the following options:

- **Word Wrap**—When this is checked, code wraps to the next line when it reaches the end (right edge) of the Document window.

- **Line Numbers**—When this is checked, line numbers appear in the leftmost gutter (highlighted as blue).

▶ **Hidden Characters**—When this option is selected, line breaks, similar to those within a word processor, are displayed within the code. Although hidden characters are visible in Code view, they are not shown within the browser.

▶ **Highlight Invalid Code**—When this is checked, all invalid code is highlighted in yellow.

▶ **Syntax Coloring**—Checking this option enables various colors to be associated with different tags. You can configure these colors within the Code Coloring category of the Preferences dialog, also covered in Appendix C.

▶ **Auto Indent**—Checking this option automatically causes child tags to indent from their parent tags. A perfect example of this is the `<table>` tag. Because this tag has two child tags: the `<tr>` and `<td>` tags, these tags will be indented to make them easier to spot when you're glancing at a page full of code. This automatic indentation of tags is Dreamweaver's way of formatting your code on-the-fly and is also known as *auto formatting*.

▶ **Syntax Error Alerts in Info Bar**—Enables or disables syntax error alerts within Dreamweaver's Info Bar.

The View Options menu configures itself to display the following features:

▶ **Head Content**—When this is selected, the Head Content list appears just below the Document toolbar. The Head content list, discussed later in this chapter, allows you to add and customize `<head>` tag-specific items such as the title, scripts, styles, meta tags, and so on.

▶ **Rulers**—When this is selected, rulers become visible on the page. Working with rulers makes it easier to see and work with pixel-based dimensions of the page. It's also useful for lining up various elements with each other.

▶ **Grid**—Selecting this option displays a grid within the background of the current page. This is a visual feature that makes positioning of elements easier to a developer.

▶ **Guides**—When rulers are visible, you can use this option to drag visual guides into the Document window. Similar to image editing and print publishing programs, guides are a handy feature that allow you to position elements on the page so that they line up with a particular guide.

▶ **Tracing Image**—Discussed in greater depth in Chapter 4, "Web Page Structuring Using Tables," a Tracing Image is merely a completed mockup added to the page as a background to aid in the position of elements within Design view.

▶ **Design View on Top**—The Design View on Top option allows you to position Design view so that it's on the top and Code view is on the bottom, or vice versa, when you choose Split Code/Design view.

Visual Aids

The Visual Aids menu, like the View Options menu, allows you to customize how specific visual aids are displayed or not displayed within the Document window.

A *visual aid* constitutes any piece of functionality within the Document window that aids in viewing elements that would otherwise not be shown within the browser. For instance, if you create a new table within the Document window with a border of 0 pixels, it would be difficult to add elements within the cells of that table because a border doesn't exist to allow you to see the boundaries of the specific cells. As an aid, Dreamweaver adds a temporary border at design time to allow you to see the outlining boundaries of the table's cells. In the browser, however, your table will still appear borderless. This temporary border that Dreamweaver adds is considered a visual aid.

Dreamweaver includes several visual aids that you can use depending on functionality. These visual aids are enabled/disabled within this menu and are outlined here:

- ▶ **Hide All Visual Aids**—Select this option to hide all visual aids within the Document window.

- ▶ **CSS Layout Options**—As you will see in Chapter 5, "Page Formatting Using Cascading Style Sheets," Dreamweaver uses what are known as *AP Elements* to allow you to position content (text, images, and so on) anywhere on your page by dragging the AP Element around within the Document window. Specifically, AP Elements are `<div>` tags that include the `display:block`, `position:absolute`, or `position:relative` properties and values. Although Dreamweaver provides numerous visual aids for viewing AP Elements, none are more obvious than the ones listed within this menu. For instance, you can choose the CSS Layout Outlines to show the outlines of all AP Elements on the page. You can also choose the CSS Layout Backgrounds option to show or hide the assigned background colors for each AP Element on the page. Finally, you can choose the CSS Layout Box Model option to show or hide padding, margins, and the like for a selected AP Element on the page.

- ▶ **AP Element Outlines**—Similar to the temporary border that is added to a table, you can choose this option to temporarily show or hide an outline/border for an AP Element. By default, AP Elements are borderless. This feature is merely a visual aid that helps you see the boundaries of the AP Element while you're working.

- ▶ **Table Widths**—A visual aid discussed with more detail in Chapter 4, table widths allow you to quickly see and manipulate the width of an entire table or the individual columns within a table.

- ▶ **Table Borders and Frame Borders**—As mentioned earlier in this section, choose the Table Borders option to show or hide the temporarily assigned border to a table when the border attribute is set to 0. Alternatively, you can show or hide frame borders when the border attribute of a frame is set to 0 as well.

- ▶ **Image Maps**—Choose this option to show or hide image maps on the page. This feature is discussed in more detail in the next chapter.

▶ **Invisible Elements**—Some HTML elements don't have visual representations within a browser. For example, anchor tags don't appear in browsers. However, it can be useful to be able to select such invisible elements while you're creating a page in an effort to edit them, move them, or delete them. If this is the case, you can select this option to show invisible elements and then make the necessary edits.

Validate Markup

As a mechanism for standardizing the way in which developers build web pages, the World Wide Web Consortium (W3C) created a set of *Document Type Definitions*, or *DTDs*, for developers to follow. These DTDs, which are XML-schema-based documents, outline rules for how markup languages should be written. Conveniently located at the W3C's website, the DTDs can be referenced directly by what is known as a *validator*. In the past, developers would either download a validator to their computers to perform manual checks, or they would browse to the W3C's website and enter the web page to validate within a utility provided on the web page.

Fortunately, times have changed. Dreamweaver now provides this validation utility directly from the Document toolbar. By default, when you create a new page to work with, Dreamweaver adds what's known as a *Document Type Declaration* as the very first line of code within the document:

```
<!DOCTYPE html PUBLIC "-//W3C//DTD XHTML 1.0 Transitional//EN"
"http://www.w3.org/TR/xhtml1/DTD/xhtml1-transitional.dtd">
```

As you can see, this Document Type Declaration includes numerous attributes, including the type of page (HTML), the DTD to use for validation (XHTML 1.0 Transitional), and more importantly, the location of the DTD on the W3C's website.

By default, Dreamweaver uses the HTML Document Type Declaration. However, Dreamweaver can validate documents in many languages, including HTML, XHTML, ColdFusion Markup Language (CFML), JavaServer Pages (JSP), Wireless Markup Language (WML), and XML. To give you an idea of how all this works, let's walk through a simple example together. To check the browser support for your page, follow these steps:

1. Purposely add a bogus tag to your code by switching to Code view and typing in the code `<zak>This is a bogus tag and should be eliminated</zak>` within the `<body>` tag as shown on code line 9 of Figure 1.8.

2. Now save your document by choosing File, Save. Enter a unique name for your file, followed by the `.html` extension, and place the file anywhere on your computer. Personally, I prefer the desktop or the My Documents folder in Windows.

3. Click the Validate markup icon and select the Validate current document option. Immediately, the Validation category of the Results panel, shown in Figure 1.9, appears showing the specific error, the page that the error appeared on, and even the line number.

FIGURE 1.8   Add a tag to the code that doesn't exist in HTML.

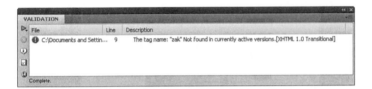

FIGURE 1.9   The Validation category of the Results panel displays the markup error.

NOTE

The Results panel, discussed later in the book, is a centralized location for performing searches, page validation, browser compatibility checks, checking links, creating site reports, and so on.

After the error appears in the Validation category of the Results panel, you need only to double-click the error. Dreamweaver will automatically open the page and even highlight the specific line that contains the error, allowing you to make changes. Of course, in our case we'd want to completely remove the invalid tag.

Check Browser Compatibility

The browser compatibility check enables you to quickly check your page against preconfigured browser types. In the past, Dreamweaver developers had to install multiple versions of every browser, open their page within those browsers, check for inconsistencies and errors, and then make tweaks to fix the problems for the particular browser type in Dreamweaver. Although it's still important to check your page on various browsers for visual layout issues, the Browser Compatibility Check built in to Dreamweaver can automatically detect CSS inconsistencies and errors that are not supported in a particular browser version. All you have to do is provide the browser version to perform the check against, save your page, and then select Check Browser Compatibility. Like the Validate Markup feature, Dreamweaver automatically checks the page against the browser rendering engines that you specify and then provides a list of errors (if any exist) within the Browser Compatibility Check category of the Results panel. It's that easy!

Configuring the browser types that you want to target is just as easy. To do this, select the Check Browser Compatibility button and choose Settings. The Target Browser dialog appears, similar to Figure 1.10, allowing you to customize which browsers to check against and, more specifically, which version of that particular browser to check.

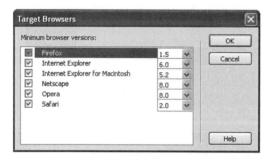

FIGURE 1.10   The Target Browsers dialog enables you to customize which browsers and browser versions to check your pages against.

NOTE

The Check Accessibility option is covered in much more detail in the online Appendix A, "Accessibility."

The Standard Toolbar

The Standard toolbar, available by selecting View, Toolbars, Standard, provides basic file-based operations such as:

- ▶ **New**—Opens the New Document dialog box, which allows you to quickly create a new document.

- ▶ **Open**—Allows you to quickly open an existing document.

- ▶ **Browse in Bridge**—Launches Adobe Bridge and allows you to navigate to, preview, organize, and/or open documents from within Bridge. Adobe Bridge is discussed with more detail in Chapter 14, "Integrating with Fireworks, Photoshop, and Flash."

- ▶ **Save**—Saves the current document.

- **Save All**—Saves all open Documents.

- **Print Code**—Prints the code as it's formatted within the Code view.

- **Cut**—When an element is selected, this option allows you to cut it.

- **Copy**—When an element is selected, this option allows you to copy it.

- **Paste**—Allows you to paste a previously cut or copied element.

- **Undo**—Undoes the last operation.

- **Redo**—Redoes the previous operation.

An example of the Standard toolbar is shown in Figure 1.11.

FIGURE 1.11   The Standard toolbar allows for quick and visual selections of file-based operations such as Open, Save, Cut, Copy, Paste, and so on.

TIP

Screen real estate is a developer's best friend. I typically turn this toolbar off because its options are also available from either the File or Edit menus, as well as easy, standardized, keyboard shortcuts.

The Style Rendering Toolbar

The Style Rendering toolbar, available by selecting View, Toolbars, Style Rendering, contains buttons that let you see how your design would look with different CSS stylesheets that include media types, including (from left to right):

- **Screen**—When enabled, this button shows you how your page will look on a typical computer screen. This is the default option.

- **Print**—When selected, this button shows you how your page will look on a printed piece of paper.

- **Handheld**—When selected, this button shows you how your page will look on a handheld device such as a cell phone or PocketPC.

- **Projection**—When selected, this button shows you how your page will look on a projection device.

▶ **TTY**—When selected, this button shows you how your page will look on a teletype machine.

▶ **TV**—When selected, this button shows you how your page will look on a television screen.

The Style Rendering toolbar also includes buttons that allow you to turn Cascading Style Sheets (CSS) on and off, as well as enabling and disabling Design-Time Style Sheets. These options are covered with more detail in Chapter 5.

> **TIP**
>
> Again, it's important to point out that the Standard and Style Rendering toolbars can also be quickly opened/closed by right-clicking the Document toolbar and then choosing the particular option from the context menu that appears.

The Status Bar

The status bar, located at the bottom of each Document window instance, outlines numerous features for working with the web page. Options include a Tag Selector for viewing and selecting from the hierarchy of HTML tags based on your cursor's position, a set of zoom tools for zooming in and out of the Document window, and a window size and download time indicator, which allows you to physically change the viewable size of the page and see approximately how long your page will take to view within a target audience's browser based on the total size (in kilobytes) of the elements within the page.

The Tag Selector

The Tag Selector displays a cleanly formatted hierarchical view of the tags from the position of your cursor. Think of the Tag Selector as night vision goggles while in Design view. Because in Design view you can't see the tags that you're currently working in, the Tag Selector displays them for you; even better, it allows you to quickly modify them without ever switching to the Code view. To see the Tag Selector in action, follow these steps:

1. Make sure you are in Design view and quickly insert a new table by choosing Insert, Table. When the Table dialog appears, modify some of the values and click OK. (Right now, it's not important what you add in these text boxes.)

2. With the table now in Design view, place your cursor within a cell and observe the Tag Selector. As you can see from Figure 1.12, the Tag Selector displays the hierarchical list of tags based on your cursor's position within the tag structure.

`<body> <table> <tr> <td>`

FIGURE 1.12 The tag selector displays a hierarchical list of tags based on your cursor's position within the tag's structure.

You can even use the context menu by right-clicking (Control+clicking) the tag within the Tag Selector for complete control over the selected tag, including the following:

▶ **Remove Tag**—Removes the selected tag if the selected tag isn't dependent on another tag. In our case, you wouldn't be able to remove either the `<td>` or `<tr>` tags because the `<table>` tag is dependent on those tags being present. However, you would be able to right-click the `<table>` tag to remove it.

▶ **Quick Tag Editor**—Allows you to edit attributes within a tag directly within a mini-code editor.

▶ **Set Class**—Allows you to set a CSS class to a tag.

▶ **Set ID**—Allows you to set a CSS ID to a tag.

▶ **Code Navigator**—Opens the Code Navigator that provides an interface for inspecting the structure of the CSS associated with the tag.

▶ **Convert Inline CSS to Rule**—Using inline CSS, as you will see later in the book, is not recommended best practice. To make your CSS cleaner and more organized, you can convert inline styles to CSS rules that reside in the head of the document or in an external style sheet. Again, CSS is covered in more detail in Chapter 5.

▶ **Collapse Full Tag**—Select this option to collapse the tag within Code view.

▶ **Collapse Outside Full Tag**—Select this option to collapse the parent tag of the currently highlighted tag. For instance, if my cursor is within a table's cell, selecting this option would collapse the `<body>` tag because the existing `<table>` tag is nested within it.

To show an example of how to use the context menu on a tag, I'll right-click (Control+click) the `<table>` tag and choose the Quick Tag Editor option. As you can see from Figure 1.13, the Quick Tag Editor appears complete within the tag, and attributes for the tag are prepopulated.

Next, I'll add the `bgcolor="red"` attribute and value and press Enter. The table's background color changes to red.

Zoom Tools

Just to the right of the Tag Selector hierarchy are tools that allow you to zoom in and out of the Document window. The zoom toolset includes a pointer icon, a hand tool for moving the page around within the Document window when zoomed in, a magnifying glass for zooming into and out of the page, the capability to toggle from zooming in and out by holding Alt (Option), and a zoom percentage menu that allows you to quickly zoom into a specific percentage value.

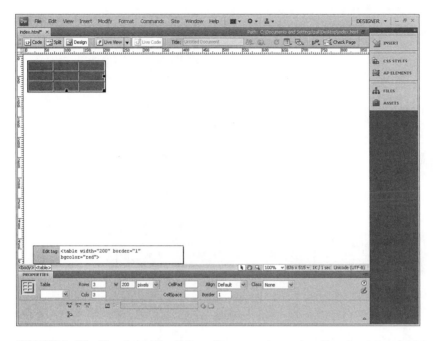

FIGURE 1.13   The Quick Tag Editor allows you to preview the structure of a tag and make quick edits.

Window Size and Download Time

You can use the Window Size option, located in the bottom-right corner of the Document window, to set the Document window's width and height in development mode according to what you think your target audience's screen resolution will be. For instance, latest browser studies have shown that as long as you develop for 800×600 screen resolutions, a large majority of your viewers will be able to see your page without scrolling horizontally. Because this is the case, you can set up your development environment to keep this size in mind. To change the Document window to accommodate 800×600 screen resolutions, follow these steps:

1. In Windows, set your Document window so that it is not maximized; select the Restore Down option in the top-right corner of the Document window.

2. With the Document window now floating, the Window Size option becomes selectable. Choose the 760×420 (800×600) option, as shown in Figure 1.14.

3. The Document window will resize itself to accommodate the new dimensions you chose.

The Download Time indicator, located just to the right of the Window Size menu, calculates the total size (in kilobytes) of text and images on the page, divides it by a specific bandwidth target, and presents the estimated download time.

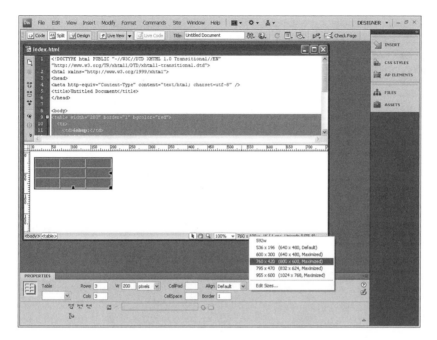

FIGURE 1.14   The window size menu allows you to configure the development environment to better target your users' browsers.

In Appendix C online, we'll review options for defining the bandwidth target as well as defining your own custom Document window sizes.

The final text label that appears just to the right of the window size and download time indicator is a simple text-based label that indicates the encoding type used by the page. This encoding type can be changed in numerous places, but none more obvious than choosing Modify, Page Properties; choosing the Title/Encoding category; and then selecting the encoding type from the Encoding drop-down menu.

Context Menus

One of the most underused features in Dreamweaver is the context menu. Context menus, as the name suggests, are context-specific menu items that appear for an element on which you right-click. Nearly every panel, toolbar, window, and so on, enables you to access a context-specific menu of options. Some of these options are more advanced features that you can select for a specific element. Others are simply items that you can find just as easily within the menu bar but that are placed within a context menu to make them easier to access.

To enable a context menu, simply right-click (Control+click) within the Document window, a toolbar, a panel, and so on. As you can see from Figure 1.15, I've right-clicked onto the Document window and instantly a centralized submenu of options appears.

Paragraph Format	▶
List	▶
Align	▶
Font	▶
Style	▶
CSS Styles	▶
Size	▶
Templates	▶
Element View	▶
Code Navigator...	Ctrl+Alt+N
Edit Tag <body>...	Shift+F5
Quick Tag Editor...	
Make Link	
Remove Link	
Open Linked Page	
Target Frame	▶
Add to Color Favorites	
Create New Snippet	
Cut	
Copy	
Paste	Ctrl+V
Paste Special...	
Design Notes for Page...	
Page Properties...	

FIGURE 1.15   The context menu allows you to quickly select options that can be performed on the selected object.

All windows, panels, inspectors, and so on have selectable options within a context menu, but none more so than the Document window. As we progress through features, we'll cover options that are available within context menus. For now, let's do a simple cut-and-paste example using the Document window's context menu. You can follow along by performing the following steps:

1. Type some text within the Document window. I'll type **Hello World**.

2. Highlight the text by selecting one end of it and dragging your mouse over to the other end.

3. Right-click (Control+click) the selected text and choose Cut from the context menu. The text disappears.

4. Now right-click (Control+click) again and choose Paste from the context menu. The text reappears.

Practice using the context menu now as we'll be using it a lot. It really is a time-saving developer's aid, as the properties that you'll be setting most for a selected item will always appear within context menus. It's extremely handy to simply right-click on an object and quickly choose what you need rather than trying to find something from the myriad of menu and submenu selections in the Menu bar or Properties inspector.

The Insert Panel

The Insert panel, similar to the Insert menu in the Menu bar, is a visual representation of elements that can be inserted into the Document window (see Figure 1.16).

FIGURE 1.16   The Insert panel is a visual representation of elements that can be inserted into the Document window.

In previous versions of Dreamweaver, the Insert panel was instead an Insert bar that was usually either free floating to allow quick, visual access to items that you would otherwise have to find from the Insert menu in the Menu bar, or it was positioned just underneath the Menu bar, agiiain to allow quick, visual access to items that you'd insert into the Document window most. In this newest version of Dreamweaver, the Insert bar has been relegated to becoming a panel and is usually found among the other panels, positioned on the right side of the Dreamweaver interface. You can open the Insert panel to see the categories (and items within those categories) by choosing Window, Insert (Ctrl+F2 in Windows or ⌘ on a Mac). As you'll see when the Insert panel is open, the panel menu (available by clicking the small expander arrow icon located just to the right of the category label) allows you to choose from the following seven categories:

▶ **Common Objects**—Allows you to quickly insert objects that you'll work with most often, such as hyperlinks, tables, and images.

▶ **Layout Objects**—Allows you to quickly insert layout and formatting objects such as tables, <div> tags, AP Elements, Spry objects, and more. After a layout object has been inserted, Dreamweaver allows you to switch between Standard and Expanded modes. Standard versus Expanded modes will be covered with more detail in Chapter 4.

▶ **Form Objects**—Use the Form category to select from and insert various form elements such as text fields, check boxes, radio buttons, lists, menus, and buttons into your page.

▶ **Data Objects**—When working with server-side applications, use this category to quickly insert dynamic objects based on the technology that you're using.

▶ **Spry Objects**—One of the newest additions to the Insert panel (as of the previous version of Dreamweaver), uses the Spry category to choose from a variety of Spry objects, including Spry data objects and widgets. Spry is covered with more detail in Chapter 24, "Working with the Spry Framework for Ajax."

▶ **Text Objects**—If you need to insert special characters, headings, copyright and trademark symbols, and so on, choose Elements from this category.

▶ **Favorites**—Select from a preconfigurable list of favorite objects.

You'll notice from Figure 1.17, the Insert panel features a unique selectable drop-down menu for switching between categories. You can also choose to display the Insert panel without labels—that is, just the icons without text labels describing what each icon is for.

FIGURE 1.17   The Insert panel shown without text labels.

Common Objects

You can choose options from the Common Objects category to quickly insert objects that you'll work with most often, including

▶ **Hyperlink**—This object provides a dialog box that contains options for creating hyperlinks within your HTML documents.

▶ **Email Link**—This option launches a dialog box providing two text fields: one to type text that will be hyperlinked, and the other to type the hyperlink itself.

▶ **Named Anchor**—The Named Anchor object enables you to create HTML anchors. Named anchors act as reference points for hyperlinks to link to an exact location on the page.

▶ **Horizontal Rule**—Clicking this icon inserts a simple horizontal line represented by the `<hr/>` tag in HTML.

▶ **Table**—Selecting this object opens the Table dialog box, which allows you to customize properties such as rows, columns, and widths before inserting a table.

▶ **Insert DIV Tag**—Inserts the Layout Block `<div>` element within the page.

▶ **Image Menu**—Use this menu to choose from various types of image options, including the following:

  ▶ **Image**—Opens a dialog box that allows you to choose from an image on your computer to insert into your document.

  ▶ **Image Placeholder**—Allows you to quickly insert an image placeholder. This can come in handy when you want to start laying out a page but haven't quite finished the graphics.

  ▶ **Rollover Image**—Choosing this option opens the Rollover Image dialog box allowing you to quickly and easily create JavaScript-based rollovers without manually having to code anything.

  ▶ **Fireworks HTML**—Adobe's Fireworks enables you to quickly create buttons, image maps, and so on that can be inserted into Dreamweaver. Selecting this option allows you to quickly insert that code. This feature is covered with more detail in Chapter 14.

  ▶ **Navigation Bar**—The Navigation Bar option picks up where the Rollover Image option leaves off. Choose this option to create a full-featured navigation bar with up to four states per button, including the Up, Over, Down, and Over While Down states.

  ▶ **Hotspot Drawing Tools**—When working with image maps, use these options to create linkable rectangular, oval, or polygonal hotspots within an image.

▶ **Media Menu**—Choose options from this menu when you want to insert Flash (SWF), FlashPaper, Flash video (FLV), or Shockwave Director (SWD) movies, ActiveX components, Java applets, or generic plugins within your page.

▶ **Date**—Opens the Insert Date dialog box, which enables you to choose from a list of preconfigured date and/or time stamp options.

▶ **Server-Side Include**—Select this button to open the Select File dialog box. Use this box to browse for and select a server-side include to use within your page. As you'll see later in the book, *server-side includes* are web pages that can be inserted into other web pages, making global changes easier and much more efficient.

▶ **Comment**—A programmer's friend, you can quickly insert comments directly into your HTML code by selecting this option. Comments aren't visible to users in the browser but are visible to you, the developer, within the Code view.

▶ **Head Tags**—This submenu allows you to pick from various head objects, including the following:

   ▶ **Meta Tags**—Meta tags are typically used to describe the contents of the web page. This can be especially useful with HTML validators.

   ▶ **Keywords**—Similar to the way meta tags describe the page, keywords describe the page and its content for search engines. If you create a site and never register or submit it to any search engine or web directory, you might still get a listing. The reason is that search engines run programs called *spiders*, which gather meta information, including keywords from different websites.

   ▶ **Description**—Use the Description meta tag in conjunction with the Keyword meta tag to provide a brief description to potential clients as to what your web page is about. The description you type will show up directly underneath your hyperlink in the results page of the search engine.

   ▶ **Refresh**—There are different uses for the Refresh meta tag. Simply put, Refresh causes the page to refresh itself. This is useful if you were displaying live sports scores on your page, for example. You could include a Refresh meta tag so that the sports scores refresh every 30, 60, or 90 seconds, for instance. This would offset the user needing to click the browser's Refresh button.

   ▶ **Base**—You can use the Base tag as a way to point all link references on your page to a single relative address.

   ▶ **Link**—Most commonly used with external style sheet and JavaScript files, you can use the Link tag as a way to directly link an external file into your document.

▶ **Script**—Select an option from this menu to insert a script block into your page's code. Selecting the Script option launches the Script dialog box. Within this dialog box, you can either type the script code or point the script dialog box to an external script to use instead. A second option within the Script menu is the No Script option. Choosing this option adds the `<noscript>` tag to your code. Within this tag you are able to add content targeting browsers that have scripting disabled.

▶ **Templates**—Use the Templates menu to choose objects for working with Dreamweaver templates. Templates are covered in greater detail in Chapter 12, "Working with Templates and Library Items."

▶ **Tag Chooser**—Choose this option to open the Tag Chooser dialog box. The Tag Chooser is a handy window that allows you to select and subsequently insert any element from the library of HTML, CFML, ASP, ASP.NET, JSP, Jrun, PHP, and WML tags.

Layout Objects

As you begin to familiarize yourself with table-based web page design (covered in greater detail in Chapter 4), you'll use the layout objects with more regularity. The Layout category is broken up into two modes: Standard mode allows you to work with tables, <div> tags, and AP Elements freely, and Expanded mode, which temporarily adds padding to tables, making them easier to work with. A complete list of features, beginning from left to right, follows here:

▶ **Insert Div Tag**—Opens the Insert Div Tag dialog box, which enables you to customize options for the insertion of a new <div> tag within the Document window.

▶ **Draw AP Div**—Enables you to freely draw an AP Div (AP Element) onto the Document window.

▶ **Spry Objects**—Enables you to quickly insert Spry elements, including the Spry Menu Bar, Spry Accordion, and Spry Tabbed and Collapsible Panels.

▶ **Insert Table**—Opens the Insert Table dialog box, which enables you to customize further options for the insertion of a new table within the Document window.

▶ **Insert Row Above**—Inserts a row above a cell within a table.

▶ **Insert Row Below**—Inserts a row below a cell within a table.

▶ **Insert Column to the Left**—Inserts a column to the left of a cell within a table.

▶ **Insert Column to the Right**—Inserts a column to the right of a cell within a table.

▶ **IFrame**—Click this button to insert the <iframe> tag into your code. IFrames (inline frames) are used as way of embedding the content of a secondary page within your page within a small scrollable window. It's important to note, however, that the IFrame is deprecated, and it should be replaced whenever possible with the much more flexible <div> tag.

▶ **Frames Menu**—Opens the Frameset submenu, which enables you to pick from various options for splitting the Document window into frames. Frames are covered in more detail in the online Appendix D, "Working with Frames and Framesets."

Form Objects

Covered in much more detail in Chapter 7, "HTML Forms," form objects facilitate interactivity between your users and your dynamic web applications. Aside from adding form objects by using the Insert, Form menu, you can visually add form objects from this category.

The list of available objects includes Form, Text Field, Hidden Field, Textarea, Checkbox, Radio Button, Radio Group, List/Menu, Jump Menu, Image Field, File Field, Button, Label, Fieldset, and various Spry validation elements including Spry Validation Text Field, Spring Validation Textarea, Spry Validation Checkbox, and Spry Validation Select.

Data Objects

Throughout the second half of this book, you will become increasingly familiar with data objects. Depending on what server technology you're using, the Data category of the Insert bar will tailor itself to accommodate features and functionality of a specific technology. To prove this point, I'll briefly create a sample PHP page. As you can see from Figure 1.18 (before) and Figure 1.19 (PHP page), the category list looks slightly different before I created the PHP page than it does afterward. The reason for this is simple; Dreamweaver doesn't need the data object-specific options when working with standard web pages, so it simply decides not to show them initially. It's not until you create a dynamic page (ASP, CFM, PHP, etc.) that Dreamweaver will decide to show data objects. Because dynamic pages rely on the options outlined within the data objects tab, they're shown when a page that supports them is created.

FIGURE 1.18   The categories of the Insert panel when you're working with a normal HTML file.

FIGURE 1.19   The categories of the Insert panel when you're working with a PHP file. Also notice the new PHP category.

It's also important to notice that depending on the server technology you decide to use, a new category will appear to support development for that particular technology. In my case, because I created a new PHP page, a new PHP category appears, complete with elements that I can use for that technology. Again, server technologies will be covered in much more detail in the second half of the book.

Spry Objects

The Spry framework is a JavaScript library that provides designers and developers with the capability to build web pages that offer richer experiences to their site's visitors. With Spry, you can use HTML, CSS, and a minimal amount of JavaScript to incorporate and visually work with XML data in your HTML documents. With various "widgets" such as accordions, menu bars, validation elements, effects, and more, it has never been easier to work with external XML data in an HTML-based web page.

Although we'll cover the Spry framework in more detail later in the book, for now, note that the Spry category in the Insert panel outlines various Spry elements that you may decide to use within your web pages.

Text Objects

As you can see from Figure 1.20, the text objects category provides a section from the Insert panel from which text can be easily formatted.

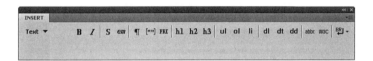

FIGURE 1.20   Use text objects when manipulating the look of text within the Document window.

Text objects can be broken into the following categories (moving from left to right):

▶ **Font Weights and Styles**—Allows you to add a bold (`<b>`) or strong (`<strong>`) tag, as well as an italic (`<i>`) or emphasis (`<em>`) tag.

▶ **Paragraph, Blockquote, & Preformatted**—Allows you to format blocks of text with the paragraph (`<p>`) tag, indent text with the blockquote (`<blockquote>`) tag, or preserve the formatting of content with the preformatted (`<pre>`) tag.

▶ **Headings**—Provides three heading options (H1, H2, H3) for your text.

▶ **Lists**—Allows you to pick from three types of lists: ordered list (numbered) and unordered list (bulleted) and the required tags within these two types of lists: list item (li). Also shown is the definition list (dl) including tags contained within the definition list including definition title (dt) and dictionary definition (dd).

▶ **Abbreviations and Acronyms**—Assign the abbreviation or acronym tag to text within your page.

▶ **Characters (BR submenu)**—Select from a group of predefined special characters from this menu. The most obvious are listed (line break, Non-Breaking Space, left and right quote, dash, pound, euro, yen, copyright, registered trademark, and trademark. You can also choose from a character map by selecting the Other Characters option. Doing so launches the Insert Other Characters dialog box, which allows you to choose from a map of characters supported on your computer.

It's important to note that most text-based formatting features are also available from the Property inspector, the context menu when right-clicking onto a text element, and by choosing a specific submenu from the Format menu in the Menu bar. Like most of the other features within the Insert bar, the Text category provides a simpler, visual method for applying text-based formatting.

Favorites

As you familiarize yourself with using the various categories of the Insert panel, you'll quickly begin to realize that you're using some objects more than others. When this happens, you might want to group some of your favorite objects within the Favorites category, making them quicker and easier to reference. To add an object to the Favorites category of the Insert panel, follow these steps:

1. Switch to the Favorites category of the Insert panel. A message within the category will instruct you to right-click (Control+click) the panel to customize your favorite objects.

2. Right-click (Control+click) the panel as the instructions indicate and select Customize Favorites.

3. The Customize Favorite Objects dialog box panel will appear.

4. Select your favorite objects from the Available Objects section on the left and add them to the Favorite Objects section on the right by clicking the double-arrow button in the center (see Figure 1.21).

5. Click OK.

FIGURE 1.21   Add your favorite objects from the Available Objects list to the Favorite Objects list.

Your new favorite objects will now be added to the Favorites category of the Insert panel. If you'd like to remove favorite objects, simply select each favorite from the Favorite Objects list in the Customize Favorite Objects dialog box and choose the trash can icon.

The Property Inspector

If you haven't noticed by now, the Property inspector is the horizontal pane located directly underneath the Document window, as shown in Figure 1.22.

HTML-specific options

CSS-specific options

FIGURE 1.22   The Property inspector adjusts its editable properties based on the task at hand.

The Property inspector—unlike any other piece of Dreamweaver's user interface—is context-sensitive and, therefore, automatically tailors itself to the task at hand. For instance, up to this point I've demonstrated simple "Hello World" examples using both plain text and tables. Although we won't begin to cover the concepts until later chapters, this is the perfect opportunity to discuss the adjustments that the Property inspector will make for each element, and subsequent other elements, that you will work with throughout the book.

> **TIP**
>
> If the Property inspector is not visible, you can always make it visible by selecting Window, Properties.

So far you might have noticed that the Property inspector provides options for editing fonts, colors, indentation, alignments, and so on by placing your cursor within a blank Document window. This is known as a text-based Property inspector. Although we'll be using the Property inspector for a lot of the examples within the book, it's important to note the changes that the Property inspector makes when working with other elements. To demonstrate this, I'll quickly add a table to the Document window by selecting Insert, Table, modifying some of the options from the Insert Table dialog box, and choosing OK. With the Table now within the Document window, try placing your cursor somewhere inside the table. As you'll see, the Property inspector changes to accommodate editable properties for a cell. Now let's try using a feature that you've already learned: the Tag Selector. This time with your cursor inside the table, select the `<table>` tag from the Tag Selector. Again, as you can see from Figure 1.23, the Property inspector changes, this time to the Table Property inspector.

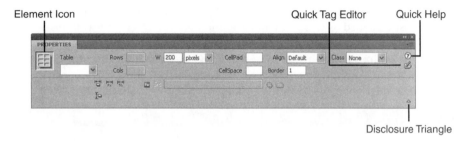

FIGURE 1.23   Selecting the table tag from the Tag Selector causes the Property inspector to change to the Table Property inspector.

The important concept to remember here is that the Property inspector will change to accommodate any selected element. Because there are so many elements to work with in Dreamweaver, the Property inspector can be deceptively tough to figure out—especially if you're working with an element that you're unfamiliar with. Just remember—if you're working with the text, the Property inspector will accommodate text; if you're working with tables, the Property inspector accommodates tables, and so on.

A couple of other elements that are worth mentioning appear within the Property inspector no matter what element is selected. These four elements are also highlighted in Figure 1.23 and are described with more detail next:

▶ **Element icon**—Every possible HTML element that can be modified within the Property inspector is represented by its own icon.

▶ **Quick Help**—Opens the Dreamweaver help menu with the element you're working with as the indexed topic.

▶ **Quick Tag Editor**—Similar to right-clicking (Control+clicking) a tag within the Tag Selector and choosing Edit Tag, the Quick Tag Editor allows you to quickly format attributes and values for a tag without having to switch to Code view.

▶ **Disclosure triangle**—If you haven't noticed yet, the Property inspector is divided into two sections by a horizontal line running down the middle. The basic properties (located in the top half) and advanced properties (located in the bottom half) can be collapsed and expanded by selecting this icon.

It's also important to mention a feature that was recently added to this newest version of Dreamweaver. As you can see from Figure 1.22, the Property inspector (particularly when it's in Text mode), displays two buttons: HTML and CSS. As a new addition, the Property inspector can now accommodate property modifications that are specific to either HTML (where a property modification would be added as an attribute to an HTML tag) or CSS. In Dreamweaver's quest to be as standards-compliant as possible, some of the features that used to reside in the Property inspector as simple HTML additions can no longer be added this way because the tags that they would create are considered deprecated. Instead, CSS must be relied upon to make these kinds of changes. Specifically, font faces, sizes, colors, and alignments must be added as CSS rules and are initiated in numerous ways, the simplest being from the CSS category in the Property inspector. And although we'll certainly cover these options more in Chapter 5, it's important to understand this major switch from non-standards-compliant support to standards-compliancy.

> **NOTE**
>
> As you'll see in the next chapter, you're not completely out of luck if you prefer to not use CSS. Although CSS is certainly advantageous to learn and is recommended whenever possible, the technology can sometimes become overwhelming, especially for newer web developers. Because we won't be discussing CSS until Chapter 5, we'll rely on alternative methods (Format menu, context menu, and so on) to circumvent the necessity of CSS, as is the case with the Property inspector.

Panels

Dreamweaver contains many panels, toolbars, inspectors, and menus to aid in the development of your web pages. Although we've talked about a select few options centralized within and around the Document window, this section focuses on the myriad of other panels that are also at your disposal.

Interacting with Panels

Dreamweaver includes a library of panels, all of which are readily available from the Window menu. Opening a panel is a simple matter of choosing the panel you want from the Window menu. For instance, because we'll be talking about the CSS Styles panel shortly, I'll select it from the Window menu. As you can see from Figure 1.24, the panel, along with the AP Elements panel, opens as a group, docked above the Files and Assets panel group.

You can also undock panels by dragging them out of their docked state (available in Windows only). For instance, if I wanted to make the CSS panel a free-floating panel, I would simply click, hold, and drag from the heading similar to Figure 1.25.

The reverse is also possible by dragging the panel back into the list of panels on the right side of the development area. You can also minimize and maximize (open panels) by double-clicking the name on the panel's tab.

Every panel supports its own unique functionality. This is made obvious by the small icons located on the bottom right of the panel. Advanced options for every panel are also available from the panel Options menu, easily accessed by selecting the icon located on the upper right of the panel (and just below the close icon); these are shown selected in Figure 1.26.

FIGURE 1.24   The CSS Styles panel can be opened by selecting CSS Styles from the Window menu.

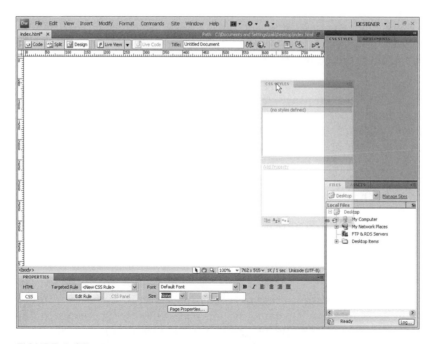

FIGURE 1.25   Panels can be docked and undocked freely.

FIGURE 1.26   Every panel features a panel Options menu that includes advanced features related to the specific panel.

At the bottom of every panel Options menu, you'll see a Help option. As you probably know by now (from the Help bullet point when describing the Property inspector), selecting this option opens the Dreamweaver Help index with the selected panel as the selected topic.

Context menus are also available on panels. If you right-click the development area of the panel, you'll notice similar (if not the same) options as were available within the panel Options menu. If you right-click the header of the panel, however, a different set of options appears that is consistent with all panels in Dreamweaver. These options are as follows:

▶ **Close**—Closes the panel when selected. You can always reopen it by selecting the specific option from the Window menu.

▶ **Close Tab Group**—Closes the group that the panel belongs to, but only when it's docked with that group. You can always reopen it by selecting the specific option from the Window menu.

▶ **Minimize/Restore Group**—Minimizes or restores the panel group.

▶ **Collapse to Icons/Expand Panels**—New to the Dreamweaver interface is the integration with the OWL interface (Operating system Widget Library) that has become commonplace in other popular Adobe programs. You can take advantage of this interface by choosing this option, which immediately collapses the panel into an icon that can then be docked onto Dreamweaver and then clicked on to re-expand. When collapsed to icons, choose the Expand Panels option to restore the panel back to its normal state. Alternatively, you can also choose the small double-arrow icon that appears just to the left of the Close icon in the upper-right corner of the panel. Clicking this arrow will also collapse to icons and expand the panel.

▶ **Auto-Collapse Iconic panels**—When the panel is collapsed to icons, choose this option to force Dreamweaver to automatically collapse the panel when it's not in use.

▶ **Auto-Show Hidden panels**—Enable this option to have any hidden panels automatically appear.

▶ **Interface Preferences**—Launches the Preferences dialog, covered with more detail in the online Appendix C. It's from this dialog box that you can customize numerous Dreamweaver preferences.

The CSS Styles Panel

The CSS Styles panel allows you to create and work with styles and style sheets. You can make the CSS Styles panel visible or hide it by selecting CSS Styles from the Window menu.

The CSS Styles panel will be covered in greater depth in Chapter 5.

The AP Elements Panel

The AP Elements panel allows you to name and change the stacking order and visibility of AP Elements within the Document window after they've been added. You can make the AP Elements panel visible or hide it by selecting AP Elements from the Window menu or by pressing the F2 shortcut key.

The AP Elements panel will be covered in greater depth in Chapter 6, "Page Structuring Using Cascading Style Sheets."

The Application Tab Group

As you begin to build dynamic applications toward the second half of the book, the Application tab group will become your best friend. The Application tab group, which includes the Databases, Bindings, Server Behaviors, and Components panels will be covered extensively in the second half of the book.

The Files Panel

Covered with more detail in the next chapter, the Files panel is a centralized repository for managing sites and files within sites. At its most basic level, the Files panel acts similar to your operating system's file explorer in that it allows you to browse your computer, network, and desktop. It also lists FTP and RDS servers, again, covered in more detail in the next chapter. You can make the Files panel visible or hide it by selecting Files from the Window menu or by pressing the F8 key.

The Assets Panel

The Assets panel is an integrated image, color, URL, Flash, Shockwave, movie, script, template, and Library Item management window. From this panel you have various options for managing and working with the features listed previously as well as adding and customizing favorites you use most often. You can make the Assets panel visible or hide it by selecting Assets from the Window menu or by pressing the F11 (Option+F11) key. The Assets panel is covered in more detail in Chapter 11, "Enhancing Workflow."

The Snippets Panel

The Snippets panel allows you to create and store scripts, markup, and notes that you use and reuse most frequently while developing web pages. Dreamweaver ships with a set of snippets that include text, navigation, meta (which includes meta tags), JavaScript, header, form, footer, content table, comment, and accessibility snippets. You can make the Snippets panel visible or hide it by selecting Snippets from the Window menu. The Snippets panel is covered in much more detail in the next chapter.

The Tag Inspector Panel

The Tag Inspector panel is a handy panel to use for setting various attributes of selected HTML tags and styles. Although the true benefits of this panel set will become more obvious as the book unfolds, you can see the power of the Attributes panel immediately by placing your cursor within the code of your page and then expanding the nodes within the Attributes category. As Figure 1.27 illustrates, various attributes and their values associated with a selected tag are outlined within the panel.

FIGURE 1.27   The Attributes panel outlines attributes and their values for a selected tag.

You can begin to see that the Attributes panel mirrors functionality in the Property inspector. The obvious difference, however, is that the Attributes panel is a more technical and less visual approach to the attributes of a specific tag. You can also switch between a categorized and list view by selecting the appropriate button located just under the tab itself. You can make the Tag Inspector panel visible or hide it by selecting Tag Inspector from the Window menu or by pressing F9 (Option+Shift+F9).

The Behaviors Panel

The Behaviors panel allows you to work with a myriad of prebuilt JavaScript behaviors. With a single click of the Add (+) button, a list of behaviors are immediately available to your web pages. You can make the Behaviors panel visible or hide it by selecting Behaviors from the Window menu or by pressing Shift+F4.

The Behaviors panel will be covered in greater depth in Chapter 8, "Using Behaviors."

The History Panel

At its most basic functionality, the History panel provides a visual historical list of steps performed. The panel features a slider that you can use to scroll through steps in the history. In contrast to selecting Edit, Undo, or pressing Ctrl+Z numerous times, the History panel also allows you to select a specific point in time to which you can return. Other features include the capability to create commands by highlighting a set of steps, right-clicking (Control+clicking), and choosing Save As Command. Commands are covered in much more detail in Chapter 11. You can make the History panel visible or hide it by selecting History from the Window menu.

The Frames Panel

You can use the Frames panel when working with frames and framesets, covered in more detail in the online Appendix D. You can make the Frames panel visible or hide it by selecting Frames from the Window menu or by pressing Shift+F2.

The Code Inspector

As you can see from Figure 1.28, the Code inspector is a detached code window.

The only real difference between the Code inspector and Code view is that the Code inspector lets you continue working within the Design view, at the same time offering a detached, floating code window—perfect for dual-monitor environments. You can make the Code inspector visible or hide it by selecting Code inspector from the Window menu, or by pressing F10 (Option+F10).

The Results Tab Group

As mentioned in an earlier section, the Results set of panels is a centralized location for performing searches, opening a reference, performing page validation, browser compatibility checks, checking links, creating site reports, checking an FTP log, and so on. You can easily interact with the Results set of panels. Simply navigate to Window, Results and then choose the particular panel that you would like opened.

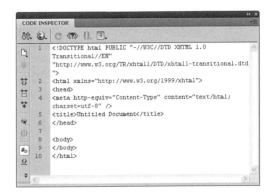

FIGURE 1.28   The Code inspector is a detached code window that mirrors the functionality and look of Code view.

The true power of these panels will become evident as the book unfolds.

Workspace Layouts

Whereas older versions of Dreamweaver allowed Windows users to select from two predefined workspace layouts (coder and designer), Dreamweaver CS4 affords the opportunity to choose from other, more specific window layouts and offers both Windows and Mac users the capability to create your own. Available by choosing one of the eight options from the Workspace Layout submenu, you can easily choose from a preconfigured layout style including App Developer, App Developer Plus, Classic, Coder, Coder Plus, Designer, Designer Compact, and Dual Screen. Choosing one of these options configures the panels and windows according to the predefined layout. Feel free to select between these eight layouts and decide for yourself which one will work best for you.

Of course, if you don't prefer to use the out-of-the-box layouts, you might decide to create your own layout instead. To create your own workspace layout, follow these steps:

1. Organize windows and panels within Dreamweaver according to how you would like to work.

2. Choose Window, Workspace Layout, New Workspace. The New Workspace Layout dialog box appears.

3. Enter a name for your new layout and click OK. The new layout will appear within the Workspace Layout submenu.

If you want to delete a workspace layout, choose Window, Workspace Layout, Manage Workspaces. Select the layout name you want to remove and click Delete. The saved workspace layout will be removed from the list. Of course, you can also rename a layout by choosing the layout and then selecting the Rename button. This launches the Rename Workspace Layout dialog box, in which you can rename your layout and then click OK to apply the changes.

It's important to point out that workspaces layouts can also be selected, created, and managed from the Workspace layout submenu that appears in the upper-right corner of the Dreamweaver interface. As Figure 1.29 indicates, the submenu is readily available, and because my layout is currently configured to use the Designer layout, it's the name that appears.

FIGURE 1.29　Workspace layouts can also be selected, created, and managed directly from the workspace layout submenu that appears in the upper-right corner of the Dreamweaver interface.

The Menu Bar

The last development-related component to be covered is arguably the most obvious, the Menu bar. Although Dreamweaver offers an assortment of panels, toolbars, and inspectors, the Menu bar always remains consistent and never needs to be hidden or made to be visible. Just about every feature we've covered thus far can be inserted, modified, or referenced through the Menu bar, with few exceptions. A generic list of menu items is listed next, complete with highlights:

▶ **Dreamweaver**—This Mac-only menu, also referred to as the Application menu, contains the About, Keyboard Shortcuts, Preferences, and Quit menu options for Mac users.

▶ **File**—Contains common file-based operations such as New, Open, Close, Save, and Revert. Highlights include the capability to preview your page in the browser, check your page against a validator or target browser, and maintain Design Notes.

▶ **Edit**—Allows you to perform common editing tasks such as undo, redo, cut, copy, paste, and select all. Highlights include the capability to set user preferences for Windows users.

▶ **View**—Anything associated with Document window viewing preferences can be found here, including visual aids; rulers; grid; the Code, Split, and Design views, and head content.

▶ **Insert**—Anything that can be inserted into your document can be found within this menu. Alternatively, you can access these options visually by way of the Insert panel by choosing Window, Insert or pressing Ctrl+F2 (⌘-F2).

▶ **Modify**—After you've inserted objects, you'll want to have the capability to manipulate them somehow. Although most properties can be changed through panels or the

Property inspector, the Modify menu is a much more thorough list of modifiable properties.

▶ **Format**—Manipulate text objects through this menu. Highlights include the capability to check your spelling.

▶ **Commands**—Commands are similar to plugins or macros. They are prebuilt components that execute or insert content within the Document window. We'll discuss Commands in much more detail in Chapter 11.

▶ **Site**—Create new or manage existing sites within this menu. After you've defined a site, all site-related options can be found here, as well. Highlights include the capability to scan your site for broken links, change links, and even generate site reports.

▶ **Window**—All panels can be opened through the Window menu. Highlights include the capability to hide all panels (F4) or to cascade and tile (vertically or horizontally) open Document window instances.

▶ **Help**—Access the Dreamweaver, Spry, ColdFusion, and other help-based windows from this menu. Highlights include access to the built-in tutorials, forums, the CSS Advisor and support center, as well as activating or deactivating the program.

Summary

As you've seen in this chapter, Dreamweaver provides numerous panels, windows, inspectors, toolbars, and menus for making development easier. The challenge is now putting everything together that you've learned conceptually about the myriad of panels and windows so that they make sense in practice. In the next chapter, we'll begin the transition by creating a simple web page. As you'll see, the panels, inspectors, and windows will make much more sense after you've started putting the concepts you've learned here into production.

Building a Web Page

In the previous chapter, you learned about the many windows, bars, panels, and menus that Dreamweaver includes to aid you in the development of your web pages. You learned that the Document window is the heart of Dreamweaver and where most of your creative energy will be focused. You also learned that the Document window is surrounded by a myriad of panels contained within user customizable groups that facilitate the addition of functionality for your pages, a feature-rich inspector to assist you in the addition of properties for elements within the Document window, and a complete Menu bar that structures every Dreamweaver feature into an easy-to-use grouped list of options, all of which accommodate users while in both Code or Design view.

Beyond the simplicities of learning the user interface lies creating an actual web page. In this chapter, you'll take the foundation that you gained in the previous chapter and build on it to create a simple web page. Using the many panels, inspectors, and windows that you explored in the previous chapter, you'll create a new page in Design view, work with text within the Document window, add images to your web page, examine linking using hyperlinks, and finally, create a full-featured navigation bar with minimal effort.

You can work with the examples in this chapter by downloading the support files from the book's website. You'll want to save the files contained within the Exercises\ Chapter02\Beginning\ folder in an easy-to-find location on your computer. I'll place mine in C:\VectaCorp\ where VectaCorp represents the fictitious website we'll be building throughout the book.

Creating a New Document

In the previous chapter, you learned that the Welcome screen is a handy window used to open new, existing, or recently accessed documents. Although the Welcome screen will work fine when Dreamweaver has been opened for the first time, it does little good if we need to create a new document when document window instances are already open. In such cases, you'll want to use the New Document dialog box. Accessible by selecting File, New, and shown in Figure 2.1, the New Document dialog box enables you to create new documents based on an existing predefined skeleton file, create new documents based on a prebuilt template, and so on.

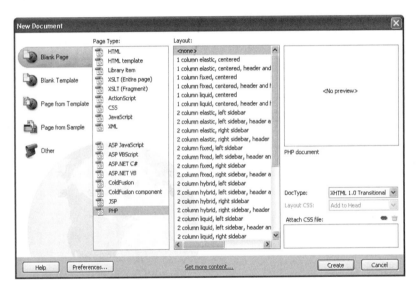

FIGURE 2.1   The New Document dialog box enables you to open new documents, new preconfigured documents, and ready-made templates.

NOTE

You can also create a new document by right-clicking (Control-click) the defined site (covered in greater depth in the next chapter) in the Files panel and selecting the New File option from the context menu. This method simply creates a new document within the Files panel but does not open it automatically within the Document window; by clicking the Files panel options menu and selecting File, New File; by using the keyboard shortcut Ctrl+N on Windows and ⌘-N on a Mac; or by using the New File object on the Standard toolbar.

NOTE

You're probably wondering why there are so many different types of files to choose from in the New Document dialog box. The reason is simple. Because all web pages require a minimum set of tags, Dreamweaver provides what are known as *skeleton files*. The skeleton files that you see in the New Document dialog box help get you started by including tags that the developer must add anyway. For instance, all HTML pages require <html>, <head>, <body>, and <!doctype> tags. Because this is the case, choosing the HTML option from the Blank Page category results in the creation of a new Document window instance, complete with the required tags inserted within Code view.

As you can see from Figure 2.1, the New Document window outlines the following features:

▶ **Category list**—This list includes all selectable page categories.

▶ **Page Type list**—After an option has been selected from the Category list, the Page Type list will display all selectable skeleton files that coincide with the particular category type.

▶ **Layout list**—Available when most Blank Page types and Blank Template types are selected, the Layout list outlines numerous CSS-based layouts that you might want to take advantage of for structuring your web pages. These options will be covered in greater depth in Chapter 6, "Page Structuring Using Cascading Style Sheets." When the Page from Sample category is selected, this list displays a set of prebuilt Adobe web page layouts instead.

▶ **Preview pane**—When a preview is available, the Preview pane displays a small thumbnail of the selected page type.

▶ **Description pane**—When necessary, the Description pane outlines the features and benefits of the selected page type.

▶ **Document Type (DTD)**—This menu allows you to pick from a predefined list of DTDs for your document. A *DTD* states what tags and attributes are used to describe content within an XML or HTML document, where each tag is allowed, and which tags can appear within other tags. Remember, these rules are outlined by the World Wide Web consortium (W3C) and are outlined within a Document Type Definition on W3C servers. When you run Dreamweaver's built-in page validator, the page is validated against the DTD you select here. Options within this list include None, HTML 4.01 Transitional, HTML 4.01 Strict, XHTML 1.0 Transitional, XHTML 1.0 Strict, XHTML 1.1, and XHTML Mobile 1.0.

▶ **Layout CSS**—With this and the previous version of Dreamweaver, the product team made a serious push toward integrating more CSS-based page structuring features. You might have noticed that the Layout category outlines numerous CSS-based page layouts that you can take advantage of. As you will see in Chapter 6, the Layout CSS menu allows you to choose options that place the CSS code within the <head> tag of the page, in an external CSS document, or as a link in your own styles from an existing CSS file.

▶ **Attach CSS File**—Click the Attach Style Sheet icon to launch the Attach Style Sheet dialog box. You can choose this option when you have a prebuilt CSS document that you'd like to link into the newly created page.

▶ **Help**—The option launches Dreamweaver's Help window with the New Document dialog box as the indexed selection.

▶ **Preferences**—This option launches the Preferences dialog box with the New Document category selected. Use this option to change preferences for creating new documents. These options will be covered in the online Appendix C, "Defining Preferences."

▶ **Get More Content**—This option launches the Dreamweaver Exchange. Use this feature to search for more prebuilt skeleton, page design, and template pages.

The focal point of the New Document dialog box lies in the categories and associated page types:

▶ **Blank Page**—Includes skeleton files for creating new HTML, HTML Template, Library Item, XSLT, ActionScript, CSS, JavaScript, XML, ASP JavaScript, ASP VBScript, ASP.NET C#, ASP.NET VB, ColdFusion, ColdFusion Component, JSP, and PHP pages.

▶ **Blank Template**—Includes skeleton files for creating new dynamic template pages for ASP JavaScript, ASP VBScript, ASP.NET C#, ASP.NET VB, ColdFusion, HTML, JSP, and PHP.

▶ **Page from Template**—Choose this category to browse templates that you build. As you'll see in Chapter 3, "Dreamweaver Site Management" and Chapter 12, "Working with Templates and Library Items," user-built templates are stored within defined sites. When this option is selected, the Page Type category outlines your list of defined sites. Choosing a defined site will reveal any templates associated with that site within the Template for Site "<selected site>" list.

▶ **Page from Sample**—Select this option to reveal a subcategory of prebuilt CSS and Frameset starter pages. Choosing a folder from the Sample Folder list reveals numerous prebuilt pages within the Sample Page list. The two types of sample folders that you'll see here are outlined in the following list:

    ▶ **CSS Style Sheets**—Includes a myriad of prebuilt style sheets that you can use to add style and flare to your web pages. We'll cover this topic in more depth in Chapter 5, "Page Formatting Using Cascading Style Sheets."

    ▶ **Framesets**—Includes a number of prebuilt frameset pages that you can use. We'll cover this topic in more depth in the online Appendix D, "Working with Frames and Framesets."

► Other—Includes skeleton files for creating new ActionScript communications, ActionScript remote, C#, EDML, Java, Text, TLD, VB, VBScript, and WML pages. Because these files are seldomly created in Dreamweaver, they're placed into the Other category.

Now that you've gotten a thorough tour of the New Document dialog box, let's use it to create a new HTML page that we can use throughout the chapter. To create a new HTML page, follow these steps:

1. Choose the Blank Page option from the Category pane.

2. Choose the HTML option from the Page Type list.

3. Choose the <none> option from the Layout list, and then click the Create button. The New Document dialog box will close and a new HTML Document window instance will appear, similar to Figure 2.2.

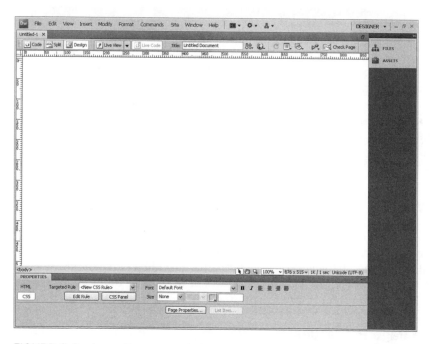

FIGURE 2.2   A new Document window instance can be created from the Blank Page, HTML category within the New Document dialog box.

NOTE

You'll notice that I've collapsed my panels to icons. As was mentioned in the previous chapter, this is a personal preference and can be easily accomplished by either right-clicking onto the panel's heading and choosing Collapse to Icons or by clicking the disclosure triangle that appears just to the left of the Close icon within the tab group. Although I might not always show Dreamweaver in this view, it's done here so that the Document toolbar is not cut off from view.

4. If necessary, switch to Design view by clicking the Design button within the Document toolbar and then immediately save your document (choose File, Save) to the folder that contains the examples for this chapter (C:\VectaCorp\). I'll call mine index.html.

TIP

Most web-hosting providers accept default files named index.html, home.html, and default.html. Naming your starting page with one of these three names guarantees that you won't have to type a fully qualified path such as http://www.vectacorp.com/mystartpage.html. Instead, because I've saved my filename with a standard default page name (index.html), and I can limit the URL reference to www.vectacorp.com. Again, because most web-hosting providers use *index*, *home*, and *default* as standard start page names, falling in line with this naming convention makes referencing your domain easier in the long run.

Working with a New Document in Design View

With a new document window open, we're ready to start working. Throughout this section, we'll explore topics for building a new web page visually within Dreamweaver. Specifically, we'll look at modifying generic page properties including background color, font color, link colors, and more. We'll also look at ways of adding text to the page, formatting it using the Property inspector, checking your spelling, working with lists, and more.

Modifying the Page Properties

Before you begin building a web page, you might want to think about how you want your page to look. Typically, most developers already have a basic idea for the appearance or the color scheme of their web page. I'm sure you're thinking about these options, right? Because you are, Dreamweaver provides properties that you can set for the page. Options such as the page's background color, link colors, margin sizes, encoding, and so on are all accessible from the Page Properties button located within the Property inspector by right-clicking within the Document window and choosing Page Properties, or by selecting Modify, Page Properties (alternatively, press Ctrl+J or ⌘-J on the Mac). When the Page Properties dialog box appears, it is separated into the following categories:

▶ **Appearance (CSS)**—This category contains CSS-specific options for adding a page background, changing the background color, modifying text and link colors, and setting margin widths and heights. These options will be covered with more detail in Chapter 5.

▶ **Appearance (HTML)**—This category contains options for adding a page background, changing the background color, modifying text and link colors, and setting margin widths and heights.

▶ **Links (CSS)**—This category contains CSS-specific options for setting the link font face, size, and color. Additionally, options exist within this menu to set the visited, active, and rollover state of hyperlinks, as well as the decoration style of a hyperlink (whether a hyperlink should be underlined). These options will be covered with more detail in Chapter 5.

▶ **Headings (CSS)**—This category outlines options for redefining the font face, size, and color for the <h1>, <h2>, <h3>, <h4>, <h5>, and <h6> tags. These options will also be covered in more detail in Chapter 5.

▶ **Title/Encoding**—Choose this category to change the title of your document, the DTD for the page, the default encoding type of the page, and the unicode normalization form.

▶ **Tracing Image**—A unique feature to web design, a tracing image makes it possible for you to add a slightly transparent complete version of your web page (as an image) so that you can design the structure of your layout while having the complete version faintly visible in the background to reference.

As I'm sure you've noticed, options within the Page Properties dialog box differ depending on which mode of development you plan on implementing, either HTML or CSS. Whereas CSS is definitely the standard to follow, there's more of a learning curve than is the case with traditional HTML. For this reason HTML-based categories within the Page Properties dialog box are mentioned in this chapter. As we begin to move into Chapter 5, coverage of formatting techniques will begin to transition from HTML-based formatting techniques to CSS-based ones.

Modifying the Appearance

The Appearance (HTML) category enables you to perform numerous tasks associated with modifying the overall look of the page, including setting a background image, changing the background color, choosing text and link colors, and setting margin width and heights. The following is a detailed list of features:

▶ **Background image**—Sets a background image for the page.

▶ **Background**—Choosing this little square icon displays a color palette that allows you to select from one of the 216 web-safe or system colors. Select this option now, choose a color, and then click the Apply button. You'll see that the Document window's entire background changes to the color you selected. You can change this color back to the default of white by clicking the little square icon again and this time choosing the white square with the red line crossed through it within the color palette that appears. This color palette is covered in much more detail later in this chapter.

▶ **Text**—Choose this option to change the default text color of the page. Black is the default.

▶ **Links**—Choose this option to change the default link color within the page. Blue is the default.

▶ **Visited links**—Choose this option to change the visited links color of the page. A *visited link* is the color that appears when a user clicks your link and then revisits the page. Purple is the default.

▶ **Active links**—The *active link* color is the color that appears just as a user's mouse clicks a hyperlink. Black is the default.

▶ **Left margin**—Set a value to change the size of the left margin within the Document window. All browsers except for Netscape 4 use this property.

▶ **Top margin**—Set a value to change the size of the top margin within the Document window. All browsers except for Netscape 4 use this property.

▶ **Margin width**—Set a value to change the size of the left margin within the Document window. The margin width feature is specific to Netscape 4 only.

▶ **Margin height**—Set a value to change the size of the top margin within the Document window. The margin height feature is specific to Netscape 4 only.

NOTE

The biggest difference between the two Appearance categories (HTML and CSS) deals mostly with how the appropriate code is added to the document. When setting the Appearance (HTML) properties, modifications are added to the page as attributes within the <body> tag. When setting the Appearance (CSS) properties, modifications are added by default to a body tag redefinition outlined within a <style> tag contained within the head section of the page. As you'll see later in the book, this is known as a document-wide style sheet.

Now that you have an idea as to the properties of the Appearance (HTML) category, let's set some of these values for our page. Go ahead and change the properties so that they look similar to Figure 2.3.

As you can see, we've changed the background of the page to use the header_bg.gif image located within the Images folder of the files that you downloaded. Additionally, we changed the default Text, Link, and Visited Link colors of the page and modified the top margin and left margin properties for the page to 15 and 0 pixels, respectively. If you click OK, you can see that the page is formatted based on the background image I specified.

You'll also notice that your cursor is blinking with no room to spare at the top of the browser but has about 15 pixels as a margin from the left side of the browser. The text and link modifications will become evident as the chapter unfolds.

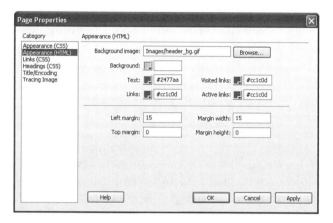

FIGURE 2.3   Modify the appearance of the page.

Looking at the background image in the browser reveals an image that is 1 pixel wide by 1,050 pixels high. The color you see near the top of the page is the image spanning only 142 pixels of the 1,000. The rest of the image is just plain white. This arrangement allows us to fill the Document window with a background image that consumes only the top portion of the page, leaving the rest white for text. You'll also notice that the entire page is consumed by this 1-pixel-wide background image. By default, background images tile horizontally and vertically. So in our case, the 1-pixel background image tiles across the page even if the user expands and contracts the browser window. The image never gets to tile vertically, however, because the image—at 1,050 pixels—is just too large. Even if a user maximized the browser window, it still wouldn't tile unless the screen resolution exceeded that 1,050 pixel depth, or if there were so much text on the page that it would leave no choice than to tile. While this method will serve us well now, best practices dictate using either tables or CSS to limit the size of the image so that it never has a chance to tile. More on this in later chapters.

Title/Encoding

The second selectable option within the Category pane is Title/Encoding. We've covered the topic of titles already (in the previous chapter when we discussed the Title text box in the Document toolbar), and you can also use this category to set the document's encoding type, change the preset DTD, and even change the Unicode normalization form. Because we've covered the DTD topic already (again, this was covered in the previous chapter), let's discuss encoding now. *Encoding* is a system for electronically displaying appropriate characters for different languages in a similar way. Basically, by setting the encoding type, HTML code is added to the page that tells both Dreamweaver and the browser which character set should be used to display the page. In Dreamweaver, the default encoding type used is Unicode (UTF-8)—the most commonly used Unicode format. For the sake of simplicity, we won't be changing that option here. For more information on Unicode however, including a detailed description and history, visit the following Wikipedia page: en.wikipedia.org/wiki/UTF-8.

The next option is Unicode Normalization Form. Available only when Unicode (UTF-8) is selected from the Encoding menu, *Unicode normalization* is the process of making sure all characters that can be saved in different forms are saved using the same form. For example, characters in languages that include emphasis, like Spanish, will all be saved using a similar normalization form. In general, there are four normalization forms: Normalization Form Canonical Decomposition (NFD), Normalization Form Canonical Composition (NFC), Normalization Form Compatibility Decomposition (NFKD), and Normalization Form Compatibility Composition (NFKC). Again, because Unicode normalization isn't as captivating as building a web page, I'll defer to Wikipedia for the details on this topic. For more information, visit the following Wikipedia page: en.wikipedia.org/wiki/Unicode_normalization.

Just below the Unicode Normalization Form menu is the Unicode Signature check box. Click this check box to set the Byte Order Mark (BOM). More information on the BOM can also be found at the following page: en.wikipedia.org/wiki/Byte_Order_Mark.

As you can see, the Title/Encoding section of the Page Properties dialog box can become fairly technical. For our purposes however, we'll use this screen to set the title of the page. As we did from the Document toolbar within the Document window, we'll now change the text that currently reads Untitled Document to The Vecta Corp Company Intranet, as shown in Figure 2.4.

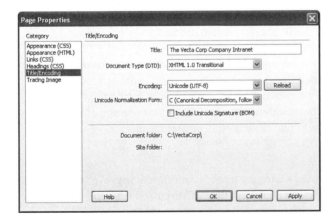

FIGURE 2.4   Change the title of the page.

Again, you can click Apply to see this change applied to your page, or simply click OK to commit the changes to your page and close out the Page Properties dialog box.

The last two text labels that you'll see within this screen outline the document and defined site folders for your project. They are merely read-only labels that you can use as a point of reference.

Tracing Image

The third option available within the Category pane is Tracing Image. As I mentioned earlier, you can use the Tracing Image option to set a temporary background image on the page, set its transparency, and then build your web page on top of the background while using it as a reference or guide for laying out your design. Because of the transparency setting, you can use Dreamweaver elements, such as AP Elements, to design your web page on top of the tracing image as if you were drawing on tracing paper sitting on top of an original document. We'll cover this option with much more detail in Chapter 6.

Working with Text

Now that you've successfully set the properties for the page, it's time to start adding content to it. This next section is devoted entirely to text formatting within the Document window. Although most features are derived from and might seem similar to popular word processing programs, you'll definitely find limitations and workarounds a necessity in some cases.

Copying and Pasting Text from External Sources

The first step in working with content in Dreamweaver is actually getting that content into the development environment. Technically you could just place your cursor into the Document window and begin typing. Although this method will work just fine, a more realistic approach would be to have a content manager within your organization write the content for you. Then, as a developer, you would copy the contents from an external source (such as a text file) and paste it into the Document window. Going with this approach, let's assume that our fictitious Vecta Corp company employs a content manager named Cammy who just happens to be responsible for creating all corporate content. After the content has been written for a specific page, Cammy the content manager emails you the text files for placement on the website. After you have those files, you immediately place them within an Assets folder. What next?

NOTE

If you've looked at the folder for the files that you've downloaded, you'll notice that an Assets folder is already included for you. You'll also notice that I've placed some files in the Assets folder that we'll be referencing throughout the chapter. The two text files, `home.txt` and `footer.txt`, closely resemble text files that a content manager might provide.

Again, you could just print out the content Cammy sent you, tape it to your computer screen, and key what appears on the printed page into the Document window. Not likely, right? Fortunately Dreamweaver includes numerous options for easily adding content to your page from external sources. The most obvious option is to open the text file within Dreamweaver, select all the text (choose Edit, Select All), copy the text (choose Edit, Copy), and then paste it into the page (choose Edit, Paste). Before we jump ahead, however, note that other options for pasting text into your page also exist (within the Edit menu), including the following:

▶ **Paste**—Pastes the copied text into the page with minimal formatting. Formatting is limited to paragraph breaks.

▶ **Paste Special**—When this option is selected, the Paste Special dialog box appears. From this dialog box, you have the option of pasting the raw, unformatted text only (shows as a giant paragraph with no formatting or line breaks), text with structure (includes paragraphs, lists, tables, and so on), text with structure and basic formatting (includes bold, italic, and so on), and text with structure plus full formatting (includes bold, italic, styles, and so on). From this dialog box, you also have the option of deciding to retain any line breaks that are added to the text by the source text editor. And, if you're copying directly from Microsoft Word, you have the option of allowing Dreamweaver to automatically clean up Word's paragraph spacing.

As an example, try opening home.txt from the Assets folder. Next, copy the text from the file (by choosing Edit, Select All and then Edit, Copy), switch back to your Web page, and choose Edit, Paste. As Figure 2.5 shows, the text is inserted into the page with minimal formatting; essentially only line breaks and paragraph breaks are preserved.

Now let's try the Paste Special option. Before you do, undo what you've just pasted in by choosing Edit, Undo Paste as Text. Now to demonstrate the Paste Special option, open the file home.doc, again located within the Assets folder. The file should open directly in Microsoft Word (or a compatible rich text editor). You'll immediately notice that the text includes some basic formatting, including font face, size, color, and a heading for the title. Again, select all of the text and copy it. Now switch back to Dreamweaver and try pasting the text into the Document window using Edit, Paste. You'll notice that the font face, size, and colors are lost when using this option. Clearly we need an alternative method—specifically one that preserves the formatting that was created within our rich text editor. To fix this issue, you'll want to use the Paste Special option. Undo the text you've just pasted in by choosing Edit, Undo Paste as Text. Now select Edit, Paste Special. The Paste Special dialog box will launch, similar to Figure 2.6.

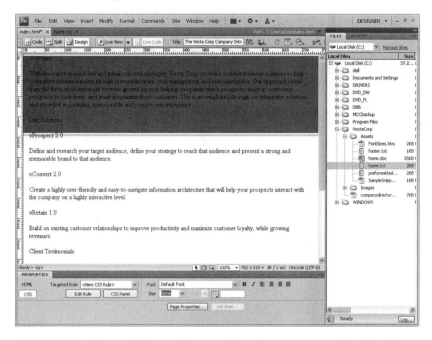

FIGURE 2.5   The copied text is inserted into the web page with minimal formatting.

FIGURE 2.6   The Paste Special dialog box enables you to choose from various formatting options to be applied to text that's being copied from an external source.

Choose the Text with Structure Plus Full Formatting (Bold, Italic, Styles) option and click OK. As you can see from Figure 2.7, for good or bad, the font face, font color, and the font sizes are the same as the original document.

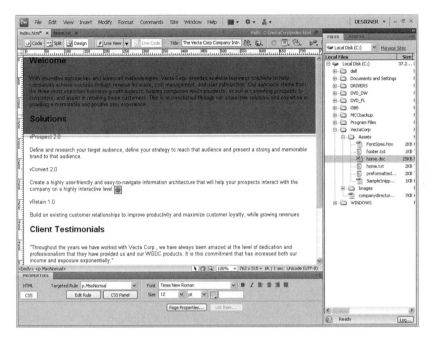

FIGURE 2.7   Formatting including font face, size, and color are retained from the external source.

Be extremely careful when copying and pasting content from a rich text editor such as Word. Rich text editors, Word especially, use a combination of inline and document-wide styles that control the look of a page. To prove this point, try switching over to the Code view now. You'll notice a ton of perplexing code that almost certainly doesn't need to be there for a basic document such as this. Formatting a page that has been pasted in from a copied Word document is very tricky and can become extremely tedious to clean up. Because this is the case, we'll use an alternative method (covered next) for our project. Go ahead and switch back to Design view now and then choose Edit, Undo to revert back to a blank page. Although copying and pasting text into your web pages seems easy enough, it gets easier. You can add text directly into your page without ever having to open the original file in a text editor. To do this, drag the text file titled home.txt (from your file explorer) into your Document window (supported only on a PC). Immediately, the Insert Document dialog box appears, similar to Figure 2.8.

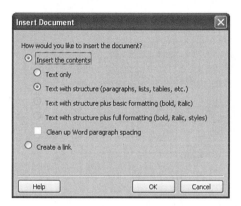

FIGURE 2.8   Make copying and pasting easier by dragging the text file into the page.

The Insert Document dialog box allows you to insert the contents of the file directly into the page or create a link on the page to the text document. Choosing the Insert the Contents option and then choosing the Text Only option results in the text being added to the page as one giant block of text. I know this looks ugly, but don't worry—this is what we want, as it leads into the next topic: text formatting.

> **TIP**
>
> If you're using a Mac and the drag-and-drop method is not possible, simply open the text file, copy the content out of it, revert back to the `index.html` file, select Edit, Paste Special, choose the Text only option, and then click OK.

Text Formatting

Now that the text is on the page, we'll want to format it so that it looks somewhat presentable. For instance, we might want to create headers to separate the text into three distinct parts: Welcome, Our Solutions, and Client Testimonials. Also, you'll notice that our text gets lost at the top of the page because the text color closely matches the color contained within the background image. To fix this problem, we could use paragraph breaks and line breaks to cleanly divide the text into legible sections and at the same time, move it down from the top of the page.

As a start, let's look at line breaks. Line breaks, inserted onto the page by selecting Insert, HTML, Special Characters, Line Break, or by pressing Shift+Enter for Windows or Shift-Return on a Mac, allow you to break one line into two. In our case, we'll use the line break to force breaks into our page, cleanly separating the text from the top of the page until the first sentence is clear of the background. To do this, place your cursor just before the first line of text and press Shift+Enter for Windows and Shift-Return on a Mac 11 times. As you can see from Figure 2.9, the text now clears the background and is much more legible on the white background.

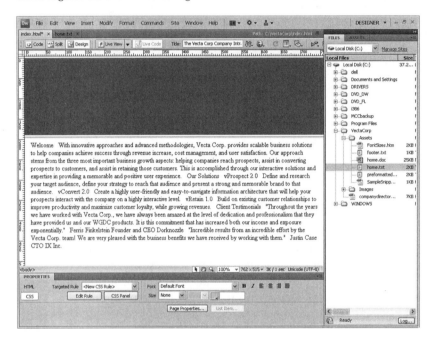

FIGURE 2.9   Use a line break to force text to shift down a few lines.

Alternatively, you could use a paragraph break to divide two or more portions of text into sections that can be easily formatted using various other paragraph-based formatting tools. For instance, alignments, lists, and indenting can be performed only on sections of text that are marked as paragraphs. To give you an idea as to the difference between line breaks and paragraph breaks, try using two more line breaks on your text, randomly placing your cursor within the text and pressing Shift+Enter (Shift-Return on a Mac) twice each time. This will effectively divide your text into three sections similar to Figure 2.10.

Now highlight the first paragraph (beginning with "With innovative approaches..."), right-click it to access the context menu, and choose Align, Center. Now all the text is centered, rather than just the highlighted section.

To correct this problem, we'll choose Edit, Undo Text Alignment until we return to where we started (with one big block of text beginning with "Welcome" just below our background image). Now, instead of using line breaks, use paragraph breaks to divide your text into three sections. This can be accomplished by placing your cursor at the point of the text block where you want to create a paragraph break and pressing Enter once. Repeat this step until your text block has been formatted into three distinct paragraphs similar to Figure 2.11.

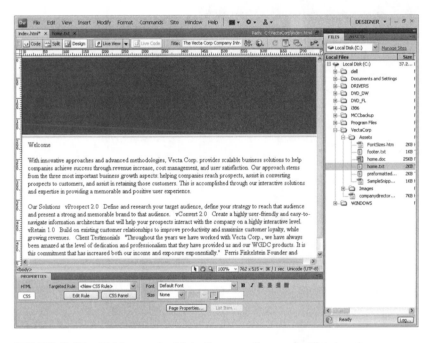

FIGURE 2.10   Divide your text into three sections using line breaks.

Now highlight the first section of text, right-click the highlighted section to access the context menu, and choose Align, Center. This time, only the highlighted section of text is center-aligned.

Whereas line breaks are advantageous in that you can cleanly shift your text down to the next line, paragraph breaks offer much more flexibility because each section that is defined as a paragraph can be formatted independently of other paragraphs.

Another simple formatting technique comes by way of headings. Available from the HTML section in the Property inspector, selectable from the context menu under Paragraph Format, or by choosing Format, Paragraph Format, headings are a generic method for quickly applying formatting to text-based elements on a web page. If you look closely at the Format drop-down menu within the Property inspector for instance, you'll notice that Paragraph is currently selected. Believe it or not, the paragraph break is actually considered a formatting option, whereas the line break is considered a special character (which is why the line break appears within the Special Characters submenu). The advantage is that we can remove the paragraph formatting from a section of text by highlighting it and then choosing None from the Format drop-down menu. Of course, we don't want to do that at this point; instead, we want to review the remaining options within the Format menu, specifically Heading 1 through Heading 6.

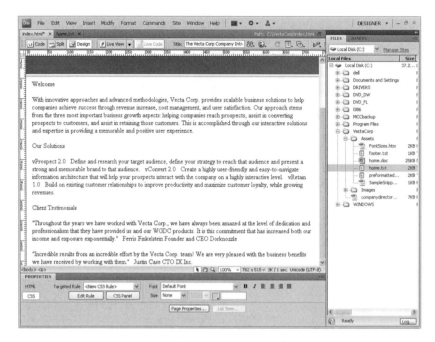

FIGURE 2.11   Paragraph breaks cleanly divide our text into much more easily editable sections.

You can use the six headings available from the Format menu as a way of adding a preconfigured style to text within your page. The browser renders each of the heading options differently, so it's wise to experiment with all of them, so you get an understanding as to the relative dimensions of each. For our example, however, we'll use Heading 3. To demonstrate this heading, we'll highlight the Welcome text and then choose Heading 3 from the Format menu. Repeat this step for the Our Solutions and Client Testimonials text elements. When you're finished, the formatted text will resemble Figure 2.12.

TIP

In HTML, headings (along with other HTML tags) have a predetermined font face, color, and size. As you'll see in Chapter 5, CSS allows for you to override these default properties with your own. Otherwise known as a type selector or tag redefinition, CSS allows for you to literally change the browser rendering engine's default interpretation of the tag to what you outline using CSS!

The final option within the Format menu is the Preformatted option. You'll want to use this option in cases where you have text that was formatted in one editor and you want to preserve the formatting when adding the text within Dreamweaver. To demonstrate this option, follow these steps:

1. Create a new blank HTML document by selecting File, New. Choose the HTML option from the Page Type category, choose None from the Layout category, and click Create.

2. Open the text file titled `preformatted.txt` located in the Assets folder, choose Edit, Select All, and then choose Edit, Copy. Now close the text file.

3. Now place your cursor within the new document and choose Edit, Paste. The text is broken apart and illegible.

4. To fix this and preserve the formatting from the previous editor, press Ctrl+Z (⌘-Z on a Mac) to undo the paste. Next choose the Preformatted option from the Format menu.

5. Immediately choose Paste. This time, the text formatting is preserved.

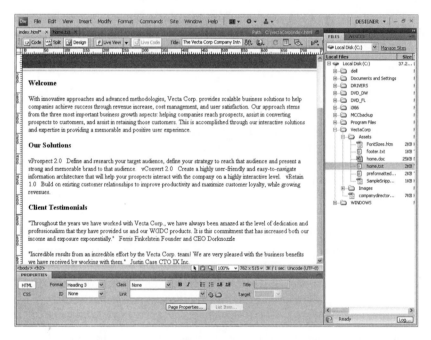

FIGURE 2.12   Choose one of the six Heading options to add a preformatted style to your text.

Choosing Typefaces

Up to this point, you'll notice that our text appears as Times New Roman. Without choosing a font, Dreamweaver defaults to the browser default, which is (in most cases)—you guessed it, Times New Roman. You're not limited to this font, but you *are* limited in terms of how many fonts you can use. Unlike print publishing programs that support thousands of different fonts and type faces, browsers, by default, recognize a select few to maintain maximum viewability across millions of potential web visitors. These few include Verdana,

Georgia, Courier, Courier New, Arial, Helvetica, Tahoma, Trebuchet MS, Arial Black, Times New Roman, Palatino Linotype, Lucida, MS Serif, Lucida Console, Comic Sans MS, as well as slight variations to each.

NOTE

To understand why we're limited in terms of fonts, it is important to understand how browsers identify fonts. Unlike print publishing programs, in which fonts can be bundled with the file for final production, web pages use references to the appropriate type faces on the user's computer. Essentially, you are betting that users viewing your web page also have on their computers the font you are referencing within your page. If they do, the font is loaded and users can view the page as you intended. If they don't, the browser defaults to the font that is set as the default within the browser. Again, this font is usually a serif font such as Time New Roman. Browsers use the previously mentioned fonts as defaults because the majority of Internet users, regardless of platform, have these fonts loaded on their computers.

Dreamweaver allows you to choose from these fonts using various methods. If you're using CSS (which we will, later in the book), you might opt for the CSS section of the Property inspector. Because we're not at that point yet, we'll use other options, specifically the Font category within the context menu that's available by right-clicking on the selection on the page, or by choosing Format, Font. To demonstrate the application of a font, try selecting all the text within the page, right-click on the section, and then choose the Arial, Helvetica, Sans-serif option from the Font submenu. All the text then changes from Times New Roman to Arial.

The next question is, why are three fonts grouped into one option? By default, Dreamweaver organizes sets of fonts into what are known as *font families*, or *font groups*. This is beneficial in the sense that if a user's browser doesn't have the first font in the family (Arial), it defaults to the next font in the family (Helvetica). If a user doesn't have that font either, the browser simply defaults to the next best sans-serif font, the last option within our family.

With all this said, you're not completely out of luck in terms of fonts. For instance, if you're working in an Intranet environment where everyone's computer within your organization is configured the same way, go ahead and use your own fonts. Because the font you'll likely choose will be loaded on the users' computers within your organization, everything should function smoothly. But, how exactly do you incorporate your own fonts? You can create your own font families again by right-clicking on the selection and then choosing Font, Edit Font List, which opens the Edit Font List dialog box shown in Figure 2.13.

As you can see from Figure 2.13, the dialog is broken up into three panes. The first pane, Font List, shows you a list of currently configured font families. The second pane, Available Fonts, shows you a list of all fonts installed on your computer. You can move available fonts into the third pane, Chosen Fonts, to create a font family. To do this, just find fonts that you want to use within the Available Fonts pane and click the twin arrows button to move them over to the Chosen Fonts pane. You'll see the font family build within the Font List pane as you add them to the Chosen Fonts pane. When you've finished configuring your font family, click OK. Now look in the Font menu. The new font family appears within the Font submenu.

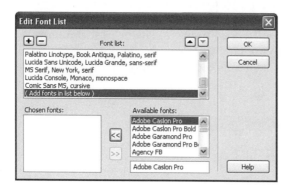

FIGURE 2.13   The Edit Font List dialog box enables you to create your own font families.

TIP

Again, unless you're working in an intranet environment in which you know everyone has the same font installed, you're better off using the default font families referenced within Dreamweaver.

Text Colors

Yet another frustrating topic in web development is that of choosing the right colors for your website. Unlike in print publishing programs or word processing programs, where you can choose from a color palette containing millions of colors, browsers choose from a web-safe color palette of 216 colors that are common to all computers. This guarantees that the colors we choose will be accurately viewed on browsers, independent of platform or operating system.

TIP

Web safe refers to the spectrum of 216 colors that are guaranteed to work on a 256-color (8-bit) computer. When colors were introduced to the Web in the early to mid 1990s, the majority of developers were designing their web pages on antiquated systems that, at best, had an 8-bit video card installed. Because the hardware couldn't support a range beyond 256 colors, a web-safe spectrum of 216 colors was introduced to make web page colors as compatible across the board as possible. Today, these systems are rare, and the need to rely on the web-safe color spectrum has diminished greatly. Realistically, the only time you'd need to rely on the 216 web-safe colors is when development is targeted to small form factor devices, such as a PDA or a cell phone.

Dreamweaver organizes web-safe colors within the Text Color palette available just to the right of the Size menu in the Property inspector (when the CSS category is selected). Additionally, you can modify the color for all of the text on the page in one shot by modifying the Text color property from the Page Properties dialog box. Select this option now by choosing Modify, Page Properties. Notice the Text Color palette icon located just to the right of the Text, Link, Visted Link, and Active Link text labels. Selecting the Text Color palette icon immediately opens the Color palette, also shown in Figure 2.14, and turns the pointer into an eyedropper, allowing you to not only sample colors from within Dreamweaver's interface but also from any other application or image that is visible on your screen.

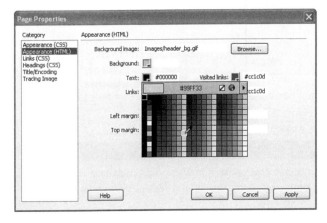

FIGURE 2.14   The Color palette opens, allowing you to sample from a list of colors directly from Dreamweaver's interface—or anything else on your screen.

Here's a complete list of features supported by Dreamweaver's Color palette:

▶ **Color Cubes**—Displays a list of web-safe colors organized within cubes, starting with Black cubes on the left, followed by grayscale cubes, RGB cubes, CMYK cubes, and so on.

▶ **Color Preview**—Displays a larger preview of the color when your mouse rolls over a color cube.

▶ **Hexadecimal Value**—Displays the hexadecimal value of the color when your mouse rolls over the color cube. Explaining the concept of hexadecimal values can be a lengthy topic. For this reason, additional information can be found at the following page: en.wikipedia.org/wiki/Hexadecimal_color.

▶ **Default Color**—Choosing this option returns the selection back to its default color.

▶ **System Color Palette**—Choose this option to select from your system's color palette. The system color palette is a predefined color palette that allows you to choose from millions of colors, rather than the 216 web-safe colors that you get from the standard color cubes.

▶ **Options Menu**—Click this arrow icon for additonal options, including displaying Color Cubes (default), Continuous Tone, Windows OS, MAC OS, and Grayscale.

▶ **Esc**—Press the Esc key on your keyboard to cancel out of the color palette.

> **TIP**
>
> In this example, we used the Text color option within the Page Properties dialog box to set the text color for all of the text on the page. You could, of course, highlight a portion of text on the page and then choose Format, Color to launch the system color palette directly. Doing so allows you to set the font color for a selected element.

> **NOTE**
>
> In this example we relied on HTML-based formatting options for setting the text color. Again, as you'll see in Chapter 5, setting the text color can also be accomplished from the Text Color palette option from the CSS category of options in the Property inspector.

Text Styles

Just to the right of the class menu within the HTML-based Property inspector lie two options for modifying the weight (Bold(B)) and style (Italic(I)) of text in your pages. Bold and italic are two options that you can use in your web pages, but you're certainly not limited to these two. In fact, you can expand the Styles menu by choosing Format, Style to see a complete list of options. Most of the text styles within this list are deprecated, meaning the World Wide Web Consortium doesn't recommend their use because they have been replaced, in most cases by options within CSS. Bold and italic, however, are still common options. To demonstrate how bold can be used, create a few line breaks for each of the three Vecta Corp solutions. Next, select each solution and then click the Bold (B) button within the Property inspector. The text will become bolded, similar to Figure 2.15.

Text Alignment and Indentations

Similar to a word processor, Dreamweaver includes the capability to align your text. Four alignment options are available, including left align, center align, right align, and justify. These options are represented by the four buttons just to the right of the Italic button within the Property inspector when in CSS mode. Additionally, you can choose Format, Align, or right-click the text to access the context menu and choose one of the four options from the Align submenu that appears. To see the alignment features in action, open the text file titled `footer.txt` located in the Assets folder, select all the text, copy it, and paste it somewhere near the bottom of the web page within Dreamweaver. You might have to include more paragraph breaks to force the cursor near the bottom of the page. You might want to enhance this small footer by implementing features that you've already learned, such as changing the font face, font size, and color. When you're done, center the text by right-clicking on the selection to access the context menu and choose Align, Center. The result is shown in Figure 2.16.

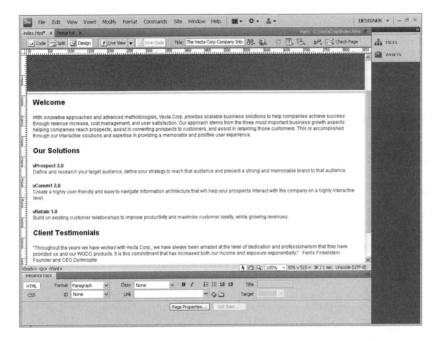

FIGURE 2.15   Vecta Corp solutions become bolded when you highlight them and then click the bold button within the HTML-based Property inspector.

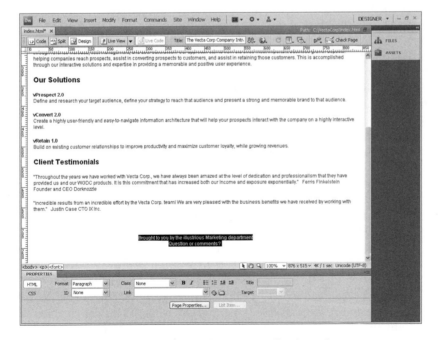

FIGURE 2.16   Format the text and then center-align it on the page.

You can also indent your text by using the Text Indent and Text Outdent buttons located just to the left of the currently disabled Title text box within the HTML-based Property inspector. Additionally, you can select these options by right-clicking on the selection to access the context menu and then choosing List, Indent or Outdent, or select Format, Indent or Format, Outdent to accomplish the same task.

To demonstrate the use of indenting in Dreamweaver, let's assume that I wanted to indent the text that appears below each heading, I would simply select the text and choose Text Indent using one of the methods mentioned previously. The result will appear similar to Figure 2.17.

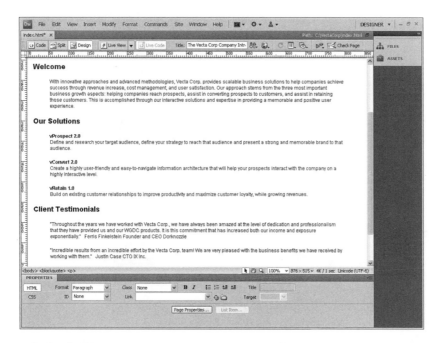

FIGURE 2.17   Choose the Text Indent option to indent your text.

Working with Lists

You can create lists easily within Dreamweaver. Although Dreamweaver supports three types of lists (Ordered, Unordered, and Definition), arguably the more popular—ordered and unordered lists—are available directly from the HTML-based Property inspector by selecting the icons just to the right of the Bold (B) and Italic (I) icons.

Often referred to as *bulleted lists*, unordered lists by default create a bullet circle to the left of the selected item, whereas ordered lists apply a number instead of a bullet to the left of the item and follow in sequential order.

Creating a list in Dreamweaver is a simple process that involves nothing more than high-lighting the text items to include in the list and choosing the appropriate option from the Property inspector. Alternatively, you can place your cursor on the page and choose the list option from the Property inspector. Immediately, a bullet or number is created. You can type your items as you go, pressing Enter to move to the next line, creating a new bullet or incrementing number as you go. To use a list, for example, highlight the three solutions (and their corresponding text): vProspect 2.0, vConvert 2.0, and vRetain 1.0. Then click the Unordered List (Bullets) button within the HTML-based Property inspector. The three Vecta Corp solutions will now be bulleted, similar to Figure 2.18.

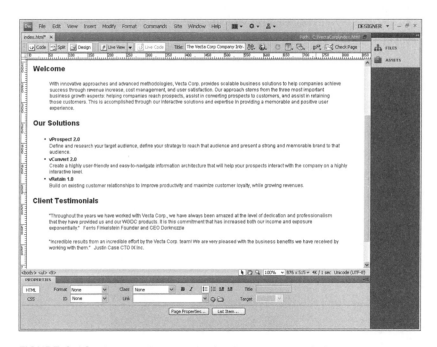

FIGURE 2.18   Create a bulleted list for the company solutions.

To see what the ordered list looks like, highlight the three solutions again and click the Ordered List icon within the Property inspector. As you'll see, the bullets become numbers.

You're not limited to plain bullets or numbers when working with lists. For instance, you can format your lists so that the bullets show as squares and the numbers show as letters or Roman numerals, or even format a specific list item rather than the list as a whole. This can be accomplished by placing your cursor on a list item and clicking the List Item button within the Property inspector. Alternatively, you can right-click the list item to access the context menu and then choose List, Properties or select the bulleted item and choose Format, List, Properties. Choosing this option opens the List Properties dialog box, as shown in Figure 2.19. *This applies only to an already bulleted item. So, Bullet it. Then right click it.*

As you can see from Figure 2.19, the dialog is separated into two parts. The top part enables you to modify the properties of the list as a whole. For instance, with Bulleted List selected in the List type menu, choose Square from the Style menu and click OK. You'll notice that all the bullets for the list items are changed to squares. The second half of the dialog (List Item) enables you to modify the properties of an individual list item rather than the list as a whole. You can choose to work with Roman numerals or letters by selecting Numbered List from the List Type menu and choosing the appropriate option from the Style menu. After you've done this, you can even create a starting number by entering that value within the Start Count text box.

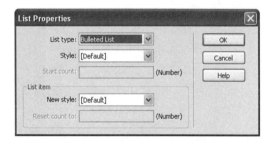

FIGURE 2.19   You can modify list item properties by opening the List Properties dialog.

The third type of list supported by Dreamweaver is the Definition list. Available by selecting Format, List, Definition List, the Definition list enables you to create a list that resembles a dictionary definition—where a definition appears indented below the term. To create your own Definition list, follow these steps:

1. Create a new blank page for testing purposes.
2. Copy the welcome text (the Welcome header and its corresponding text) from the previous page (`index.html`) and paste it into the new testing page.
3. Highlight the text and choose Definition List from the List submenu of the Text menu.
4. Place your cursor just before the second sentence, choose Backspace, and press Enter.

The "definition" is indented, and the list looks very similar to a dictionary definition.

Using Special Characters

Dreamweaver includes a library of special characters that you can use within your web pages. *Special characters* are text elements that must be inserted using special code because a keyboard key doesn't exist for it. For instance, left and right quotes, dashes, the euro symbol, the English pound sterling symbol, the Japanese yen symbol, copyright symbols, registration marks, trademarks, and more are all considered special characters and must be inserted using the Text category within the Insert panel (see Figure 2.20).

TIP

Special characters are also available from the Insert, HTML, Special Characters submenu.

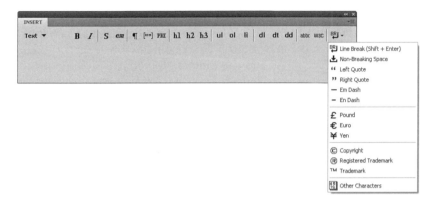

FIGURE 2.20   The text category of the Insert panel contains a submenu of special characters.

You're also not limited to the special characters outlined within this list. For instance, Dreamweaver includes a character map that provides numerous other special characters that you can insert into your page. To open the character map, choose the Other Characters option from the Special Characters submenu. As you can see from Figure 2.21, the Insert Other Character dialog box appears with numerous other special characters.

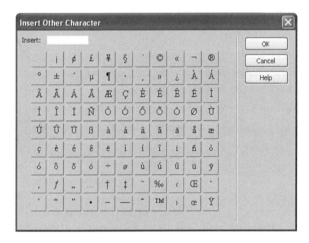

FIGURE 2.21   Use the Insert Other Character dialog box to insert characters other than those listed within the submenu.

The last special character that you can insert is the Non-Breaking Space. The Non-Breaking Space, which is similar to pressing the spacebar in most word-processing programs, simply inserts a space. By default, browsers ignore more than one blank space within HTML code. Therefore, a Non-Breaking Space, represented by the special character , must be inserted to alert the browser that a space should be recognized.

Unfortunately, Dreamweaver doesn't map the spacebar to automatically insert a Non-Breaking Space. Instead, you have to press Ctrl+Shift+Space/⌘-Shift-Space to insert this special character. If you want to make inserting a Non-Breaking Space easier, you can modify Dreamweaver Preferences to automatically insert a Non-Breaking Space when you press the spacebar. To do this, choose Edit, Preferences. From the General category, enable the Allow Multiple Consecutive Spaces option and click OK. To test the functionality, place your cursor anywhere on the page and press the spacebar repeatedly. You'll quickly notice the advantage.

Checking Your Spelling

One of the last things that I like to do before calling a web page finished is to check the spelling. Dreamweaver integrates a spell-checking engine that functions similar to those found in popular word processing programs. To use the spell checker built into Dreamweaver, select the Check Spelling option from the Commands menu or press Shift+F7. The Check Spelling dialog box appears. The Check Spelling dialog includes the following functionality:

▶ **Word not found in dictionary**—As Dreamweaver scans your document, words that are not found within Dreamweaver's dictionary are listed here one at a time.

▶ **Suggestions and Change To**—When the spell checker has located a word that is not in Dreamweaver's dictionary, it makes a list of suggestions. You can select a word from this suggestion list and click Change to replace your word with the word highlighted within the Change To text box.

▶ **Add to Personal**—You can add a word to your personal dictionary so that Dreamweaver doesn't detect it as a misspelled word the next time you run the spell checker.

▶ **Ignore**—Ignores and skips over the selected word.

▶ **Change**—Changes the word within the page to the suggested word.

▶ **Ignore All**—Ignores all instances of a selected word.

▶ **Change All**—Changes all instances of a selected word.

When you've finished performing a spell check, you can click Close to return to the Document window.

Inserting the Time and Date

Dreamweaver includes functionality for inserting a time and date stamp. Available from the Insert menu (or the Common category in the Insert panel), the Date option opens the Insert Date dialog box, as shown in Figure 2.22.

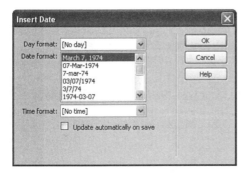

FIGURE 2.22   The Insert Date dialog box enables you to insert a time and date stamp.

As you can see from Figure 2.22, the Insert Date dialog box enables you to choose a day format represented by the Day Format menu, a date format represented within the Date Format menu, and a time format represented by the Time Format menu. You can also allow Dreamweaver to automatically modify the time and/or date stamp when the document is saved. To insert a time and date stamp within our project, follow these steps:

1. Insert the text **Page Last Updated:** just below the footer. You might need to format the text according to the modifications that you've made on the page thus far.

2. Place your cursor to the right of the text you just added and choose Insert, Date. The Insert Date dialog box will appear similar to Figure 2.22.

3. Pick a date format from the Date format list, check the Update Automatically On Save check box, and choose OK. The date will appear next to the text.

4. Format the text, applying a font, size, and color so that it appears similar to Figure 2.23.

Inserting a Horizontal Rule

Another simple design element that you can add to your web pages is the horizontal rule. Available from the Insert, HTML menu, the horizontal rule adds a straight horizontal line across the page. To demonstrate the horizontal rule, I'll place my cursor just before the footer that we inserted at the bottom of the page. Next, I'll add the horizontal rule by choosing Insert, HTML, Horizontal Rule. Shown in Figure 2.24, the horizontal rule adds a straight line across the page at a width of 100%.

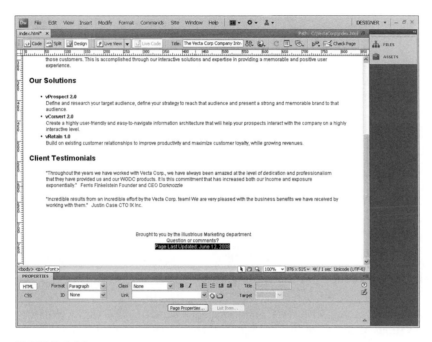

FIGURE 2.23   Insert a date and/or time stamp within your page.

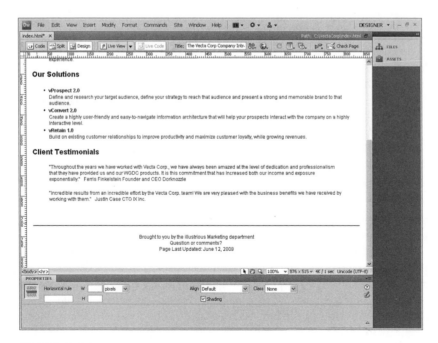

FIGURE 2.24   A horizontal rule is added to the page at a default width of 100%.

Select the horizontal rule and, in the Horizontal Rule Property inspector, you can now make the following property modifications:

- **ID**—Uniquely identifies your horizontal rule. The ID is useful in this case in scenarios where you wanted to maybe control the visibility of the horizontal rule using JavaScript and/or CSS. Without unique identifying the rule, this would not be possible.

- **Width**—Changes the width in either pixels or percent for the horizontal rule. The default is 100%.

- **Height**—Sets the height in pixels for the horizontal rule. The default is 2 pixels.

- **Align**—Aligns the horizontal rule left, center, or right on the page. The default is center.

- **Shading**—Enables or disables shading on the horizontal rule. Disabling this box causes the horizontal rule to be a solid, flat line.

- **Class**—Assigns a CSS class to your horizontal rule.

Go ahead and familiarize yourself with the Horizontal Rule Property inspector by experimenting with the various settings. For our example, I'll change the width to 300 pixels, height to 1 pixel, and uncheck the Shading check box.

Working with Images

One of the more convoluted topics as it relates to the web is that of images. As with fonts, colors, and file sizes, you're limited in the types of images you can use. In addition, because you're dealing with the Web, bandwidth becomes an issue. For this reason, images must usually remain small, resulting in degradation of quality and loss of color variation. Although print publishers have a wide array of image choices—including EPS, TIF, JPEG, BMP, PCX, PICT, PNG, and so on—and are not limited by file size, web developers are limited to working with GIF, JPEG, and PNG, and must use tools to optimize the images before they're generally ready for use within web pages. Knowing what types of images to use can also become an important factor as you design for the Web. As a general rule, GIF, JPEG, and PNG files should be used as follows:

- **GIF**—Graphical Interchange Format (GIF) is used for images or graphics with smaller amounts of color and graphics without much tonal range. Because GIFs read color in a horizontal line, the more color the format encounters when reading, the larger the file size. Also, because GIFs read color in a horizontal line, too much color gradation can result in *banding*—the process of gradients being broken up into bands representing a lower dimension of color variation. GIFs also have a color table attached to them that dictates to the graphic how many colors and which colors can be used in the artwork. More colors in the color table yield larger file sizes. GIFs can also store transparencies and animations but are ideal when used for flat, lower-colored graphics such as cartoons or clip art.

▶ **JPEG**—Joint Photographic Experts Group (JPEG or JPG) is a lossy compression standard used on graphics with high tonal ranges, such as photographs. This compression standard removes pixels from an image to reduce the file size. Too much compression can result in artifacts, which causes the image to look blurry and unclear. As a general rule, use the JPEG file format when adding pictures that contain a lot of gradation, such as family photos, to your websites.

▶ **PNG**—Portable Network Graphics (PNG) were introduced as a replacement to GIF in the mid-1990s and was supported by the W3C as a proposed web standard in late 1996. As an example of the flexibility of the PNG format, Adobe Fireworks adopted this format as its native file type. PNG holds a number of advantages over GIF files on the Web. First, color features are greater in that PNG supports photorealistic color depths, like JPEG, as well as alpha transparencies, which means you can have 256 levels of transparency instead of just on and off as in GIF; cross-platform control of image brightness; and two-dimensional interlacing (a method of progressive display that is similar to JPEG). PNG also compresses 5%–25% better than GIF, making it an attractive format for web developers. The only thing holding back the widespread use of PNG files on the Web was the poor level of support in older versions of Microsoft's Internet Explorer. As of the 2006 release of IE7, the main issues with displaying PNG files have been addressed, making the use of this format much more viable.

As a general rule, if you're working with flat, solid images, use GIF. However, if you're working with images with a lot of color gradation, such as photographs, use JPEG. If you are working with photographic-type images that require multiple levels of transparence, use PNG.

Inserting Images into a Dreamweaver Document

The traditional Dreamweaver method of inserting an image is to use the browse-to-file method, in which you select Insert, Image, browse to your file, and click Open to insert the image within the page. However, Dreamweaver also features a drag-and-drop method of inserting images directly from the File list. Before we jump ahead of ourselves, however, let's review the process of inserting an image by browsing to the image file using the Select Image Source dialog box. To use this method, follow these steps:

1. Start by placing your cursor at the top of the page.

2. Choose the Image option from the Insert menu or select the Image icon from the Images submenu of the Common category within the Insert panel. Either method will open the Select Image Source dialog box.

3. Now browse for the file `header.gif` located within the Images folder of the project files that you copied over (located within `C:\VectaCorp\Images`). As you can see from

Figure 2.25, the filename, an image preview, and the dimensions in terms of size and approximate download time based on file size are displayed within the dialog box.

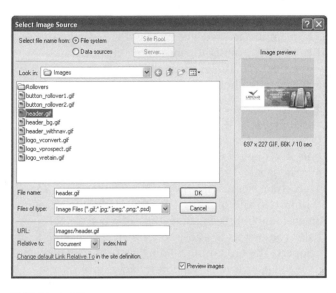

FIGURE 2.25   Browse to `header.gif` so that you can see the filename and the image preview.

4. Aside from simple browsing and previewing, the Select Image Source dialog box also includes the capability to browse by file type, enable and disable image previewing, and allows you to set the file path method (document or site root relative) for the file. For our example, simply click OK.

NOTE

After you click OK, the Image Tag Accessibility Attributes dialog box appears. Because accessibility is addressed extensively in the online Appendix A, "Accessibility," for now just click the Change the Accessibility Preferences link located at the bottom of the dialog box. The Preferences dialog box will appear with the Accessibility category selected. Uncheck all four check boxes (Form Objects, Frames, Media, and Images) and click OK. Click Cancel to close the Image Tag Accessibility Attributes dialog box.

The image is inserted at the top of the page and blends in nicely to our background image. You might need to remove extra line breaks between the image and the Welcome heading (place your cursor just before the Welcome heading and press Backspace on your keyboard nine times) to get your design to look like Figure 2.26.

FIGURE 2.26   The inserted header image blends in nicely to our background image.

A second option for inserting images is to drag-and drop the images directly from the Files panel. Unfortunately, this method works only when you have a defined site. Because we won't be working with defined sites until the next chapter, we'll defer discussion of this method until later.

Formatting Images Within a Document

Like every other element that can be inserted into your web pages, images allow you to format numerous properties directly from the Property inspector. As an example, highlight the three solution elements and then uncheck the Unordered List button to remove the bulleted listing. Now place your cursor to the immediate left of the first item (vProspect 2.0) and choose Insert, Image. When the Insert Image dialog box appears, browse to the logo_vprospect.gif image and click OK. The image will be inserted next to its associated text blurb. Repeat this process for the other two solution elements. Your page should currently resemble Figure 2.27.

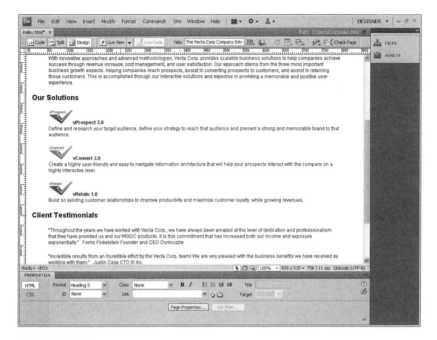

FIGURE 2.27   Remove the list formatting for the three solutions and then add each solution's representative image.

Immediately, you'll notice that the text doesn't wrap nicely around the images. Setting the text alignment is just one of the many features outlined within the Property inspector. A detailed list of each feature, moving from left to right and from basic to advanced is outlined next:

▶ **Image Thumbnail**—Shows a small thumbnail of the selected image.

▶ **Image Size**—Displays the selected image's size in kilobytes.

▶ **ID**—Provides a method for uniquely identifying the selected image.

▶ **W and H**—Shows the width and height of the image, as defined by the binary makeup of the image. You may change these values, in which case Dreamweaver will stretch the dimensions of the image (values will be shown in boldface). However, I don't recommend stretching an image because it degrades the quality of the image substantially. Instead, resample an image using an image editor such as Photoshop or Fireworks.

▶ **Src**—Short for *source*, this is the file path to the image on your computer. This value can also be an external web address, in which case the image shows broken until viewed within the browser.

▶ **Link**—Add a hyperlink to your image here. Hyperlinks are outlined with more detail later in this chapter.

▶ **Alt**—For accessibility purposes, you'll want to enter alternate text here. Entering alternate text is beneficial for a variety of reasons. First, it allows text-to-speech readers to present the alternate text to visually impaired users. Second, in Internet Explorer, a yellow ToolTip appears with the alternate text when a user hovers over the image. Finally, on slower connections, the alternate text appears first while the image is loading. See online Appendix A for more about alternate text.

▶ **Edit**—Dreamweaver incorporates minimal editing functionality within this group of icons. For instance, you can open the selected image directly in Photoshop or Fireworks for editing or optimizing. You can also launch the image optimization window (covered in more detail later in the chapter), or if you're using Smart Objects, you can click the Update from Original button to update the included image based on a modified original PSD file. This integration is covered with more detail in Chapter 14, "Integrating with Photoshop, Fireworks and Flash."

▶ **Class**—Allows you to apply a CSS class to your image.

▶ **Image Map**—Discussed in more detail later in this chapter, an *image map* is a method for creating multiple hyperlinked hotspots within a selected image.

▶ **V Space and H Space**—Enter values here to create vertical and horizontal spacing in pixels around your image.

▶ **Target**—When a value is added to the Link text box, this menu becomes enabled. Targets, as you will see, provide a method for targeting browser windows when a user is linked from one web page to the next.

▶ **Original**—Use this feature when you want to associate an image file with an original PDF or PNG file. Doing this is ideal in roundtrip graphics editing scenarios. Covered in more detail later in the book, *roundtrip graphics editing* refers to the process of associating an image file with its original layered PSD or PNG file. This way, when changes need to be made to the image, you can simply select the image and click an icon to launch the original version in the image editing program. You can then make your necessary modifications and click the Done button, at which point the original PSD/PNG file is saved, the image editing program closes itself, and the exported file within Dreamweaver is updated. This Original path is required when working with true roundtrip graphics editing.

▶ **Border**—Use the Border text box to add a border around your image in pixels. The color of the border depends on the default text color within the page and cannot be independently changed.

▶ **Crop, Resample, Brightness/Contrast, Sharpen**—Click one of these four buttons to quickly crop, resample, sharpen, or change the brightness and/or contrast of a selected image. Be extremely careful when using this option, as changes you make using these buttons result in permanent modifications. Personally, I would recommend not using these features and instead, use software that is devoted to image editing tasks such as Photoshop or Fireworks.

▶ **Align**—Provides options for aligning the text around an image. Options include Baseline, Top, Middle, Bottom, TextTop, Absolute Middle, Absolute Bottom, Left, and Right. The default is Bottom.

Although we'll eventually use most, if not all, of these features throughout the book, for now, format the properties of the image so that you've selected the Left option from the Align menu for each image. The result will resemble Figure 2.28.

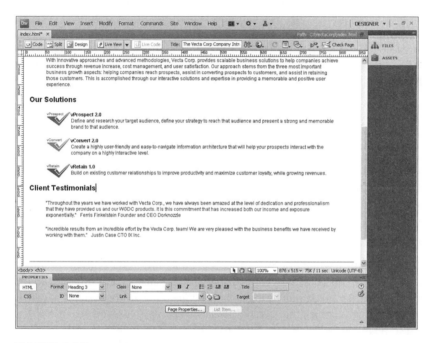

FIGURE 2.28   Modify the alignment of the image.

You'll notice that the text wraps nicely around the right side of each image.

Image Placeholders

Image Placeholders are handy to use in prototyping scenarios, or in cases in which you as a developer are relying on a graphic designer to provide imagery. Image Placeholders, as their name implies, are temporary image references that represent the dimensions of the finished product and are simply meant to show that something (an image) will end up taking its place. After you've inserted an Image Placeholder, you can easily adjust width and height dimensions and color to your liking. When you're content with the dimensions, you can then select the Create option from the Property inspector to launch Fireworks or Photoshop and begin creating the "real" image that will take the Placeholder's place. To see how Image Placeholders work, follow these instructions:

1. Place your cursor just before the Welcome text and choose Insert, Image Objects, Image Placeholder.

2. The Image Placeholder dialog box appears, allowing you to give your placeholder a name, width, height, color, and for accessibility reasons, the option to insert alternate text. For our purposes, name the placeholder **SamplePlaceholder**, and assign the dimensions of 300 for width and 50 for height. Change the color to the blue color within the background header bar, and click OK.

3. The temporary Image Placeholder appears on the page as a solid color image similar to Figure 2.29.

FIGURE 2.29   The Image Placeholder appears on the page as a solid color image.

You'll notice that the Image Placeholder includes the name and dimensions. Selecting the Image Placeholder reveals the Image Placeholder Property inspector (which is similar to the Image-Based Property inspector), which allows you to freely modify the width, height, and color. The Image Placeholder Property inspector also features the Create button, which, when clicked, opens Adobe Fireworks (assuming it is installed), complete with a new document that is sized according to the Image Placeholder dimensions. We'll be discussing Dreamweaver and Fireworks integration in more detail in Chapter 14. Again, the idea behind the Image Placeholder is that it allows you to begin the layout of the page without having all the images at hand. You can use Image Placeholders and then replace the placeholders with the final images when they become ready.

Rollover Images

Creating images that change appearance when a user's cursor rolls over the image, otherwise known as *rollover images*, have traditionally been a tricky task for web developers. In
the past, web developers begged, borrowed, and stole JavaScript code that they could
"plug into" their websites to perform this operation. Fortunately for you, Dreamweaver
includes an intuitive Insert Rollover Image dialog box, available by choosing Insert, Image
Objects, Rollover Image. As long as you supply the images, Dreamweaver will supply the
code to get your image rollovers to work. To insert a rollover image within the page,
follow these steps:

1. Place your cursor just above the horizontal rule located near the bottom of the page.

2. Select Insert, Image Objects, Rollover Image. The Insert Rollover Image dialog box
   appears.

3. Format the Insert Rollover Image dialog box similar to Figure 2.30, giving your
   image a unique name, choosing the button_rollover1.gif image for the original
   image and button_rollover2.gif for the rollover image. Again, these images are
   contained within the Images folder for the project files that you downloaded at the
   beginning of the chapter.

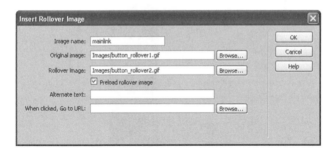

FIGURE 2.30   Give your rollover image a unique name and then assign GIF images for the original and rollover states.

4. As you can see from Figure 2.30, the dialog box allows you to insert an image name,
   assign two image states (typically these two images will have the same size and text
   but will differ in color), alternate text, and a hyperlink. The dialog box also allows
   you to add functionality that forces the browser to preload both images before the
   original is loaded. After you've formatted the properties, click OK.

When the rollover appears, immediately center the image so that it lines up with the
footer. The placement should resemble Figure 2.31.

Now try viewing your page in the browser by choosing the Preview in Browser option
from the Document toolbar (as was discussed in the previous chapter), or by pressing F12
(Option-F12). Within the browser, try moving your cursor over the new image. You'll
notice that the original image (button_rollover1.gif) changes color to its rollover state

(`button_rollover2.gif`) when your mouse moves over the image. Alternatively, you could use a new Dreamweaver CS4 feature in Live View to preview your page without having to use the preview in browser option. To use the Live View feature now, click the Live View button. Dreamweaver will switch to its Live View mode. Again, try rolling over the image. Your rollover should function exactly as it did within the browser.

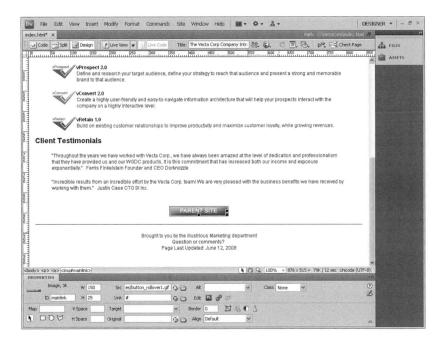

FIGURE 2.31   The original image appears just above the horizontal rule.

There are numerous methods for creating rollover images. As the book unfolds, we'll look at others. For now, this is the simplest method that Dreamweaver offers.

Working with Hyperlinks

One of the basic premises of working with the Web is that we can create pages that link. This concept, known as *hyperlinking*, is the foundation behind the Hypertext Markup Language (HTML). By adding some text to the page and then associating a link with that text, we can allow our users to interact with multiple pages within a website, rather than being confined to a single page. Like other web features, Dreamweaver has excellent support for creating and working with the following types of links:

- ▶ Text links
- ▶ Email links
- ▶ Image links
- ▶ Image maps

▶ Named anchors

▶ Navigation bars

Before we jump directly into linking, however, it's important to discuss the concept of paths and targets. Creating a hyperlink is merely the process of assigning a path to the hyperlink reference (href) of text, images, hotspots within image maps, or anchors. When you assign a path to one of these elements, you are making a link available from your linked element to the endpoint via the path. When it comes to paths, developers have three to work with:

▶ **Document Relative**—Possibly the easiest type of path to work with, Document Relative paths require little more than the path from the current file to the target file. For instance, if I am working with a file located in the folder VectaCorp\Departments\Marketing\Press Releases\ and I need to link to a file called marketing.htm within the Marketing folder, I would simply use ../../marketing.html as my path. The ../ essentially forces the browser to back out of the current folder. The same holds true if I am working with a file within the same Press Releases folder and I need to reference an image within the Images folder located within the Press Releases folder. In that case, my path would resemble Images/file.gif. Simple enough, right? The downside to working with Document Relative paths is that you can back out of only so many folders (two) before it becomes impractical. If you're working within a lengthy folder structure, the Site Root Relative path might be your answer.

▶ **Site Root Relative**—The upside to Site Root Relative paths is that they have no limit to folder depth. For instance, the example in the Document Relative path description references the path VectaCorp\Departments\Marketing\Press Releases. If I am working with a file within the Press Releases folder and need to link to the file index.html within the VectaCorp folder root, I could use a Site Root Relative path to reference the path /index.html. The / instructs the browser to find the site root and then retrieve index.html.

NOTE

By default, Dreamweaver works with Document Relative paths. If you want to work with Site Root Relative paths, you'll have to configure it when you define a site. This is covered in more detail in the next chapter.

▶ **Absolute**—You can use Absolute paths when referencing files located in paths that don't change. For instance, the domain name www.vectacorp.com or www.dreamweaverunleashed.com will never change. They are said to be *absolute*. Because this is the case, I could assign these domain names as my Absolute paths. Furthermore, I could also use a specifc folder within that domain. For instance, if I wanted to reference an image within the Images folder of the www.vectacorp.com site, I could reference its Absolute path as follows: www.vectacorp.com/Images/image.gif.

After you've assigned a path to an element within your web page to create a link, you might also want to declare a target. A *target* exists as a way of instructing the browser how to open the path. For instance, the following four targets can be assigned when you're working with hyperlinks:

▶ **_self**—Opens the path within the same browser window as the original page. This target is the default.

▶ **_blank**—Forces the browser to open the path within a new browser window instance. This keeps the original page in the background.

▶ **_parent**—When working with frames, choose this option to load the linked document in the parent frame or parent window of the frame that contains the link. If the frame containing the link is not nested, the linked document loads in the full browser window.

▶ **_top**—When working with framesets, choose this option when you want to load a linked document in a full browser window, thereby removing all frames.

> **NOTE**
>
> The Target drop-down menu is always located near the Link text box within the Property inspector, regardless of whether you're working with text-based links, image-based links, and so on.

Linking Text

Arguably the easiest form of hyperlinking, creating text links, can be performed in one of three ways. First, we can type the text onto the page, highlight it, and then enter a path into the Link text box within the Property inspector. Second, we can place our cursor where we want the link to appear on the page and select Insert, Hyperlink. This method generates the text and link at the same time. Finally, we can highlight existing text on the page, right-click (Control-click) to access the context menu, and choose the Make Link option. Either of these three methods performs the same task.

Although we will not walk through each method, it's important to note that each functions in a similar manner. When you've got one method down, the other two are just as simple. For now, we'll focus on creating text links by typing text onto the page and generating a link within the Property inspector (as you'll be using this tool most often for other operations, anyway). To do this, follow these steps:

1. Highlight the text Vecta Corp. on the first line of the opening paragraph.

2. Enter the absolute path **http://www.vectacorp.com** into the Link text box within the Property inspector and press Enter/Return to commit the change. You'll immediately notice that the text is underlined and becomes a redish color similar to Figure 2.32. The text is Red (#cc1c0d) because that was the color we assigned it when

we defined our link colors in the Page Properties dialog box earlier in the chapter, and it's underlined because that's the default style that is automatically applied to hyperlinks.

FIGURE 2.32   A link is created from the highlighted text.

3. With the link now created, preview your page in the browser by selecting Preview in Browser from the Document toolbar or choose F12 (Option-F12). As you'll see, clicking the link redirects the user to the real Vecta Corp website.

You can also change the target of the link to _blank, thus forcing the Vecta Corp website to open within its own browser window instead of replacing the existing site.

Another method for inserting hyperlinks is to choose the Hyperlink option from the Insert menu. Choosing this option launches the Hyperlink dialog box, as shown in Figure 2.33.

As you can see from Figure 2.33, the dialog box supports the following properties:

▶ **Text**—Enter the text that should be linked here.

▶ **Link**—Enter or browse to the path of the link here.

▶ **Target**—Choose a target (_blank, _parent, _self, or _top) from this menu.

FIGURE 2.33 The Hyperlink dialog box enables you to create a hyperlink on the page.

▶ **Title**—Whereas setting the Alt attribute displays a yellow ToolTip in Internet Explorer and nothing in Firefox, when the user's mouse rolls over the hyperlink, the Title attribute displays the yellow ToolTip in all browsers. Technically, the Title attribute is the standards-compliant method for titling a hyperlink.

▶ **Access Key**—Use this attribute to set a shortcut key for the hyperlink. For instance, entering the letter **M** here allows me to press Alt+M to highlight and ultimately trigger the hyperlink within the browser.

▶ **Tab Index**—Set this text box to a numeric value when the current hyperlink appears within a long list of hyperlinks. Doing this will set the numeric order when a user tabs through links.

As you can see, this technique provides a more complete method for creating a text-based hyperlink.

Email Links

Aside from linking directly to external websites or to files located within the same folder, you can also use the Link text box within the Property inspector to provide a link for users to send email. For instance, the footer of our page has a sentence that reads Questions or Comments. We could turn this sentence into a link that, when clicked, opens the user's default email program complete with an email address, subject, and so on. To do this, follow these instructions:

1. Highlight the text "Questions or Comments?" as if you were creating a hyperlink.

2. Enter the text **mailto:** followed by the email address that you want to appear in the To: field of the email program within the Link text box in the Property inspector. For instance, I'll type **mailto:webmaster@vectacorp.com.**

3. If you would like a subject to appear when the email program is launched, enter the email address, followed by a **?Subject=**, and then the subject text you would like to appear. For instance, I'll type **mailto:webmaster@vectacorp.com?Subject=Question about the site.**

> **TIP**
>
> Although we've used Subject as an example here, you could also prefill the Body, CC, and/or BCC fields within the new email message. To do this, simply append the `mailto:` link with the appropriate field. For instance, if we wanted to add CC, the formatted link would resemble this: **mailto:webmaster@vectacorp. com?Subject=Question about the site&CC=webdev@vectacorp.com**.

4. Save your work and test the results in the browser by selecting the Preview in Browser option from the Document toolbar or press F12 (Option-F12). After the page appears in the browser, select the link to launch the email program complete with the To and Subject fields prepopulated, similar to Figure 2.34.

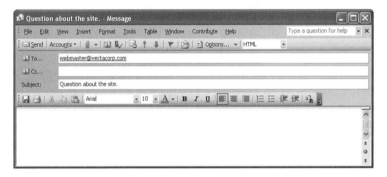

FIGURE 2.34   Use the mailto: option within the Link text box to create an email link on your web page.

To accomplish the same task, you could also choose Insert, Email Link. The Email Link dialog box allows you to enter the text to appear on the page and the email address to be associated with the text.

Linking Images

Aside from linking text, you can also create links from images. Selecting an image reveals the image-based Property inspector, which, like the text-based Property inspector, features a Link text box and a Target menu. To learn how to create a link from an image, follow these steps:

1. Select the vProspect image that you added earlier within the Our Solution section.

2. Type **http://www.vectacorp.com/vc/solutions.html** into the Link text box on the Image Property inspector and press Tab. Repeat steps 1 and 2, adding links for the vConvert and vRetain images as well.

3. Save your work and then select the Preview in Browser option from the Document toolbar to test the results within a browser window.

In this case, you created a link for an image to a page that currently exists (the finished fictitious Vecta Corp site). As you progress through the book, you'll be linking to a page within your project folder (otherwise known as a defined site). For now, because we haven't built many pages, we're merely experimenting with a page that already exists.

Image Maps

The third method of linking is to define an image map. An *image map* can be defined as a series of hot spots within an image that, when clicked, navigate the user to the specified page. For our image map, we'll use a different header image called `header_withnav.gif`, essentially replacing our existing `header.gif` image with this version. To replace our existing `header.gif` image with the `header_withnav.gif` image, start by selecting the header image within the page. Next, click the yellow folder icon next to the Src text box on the Property inspector. The Select Image Source dialog box will appear. Now browse to the `header_withnav.gif` image, select it, and click OK (Choose). The existing header image will be replaced with this newest version, also shown in Figure 2.35.

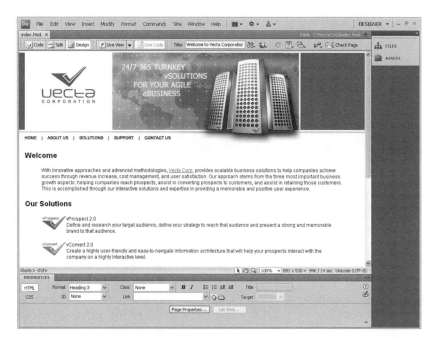

FIGURE 2.35   The newest header image contains text in the image, made to simulate the look of a link.

As you can see, the new image contains links that were created within an image editor to simulate text links. We'll want to define areas within the image so that the linking experience is as seamless as possible. This can be done by creating an image map. You can define an image map within the new image by following these steps:

1. Select the image.

2. The bottom-left corner of the Image Property inspector defines options for working with image maps and hot spots, including the Map Name text box, the Pointer Hotspot tool, the Rectangular Hotspot tool, the Oval Hotspot tool, and the Polygon Hotspot tool. Select the Rectangular Hotspot tool.

3. The pointer now becomes a crosshair, which allows you to draw a square hot spot around an image. Draw a square hot spot around the Home link within the new header image.

4. As you've probably noticed, the Image Property inspector now becomes the Hotspot Property inspector, which allows you to define the map name, choose a link, select a target, and add some alternate text. For our example, simply add the text index.html within the Link text box and press Tab.

5. Repeat steps 2 through 4, adding rectangular hot spots around the remaining links. Be sure to associate these hot spots with the paths aboutus.html, solutions.html, support.html, and contactus.html, pages that we'll create in the next chapter. The resulting formatted page should look like Figure 2.36.

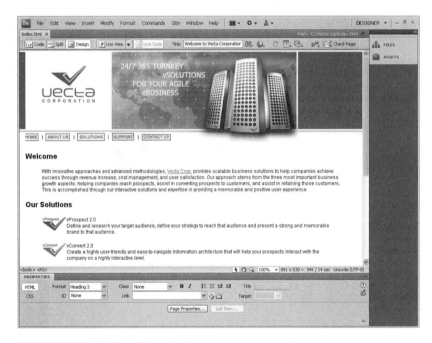

FIGURE 2.36   Add a link and alternate text to your hot spot.

When you've finished, save your work and preview the result within the browser by selecting the Preview in Browser option from the Document toolbar or by pressing F12 (Option-F12). When the page opens in the browser, try rolling over the hot spots. As you'll notice, only the areas where you defined the hot spots should be clickable.

Named Anchors

The final type of linking element that you can add to your web pages are *named anchors*. Adding named anchors on a page allows you to create hyperlinks that link to specific areas within a page. Although you can also use named anchors to link a user to a specific spot on another page, named anchors are generally reserved for pages that contain an excessive amount of content, such as an index, a glossary, or a series of frequently asked questions. In this situation, a small subnavigation menu can be created that links the user to specific spots (named anchors) on the page. Subsequently, you can add a Back to Top link at the point on the page where the user was linked to; when the Back to Top link is clicked, the user is returned to the top of the page. So that you understand how named anchors work, follow the steps outlined next:

1. Open the file `companydirectory.html`. As you've probably noticed, this file was included for you within the chapter files that you downloaded from the book's website.

2. As you will see, the company directory page contains 10 management bios for employees at our fictitious company. Near the top of the page, you'll see a menu bar that contains a horizontal list of all the employees shown on the page. Rather than forcing users to scroll down the page until they find the desired bio, you can link the names at the top so that when they are clicked, the browser automatically jumps down the page to the appropriate bio. To create the named anchor, place your cursor next to the first name in the list and select Insert, Named Anchor. The Named Anchor dialog box will appear, as shown in Figure 2.37.

FIGURE 2.37   The Named Anchor dialog box allows you to create a named anchor within the page.

3. Within the dialog box, enter the name of the first employee, **Ada**, and click OK.

4. The yellow named anchor icon will appear next to Ada's name. Because this named anchor icon is considered an invisible element, you may or may not be able to see it. If you're not able to see what appears to be a yellow anchor icon, you'll need to enable invisible elements. To enable it, make sure the Invisible Elements option is checked within the Visual Aids submenu in the Document toolbar.

5. The next step is to create a hyperlink to the named anchor for Ada's name within the horizontal menu. Begin by highlighting Ada's name in the Menu bar.

6. Place your cursor within the Link text box in the Property inspector and type **#Ada**. The # symbol represents an anchor name and Ada represents the name itself. Note the invisible element for the anchor next to Ada's name; Ada's name in the submenu is hyperlinked, and the code #Ada appears within the Link text box in the Property inspector.

7. Repeat this process, creating a new anchor for each name within the page and then linking each name within the menu to its corresponding anchor. When finished, the design should resemble Figure 2.38.

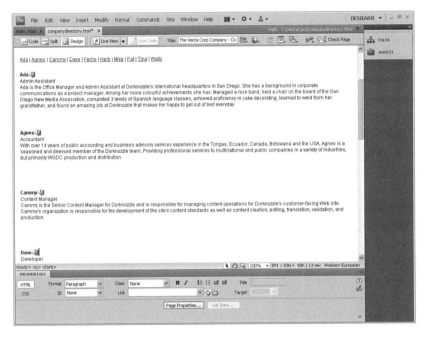

FIGURE 2.38   Create a hyperlink from the horizontal menu to the new named anchor.

Now preview your work in the browser by selecting the Preview in Browser option from the Document toolbar or press F12 (Option-F12). When the page opens in the browser, select Ada's name from the horizontal menu. The browser should advance the page down to Ada's name.

Our next step is to add the Back to Top functionality. You can add this by following these steps:

1. Place your cursor next to Ada's name in the submenu bar and choose Insert, Named Anchor. When the Named Anchor dialog box appears, enter the text **top** and click OK. A new named anchor invisible element should appear next to Ada's name in the subnavigation menu.

2. Next, add the text **(Back to Top)** next to Ada's name, and just to the right of the existing invisible element.

3. Highlight the (Back To Top) text and enter the **#top** text in the Link text box within the Property inspector.

4. Either repeat this process for the rest of the names in the list or simply copy the existing hyperlink and paste it nine times next to each person's name in the directory. The result should resemble Figure 2.39.

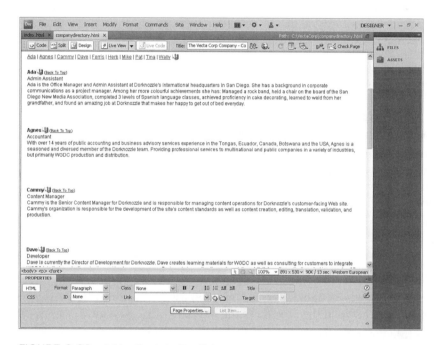

FIGURE 2.39   Add a Back to Top link to your page.

5. Preview your page in the browser by selecting the Preview in Browser option from the Document toolbar or by pressing F12 (Option-F12). This time when the page links down to Ada's name, try choosing the Back to Top link. The page should move back to the top of the page.

TIP

Another way of linking to an existing named anchor is to use the point-to-file icon located just to the right of the Link text box within the Property inspector. This little icon (which looks like the crosshairs on a small target) can be dragged over and onto an existing named anchor. When you let go, Dreamweaver will automatically produce the anchor code required within the Link text box. You don't have to use the point-to-file icon specifically for named anchors. You could also drag the point-to-file icon into the Files panel to create links to existing documents. More on this in the next few chapters.

Creating a Navigation Bar

You've already seen how to create a rollover image using the Rollover Image dialog box located within the Image Objects subcategory of the Insert menu. Aside from creating an image that, when rolled over, changes to a new version of the image, the Image Object subcategory also lists the Navigation Bar option. This feature, like the Rollover Image option, allows you to create a series of rollover images that resembles the look and functionality of a typical website navigation bar. To use the Navigation Bar option from the Image Objects subcategory, assume for a moment that the header image of our website didn't have the image map; instead, we had to build our own navigation menu from scratch. To build the navigation bar, follow these steps:

1. Create a new blank HTML page by choosing File, New. Choose the HTML option from the Page Type category, with a layout of None, and click Create. Immediately save the page as navbar.html.

2. Choose Insert, Image Objects, Navigation Bar. The Insert Navigation Bar dialog box appears. The Insert Navigation dialog exposes the following functionality:

   ▶ **Nav bar elements**—Lists the navigation bar elements. Select the Add Item (+) icon to create a new navigation bar element, the ⊡ icon to remove one, and the up and down icons to position or reposition navigation elements within the list.

   ▶ **Element name**—Give the navigation bar element a unique name. This option is required, and names cannot start with a number or contain a space.

   ▶ **Up image**—Enter or browse for the image to use for the up state.

   ▶ **Over image**—Enter or browse for the image to use for the rollover state.

   ▶ **Down image**—Enter or browse for the image to use for the down state. This image will appear when the user clicks the navigation bar element.

   ▶ **Over while down image**—Enter or browse for the image to use when users roll their mouse over the section of the navbar that is already in its down state.

   ▶ **Alternate text**—Enter the Alternate (Alt) text here.

   ▶ **When clicked, Go to URL**—Enter the path that the image link will go to when clicked.

   ▶ **In menu**—Choose the target to be associated with the link. Normal targets do not appear here. However, frame names will appear here as targets when applicable.

   ▶ **Options**—Choose the Preload images option to force the browser to preload all images before the page loads. Optionally, you can also force the browser to display a specific image's down state when the page loads. This great usability feature alerts users as to which page they're currently on.

   ▶ **Insert**—Choose an option from this menu to display the navigation bar horizontally or vertically.

   ▶ **Use tables**—Enable this check box to position the navigation bar using tables. Using tables provides more flexible positioning and spacing options.

3. To begin using the Insert Navigation Bar dialog box, start by choosing a name for the first rollover image within the Element Name text box. For the first image, you might want to enter the text **Home.**

4. Located inside the Navigation Menu folder within the Images folder, you'll find a series of images labeled with the name of the image followed by up, over, and down. Browse to those files using the appropriate text box's Browse button. For our example, you should use home_up.gif, home_over.gif, and home_down.gif. Leave the Over While Down Image text box blank.

5. Enter **Home** within the Alternate text box.

6. Enter or browse to index.html within the When Clicked, Go to URL text box.

7. Disable the Use Tables check box.

When you've finished, the dialog box should resemble Figure 2.40.

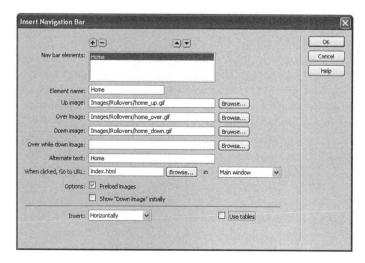

FIGURE 2.40   Enter the appropriate values to create a fully functioning navigation bar.

Unlike the Rollover Image dialog box (which allows you to create only one rollover image), the Navigation Bar dialog box enables you to create multiple rollover images by clicking the Add Item (+) icon. After you've finished entering the properties for the Home image, click the Add Item (+) icon again to set the Home navigation bar element and to clear the values of the text boxes so that you can enter new values for a second navigation bar element. Repeat this process until you've added all the navigation elements. When you've finished, preview the result in the browser by choosing the Preview in Browser option from the Document toolbar or by pressing F12 (Option-F12). Within the browser, the navigation bar should resemble Figure 2.41.

FIGURE 2.41   The navigation bar within the browser.

Summary

As you have seen, building web pages in Dreamweaver is extremely intuitive and quick to pick up. Flanked by key panels and inspectors, building web pages in Dreamweaver is merely a matter of dragging and dropping objects onto the development environment and formatting attributes using the Property inspector. This introductory chapter opened a new world to some important features within Dreamweaver and should serve as a foundation for future development. In the next few chapters, we'll step away from development for a bit and discuss one of the most important topics as it relates to Dreamweaver—site management.

Dreamweaver Site Management

In the previous chapter, you learned how to build a simple web page within Dreamweaver. Some of the more notable concepts that you learned were page formatting, handling images, and linking. Although it seems obvious that Dreamweaver's sole purpose is to create web pages, think again. What makes Dreamweaver truly unique and powerful at the same time are features and functionality built into its framework for managing your web pages, and more importantly, your websites.

Site management, you ask? Arguably the most important aspect of Dreamweaver, regardless of version, is site management—the process of administering websites within the framework of Dreamweaver. Site management affords developers many benefits, including, but not limited to, the capability to

▶ Change website links across an entire site.

▶ Check for and fix broken links across an entire website.

▶ Establish a connection and upload files to a remote web hosting provider.

▶ Work with visual site reports.

▶ Build and apply site templates. As you will see throughout this chapter, by simply establishing a *reference* (defining a site) between Dreamweaver and the files on your computer, Dreamweaver greatly expands its feature set to include functionality to help you manage your web pages and websites.

You can work with the examples in this chapter by downloading the files from www.dreamweaverunleashed.com.

You'll want to replace the files for Chapter 2, "Building a Web Page," in your working VectaCorp folder with the files for Chapter 3, "Dreamweaver Site Management." Again, I'll place mine in `C:\VectaCorp\`. For this chapter, six files (`index.html`, `aboutus.html`, `companydirectory.html`, `solutions.html`, `support.html`, and `contactus.html`) have been included for you.

The Importance of Defining Sites in Dreamweaver

As I briefly highlighted in the introductory paragraph of this chapter, site management—beginning with defining a site—presents numerous benefits to a developer. But you still might be asking yourself, "Why do I need to manage a site within Dreamweaver? I can manage my site within the file browser included with my operating system." To a certain extent this is true. However, the significance and importance of managing a site within Dreamweaver's framework goes far beyond simple drag and drop to include the following beneficial features:

> ▶ **A clean method of organizing content and assets**—Managing a site within Dreamweaver begins with defining a site (discussed in the next section). After you've defined a site, Dreamweaver cleanly organizes your files within the Files panel. As you can see from the predefined sample site in Figure 3.1, the Files panel can organize assets, images, and at the root of the directory, web pages. Additionally, your defined site might include media files, scripts, Dreamweaver templates, and more.

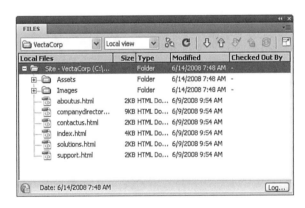

FIGURE 3.1   The Files panel cleanly organizes files.

NOTE

It's important to mention that a certain level of effort is required by you in terms of document structuring. Although Dreamweaver will automatically create some folders for you (_notes, Scripts, Templates, and Library), you're responsible for creating the rest.

In the previous chapter, we didn't define a site. Instead, we had to navigate the entire directory structure to work with our files. By defining a site, Dreamweaver conveniently isolates the folder referenced when the site was defined.

▶ **A site cache, which guarantees link integrity**—After you've defined a site, a reference is established between Dreamweaver and the files on your computer. Dreamweaver then takes a snapshot of those files and caches them. The cache acts as a digital memory of sorts for the files that Dreamweaver needs to work with. Because Dreamweaver now remembers the organizational structure, link, and path makeup of your files, if changes are made that break that structure, Dreamweaver automatically detects the changes, alerts you to them, and then fixes them, if you so choose.

▶ **A built-in FTP client**—One of the most common questions asked by beginning developers is "After I've finished developing my web pages in Dreamweaver, how do I upload them to my web hosting provider so that everyone can see them?" The answer to this question is simple. Dreamweaver provides a built-in File Transfer Protocol (FTP) client that you can use to easily drag and drop files from your local computer (the computer that you do your work on) to the remote computer (the computer that everyone can access to see your web pages).

▶ **A quick method for "getting" and "putting" files**—Even easier than dragging and dropping your files from the local computer to the remote computer is the concept of Get and Put. After you've established a connection to your remote computer using the built-in FTP client, retrieving files from the remote computer is as easy as clicking the Get button. Alternatively, you can easily send files to the remote computer by clicking the Put button.

▶ **A centralized client for managing files within teams**—As we'll explore in Part III, "Team Collaboration and Task Automation," Dreamweaver's support for working within teams is unparalleled. Facilitated by a defined site, collaborative teams can manage sites in Dreamweaver through a variety of channels, including Check In/Check Out, Subversion integration, Design Notes, site reports, source control programs such as Microsoft's Visual SourceSafe, WebDAV, and Adobe Contribute.

▶ **The capability to generate site reports**—From an organizational management perspective, defining a site within Dreamweaver provides the capability to generate site reports. Workflow statistics in terms of files that are checked out and recently modified can be generated. Additionally, you can create HTML reports that include analysis of various accessibility and usability flaws within your web pages or website.

▶ **A site synchronization utility**—Site synchronization is the process of synchronizing multiple local copies of your site with one remote copy. As Figure 3.2 illustrates, you can sync files between your local home computer and your remote server. Then, when you go to work, you can synchronize your server with your local work computer. This ensures that you're consistently working on the most up-to-date files and prevents file overlaps.

FIGURE 3.2   Use the site synchronization features built into Dreamweaver to synchronize your files between multiple computers running Dreamweaver and the version of your site on your remote server.

▶ **The capability to work with templates and library items**—Covered in more depth in Chapter 12, "Working with Templates and Library Items," templates and library items are managed, added, and edited via a defined site. Without a defined site, these added features are unusable.

As you can see from the list, there are numerous benefits to site management in Dreamweaver. Although these benefits won't appear obvious at first glance, they will become apparent as you gain experience working with Dreamweaver site management throughout this chapter and the remainder of the book.

Defining a New Site in Dreamweaver

Site management in Dreamweaver begins with defining a site. When you define a site in Dreamweaver, you're essentially establishing a reference between Dreamweaver and the files on your computer. Dreamweaver then takes a digital snapshot of the files in your project folder and caches them. By caching the files, Dreamweaver can automatically detect whether changes are made to image paths, links, and so on, and can automatically fix them for you. We'll get to all this as we progress through the chapter. For now, just keep in mind that everything begins with defining a new site. You can begin the process of defining a site by selecting Manage Sites from the Site menu. The Manage Sites dialog box will appear similar to Figure 3.3.

FIGURE 3.3   The Manage Sites dialog box allows you to create new sites or edit existing ones.

As you can see from Figure 3.3, the Manage Sites dialog box includes various buttons, each constituting specific functionality:

▶ **New**—Selecting this option opens a submenu that allows you to choose from either Site or FTP & RDS Server options. For our examples, we'll use the Site option from this submenu. In Chapter 19, "Working with Dynamic Data," we'll review the FTP & RDS Server option in more detail.

▶ **Edit**—Choose this option to edit a site that's already been defined. Selecting this option opens the Site Definition for the <site name> dialog box.

▶ **Duplicate**—Allows you to duplicate a site and its configured settings. This option is useful if you've preconfigured numerous options (FTP host, username, password, and so on) and would like to reuse them on a new site.

▶ **Remove**—Permanently deletes a site from Dreamweaver. It's important to note that choosing this option removes only the Dreamweaver reference to files on the computer, not the actual files on your computer.

▶ **Export**—Use this option when migrating sites from one computer to another. This option creates an .STE file that can be backed up and later imported on the new Dreamweaver installation using the Import button.

▶ **Import**—Use this option to import backed up sites (.STE files) into the Manage Sites dialog box.

▶ **Help**—Choosing this option opens the Dreamweaver Help window with the Manage Sites dialog box indexed.

▶ **Done**—Closes the Manage Sites dialog box.

Now that you have an idea as to how the Manage Sites dialog box works and the functionality it encapsulates, let's actually create a new site. Choose the Site option from the New button's submenu. The Site Definition window will appear similar to Figure 3.4.

As you can see from Figure 3.4, the Site Definition window is split into two tabs: Basic and Advanced options. The next section aims to shed some light on each.

With the Site Definition window open, you can use either the Basic or Advanced tab to define a new site; however, the options provided within each tab are dramatically different. If you're a beginning web developer who doesn't understand the myriad of terms and acronyms, then the Basic tab, which guides you through an easy-to-understand wizard, is probably for you. If, however, you're a seasoned veteran who wants fine control over your site management experience, the Advanced tab should be the selection you'll pick. Don't worry if you're unsure of which one best suits your needs; we'll walk through both options starting with the Basic tab.

You'll notice that when the Site Definition window opens for the first time, it defaults to the Basic tab. The Basic tab provides an easy-to-use and easy-to-understand wizard that gently guides you through the site definition process. As you can see from Figure 3.4, the first window that appears simply asks you for the site name. By defining a site, we're creating only a reference between Dreamweaver and the files on the computer so that Dreamweaver can help you manage those files better than the operating system can. The name you enter here is merely a unique name for that reference, nothing more. I'll enter **VectaCorp.** Below the name option, you'll find a text box that refers to the URL of your site. If the site you're defining contains a valid HTTP address (for example, http://www.vectacorp.com/vc/), enter that here. In the long run, entering the HTTP address for your website helps Dreamweaver manage site root relative links and absolute links (those that refer to your website) through its link checker. After you've finished entering these values, click Next.

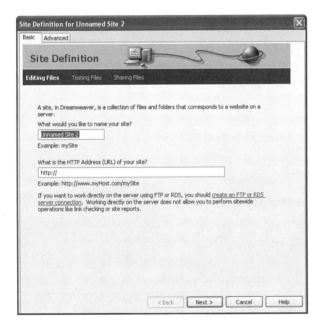

FIGURE 3.4   The Site Definition window features a wizard that guides you through the process of defining a new site.

Clicking Next causes the second dialog box of the Basic wizard to appear. Within this dialog box, you'll choose either to work with a server technology or not. Although we'll be working with server technologies in Part V, "Dynamic Web Page Development," for now we'll choose the option button titled No, I Do Not Want to Use a Server Technology and click Next.

Clicking Next again opens the third part of the Basic wizard (see Figure 3.5).

As I mentioned earlier, the practice of defining a site is the process of establishing a reference between Dreamweaver and the files on your local computer. In this screen you essentially tell Dreamweaver where those files are located. You'll want to choose the option Edit Local Copies on My Machine, Then Upload to Server When Ready. Next, use the folder icon to browse to the folder where your files are located. If you've been working out of the same location I have, your text box should have the path C:\VectaCorp (Macintosh: HD/VectaCorp) populated. You don't have to use the same path I do, but it is recommended so that we're on the same page (no pun intended) throughout the book.

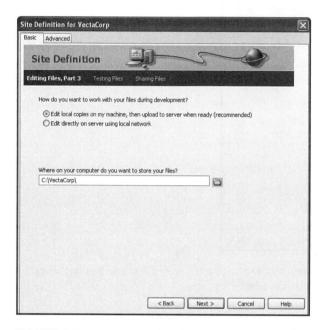

FIGURE 3.5   The third window allows you to set a path to the files on your local computer.

NOTE

The second option button allows you to work with files directly off the network. Assuming your organization's web server physically resides on the network and you don't feel the need to test your work before uploading to the web server, go ahead and check this option. Then point the path to the location of the files on the web server. I don't recommend this kind of editing for anyone except an advanced user, as one mistake can lead to a nonfunctional site.

After you've configured the dialog box, click Next. Assuming you're not using a server technology (in which case, the submenu skips over Testing Files and goes directly to Sharing Files), the fourth part of the Basic window appears, as shown in Figure 3.6.

Now that you've set the path to the files on your local computer, it's time to set the path and connection settings to the remote server. Remember, Dreamweaver's built-in FTP client allows you to transfer files between your local computer and the remote computer (typically a web server that can be accessed by the general public). For this reason, you'll want to configure this screen by selecting an option from the Remote Server menu by choosing one of the following:

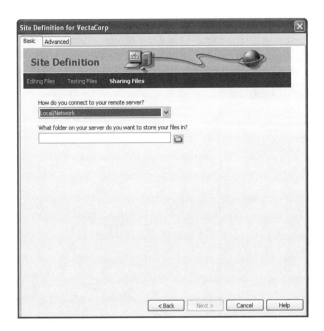

FIGURE 3.6   The fourth part of the Basic window allows you to set the properties, including path and connection options to the remote computer.

▶ **None**—Choose None if you don't want to use the built-in FTP client to upload files to a remote computer. Choosing this option assumes that you're defining a site purely for the site management features in Dreamweaver and not for the FTP capabilities.

▶ **FTP**—The most common option, FTP allows you to configure connection and login properties to a remote computer. After the connection and login properties have been established, you can use Dreamweaver's built-in FTP client to transfer files between your local computer and the remote computer.

▶ **Local/Network**—Assuming your web server is accessible on your organization's network, you'd want to choose this option to configure the path to the folder that contains the files (residing on the web server within your network).

▶ **WebDAV**—Short for Web-based Distributed Authoring and Versioning, WebDAV allows teams to collaboratively edit and manage files on remote web servers. WebDAV includes numerous versioning and control features such as file locking, which prevents multiple authors from overwriting each other's changes, as well as remote file management, versioning, and so on.

▶ **RDS**—If you've configured ColdFusion as your server technology of choice, you can use the RDS option to easily and more intuitively connect to the ColdFusion application server. This is discussed with more detail in Part V.

▶ **Microsoft Visual SourceSafe Database**—Microsoft's Visual SourceSafe is a versatile source control and version program that relies on a self-contained database for the management of files within teams. Select this option and configure the settings when working with SourceSafe instances. This feature is discussed in much more detail in Chapter 9, "Building Dreamweaver Websites Within Teams."

Although we could easily get away with choosing None for most of our examples, it would defeat the purpose of learning about one of the more important features built into Dreamweaver: the FTP client. For this reason, I'll choose FTP. However, unless you've purchased web space from a third-party web-hosting company, you might want to choose None and rereference the FTP sections of this chapter when you can follow along with your own settings.

TIP

One of the most frequently asked questions from beginning web developers deals with recommending a web host provider. Although there are literally thousands of web host providers to choose from, I recommend one. You can visit the support website at www.dreamweaverunleashed.com for information on a web hosting provider that I recommend and even a video-based tutorial on how to upload your files to that web hosting provider after you've signed up.

After you've selected the FTP option from the Access menu, the screen will tailor itself to allow you to configure path and connection details for your remote computer, similar to Figure 3.7.

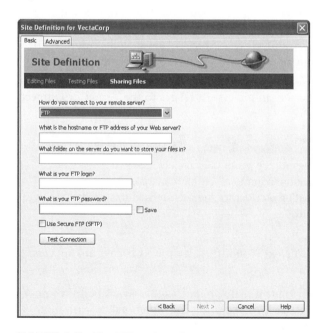

FIGURE 3.7   The FTP option allows you to set a remote path and connection information.

As you can see from Figure 3.7, the screen outlines the following options:

▶ **Hostname**—Enter the physical path of the remote computer here. I'll enter **www. vectacorp.com.**

▶ **Hostname Folder**—If you're working within a specific folder on the remote computer, enter that here. In my case, my web-hosting provider places web files in a folder called webroot/vc, so, I'll enter that here. You'll need to check with your web-hosting provider's documentation to find out whether it requires a hostname folder.

▶ **FTP Login**—Enter your login name here.

▶ **FTP Password**—Enter your password here.

▶ **Save**—If you don't want to type your password every time you want to transfer files to the remote computer, choose this check box.

▶ **Use Secure FTP**—Secure File Transfer Protocol (SFTP) is the newest standard for transferring files between local and remote computers securely. Whereas normal FTP transfers your data in an unencrypted format, SFTP encrypts data using DES, TripleDES, Blowfish, RSA, and similar encryption algorithms. But don't think you can just select this option to begin using SFTP; SFTP relies on third-party software running on the web server to facilitate the secure interaction between the local and remote computers. You'll need to check with your web-hosting provider's documentation to find out whether it supports SFTP. If it does, it's to your benefit to take advantage of it.

▶ **Test Connection**—After you've configured the options on this screen, click this button to test the connection. If everything goes well, you should receive a dialog box stating that the connection to the web server succeeded. If the connection doesn't succeed, however, review your settings. Typical issues include inputting the wrong hostname, a bad username, or even a forgotten password.

Figure 3.8 shows a typical configured screen. In my case, it relates to the Vecta Corp project.

NOTE

In this example I've defined FTP settings for the Vecta Corp project. Because there's no practical way for me to share my FTP information to all of the readers of this book, you'll be on your own to find a web-hosting provider for the examples in this chapter.

After you've configured the screen, click Next. The fifth part of the Basic wizard appears, similar to Figure 3.9.

As you might have guessed from reviewing this dialog box, Dreamweaver's built-in source control features can be configured here. We'll be exploring this functionality with more detail in Chapter 9, so for now click the option button titled No, Do Not Enable Check In and Check Out and click Next.

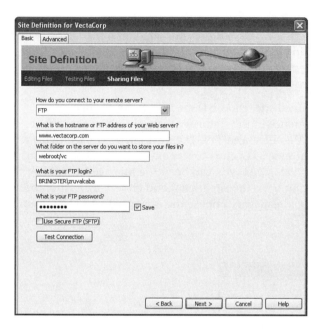

FIGURE 3.8   Configure the properties to your remote computer so that you can transfer files back and forth using FTP.

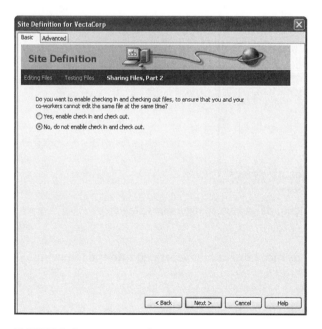

FIGURE 3.9   Configure this dialog box to enable Dreamweaver's built-in source control features.

Finally, the sixth dialog box appears, allowing you to review the settings that you've made within the wizard. If you see errors, click the Back button until you get to the dialog box that contains the problems. If everything looks good, choose Done. When you click Done, Dreamweaver scans the folder and file structure of your local files, caches them, and then adds the site reference within the Manage Sites dialog box.

To begin working with your newly defined site, choose Done to close the Manage Sites dialog box. You probably noticed a sentence in the summary dialog box that reads Your Site Can Be Further Configured Using the Advanced Tab. The next few sections provide a detailed look at the Advanced tab's features. To open your site and use the Advanced tab, select your site from the Manage Sites dialog box (you can open the Manage Sites dialog box by choosing the Manage Sites option from the Site menu) and choose Edit. After the Site Definition for Vecta Corp dialog box reappears, choose the Advanced tab. The screen will resemble Figure 3.10.

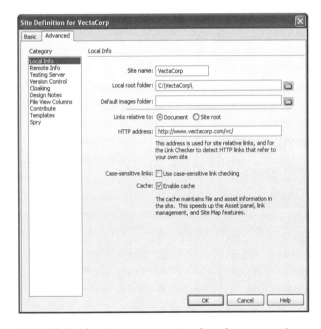

FIGURE 3.10   The Advanced interface features various configurable categories.

As you can see from Figure 3.10, the Advanced interface is separated into the following configurable categories:

- ▶ Local Info
- ▶ Remote Info
- ▶ Testing Server
- ▶ Version Control

> ▶ Cloaking

> ▶ Design Notes

> ▶ File View Columns

> ▶ Contribute

> ▶ Templates

> ▶ Spry

Let's review each.

The Local Info Category

Similar to the first two dialog boxes within the Basic wizard, the Local Info category, also shown in Figure 3.10, enables you to configure the following information:

> ▶ **Site name**—Creates a name for your defined site. Remember, this is merely a name for the reference made between Dreamweaver and the files on your local computer.

> ▶ **Local root folder**—Add the path to the files on your local computer here.

> ▶ **Default images folder**—You can set a default images folder when you have two or more defined sites that share a common images folder. This prevents you from having to make duplicate image folders for multiple defined sites.

> ▶ **Links relative to**—If you want to change the relative path of the links you create to other pages in the site, select a Links Relative To option. By default, Dreamweaver creates links using document-relative paths. You could select the site root option to change the path setting for the entire site to use site root-relative paths as discussed in detail in the previous chapter. If you select the site root option, make sure you specify the HTTP address in the next option. I recommend leaving this setting as it is.

> ▶ **HTTP address**—Specify the complete web address to your site here (for example, www.vectacorp.com/vc/). This allows Dreamweaver to verify links to absolute URLs. Dreamweaver also uses this address to make sure site root-relative links work on the remote server, which might have a different site root. For instance, I keep my Vecta Corp files within a folder called vc/ on the remote web server. So when I reference www.vectacorp.com, I have a redirect that automatically takes me to www.vectacorp. com/vc/ because all my files are contained within this vc/ folder. If I'm working with site-root relative paths, it's crucial that the full path www.vectacorp.com/vc/ is added within the HTTP address. Otherwise, Dreamweaver assumes that the site root is / as opposed to vc/ and would produce broken references when establishing paths to pages, images, and media elements within my site. If you're using document-relative paths as I'm doing, setting this text box is purely optional.

> ▶ **Case-sensitive links**—Enabling this check box guarantees that Dreamweaver checks case when checking links throughout your site.

> ▶ **Cache**—Ensure that this option is selected so that Dreamweaver can take a snapshot of your folder and file structure. You'd want to disable this check box only when

your folder and file structure is so massive that having Dreamweaver cache your files each time you make a change produces sluggish results. Instances like this will be extremely rare because you'd be looking at sites with hundreds, if not thousands, of pages.

Because we've already configured most of these options within the Basic tab, I'll leave the configuration alone and move directly to the Remote Info category.

The Remote Info Category

Similar to the Remote Configuration screen within the Basic tab, the Remote Info category, shown in Figure 3.11, allows you to further configure remote computer options such as firewall settings, passive FTP, and the like—essentially advanced options that Dreamweaver doesn't bother you with in the Basic wizard.

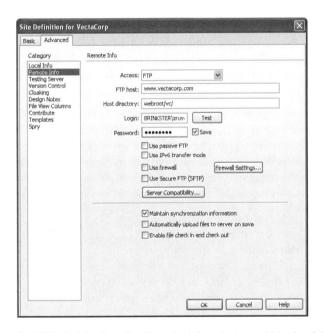

FIGURE 3.11   Use the Remote Info category within the Advanced tab to configure further options such as firewall settings, passive FTP, and more.

A detailed list of features and functionality is listed here:

▶ **Access**—Choose from a list of access methods from this menu. These options include None, FTP, Local/Network, WebDAV, RDS, and Microsoft Visual SourceSafe. In most scenarios you'll use the FTP option. When this option is selected, the options listed next are present.

NOTE

As we progress through the book, we'll discuss the other options within the Access list. For instance, in Chapter 9, we'll discuss both the WebDAV and SourceSafe options. Similarly, in Chapter 16, "Working with Server-Side Technologies," we'll discuss the Local/Network option.

▶ **FTP host**—Enter the FTP path to the remote computer here. In most cases you would simply use the URL of the site as the web host. If you're pointing directly to an FTP server, an IP address might be used instead.

▶ **Host directory**—If you're working within a folder on the remote computer, enter that here. Again, my web-hosting provider places all web pages within a webroot folder. Additionally, because I host many websites on the same server, I create additional folders within the webroot. For the Vecta Corp project, I created a folder within the webroot folder called vc/. Because this is the case, my host directory becomes webroot/vc/.

▶ **Login**—Enter the login name for your remote computer here.

▶ **Password**—Enter the password for your remote computer here.

▶ **Use passive FTP**—By default, Dreamweaver uses what is known as *Active FTP*. Simply put, Active FTP allows the remote server to configure FTP access to it. *Passive FTP*, on the other hand, is a more secure form of data transfer in which the flow of data is set up and initiated by Dreamweaver's FTP client rather than by the remote server. As a general rule, most organizations that are behind a firewall prefer passive FTP because they only recognize input from the outside in response to user requests that were sent out requesting the input. The use of passive FTP ensures all data flow initiation comes from inside the network rather than from the outside.

▶ **Use IPv6 transfer mode**—Internet Protocol version 6 (IPv6) is a network layer protocol designed to succeed IPv4, the current version of the Internet Protocol, for general use on the Internet. If you are using an IPv6-enabled FTP server, check this box.

▶ **Use firewall**—Choose this option if you connect to the remote server from behind a firewall.

▶ **Firewall Settings**—If you've checked the Use Firewall check box, your next step will be to configure firewall settings. Clicking this button launches the Site category within the Preferences dialog box. We'll discuss these options in more detail in online Appendix C, "Defining Preferences."

▶ **Use Secure FTP (SFTP)**—As I mentioned earlier, files are transferred from the local and remote computer in a nonencrypted format. If your remote computer has SFTP software installed, you can check this option to use a secure, encrypted format in Secure FTP instead of the normal, less-secure FTP option.

▸ **Server Compatibility**—Select this option to further maximize the compatibility between Dreamweaver and your remote computer. Selecting this option launches the Server Compatibility dialog box, which includes options for FTP performance optimization as well as the option for using a different method of rolling back files when check in and check out is enabled.

▸ **Maintain synchronization information**—Select this check box if you want Dreamweaver to keep record of important synchronization information. When this check box is selected and at least one synchronization is performed, Dreamweaver creates a hidden file (dwsync.xml) and places that file within a _notes folder in your site root. This information is merely a file used by Dreamweaver to improve performance when synchronizing files.

▸ **Automatically upload files to server on save**—A dangerous option, checking this box gives Dreamweaver free rein to upload files to your remote computer as soon as you save the file locally. I don't typically recommend checking this option.

▸ **Enable file check in and check out**—If you're working in a collaborative team environment, check this option to allow other developers in your workgroup to check in and check out files. This option effectively enables the source control functionality built into Dreamweaver. We'll discuss this option in more detail in Chapter 9.

Again, we managed to configure most of the options that we've needed up to this point from within the Basic tab. For now, I'll leave the configurations alone and move onto the Testing Server category.

The Testing Server Category

After you start working with server-side technologies (ASP, ColdFusion, or PHP, to name a few), the Testing Server category, shown in Figure 3.12, will become more useful.

A detailed list of features and functionality exposed by the Testing Server category is presented here:

▸ **Server model**—Choose an option from this menu to set the server technology for the site. Options include ASP JavaScript, ASP VBScript, ASP.NET C#, ASP.NET VB, ColdFusion, JSP, and PHP MySQL. We'll begin to discuss the various server technology options in Part V.

▸ **Access**—The second menu available within this screen is the access method used to connect to the testing server. Options include FTP, Local/Network, WebDAV, and RDS (available only if RDS is selected as the Access option from the Remote Info category). Because the testing server can also be the local computer, it is possible to select a server technology without specifying an access method.

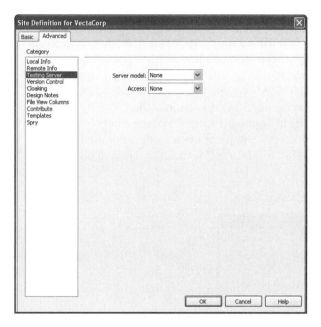

FIGURE 3.12   The Testing Server category allows you to choose a server technology and an access method.

Because we're not working with server technologies just yet, I'll keep the option set to None for both the Server model and Access menus.

The Version Control Category

A new category to Dreamweaver CS4, the Version Control category allows you to enable and configure Subversion software integration within Dreamweaver. As mentioned in the new features section in Chapter 1, "The Dreamweaver CS4 Interface," and covered with much more detail in Chapter 9, Subversion is an open source version control software package currently being integrated by various projects and organizations, including Dreamweaver, Google, Ruby, Mono, SourceForge, GNOME, Apache Software Foundation, and more. Subversion is unique in that it can be installed and used on virtually any type of server and environment. Whether your using Windows, UNIX, Linux, Mac OS X, etc., Subversion can be installed and implemented with Dreamweaver very easily. Additionally, Dreamweaver has full support for Subversion, allowing you to maintain copies of all of your project files, maintain backups of project files, perform comparisons of multiple files, check files in and out, and more. Subversion is also ideal in single developer scenarios as it allows you to maintain project histories, separating each version of a project so that you can roll back/recover a previous version of a project with ease. More information on Subversion can be found in Chapter 9.

The Cloaking Category

As we progress through the chapter, you'll learn about features such as site synchronization, file get and put, and more. While you work with some of these operations, you might decide that you'll need to exclude files in an effort to improve the performance of Dreamweaver's site scanning capabilities. Furthermore, you might decide to explicitly exclude certain files from consideration during these operations. The Cloaking category exists specifically for this reason. Shown in Figure 3.13, the Cloaking category allows you to hide certain file types, even entire folders, to prevent them from being used within a variety of Dreamweaver operations, including site synchronization, get and put, find and replace, and more.

FIGURE 3.13   The Cloaking category allows you to enable or disable cloaking, allowing you to cloak files with specific extensions or, later from the Files panel, whole folders.

The Cloaking category provides the following functionality:

▶ **Enable cloaking**—Enables or disables cloaking.

▶ **Cloak files ending with**—When the Enable Cloaking option is enabled, this check box also becomes enabled. You can then click this check box to enter specific file extension types separated by spaces. Doing this will automatically cloak files with the specific extension type.

Because we'll be discussing cloaking in more detail later in the chapter, make sure that the Enable Cloaking check box is selected.

The Design Notes Category

Covered in more detail in Chapter 9, Design Notes let you share and edit information about pages within a site with members of a team. By enabling Design Notes within the screen shown in Figure 3.14, you can create text-based notes (.MNO files) which are in turn saved to a _notes folder within the site's root.

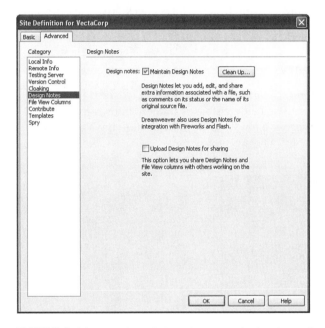

FIGURE 3.14   Enable collaborative note sharing for a site using Design Notes.

Here's a complete list of features available through the Design Notes category:

▶ **Maintain Design Notes**—Enables or disables Dreamweaver's capability to keep Design Notes.

▶ **Clean Up**—As you will see, Design Notes are associated with pages. If you have pages that are no longer needed or have been deleted, Dreamweaver doesn't necessarily delete its respective Design Notes. Click this button to manually delete Design Notes that are either no longer needed or are associated with pages that no longer exist.

▶ **Upload Design Notes for sharing**—Check this option to make Design Notes available to other members of your collaborative team. If this option is selected, Design Notes are automatically transferred to the remote computer. If you want to maintain Design Notes just for yourself, uncheck this option.

NOTE

Design Notes are also created and used by other Adobe applications to keep track of information relating to file paths of source and output files. An example of this is when doing round-trip editing of graphics between Fireworks or Photoshop and Dreamweaver. This is covered more in Chapter 14, "Integrating with Photoshop, Fireworks, and Flash."

Although we won't be discussing Design Notes until Chapter 9, it won't affect our work by enabling these options now. So make sure that the Design Notes check box is selected and that the Upload Design Notes for sharing check box is selected as well.

The File View Columns Category

Like your operating system's file explorer, Dreamweaver's Files panel (covered later) supports the customization of columns to be made visible or hidden. Shown in Figure 3.15, the File View Columns category allows you to show or hide the Name, Notes, Size, Type, Modified, and Checked Out By columns.

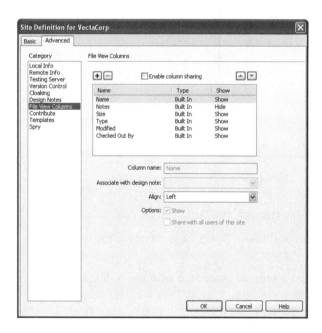

FIGURE 3.15   Use the File View Columns category to show or hide columns within the Files panel.

The File View Columns category can be broken down into the following list of features:

▶ **Enable column sharing**—Check this box to share file view columns and custom file view columns with other members of a collaborative team.

▶ **Add (+)/Remove (–)**—Allows you to add a custom view column. After you've added the custom column, you can associate the column with an option from the Associate with Design Note menu. Select the Remove icon to remove a custom column. Dreamweaver does not allow you to remove built-in columns. They can only be hidden.

▶ **Move Up/Move Down**—Select the Move Up or Move Down icons in the top-right of the screen to reposition the file view columns. Repositioning the columns changes the arrangement of the columns within the site management window moving left to right. Built-in columns cannot be repositioned.

▶ **File View Columns list**—Lists built-in and customized file view columns. Select a file view column from this list to interact with other configurable options within the screen.

▶ **Column name**—Allows you to name a custom file view column. Built-in file view columns cannot be renamed.

▶ **Associate with design note**—Custom file view columns must be associated with Design Notes. After you've created a custom file view column, select an option from this list to associate a Design Note property with the custom file view column. Default options within this list include Assigned, Due, Priority, and Status. We'll cover this topic in much more detail in Chapter 9.

▶ **Align**—Sets the alignment of text within the file view column. Options include Left (default), Center, and Right align.

▶ **Show**—Enable or disable this check box to show or hide a file view column. The Name column is the only column that may not be hidden.

▶ **Share with all users of this site**—Allows you to share custom file view columns with other members of the collaborative team.

You'll notice that Notes currently show as hidden. This is fine because we won't be working with Design Notes until Chapter 9. Also, because we won't be using the Check In and Check Out functionality until Chapter 9, go ahead and select that column name within the File View Columns pane and uncheck the Show check box.

The Contribute Category

Adobe Contribute makes it easy for content managers within an organization to add and modify content on a website without the need to know Dreamweaver. You can make your site accessible via Contribute by enabling the check box within the Contribute category screen, shown in Figure 3.16.

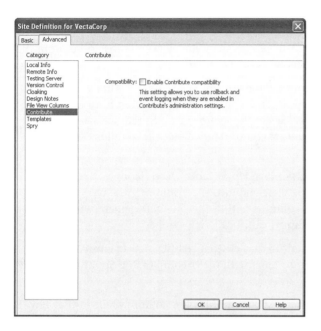

FIGURE 3.16   Enable Contribute compatibility for your defined site by enabling this check box.

It's important to note, however, that Dreamweaver will not allow you to select this option if an Access method has not been chosen first. Contribute is covered with much more detail in Chapter 10, "Managing Website Content Using Contribute."

The Templates Category

As you'll see in Chapter 12, when you create a template file by saving an existing page as a template, the new template (which resides in a Templates folder that Dreamweaver automatically creates) and any links in the file are updated so that their document-relative paths are correct. Later, when you create a document based on that template and save it, all the document-relative links are updated again to continue to point to the correct files. When you add a new document-relative link to a template file, it's easy to enter the wrong pathname if you type the path into the Link text box in the Property inspector. The correct path in a template file is the path from the Templates folder to the linked document, not the path from the template-based document's folder to the linked document.

Previous to Dreamweaver 8, Dreamweaver did not update links to files that resided in the Templates folder. For example, if you had a file called styles.css in the Templates folder and had written href="styles.css" as a link in the template file, Dreamweaver would not update this link when creating a template-based page. Some users took advantage of the way Dreamweaver treated links to files in the Templates folder and used this inconsistency to create links that they intentionally did not want to update when creating template-based pages. In Dreamweaver 8, however, this behavior was changed so that all document-relative links are updated when creating template-based pages, regardless of the apparent location of the linked files. This update in Dreamweaver 8 broke links in pages created by those designers who had taken advantage of Dreamweaver's former practice of not updating links to files in the Templates folder.

With the Dreamweaver 8.01 patch, Dreamweaver provided this check box, which enables you to turn the update relative links behavior on and off. This special preference applies only to links to files in the Templates folder, not to links in general. The default behavior is to not update these links, but if you want Dreamweaver to update these kinds of links when creating template-based pages, you can deselect the preference.

The Spry Category

As you'll see in Chapter 24, "Working with the Spry Framework for Ajax," Dreamweaver must use a collection of JavaScript libraries that are referenced by every page that contain Spry elements. These JavaScript libraries, or assets, must be placed somewhere within your defined site. This text box allows you to define the folder where your Spry assets should be stored. By default, Dreamweaver creates a folder called SpryAssets within your site root; however, feel free to customize the name of this folder to your liking.

Now that you have a general understanding of what each category within the Site Definition dialog box does, go ahead and close it now by choosing the OK button. The Site Definition dialog box will close and you'll be returned to the Manage Sites dialog box. Because we're finished defining sites, click the Done button.

Managing a Website in Dreamweaver

Defining a site is the first step to managing a website within the framework of Dreamweaver. Now that you've learned about the site definition features built into both the Basic and Advanced screens, let's take a look at the features built into Dreamweaver to help you manage your website.

Managing a site within Dreamweaver begins with the Files panel. Shown with detailed callouts in Figure 3.17, the Files panel outlines folders and files within your defined site. It allows you to manipulate filenames and placement as you would be able to within your operating system's file explorer. It features views for local, remote, and testing servers, allows you to quickly get and put files, and even allows you to check out files if you're working within teams.

A complete list of features within the Files panel is detailed next:

▶ **File menu**—Displays a list of drives and defined sites. Although most of the icons will appear similar to your operating system's file browser, Dreamweaver includes green folder icons near the bottom of the list to represent defined sites. Also at the bottom of the list is the selectable option Manage Sites, and when it is clicked, it launches the Manage Sites dialog box.

▶ **View menu**—Use the View menu on the Files panel to select among Local, Remote, Testing Server, and Repository Server views. The Local view will always be shown at the moment that it is selected from the menu. Testing Server, Remote, and

Repository views appear when they are selected and the Connect button is pressed. (Windows only; Mac users need to access this View menu from the Files panel and Options menu).

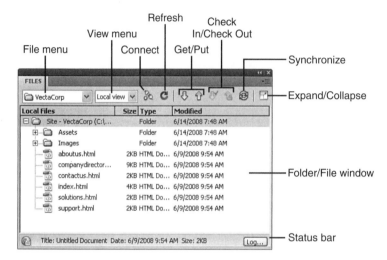

FIGURE 3.17   The Files panel outlines various features for working with a defined site.

▶ **Connect**—Clicking this button connects to the Remote, Testing, or Repository server assuming that the connection, login, and password are valid. To connect, Testing Server, Remote, or Repository views must be selected from the View menu first. Furthermore, the testing, remote, and/or repository servers must be configured within the Site Definition dialog box.

▶ **Refresh**—You can click this button to refresh the folder and file list. This is especially important if you manipulate files (perhaps delete a file or add a new file) within the Files panel outside of Dreamweaver (perhaps using your computer's file explorer). If changes occur outside of Dreamweaver, Dreamweaver might not automatically pick up on these changes. Clicking the refresh button forces Dreamweaver to refresh its view within the Files panel. It's important to note, that making changes outside of Dreamweaver is not recommended.

▶ **Get/Put**—Allows you to quickly upload to and download files from the remote, testing, or repository server. We'll discuss this option later in the chapter.

▶ **Check In/Check Out**—Allows you to quickly check in and check out files, assuming that this option was enabled when the site was defined. If it weren't, selecting this option now provides you with a dialog box that asks you to enable it.

▶ **Synchronize**—Click this button to launch the Synchronize Files dialog box. The Synchronize Files dialog box is the first step to site synchronization, covered in more detail later in the chapter.

▶ **Expand/Collapse**—Expands the Site File list to its advanced and more detailed state. We'll be discussing this option next.

▶ **Folder/File window**—Lists all folders and files within the defined site. Recall that we discussed the topic of File View Columns. Looking at this list, you can see file view columns for Name, Size, Type, and Modified.

▶ **Status bar**—Subtly located at the bottom of the Files panel, the status bar displays the title of the page as your cursor rolls over it. After a file has been selected, the status bar displays the size of the file in bytes. Also available within the status bar is a small globe icon and Log button. Clicking the Log button opens the FTP log and displays detailed messages as to the status of activity on the FTP server. Clicking the globe icon (which animates when file activity is occurring) displays the Background File Activity dialog box, which provides a detailed list of files currently being transferred.

Now that you've seen the feature list within this panel, let me offer a taste of the power behind site management in Dreamweaver—more specifically, link validation. To see this in action, try selecting an important file within our list, such as `index.html`, and drag it into the Assets folder. Immediately, the Update Files dialog box appears, similar to Figure 3.18.

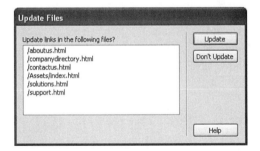

FIGURE 3.18   Dreamweaver detects that a file is being moved to a new folder and immediately asks you to update all references to and from that file.

As you can see from the dialog box, Dreamweaver detects that you're trying to move a file from one location to another. Because references exist to and from that file, Dreamweaver will detect this and ask you whether you want to update all files that make references to and from `index.html`. Because all these files assume that `index.html` is in the root directory, if this feature didn't exist, references to this file would either be broken, or we'd have to manually open all files within our site, search for all references within each page, and manually correct them. By clicking the Update button, Dreamweaver scans all files within the list and then fixes all the references to and from that file automatically. To move the file back to the root, drag it back from the Assets folder into the root of the defined site. The same process of detecting and fixing the references will occur.

CAUTION

After you've defined a site, it's important that file movement be done through the Files panel rather than through the operating system's file explorer. Doing this will ensure that file references are always tracked and automatically updated by Dreamweaver. If you move files using the operating system's file explorer, Dreamweaver never gets a chance to detect reference changes, and ultimately you'll end up with broken links and references within your site.

This is only the tip of the iceberg. You can begin to see more options available from the Files panel by selecting the Expand/Collapse icon to expand the panel into a larger window. As you can see from the callouts in Figure 3.19, additional features become available and the Files panel becomes much more useful.

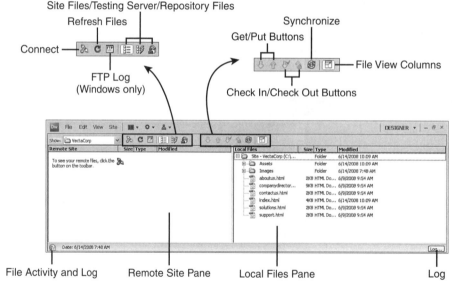

FIGURE 3.19   The Files panel provides advanced features for managing defined sites, including the capability to drag and drop files to and from the remote and local files panes.

The list of additional features is highlighted here:

▶ **View Site FTP Log**—Clicking this options opens the FTP Log within the Results window and displays a text-based log of FTP activity for your defined site.

▶ **Site Files View**—Choose this option to display a list of local files in the right pane and remote files on the left pane. The is the default view.

▶ **Testing Server View**—Choose this option to display a list of local files in the right pane and testing server files on the left pane.

▶ **Respository Files View**—Choose this option to display and manage files contained within the repository server. We'll discuss this feature with more detail in Chapter 9.

When the Files panel is expanded, it's easier to see the changes to the available columns that we configured when we defined the site. As you can probably tell from Figure 3.19, our Notes and Checked Out By columns are hidden. If you decide that you want to view those columns again, you can revisit the File View Columns category for the defined site by selecting Manage Sites from the Site List drop-down menu.

Uploading Your Files to a Remote Server

Although the Files panel includes advanced features for managing your defined site, its true power lies in the fact that it's actually a built-in FTP client. Because this is the case, we can easily connect to our remote server and transfer files by dragging from the Local pane and dropping the files into the Remote pane. Assuming that you have a remote server defined, follow these steps:

1. With the Files panel expanded, click the Connect button. Assuming your connection, login, and password are valid, your remote site files will appear in the left (Remote Site) pane, and the Connect icon will display a green light similar to Figure 3.20.

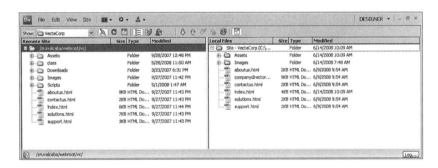

FIGURE 3.20 After you connect to the remote server, the Connect icon will display a green light, and the remote folder and file list will display in the left pane.

2. Select and drag a file from the Local Files pane into either a folder or the root within the Remote Site pane. Immediately, the Dependent Files dialog box will appear. What you're seeing is yet another site management gem. All we've done is drag over one file from the Local Files pane. Dreamweaver, recognizing that the HTML file being transferred includes dependent images, alerts you of this. By choosing Yes from the dialog box, Dreamweaver will automatically transfer all these files for you, sparing you the trouble of manually locating all images, media elements, and so on that might also need to be transferred manually.

3. The Background File Activity dialog box displays with a progress indicator showing the status of the file transfer. The dialog box initially shows minimized, but you can expand the Details pane by clicking the small arrow icon next to the Details text label to reveal a detailed file transfer list similar to Figure 3.21. The real beauty in this dialog box, however (previous Dreamweaver users will attest to this), is that it can be minimized. If you're transferring a lot of files and you have other work to do in the meantime, you can choose the Hide button to minimize the Background File Activity dialog box to the taskbar. Previous versions of Dreamweaver (pre-Dreamweaver 8) forced you to wait for the file transfer to complete before you could move on with other work.

NOTE

The Background File Activity dialog box allows you to minimize Dreamweaver and resume working with your operating system. However, you will not be able to continue working with files in your defined site while there is file transfer activity.

FIGURE 3.21   The Background File Activity dialog box displays a detailed list and progress indicator for the overall transfer process.

4. To see the files that were copied over, all I have to do is open a web browser and browse to the URL where the file exists. Because I've dragged the file called index.html into the Scripts folder, I need only to reference the URL www.vectacorp.com/vc/scripts/ to see the newly transferred page. Figure 3.22 shows the file and URL within the address bar as it appears within the browser.

The same process, selecting files from the Remote Site pane and dragging them into the Local Files pane, is also possible.

For all the simplicities that this built-in FTP client offers, it's still somewhat of an involved method. The next section will introduce you to the same process of transferring files, but this time we'll use the Get and Put options.

Getting and Putting Files

The downside to using the Files panel is that you have to manually connect to your remote site and then drag and drop files over. It's distracting to your workflow because you have to expand the Files panel first, essentially taking you away from your work. A simpler method of transferring files from your local computer to your remote computer is

that of getting and putting files. By using the Get and Put (Ctrl+Shift+D and Ctrl+Shift+U
⌘-Shift-D and ⌘-Shift-U) options located in the File management submenu within the
Document toolbar, you can easily transfer files that you are working on to and from your
remote server with the simple click of a button. As an example, I'll open the index.html
file. Next, I'll select the Put option from the File management submenu within the
Document toolbar, also shown in Figure 3.23.

FIGURE 3.22   The index.html page appears within the browser after I manually dragged it
from the Local Files pane to the Scripts folder in the Remote Files pane.

FIGURE 3.23   Use the Put option to quickly transfer an open file without disrupting your
workflow.

As you'll notice, Dreamweaver automatically connects to your remote server and then
presents the same dialog box asking whether you want to upload dependent files.

Choosing Yes uploads index.html, as well as all files associated with index.html. Also, Dreamweaver remains connected to your remote server. You can see that by the green connect icon within the Files panel.

You can use the Get and Put options directly from the Files panel as well. By simply selecting a file and choosing the Put icon (represented by the up-arrow button) from the Files panel, the same functionality can be achieved. Furthermore you might decide to use the Get and Put options available from the context menu. To do this, simply right-click (Control+click) onto the file in the Files panel and choose either Get or Put to perform the same operation.

Synchronizing Local and Remote Files

Although it's great to be able to transfer files from your local computer to your remote computer, the truth is that most people work in an environment where a local computer can be represented by two computers. In this scenario, keeping accurate folder and file structures between two local computer instances can be extremely difficult. For instance, earlier in the chapter I used the example of having two working locations. Assuming you do work at home and at the office, you would have two local computers—one for your office and one for your home. Figure 3.24 clearly demonstrates this model.

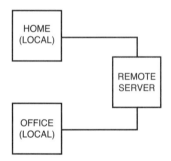

FIGURE 3.24   Your workflow could be such that you work from both your home and the office.

You could potentially do work from home, upload your files to the remote server, go to the office, do some more work, and then accidentally upload over files that you had done work on from home. To prevent any such disasters from occurring, you could use the site synchronization feature built into Dreamweaver. Available from either the Files panel's Options menu or the Site menu, the Synchronize option launches the Synchronize Files dialog box similar to Figure 3.25.

The Synchronize Files dialog box displays the following features:

- ▶ **Synchronize**—This menu includes two options. Choose between synchronizing the entire site or selected files within a site.

- ▶ **Direction**—This menu includes three options. Choose between putting newer files to remote, getting newer files from remote, or getting and putting newer files. It's important to note that the synchronization process transfers only the newest files. This assures that your remote or local files are consistently updated based on the newest possible files from the respective computer.

▶ **Delete remote files on local drive**—Select this option to delete the files on the destination site that don't have counterparts on the original site. This check box is disabled if you select the Get and Put newer files option.

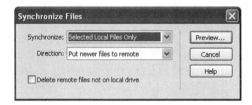

FIGURE 3.25   The Synchronize Files dialog box facilitates the synchronization process between the local and remote computers.

Because I've uploaded only the `index.html` file and associated images, I'll choose the Entire Vecta Corp Site option from the Synchronize menu, choose the Put Newer Files to Remote option from the Direction list, and click Preview. Dreamweaver then scans the folder and file structure on both the local and remote computers, compares the two, and then presents a list within the Synchronize window (see Figure 3.26) of newer files that need to be uploaded to the remote computer.

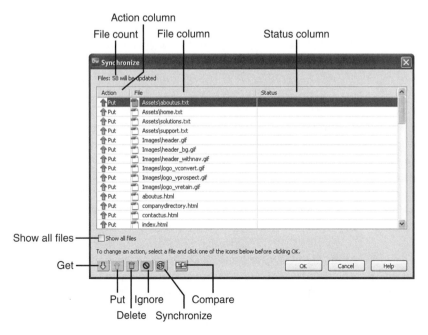

FIGURE 3.26   Dreamweaver presents a list of newer files that need to be transferred.

As you can see from the callouts in Figure 3.26, the Synchronize window includes numerous features for managing the synchronization of files, including the following:

▶ **File Count**—This label displays a count of files that will be updated.

▶ **Action column**—Based on the Direction that you pick from the previous menu, this column displays either a Get or Put text label and associative icon. Furthermore, if you mark files as Ignore or Delete, this column will display the associative icon and text label, also shown in Figure 3.26.

▶ **File column**—Displays the filename that will be updated.

▶ **Status column**—Displays the status of the file whose properties you decide to manipulate using the button bar near the bottom left of the window.

▶ **Show all files**—Displays all files regardless of synchronization necessity.

▶ **Get**—When a file's action has been changed to Ignore, click this button to return the action to Get.

▶ **Put**—When a file's action has been changed to Ignore, click this button to return the action to Put.

▶ **Mark for Deletion**—Marks a specific file for deletion.

▶ **Ignore**—Changes the action for a file from Get or Put to Ignore. This allows you to change your mind about a file at the last minute without having to cancel out of the Synchronize window.

▶ **Mark as Synchronized**—Sets the action of a file to Synchronized and immediately removes it from the File list.

▶ **Compare**—Uses the "diff" program you specify within the File Compare category in the Preferences window to compare a particular file on the remote server with one on the local server. More on setting up a file comparison program is provided in online Appendix C.

When you're happy with the options in the Synchronize window, click OK to begin the update. Immediately, the Synchronize window closes and the Background File Activity window opens displaying the status of the transfer. When the update completes, click the Close button to close the Background File Activity window. To verify the successful transfer of files, try running the site synchronization feature one more time. This time when you run it, a dialog box stating that a synchronization is not necessary will appear.

Cloaking Files

Cloaking files is the process of hiding files from typical Dreamweaver operations such as global find and replace, site synchronization, and so on. For instance, you might decide to keep original Photoshop .psd files, Fireworks .png files, Illustrator .ai files, Flash .fla files, and so on within your Assets folder. Although files such as these are important to the overall design of your site, they serve little purpose in terms of how your pages function. In this situation you might want to cloak the entire Assets folder in an effort to speed up search features such as site synchronization. Dreamweaver will ignore anything that is cloaked. Cloaking files in Dreamweaver is easy and can be done directly within the Files panel. Select the folder (I'll choose Assets), right-click (Control-click) to access the context menu, choose the Cloaking submenu, and select Cloak. After you've cloaked the folder, the icon changes to a green folder with a red line through it. This means the folder is cloaked. You can also use the Files panel Options menu to cloak and uncloak files. This time let's use this method to uncloak the Assets folder. Select the Assets folder, click the Files panel Options menu, choose Site, Cloaking, Uncloak (see Figure 3.27).

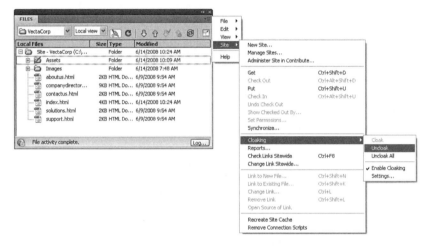

FIGURE 3.27   Choose Site, Cloaking, Uncloak from the Files panel Options menu.

Now if you perform the site synchronization feature again, the Assets panel will be included in the search. You can also cloak all files with specific extensions by checking the Cloak Files Ending With option within the Cloaking category of the Site Definition dialog box when you define your site. With this check box selected, you then have the option of creating a space-delimited list of files that should be cloaked sitewide. By default, all .png and .fla files are cloaked.

NOTE

Globally cloaking .png files will cloak Fireworks source .png files but will also cloak standard .png files that you might be using as images in your site. If you want to keep your Fireworks source files within your site and don't want them uploaded to your server where people could potentially access them, you could create a folder called Fw Source (or whatever name you prefer) within your site, save your Fireworks source .png files there, and cloak the whole Fw Source folder instead of specifying .png as a cloaked extension.

Checking Links Sitewide

By far one of the biggest benefits of defining a site in Dreamweaver is so that Dreamweaver can verify and fix links for you automatically. As your sites grow in proportion, so will the number of internal and external links on the site. By using the Site, Check Links Sitewide option, you can check the integrity of all paths to links and files within your site. In fact, Dreamweaver's link checker can verify the following:

▸ **Broken Links**—Broken links are hyperlinks that are not referenced properly. They generally will be linked to a file that does not exist in a particular directory or that in most cases is misreferenced.

▸ **External Links**—This report is a list of external path references within your site. Because Dreamweaver has no way of checking for external links, it will, at the very least, list them out so that you can check them manually in one short concise list.

▸ **Orphaned Files**—Orphaned files are files that exist within folders in your site but that are not directly referenced by your web pages. Assets, for instance, will always appear within this list even when cloaked. Dreamweaver is providing a list so that later you can go into your site and perform a manual cleanup of unused files.

Before we demonstrate the process of checking links, let's actually create a broken link within a new page. You can do this quickly by first choosing File, New. Choose Blank Page, HTML, <none>; then click Create. This will create the new web page. Now place your cursor on the page and choose Insert, Hyperlink. When the Hyperlink dialog box appears, enter the value `Fake Link` within the Text text box and then enter a broken path in the Link field, perhaps `homepage.html`. Remember, homepage.html doesn't actually exist. We're purposely creating a broken reference here to test the functionality. Click OK and save the page as `sample.html`. Now we're ready to check for bad links. Checking links within your site can be accomplished using one of two methods. First, you can check the links for an individual file; and second, you can check links for an entire defined site. Because the process for both is similar, I'll demonstrate the Check Links Sitewide feature for an entire site here. You can do this by following these steps:

1. Within the Files panel, select the defined site, right-click (Control-click) to access the context menu, and choose Check Links, Entire Local Site. The Results panel will appear with the Link Checker tab highlighted, similar to Figure 3.28.

FIGURE 3.28   Open the Link Checker by choosing Check Links, Entire Local Site.

As you saw, the Check Links submenu also features the Selected Files/Folders option. If you didn't need to check the links for the entire site, you could highlight the files and/or folders and choose this option. Also, the path we took to open the Link Checker is merely one method. Like every other feature in Dreamweaver, the Check Links feature can be accessed using numerous methods: the Link Checker can also be accessed directly from the Site menu by choosing Check Links Sitewide. Alternatively, you can choose the Check Links Sitewide option from the Site submenu located within the Files panel Options menu.

2. With the Link Checker tab open, you'll notice a few options. First and foremost, in the top-left corner is the Show drop-down menu that offers the three available options for link checking reports (Broken Links, External Links, and Orphaned Files). Also, you'll notice that the Link Checker tab is divided into two columns; the left side is where problematic files will be listed, and on the right is the link that is causing the problem.

3. To fix the broken link, double-click the document on the left side of the pane within the Files column. This opens the document and highlights the problematic link. Within the Property inspector, change the link in the Link text field to something that you know is valid, such as **index.html**. Alternatively, you could click the troubled link on the right side of the dialog box within the Broken Links column. Here you can either type in the link manually or click the folder icon to search for the appropriate file. After the file is found, the correct path is added and the reference to the broken link disappears within the Link Checker menu.

You can also check the external links within your site by choosing the External Link option from the Show menu. As you can see from Figure 3.29, the Link Checker pane lists all the external link references, including the link to the public website as well as the mail link that we created in the previous chapter.

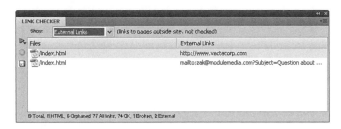

FIGURE 3.29   Check the external link references within your site by choosing the External Links option from the Show menu.

You can change the link references within this list, but they won't ever be removed. Dreamweaver will always list all external links regardless of whether you know they're correct.

Finally, you can view orphaned files, files that are in your site but that aren't linked to any pages, by choosing the Orphaned Files option from the Show menu. As you can see from Figure 3.30, all files not directly referenced from an HTML file are shown as orphaned.

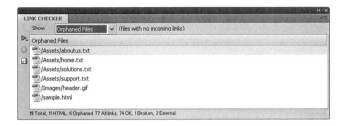

FIGURE 3.30   Orphaned files are listed after you select the Orphaned Files option from the Show menu.

If you've determined that a file is no longer needed, you can select it within the list and click the Delete key on your keyboard. Doing this permanently deletes the file.

Additional options provided by the Link Checker include the following:

▶ **Play button**—Although the Play button exists as a way to rerun the Link Checker, holding down the icon displays options for checking links for the current document, the entire site, or selected files and folders within the site.

▶ **Stop button**—As your site grows in size, so will the search time. If the search becomes excessively long, click this button to stop the link checker's search.

▶ **Save button**—Click this button to save a text-based report of broken links, external links, and orphaned files for later reference.

▶ **Status bar**—Click the status bar, located at the bottom of the Results panel, to see a total count of files scanned as well as a breakdown of total broken, external, orphaned files, and so on.

When you're satisfied with results, close the panel or choose Close Panel Group from the Results panel Options menu.

Changing Links Sitewide

One of the simplest and most time-efficient methods of managing links within your site is the Change Links Sitewide feature. This feature, available by choosing Site, Change Links Sitewide, allows you to quickly change the name of all instances of a specific link referenced within your site. To demonstrate this feature, let's assume that Mike in Marketing decided he no longer wants the navigation item Company Directory but instead wanted it to read Employee Directory. Aside from changing the text on every page, you would also have to rename the file, essentially breaking all references to that file. A quick way to fix this without launching the Link Checker, is to use the Change Link Sitewide feature, shown in Figure 3.31, to change all link references from `companydirectory.html` to `employeedirectory.html`.

When you click OK, Dreamweaver scans and fixes all instances of the file.

FIGURE 3.31   Use the Change Link Sitewide feature to quickly change references of a link.

Creating Site Reports

One of the basic premises behind site management is having the capability to check your work against various factors before considering your site done. Are you sure every page has a title? Did you add alternate text to all your images for accessibility's sake? Is your HTML clean enough to be considered valid? These questions and more can be answered by running site reports on your site. Available by selecting Site, Reports, the Reports dialog box (shown in Figure 3.32) features numerous options for customizing Dreamweaver's reporting capabilities.

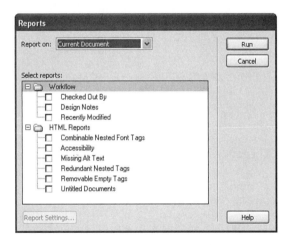

FIGURE 3.32   Use the Reports feature to run checks on HTML and workflow processes.

As you can see from Figure 3.32, the dialog box is split into two parts. The first part, the Report On list allows you to choose whether to run site reports on the current document, the entire current local site, selected files within the site, or a specific folder. The second part of the dialog box is the Select Reports pane. Within this pane, you'll choose the options for reporting. These options include the following:

▶ **Checked Out By**—When Checked Out By is selected, the Report Settings button in the bottom-left corner of the dialog box becomes active. Click the button to search for an individual who might have files checked out. It's important to know that this value is case-sensitive; however, you don't need to type in someone's entire name. For example, if you were looking for Zak Ruvalcaba, you could simply type in **Zak**, **zak**, or even **Ruvalcaba.**

▶ **Design Notes**—When this option is selected, the Report Settings button also becomes active. Click it to bring up the Design Notes dialog box, in which you can enter the design note to search for and how to search for it. When searching for a design note, you must enter in a condition, such as contains, does not contain, is, is not, and so on, for the search to meet.

▶ **Recently Modified**—Again, choosing this option makes the Report Settings button active. Click the button to launch the Recently Modified dialog box, which allows you to customize time ranges, modified by, and server location filters for recently modified files.

▶ **Combinable Nested Font Tags**—Use this option to perform searches for unnecessary uses of multiple Font tags. If for some reason there is more than one Font tag around a particular area of text, most likely it's because each Font tag has a different attribute. For example, the following Font tags `<font size="3"><font face="Arial"></font></font>` could be combined to read `<font face="Arial" size="3"></font>`. This option would alert you of this.

▶ **Accessibility**—As you'll see in Appendix A, "Accessibility," this option reports on glaring accessibility issues. Checking this option also makes the Report Settings button available, which, when selected, allows you to configure various potential accessibility issues to report on.

▶ **Missing Alt Text**—This option searches all `<img>` tags within your document to find missing `Alt` attributes.

▶ **Redundant Nested Tags**—This option checks to see whether tags are nested inside themselves and removes them as necessary. For instance, `<em>Visit Vecta Corp's website<em>today!</em></em>` could be combined to read `<em>Visit Vecta Corp's website today!</em>`. This option would alert you of this.

▶ **Removable Empty Tags**—Use this option to report on any tags within your web pages that do not contain anything. An example of an empty tag looks like this: `<font></font>`. Because the tag doesn't contain anything, it's not needed and should be removed.

▶ **Untitled Documents**—Use this handy option to run reports on duplicate titled documents, nontitled documents, and documents titled as the Dreamweaver default of Untitled Document.

To run a site report, follow these steps:

1. Choose Site, Reports to open the Reports dialog box.

2. In the Report On list, you can choose the current document (if a document is open), the entire current local site, any file you might have selected in the Files panel, or a selected folder. For this example, I'll choose the Entire Current Local Site option.

3. Now that you've selected what you're going to report on, the next thing to choose is what report you want to build. You can choose from any one of the options discussed in the preceding bullet points. I'll choose all the HTML reports except for Accessibility.

4. Click the Run button to generate the report.

5. Dreamweaver scans the documents and presents the site report as a list in the Site Reports tab of the Results panel similar to Figure 3.33. As you can see, Dreamweaver displays an icon symbolizing the severity of the error. (Question mark means minor or the user might need to provide more info, a yellow warning means slightly higher than minor and that the page might fail in certain aspects when validation is performed, and the red x means a critical error or that the page will fail if validation is performed.) The results also display the filename in which the error appears, the line number of the code in which the error appears, and a description of the actual error.

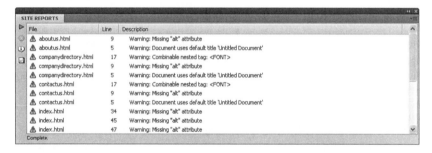

FIGURE 3.33   Site report results are displayed within the Site Reports tab in the Results panel.

6. Similar to the functionality within the Link Checker, you can double-click the error within the Results panel. Dreamweaver will automatically open the document (in Code view) and have your cursor focused on the exact line that contains the error.

7. You can also save the report for later use. To do this, choose the Save button (floppy disc icon). Dreamweaver will save the file in XML format, allowing you to later format the report into a web page, a spreadsheet, or a database.

After you've fixed the errors, you can run the report again by selecting the Play button to reopen the Reports dialog box.

Using Advanced Site Management Options

Although it seems we've run the gamut in terms of site management functionality, Dreamweaver includes a few more features that can only be categorized as advanced site-management options. Available by choosing Site, Advanced, these advanced features include the following:

▶ **FTP Log**—While transferring files using the built-in FTP client, Dreamweaver records all activity. If an error occurs when you are transferring a file using FTP, the FTP log can help you determine the problem. Select this option to present the text-based log within the FTP Log tab in the Results panel.

▶ **Recreate Site Cache**—You might remember from the beginning of the chapter that we discussed the cache. I mentioned that Dreamweaver takes a snapshot of your folder and file structure and *caches* it. In most cases, this cache is automatically generated, and in some cases, when changes are made within Dreamweaver, regenerated. If for some reason you make changes to the folder and file structure outside of Dreamweaver (not recommended), run this handy utility to re-create Dreamweaver's cache for the site.

▶ **Remove Connection Scripts**—When connecting to databases, Dreamweaver relies on a connection script built into a file and placed within a Connections folder on your site. If you've begun working with databases, this file is automatically created for you. Unfortunately, Dreamweaver doesn't know when you're no longer working with databases and will not automatically delete the files it no longer needs. You can minimize the security risk of someone tampering with your databases (if they found this file and were able to decipher the connection string information) by choosing this option to have Dreamweaver remove these connection scripts for you.

▶ **Deploy Supporting Files**—When working with dynamic web applications, Dreamweaver relies on prebuilt files and scripts (such as connection scripts) to create the functionality that you'll ultimately interact with. In most cases, Dreamweaver will automatically create a folder within your site for these files. If for some reason the folder isn't created, you can select this option to force Dreamweaver to do so. This option will be covered in more detail in Part V.

Summary

As you've seen in this chapter, Dreamweaver includes numerous options for managing a site. By defining a site first, you can take advantage of various features outlined within Dreamweaver's framework, including caching, link verification, file transfer using FTP, site maps, and so on. Now that you have a foundation in terms of Dreamweaver's user interface, managing a site, and building a simple web page, let's go beyond the simple web page that we've built and look at how to use formatting and structuring techniques such as tables and even CSS to create richer and standards-compliant websites.

PART II

Static Web Page Development

IN THIS PART

Web Page Structuring Using Tables

One of the biggest complaints print designers have when moving from print design to web design is the fact that HTML is so finicky. More specifically, the placement of elements within your web pages is limited because of the lack of support (within browsers) to control the organization of text, images, and media within the page. Although this might be true to a certain extent, HTML is, in fact, extremely flexible and offers many rich elements that can be used to control the organization of components. As the book unfolds, you'll learn about various elements and technologies Dreamweaver offers to control the pinpoint accurate placement of elements on your page. Technologies such as CSS and options such as AP Elements and tables can be used by web developers who strive for the fluid look print design programs have offered for years. The trick is learning the intricacies of the elements and how Dreamweaver allows you to work with them within its framework.

In this chapter, we'll begin to move from the simplicities of inserting and modifying elements on the page to a richer topic that involves structuring and placing elements on the page using HTML tables. As you'll begin to see, tables offer a flexible and simple alternative to the basic formatting techniques we've covered thus far for controlling the placement of elements within your web pages.

To work with the examples in this chapter, visit the book's website to download the exercises files used in this and other chapters. You'll want to replace the files for Chapter 3, "Dreamweaver Site Management," in your working VectaCorp folder with the files for Chapter 4, "Web Page Structuring Using Tables." Again, I'll place mine in `C:\VectaCorp\`.

Inserting and Working with Tables

If you remember, in Chapter 2, "Building a Web Page," the development of our Vecta Corp web page was severely limited to inserting text and images in a vertical, linear fashion. Elements on the page were organized so that we inserted text and images, followed by a line break, then either more text or another image, and then repeated the process until the page looked somewhat presentable. Although this process might work for simple web pages, it reveals drawbacks that become immediately obvious when large amounts of text are added to the page. As you can see from Figure 4.1, the background image that we added to the page begins to repeat itself near the bottom of the companydirectory.html page.

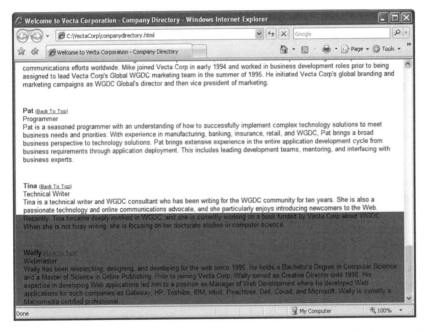

FIGURE 4.1   The background image begins to repeat itself near the bottom when there's too much text on the page.

The reason for this flaw might not seem immediately clear, but it begins to reveal itself with some explanation. The image we used for the background (header_bg.gif) is 1 pixel wide by 2,000 pixels high. The positive side is that the image always tiles horizontally no matter how wide we make the page. The downside is that the image is 2,000 pixels high, and because the natural viewing of pages is such that users navigate up and down, if the page exceeds that 2,000 pixel height, the image will tile vertically as it does horizontally. Another problem, visible in Figure 4.2, is that no definitive break exists between paragraphs. Depending on how the page's width is resized, the text and images might run together.

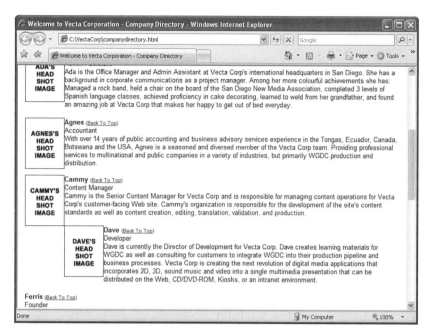

FIGURE 4.2   Because there's no definitive break between paragraphs, text and images might run together.

Although these design flaws are minor, they begin to demonstrate the complexity that our designs could potentially hold. As your web pages become more intricate and complex, structuring your web pages using elements such as tables becomes a viable alternative.

Working with tables in Dreamweaver can be a complex process depending on how intricate your design becomes. To walk you through all the table-based features exposed by Dreamweaver, we'll rebuild our Vecta Corp website from scratch. Not only will this help you understand all the features available for working with tables in Dreamweaver, but it will also show you how the small design flaws mentioned previously can be avoided by using tables to structure your pages instead. To insert a new table, create a new blank HTML page and then choose Insert, Table. The Table dialog box appears similar to Figure 4.3.

The features outlined within the Table dialog box should start looking relatively familiar. If you've used word-processing, database, or spreadsheet programs, the concept of rows, columns, and headers should be recognizable.

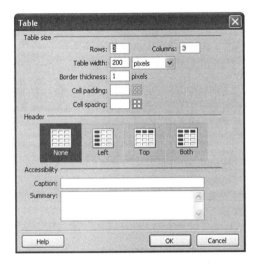

FIGURE 4.3   Insert and format basic properties for a table from the Table dialog box.

NOTE

Tables were never meant to be a way to lay out and position HTML elements on the page; they were meant to be a means of structuring large amounts of tabular data in a well-formed and ordered format. Over time, web designers realized that the concept of rows and columns could easily structure images, text, and media elements within a page. Although this method has stood the test of time and still remains the most consistent and backward-compatible format, newer methods in CSS have become more prominent and are slowly becoming the new standard for structuring elements within your web pages. We'll cover using CSS to structure web pages in the next chapter.

The features provided for working with tables in HTML go far beyond the simplicities of rows and columns. The Table dialog box displays a few options, separated into three parts: Table Size, Header, and Accessibility. A detailed list of the features outlined within these three parts is given next:

▶ **Rows**—Enter a number within this text box to set the number of rows the table will contain.

▶ **Columns**—Enter a number within this text box to set the number of columns (cells within a row) the table will have.

▶ **Table width**—Enter a number within this text box to set the width, in either pixels or a percentage, a table will have.

▶ **Border thickness**—Enter a number within this text box to set the thickness of the border in pixels that the borders will have. If you don't enter a value here, browsers will interpret the border thickness as 1. To avoid this problem, either enter a numeric value greater than 0, or if you don't want a border, enter 0.

▶ **Cell padding**—Enter a number within this text box to set the padding value between the contents of a cell and the cell border. If you don't enter a value here, browsers will interpret the cell padding as 1. To avoid this problem, either enter a numeric value greater than 0, or if you don't want cell padding, enter 0.

▶ **Cell spacing**—Enter a number within this text box to set the spacing between cells. If you don't enter a value here, browsers will interpret the cell spacing as 2. To avoid this problem, either enter a numeric value greater than 0, or if you don't want cell spacing, enter 0.

▶ **Header**—Headers are a quick way of formatting rows within a table so that the contents within the header are centered and boldface. Four options exist when working with Headers. Choose None (the default) if you don't want a header within your table. Choose Left if you'd like to have the left column of the table designated as a header, choose Top if you'd like to designate the top row of the table as a header, and choose Both if you'd like to designate both the top and left portions of the table as headers.

▶ **Caption**—Enter a value within this text box to have text appear outside of the table describing contents within it. More on this feature can be found in the online Appendix A, "Accessibility."

▶ **Align caption**—Choose an option from this menu to set the alignment of the caption in relation to the table. Five options exist within this list, including Default (Center), Top, Bottom, Left, and Right. More on this feature can be found in Appendix A.

▶ **Summary**—An important accessibility option is the summary attribute of the table. Because screen readers cannot decipher the contents within a table accurately, entering a brief description here ensures that users with screen readers can get a clear portrayal of the contents of your table. More on this feature can be found in Appendix A.

Accepting the default properties already in the Insert Tables dialog box, go ahead and click OK now to insert the new table into the page. The new table should resemble Figure 4.4 within the Document window.

Selecting Table Elements

Before we begin formatting the page using a table, it's important to touch on some important concepts, including a topic as simple as selecting the table and elements such as rows and cells within the table. As your designs become more and more complex, you'll begin to work with numerous tables within a page, including tables within table cells, also known as *nested tables*. When that time comes, the skills you learn within this section will become invaluable.

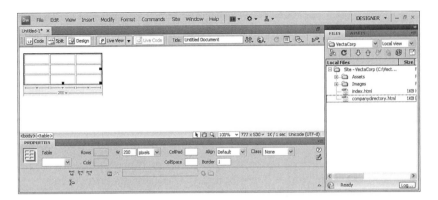

FIGURE 4.4   The new table is inserted into the page.

There are numerous ways to select a table:

▶ You can select the table by clicking, holding the cursor on the page, and then dragging it into the table.

▶ You can place your cursor into any cell within the table, at which point the Table Widths Visual Aid appears. From the Table Widths Visual Aid's menu, you can choose the Select Table as shown in Figure 4.5.

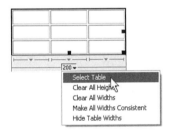

FIGURE 4.5   Choose the Select Table option from the Table Widths Visual Aid's list.

TIP

You can hide the Table Widths Visual Aid by selecting View, Visual Aids, Table Widths or by clicking Visual Aids on the Document toolbar and selecting the Table Widths option from the list.

▶ You can place your cursor within a cell and choose the `<table>` tag from the Tag Selector within the Document window's status bar.

▶ You can right-click (Control-click) within a cell to access the context menu and then choose the Select Table option from the Table submenu shown in Figure 4.6.

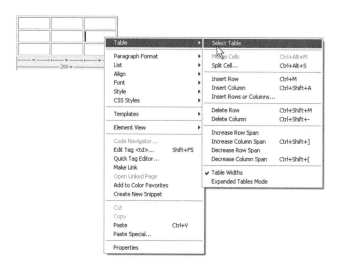

FIGURE 4.6   You can select a table by choosing Table, Select Table option from the contextual menu.

▶ You can choose Modify, Table, Select Table.

▶ You can hold down the Ctrl (⌘) key and select the outer border of the table. You'll notice that as you roll over the outer border of the table, it highlights red. Clicking after you've rolled over it will select the table.

Whatever method you choose from the preceding list, the result is the same—the table is selected. This is obvious because of the black border that is placed around the table. You can also select individual rows and columns by choosing from one of the following methods:

▶ By placing your cursor either just to the left of the table row or just above the table column, you can select a row or column, respectively. Doing so changes the cursor to a black arrow and also highlights the row or column in red. A column has been selected in Figure 4.7. Clicking the mouse will select the row or column and highlight the element(s) with the same black border you saw when you selected the table.

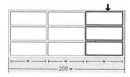

FIGURE 4.7   Place your cursor just to the left of the row to select a row or just above the column to select a column. The cursor will change to an arrow, and the row or column will be highlighted.

▶ By placing your cursor within any cell and choosing the <tr> tag from the Tag Selector, you can select that row. You can also select an individual cell by placing your cursor within the cell and choosing the <td> tag from the Tag Selector.

▶ Hold down the Ctrl (⌘) key and select an individual cell. You'll notice that as you roll over a cell, it highlights red. Clicking the cell after you've rolled over it will select it.

It's important to note that the previous methods will also work for selecting multiple rows, columns, and cells. For instance, if you'd like to select 3 rows, you can place your cursor just to the left of the first row you want selected, click, hold, and then drag either up or down to select multiple rows. The same method works for selecting multiple columns as well. Additionally, you can select multiple cells by holding the Ctrl key and then choosing the cells that you want selected.

Modifying Table Properties Using the Property Inspector

For precise formatting of tables, it's essential that you become familiar with the options revealed by the Table Property inspector. Shown in Figure 4.8, this Property inspector becomes available when the table is selected (for more on selecting tables, see the previous section).

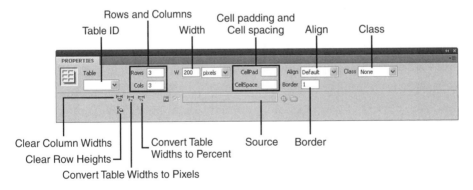

FIGURE 4.8   Format table attributes from within the Table Property inspector.

As you can see from the callouts in Figure 4.8, the Table Property inspector allows you to set/customize the following attributes (moving from left to right):

▶ ID

▶ Rows and Columns

▶ Width

▶ Cell Padding and Cell Spacing

- ▶ Alignment

- ▶ Border

- ▶ CSS Class

- ▶ Clear Column Widths or Heights

- ▶ Convert Table Widths to Pixels

- ▶ Convert Table Widths to Percent

- ▶ Source

To demonstrate the use and functionality of these attributes and formatting options, let's rebuild the main page (index.html) of the Vecta Corp site.

If you open the index.html file for this chapter, it'll appear to be a blank document, but a couple of minor changes have been made. First, the title and background color have been preset for you. Second, the header_bg.gif image isn't included. As a matter of fact, this clunky (1 pixel by 2,000 pixels) image is no longer needed; it's being replaced altogether by a centered, cleaner design.

To begin this exercise, insert a new table into the Document window by selecting Insert, Table. When the Table dialog box opens, format the options in the table dialog box so that it contains one row, one column, has a width of 100%, contains no border, no cell padding, and no cell spacing. The configured Table dialog box will look like Figure 4.9.

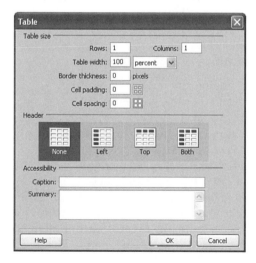

FIGURE 4.9   Format the new table so that it contains one row, one column, has a width of 100%, contains no border, no cell padding, and no cell spacing.

Click OK to insert the new table into the Document window. With the table now in the Document window, you'll notice a few details. First and the most obvious is that the table spans the entire width of the Document window. Remember, this table is set to 100%. What that means is that no matter how I stretch the Files panel group on the right, the table will always automatically adjust to accommodate the width of the Document window—as it will do in the browser window as well. Second, you'll notice that the Table Widths Visual Aid displays the width of the table as a percentage, but just to the right of that figure displays the current width in pixels within parentheses. This value is simply for your information and is useful to reference in case you ever need to convert the table's percentage to a pixel value instead. Finally, you'll notice that even though we didn't specify a border, the table appears to contain a dotted border surrounding the perimeter of the table. This is actually a visual aid and not a border. This visual aid, which can be disabled by clicking the Visual Aids button on the Document toolbar and unchecking the Table Borders option, won't show in the browser.

With the table selected, you can now begin modifying various attributes within the Property inspector. Let's begin.

The Table ID

An attribute seldom used (unless you're working with JavaScript and/or CSS), the Table ID attribute allows you to uniquely identify the table so that it can be referenced from scripting languages. This attribute is entirely optional and will have no effect on the table if left empty. We'll use the Table ID as a simple way of identifying the tables throughout the chapter. If I say *select the content table*, you'll know what table to select. If I indicate *select the header table*, again, you'll know what table to select. With our existing table selected, enter the value **header** into the Table ID text box and press Enter (Return).

Adding and Removing Rows and Columns

As you might expect, there are numerous ways for adding and removing rows and columns after you've inserted a table. You could delete the table and reinsert it if you really wanted to, but there are simpler methods. For instance, to add a row, you could place your cursor within the last cell of the last row and press the Tab key. Doing this adds a new row. Alternatively, you could use the Insert Row option (press Ctrl+M/⌘-M) available from the Table submenu within both the context menu, invoked by right-clicking (Control-clicking) the table, and the Modify menu. After the new row has been inserted, you can easily remove it by accessing the Delete Row option (press Ctrl+Shift+M/⌘-Shift-M) from the Table submenu within either the context menu or the Modify menu. Another, more flexible, alternative for inserting rows is to use the Insert Rows or Columns dialog box available from the Table submenu in both the context menu and the Modify menu. Choosing this option opens the Insert Rows or Columns dialog box (see Figure 4.10).

With the dialog box open, you'll immediately notice that you can not only insert a new row below the existing row, but can also insert a new row above the existing row. Even better, you have the option of inserting new columns before or after the column where your cursor is currently focused. Try entering the number **5** within the Number of Rows text box and click OK. As you can see from Figure 4.11, the rows are added to the table.

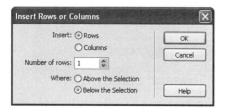

FIGURE 4.10   Use the Insert Rows or Columns dialog box as an alternative method to inserting rows or columns within your table.

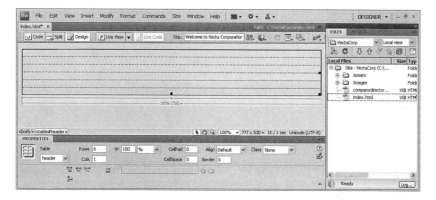

FIGURE 4.11   New rows are added to the table using the Insert Rows or Columns dialog box.

It's important to note that the previous methods work only when your cursor is focused within a cell. You can change the overall count of rows and columns for the table from the Property inspector by selecting the table and changing the text box values for Rows and Cols. To return my table back to its original state, I'll enter **1** within the Rows text box and press Enter (Return). The table will return to its original state.

Changing Table Sizes

Aside from adding and removing rows and columns, you also have the capability to change the width of the table directly from the Property inspector. You already saw how you can use the Table dialog box to initially set the width of the table (we set it to 100%); alternatively, you can set the width of the table directly within the Property inspector. Because I know that the image header.gif will reside within this table, and I know that the width of the image is 697 pixels, I'll change the width of the table now to this number by placing my cursor within the W text box, typing **697**, making sure *pixels* is selected from the menu, and pressing Enter. As you can see from Figure 4.12, the width of the table is affected.

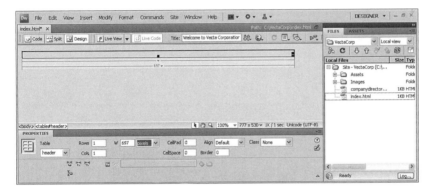

FIGURE 4.12   Change the width of the table to 697 pixels from within the Property inspector.

NOTE

You'll notice that there isn't an option for setting the height of the table. Whereas previous versions of Dreamweaver supported a height text box just underneath the width text box, newer versions of Dreamweaver exclude it. The height attribute is considered a deprecated property and is no longer supported in browsers other than Internet Explorer.

NOTE

Even though you can't set the height of the table, you'll notice that the table's height never fully collapses to nothing. By default, Dreamweaver inserts a nonbreaking space ( ) (visible only in Code view or the Code inspector) character into each cell to make it easier for you to place your cursor into the cell and begin working. If that nonbreaking space wasn't there, the table's height would collapse and make it impossible for you to place your cursor within the cell to work.

As your web pages become increasingly complex, you'll begin to realize that keeping track of your table's dimensions can get out of hand. If you ever feel like starting over, you can clear all widths and heights from both the table and cells within the table using the Clear All Widths and Clear All Heights options. You can access these options in one of three ways: First, you can choose these options from the Table Widths Visual Aid's list, as shown in Figure 4.13.

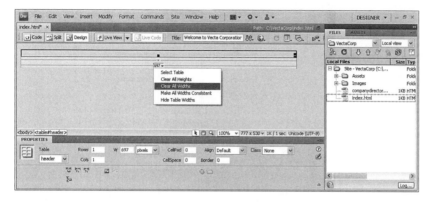

FIGURE 4.13   Select the Clear All Widths or Clear All Heights options to clear table or cell widths, respectively.

Second, you can clear column widths and column heights by clicking the Clear Column Widths and Clear Column Heights buttons located just below and to the right of the Table ID field on the Property inspector. Finally, you can perform the same operation by choosing the Clear Cell Heights and Clear Cell Widths options located in the Modify, Table submenu. Whichever method you choose results in the same action: either the height (for cells) or width is removed.

> **NOTE**
>
> Unlike other table options such as cell padding, cell spacing, and border, leaving the W text box empty in the Property inspector results in the browser interpreting the value as 0.

Modifying Cell Padding and Cell Spacing

Although it might not seem like it, the structure of our new Vecta Corp page is coming along nicely. As I'm sure you can tell, we're outlining the various properties outlined by the Table Property inspector while at the same time designing the header for our table-based page. And while there's still a lot to be done, let's move forward by adding the main header image to the cell within the header table. This can be done by locating the `header.gif` image within the Images folder of our defined site, selecting it, and dragging it over and into our table's cell. The result will appear similar to Figure 4.14.

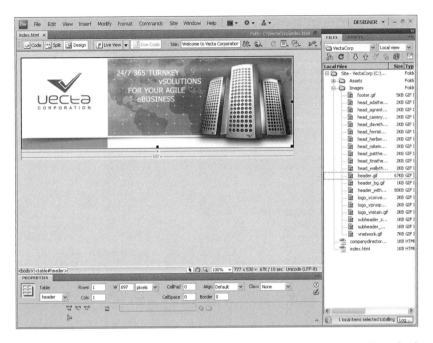

FIGURE 4.14   Drag the header graphic into the table's cell to round out the heading for our web page.

Now that you have the header of the page squared away, it's time to build the bottom portion of the site. Yes, we could insert the contents of home.txt (located within the Assets folder) directly underneath the existing table; unfortunately, doing this would cause the text to align flush against the edge of the Document window as our margins are currently set to 0 pixels. Although we could fix this by adding a margin width, doing that would cause our table at the top of the page to shift to the right to compensate. Instead, we could create a table below our existing table and adjust its cell spacing or cell padding to make up for the necessary spacing. To do this, we'll begin by adding a new table. Begin the process by following these steps:

1. Place your cursor just to the right of the header table.

2. Choose Insert, Table. The Table dialog box appears.

3. Give your new table 2 rows, 2 columns, a width of 697 pixels, a border thickness of 0, a cell padding of 0, and a cell spacing of 4.

4. Click OK. Your new table will be inserted into the Document window, below the header table, and will look similar to Figure 4.15.

5. Assign your table the ID content within the Table ID text box in the Property inspector (shown in Figure 4.15).

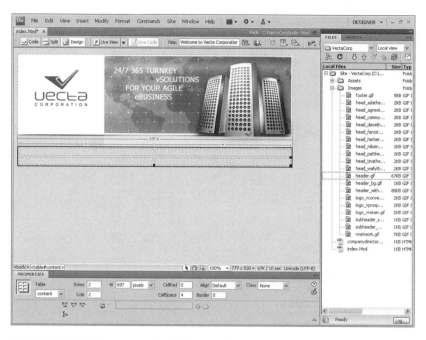

FIGURE 4.15 The new table is inserted and includes cell spacing to protect the content from the left edge of the page.

Now that the table is firmly in place, you can see that the cell spacing is available. Unlike the header table, which doesn't contain spacing around the edges of the table, our content table contains spacing around the table and between cells. This will become more obvious later, when you insert text into a cell.

TIP

As you've seen, manipulating the table's cell spacing and cell padding is easy using the Insert Table dialog box. Modifying cell spacing and cell padding using the Property inspector is also possible. Just to the right of the W text box, you'll notice text boxes for CellPad (cell padding) and CellSpace (cell spacing). The cell padding and cell spacing of a table can also be adjusted here.

Table Alignment

Now that we have both a header and a content table within our page, let's finish off the table structure by aligning both tables to the center of the page. To do this, select each table and then choose the option Center from the Align menu in the Property inspector so that each of your two tables is center-aligned on the page, similar to Figure 4.16.

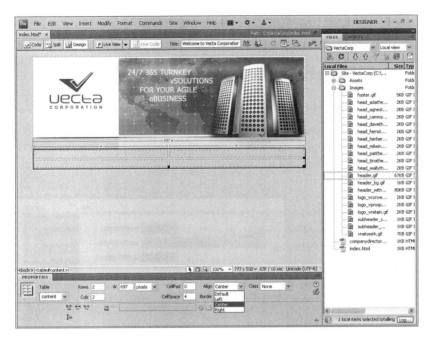

FIGURE 4.16   Select each table and center align them on the page.

It's important to note that this option aligns only the table on the page, not the content within the table. To align the content within the table, you'll still need to select any content that you add within the table and choose the center align option from the Text Property inspector.

Working with Table Borders

There are a couple of methods for adding borders to your existing tables, but none more obvious than the Border text box option located within the Property inspector. Selecting a table and adding a value here (other than 0) creates a traditional, ordinary looking border. Nothing fancy here! We'll discuss a second option for adding borders in CSS in the next chapter.

Converting Table Widths to a Percentage or Pixels

Every now and then you might find the need to convert an existing table that was created using pixels into a percentage value or vice versa. For instance, our content table is displayed at the bottom of the page and has a fixed width of 697 pixels. Looking at the table and its width within the page, it appears to take up roughly 80% of the page. If I like this width, but prefer the width to be expressed in percentages as opposed to pixels, I can easily perform a conversion with a simple click of a button. To do this, I can select the table and choose Modify, Table, Convert Widths to Percent (shown in Figure 4.17).

Although you won't notice a significant difference initially, the Table Widths Visual Aid does, in fact, display the table width as a percentage followed by the pixel width within the parentheses. Just below that value is the width of the cell expressed as a percentage, again followed by the pixel width in parentheses.

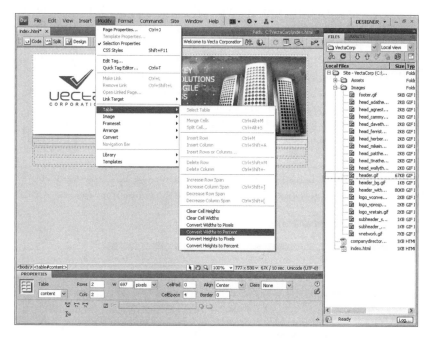

FIGURE 4.17   Convert table widths to percentages.

NOTE

While using pixel-based dimensions certainly allows you to keep your designs within a fixed width, you shouldn't discount the use of percentages for setting the dimensions of a web page. Percentages allow you to build "liquid" designs. That is, a design that constantly adjusts to the width (and sometimes height) of the user's screen resolution. Assuming you built a table that stretched 100% of the page width, the design would appear equally to users who have their screen resolutions set to 800x600 or 1024x768 for instance.

Other options exist from the same menu, including Convert Widths to Percent, Convert Heights to Pixels, and Convert Heights to Percent. Furthermore, you can access these options directly from the Property inspector by choosing the icons located to the bottom-left of the Property inspector, just underneath the Table ID text box.

Modifying Cell Properties Using the Property Inspector

As you've seen thus far, numerous options exist for modifying properties associated with a table. You've seen the basic properties that exist when a table is initially inserted from within the Table dialog. You've also seen that when you select a table, the Property inspector tailors itself to accommodate the modification of attributes associated with the table.

Just as there are many options for modifying properties associated with a table, so too are there many options for modifying the cells within that table. In fact, different properties exist for the table, as opposed to cells within the table. Cells can be merged, split, vertically-aligned, horizontally-aligned, and so on. Also, content within cells can be formatted using text formatting properties that you learned in Chapter 2. The content can also be aligned within the cells, prevented from wrapping within the cells, or even converted to a header. The table, on the other hand, doesn't support a lot of these properties. For instance, the content as a whole can't be formatted, cells can't be manipulated, and so on. In general, it's safe to say that the properties exposed by the table are broad and specific to the table as a whole, whereas properties provided for individual cells are more refined and thorough—and allow for cells to be formatted independently of one another. As you can see from Figure 4.18, you can access the Table Cell Property inspector by placing your cursor within a cell.

As you can see from the callouts in Figure 4.18, the upper half of the Property inspector reveals simple text-based formatting options covered in Chapter 2, but the bottom

Text-based formatting options

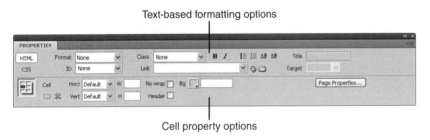

Cell property options

FIGURE 4.18   The Table Cell Property inspector becomes available when you place your cursor into a cell.

portion outlines key properties (moving from left to right) supported by table cells, including the following:

- Merging and Splitting Cells

- Horizontal and Vertical Alignment

- Width and Height

- No Wrap

- Header

- Background Color

- Page Properties

To demonstrate these properties, let's format the cells within the content table.

Changing Cell Widths and Heights

So far you've seen how to manipulate the width of the table as a whole. The cells within a table, however, function somewhat differently. If you recall, earlier in the book we selected the content table and assigned it a width of 697 pixels. The table is inserted at the 697 pixel width; however, by default the width of each cell is given a width equal to the width of the table divided by the number of cells within the specific row. So in our case, the cells appear to have a width of roughly 348–349 pixels each. Although this might have seemed to be the case, in fact, inserting the image subheader_welcome.gif into the first cell of the second column reveals otherwise. As you can see from Figure 4.19, inserting content into the cell shifts the cells out of proportion.

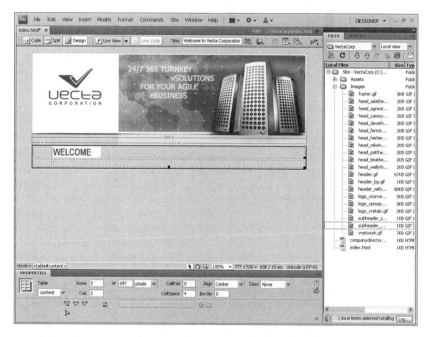

FIGURE 4.19   Insert an image into the cell to see the cells shift out of proportion.

Although Dreamweaver initially makes an attempt to proportionately size your tables, it will always rely on you to manually set the size of the cells individually. Because we didn't set the size of each cell, Dreamweaver accommodates the addition of content within the second cell by automatically moving the cells over to the left (or right, had we inserted the image in the left column), essentially freeing up room for you to work.

The lack of cell widths is also evident from the Table Widths Visual Aid. As Figure 4.19 also indicates, although a set width exists for the table as a whole, the two individual width values for the columns are empty. Setting the width of columns, which sets the width of each cell within the column within the Property inspector is just as simple as it was for the table. To set the widths of our two columns, follow these steps:

1. Place your cursor into the first cell within the first column. Immediately the Table Widths Visual Aid becomes available.

2. Choose the Select Column option from the cell menu, similar to Figure 4.20.

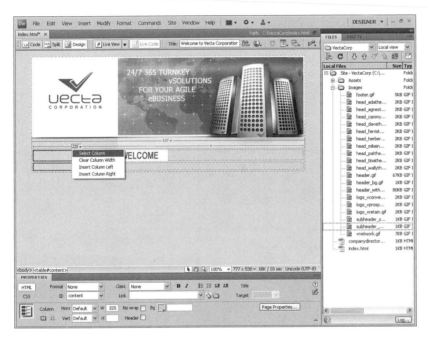

FIGURE 4.20   Choose the Select Column option from the cell menu in the Table Widths Visual Aid and then change the width of the cell to 220 pixels.

3. Within the Width (W) text box in the Property inspector, enter the value **220** and press Enter. The table's column will resize accordingly.

4. To make the table functionally correct, we'd now have to set the width on the second column. Rather than trying to figure out what 697 pixels minus 220 pixels is, we can take a shortcut. From the Table Widths Visual Aid menu, select the Make All Widths Consistent option. Immediately you'll notice that a value of 465 pixels is assigned to the second column.

When you're finished, the table will be resized proportionally, and the Table Widths Visual Aid will contain width values for the each column similar to Figure 4.21.

If you need to clear the widths for a column, you can do one of two things. First, you can select the entire column, which also selects every cell within that column, and physically remove the numeric pixel value within the Width (W) text box in the Property inspector.

Second, you can easily remove the width of a column by accessing the column-based menu from the Table Widths Visual Aid and choosing the Clear Column Width option.

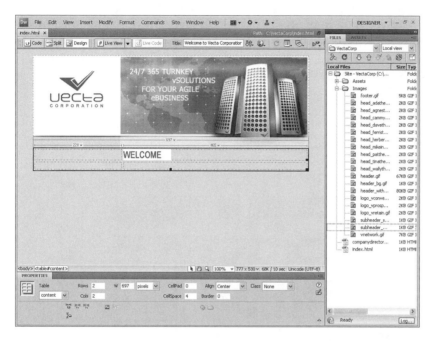

FIGURE 4.21   The cells are resized proportionally and the Table Widths Visual Aid includes cell widths as well.

TIP

You might be thinking that 697 pixels (the width of the table) minus 220 pixels (the width of the first column) doesn't equal 465 pixels, but instead 477. When sizing columns, it's important to take cell spacing and cell padding into consideration. If you have cell padding and cell spacing (as we currently do), those values must also be deducted from the total size of the table; otherwise, the dimensions will be slightly off.

Cell heights can also be modified. The reason it has not been covered with more detail is twofold. First, it's just as simple to modify a height as it is to modify the width. After you've learned how to modify the width, modifying the height on your own should be easy. Second, it's not important that you set a cell height. Generally, you'll allow the contents within the cell to govern the height for you.

Splitting and Merging Cells

After you've inserted a table onto the page, you'll often need to merge cells to create more space within the table. For instance, although you might need to work with two independent cells within a row, you might have a bigger image that needs more space than what has been allotted for the columns. Instead of creating a whole new table, you can merge the cells within an existing row into fewer cells, essentially freeing up the needed space.

To merge two or more cells within a table, you would highlight by clicking, holding, and dragging the cells that you want to merge. With the cells highlighted, you can merge the cells by either choosing the Merge Cells icon within the Property inspector, selecting the Merge Cells option from the Table submenu within the context menu, or by choosing Modify, Table, Merge Cells. Any method you choose merges the cells.

Let's try it out on our example using one of these methods. Left-click, hold, and drag across from the first cell in the second row over to the second cell of the same row. Choose Modify, Table, Merge Cells. The cells will merge into one cell. Now find the footer.gif image located within our Images folder and drag it into the newly merged cell. The result of the merger and image addition will resemble Figure 4.22.

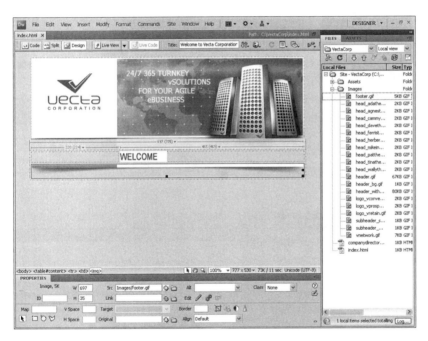

FIGURE 4.22   Highlight the cells that you want to merge by clicking, holding, and dragging over from the first cell over to the second cell.

In addition to merging cells, you can also split bigger cells up into smaller cells. For instance, I can place my cursor within a recently merged cell and click the Split Cell icon from the Property inspector. Doing this opens the Split Cell dialog box, as shown in Figure 4.23.

As you can see from Figure 4.23, the dialog box defaults to the Split Cell into Columns option. You can enter a value to split the cell into columns and then click OK to commit the changes.

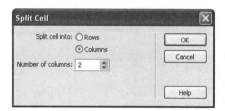

FIGURE 4.23   The Split Cell dialog box allows you to split cells into smaller individual cells.

> **NOTE**
>
> Dreamweaver's Split Cell dialog box always defaults its values to the natural develop-
> ment of the table. Because the table's structure appears to contain two columns over-
> all, Dreamweaver will default to a two-column split. Also, entering a number greater
> than the column count of the table results in the split occurring within the left-most
> cell. Try it on your own to see the results.

The Split Cell option is also available from the Table submenu in both the context and
Modify menus.

An alternative way of splitting and merging cells and rows is to choose Modify, Table,
Increase/Decrease Row and Column Span. To use these options, place your cursor in the
cell that has been merged and select Decrease Column Span. To split the same cells back
up, choose the Increase Column Span option. These methods are quick alternatives to
using the Split and Merge Cell features.

Setting Horizontal and Vertical Alignments

You can specify horizontal and vertical alignments for a cell by choosing from options
available within the Horizontal (Horz) and Vertical (Vert) menus in the Property inspector.
To demonstrate alignments, I'll add a navigation menu to the first cell. To do this, place
your cursor within the first cell and enter the text **Home** followed by a line break
(Shift+Enter or Shift-Return). Repeat this process, adding **About Us**, **Solutions**, **Support**,
and **Contact Us** navigation items to the cell. You might also want to format the font for
the navigation menu by selecting all the text, right-clicking, and then choosing Font,
Arial, Helvetica, San-serif from the context menu that appears.

As you would expect, the text looks fine within the cell. The same can't be said after I
insert the welcome text (available by opening home.txt, selecting all the content, copying
it, and then pasting it) into the second cell (the cell next to the one that contains our
navigation menu). As you can see from Figure 4.24, the navigation is shifted to the vertical center of the cell.

FIGURE 4.24   Inserting text into one cell causes elements within a second cell that are shorter to align to the vertical center of the cell.

Although this result is perfectly normal, it might not be what you intend. A more desirable result would be to align the navigation menu to the top of the cell so that it appears as though the welcome text and navigation menu are both aligned to the top of their respective cells. To do this, place your cursor into the cell that contains the navigation menu and select the Top option from the Vert menu (located within the bottom half of the Table Cell Property inspector just to the right of the split and merge cells icons). The navigation menu text will shift to the top of its cell. You might also want to do this for the cell that contains our welcome text. You never know when you'll have a page that contains text that results in a cell that is smaller than the navigation menu.

Of course, if you ever want to horizontally align content within the cell, you can select from one of the options in the Horz menu. To give you an idea as to how this works, place your cursor within the navigation menu's cell and choose the Center option from the Horz menu in the Cell Property inspector. Your navigation menu will immediately center itself within the cell.

You might want to round out the design by creating hyperlinks for each navigation menu item: index.html for the Home menu item, aboutus.html for About Us, solutions.html for Solutions, support.html for Support, and contactus.html for Contact Us.

Setting the Background Color and Cell Wrapping

Looking at the welcome text, you can see that the text is cleanly formatted with spacing and line breaks. We didn't add the spacing or the line breaks at the end of each line, Dreamweaver does it automatically for us. When a line reaches the end of the cell, the text breaks and keeps going on to the next line, as you might expect. But what if you didn't want that to happen? What if you wanted the text to keep going and automatically stretch the width of the table regardless of the pixel size we explicitly set? A good way to prevent text within a cell from wrapping is to use the No Wrap check box within the Property inspector.

The question becomes, "Why would I want to prevent the text from wrapping within the cell?" Assume for a moment that you had a website that contained a tabbed navigation bar at the top of the page. Depending on the page you happened to be on, those tabs changed and varied based on the page and the content within the page. Assuming you had a few dozen web pages within your site, your tabs could number in the hundreds. Would you want to create a few hundred different images for every tab in your website? Probably not, right? Instead, you could create dynamic tabs that stretched (using the No Wrap option) based on the content within the cell. This way, you're creating the tab structure only once, and the text within the tab is the only part that changes. Doing this would make your tabbed navigation much easier to manage. To demonstrate my point, let's do a quick example. To follow along, review these steps:

1. Create a new blank HTML page by choosing File, New. Choose HTML from the Blank Page category, choose the <none> option from the Layout category, and click Create. The new blank page appears. Immediately save your work as `nowrap.html`.

2. Create a new table by choosing Insert, Table. When the Table dialog box appears, create a table with 1 row, 3 columns, a width of 150 pixels, a border thickness of 0, cell padding of 0, and cell spacing of 0; then click OK. The new table appears within the page.

3. Resize the first column to 24 pixels and the third column to 30 pixels. Again, this can be accomplished by placing your cursor within the specific cell and adding the value to the W text box within the Table Cell Property inspector.

4. Locate the images `lefttab.gif` and `righttab.gif` located within the `Assets\NoWrapExample` folder for the exercise files that you downloaded for this chapter. Insert (by either dragging the image from the Files panel or by choosing Insert, Image) the specific image into its respective cell (`lefttab.gif` will go in the first cell and `righttab.gif` will go in the third cell.)

5. Use the Tag Editor (covered in more detail later in the book) to set the middle column's background image to `bg.gif`. You can do this by right-clicking within the middle cell and then choosing Edit Tag <td>. The Tag Editor dialog box will appear. Select the Browser Specific category and then click the Browse button located just to

the right of the Background Image text box. Find `bg.gif` located within the same folder that contained our two tab images. Click OK to close the Tag Editor. Now the table should resemble Figure 4.25.

FIGURE 4.25   Create a table to resemble the functionality and look of a tab.

6. With your cursor still focused within the middle cell, choose the Center option from the Horz menu and the Bottom option from the Vert menu within the Property inspector.

7. Select the table, select the Copy option from the Edit menu, place your cursor just after the table, press Enter to create a paragraph break, and click the Paste option from the Edit menu. Now you'll have two tables that look like tabs.

8. Place your cursor in the middle cell of the first table and select Insert, Hyperlink. When the Hyperlink dialog appears, enter the text **Option 1** and type the # (to create an anchor with no link) symbol within the link text box. Click OK.

9. Place your cursor in the second cell of the second table, select Insert, Hyperlink. When the Hyperlink dialog appears, enter the text **This is a really long Option** and type the # symbol within the link text box. Click OK.

With everything done, the two tabs should resemble Figure 4.26.

FIGURE 4.26   One tab has little text and fits perfectly in the tab. The second tab contains long text that wraps.

As you can see from Figure 4.26, because of the fixed width of the table, the second cell within the second table automatically wraps the contents within it. To allow the tab's size to fluctuate, place your cursor within the middle cell of the second table and choose the No Wrap check box. As you can see from Figure 4.27, the tab's size automatically adjusts.

FIGURE 4.27   The No Wrap check box within the Property inspector prevents the table's cell from wrapping to the next line.

The upside to this method is that no matter how short the contents, the tabs will never be smaller than 150 pixels, and you can guarantee that only three images will be used. The contents within the cells are all that change.

Aside from setting the No Wrap option within the Property inspector, you also saw how to use the Tag Editor to set the Background Image (Bg) within a cell.

Although a cell's background image can be set from the Tag Editor dialog box, the background color for a cell can be set directly from the Cell Property inspector. To demonstrate this feature, follow these steps:

1. Select the content table and change the cell spacing from 4 pixels to 0 pixels. This will eliminate the cell spacing, as it's no longer needed. You might need to readjust the cell's columns so that the first column is set to 220 pixels and the second column is set to 477 pixels, as opposed to the 465 pixels that we set previously.

2. Place your cursor within the table's first cell and add a background color by clicking the Bg color picker option from the Cell Property inspector. When your cursor changes to an eyedropper, sample the dark gray color from either the header or the

footer images to make the navigation menu's background color appear to continue from the header down to the footer.

3. Repeat this process for the cell that contains the welcome text. Rather than sampling a color from the interface, simply select white, as this is the color that we need to make the design blend together. The result will look similar to Figure 4.28.

FIGURE 4.28   Add background color for both the navigation cell and the welcome text's cell.

Converting a Cell to a Header

You've already seen how to work with headers within the Table dialog box. Dreamweaver also supports the capability to convert an existing cell into a table header through the use of the Header check box within the Property inspector. To use this functionality, place your cursor within a table cell and enable the Header check box. The cursor within the cell will then be centered, and any text typed into the cell will be made bold.

Why a Separate Tag for a Table Header?

Tables without headers are inserted with the following code:

```
<table>
<tr>
<td colspan="2">Header cell</td>
</tr>
<tr>
```

```
<td>Cell 3</td>
<td<Cell 4</td>
</tr>
</table>
```

In this case, the table has two rows (represented by <tr>) and three cells (represented by <td>). The first cell uses the colspan attribute to merge the cells into one cell that spans the width of the bottom two cells. Converting a cell into a header removes the row and cell containing the colspan and replaces it with a <th> tag as follows:

```
<table>
<th>Header cell</th>
<tr>
<td>Cell 3</td>
<td<Cell 4</td>
</tr>
</table>
```

As you can see, the addition of the table header results in cleaner and more concise code, which ultimately means faster loading of the web page by the browser. Try both code blocks in Dreamweaver on your own to see the effects.

Nesting Tables

As you can see from the design thus far, our page is becoming relatively complex in its structure. So far we have two tables: one for the header and one for the content that also contains a footer. Obviously, it doesn't have to stop there. Let's assume we wanted to add a third table to structure the company's solution offerings underneath the welcome text. If that's the case, we'll need to add a *nested* table. A nested table as the name implies, is a table that nests within a cell of an existing table. Our solutions table is a perfect example of a nested table within a cell. Because we have three solutions, complete with an icon, a title, and descriptive text, we'll need to add another table to structure that content so that its presentation is cleaner than the bulleted list we used in Chapter 2. To create the nested table, follow these steps:

1. Place your cursor after the welcome text and click Enter (Return) to insert a paragraph break. Drag the subheader_solutions.gif image located within the Images folder over to the cell. Now place your cursor just to the right of the solutions image and click Enter (Return) one more time to create a paragraph break.

2. Create a new table by choosing Insert, Table. When the Table dialog box appears, create a table with 5 rows, 2 columns, a width of 450 pixels, a border thickness of 0, cell padding of 0, and cell spacing of 0; click OK. The new table will appear nested within the cell.

3. Resize the first column to 70 pixels and the second column to 380 pixels.

4. Add the `logo_vprospect.gif`, `logo_vconvert.gif`, and `logo_vretain.gif` images to the first, third, and fifth cells of the second column.

5. Open the `solutions.txt` file located within the Assets folder and copy each solution's representative description and paste it into its respective cell within the nested table. When you've finished, the table should resemble Figure 4.29.

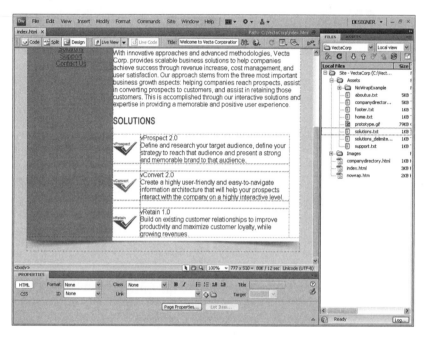

FIGURE 4.29   Add the images and respective descriptions to each cell.

As you can see, nesting tables provides us with much more flexibility in our design. Because of nesting, we're no longer limited to a stringent design. Instead we now have the opportunity to fine-tune and precisely position elements within our page.

Working with Tables in Expanded Tables Mode

Up until this point, we've focused on one mode of development: the Standard mode. The Standard mode, which is the default form of development, allows you to add and work with tables as you have done so far. It's important to note, however, that one other mode exists: the Expanded Tables mode.

As you can see, our table structure has gotten somewhat complex, especially now that we have a nested table. You've probably noticed that selecting rows, cells, and even the nested table is a bit more difficult than it was at the beginning of the chapter when we were working with just one table. Although it certainly might seem frustrating to get your cursor in the right place in between nested tables and cells, it's important to note that there is relief via the Expanded Tables mode. The Expanded Tables mode, available from the Layout category in the Insert panel, temporarily adds cell spacing and cell padding to your cells within Design view, essentially making it easier for you to place your cursor in between and work with cells and nested tables. You can use the Expanded Tables mode by clicking the Expanded button located within the Layout category of the Insert panel. After you've clicked the button, Dreamweaver provides you with a Getting Started in Expanded Tables Mode dialog box to explain the mode. Click OK to close the dialog box and return to your page. As you can see from Figure 4.30, the Expanded Tables mode created spacing between cells, essentially allowing for the easy placement of the cursor between cells and nested tables.

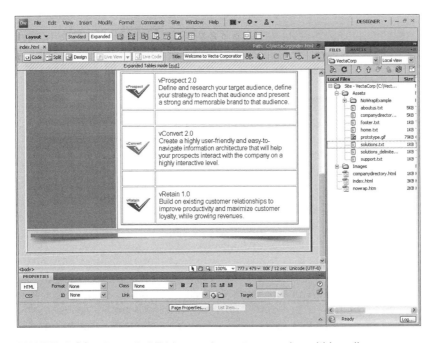

FIGURE 4.30   Expanded Tables mode creates spacing within cells.

To exit the Expanded Tables mode, click the exit link located within the temporary blue shaded menu bar located just below the Document bar. Your page will return to Standard mode. You can also click the Standard button (located to the left of the Expanded button) in the Layout category of the Insert panel to return the layout back to Standard mode.

Importing Tabular Data

Earlier in the chapter, we built a table within `index.html` to hold the company's solution offerings. Remember that we created a table with six rows and three columns and then manually added solutions images and descriptive text. Numerous options exist for making this solution more dynamic. One solution, using a database to feed solution offerings to a table within the main page, will be discussed in Part V, "Dynamic Web Page Development." For now, let's discuss a simple alternative: the Import Tabular Data feature, available within Dreamweaver's Insert menu.

The Import Tabular Data option, available by choosing Insert, Table Objects, Import Tabular Data enables you to quickly build an HTML table based on preformatted tab-, comma-, semicolon-, or colon-delimited files. This means that Mike over in Marketing can maintain a spreadsheet of the company's solution offerings. When he's ready to have a set of new offerings posted on the website, he can export his spreadsheet to one of the delimited options and then send it to Wally the webmaster for quick import via the Import Tabular Data feature.

For our example, we'll use a tab-delimited file located within the Assets folder called `solutions_delimited.txt`. Opening the file reveals that the text within the file is separated by tabs similar to Figure 4.31.

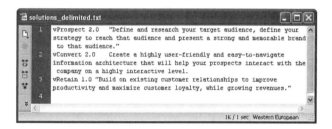

FIGURE 4.31   A tab-delimited file contains text separated by tabs.

Dreamweaver, recognizing that the file is separated by tabs, will pick apart all text elements within this file and place them into their own cells within a new table. To see this feature for yourself, first open `index.html`, remove the existing company events table, leaving your cursor within the cell, and choose Insert, Table Objects, Import Tabular Data. The Import Tabular Data dialog box will appear (see Figure 4.32).

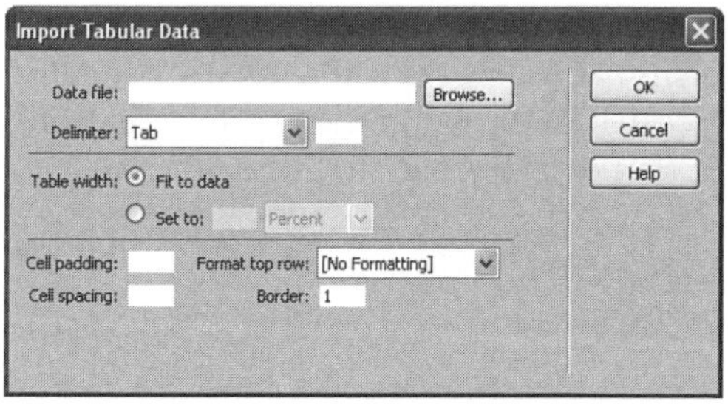

FIGURE 4.32   The Import Tabular Data dialog box allows you to import a file based on a delimiter option and then format the table that will be created for the content.

Looking at the dialog box, you'll notice that it contains options for importing the file to use, choosing a delimiter option, and then formatting the table that will be created for the content. The complete list of functionality exposed by the dialog box is outlined here:

▶ **Data file**—Click the Browse button from this file field to look for and select the file to use. For our example, browse to the `solutions_delimited.txt` file located within the Assets folder.

▶ **Delimiter**—Choose a delimiter option. Options include Tab, Comma, Semicolon, Colon, and Other. Choosing Other enables a text box allowing you to type in the delimiter symbol. For our example, choose Tab.

▶ **Table width**—Choose the Fit to Data option button to have the newly generated table added to the page with no widths specified. Because no widths will be specified, the table will be as wide as the longest text element within the cells. You can also choose the Set option to manually specify a width in either pixels or a percentage. For example, choose the Set to Radio button, type the value **100** into the text box, and choose the Percent option from the menu.

▶ **Cell padding and Cell spacing**—Assigns a cell padding or cell spacing (or both) to your table. For our example, enter **2** for cell padding and **0** for cell spacing.

▶ **Format top row**—Select an option from this menu to format the top row of your table if you have one. Options in this list include Bold, Italic, and Bold and Italic. For our example, leave this as is.

▶ **Border**—Enter a value within this text box to assign a border to your table. For our example, enter **0**.

When you've finished reviewing the options and have made the appropriate additions and selections, click OK. The new table will be added to your page. The page should look like Figure 4.33.

The final tasks are to set the font for the text in the table, add a new column in front of the existing content for the product logos, add the logos to the cells within the new column, and then set pixel widths for each of the three columns within the table. When you're finished, the table might resemble Figure 4.34.

Sorting Tables

In the previous section, we imported data that created a table with three rows of content. Imagine that instead you imported data that created hundreds of rows within a table. Even worse, imagine that all your rows were unsorted within the table. Trying to manually sort a table that contained hundreds of rows could take hours. Instead, you can use the Sort Table command to have Dreamweaver automatically sort the table based on a column that you choose. To use this feature, select the newly created solutions table and choose the Sort Table command available from the Commands menu. The Sort Table dialog box will appear similar to Figure 4.35.

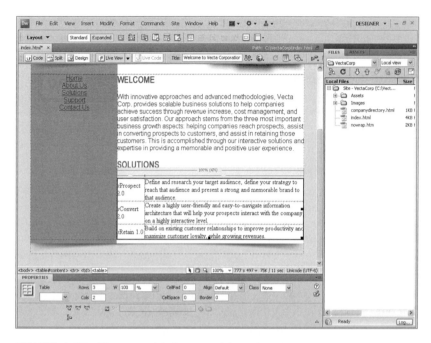

FIGURE 4.33   The new table is created based on the content within our tab-delimited file.

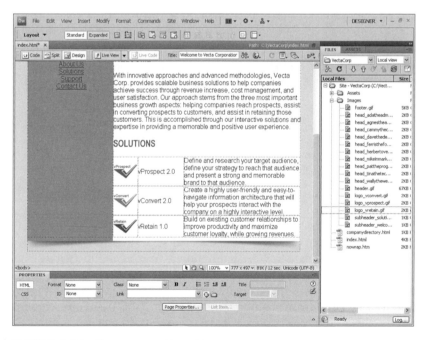

FIGURE 4.34   Format the table, add a new column before the content, and add the product icons to the cells within the new column.

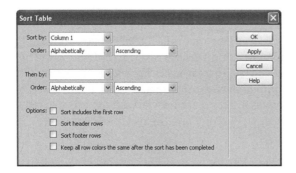

FIGURE 4.35   The Sort Table command allows you to sort a table based on a prespecified column.

As you can see from Figure 4.35, the Sort Table command allows you to sort the table based on a primary and secondary column. A complete list of features is outlined here:

▶ **Sort by and Order**—Choose an option from the Sort list to specify which column from the table the sort will be performed on. Furthermore, you can select options from the Order menus to specify how the sort should be performed. You can perform alphabetic and numeric sorts and then choose whether to sort the values in the column in an ascending or descending order.

▶ **Then by and Order**—Choose a column from the Then By list when you want to perform a sort on a second column after the primary sort has been complete. Again, you can set the order of the sort on the secondary column.

▶ **Sort includes the first row**—Generally the first row of a table contains a header describing the content within the columns. If your table doesn't, you can include the first row in the sort by choosing this check box.

▶ **Sort header rows**—Check this option to sort all the rows in the table's <thead> section (if it exists) using the same criteria as the body rows.

▶ **Sort footer rows**—Check this option to sort all the rows in the table's <tfoot> section (if it exists) using the same criteria as the body rows.

▶ **Keep all row colors the same after the sort has been completed**—Check this option so that the table row attributes (such as color) remain associated with the same content after the sort. For instance, if your table rows are formatted with two alternating colors, do not select this option to ensure that the sorted table still has alternating-colored rows.

For our example, choose the Column 2 option from the Sort By list and click OK. Immediately the dialog box closes, and the table is sorted based on the solution name.

Tracing Images

Many times, our design prototypes become so complex that it becomes difficult to figure out exactly how to structure the page with tables using Dreamweaver. To aid you with this obstacle, Dreamweaver allows you to include a tracing image. *Tracing images* allow you to build your page prototype within your favorite image-editing program, save the prototype as a GIF or JPEG image, and then lay it down as a temporary background to your page so that you can build your page structure over it. To demonstrate the use of tracing images, follow these instructions:

1. Create a new blank page by choosing File, New or by pressing Ctrl+N (⌘-N). When the New Document dialog box appears, choose the HTML page type from the Blank Page category, choose the <none> option from the Layout category, and click Create. A new blank page is created. Immediately save your page as `tracingimage.html`.

2. With the page now open, select the Page Properties option from the Modify menu or by pressing Ctrl+J (⌘-J). The Page Properties dialog appears.

3. Enter **0** for each of the Left Margin, Top Margin, Margin Width, and Margin Height text boxes within the Appearance (HTML) category.

4. Switch to the Tracing Image category. As you can see, the Tracing Image category outlines two options: first, a file field that allows you to select the tracing image to use, and second, a transparency slider to select the opacity of the tracing image within the Document window.

5. In the Tracing Image text box, browse to the `prototype.gif` image located within the Assets folder.

6. Slide the Transparency slider to 30% and click Apply. As you can see from Figure 4.36, the prototype design is faintly visible in the background.

7. Click OK to close the Page Properties dialog box.

With the prototype faintly visible in the background, you can now add and manipulate tables to create a design using the background tracing image as a reference.

When you've finished creating the structure based on the tracing image, you can revisit the Tracing Image category within the Page Properties dialog box and remove it.

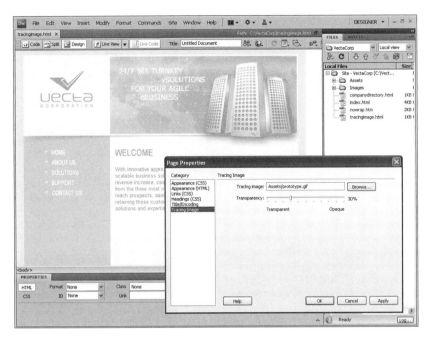

FIGURE 4.36   The tracing image is faintly visible in the background of the page.

Summary

As you have seen, tables provide flexibility when working with your page designs in Dreamweaver. In Chapter 2, we used simple page-formatting techniques such as line breaks, paragraph and heading formatting, paragraph breaks, lists, and so on to create designs that were limited in the layout and placement of elements within the page.

In this chapter, tables were introduced as an alternative and more realistic method. Tables provide a rich and welcome approach to layout design using a myriad of options available within the Property inspector. In the next chapter, we'll explore other options for structuring and formatting our designs using a more standards-compliant approach in Cascading Style Sheets, more commonly referred by its acronym, CSS. As you will see, CSS provides tremendous flexibility for creating rich layouts and clean page designs.

CHAPTER 5

Page Formatting Using Cascading Style Sheets

As you have seen, HTML is extremely restrictive when it comes to web page formatting, but this is by no means a fault of the language. Unfortunately, many beginning developers who are expert designers in the print industry jump to web development thinking that visual web editors function the same way as popular print design programs, such as InDesign and Quark. They think visually rather than practically, which results in "hacked" code, mediocre page structures, and poorly designed pages that leave many people with a sour attitude toward web development and HTML in general.

A better solution is available. Cascading Style Sheets (CSS) provide what many designers and developers have asked for over the years: more control, more flexibility, and more pizazz to the overall look of their pages. How? CSS has endless support for font styles, sizes, and weights. It supports tracking, leading, text indenting, and paragraph spacing. Tables don't have to have cell padding and cell spacing around the entire table; instead, tables can contain cell padding and spacing on just one side of the table, independent of the other sides. Form elements can contain background colors, borders, and styles. With CSS you can now use your own custom images for bullets. Additionally, you can even control the structure of your page using various positioning attributes outlined through CSS. With increasing browser support for the newest CSS specifications, CSS makes a huge difference in the way developers create web pages now and in the future.

An Introduction to CSS

Imagine for a moment that our fictitious Vecta Corp website uses the same font, color, and size consistently throughout the site. Also imagine that the Vecta Corp site consists of 300 pages, and you need to change the fonts from Arial to Verdana and the color from black to gray throughout the site. You can imagine how frustrating it would be to open every one of those 300 files and have to manually change every place where a font is applied to a section of text. At its foundation, CSS solves this dilemma. With CSS you can create one file (`styles.css`) and apply style rules within that CSS file that dictate how the text within your website should look. If the time ever comes to change the font properties, you can do it in that one CSS file, and your changes will appear throughout the entire site.

But how does this work? Style sheets are usually contained within an external CSS file (but they don't have to be) and are linked in to every web page that you are working with by adding the `<link>` tag within the `<head>` tag of your document. Therefore, any and all styles from that CSS file can be applied to the web pages that you are working with, ultimately providing you with the flexibility to quickly and easily modify one CSS file that propagates changes to all web pages that share the CSS file.

Although I've mentioned one way of creating style sheets (external CSS file), there are, in fact, three standard ways of creating them:

▶ **External file**—Arguably the most popular and time-efficient way to create style sheets is by using an external CSS file. You can link an external style sheet file to any and all of your web pages using the `<link>` tag and placing it within the `<head>` tag of your web pages. Later, when the time comes to make changes, you can make modifications on the one CSS file, and all the pages of your website change accordingly.

▶ **Document wide**—Another efficient way to create styles is by adding them straight to your web page using the `<style>` tag and placing it within the `<head>` tag of your page. Using a document-wide style sheet doesn't afford you a global repository for styles within your site, but it does allow you to create styles that can be used throughout the page.

▶ **Inline**—Inline styles allow for quick additions of styles within a tag. An example of an inline style could look similar to this:

```
<input type="text" style="border-style:groove;" />
```

This would effectively add a border to a text field on your web page. The downside to using inline styles, however, is that they are difficult to manage and are ultimately specific to a tag rather than the page or the site.

Now that you have an idea as to how style sheets can be created, let's take a look at how styles are defined within style sheets. A *Cascading Style Sheet,* or a *CSS* file, consists of numerous parts working together to form *rules* in an effort to enhance the look of your web pages. These rules can consist of font properties, positioning properties, border properties, and more. Figure 5.1 shows what a typical CSS file might look like.

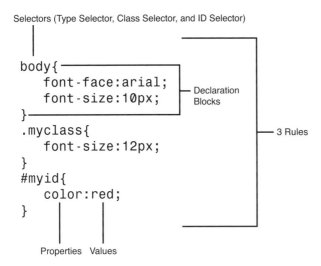

FIGURE 5.1   A typical CSS file.

As you can see from the callouts, a typical CSS file contains declaration blocks, properties, values, and more importantly, selectors. All of these are organized to form style rules. These rules are typically structured within an external file or document-wide `<style>` tag to form a style sheet. Although style sheets are integral when formatting HTML pages, CSS would be relatively useless without selectors. *Selectors*, as the name implies, are used to select elements on an HTML page in an effort to associate a particular element with the rule that you're defining. Although many different types of selectors exist, arguably the most important are the folllowing:

▶ **Class selectors**—Possibly the most popular way of outlining rules within a style sheet, class selectors allow you to set up a custom style and use the class selector name as an attribute value later in the tag. For instance, if you were to set up a class selector named `.myclass` and give it the appropriate properties and values, you could later add the class selector reference to a paragraph of text as follows:

```
<head>
<style>
.myclass {font:Arial;}
</style>
</head>


<body>
<p class="myclass">Vecta Corp</p>
</body>
```

In this case, the rule is defined (as a document-wide style sheet) so that a class selector is set with the font property. The property value is set to Arial. The paragraph <p> tag references the class selector, accessing it with the `class` attribute, and renders the text *Vecta Corp* as Arial within the browser.

▶ **Pseudo-classes**—Pseudo-classes are similar to classes in that they define rules for use on your web pages. The difference between classes and pseudo-classes, however, is that pseudo-classes aren't applied to elements in your web pages as classes are. For the most part, pseudo-classes are reserved for modifying links, visited links, active links, and hover states for links. Here is an example of pseudo-classes in use:

```
<head>
<style>
a.link {font:Arial; color:blue;}
a.hover {color:Red;}
</style>
</head>


<body>
<a href="index.html">Home</a>
</body>
```

In this case, the `link` and `hover` pseudo-classes are used to define the font and color of all hyperlinks on the page. Pseudo-classes are discussed in greater detail later in the chapter.

▶ **ID selectors**—Generally used when working with JavaScript and CSS together, an ID selector allows you to set up a custom style as well as reference the uniquely named element from JavaScript. For instance, if you were to set up an ID selector named `#myclass` and give it the appropriate properties, you can later add the ID to your code and have it referenced within JavaScript as follows:

```
<head>
<script>
function alertme() {
    window.alert(document.form1.mytextbox.value);
}
</script>


<style>
#mytextbox {background-color:silver;}
</style>
</head>
```

```
<body>
<form name="form1">
<input type="text" id="mytextbox" />
<input type="button" id="btnSubmit" value="Click Me" onClick="alertme()" />
</form>
</body>
```

In this example, I've created a text box with an ID named mytextbox. This uniquely identifies the element, and it also allows me to set its style using the # identifier (used when working with ID selectors) within the document-wide style sheet. Even better, I can reference the same ID within JavaScript to extract the value and present it within an alert dialog box when the button is clicked. It's safe to say that by using ID selectors, you are effectively "killing two birds with one stone."

▶ **Type selectors**—Type selectors are an excellent way to redefine the properties of HTML tags as they are defined within the browser. For instance, Heading 1, represented by the <h1> tag, is generally defined by the browser as having a font size of 7, a Times New Roman font (depending on user settings within the browser), and a color of black. You could change the way the tag appears in the browser by redefining the tag using a type selector as follows:

```
<head>
<style>
h1 {font:Arial;font-size:12px;color:red;}
</style>
</head>



<body>
<h1>Welcome to Vecta Corporation!</h1>
</body>
```

In this scenario, the <h1> tag is redefined with properties of Arial for the font, 12 pixels for the size, and red for the color. In the body, we do little more than wrap the literal text with the <h1> tag. In the browser, our text is defined with the properties we set in the document-wide CSS style sheet.

▶ **Descendant selectors**—Descendant selectors, also known as compound selectors, are a handy way of selecting and changing the style for an element that is a direct descendant of another element within the web page's hierarchy of tags. For instance, assume that you want to stylize the italic tag <em>, which is directly nested within a Heading 1 tag <h1>. You can change the way the tag appears in the browser by writing the following code:

```
<head>
<style>
h1 em {font-weight:bold;font-size:10px;color:blue;}
</style>
```

```
</head>


<body>
<h1>Welcome to <em>Vecta Corporation!</em></h1>
</body>
```

In this scenario, the <em> tag is redefined with the properties of bold font weight, 10 pixels for the size, and blue for the color. As you can see from the code, spaces exist between the h1 selector and the em selector. This is recognized as the <em> tag, which is nested within the <h1> tag, and should have its properties redefined based on what I outline.

As you can see, the power of CSS is virtually limitless. With three methods for creating style sheets and numerous methods for outling selectors for rules within those style sheets, you now have an opportunity to greatly improve the look and general feel of your website using a flexible and robust environment. But you might still be in the dark as to the differences between HTML formatting techniques and those implemented using CSS. In the next section, we'll dissect the differences.

CSS Versus HTML

Although CSS properties can create the same types of presentation effects as HTML tags and attributes, CSS styles go far beyond the restrictive aspects of HTML, enabling you to create stunning effects that ordinarily wouldn't be possible using HTML. Beyond simple text effects, CSS styles can also be used to lay out the entire page, entirely avoiding the use of HTML tables. This allows HTML to be used for its primary purpose of conveying the structure of the content, while the style sheet defines the presentation and overall "look." A detailed list of differences is given in Table 5.1.

TABLE 5.1   Comparisons of HTML and CSS

Element	HTML	CSS
Font	No change.	No change.
Font Size	Limited to absolute sizes of 1–7 and relative sizes of +1–+7 and –1–5.	Virtually limitless. You can use pixels, points, picas, inches, centimeters, metric, and so on. Even better, the size is limited only by the space available on your page. Therefore, you can use 11.25 points, 2.25 inches, and so on.
Color	No change.	No change.
Font Weight	Limited to <strong> and <em>.	Options include Bold, Bolder, Normal, Light, Lighter, and weight values of 100–900.

TABLE 5.1   Comparisons of HTML and CSS

Element	HTML	CSS
Case	No automatic conversion to uppercase or lowercase.	Supports automatic conversion of uppercase and lowercase and even the capability to capitalize the first letter in the word.
Text Decoration	Supports underline and strikethrough.	Supports underline, strikethrough, overline, and can even remove underlines from links using the None property.
Link Rollovers	Not supported.	Using psuedo-class selectors such as Hover, you can have links within the page that change color when a user rolls over them.
Background Color and Images	Can set the background color of the page, tables, cells, and AP Elements. Unfortunately, background images will always tile.	Supports background color for the page, tables, cells, AP Elements, and even text. Tiling can be limited to tiling vertically, horizontally, or can be prevented from tiling at all.
Block Formatting	Limited to nonbreaking spaces, paragraph breaks, and line breaks. Text indenting is limited to `<blockquote>`.	Properties exist to control word spacing, letter spacing, vertical alignments, text indenting using pixel spacing, and so on.
Table Formatting	Cell padding and cell spacing must be defined for the entire table. Thus, padding and spacing appears around all edges of the table and cell.	Cell padding and cell spacing can be adjusted on each side of the table independent of other sides. This means that the left edge of all tables and cells can have a spacing and padding of 0, while other sides can have a spacing or padding of 5.
Borders	Tables, AP Elements, images, and cells can contain simple borders.	Sizes are controlled by pixel, and the color is limited depending on element type. All elements (including text) can have borders. Even better, border styles can be set, widths can be set in pixels, percentages, inches, and so on, and the color can be customized as well.

5

TABLE 5.1   Comparisons of HTML and CSS

Element	HTML	CSS
Lists	Lists are limited to bullets, squares, numbers, and roman numerals.	All options available in HTML are relevant in CSS including the capability to customize your own image to use with the list item and also to control the positioning of the image within the list item.
Positioning	Limited to using tables to control the placement of elements on the page.	CSS positioning properties in conjunction with the `<div>` HTML tag expose functionality for creating draggable and precisely positioned elements in the Document window and, ultimately, the browser. This feature set closely resembles the functionality of print design programs.
Cursor Customization	Not supported.	Cursor can be customized to 14 different icon types.

Although we're merely scratching the surface in our comparison of HTML and CSS, you can begin to see the overall benefits that CSS has over HTML. To further elaborate on the differences between the two, I need only to point to the structure of properties that control the look on the page. For instance, Figure 5.2 shows a typical formatted page using HTML formatting elements.

As you can see from Figure 5.2, elements formatted using HTML are difficult to pick out because of the abundance of code. Even worse, all elements on the page are formatted independently of one another, making global changes nearly impossible. Alternatively, take a look at Figure 5.3, which shows a similar page formatted using CSS.

As you can see from Figure 5.3, CSS cleanly separates the formatting of the page into a separate file, effectively making your HTML cleaner and easier to manage. Furthermore, separating the formatting of the page into a separate file that uses the power of CSS enables you to work with that file throughout your entire website.

Although I've attempted to shed some light on the differences between HTML and CSS formatting, the real comparison will be made by you as the chapter unfolds.

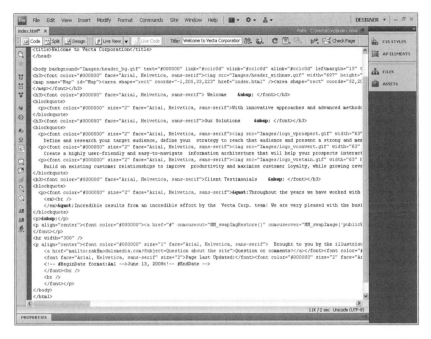

FIGURE 5.2   Elements formatted using HTML are hard to spot because of the abundance of code.

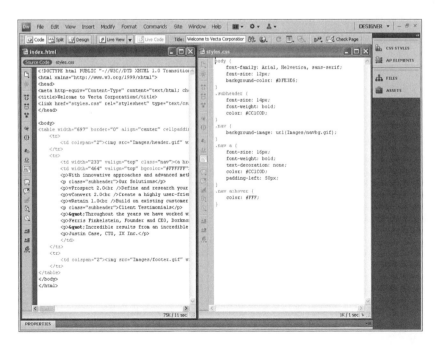

FIGURE 5.3   CSS cleanly separates formatting elements into a separate page. This causes the HTML code to appear cleaner and makes it easier to manage.

Browser Support for CSS

CSS has been around for a decade or so, but it's only been recently that widespread support for CSS has been integrated into browsers. Early implementations of CSS, notably Internet Explorer 3 and Netscape 4, were well meaning, but left much to be desired. To that end, most web developers wisely avoided using CSS until browsers could correctly interpret their designs.

The listing of browser versions in Table 5.2 should give you a rough idea as to the widespread adoption of CSS. This is just a representative sample of the most common browsers and doesn't include many of the other browsers out there.

The good news is that CSS support continues to improve, and the newest browser versions are quite good at displaying most CSS styles. The bad news is that older browsers are still out there. This means you need to be sure to test pages you've designed using CSS in as many browsers as you can, and more importantly depending on your target audience, try to come up with alternative methods of displaying your pages in an effort to make them backward-compatible.

TABLE 5.2   A Comparison of Browsers and Their Support for CSS

Browser and Version	CSS Implementation
Internet Explorer 3	Poor
Internet Explorer 4	Fair
Internet Explorer 5 (Win)	Good
Internet Explorer 5 (Mac)	Good
Internet Explorer 6	Exceptional
Internet Explorer 7	Exceptional
Lynx	None
Netscape 3	None
Netscape 4	Poor
Netscape 6	Great
Netscape 7	Exceptional
Netscape 8	Exceptional
Opera 3	Fair
Opera 4	Good
Opera 5	Good
Opera 6	Great
Opera 7	Excellent
Opera 8	Excellent
Opera 9	Exceptional
WebTV	Fair
Firefox 1 (Mozilla)	Exceptional
Firefox 2 (Mozilla)	Exceptional
Safari	Exceptional

NOTE

Several newer browsers have a special compatibility mode for HTML and CSS, in which they adhere more closely to the published standards. Firefox, Netscape 6+, and Internet Explorer 6+ turn on this mode when they encounter a valid DOCTYPE for HTML Strict and for a few other DOCTYPE declarations; other pages are done in a "quirky" mode for backward-compatibility with older browsers. For more information, visit http://developer.mozilla.org/en/docs/Mozilla's_Quirks_Mode or http://msdn2.microsoft.com/en-us/library/bb250395.aspx.

Now that you've seen the CSS support by browsers, let's divert our attention to the support of CSS within Dreamweaver. As you know, Dreamweaver is merely a development tool for web pages that will ultimately be viewed within the browser. Your designs will be limited only by your knowledge of CSS—and ultimately your knowledge of Dreamweaver's CSS support and formatting capabilities.

Designing CSS Using Dreamweaver and the CSS Styles Panel

In the previous sections, we looked at the various methods for defining style sheets. We also reviewed the different types of selectors that you might decide to use to style HTML elements when defining style rules. As you've seen, there's a lot to learn as it relates to CSS, and we've really only scratched the surface. The benefit to using Dreamweaver is that you don't have to know how to code HTML or CSS. As long as you understand the terminology, you can instead interact with the windows, panels, and inspectors to run through the functionality that you would otherwise have had to add manually within code. Working with CSS in Dreamweaver is easy and begins with the CSS Styles panel, available by choosing Window, CSS Styles. The CSS Styles panel will appear with the Current button depressed. Although we'll certainly discuss this view, for now, immediately click the All button so that the CSS Styles panel appears in the All view, as shown in Figure 5.4.

The CSS Styles panel has two buttons that represent two distinct CSS Styles panel views. We'll discuss the Current view later in this section, but for now notice from the callouts in Figure 5.4 that the CSS Styles panel exposes the following functionality in the All view:

▶ **Panel Options menu**—Options from this menu include some of the more popular and widely used CSS operations. For instance, you can create a new style sheet, edit an existing style sheet, delete a style sheet, export a style sheet, add a design-time style sheet, and so on from this menu.

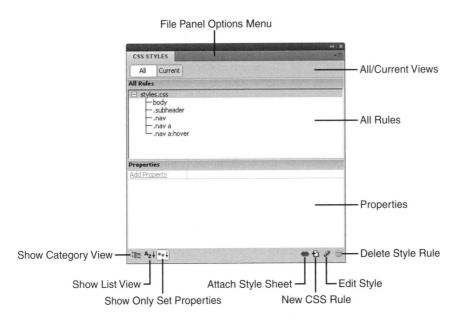

FIGURE 5.4 The CSS Styles panel allows you to interact with styles in Dreamweaver.

▶ **All/Current Views**—Use these buttons to switch between the All and Current views. In the All view, the CSS Styles panel displays all document-wide and external style sheets as well as rules set out for the entire defined site. In the Current view, however, the CSS Styles panel displays detailed style information for a selected element.

▶ **All Rules**—After styles have been created, they are listed here. External style sheets appear with the name of the external style sheet file (for example, `styles.css`). Document-wide style sheets appear as `<style>`. You can expand the style sheet to see all class selectors, pseudo classes, ID selectors, type selectors, and more within your style sheet.

▶ **Properties**—Use this menu to display a complete or filtered list of properties for a specific style rule. Depending on the view you choose from the Show Category or Show List View button, this list is customized to display either a Category or List view of all available properties for a style rule or filtered to display only properties that have been set for a selected rule.

▶ **Show Category View**—Click this button to display a categorically sorted view of available properties for a selected style rule. After you've selected this button, the Properties list will change similar to Figure 5.5.

▶ **Show List View**—Click this button to display a complete List view of available properties for a selected style rule. After you've selected this button, the Properties list will appear similar to Figure 5.6.

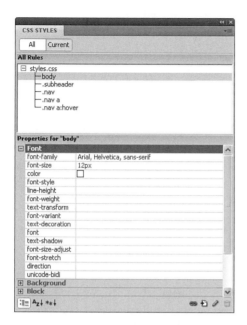

FIGURE 5.5   Use the Show Category View button to display a categorically sorted view of available properties for a style rule.

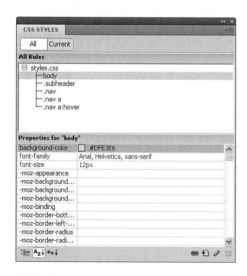

FIGURE 5.6   Use the Show List View button to display a complete List view of available properties for a style rule.

▶ **Show Only Set Properties**—Click this button to display only properties that have already been set for a style rule. You can still add properties from this view by clicking the Add Property link. Selecting this link displays a list of available properties for the style rule, similar to Figure 5.7.

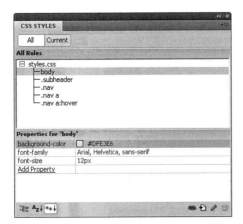

FIGURE 5.7   Use the Show Only Set Properties view to display only properties that have already been set for a style rule.

- ▶ **Attach Style Sheet**—Selecting this option opens the Attach External Style Sheet dialog box. From this dialog box you can browse to and include existing external style sheet files within your document. This option will be covered in more detail later in the chapter.

- ▶ **New CSS Style**—Selecting this option opens the New CSS Rule dialog box. Within this dialog box you will initiate the process of creating a new style sheet complete with class selectors, pseudo-classes, ID selectors, and type selectors for your documents.

- ▶ **Edit Style**—Select this option to edit a style sheet or properties for a class selector, pseudo-class, ID selector, or type selector within a style sheet. The appropriate dialog box opens, depending on what you select from the Style list. Selecting the style sheet (represented by either <stylesheetname>.css or <style>) within the Style list opens the Style Sheet Editor dialog box; selecting a style within the style sheet opens the CSS Rule Definition dialog box.

- ▶ **Delete CSS Rule/Unlink CSS Stylesheet**—Select the Delete CSS Rule icon to remove a selected rule. When a style sheet is selected, this icon becomes the Unlink CSS Style Sheet icon. Select this icon to unlink (not delete) a style sheet's reference from the page.

Now that you have an idea as to how the All view for the CSS Styles panel functions, let's divert our attention to the Current view. As you can see from Figure 5.8, the Current view can be used to inspect styles that are associated with a selected element on the page.

As you can see from the callouts in Figure 5.8, the following features are revealed within the Current view:

- ▶ **Summary for Selection**—This menu displays a list of style properties attached to the current selection. As you'll see later in the chapter, you can double-click a specific property to open the CSS Rule Definition dialog box to make edits to the current selection.

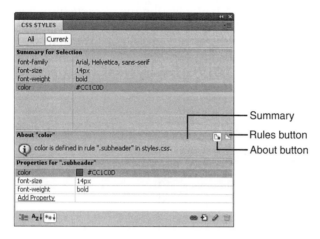

FIGURE 5.8   Use the Current view to display a list of styles applied to a current selection.

▶ **About**—Clicking this button changes the pane to display information that coincides with the selected style rule.

▶ **Rules**—Click this button to display the cascade of rules for the particular selection. Rolling over the selection, also shown in Figure 5.9, displays the specificity of the rule, as well as where the rule is defined within the page.

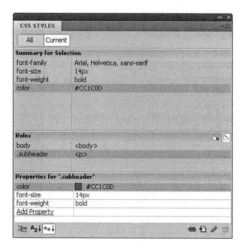

FIGURE 5.9   Click the Rules button to display the cascade of rules for a particular selection.

Although the CSS Styles panel is certainly integral to CSS development in Dreamweaver, it's also important to understand that the Property inspector is a viable alternative for working with CSS on-the-fly. As shown in Figure 5.10, the Property inspector is divided into two sections: HTML and CSS. Choosing the CSS button within the Property inspector prompts it to outline commonly used properties that you might want to set for an element. Core text-based properties such as font face, size, color, weight, and alignments are outlined and may be quickly selected from the CSS Property inspector. Furthermore, as you'll notice from Figure 5.10, the CSS Property inspector outlines a couple of buttons and a menu that facilitate the creation of styles.

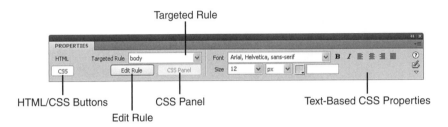

FIGURE 5.10   The new CSS Property inspector facilitates working with CSS including creating new styles, new inline styles, removing styles for an element, opening the CSS Styles panel, editing rules, and applying basic font-based properties.

As you can see from the callouts in Figure 5.10, the following features are revealed within the CSS Property inspector:

▶ **HTML/CSS buttons**—Click either one of these buttons to switch the interface for the Property inspector to support either HTML- or CSS-specific property modification.

▶ **Targeted Rule**—A handy and feature-rich menu, the Targeted Rule menu initially allows you to create a new document-wide or external style sheet by choosing the <New CSS Rule> option and clicking the Edit Rule button; to create a new inline style rule by choosing the <New Inline Style> option and clicking the Edit Rule button; or to remove an applied class by selecting the element on the page and choosing the <Remove Class> option from the menu. Beyond these simple options, the Targeted Rule menu will also outline classes as you create them, which you can choose from at the bottom of the menu, as well as cascading styles (compound/ descendant selectors) near the top of the menu.

▶ **Edit Rule**—Click this button to launch the New CSS Rule dialog box when the <New CSS Rule> option is selected from within the Targeted Rule menu. Clicking this button when the <New Inline Style> option is selected from within the Targeted Rule menu causes the CSS Rule Definition for <inline style> dialog box to appear instead.

▶ **CSS Panel**—Click this button to open the CSS Styles panel with the Current view selected. This button will only become enabled when the CSS Styles panel is either minimized or closed.

▶ **Text-Based CSS properties**—Choose from this group of properties to quickly format an element's font face, font size, color, font weight, or alignment. Selecting one of these options for an element that doesn't already have a selector applied to it causes the New CSS Rule dialog box to open, in which case you're guided through the process of creating a selector and style sheet definition for your new style. When a selector is already applied to an element, these properties simply outline the basic text-based properties that are applied to the element.

Now that you have an idea as to the basic premise behind CSS and understand the features outlined within the CSS Styles panel and the CSS Property inspector, let's begin working with CSS in the context of our Vecta Corp project. You can download these and other project files from the book's website. You'll want to replace the files in your working folder `C:\VectaCorp\` with the exercise files contained in `Exercises\Chapter05\` `Beginning`. For this chapter, two files (`index.html` and `companydirectory.html`) exist with slightly modified table and navigation structures to coincide with the examples. As you can probably tell, we're going to format the look of these pages using CSS.

Creating a Type Selector Within an External Style Sheet

As we mentioned earlier in the chapter, creating styles within an external style sheet file is the ideal way to work, especially if you're dealing with a site that consists of numerous pages. This makes overall maintenance of the site simpler and much more flexible. You can create a new external style sheet file by following these steps:

1. Open the `index.html` file that was included with the files that you've downloaded for this chapter. As you'll see, the overall structure of the page has been created for you. However, the page contains little to no formatting. Remember, we're going to use CSS from here on out to handle the formatting of the page.

2. With the CSS Styles panel open, click the New CSS Rule icon located second from the left in the icon group near the bottom-right of the CSS Styles panel. Immediately, the New CSS Rule dialog box appears (see Figure 5.11).

NOTE

Alternatively, you can open the New CSS Rule dialog box by right-clicking (Control-clicking) in the CSS Styles panel to access the context menu and choosing the option New. Furthermore, you can access the New option from the CSS Styles submenu in both the context and Modify menus. Finally, you can choose the New option from the CSS Styles panel Options menu located to the right in the blue title bar for the panel group.

---

3. As you can see from Figure 5.11, the dialog box reveals the following functionality:

▶ **Selector Type**—Allows you to pick the type of selector to use for your new CSS rule. Options include Class, Tag (type selector), ID, and Compound (descendant selector).

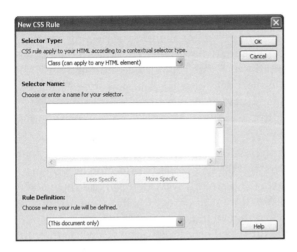

FIGURE 5.11   The New CSS Rule dialog box allows you to create new styles and style sheets.

> ▶ **Selector Name**—Depending on the option you select within the Selector Type
>   menu, this menu changes its functionality to support the addition/selection of
>   a class, ID, tag, decendant tag, or pseudo-class. For our example, choose the
>   Tag option from the Selector Type menu and then select the <body> tag from
>   this menu. You've probably guessed that we're going to start off by redefining
>   the look of the page via the <body> tag.
>
> ▶ **Rule Definition**—The first option, New Style Sheet File, opens the Save Style
>   Sheet File As dialog box, effectively allowing you to create a new external style
>   sheet file based on the name you specify. The second option, This Document
>   Only, creates a new document-wide style sheet within the <head> tag of the
>   existing page. For our example, make sure the New Style Sheet File option is
>   selected.

4. Click OK. When the Save Style Sheet File As dialog box appears, navigate to the root
   of your project (it should already be within the root if you defined your site
   correctly), and enter the name **styles** within the File name text box.

5. Click Save. Immediately the CSS Rule Definition dialog box appears, as shown in
   Figure 5.12.

Now that you have a new style sheet file created (`styles.css`) and you've effectively
created a type selector to redefine the <body> tag within that style sheet file, it's time to
start assigning properties for the new rule. You can see from Figure 5.12 that the CSS Rule
Definition dialog box enables us to set properties for the following categories:

▶ Type

▶ Background

▶ Block

▶ Box

- ▶ Border

- ▶ List

- ▶ Positioning

- ▶ Extensions

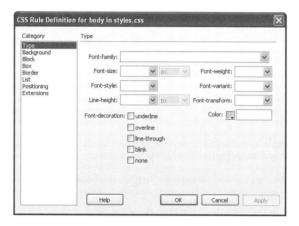

FIGURE 5.12   The CSS Rule Definition dialog box allows you to define properties for your new class.

NOTE

It's important to understand that the CSS Rule Definition dialog box is only one method for modifying properties within a style rule. As you'll see throughout the chapter, the CSS Styles panel exposes a Category and List view, as well as an Add Property link within the Properties list that enables you to quickly define properties for a rule directly from the CSS Styles panel without having to open the CSS Rule Definition dialog box.

Let's discuss each category before we make any adjustments to our type selector.

Type Options

The Type category, shown in Figure 5.12, provides you with the capability to format text-level elements including their face, size, decoration, weight, color, and so on.

The following is a detailed list of properties exposed by the Type category:

- ▶ **Font-Family**—Use this menu to select from one of 13 available font families. If you're working within an intranet environment, you might even decide to create your own font family by choosing the Edit Font List option. For our project, choose the Arial, Helvetica, Sans-serif font family.

- ▶ **Font-Size**—Allows you to select from a list of preset values. You can also enter any number you choose and then select from the menu to the right to select a measurement type. Options include Pixels, Points, Inches, Centimeters, Millimeters, Picas, and so on. For our example, enter **12** and choose the option Px (pixels) from the measurements menu.

▶ **Font-Weight**—This menu includes numerous options for controlling the weight of text on the page. Options include various bold properties as well as numeric weight values from 100–900.

▶ **Font-Style**—Choose from any one of the options within this menu to control the style of text on your page. Options include Normal, Italic, and Oblique.

▶ **Font-Variant**—Choose from one of two options in this menu to set the variant on text to either Normal or Small Caps.

▶ **Line-Height**—Traditionally referred to as *leading*, enter a value here to set the height of the line on which the text is placed.

▶ **Font-Transform**—Choose an option from this menu to capitalize the first letter of each word in the selection or to change all selected text to uppercase or lowercase.

▶ **Font-Decoration**—Choose options from this check box group to underline text, overline text, strike through text, or cause text to blink. The blink property is not supported by Internet Explorer. The default option for text is None, and the default option for links is Underline.

▶ **Color**—Use the color picker to choose from a palette of 216 web-safe colors, including colors from your operating system's color palette. Because the default text color is black, we'll leave this option as is.

After you've completely formatted the Type category, you're ready to move on to the Background category.

Background Options

The Background category of the CSS Rule Definition dialog box, shown in Figure 5.13, provides you with the capability to customize backgrounds for elements and text. Modifying these values gives you control over the color, image, whether you want to repeat an image, and so on.

The following is a detailed list of properties exposed by the Background category:

▶ **Background-Color**—Use the color picker to choose from a palette of 216 web-safe colors, including colors from your operating system's color palette. This option effectively sets the background color of the element. Because we're redefining the look of the <body> tag, and because it's the <body> tag's responsibility to set the background color of the page, enter the hexadecimal value of **#DFE3E6** now.

▶ **Background-Image**—Use the Browse button to locate an image within your site to use as the background image for the element.

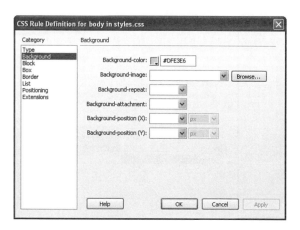

FIGURE 5.13   Use the Background category to set a background color or image for elements and text within your page.

▶ **Background-Repeat**—Select an option from this menu to set the tiling of the background image on the element. Options include No-repeat, Repeat, Repeat-x, Repeat-y. The default value is Repeat. The No-repeat option places the image as the background to the element but will prevent it from repeating horizontally and vertically. The Repeat-x option will repeat only horizontally, whereas the Repeat-y option causes the image to repeat vertically.

▶ **Background-Attachment**—Use the attachment option to force a background image to its fixed position or to allow it to scroll along with the content. The scroll option is supported by Internet Explorer but not Netscape.

▶ **Background-Position (X)**—Select an option from this menu to specify the initial position of the background image in relation to the element it is attached to. This can be used to align a background image horizontally to either the left, center, or right of the page. If the attachment property is Fixed, the position is relative to the element, not the document. Again, this property is supported by Internet Explorer but not Netscape.

▶ **Background-Position (Y)**—Select an option from this menu to specify the initial position of the background image in relation to the element it is attached to. This can be used to align a background image vertically to either the top, middle, or bottom of the page. If the attachment property is Fixed, the position is relative to the Document window, not to the element. Again, this property is supported by Internet Explorer but not Netscape.

Block Options

The Block category of the CSS Rule Definition dialog box, shown in Figure 5.14, provides you with the capability to define spacing and alignment settings for elements within your web pages.

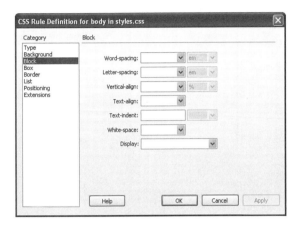

FIGURE 5.14   Use the Block category to modify spacing between paragraphs, lines of text, and so on.

Here's a list of properties exposed by the Block category:

▶ **Word-Spacing**—Enter a value within this text box to set the spacing between words. After you've entered a value, you can choose from one of the measurement options from the menu just to the right. Negative numbers are also allowed, but the appearance depends on the browser.

▶ **Letter-Spacing**—Enter a value within this text box to increase (represented by a positive value) or decrease (represented by a negative value) space between letters or characters.

▶ **Vertical-Align**—Select an option from this menu to specify the vertical alignment of the element to which the selector is applied. Dreamweaver displays this attribute in the Document window only when it is applied to an image.

▶ **Text-Align**—Sets the alignment of text on the page to left, right, center, or justify.

▶ **Text-Indent**—Enter a value within this text box to have the first line of text in your paragraph indent. You can also enter a negative number to outdent, but the appearance depends on the browser.

▶ **White-Space**—Select an option from this menu to specify how whitespace within the selected element is handled. Options within this menu include Normal, Pre, and Nowrap. Choose Normal to collapse whitespace. Choose Pre to retain all whitespace, including spaces, tabs, and returns. Choose Nowrap to specify that text wraps only when a line break (<br />) is encountered.

▶ **Display**—Choose an option from this menu to specify whether an element is displayed, and if so, how it is displayed. For example, you can mimic the look and functionality of a table-based structure by using various properties offered within this menu, such as table, table-column, table-row, table-cell, and so on. These properties will become useful in the next chapter as we discuss page structuring techniques using CSS. Detailed descriptions of each option within this menu are listed next:

- **None**—The element will not be displayed.

- **Block**—The element will be displayed as a block-level element, with a line break before and after the element.

- **Inline**—This is the default. The element will be displayed as an inline element, with no line break before or after the element.

- **List-item**—The element will be displayed as a list.

- **Run-in**—The element will be displayed as a block-level or an inline element, depending on context.

- **Inline-block**—The element is placed inline (on the same line as adjacent content), but it behaves as a block.

- **Compact**—The element will be displayed as a block-level or an inline element, depending on context.

- **Marker**—Used to specify the nearest border edges of a marker box and its associated principal box. Many browsers still do not support this property.

- **Table**—The element will be displayed as a block table (such as `<table>`), with a line break before and after the table.

- **Inline-table**—The element will be displayed as an inline table (such as `<table>`), with no line break before or after the table.

- **Table-row-group**—The element will be displayed as a group of one or more rows (such as `<tbody>`).

- **Table-header-group**—The element will be displayed as a group of one or more rows (such as `<thead>`).

- **Table-footer-group**—The element will be displayed as a group of one or more rows (such as `<tfoot>`).

- **Table-row**—The element will be displayed as a table row (such as `<tr>`).

- **Table-column-group**—The element will be displayed as a group of one or more columns (such as `<colgroup>`).

- **Table-column**—The element will be displayed as a column of cells (such as `<col>`).

- **Table-cell**—The element will be displayed as a table cell (such as `<td>` and `<th>`).

- **Table-caption**—The element will be displayed as a table caption (such as `<caption>`).

- **Inherit**—Inherits display properties from the parent element.

Don't be alarmed by the overwhelming list of properties contained within the Block category. This is merely an overview and reference. The next chapter will put a lot of these properties into perspective.

Box Options

The Box category of the CSS Rule Definition dialog box, shown in Figure 5.15, provides you with the capability to change and customize attributes within tables and the page itself. If you need to modify the width, height, padding, and spacing on a table, row, or cell, you would modify elements within this category. Furthermore, you can set the margins for the page by using the margin properties.

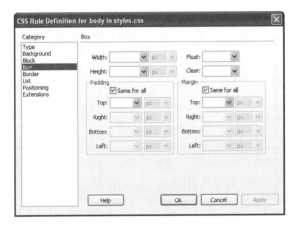

FIGURE 5.15   Use the Box category to modify width, height, padding, and spacing for tables, rows, and cells.

The following is a list of properties exposed by the Box category:

▶ **Width and Height**—Enter a value and then select a measurement to set the width and height of the element. These properties are especially useful when working with page-structuring techniques in CSS, which we'll be covering in the next chapter.

▶ **Float**—Choose an option from this menu to set which side elements, such as text, AP Elements, tables, and so on, will float around an element.

▶ **Clear**—Choose an option from this menu in cases in which you are inserting images or need to place a description next to the image but still need to add more text under the image.

▶ **Padding**—Use this group of options to specify the amount of space that should be added in between an element and the element's border. Unlike HTML, which forces you to enter one value for all sides, you can enter separate values followed by the measurement unit independently for each side. If you'd like to use the same value for all sides of the element, check the Same For All check box.

▶ **Margin**—Use this group of options to specify the amount of space that should be added between elements, such as cells within a table or the margins for the entire page. Unlike HTML, which forces you to enter one value for all sides, you can enter separate values for all sides. If you'd like to use the same value for all sides of the element, check the Same For All check box.

Border Options

The Border category of the CSS Rule Definition dialog box, shown in Figure 5.16, provides you with the capability to make changes to borders. This feature works only on items that accept borders for attributes, such as text boxes, tables, AP Elements, and so on.

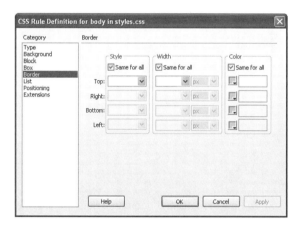

FIGURE 5.16   Use the Border category to make border adjustments to elements that support borders such as tables, text boxes, AP Elements, and so on.

Following is a list of properties exposed by the Border category:

▶ **Style**—Use this group of options to specify the style of the border. Options include dotted, dashed, solid, double, groove, ridge, inset, and outset.

▶ **Width**—Select or enter a value within this text box to set the width of the border. Selectable options include thin, medium, and thick. You can also enter your own numeric value followed by the measurement type.

▶ **Color**—Use the color picker to select from a palette of 216 web-safe colors or choose from your operating system's color palette. Unlike HTML, where border colors are limited depending on the element used, border colors for all elements that support borders can be set independently of one another here.

As with options in the Box category, all options within the Border category have the optional Same for All check box to apply identical values to the top, bottom, left, and right sides. By unchecking this box, you can enter separate values followed by the measurement independently of other sides. If you'd like to use the same value for all sides of the element, check the Same for All check box.

List Options

The List category of the CSS Rule Definition dialog box, shown in Figure 5.17, provides you with the capability to customize the way lists are created within Dreamweaver. You can customize options for bullets and numbers, even providing your own custom image to replace the standard bullets.

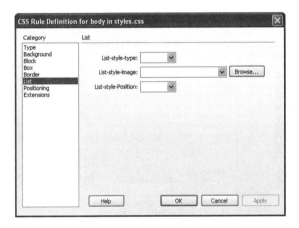

FIGURE 5.17   Use the List category to customize how ordered and unordered lists are created within Dreamweaver.

Following is a list of properties exposed by the List category:

- **List-Style-Type**—Choose from one of the eight options in this list to identify the type of list that should be applied to the selected element. Options include Disc, Circle, Square, Decimal, Lower-roman, Upper-roman, lower-alpha, Upper-alpha, and None (the default).

- **List-Style-Image**—Use the Browse to button to select a custom image to use in place of bullets.

- **List-Style-Position**—Select an option from this menu to set whether list item text wraps and indents (outside) or whether the text wraps to the left margin (inside).

Positioning Options

The Positioning category of the CSS Rule Definition dialog box, shown in Figure 5.18, provides you with options that enable you to position <div> and <span> tags freely on the web page. Otherwise known as AP Elements in Dreamweaver, the positioning properties allow for pinpoint accurate movement and placement of various elements within your web pages.

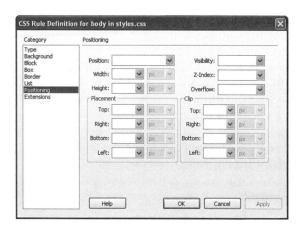

FIGURE 5.18   Use the Positioning category to set placement properties for `<div>` and `<span>` tags.

The following is a list of properties exposed by the Positioning category:

▶ **Position**—Choose one of four options in this menu to set the type of positioning an AP Element should have in the browser. Options include Absolute, Fixed, Relative, and Static. Setting the type to Absolute guarantees that the AP Element's positioning is governed by the top-left corner of the nearest absolutely positioned element. If none is specified, it uses the page as a reference. Choose Fixed to set an AP Element's positioning relative to the top-left corner of the browser. The content will remain fixed in this position as the user scrolls the page. Choose Relative when you want to position an element relative to another element's flow within the document. Finally, choose Static when you want to place the AP Element in a fixed position within the text flow. This is the default position of all positionable HTML elements.

▶ **Width and Height**—Sets the width and height of the AP Element based on the value you enter and the measurement type you select.

▶ **Visibility**—Choose an option from this menu to set the display condition of the AP Element within the page. Options include Inherit, Visible, and Hidden. Inherit guarantees that a nested AP Element will inherit the visibility properties of its parent AP Element. If it has no parent AP Element, the visibility will default to Visible. Choose the Visible option when you want to show the AP Element regardless of the parent value. Choose the Hidden option when you want to hide the AP Element regardless of the parent value. We'll discuss visibility in more detail later in the book.

▶ **Z-Index**—One interesting aspect of AP Elements is that they can be stacked and overlapped. Use the Z-Index property to set the stacking order of AP Elements. Higher z-indexed AP Elements appear above lower z-indexed AP Elements. .

5

▶ **Overflow**—Choose an option from this menu to set how content within the AP Element should be treated if it exceeds the width and/or height of the AP Element. Options include Visible, Hidden, Scroll, and Auto. Choose Visible when you want the AP Element to automatically resize if the content exceeds the width and/or height of the AP Element. Choose Hidden when you want the content within the AP Element to appear hidden if it exceeds the width and/or height of the AP Element. Alternatively, you can choose Scroll to automatically have scrollbars appear to the right and bottom of the AP Element, allowing you to scroll the content within the AP Element. This option will display scrollbars even if the content doesn't exceed the width and/or height. Finally, choose Auto when you want to display scrollbars within the AP Element only when the content exceeds the width and/or height of the AP Element.

▶ **Placement**—Enter values within these text boxes to set the physical location of the positionable element on the page. Although the default measurement is represented by pixels, you can also choose to use picas, points, inches, millimeters, centimeters, percentages, and more by selecting the appropriate option from the measurement type menu.

▶ **Clip**—Enter a value within this series of text boxes to define the part of the positionable element that is visible. You can use these properties in conjunction with JavaScript to create visual effects such as transitions.

Extensions

The Extensions category of the CSS Rule Definition dialog box, shown in Figure 5.19, provides you with advanced CSS functionality. Modifying extensions allows you to make changes to the way page breaks are handled, customize cursors, create opacities and glows, and so on.

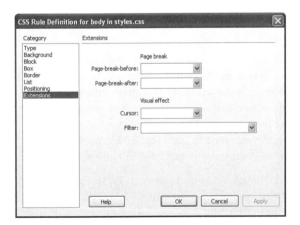

FIGURE 5.19   Use the Extensions category to work with advanced CSS features such as customized cursors.

The following is a list of properties exposed by the Extensions category:

- ▶ **Page-Break-Before/Page-Break-After**—Choose options from these menus to force a page break during printing either before or after the element controlled by the style. This property is supported only by Internet Explorer browser versions 5.5 and later.

- ▶ **Cursor**—Choose an option from this menu to change the pointer image when the pointer is over the element controlled by the style. There are 14 cursor options to choose from.

- ▶ **Filter**—Select an option from this menu to apply special effects to the element controlled by the style. Most of the options within this list are supported only by Internet Explorer 4 and later and are not covered in this book.

With your font and background properties defined for your type selector, go ahead and click OK now to close the CSS Rule Definition dialog box and commit your changes to your newly created external style sheet. After you've clicked OK, you'll notice a few changes. First, the look of the page has changed—all of your text is now Arial and the size is now 12 pixels. Also, the background color of the page has changed to the hexadecimal value #DFE3E6, which we defined within the Background category. It's important to understand that because we redefined the look of the <body> tag by way of a type selector, nothing needed to be applied. Because a <body> tag exists on every HTML page, the properties that we outline are automatically applied. Another thing you'll notice is the new styles.css file at the root of your project/defined site within the Files panel. Finally, notice the new style sheet reference and type selector that displays within the CSS Styles panel.

Now that you have a good idea as to where the CSS Styles panel is and how it can be used to create new selectors and style sheets, and you're familiar with the various properties for defining CSS rules, let's build on that knowledge to create a new class selector.

Creating a Class Selector

In the previous section, we walked through the process of creating a type selector. We redefined the <body> tag so that the text on the page defaults to Arial, has a size of 12 pixels, and set the background color of the page to a hexdecimal value of #DFE3E6. As soon as we clicked OK in the CSS Rule Definition dialog box, the properties were automatically applied to our page. Because we redefined the <body> tag via a type selector, there was nothing for us to physically apply—Dreamweaver applies it for us automatically because every HTML page must have a <body> tag. Class selectors, on the other hand, work a bit differently. With class selectors you're responsible for creating the class, setting the properties, and then applying the class to every element on the page to which you want the properties applied. Although the process of creating a class selector is very similar to that of a type selector, the application of the class selector is different. Before we jump ahead of ourselves, let's walk through the process of creating a class selector.

To create a class selector, follow these steps:

1. Create a new style rule within your external `styles.css` file by choosing the New CSS Rule icon, located in the icon group second from the left, in the bottom-right of the CSS Styles panel. The New CSS Rule dialog box appears.

2. Choose the Class option from the Selector Type menu.

3. Enter the name **`.subheader`** within the Selector Name text box.

4. Make sure the `styles.css` option is selected in the Rule Definition menu and click OK to close the New CSS Rule dialog and open the CSS Rule Definition dialog box.

5. Change the font size to 14 pixels, select the `Bold` option from the Font Weight menu, enter the hexadecimal value **`#CC1C0D`** within the Color Text box, and click OK to finish off your new style rule.

You should now see the new class selector appear within the CSS Styles panel, as shown in Figure 5.20.

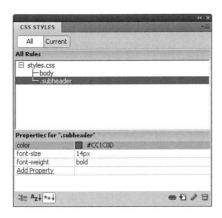

FIGURE 5.20   The new style class appears within the CSS Styles panel.

Looking at the CSS Styles panel in Figure 5.20, you'll notice a few interesting points. First, the style is defined as a class selector. You can tell it is a class selector because it appears with a period (.) before the name in the CSS Styles panel. Second, you can see the properties of the class selector listed below the All Rules list, within the Properties for `.subheader` list. Finally, you can see that the rules (both for the class selector we just created and the type selector we created in the previous section) are actually a part of an external style sheet defined by `styles.css`. Hierarchically, the class and type selectors appear under, or within, the external style sheet file. If we were using a document-wide style sheet, the selectors would appear under the heading `<style>`.

> **NOTE**
>
> The CSS Styles panel allows you to work with external style sheets and document-wide styles within the same page. An external style sheet is defined by `styles.css` within the CSS Styles panel, whereas a document-wide style is defined with the `<style>` tag. All selectors are hierarchically listed under their respective style sheet reference.

Because we've created a class named `.subheader`, this should tip you off to the fact that we've just created a style to handle each subheading (Welcome, Solutions, and Client Testimonials) within our page. To apply the new style to a subheader, highlight the subheader (in this case, Welcome) and choose the `Subheader` option from the Targeted Rule menu within the CSS Property inspector, as shown in Figure 5.21.

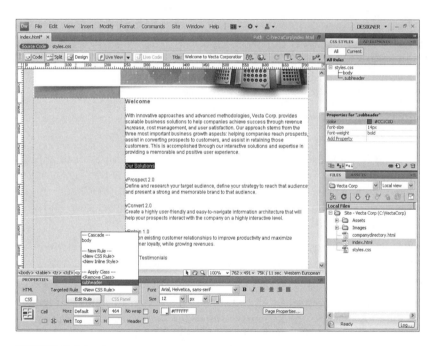

FIGURE 5.21   Select the `Subheader` option from the Targeted Rule menu to apply the class selector to an element on the page.

After you select the style from the list, you'll notice that the Welcome text changes, based on the properties we defined within the CSS Rule Definition dialog box. Now select each of the other subheaders (Solutions and Client Testimonials) and apply the same `Subheader` class selector by choosing it from the Targeted Rule menu in the CSS Property inspector. When you're finished, the page will resemble Figure 5.22.

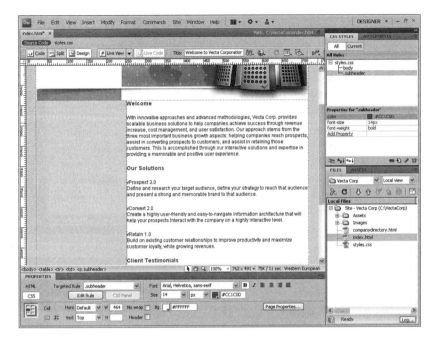

FIGURE 5.22   Apply the .subheader class selector to all the subheaders within the page.

Although we've used the Targeted Rule menu within the CSS Property inspector to apply a class selector, there are other ways. For instance, you might decide to use the Tag Selector instead of the Targeted Rule menu to apply a class. To do this, highlight the Client Testimonials subheader, right-click (Control-click) the <p> tag in the Tag Selector, and choose the Subheader option from the Set Class submenu (see Figure 5.23).

You can remove a style class by choosing the None option from the Set Class submenu by right-clicking (Control-clicking) the tag within the Tag Selector. Alternatively, you can choose the Remove Class option from the Targeted Rule menu in the CSS Property inspector.

Now that you have an idea as to how selectors and style sheets are created and you know how to apply class and type selectors to elements within your web pages, let's direct our attention to working with descendant selectors. In the next section, we'll build the navigation menu by first developing a class to set the background image of the navigation cell. Then we'll use a descendant selector to redefine the <a> tag within that cell.

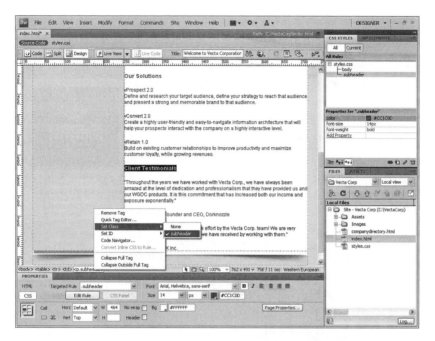

FIGURE 5.23   Apply the class selector directly from within the Tag Selector.

Working with Descendant Selectors

A third type of selector that you might decide to take advantage of are descendant selectors, also known as compound selectors in Dreamweaver. As mentioned previously, descendant selectors are ideal in scenarios where perhaps you'd like to redefine the look of a tag that is nested within a second tag. In our page, we'll use a descendant selector to redefine the <a> tag, which we'll create within the navigation cell in our web page's table. Rather than redefining every <a> tag for our site, you'll see how a descendant selector can be used to redefine just the <a> tags that are nested within a cell that'll have a class selector applied to it.

Before we get too far ahead of ourselves with descendant selectors, let's begin by creating a simple class to set the background image for the navigation cell. You can follow along by performing these steps:

1. Create a new style rule within your external styles.css file by choosing the New CSS Rule icon located in the icon group second from the left, near the bottom-right of the CSS Styles panel. The New CSS Rule dialog box appears.

2. Choose the Class option from the Selector Type menu.

3. Enter the name .nav within the Selector Name text box.

4. Make sure that `styles.css` is selected from the Rule Definition menu.

5. Click OK. The CSS Rule Definition dialog box appears.

6. Switch to the Background category and click Browse from within the Background-Image text box to open the Select Image Source dialog box. Locate the `navbg.gif` image located within the Images folder of the defined site and click OK to select the image and close the Select Image Source dialog box.

7. Click OK to close the CSS Rule Definition dialog box and return to your workspace.

8. To apply the `.nav` class selector that you've just created, place your cursor within the navigation cell in the table, right-click the `<td>` tag within the Tag Selector, and choose the `.nav` option from the Set Class submenu. The table's cell will instantly have the background image applied to it and will appear similar to Figure 5.24.

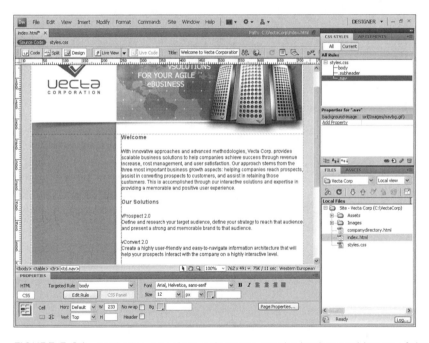

FIGURE 5.24   Apply the .nav class selector to set the background image of the table's cell.

Of course, up until this point we've done nothing more than create a class selector that sets the background image for our navigation cell. This is where descendant selectors come in. Before we get to building the actual selector, let's begin by outlining the navigation menu:

1. Place your cursor within the navigation cell and add the text **Home**, followed by a line break (Shift+Enter/Shift-Return).

2. Repeat step 1 until the text elements "About Us," "Solutions," "Support," and "Contact Us" are all added to the cell.

3. Highlight each text element and apply a link from within the HTML Property inspector. Enter **index.html** for Home, **aboutus.html** for About Us, **solutions.html** for Solutions, **support.html** for Support, and **contactus.html** for Contact Us. After you've finished, the beginnings of your navigation menu will resemble Figure 5.25.

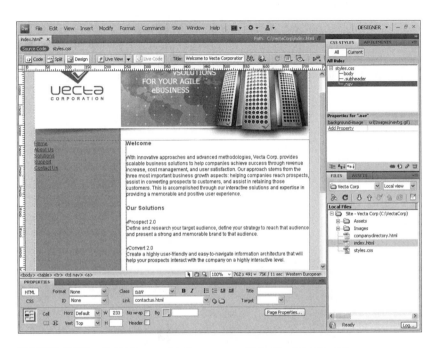

FIGURE 5.25   Build the navigation menu within the table's cell.

Now we're ready to build the descendant selector to define the look of the hyperlinks, but only within the cell that has the .nav class selector applied to it:

1. Place your cursor onto one of the hyperlinks that you've just created—it doesn't matter which one.

2. Create a new style rule within your external styles.css file by choosing the New CSS Rule icon located in the icon group second from the left, near the bottom-right of the CSS Styles panel. The New CSS Rule dialog box appears.

3. When the New CSS Rule dialog box appears, you'll notice the Compound option has already been chosen for you from within the Selector Type menu, and Selector Name text box has the .nav a value entered for you. As you can see, Dreamweaver is smart enough to detect that because you have an <a> tag selected on the page, you must be trying to create a descendant selector, which will redefine the look of the <a> tag, but only for <a> tags positioned within the .nav selector in the cell's hierarchy. You'll even see that Dreamweaver adds the descriptive text "This selector name will apply your rule to all <a> elements that are within any HTML elements with class

"nav"." within the Selector Name's description text box. Additionally, if Dreamweaver picks up too many or too few tags when building descendant selectors, you can always click either the Less Specific or More Specific buttons. For our purpose, everything is perfect. Go ahead and click OK now to close the New CSS Rule dialog box and open the CSS Rule Definition dialog box.

4. Select 16 pixels from the Font-Size and Measurement Type menus. Click Apply to see the change take place as you set properties. Choose Bold from the Font-Weight menu and again click Apply. Click the None option from the Font-Decoration check box group. Enter the hexadecimal value **#CC1C0D** in the Font-Color text box and click Apply.

5. Now switch to the Box category and uncheck the Same For All check box for padding. Enter **50** pixels within the Left text box and click Apply to see the change. Click OK to close the CSS Rule Definition dialog box and return to your workspace. As you'll see in Figure 5.26, the navigation menu is now completely formatted because of the descendant selector that we just built.

FIGURE 5.26   Redefining the <a> tag as a descendant selector allows us to redefine the look of the hyperlinks positioned within the navigation cell.

Descendant selectors can be highly advantageous to use in scenarios where you'd like to redefine a tag but don't necessarily want to redefine all the tags for the site. In this example, we used a descendant selector to redefine the hyperlinks contained within the navigation cell that had the `.nav` class selector applied to them. In the next section, we'll look at pseudo-class selectors as a way of defining the behavior of those hyperlinks when the user's cursor rolls over them.

Working with Pseudo-Classes

You can use pseudo-classes to define styles for hyperlink states. The difference between normal class selectors and pseudo-class selectors is that pseudo-classes must be associated with an already defined class/type selector and are "attached" to the existing selector by a colon. For instance, we've redefined the look of the <a> tag using a descendant selector within our navigation menu. We can use the `hover` pseudo-class to assign styling to the rollover state of the hyperlinks within our navigation menu as follows:

`.nav a:hover`

This code would effectively allow us to redefine the rollover state of the hyperlinks within our navigation menu. It's important to note that pseudo-classes already have predefined names, in contrast to classes, which you name yourself. The most common pseudo-classes are those that specify styling for hyperlinks. These include the following:

- **a:link**—The styling given to all unvisited links.
- **a:visited**—The styling given to all links that have already been clicked.
- **a:hover**—The styling given to all links when the cursor rolls over them.
- **a:active**—The styling given to all currently selected links.

For the most part, pseudo-classes, as they are supported within Dreamweaver, are associated with the <a> tag. (Although this is not always the case when hand-coding pseudo-classes.) For this reason, they are listed with the <a> tag followed by a colon and then the pseudo-class type. However, pseudo-classes can also be associated with existing classes. Assuming that we created a class selector called `.link` for our navigation items instead, we could easily associate the hover pseudo-class to the `.link` class as follows: `.link:hover`. For our purposes however, we'll apply styling to our already redefined <a> tags within our navigation menu. To do this, follow these steps:

1. Place your cursor onto one of the hyperlinks within our navigation menu. Now create a new style within your external `styles.css` file by choosing the New CSS Rule icon located in the icon group second from the left, near the bottom-right of the CSS Styles panel. The New CSS Rule dialog box appears.

2. Notice that the `.nav a` descendant selector is chosen for you within the Selector Name text box.

3. Expand the Selector Name menu to reveal the four pseudo-classes mentioned previously. Your dialog box will resemble Figure 5.27.

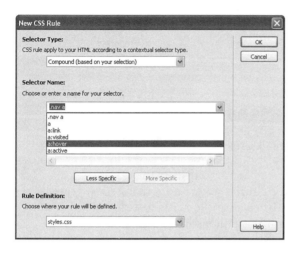

FIGURE 5.27   Pseudo-classes are listed within the Selector Name menu when the Compound option is selected from the Selector Type menu.

4. Rather than selecting one of these options (which would replace what was automatically added for us within the Selector Name menu), instead simply append the :hover pseudo-class manually to the end of the .nav a string within the Selector Name text box. Click OK. The CSS Rule Definition dialog box for .nav a:hover in styles.css appears.

5. This time, change only the Color. Sample (using the eyedropper tool that appears) the white color (#FFF) from the color palette that appears.

6. Click OK. The new pseudo-class appears within the CSS Styles panel.

Again, like type selectors, you don't select and apply pseudo-classes the same as you would a normal class selector. Instead, pseudo-classes are associated with existing class or type selectors and their functionality is automatically applied in the browser. In our case, our pseudo-class is associated with the existing .nav a descendant selector. This means all links within our navigation menu will take on the properties defined by the pseudo-class's properties. Essentially as soon as the user's cursor rolls over them, they will take on any properties that derive from those defined within the normal class, or in our case, the color defined within the pseudo-class hover. Save your work and preview the page in the browser. As Figure 5.28 shows, the link color changes when the cursor rolls over it.

We've merely scratched the surface of our discussion of pseudo-classes. We could also define properties for the other pseudo-classes, such as link, visited, and active. Experiment with the others at your leisure to see how they work.

FIGURE 5.28   The link changes color when the cursor rolls over it.

Attaching a Style Sheet

Rest assured the time will come when you'll work on a site that contains numerous files edited using traditional HTML instead of CSS. The files might exist in a project folder that already contains an external style sheet file. In this scenario, you'll want to remove HTML formatting from all pages and attach an existing, prewritten CSS style sheet to each page within the project folder. You can attach an existing style sheet file to a web page using the Edit Style Sheet dialog box. To demonstrate the process, follow these steps:

1. Open the `companydirectory.html` file from the Site Files list. As you can see, the page contains structure but no formatting.

2. Select the Attach Style Sheet option from the Style menu in the Property inspector. The Attach External Style Sheet dialog box appears, similar to Figure 5.29. Alternatively, you could also select the Attach Style Sheet icon located first from the left in the icon bar located in the bottom-right of the CSS Styles panel.

FIGURE 5.29   The Attach External Style Sheet dialog box allows you to browse to and select an existing style sheet to link into a web page.

3. With the Link option selected from the Add As option button, browse to the styles.css file located within the root of your project folder. Leave the Media menu as is, and click OK to close the Attach External Style Sheet dialog box.

4. The page will reformat slightly. Essentially, all the properties defined for the <body> tag redefinition and our navigation menu are automatically applied. You'll still need to add the .nav class to the cell that contains the navigation menu. In any case, you've just successfully attached a style sheet file to an existing web page.

You probably noticed other options within the Attach External Style Sheet dialog box. For the sake of completeness, let's discuss those options:

▶ **File/URL**—As you have seen, you can use the Browse button to browse to and select an external style sheet file for attachment to the existing web page.

▶ **Add as: Link**—Select this radio button to attach the style sheet using the <link> tag within the <head> tag of the page. In most cases, this is the option you'll use.

▶ **Add as: Import**—Click this option to attach the style sheet using the following code within the <head> tag of the web page:

```
<style type="text/css">
<!—
@import url("styles.css");
—>
</style>
```

The only real advantage to using Import over Link is that older browsers don't recognize the Import keyword. Because this is the case, you can prevent CSS from being loaded in older browsers if you choose. The downside to using Import is that Internet Explorer 6 tends to produce a momentary flash of unstyled page content before actually loading the stylized page. You can read more about this oddity by visiting the following URL: http://www.bluerobot.com/web/css/fouc.asp.

CAUTION

One of the topics we have not yet discussed is that of bandwidth usage as it relates to CSS files. It's important to understand that CSS files are separate files from the HTML file but are ultimately used, potentially, by all HTML files in your site. This means, in terms of size, that if you had a 5KB HTML file and a 5KB CSS file, the total download size for both files would be equivalent to 10KB. Keep this in mind when you're designing CSS files. Try to avoid storing unneeded style rules within the file and maintain only style rules that you think you'll use often.

▶ **Media**—Use options from this menu to specify the target medium for the style sheet. For more information on media-dependent style sheets, visit the following URL: www.w3.org/TR/CSS21/media.html.

▶ **Preview**—Click this button to preview the selected style sheet within the page. Clicking the Cancel button reverts the page back to its original state before the Preview button was clicked.

▶ **Sample Style Sheets**—Clicking this hyperlink opens the Sample Style Sheets dialog box, as shown in Figure 5.30.

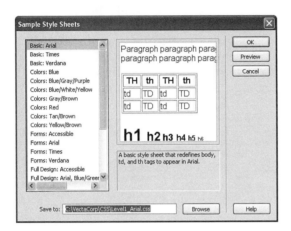

FIGURE 5.30   Use the Sample Style Sheets dialog box to browse through and select from a list of prebuilt style sheets.

Use this dialog box to browse through and select from a set of prebuilt style sheets that you can use within your projects. As you can see from Figure 5.30, the dialog box also features a Save To text box that allows you to save the prebuilt style sheet into your project. The Sample Style Sheets dialog box is also available by choosing File, New, choosing the Page from Sample category, and selecting the CSS Style Sheet category from the Sample Folder pane.

Using the Code Navigator

As you've worked with Dreamweaver and particularly with CSS, you might have noticed a small icon appear over elements that have styling applied to them. This icon, which is also shown in Figure 5.31, is called the Code Navigator and is a new feature in Dreamweaver CS4.

FIGURE 5.31   The Code Navigator icon appears over an element that has styling applied to it.

TIP

You can also open the Code Navigator by Alt+clicking (Option-clicking) onto any element that has a style selector applied to it.

The Code Navigator, simply put, is a small screen that appears when the icon is clicked to reveal styles that are applied directly to the element the Code Navigator was hovering over. This small window, shown in Figure 5.32, displays the style sheet that the applied style belongs to, selectors associated with the element, the actual properties and values that give the element style, and any styles applied to other tags within the hierarchy of nested tags.

FIGURE 5.32   The Code Navigator window displays the style sheet, selectors, properties, values, and more associated with a selected element.

TIP

You can disable the Code Navigator icon from appearing automatically when you hover over an element by checking the disable button when the Code Navigator window appears. If you do decide to disable the Code Navigator icon, you may still access the Code Navigator window by Alt+clicking (Option-clicking) onto an element that contains style.

You'll notice that you can roll your cursor over a selector within the Code Navigator window. While rolling your cursor over a selector displays the properties and values associated with that selector (shown in Figure 5.33), clicking on the selector also opens the style sheet with that particular selector in focus, allowing you to make quick edits without actually opening the CSS file in its own window (also shown in Figure 5.33).

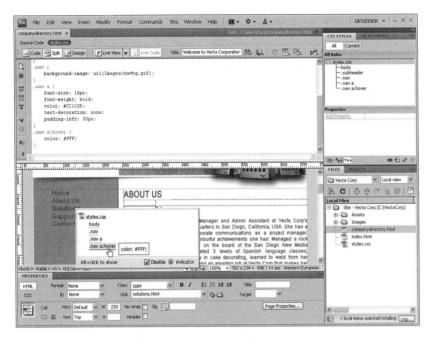

FIGURE 5.33   The Code Navigator window outlines selectors for a stylized element. Clicking the selector opens the style sheet in Code view for you to inspect and make edits.

Validating Your CSS

Dreamweaver enables you to check your HTML code for validity and conformance to accessibility standards. Unfortunately, it doesn't currently provide the same capability for style sheets.

Instead, you can use the W3C's CSS validator to check your CSS for code mistakes or omissions. You can verify your style sheet by going to jigsaw.w3.org/css-validator. As you can see from Figure 5.34, three options exist to validate your document.

The first option allows you to validate your CSS by inputting the full URI of your page. The second option allows you to browse to and select the CSS file on your computer, and the third option allows you to write CSS code directly into a text box for validation. To demonstrate this interface, I'll choose the second option. First, I'll browse to and select the styles.css file and click Open. The full path will appear within the text box. Now I'll click Check. The web-based application returns the results shown in Figure 5.35 in the browser.

As you can see from Figure 5.35, the validator didn't find any errors. If you run the validator on your CSS files and no errors appear, feel free to use the W3C CSS compliancy images to show your visitors that your site maintains CSS compliancy.

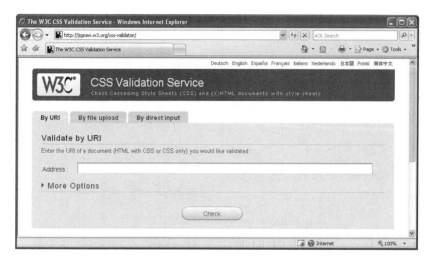

FIGURE 5.34   The World Wide Web Consortium provides a website that allows you to validate your CSS code.

FIGURE 5.35   The web-based application returns the results of CSS validation.

Using Design-Time Style Sheets

Dreamweaver enables you to specify style sheets that are displayed only while you are editing and that aren't included in the web page when it's saved or previewed. For example, you might want to create a style sheet to include or exclude the effect of a

Macintosh-only or a Windows-only style sheet as you design a page. These are called *design-time style sheets*. Design-time style sheets apply only while you are working in a Dreamweaver document; when the page is displayed in a browser window, only the styles that are actually attached to or embedded in the document appear in a browser, and everything else is ignored.

You can create a design-time style sheet the same way you create any other style sheet; however, because these style sheets are intended only for development, you won't have to worry about making them look pretty. The purpose is to make certain things stand out while you're editing. To create a design-time style sheet, follow these steps:

1. Select File, New. The New Document dialog box will appear. Select the CSS option from the Page Type list in the Blank Page category and click Create.

2. With the new CSS file open, enter the following CSS code:

   ```css
   abbr, acronym {
   background-color: silver;
   }
   .person {
   background-color: #FFCCFF;
   }
   .job {
   background-color: #66FF66;
   }
   h1, h2, h3, h4, h5, h6 {
   border: thin dotted teal;
       }
   ```

3. Save the new style sheet with the name `designtime.css`.

4. Switch back to the `companydirectory.html` page.

5. Apply the `designtime.css` file to your editing environment by choosing the Design-Time Style Sheet option from the CSS Styles panel Options menu. The Design-Time Style Sheets dialog box appears, similar to Figure 5.36.

6. Add the style sheet by clicking the Add (+) button and browsing to find the `designtime.css` file. The file will appear within the list as it does in Figure 5.36. You can also choose to hide specific style sheets while you're developing by adding them to the Hide at Design-Time list just below the Show Only at Design-Time menu widget.

7. Click OK. The design-time style sheet appears within the CSS Styles panel as a separate node.

8. To demonstrate that these style sheets are visible only at design-time, I'll highlight an entire paragraph of text and choose a style from the Targeted Rule menu in the CSS Property inspector. Notice that the background of the text is highlighted.

9. Now preview your page in the browser. The highlight is not shown.

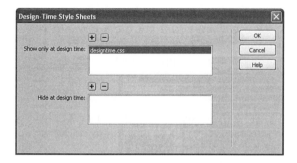

FIGURE 5.36   The Design-Time Style Sheets dialog box allows you to add and manage style sheets that will be used while developing.

Using CSS Advisor

Adobe's CSS Advisor is an Adobe-sponsored and hosted website/forum devoted to CSS compliance and standards. At its core, CSS Advisor's goals are the following:

▶ Allow web developers to quickly and easily find solutions to CSS and browser compatibility issues

▶ Allow the development community to share solutions and workarounds that they've discovered with colleagues

▶ Allow the development community to comment on and improve existing solutions

Available by browsing to the URL www.adobe.com/go/cssadvisor and shown in Figure 5.37, Adobe's CSS Advisor features a forum-like interface that allows developers to share, collaborate on, and research various CSS-related topics such as background, border, color, float, font, margin, padding, positioning, text, and dimension properties. Additionally, topics on browser quirks and workarounds also exist for Internet Explorer, Mozilla/Firefox, Opera, and Safari.

As a web developer, feel free to register on the site, submit posts, and even subscribe to the RSS feeds in an effort to stay in the loop with CSS-related compliance topics.

TIP

The CSS Advisor website can also be accessed directly from Dreamweaver by choosing either the Check CSS Advisor for New Issues or Report a Browser Rendering Issue options from the Check Page menu within the Document toolbar (shown in Figure 5.38).

Although the long-term goals of CSS Advisor are still unclear, the immediate benefit to the Dreamweaver web developer are obvious. As you progress and delve into CSS, you'll find many quirks and consistency issues, depending on the browser that you're using to display your CSS-based web page. CSS Advisor can help you stay abreast of these issues, helping you to avoid frustration down the line.

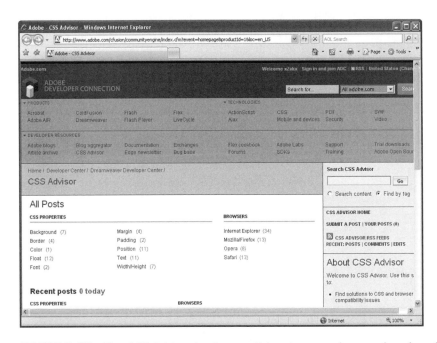

FIGURE 5.37   Use CSS Advisor to share, collaborate on, and research various CSS-related topics within a community of developers.

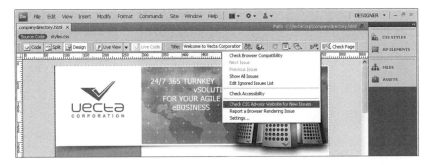

FIGURE 5.38   Access the CSS Advisor directly from Dreamweaver by choosing one of two options available from the Check Page menu in the Document toolbar.

Summary

CSS, if used correctly, can greatly extend your ability to create attractive web designs. Because current browsers have excellent support for CSS standards, CSS should be used whenever possible to create standards-compliant web pages. Dreamweaver lets you define and edit styles through a menu interface, making it easy to apply styles to text, create boxes, or even lay out an entire web page. You also learned that you can create custom class selectors, redefine the appearance of HTML tags (type selectors), or employ descendant selectors for more precise definition. From this point forward, we won't be using traditional methods of HTML formatting; instead, we will opt to use standards-compliant CSS to format the look of our pages whenever possible.

CHAPTER 6

Page Structuring Using Cascading Style Sheets

In Chapter 4, "Web Page Structuring Using Tables," you learned that using HTML tables to structure the content of elements on the page is not only easy, but also, when used correctly, extremely flexible. Unfortunately, you probably also noticed that as the site became more complex, the process of getting the tables perfectly adjusted and getting the content exactly where you wanted it to be was hit or miss at best. After fumbling with rows and columns, working with merging and splitting cells, and experimenting with horizontal and vertical alignments, you might be thinking there's got to be a better way to structure your site. There is! That is where CSS and, more specifically, AP Elements come in.

As you'll learn throughout the chapter, AP Elements, or Absolutely Positioned Elements, are nothing more than CSS-driven "containers" in Dreamweaver that can contain text, images, media elements, and more. Beyond the simplicities of being able to add content to an AP Element, you can also freely position (usually by dragging and dropping) the AP Element anywhere you want on the page. As you'll see, this is possible because AP Elements rely on standards-compliant CSS positioning properties for controlling the structuring of these unique elements. Regardless of whether you're a print designer looking for web-based structuring techniques that closely resemble print programs like InDesign or Illustrator, or a seasoned web page developer who's traditionally relied on tables for web page structuring, AP Elements are your answer!

Introduction to AP Elements

AP Elements in the world of web design mean freedom from messy table workarounds and total control of content layout. To achieve this, AP Elements outline properties for precise placement of elements on the page. Even better, AP Elements offer a third dimension called the *z-index*, ripped from geometric practices based on x, y, and z coordinates. The higher an AP Element's z-index value, the higher in the stacking order the AP Element will be. The lower the z-index value, the lower in the stacking order the element will be, resulting in an item closer to the background and possibly hidden from view.

Precise placement of elements on the page? Why would you ever fumble with tabled structures again? This is the question that plagues designers and developers. The answer lies in your user's target browser, which, for the most part, is impossible to know. For AP Elements to be visible in a browser, the browser must be a 4.0 or later version of Netscape or Internet Explorer. For advanced properties outlined by AP Elements to be viewed correctly, the browser must be a newer browser version such as Netscape 7 or later, Internet Explorer 6 or later, Firefox, Safari, Opera, and so on. Figure 6.1 shows the Vecta Corp website design using AP Elements in Internet Explorer 7.

FIGURE 6.1   The Vecta Corp site, designed using AP Elements, shown in Internet Explorer 7.

Internet Explorer 7 is considered a modern browser and supports the newest CSS specifications as they relate to the advanced positioning properties of AP Elements. The outcome would be similar if we viewed the site in Firefox, Safari, Opera, or newer versions of Netscape. However, Figure 6.2 shows the same design in Netscape 4.

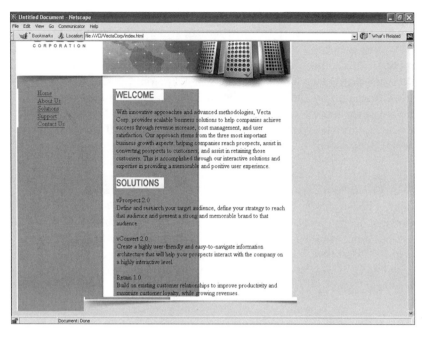

FIGURE 6.2   The Vecta Corp site, designed using AP Elements, shown in the Netscape 4 browser.

In this second scenario, the outcome is not as desirable as the first. You can see that the navigation items are falling under the icons, the bitmaps aren't being drawn correctly, and in general, the page looks bad. The reason for this is simple—and lies in the support of AP Elements by older browsers, the introduction of positionable tags with the inception of HTML 4.0, and the code generated by Dreamweaver.

Before we get ahead of ourselves, however, let's backtrack a bit by introducing and discussing the evolution of AP Elements. In the late 1990s, the W3C established a new HTML 4.0 specification that introduced radical changes to the way developers could write HTML, and even better, format that HTML using a new and more robust CSS specification. Combined with JavaScript, the phenomena was coined *Dynamic HTML (DHTML)* and thus introduced designers and developers to a new way of working with web pages. The idea was simple: DHTML was the harmonious combination of HTML, CSS, and JavaScript. Among other things, DHTML would allow developers to change the style declarations of an HTML element by means of JavaScript. Even better, through the use of absolutely positioned elements, content on the page could be precisely positioned in the browser window using absolute or relative positioning properties. As part of this transition, browsers scrambled to support what was touted as the next "big thing" in web development.

As a result, the two major browsers of the time (Netscape and Internet Explorer) ended up supporting very different extensions to the original specification. For instance, the HTML 4.0 specification brought about two tags used to generate and work with AP Elements: the <div> and <span> tags. Although Internet Explorer supported these tags, Netscape 4.0

didn't (in terms of creating AP Elements), instead opting for the proprietary <layer> and <iLayer> tags. To make a long story short, the dust settled, and a major shift in the browser industry saw users preferring Internet Explorer over Netscape version browsers. The web development trend also moved to support the more popular and much more flexible <div> and <span> tags. Newer versions of Netscape, Firefox, Opera, Safari, and Internet Explorer now fully support the use of <div> and <span> tags, and the <layer> and <iLayer> tags have since become deprecated. In fact, Dreamweaver doesn't even support the use of <layer> and <iLayer> tags, opting instead to create AP Elements using the widely adopted <div> or <span> tag.

> **NOTE**
>
> Although Dreamweaver no longer supports the <layer> and <iLayer> tags in its visual environment, that doesn't mean that you can't use these tags. If you're adamant about supporting older versions of the Netscape browser, you can still find the tags in the Code Hints menu in Code view. This means that if you plan to support older versions of Netscape and you must use AP Elements in your site, you'll end up writing a lot of the code by hand.

In short, you must be aware of your target audience. If your organization is structured so that your livelihood depends on your next online sale, tables are probably your best bet because they are supported by a much greater array of browsers and are backward-compatible. If, however, you've developed a new media site to market development services or your aim is to comply with forward-thinking practices, you might opt for a more standards-compliant alternative in AP Elements to impress, show off design and development capabilities, and just plain have a faster loading site. Be aware though, that if the end user is viewing your site with a web browser that is not compatible with AP Elements written using the <div> or <span> tags, the result will be detrimental to the look of the site, as you saw in Figure 6.2. In the end, it's crucial to be aware of your target audience when using AP Elements in your site.

Working with AP Elements

Now that you have a formal understanding of the power AP Elements are meant to provide, let's actually insert and work with them in Dreamweaver. In the following sections, you'll learn about the various techniques for inserting AP Elements, modifying AP Element properties through the Property inspector and the AP Elements panel, building a tableless web page using AP Elements and CSS positioning properties, and how to use built-in CSS page layouts.

To begin working with the examples in this chapter, you'll need to download the support files online. You can download these and other project files from the book's website. You'll want to replace the files in your working folder C:\VectaCorp\ with the exercise files contained in Exercises\Chapter06\Beginning.

Inserting an AP Element

You have a couple options for inserting AP Elements into a web page; the method you use depends on your needs and skill set. By far the easiest method for inserting an AP Element is to use the AP Element option in the Insert, Layout Objects submenu. To use this method, follow these steps:

1. Create a new HTML page by choosing File, New. When the New Document dialog box appears, select the HTML option from the Page Type category, choose the <none> option from the Layout list, and click Create.

2. Place your cursor on the page and select Insert, Layout Objects, AP Div. The new 200 pixel by 115 pixel AP Element appears on the page similar to Figure 6.3.

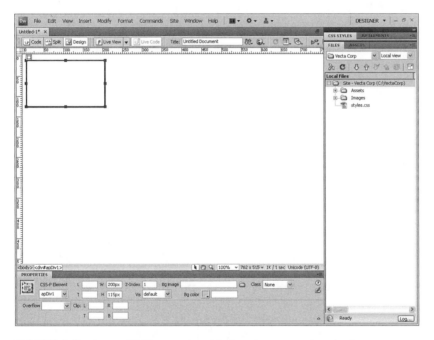

FIGURE 6.3   A new AP Element is added to the page using the Insert menu.

Initially, you'll notice that the AP Element appears as a box with a border surrounding it. You can easily select the AP Element by rolling your cursor over the border of the AP Element until your cursor turns into the Move icon. Now click to select the AP Element. Notice that the AP Element highlights blue and displays eight small blue squares, otherwise known as *resize handles*, at each point and in the middle of each line. Also notice that a handle appears in the top-left corner of the AP Element, also shown in Figure 6.3.

You can use the small resize handles to click, hold, and drag out to resize the AP Element vertically, horizontally, or both. Furthermore, you can use the top-left handle to select and move the AP Element anywhere you want on the page.

Dreamweaver also allows you to select an AP Element by its border and move it around on the page. If you use this method, make sure that you don't accidentally select a resize handle, or you'll find yourself resizing the AP Element instead of moving it.

Drawing an AP Element

Another simple alternative for adding an AP Element to the page is to use the Draw AP Element method. With this method, you can easily click and draw an AP Element in the page to any dimensions that you want. To use this method, follow these steps:

1. Switch to the Layout category of the Insert panel.

2. Select the Draw AP Div icon, the second icon to the right of the Standard and Expanded buttons in the Insert panel.

3. Place your cursor on the page; click, hold, and drag out to draw the AP Element in the Document window.

The AP Element is eventually created to look similar to the one created with the first method. The only difference is that by drawing an AP Element, you can set the initial dimensions to anything you want instead of setting them at the default 200 pixels by 115 pixels. We'll use this method, in conjunction with the Grid and Guides (explained later in the chapter), to draw AP Elements when we build the tableless version of the Vecta Corp site.

Inserting Content into AP Elements

Inserting content into an AP Element is just as easy as it is to insert content into the cell of a table. To demonstrate this, I'll insert text into the first AP Element (the one at the top-left of the page) and insert an image into the second AP Element (the one on the center of the page that we just drew). To insert text into the first AP Element, place your cursor into the AP Element and start typing the text **Ada the Admin Assistant**. Now let's insert Ada's headshot photograph into the second AP Element. To do this, drag the head_adatheadminassistant.gif image (located in the Images folder of our defined site in the Files panel) into the AP Element. When you've finished, the page will resemble Figure 6.4.

Notice that the text and the image are slightly undersized compared to the size of the AP Elements. To resize the AP Elements to correspond with their content, click, hold, and drag the resize handle located in the bottom-right of each AP Element to resize the AP Element to the size of the content within it. Finally, move the AP Element that contains the headshot photograph and place it just underneath the text AP Element. The result looks like Figure 6.5.

You'll begin to notice the flexibility that AP Elements reveal: Adding them to the page is easy, moving them is easy, and resizing them respective to the content within them is easy. In the next few sections, we'll discuss the various properties you can set using the Property inspector and the AP Elements panel.

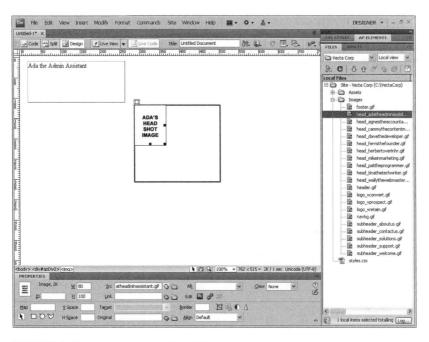

FIGURE 6.4   Add text to the first AP Element and drag an image into the second AP Element.

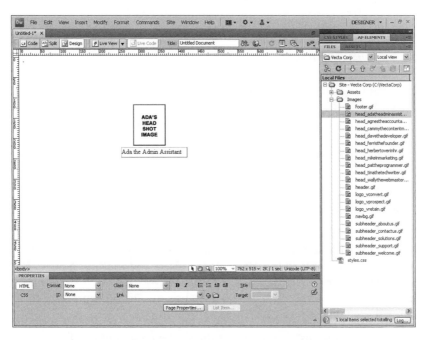

FIGURE 6.5   Resize the AP Elements so that they match the size of the content within them and drag the headshot AP Element so that it sits just above the text AP Element.

Modifying AP Element Properties with the Property Inspector

Like every feature in Dreamweaver, AP Elements have properties you can customize using the Property inspector. If you haven't noticed, the AP Elements Property inspector becomes available when you select an AP Element. As you can see in Figure 6.6, the Property inspector outlines properties that uniquely identify the AP Element, set the dimensions of the AP Element, set the stacking order or Z-Index of the AP Element, and so on. Also notice that moving your cursor just over the AP Element displays properties already set for the AP Element within a ToolTip.

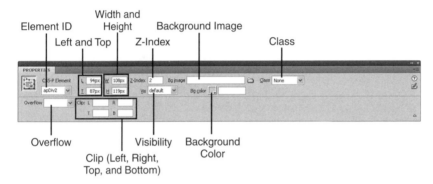

FIGURE 6.6   The AP Element Property inspector outlines numerous customizable properties.

A complete list of customizable properties outlined includes the following:

▶ **Element ID**—Add a value in this text box to uniquely identify the selected AP Element. By default, Dreamweaver adds the values apDiv1, apDiv2, and so on as you add AP Elements to the page. However, the default names mean little to us, so we'll change them. To demonstrate this, select each of the two AP Elements and name them **AdaImage** and **AdaText**, respectively. Also note that you can use only standard alphanumeric characters when naming an AP Element. Spaces, hyphens, slashes, and periods are not allowed.

▶ **L and T**—Enter values into these text boxes to set the position of the AP Element from the Left and Top of the browser. The Left and Top values are measured from the top-left point of the AP Element. If you're working with nested AP Elements, the Left and Top values are measured from the top and leftmost corner of the parent AP Element.

▶ **W and H**—Enter values into these text boxes to set the width and height of the AP Element in pixels. If the content in the AP Element exceeds the width or height of the AP Element, Dreamweaver automatically stretches the AP Element to accommodate the content within it. As you'll see, you can change the Overflow property to set how the browser handles the excess content in the browser.

▶ **Z-Index**—Enter a value into this text box to set the stacking order of the AP Element. The lower the number, the lower the AP Element appears in the stacking order. The higher the number, the higher the AP Element appears in the stacking order. To demonstrate this property, select the AdaImage AP Element and change the Z-Index to **2**. Now select the AdaText AP Element and change that Z-Index to **1**. Position the AdaImage AP Element over the AdaText AP Element. As you can see from Figure 6.7, the AdaImage AP Element partially hides the AdaText AP Element. You know this is possible because the AdaImage AP Element has a higher Z-Index (2) than the AdaText AP Element (with a Z-Index value of 1).

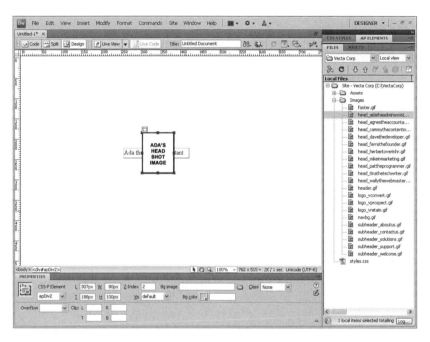

FIGURE 6.7 AP Elements with higher Z-Indexes appear above AP Elements with lower Z-Indexes.

▶ **Vis**—Select from the four options in this menu to set the visibility of the AP Element. Options include Default (which is essentially the same as Inherit), Visible (which makes the AP Element visible), Hidden (which hides the AP Element and the content within it), and Inherit (which assumes the visibility property of the parent AP Element when the AP Element is nested). If an AP Element is not nested within another AP Element, the default of Visible kicks in. When an AP Element is hidden, you'll want to use a scripting language such as JavaScript (the Show/Hide AP Element behavior in Dreamweaver's case) to dynamically set the visibility property of the AP Element.

▶ **Bg image**—Use the Browse for File icon to find and select an image to use as the AP Element's background. Background images in AP Elements are treated the same as the page and tables, in that images smaller than the size of the AP Element end up tiling. However, you can always use the Repeat property in CSS to set how the background image for an AP Element tiles or repeats.

► **Bg color**—Choose a color from this color picker to set the background color of the AP Element. Leave this option blank to make the AP Element transparent.

► **Class**—When defining custom class selectors in CSS, pick a class from this menu to change the style of the AP Element according to the properties set out within the style rule.

► **Overflow**—Select an option from this menu to set how the browser should treat an AP Element when the content exceeds the width or height of the AP Element. Options include Visible, Hidden, Scroll, and Auto. Choosing Visible forces the browser to stretch the AP Element to accommodate the content in the AP Element. Choosing Hidden forces the browser to automatically crop the excess content when it exceeds the width or height of the AP Element. Choosing Scroll forces the browser to automatically add a scrollbar at the right and bottom of the AP Element. These scrollbars appear even if the content in the AP Element doesn't exceed the width or height of the AP Element. Choosing Auto forces the browser to automatically add a scrollbar at the right of the AP Element only if the content exceeds the height of the AP Element and to add a scrollbar to the bottom of the AP Element only if the content exceeds the width of the AP Element.

► **Clip**—Enter values into these text boxes to define the visible area of the AP Element. You can specify values for the Left, Top, Right, and Bottom coordinates to "clip" off content within the AP Element in the same way you'd crop an image in Fireworks or Photoshop.

As you'll see throughout the chapter, an AP Element is nothing more than a `<div>` or `<span>` tag complete with a unique ID and a document-wide style rule (by default). Modifying properties in the Property inspector changes the document-wide style rule accordingly. To demonstrate this, switch to Code view. As you can see from Figure 6.8, each AP Element is nothing more than a `<div>` tag with an ID and a document-wide style rule.

You're probably thinking that document-wide styles aren't the best way of manipulating properties for AP Elements. If that's what you're thinking, you're right! Assuming that you were developing your site entirely in AP Elements, changing all the AP Element's properties in your site would be a nightmare if all the styles were developed within individual pages. A much better alternative is to create an ID within a style sheet that defines AP Element properties globally. When you want to make property adjustments (such as positioning properties), you make them once in the style sheet, and instantly those changes are propagated to all of the pages that make use of the style properties. We'll demonstrate this process later in the chapter.

Modifying AP Element Properties with the AP Elements Panel

Another option for customizing AP Element properties is the AP Elements panel. You can use the AP Elements panel as a way to set an AP Element's ID, Visibility properties, Z-Index, and whether AP Elements can overlap one another. The AP Elements panel, shown in Figure 6.9, can be selected directly from the CSS Styles panel group or by choosing the AP Elements option from the Window menu or by pressing F2. Alternatively, you can right-click (Control-click) an AP Element's border to access the context menu and choose the AP Elements Panel option to open the AP Elements panel.

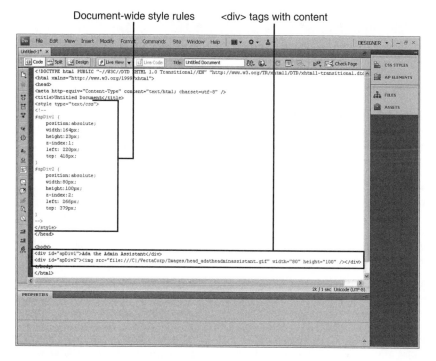

FIGURE 6.8   AP Elements are nothing more than a `<div>` or `<span>` tag complete with a unique ID and an inline style rule.

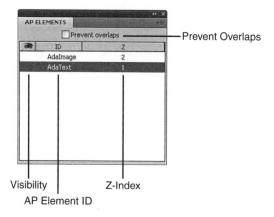

FIGURE 6.9   Use the AP Elements panel to visually set visibility, Z-Index, ID, and overlapping properties.

With the AP Elements panel open, notice that the style and overall appearance is strikingly familiar, looking much like the Layers panel does in an image-editing program such as Fireworks or Photoshop. For instance, you can drag AP Elements above or below other AP Elements, effectively changing the Z-Index of the AP Elements on the page.

TIP

If you drag an AP Element in the Document window that doesn't contain a Z-Index, Dreamweaver automatically adds one for you.

You can also click in the eyeball column to change the initial Visibility property for an AP Element. Finally, you can double-click in the ID column to change the ID of the selected AP Element. All this and more is possible through the AP Elements panel. The following customizable properties are revealed within the AP Elements panel:

▶ **Visibility**—You can click in this column for a particular AP Element to change the Visibility property. Icons include a closed eye (which represents Hidden), an open eye (which represents Visible), and no eye, the default (which represents Inherit).

▶ **AP Element ID**—You can double-click the AP Element's ID in this column to change the ID for the specific AP Element.

▶ **Z-Index**—You can double-click the AP Element in this column to change the Z-Index (stacking order) for the specific AP Element. You can also drag and drop AP Elements above or below one another to accomplish the same task.

▶ **Prevent overlaps**—When designing AP Element-based sites, click this button to prevent AP Elements from overlapping each other. This is important when you want to work with two AP Elements next to each other but want to prevent them from falling into an area used by another AP Element. We'll discuss this option further in the next section.

It's important to understand the place of the AP Elements panel. Sure, most of these properties can be set by selecting the AP Element and making the necessary change in the Property inspector. The difference between the Property inspector and the AP Elements panel, however, is that the AP Elements panel allows you to work with AP Elements even when they're hidden from view. Because the Property inspector becomes available only when an AP Element is selected, there is no way of changing the Visibility of an AP Element back to Visible after it's been Hidden without the use of the AP Elements panel. Also, it's important to note that the AP Elements panel represents the collection of AP Elements on the page, in contrast to the single AP Element that is covered by the Property inspector.

Preventing AP Elements from Overlapping

As mentioned in the previous section, you can use the Prevent Overlaps check box in the AP Elements panel to prevent all AP Elements on your page from accidentally overlapping each other when you position them. To demonstrate this feature, follow these steps:

1. Click the Prevent Overlaps check box in the AP Elements panel.

2. Try to drag the AdaImage AP Element above the AdaText AP Element as you did earlier in the chapter. You'll quickly notice that Dreamweaver prevents you from doing that.

3. To disable the feature, uncheck the Prevent Overlaps check box.

Remember, this feature comes in handy when designing AP Element-based websites because it can prevent you from accidentally moving an AP Element above or below another AP Element.

Nesting AP Elements

Similar to the process of nesting tables within a cell of another table, AP Element nesting is the process of placing an AP Element within another AP Element. By default, Dreamweaver doesn't automatically nest AP Elements; instead, Dreamweaver allows you to enable this option in the AP Elements category of the Preferences window. To enable AP Element nesting in your site, follow these steps:

1. Select Edit, Preferences (Dreamweaver, Preferences), or press Ctrl+U (⌘-U). The Preferences dialog appears.

2. Select the AP Elements category.

3. Enable the Nesting: Nest When Created Within an AP Div check box.

4. Click OK.

With that preference set, you can now create AP Elements within other AP Elements. For the most part, the process of nesting an AP Element within a second AP Element is as simple as drawing or inserting an AP Element within another AP Element. To do this, follow these steps:

1. Insert or draw a new AP Element on the page and name it **BgAPElement**.

2. Select the AP Element and set the background color to gray by selecting a gray tone from the Bg Color field in the Property inspector.

3. Create a nested element by inserting a new AP Element within the existing BgAPElement AP Element. Name the new AP Element **NestedAPElement**.

4. Insert Agnes's headshot image into the new NestedAPElement AP Element so the result resembles Figure 6.10.

It won't be overly obvious that the new AP Element is nested within the BgAPElement AP Element. However, you can see that the AP Element is, in fact, nested by looking at the AP Elements panel, also shown in Figure 6.10. As you can see, the NestedAPElement AP Element appears as a child node beneath its parent BgAPElement AP Element. The real benefit to nesting AP Elements becomes evident when you're working with Visibility properties. Because the default Visibility property of an AP Element is Inherit, the child AP Element always inherits the properties of its parent AP Element. What this means is that all we have to modify is the parent BgAPElement AP Element. Visibility changes made to this AP Element propagate down to all child AP Elements, effectively saving us from doubling our efforts.

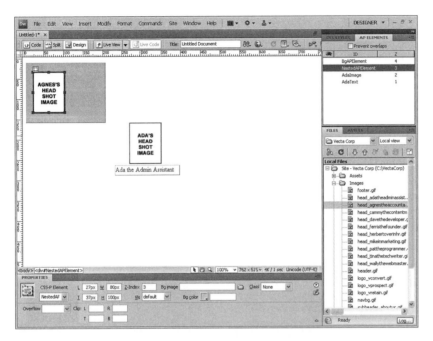

FIGURE 6.10   Nest an AP Element within an existing AP Element.

Although it would seem logical that dragging a nested AP Element out of its container AP Element would unnest an AP Element, that isn't how you unnest elements. To unnest an AP Element, you must use the AP Elements panel to drag a child AP Element out of its current position and reposition it higher in the list in the AP Elements panel.

Deleting an AP Element

If you decide that a particular AP Element is no longer needed, you can easily delete it using one of two methods. The easiest way to delete an AP Element is to select it on the page and press the Delete or Backspace key on your keyboard. This action effectively removes the AP Element and its content from the document. The second option for deleting an AP Element from the Document window is to right-click (Control-click) the <div> tag in the Tag Selector and choose the Remove Tag option from the context menu. This action removes the <div> tag but does not remove the content from the Document window. The same holds true if you right-click the actual <div> tag on the page and choose Remove Tag <div> from the context menu that appears. It's important to note however, that deleting the element does not remove the CSS positioning code from the page. Removing the code can only be accomplished from the CSS Styles panel or by going into code view and manually removing it.

Designing Tableless Web Pages Using `<div>` Tags

One of the biggest trends in web development is that of designing websites that don't use antiquated tables to control the structure of the site, but instead rely on <div> tags and CSS to control the layout and flow of web pages. In the next few sections, you'll learn how Dreamweaver—in conjunction with the <div> tag and a little CSS—can create standards-compliant web designs.

> **NOTE**
>
> The term given to the process used for handling layout in CSS-based page designs is referred to as *CSS-P (P for "positioning")*. Technically, <div> tags in Dreamweaver can use CSS-P for their positioning. In fact, if you select an AP Element in the Document window, you'll notice the label "CSS-P Element" is shown in the upper-left corner of the Property inspector.

Designing the Page Structure Using ID Selectors

In the previous sections of this chapter, you learned how easy it was to insert AP Elements using either the Insert, Layout Objects, AP Div command or the Draw AP Element option available from the Layout category in the Insert panel. Although these are viable options for designing a site using AP Elements, they aren't the best choice. The reason for this is simple: When you use either of these methods to insert AP Elements on the page, Dreamweaver automatically assigns document-wide CSS positioning properties for each AP Element. As a result, the page becomes inflexible and difficult to modify globally when numerous pages exist within the site.

A better alternative to inserting or drawing AP Elements onto the page is to create an external style sheet (which we already have for our project) and define numerous ID selectors that define the various sections of the page. For instance, if we're to rebuild the table-based Vecta Corp site, we might consider the following AP Elements to use as containers for our content:

> ▶ **Header**—We know we'll have a header that resides near the top of the page. The header will have a width of 697 pixels and a height of 227 pixels. We also know that the header will contain the `header.gif` image that defines the logo and company name.

> ▶ **Navigation**—Just under the header but to the left, we'll have a simple navigation menu. In this scenario, we can add an AP Element that will serve as a container for the five navigation links. We might decide to set a fixed width of 170 pixels and maybe even add a left margin of 50 pixels to offset the navigation menu from the left edge of the <div>.

▶ **Content**—The third major section in the page is reserved for the content. This section will reside under the header but just to the right of the navigation area. Because our navigation area has a set width of 220 pixels (170 pixels wide plus 50 pixels for a margin) and we want to keep the entire width of the page to 697 pixels, we'll set the content area's width to 457 pixels and then add 10 pixels of padding to both the left and right sides of the Content <div> (457 pixels + 20 pixels = 477 pixels, the difference between 697 pixels or the total width of the container minus the 220 pixels for the navigation <div>). Again, because a user will naturally scroll up and down the web page, the height for this section is irrelevant.

▶ **Footer**—The next area within our design will be reserved for a footer image. The footer will also have a width of 697 pixels but will have a height of 35 pixels. We'll also want to add the footer.gif image into the AP Element that we'll create for the footer.

▶ **Container**—The Header, Navigation, Content, and Footer AP Elements will all be nested within the Container AP Element. This will allow for precise placement of our four layout AP Elements without anything going awry.

Now that we've outlined the major sections for our page, let's begin outlining the CSS rules. Because we know we'll have at least five major sections in the page (Container, Header, Navigation, Content, and Footer), we can surmise that we'll need at least five CSS rules represented by five unique ID selectors titled container, header, nav, content, and footer, respectively. To begin creating these selectors, follow these steps:

1. Close the previous sample page that you've been working with. Create a new HTML page by choosing File, New. When the New Document dialog box appears, select the HTML option from the Basic Page category, choose the <none> option from the Layout list, and click Create. Immediately save the page as index.html.

2. Attach the existing styles.css style sheet by opening the CSS Style panel, selecting the Attach Style Sheet icon, browsing for the styles.css file, and clicking OK. You'll immediately notice that the background of the page and font style are preset for you.

3. Create a new CSS rule by clicking the New CSS Rule button in the CSS Styles panel. The New CSS Rule dialog box appears.

4. Choose the ID option from the Selector Type menu and then enter the name **#container** into the Selector Name text box. Remember that the pound symbol represents ID (thus, the ID selector name is *container*). When you finish making your modifications, the dialog box should resemble Figure 6.11.

5. Click OK. You're now ready to start defining the properties that will make up the container rule and ultimately define the container AP Element that we'll use as a wrapper for the remaining AP Elements.

6. Switch over to the Background category, click the Browse button Background-image, locate the navbg.gif image located within the Images folder, and then click OK to select it and return back to the CSS Rule Definition dialog box.

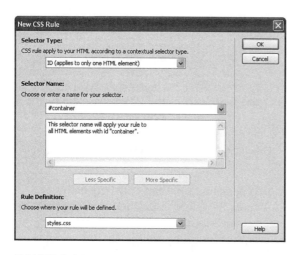

FIGURE 6.11   Create a new ID selector called #container.

7. Next switch over to the Box category. Set the width to 697 pixels, uncheck the Same For All check box for Margin, and select Auto for both Left and Right. When you finish, the Box dialog box resembles Figure 6.12.

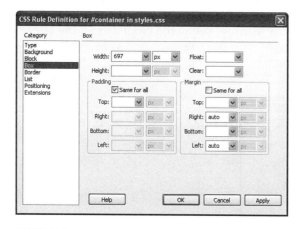

FIGURE 6.12   Modify the Box attributes for the container rule.

8. Click OK. The new ID selector (named *container*) appears in the CSS Styles panel.

That's it! You're now ready to define the style rules for the remaining AP Elements. To define the header rule, follow these steps:

1. Create a new CSS rule by clicking the New CSS Rule button in the CSS Styles panel. The New CSS Rule dialog box appears.

2. Choose the ID option from the Selector Type menu and then enter the name **#header** into the Selector Name text box. Remember that the pound symbol represents ID (thus, the ID selector name is *header*).

3. Click OK. You're now ready to start defining the properties that will make up the header rule and ultimately define the header AP Element.

4. Switch over to the Positioning category. Set the property for Width to 697 and the property for Height to 227 pixels.

5. Click OK. The new ID selector (named *header*) appears in the CSS Styles panel.

To define the navigation rule, follow these steps:

1. Create a new CSS rule by clicking the New CSS Rule button in the CSS Styles panel. The New CSS Rule dialog box appears.

2. Choose the ID option from the Selector Type menu and then enter the name **#navigation** into the Selector Name text box. Remember that the pound symbol represents ID (thus, the ID selector name is *navigation*).

3. Click OK. You're now ready to start defining the properties that will make up the navigation rule and ultimately define the navigation AP Element.

4. Switch over to the Box category. Set the property for Width to 170, uncheck the Same For All check box for Padding, enter a value of 50 pixels for Left, and then choose the left option from the Float menu. One of the options that we've yet to discuss in practice is Float. Float is used in CSS when you want to allow AP Elements to coexist side by side. Because we want the navigation <div> to reside next to the content <div>, we use Float Left. Later, when we define the properties for the content <div>, we assign it a Float Right. This way, the two <div>s can exist side by side. When you finish, the screen should resemble Figure 6.13.

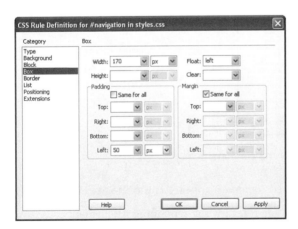

FIGURE 6.13   Modify the Box attributes for the navigation rule.

5. Click OK. The new ID selector appears in the CSS Styles panel.

To define the content rule, follow these steps:

1. Create a new CSS rule by clicking the New CSS Rule icon in the CSS Styles panel. The New CSS Rule dialog box appears.

2. Choose the ID option from the Selector Type menu and then enter the name **#content** into the Selector Name text box. Remember that the pound symbol represents ID (thus, the ID selector name is *content*).

3. Click OK. You're now ready to start defining the properties that will make up the Content rule and ultimately define the content AP Element.

4. Switch over to the Box category. Set the property for Width to 457, uncheck the Same For All check box for Padding, enter a value of 10 pixels for Left and 10 pixels for Right, and then choose the Right option from the Float menu.

5. Click OK. The new ID selector appears within the CSS Styles panel.

Almost done! To define the last ID selector for footer, follow these steps:

1. Create a new CSS rule by clicking the New CSS Rule icon in the CSS Styles panel. The New CSS Rule dialog box appears.

2. Choose the ID option from the Selector Type menu and then enter the name **#footer** into the Selector Name text box. Remember that the pound symbol represents ID (thus, the ID selector name is *footer*).

3. Click OK. You're now ready to start defining the properties that will make up the footer rule and ultimately define the footer AP Element.

4. Switch over to the Box category. Set the property for Width to 697 pixels, set the property for Height to 35 pixels, and then choose the Both option from the Clear menu. Again, like the Float menu, the Clear menu is a property that we've yet to discuss in detail. Simply put, the Clear property allows you to specify sides of a <div> that should not support other <div> tags next to it. Our footer <div> for instance, should not have allowed the content <div> nor the container <div> to appear to either the left or right side. For this reason, we use the Both property.

5. Click OK. The new ID selector appears within the CSS Styles panel.

Now that we've outlined the properties for the five major sections of the site, we're ready to insert the <div> tags that will act as containers for the content. The properties we've outlined will serve as the formatting and positioning attributes for the <div> tags we'll add next.

Inserting <div> Tags

Because we've already outlined the style rules using ID selectors in an external style sheet, we need only to insert five <div> tags into the page with IDs that match the selector names we created. To demonstrate this, let's insert a <div> for the main container portion of our page. You can do this by choosing Insert, Layout Objects, Div Tag. Alternatively, you could also click the Insert Div Tag icon (the first icon to the right of the Standard and Expanded buttons) in the Layout category of the Insert bar. Either method you choose produces the same result; the Insert Div Tag dialog box launches and appears similar to Figure 6.14.

FIGURE 6.14   Use the Insert Div Tag dialog box to create a new <div> tag in the page.

Although the dialog allows you to enter a class name and pick an insertion point for the tag, all we care about is entering the ID that represents the selector we've defined within our style sheet. Because we're creating the container of the page, select the container option from the ID drop-down menu (see Figure 6.14) and click OK. The <div> is created, complete with the dimensions and the background image we defined.

By default, Dreamweaver adds the text *Content for id "container" Goes Here* within the <div>. Select this text and delete it so that we can add the rest of the <div> tags within the container (header, navigation, content, and footer). You'll notice that the <div> tag's height will collapse down into an unworkable size. Don't worry about this, as we'll be using the Insert Div Tag dialog box from here on out.

Again, choose Insert, Layout Objects, Div Tag. The Insert Div Tag dialog box appears. This time, choose the After Start of Tag option from the Insert menu and choose the <div id="container"> option from the menu just to the right. This will force the header <div> (which we're about to add) to nest. Now choose the header option from the ID menu and click OK. Again, delete the text that reads *Content for id "header" goes here*. Now find the header.gif image located within the Images folder of the defined site and drag it into the header <div>. The result of the design resembles Figure 6.15.

Now you're ready to create the third <div> tag that will define the navigation section. Choose Insert, Layout Objects, Div Tag. The Insert Div Tag dialog box appears. This time, choose the After Tag option from the Insert menu and choose the <div id="header"> option from the menu just to the right. This will force the navigation <div> to nest within the container <div> but appear just after the header <div>. Now choose the navigation option from the ID menu and click OK. Again, delete the text that reads *Content for id "navigation" goes here* so that we can begin to define the text-based navigation menu. After the placeholder text is deleted, place your cursor within the <div> and add the text **Home** followed by a line break (Shift+Enter or Shift+Return). Repeat this process, adding the text **About Us, Solutions, Support**, and **Contact Us**. When you finish adding the navigation items, the result appears similar to Figure 6.16.

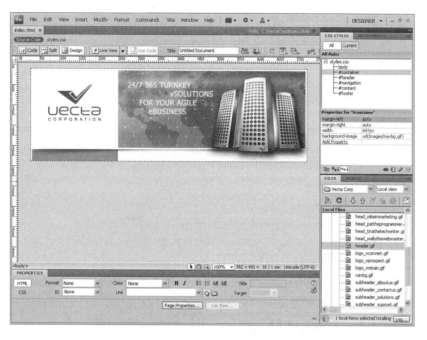

FIGURE 6.15   Add the `header.gif` image into the new header <div>.

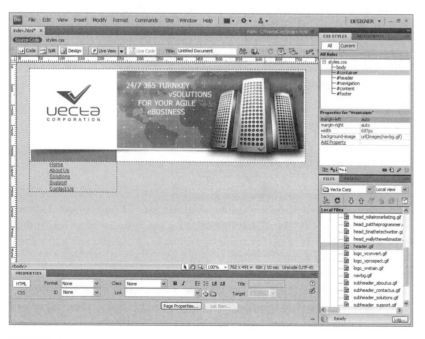

FIGURE 6.16   Add the rest of the navigational items to the navigation <div>.

Almost there! Next let's add the content section. Again, you can accomplish this task by choosing Insert, Layout Objects, Div Tag. When the Insert Div Tag dialog box appears, choose the After Tag option from the Insert menu, choose the `<div id="navigation">` option from the menu just to the right, and choose the content option from the ID drop-down menu. Click OK. The new `<div>` is added below the header `<div>` but just to the right of the navigation `<div>`. With the `<div>` firmly in place, you can add the content that will fill that area. For instance, you might want to add the subheader_welcome.gif image as the subheader within the `<div>`. You might also decide to add the text contained in the home.txt file in the Assets folder. When you've finished, the result should closely resemble Figure 6.17.

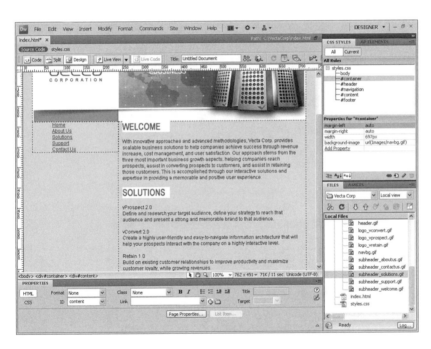

FIGURE 6.17   Add text and images to the new content `<div>`.

Finally, let's add the footer `<div>`, which will round out our design. Choose Insert, Layout Objects, Div Tag. When the Insert Div Tag dialog box appears, choose the After Tag option from the Insert menu, choose the `<div id="content">` option from the menu just to the right, and choose the footer option from the ID drop-down menu. Click OK. The new `<div>` is added below both the navigation and content `<div>`s. Now remove the text that reads *Content for id "footer" goes here* so that we can add the footer image into the `<div>`. After the placeholder text is deleted, find the footer.gif image and drag it into the newly created `<div>`. The result will appear similar to Figure 6.18.

With your design complete, test the page in a browser by pressing F12 (Option-F12). As you'll see, the design renders without problems (refer back to Figure 6.1).

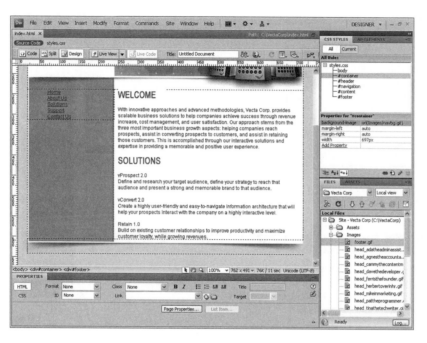

FIGURE 6.18   Add the `footer.gif` image into the newly added footer `<div>`.

Even better than the rendering of the design is what has been added to the code. Switch to Code view and notice that the code is much cleaner and is minimized to roughly 30 lines of code (mostly text for the content Div) in contrast to the 100 or so lines associated with the design when we were working with tables.

Converting Div Tags to Tables for Backward-Compatibility

In the previous sections, we used `<div>` tags to create a standards-compliant, tableless web page. Although the design was simple to create, it doesn't do us or our users much good if they're using older browser versions such as Netscape 4. As you saw back in Figure 6.2, the page doesn't look very good in Netscape 4.

To solve this problem, we have to re-create the site using a backward-compatible model in tables. Before you become frustrated at the thought of having to rebuild the page using tables, know that there's an easy and automated way of accomplishing this task in the Convert AP Divs to Tables feature. Using this feature in conjunction with the Check Browser behavior, we can guarantee that our users will see the appropriately formatted page regardless of what browser version they are using. To run through this process, choose Modify, Convert, AP Divs to Table. The Convert AP Divs to Table dialog box appears, similar to Figure 6.19.

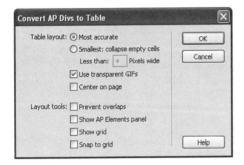

FIGURE 6.19   The Convert AP Divs to Table dialog box facilitates the process of converting our CSS-based design to one that uses tables.

NOTE

In order for the Convert AP Divs to Table feature to work, Divs cannot overlap one another. Before you choose this option, it's always a good idea to check the Prevent overlaps check box within the AP Elements panel.

The following functionality is revealed in the Convert AP Divs to Table dialog box:

- **Table Layout: Most Accurate**—Clicking this option button creates a cell for every `<div>`, plus an additional cell for any spacing required to fill out the area.

- **Table Layout: Smallest: Collapse Empty Cells**—Clicking this option button specifies that the edges surrounding `<div>` tags should be aligned if they are positioned within the specified number of pixels. We'll choose this option and leave the pixel width at the default of 4.

- **Table Layout: Use Transparent GIFs**—Checking this box ensures that the last row of the table has a 1 pixel by 1 pixel transparent GIF added to its cell. This is especially useful for guaranteeing consistent widths across all browser versions. For our purposes, make sure this check box is unchecked.

- **Table Layout: Center on Page**—Click this box to center the table on the page. Leave this option unchecked.

The rest of the features in this dialog box exist for the reverse process (that is, converting tables to AP `<div>`s). In this scenario, these check boxes merely provide viewable options such as the AP Elements panel, the grid, snapping, and so on. When you finish making the necessary adjustments, click OK. Immediately, our `<div>`-based page is converted to a table. Save your work as `index_netscape.html`. Now try testing the page in an older version of Netscape.

As you can see from Figure 6.20, the page looks as it did in newer browser versions using <div>s.

FIGURE 6.20   The page using tables looks as good in Netscape 4.7 as it did in newer browser versions using <div>s.

Built-In CSS Page Layouts

One of the hottest web-development techniques is the process of laying out web page structures using CSS instead of traditional HTML-based methods such as tables or frames. As the Web evolves, so too does the process of creating web pages. Therefore, tables are viewed as an archaic method of page structuring. As a web developer, you should be aware of that fact and begin learning and integrating standards-compliant methods into your site designs. In the previous few sections, we began to do just that. As you might recall, you looked at ways of building web pages that rely on CSS for the positioning and structuring of web pages. What little HTML we used was meant purely for integrating CSS rules or for adding imagery, media elements, and text to your pages. As you might also recall, the learning curve for creating standards-compliant CSS page designs is relatively higher as compared to tables. To help you along, Dreamweaver integrates a collection of carefully crafted and comment-rich CSS Page Layouts.

This section will get you up to speed with Dreamweaver's CSS page layouts. As you'll see, working with CSS-based structuring techniques has never been easier—thanks to this new collection of page layouts. To build a new web page based on a prestructured CSS-based layout, start by selecting File, New. The New Document dialog box appears. Select the HTML option from the Blank Page category. Up to this point in the book, we've usually selected the <none> option from the Layout list and clicked Create. This time, however, take a closer look at the additional options within the list. As you can see from Figure 6.21, additional prebuilt CSS-structured options exist.

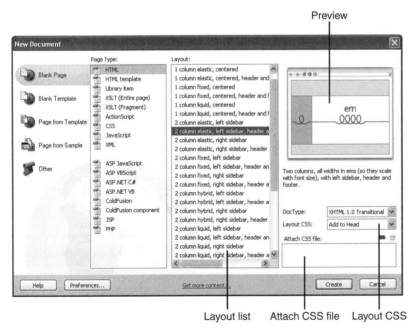

FIGURE 6.21   Choose from a list of prebuilt CSS-structured page layouts.

Numerous options exist within this dialog box for creating and handling the CSS that results, including the following:

> ► **Layout**—The Layout list contains 32 prebuilt CSS-structured layouts for you to use. For our purposes, select the 2 Column Elastic, Left Sidebar, Header and Footer option.

▶ **Preview**—The previous window displays an iconic representation of the selection you make from the Layout list. This preview is a rough approximation of what your design will be structured around.

▶ **Layout CSS**—Choose an option from this menu to instruct Dreamweaver as to how to handle the CSS that will accompany your layout. Options include Add to Head (adds all the CSS to the head of the page creating a document-wide style sheet), Create New File (adds all the CSS to a new external style sheet file), and Link to Existing File (adds all the CSS to an existing external style sheet file). When you select the Link to Existing File option, you'll be required to browse to the existing CSS style sheet using the Attach Style Sheet button, available from the Attach CSS file group of options. For our purposes, choose the Add to Head option.

▶ **Attach CSS file**—When you choose the Link to Existing File option from the Layout CSS menu, this group of options becomes immediately available. You can choose the Attach Style Sheet icon to browse to and attach an existing style sheet. Alternatively, you can delete a style sheet from this list by clicking the Remove Style Sheet icon.

Now that we have a layout selected and we've instructed Dreamweaver as to where it should place the accompanying CSS, click Create. Immediately, a new Document window is created, complete with your selected layout, similar to Figure 6.22.

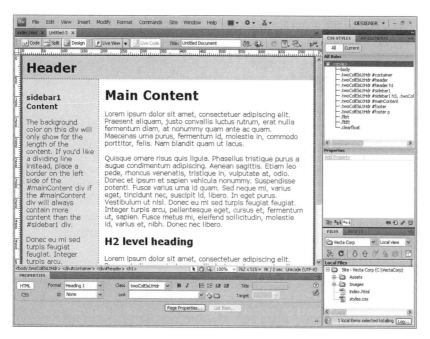

FIGURE 6.22   A new document window instance is created complete with your selected layout.

At a glance, you can see that the content is placed within <div> tags. And like you saw in the previous section, the positioning and structure of those <div> tags are controlled using a series of carefully crafted selectors, also visible in the CSS panel in Figure 6.22. Now try switching to Code view. Immediately you'll notice how many comments have been added to guide you through the relatively new process of using CSS to structure web pages. Now comes the fun part—removing the default text that appears in the <div> tags and replacing it with the Vecta Corp content. See if you can accomplish this task on your own!

Summary

As you've seen in this chapter, AP Elements/<div> tags offer a clean, standards-compliant alternative to developing websites. Using CSS in conjunction with <div> tags affords you the capability to cleanly separate positioning and formatting properties from structural code.

In this chapter, you learned about the various methods for inserting AP Elements, modifying properties outlined by AP Elements, and structuring pages using <div> tags and the CSS box model. Furthermore, you looked at some of the Dreamweaver CSS-based page layouts and how building CSS-based designs is not only easy, but also effortless when you take advantage of them.

In the next few chapters, we'll begin to shy away from CSS and take a much different direction by beginning to discuss important concepts as they relate to team collaboration and task automation.

CHAPTER 7

HTML Forms

IN THIS CHAPTER

▶ An Introduction to HTML Forms

▶ Working with Forms and Form Objects

If you've used websites such as Amazon, Yahoo!, Google, MSN, E*TRADE Financial, and eBay, chances are you've used and interacted with *forms*. Forms are everywhere on the web, and after you know what to look for, they're hard to ignore. Furthermore, they push development to a higher level by enabling interaction with the end user. Whether it's through registration forms, mailing lists, site searches, or online ordering, forms facilitate interaction between us as developers and our end users. Forms allow us to be "connected" with our end users by serving as a stepping stone to a whole new medium known as *web application development*. Covered with more detail starting in Part V, "Dynamic Web Page Development," the extremely broad and extensive topic of web application development begins with forms.

Like the rest of the chapters within this book, you can work with the examples in this chapter by downloading the files from the book's website. You'll want to replace the files within C:\VectaCorp\ with the files located in Exercises\ Chapter07\Beginning\.

An Introduction to HTML Forms

As I've just mentioned, forms are everywhere on the Web. They allow us, as developers, to collect and ultimately process data from our end users. Let's take eBay as an example. As a buyer, you visit eBay in an attempt to find a sweet deal on something you probably don't need. When you visit eBay, you don't verbally tell eBay to find an item;

instead, you interact with a form containing form objects in the shape of a search text box and a search button (see Figure 7.1).

FIGURE 7.1   eBay uses forms and form objects to collect a user's search criteria.

You enter your search criteria into the text box, click the Search button, and the results are magically returned in a clean list format that you can quickly browse through. From a development standpoint, eBay uses forms and form objects to facilitate the interaction between you and eBay's auction service. From a design standpoint, forms and form objects make it easy for me as a user to enter the criteria on which I want more information. As a buyer, you may be familiar with this process. It's straightforward, easy to use, and more important, intuitive.

From a seller's perspective, the process is slightly more complex, but again, it involves forms and form objects. When you want to sell an item on eBay's website, the first step is to register as a seller. This process is shown in more detail in Figure 7.2.

As you can see from Figure 7.2, numerous form objects exist in an effort to collect different types of information from the seller. Text boxes, like the one used in the search form, are used to collect general information such as first name, last name, address, city, email, and so on. Drop-down menus are used to allow the user to choose from a predefined set of states and countries, and from lists of months, days, and years for birthdays. In addition, if you scroll further down the page, a check box is used to collect a value indicating that yes, the user accepts the user agreement when checked; if left unchecked, it indicates that the user does not agree with the user agreement. Finally, a button object is used to submit the information to eBay for processing. (We'll get to processing the content of forms and form objects in Part V.) Both models (buyer and seller) demonstrate forms and form objects used in a real-world website that millions of people use daily. Of course, forms and form objects aren't exclusive to eBay. Companies all over the Web use forms and form objects so that users can interact with the services they offer on their websites.

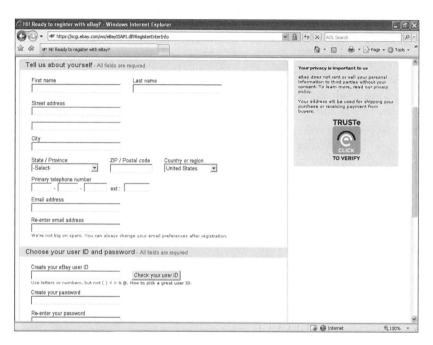

FIGURE 7.2   Potential eBay sellers use forms and form objects to register with eBay.

Even with this explanation, you still might be unclear about the differences between forms and form objects. To clear up any misconceptions between the two, think of the process of registering for a driver's license at your local Department of Motor Vehicles (DMV). You wait in line until it is your turn, you tell the usually expressionless attendant that you'd like to register to receive a new driver's license, and she hands you a form. Think about what that form contains. Paper-based forms like the one from the DMV contain places for you to enter your name, address, city, ZIP, phone number, car model, car type, and so on. The places on that registration form can be considered *form objects*. You fill out the form (that is, you fill in all the form objects, or fields) and hand it back to the attendant for processing. The Web is no different: Forms on the Web contain form objects and, in fact, are reliant on one another.

Now that you have an idea about what forms and form objects are and when and where they are used, let's actually build them within the context of our project. Throughout the rest of the chapter, we'll dissect forms and the various types of form objects you can use when working with forms in Dreamweaver.

Working with Forms and Form Objects

As I mentioned in the previous section, the addition of form objects begins with the addition of a form. You can think of the form as the container for its form objects. When the user clicks the Submit button, the entire form, along with all the data contained within the form objects in the form, is sent for processing. In fact, the form contains numerous properties that tell the browser where and how the form will be sent for processing when the Submit button is clicked. Before we jump too far ahead of ourselves, however, let's add a simple form to a web page. To do this, follow these instructions:

1. Open the `contactus.html` page located in the root of the project folder. For the most part, the design has already been created for you based on what we've learned up to this point. For now, we're concerned with adding a form and form objects so that potential customers can contact a sales representative within our fictitious company.

2. As a change of pace, we'll use the Forms category in the Insert panel to work with forms and form objects. If your Insert panel is not open, choose Window, Insert. When the Insert panel opens, switch to the Forms category.

3. Place your cursor just under the Contact Us subheader image.

4. Click the Form icon within the Insert panel to add a new form to the `contactus.html` page. As you can see in Figure 7.3, the form is indicated by the red dashed box. Because a form is considered an invisible element, you can choose to display it or hide it by enabling or disabling the Invisible Elements option located in the Visual Aids menu in the Document toolbar.

You'll also notice from Figure 7.3 that the form also changes the Property inspector. Like all elements that you add to the Document window, the Property inspector tailors itself to support property modifications for the form. The properties that become available include the following:

▶ **Form name**—Enter a value into this text box to uniquely identify your form. Although this value isn't required, it is highly recommended that you include one, especially when working with scripting languages such as JavaScript (covered in more detail as Behaviors in the next chapter). We'll leave our form name as the default **form1**.

▶ **Action**—Enter the path to the page that will process the data when the user submits the form. I'll save the long-winded explanations for Part V, but for now, know that every form's submission requires some sort of data collection endpoint. That endpoint is generally a database, text file, XML file, or even a straight email to a recipient. To get the form into that data collection mechanism, an intermediary file (containing functions with code) must process the form and perform the insertion into the data collection mechanism. For this chapter, that page has been created for you. The path, and the value you'll want to enter into this text box, is **http://www.vectacorp.com/vc/scripts/contactus.asp**.

▶ **Target**—Select one of the four options from this menu to associate the action (mentioned previously) with a particular link target. We'll leave ours blank.

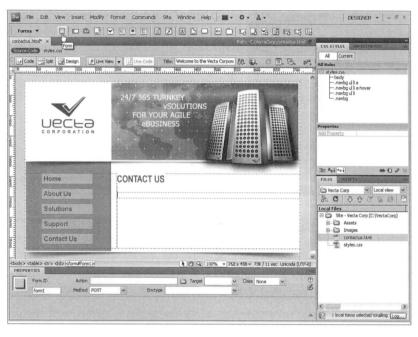

FIGURE 7.3   The form is added to the page and is evident by the red dashed box.

▶ **Class**—When working with CSS, select a class from this menu to set the overall style of the form. We'll leave ours blank.

▶ **Method**—Select one of the two options from this menu to set how the form should be sent to the intermediary file for processing. Two options are available from this menu: POST and GET. POST, which is the Dreamweaver and browser default, embeds the form within HTTP headers, essentially unseen by anyone. Nine times out of ten, you'll use POST in your development efforts because it's a much more secure alternative to GET. However, you can use GET to send the contents of all form elements within the form, appended as parameters within the URL of the page. This is beneficial when working with searches: The user can bookmark a recent search because the submitted search value is appended to the URL of the page. As you can see from the callout in Figure 7.4, AutoTrader.com uses GET when submitting searches for processing. This allows the user to later bookmark popular searches and search results and easily return to them at a later time.

Searches are about all you want to use the GET method for. Because of the potential security vulnerability and the fact that URL strings are limited to 8,192 characters, longer forms, especially those containing sensitive data such as usernames, passwords, social security numbers, and/or credit card information, should be sent using POST. We'll leave our form's method set to POST.

The Address Bar contains search criteria

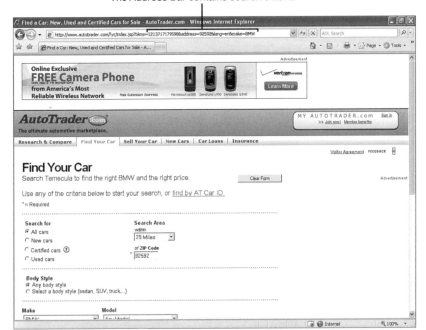

FIGURE 7.4   Use GET within search forms to allow users to bookmark recent searches.

CAUTION

Even POST isn't entirely secure. When using POST, form data is *embedded* into the HTTP headers—it is not encrypted. An attacker can still compromise sensitive information using an HTTP *packet sniffer*. For this reason, sensitive data should always be transmitted using a secure connection (SSL).

▶ **Enctype**—Choose an option from this menu to specify the MIME encoding type of the data submitted to the server for processing. By default, forms are sent using the application/x-www-form-urlencode type, but it's not uncommon to use the multipart/form-data type, especially when uploading files using the File Field form object. We'll leave this menu as is. For more information on MIME types, refer to the following formal definition at: en.wikipedia.org/wiki/MIME.

Now that you have an idea about how forms are inserted into the page, let's direct our attention to inserting form objects into the form. The form objects you can insert in Dreamweaver include the following:

▶ Text Fields, Password Fields, and Textarea

▶ Check Boxes and Checkbox Groups

▶ Radio Buttons and Radio Groups

▶ Lists and Menus

▶ Buttons

▶ File Field

▶ Image Field

▶ Hidden Field

▶ Jump Menu

Text Fields, Password Fields, and Textarea

Arguably the most widely used form object is the Text Field. Because the Text Field is so versatile, it's the perfect option when you need to create a plain text box, password text box, or a multiline text box where users can enter large amounts of information. To see the Text Field in action, follow these steps:

1. Place your cursor within the form (inside the red dashed box) and insert a new table by choosing the Table option from the Insert menu. Give the new table 13 rows, 2 columns, a width of 400 pixels, and a border thickness, cell padding, and cell spacing of 0 pixels. We'll use this table to cleanly position text labels and form objects on the page.

2. In the first six cells of the first column, add the text `Name:`, `Company Name:`, `Address:`, `City:`, `State:`, and `ZIP:`, respectively.

3. Place your cursor into the first cell in the second column and insert a new Text Field form object by clicking the Text Field icon in the Insert panel (or choosing Insert, Form, Text Field). The new Text Field will appear similar to Figure 7.5.

NOTE

After you've clicked to insert the Text Field, by default, Dreamweaver displays Accessibility options as they relate to form objects. Remember, if you don't find yourself working with Accessibility features at this point, this dialog box can be turned off by navigating to the Accessibility category of the Preferences dialog box (available from Edit, Preferences/Dreamweaver, Preferences) and unchecking the Form objects check box. More information on accessibility can be found in the online Appendix A, "Accessibility."

As you can see from Figure 7.5, selecting the Text Field within the form changes the Form Property inspector to the Form Text Property inspector. This view exposes the following customizable properties:

▶ **TextField name**—Enter a value in this text box to uniquely identify the Text Field form object on the page. Although setting a value for this field isn't required, there isn't much you can do (in terms of processing the data server-side) if you don't set a value here. The application that processes our form must reference a specific Text

Field by its unique name to grab the value it contains. For our page, we'll name this Text Field object **name** to correspond with the text label in the same row.

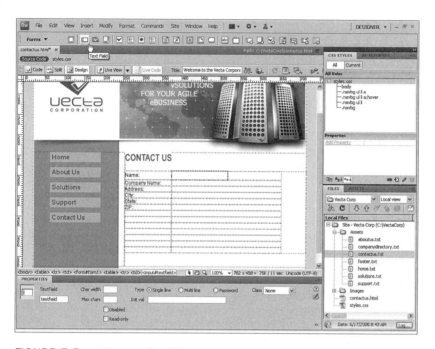

FIGURE 7.5   Add a new Text Field form object to the first cell in the second column of the table.

▶ **Char width**—Enter a value in this text box to set the width in characters for the Text Field form object. Leaving this field blank sets the default value, which is 20. We'll leave ours blank.

▶ **Max Chars/Num Lines**—Enter a value in this text box to set the maximum number of characters that this Text Field form object will accept. This is an excellent value to set when you want to limit data entry within certain fields such as ZIP code (5 characters) or age (3 characters). When working with the Multi Line type, the Max Chars text box becomes a Num Lines text box, which essentially sets the height in character lines for the Multi Line Text Field. Because we can safely assume that most people don't have names longer than 50 characters, enter **50** here.

▶ **Disabled**—Check this box to disable the initial state of the Text Field. It'll be up to you to write script (either client-side script or server-side script) to re-enable the Text Field.

▶ **Read-only**—Check this box to set the initial state of the Text Field to read-only. This is a great feature to enable when you only want users to view the value of a Text Field, rather than enter a value for submission.

▶ **Type: Single line**—Choose this option button to set the Text Field type to a standard single-line Text Field.

▶ **Type: Multi line**—Choose this option button to set the Text Field type to a multiline Text Field. You'll use this type when inserting the Questions Text Field later on in this section. This Text Field type works well for collecting large amounts of data. It also allows the user to use simple formats such as spaces and line breaks within the Text Field. The Multi Line Text Field can also be inserted by choosing Insert, Form, Textarea.

▶ **Type: Password**—Choose this option button to set the Text Field type to a password Text Field. Any text entered within a Text Field that's been assigned this type shows as asterisks (bullets on a Mac).

▶ **Class**—When working with CSS, select a class from this menu to set the overall style of the Text Field form object. We'll leave ours blank.

▶ **Init val**—Enter a value within this text box when you want a note or initial value to display within the Text Field form object when the form page is first loaded within the browser.

Now that you have an understanding of the properties associated with Text Fields, let's add five more Text Field form objects to handle the collection of the Company Name, Address, City, State, and ZIP code. Again, place your cursor within the second cell of the second column and choose the Text Field icon within the Insert panel. (You can also choose Insert, Form, Text Field.) After the Text Field appears, name the Text Field `companyname` and associate a value of `50` for the Max chars property. Repeat this process four more times, adding four more Text Fields within the third, fourth, fifth, and sixth cells of the second column and adding Text Fields. Name the Text Fields `address`, `city`, `state`, and `zip`, respectively. You might also decide to assign the Max chars value of `50` for address and city, `2` for state, and `5` for ZIP.

Finally, we'll add a seventh Text Field form object using the Textarea icon within the Insert panel. To do this, place your cursor in the eleventh cell of the first column and add the text `Questions?`. Now place your cursor in the tenth cell of the second column and choose the Textarea icon from within the Insert panel (or choose Insert, Form, Textarea). Selecting the Textarea icon inserts a new Multi Line Text Field form object within the cell.

For the Multi Line Text Field object, enter the name `questions`, assign a Char width of 30, Num Lines of 4, and set the Init Val to the text `Enter your question here`. The result of the form additions will resemble Figure 7.6.

Check Boxes and Checkbox Groups

Check boxes, like the ones that appear within the Property inspector, allow you to enable or disable selections within forms. More importantly, however, check boxes allow you to select multiple options from a group of options. For instance, in our Contact Us form, we'll ask inquiring customers to select the infrastructure of their organization. Because an organization might employ various types of operating systems, the check box becomes the perfect choice because multiple selections can be made. If the customers' organizations employ one type of operating system, fine. But at the very least, we want to provide them with the opportunity to select multiple items from a group of options. Collecting as much information as possible from potential customers will help the sales representative better assess the company's need for Vecta solutions.

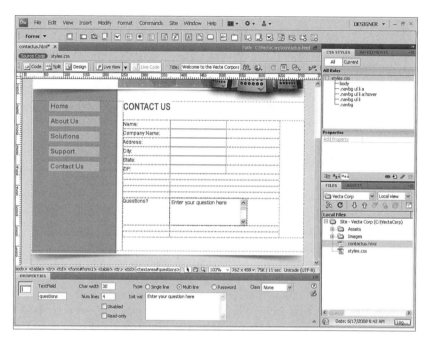

FIGURE 7.6   Insert Text Fields and a Multi Line Text Field (Textarea) onto the page.

To add and work with Check box form objects in Dreamweaver, follow these steps:

1. Place your cursor in the seventh cell of the first column and enter the text **Current Infrastructure:**.

2. Place your cursor in the seventh cell of the second column and click the Check box icon in the Insert panel to add a new Check box form object to the table's cell. You can also insert a check box by choosing Insert, Form, Check box.

3. Place your cursor to the right of the check box and enter the text **Microsoft.**

4. Repeat steps 2 and 3 three more times, entering a Check box form object and adding the text **Mac**, **Linux**, and **Unix**. After you've finished, the page should resemble Figure 7.7. Remember, you can press Shift+Enter (Shift-Return) to add a line break after the text. This will enable you to add the next check box on the next line.

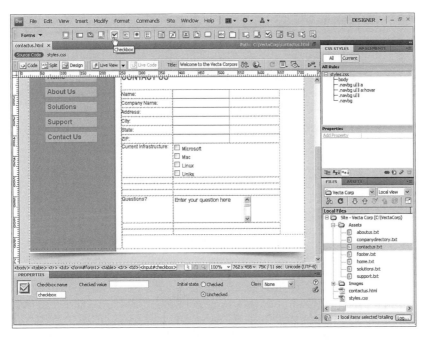

FIGURE 7.7   Add three more Check box form objects, complete with text.

You'll also notice that selecting a Check box form object reveals the following set of customizable properties in the Property inspector:

▶ **Checkbox name**—Enter the unique name of the Check box form object within this text box. In most cases, you'll want to enter the same name for all Check box form objects related to a specific group. Because we have four Check box objects that relate to infrastructure, we'll name them all **infrastructure**. This arrangement allows the application that will process this form to iterate through the Check box group and return a list of checked values, covered next.

▶ **Checked value**—The value you enter here is the value that will be sent to the server for processing. For our Check box objects, we'll want to enter values of **Microsoft**, **Mac, Linux**, and **Unix**, respectively.

▶ **Initial state**—You can set the state of the Check box form object to either checked or unchecked when the form loads for the first time. Because we can't guess which operating system the potential customer will be using, don't set an initial state for any of the check boxes.

▶ **Class**—When working with CSS, select a class from this menu to set the overall style of the Check box object. We'll leave ours blank.

> **TIP**
>
> To make it easier on you to insert large numbers of check boxes, Dreamweaver CS4 now features a Checkbox Group option, which functions similarly to the Radio Group option that has been available in Dreamweaver for quite some time. Choosing either Insert, Form, Checkbox Group or selecting the Checkbox Group icon within the Insert panel launches the Checkbox Group dialog box, which allows you to quickly add and customize large amounts of check boxes within a page. Again, the dialog box and overall feature set is exactly the same as the Radio Group option, covered with more detail in the next section.

Radio Buttons and Radio Groups

Similar to check boxes, Radio Button form objects allow users to select options within a form. The difference between Radio Buttons and check boxes, however, is that with Radio Buttons, users can select only one option from a list of options. In our example, we'll want to ask potential customers what their organizations' budgets are. Assuming that the potential customer has a set budget in mind, we can provide a list of ranges, allowing the inquiring customer to select one. This functionality can easily be accomplished by adding Radio Buttons, one for each budget range we think our inquiring customers will have.

To add and work with Radio Button form objects in Dreamweaver, follow these steps:

1. Place your cursor in the eighth cell of the first column and enter the text **Budget:**.

2. Place your cursor in the eighth cell of the second column and click the Radio Button icon in the Insert panel to add a new Radio Button to the table's cell. You can also add a Radio Button by choosing Insert, Form, Radio Button.

3. Place your cursor to the right of the Radio Button and enter the text **$1,000-$10,000**.

4. Repeat steps 2 and 3 two more times, entering a Radio Button form object and adding the text **$10,000-$50,000** and **$50,000+**. When you finish, the page should resemble Figure 7.8.

You'll also notice that selecting a Radio Button form object reveals a set of customizable properties within the Property inspector. These properties include the following:

- **Radio Button name**—Enter the unique name of the Radio Button form object within this text box. For the most part, you'll want to enter the same name for all Radio Button form objects relating to a specific group. Because we have three Radio Button objects that relate to a company's budget, we'll name them all **budget**. This arrangement allows the application that will process this form to iterate through the Radio Button group and return the checked value, covered next.

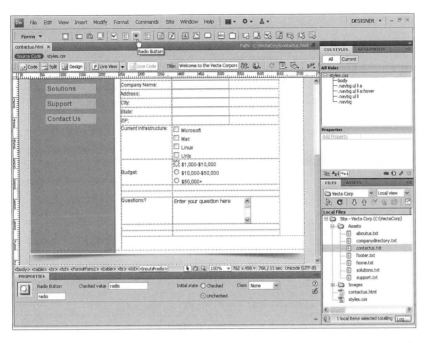

FIGURE 7.8   Add three Radio Button objects to represent a budget that an inquiring customer might have.

TIP

When working with radio buttons, it's important to understand that distinct groups of radio buttons should all be given the same name. If, by accident perhaps, you name all of your radio buttons differently, the browser will treat the radio buttons similarly to check boxes, that is, it'll allow you to select multiple radio buttons from a group. To prevent this, the Radio Group option might be a better choice. The Radio Group will automatically give each radio button within the group the same name.

▶ **Checked value**—The value you enter here is the value that will be sent to the server for processing. For our Radio Button objects, we'll want to enter values of **$1,000-$10,000**, **$10,000-$50,000**, and **$50,000+**, respectively.

▶ **Initial state**—You can set the state of the Radio Button form object to either checked or unchecked when the form page loads for the first time. Because we want to guarantee that a user selects one option, we'll make the $10,000–$50,000 Radio Button checked initially.

▶ **Class**—When you're working with CSS, select a class from this menu to set the overall style of the Radio Button form object. We'll leave ours blank.

In our example, we've added three Radio Button form objects. However, suppose that you needed to insert a large list of Radio Button objects on the page. Doing them individually would be tedious work and might discourage you from using Radio Buttons. Instead of adding Radio Buttons individually, you might want to consider using the Radio Group option available by clicking the icon next to the Radio Button icon in the Insert panel (or by choosing Insert, Form, Radio Group). Selecting this option opens the Radio Group dialog box as shown in Figure 7.9.

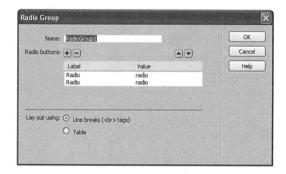

FIGURE 7.9   Use the Radio Group dialog box to add long lists of Radio Button form objects to your form.

As you can see from Figure 7.9, the Radio Group dialog box reveals the following properties:

▶ **Name**—Enter the unique name to be given to *all* Radio Buttons within this text box.

▶ **Radio buttons**—Use this pane to add new or remove and/or reposition existing Radio Buttons within the group. By default, the pane automatically includes two Radio Button form objects. To add a new Radio Button to the list, click the Add (+) icon. To remove a Radio Button from the list, click the Remove (-) icon. After the Radio Button is in the list, you can change the text label by clicking in the area of the Label column for the specific Radio Button. Furthermore, you can change the checked value by clicking within the area of the Value column for the specific Radio Button.

▶ **Lay out using**—Choose an option from this radio button group to set the layout of the Radio Button form objects on the page. Select the Line Breaks option to set the vertical positioning of Radio Buttons so that each Radio Button is spaced from the previous Radio Button using a line break (
 tag). Select the Table option to position your Radio Buttons and text labels within an HTML table.

Lists and Menus

Aside from adding Check box and Radio Button form objects, you can also add Listboxes and Drop Down Menus. The Listbox form object adds a boxed pane that contains numerous values; if you've got a lot of values and a small amount of space, you can choose to make the Listbox scrollable. Furthermore, depending on how you configure the Listbox, users navigating it can hold down the Ctrl (⌘) key and click to select multiple options within the list. Alternatively, you can use the Drop Down Menu form object as a way of storing numerous values in one expandable and collapsible menu. If you choose a Drop Down Menu, the user will click one item and be presented with as many choices as you want to make available. When the user clicks one, that choice is shown in the Drop Down Menu box and you can make only one selection. Drop Down Menus are most commonly seen when you select your State or Country on a form. To demonstrate the use of these form objects, follow these steps:

1. Place your cursor in the ninth cell of the first column and enter the text **Company Size:.**

2. Place your cursor in the ninth cell of the second column and click the List/Menu icon on the Insert panel to add a new List/Menu to the table's cell similar to Figure 7.10. You can also add a List/Menu by choosing Insert, Form, List/Menu.

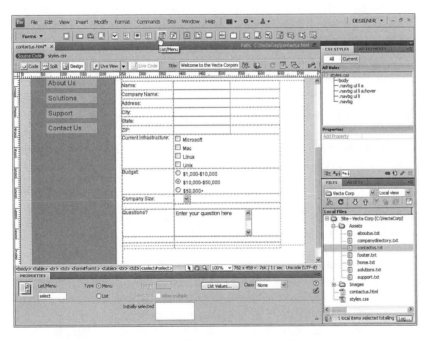

FIGURE 7.10   Add a new List/Menu form object to the page.

Because Drop Down Menu and Listbox form objects share common properties, they're added as a single object and configured as either a Drop Down Menu or Listbox in the Type radio group. However, the Type option isn't the only property outlined within the List/Menu Property inspector. The following represents a complete list of properties:

▶ **List/Menu name**—Enter the unique name to be given to the Drop Down Menu or Listbox form object in this text box. Because we're going to be creating a Drop Down Menu that should represent the size of the inquiring customer's company, let's name it **companysize.**

▶ **Type**—Select an option from this radio group to convert the form object to a Drop Down Menu or a Listbox depending on the selection. Selecting the List option enables the Height text box and Selection check box. For now, we'll keep the object we're configuring as a Drop Down Menu.

▶ **Height**—When the List Type is selected, enter a value in this text box to set the number of items displayed within the list initially.

▶ **Selections**—When the List Type is selected, enable this check box to indicate whether the user can select multiple items from the list.

▶ **List Values**—Click this button to launch the List Values dialog box. In this dialog box, you'll enter the list of items that will be displayed within the List/Menu object.

▶ **Class**—When working with CSS, select a class from this menu to set the overall style of the List/Menu object. We'll leave ours blank.

▶ **Initially Selected**—The values you add in the List Values dialog box also appear in this list box. You can set which value should be initially selected when the form page loads for the first time by selecting that value from this list.

Now that we've appropriately named our Drop Down Menu, let's add some values. To do this, click the List Values button. The List Values dialog box appears.

Similar to the Radio Group dialog box, the List Values dialog box allows you to Add (+), Remove (-), and reposition values within the list. By default, the dialog box loads with the first line in the Item Label column highlighted. You can add the first item by typing into the outlined box. I'll add the text **1-50** as the first Item Label and leave the Value column blank.

NOTE

Each item in the list has a label (the text that appears in the list) and a value (the value that's sent to the processing application if the item is selected). If no value is specified, the label is sent to the processing application instead. Values are ideal to use in situations in which the programming language can't manipulate or work with the item's label. Months of the year are a perfect example. Programming languages reference dates and times as numbers rather than text. January, for instance, will be interpreted as 1 by the programming language. If you were working with months of the year within one of these drop-down menus, you might opt to make January the item's label by making the numeric value 1, the item's value. Another example could be a drop down list that contained states. You might make the text label read California, for instance, and have its associated label be the abbreviation CA.

Now add three more items by clicking the Add (+) icon and adding the text **51-500, 501-10,000**, and **10,001+**. When you finish, the List Values dialog box will resemble Figure 7.11.

When you finish adding the values to the Drop Down Menu form object, click OK. You'll notice that the values I've added in the List Values dialog box also appear within the

Initially Selected list box in the Property inspector. It is from this menu that you're able to configure an initially selected value for the Drop Down Menu. Go ahead and select the **1-50** option now.

FIGURE 7.11   Add four total values to your Drop Down Menu.

Now that you have an idea how the Drop Down Menu form object works, let's add a Listbox form object. To do that, follow these steps:

1. Place your cursor in the tenth cell of the first column and enter the text **Product Interest:**.

2. Place your cursor in the tenth cell of the second column and click the List/Menu icon in the Insert panel to add a new List/Menu form object to the table's cell.

3. In the Property inspector, name your Listbox object **product**.

4. Check the List option from the Type radio group.

5. Enter a height of **3**.

6. Because we'll assume that an inquiring customer might have interest in all Vecta Corp solutions, also enable the Allow Multiple check box.

7. Click the List Values button to open the List Values dialog box. Add the values **vProspect 2.0**, **vConvert 2.0**, and **vRetain 1.0**.

8. Click OK. The new, populated Listbox form object appears within the page similar to Figure 7.12.

Buttons

Possibly the simplest form object to understand is the Button. Although three types of Button objects exist, the most widely used is the Submit Button. The Submit Button, when clicked, initiates the transfer of the form to the processing application outlined in the form's action. You can insert a new Button form object by simply placing your cursor into the last cell within the second column of the table and clicking the Button icon in the Insert panel. By default, a Submit Button is inserted into the page (see Figure 7.13).

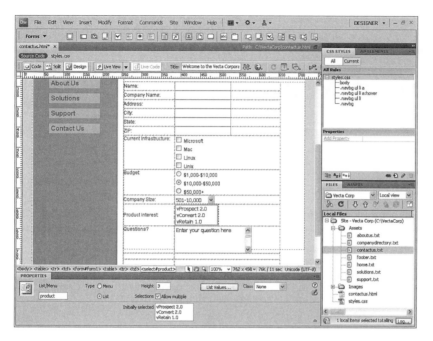

FIGURE 7.12   The new Listbox appears within the page.

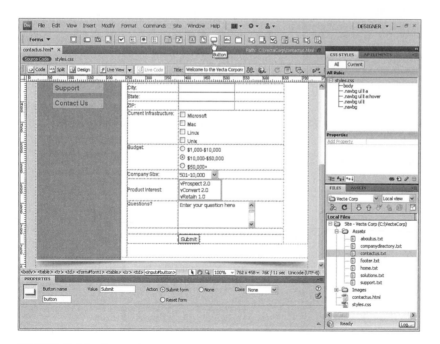

FIGURE 7.13   A new Submit Button is inserted into the page.

As you can see from Figure 7.13, selecting the Button form object changes the Property inspector to the Button Property inspector with the following customizable properties:

- ▶ **Button name**—Enter the unique name to be given to the Button form object in this text box. Because naming Button objects isn't the highest of priorities, we'll leave ours with the default value of Submit.

- ▶ **Value**—Enter a name in this text box to set the text that will appear on the button itself. Because we want to alert our users that clicking this button submits the form, we'll leave the default text (**Submit**) alone.

- ▶ **Action**—Sets what the button will do and how it will perform within the browser. For instance, the Submit form action forces the form to submit to the intermediary file specified within the Action attribute of the form when the button is clicked. The Reset action causes all form objects to reset to their initial states when the button is clicked. Finally, the None action does nothing. Typically you'd use the None action when working with Behaviors (covered in the next chapter) so that when the button is clicked, it doesn't submit or reset the form, but instead performs your custom action based on a behavior you create within Dreamweaver.

- ▶ **Class**—When you're working with CSS, select a class from this menu to set the overall style of the Button object. We'll leave ours blank.

Now that you have a Submit Button object on the page, let's add a Reset Button next to the existing Submit button. To do this, place your cursor next to the existing Submit button and click the Button icon in the Insert panel. When your new Button object appears on the page, select it and change its Action to Reset form in the Property inspector.

Test the Form

The form is taking shape nicely and is now ready for testing within the browser. To see how users will interact with your form, save your work and preview the page in the browser by pressing F12. When the page appears, fill out the form objects, entering text into the Text Fields, picking options from the Check boxes and Radio Buttons, and making selections from the Drop Down Menu and Listbox. When you've finished, click the Submit button. If you typed the path to the processing application correctly within the Action text box for the form, the page should clear itself of the form objects and display what your selections and entries were.

At first glance, what happened in the background may seem confusing. The process of sending form information to the server for processing will be cleared up in Part V. For now, we can cover the process at a basic level.

As mentioned in the beginning of the chapter, forms exist as a way for organizations to collect information from their end users (clients). By clicking the Submit button, the user can send the form and its form object values to an application (server), defined in the form's Action field, for processing. Figure 7.14 provides a visual representation of this process.

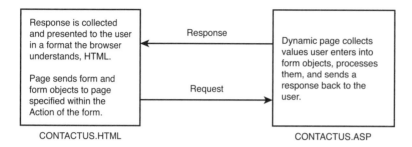

FIGURE 7.14   The form and form object values are sent to the server-side application for processing.

The approach in which you send data to a server for processing, also known as *client-server architecture*, is central to the way thousands of organizations (also known as *application service providers*) do business on the Web. In our scenario, the contactus.html form page, which is what the client interacts with, is what you've just created. The application, contactus.asp, has already been created and resides on the server (www.vectacorp.com). The application's sole purpose is to collect the values in the form objects and redisplay them in the client's browser in a readable format. As you'll learn in Part V, these applications can get much more complex than the simple example presented here. For now, this should give you an idea about the role of forms and form objects.

Image Field

The drawback to using form buttons is that they all look alike. The only way to differentiate form buttons is by their text labels. Although you can create CSS styles to reformat the look of form objects, including buttons, there is a quicker way—the Image Field form object. The Image Field form object, which is essentially an image you create and add into Dreamweaver, is treated just as a Submit Button form object would be, but is customizable based on your design standards. To add an Image Field form object to the page, follow these steps:

1. Select and delete the Submit and Reset buttons located in the last cell of the second column.

2. Click the Image Field icon located in the Insert panel (or choose Insert, Form, Image Field). Immediately, the Select Image Source dialog box appears.

3. Browse to the Images folder of the project, select the imagefield_submit.gif image, and click OK. The image appears in the cell similar to Figure 7.15.

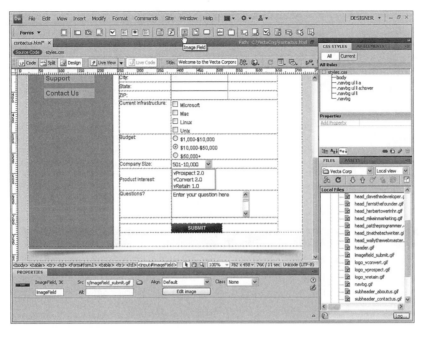

FIGURE 7.15   The Image Field form object displays a custom image but is treated as a Submit Button form object.

Selecting the button reveals the following customizable properties within the Property inspector:

▶ **Image Field name**—Enter the unique name to be given to the Image Field form object within this text box. As with Button form objects, naming Image Field objects isn't the biggest of priorities, so we'll leave ours with the default value of imageField.

▶ **Src**—Displays the source path of the Image Field form object.

▶ **Alt**—Like all images, you'll want to enter the alternative text to be associated with the Image Field form object here. We'll add the text **Click Submit**. You can find more information on Accessibility in the online Appendix A.

▶ **Align**—Select an option from this menu to set the alignment of elements around the Image Field object in relation to the Image Field. For instance, selecting Left from this menu aligns the Image Field to the Left and all elements, including text, around the Image Field's right.

▶ **Edit Image**—Click this button to launch the external editor specified for the Image Field's extension type. As you'll see in the online Appendix C, "Defining Preferences," these external editors are specified in the File Types/Editors category in the Preferences window.

▶ **Class**—When working with CSS, select a class from this menu to set the overall style of the Image Field form object. We'll leave ours blank.

File Field

One of the most underused form objects available in Dreamweaver is the File Field form object. You can use this form object as a way of enabling end users to browse their hard drives for a file in an effort to upload a file to the server for processing. The File Field object, which is really just a Text Field with a Browse Button, is shown in Figure 7.16.

FIGURE 7.16   Use the File Field form object to allow users to browse for and select files on their hard drives for uploading to the server.

> **NOTE**
>
> Initially the File Field seems like an object that would be widely adopted by web developers. The downside to the File Field is that it takes a lot of know-how and code to get it to work server-side. The difficulty in integrating the File Field with server-side applications is the primary reason this form object is rarely used.

Hidden Field

The marketing department's friend, the Hidden Field form object is a common way to persist client-side data from page to page without the end user seeing or even realizing it. I say this form object is the marketing department's friend because this form object was used to death in the late 1990s dot-com web-marketing crusade to sell unneeded and worthless software to unsuspecting Web newbies. The scam was simple and involved nothing more than forms, form objects, and a couple of Hidden Fields. Typically starting with an email (spam) advertising the next best "free" software, unsuspecting users would click the accompanying link to visit the site offering the "free" software. Initially, the offer seemed legitimate, asking the user only for their email address with a button promising that the next step was the download. The unsuspecting user would click the button to download and instantly be taken to a second page requiring more information such as name, address, and so on. The user, believing that the company already had their email address and that they would get spammed to the nth degree if they don't complete the process, cautiously enters more information and clicks yet another button that promises the next step is, in fact, the download. But to no avail; the user is now required to enter a credit card number and expiration date to purchase the $4.99 software that they initially thought was free. Fearing retaliation from the dastardly company, the user is left feeling that $4.99 and worthless software is a fair trade for not sharing the personal information they just entered into all the form objects.

We've all seen this before, right? Although not everyone is fooled into actually purchasing the software, some inexperienced Web users didn't know better and actually completed the purchase, much to their dismay. Being a culprit at one time, I can tell you that you could have easily closed the browser and been fine. The personal information was not actually sent to the server (and subsequently saved) when you clicked the Continue button to move from page to page, but was, in fact, stored in Hidden Field form objects. On the first page, the user would enter his or her email address and click Continue. The value (the email address) was stored in a Hidden Field while the user entered more values. When the user clicked Continue on that second page, the new information was stored in a new series of Hidden Field objects. The process would go on until the last page, at which time the user would finally pay for the software and then the personal information was taken from the Hidden Fields and stored by the company. Figure 7.17 diagrams the process.

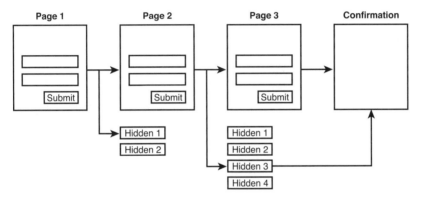

FIGURE 7.17   Hidden Fields are used to collect information from page to page of a multipage form.

Fortunately, this scam isn't widely used anymore. Now that we're in the twenty-first century, we've graduated to pop-up ads and spyware!

Jump Menu

You can use a Jump Menu to create a quick, compact navigation option for the end user. Although a Jump Menu is more of a prebuilt component than it is a form object, it does incorporate the use of the Drop Down Menu and Button form objects to aid in its implementation. With a Jump Menu, you can easily add navigation options within a Drop Down Menu that, when selected, "jumps" the page to a specified path. To insert a Jump Menu, follow these steps:

1. Create a new blank HTML page by choosing File, New. When the New Document dialog box appears, select Blank Page, HTML, <none>, and click Create. Immediately save your page as **jumpmenu.html**.

2. With your cursor on the page, click the Jump Menu icon in the Forms tab of the Insert panel (or choose Insert, Form, Jump Menu). This action launches the Insert Jump Menu dialog box, shown in Figure 7.18.

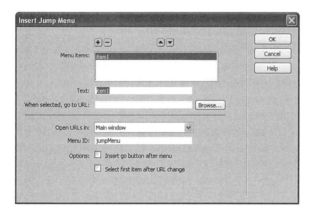

FIGURE 7.18   The Insert Jump Menu dialog box offers options to link different menu items to different pages.

3. Initially, you can add items to your new Jump Menu by clicking the Add (+) icon and typing the label of the menu item in the Text text box. I'll add the text **Go to Vecta Corp**.

4. Type the URL you'd like that menu item to link to. You can either browse for a local file or type an absolute URL. I'll add the absolute path **http://www.vectacorp.com**.

5. Repeat steps 3–4, adding a few more selectable options. When you finish, your Jump Menu may resemble mine (see Figure 7.19).

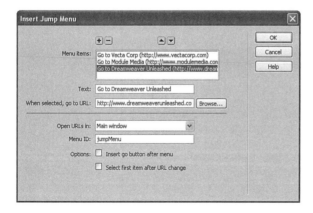

FIGURE 7.19   Add some selectable options to your Jump Menu.

6. Test your page in the browser by selecting the Preview in Browser option in the Document toolbar or by pressing F12 (Option-F12). In the browser, you should be able to select an option from the menu and automatically be redirected to the specific URL.

You might have noticed that the Insert Jump Menu component includes more customizable properties than we actually used. The following is a complete list of available options within the Insert Jump Menu dialog box (refer back to Figure 7.18):

▶ **Menu items**—Use this widget to add, remove, and reposition items within the Jump Menu. The Menu Items pane displays the text of the item complete with the associated URL in parentheses.

▶ **Text**—Enter the text to be associated with the Jump Menu item in this text box.

▶ **When Selected, Go to URL**—Enter the URL to be associated with the Jump Menu item. This is the path that the browser will navigate to when the item in the Jump Menu is selected.

▶ **Open URLs In**—Use this menu to select where you want the link to open. You can target a frame in a frameset or target the existing window (default).

▶ **Menu ID**—Enter the unique name to be given to the Jump Menu in this text box.

▶ **Options: Insert Go Button After Menu**—Select this check box to have the Jump Menu appear with a Go button next to it. The Jump Menu uses the onChange event to trigger the browser redirection that might not be supported in older browsers. The onClick event associated with the Go button, however, *is* supported in all browsers.

▶ **Options: Select First Item After URL Change**—Check this option when your Jump Menu resides in a frame and the redirection occurs in another frame. Enabling this option guarantees that the item selected is highlighted when the "jump" occurs.

Although there's no easy way to modify the Jump Menu after the Jump Menu dialog box has been configured, modifying the Jump Menu's structure isn't entirely impossible. If you need to change some of the menu items, you can highlight the Jump Menu and click the List Values button in the Property inspector. If you need to make more advanced modifications, however, use the Behaviors panel. We'll discuss this option with more detail in the next chapter.

Fieldsets

One of my favorite HTML design elements is the Fieldset. You can use the Fieldset as a handy way to group similar form objects within a bordered container. The Fieldset helps users distinguish different form objects as they relate to specific functionality on the page. To use the Fieldset, follow these instructions:

1. Switch back to the contactus.html page if it's not open already.

2. Place your cursor in the form and select the <form> tag in the Tag Selector. The entire form should be highlighted, as shown in Figure 7.20.

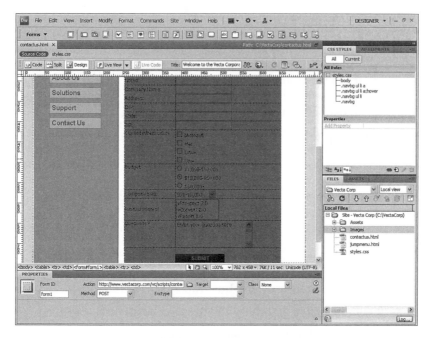

FIGURE 7.20 Select the form by clicking the `<form#form1>` tag in the Tag Selector.

3. Cut the form out of the page by choosing Edit, Cut or by pressing Ctrl+X on Windows (⌘-X on a Mac).

4. With your cursor now blinking in the cell, select the Fieldset icon from the Insert panel (or choose Insert, Form, Fieldset). Clicking this icon opens the Fieldset dialog box.

5. Within the Legend text box, enter the text **Contact a Sales Representative** and click OK. The Fieldset dialog box will close.

6. Place your cursor just to the right of the Contact a Sales Representative text (Legend) and click Enter. Immediately paste your form back into the page. You can do this by selecting Edit, Paste or by pressing Ctrl+V (⌘-V).

Preview your page in the browser by selecting the Preview in Browser option from the Document toolbar or by pressing F12 (Option-F12). As you can see from Figure 7.21, the form objects are outlined with a pane complete with the text label Contact a Sales Representative.

Labels

The final form element that you can use within your pages is the Label element available from both the Insert, Form menu and the Forms category in the Insert panel. You can use this element as a way of defining a unique association between text and a form element (usually a check box or radio button). For instance, if you haven't noticed already, the text just to the right of both the radio buttons and check boxes on our Contact Us form isn't selectable. Although this doesn't seem to pose any concerns, it does bring up a usability issue. For users to select an radio button or check box, they must select the element directly to enable/disable the radio button or check box. Selecting the text next to the element does nothing. As a usability enhancement, we might decide to make the text next to the element selectable as well. This would make it so that the text *and* the element can be selected to enable/disable the form object. Associating a Label with a form element is simple and involves nothing more than selecting both the form element and associative text and choosing Insert, Form, Label. Immediately Dreamweaver switches to Split view and adds code similar to the following boldface code:

```
<form id="form1" name="form1" method="post" action="">
    <input type="radio" name="nolabel" id="nolabel" value="No Label" />
    Does not contain a label<br />
    <label>
    <input name="infrastructure" type="checkbox" id="Microsoft" value="Microsoft" />
    Microsoft
    </label>
</form>
```

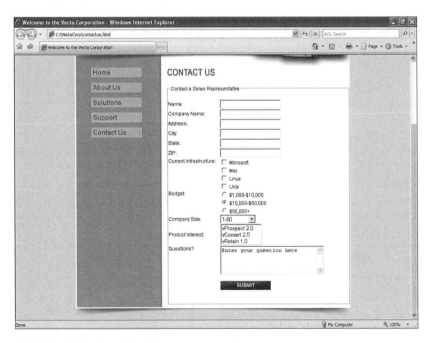

FIGURE 7.21   The Fieldset generates a clean border around your form objects.

A <label> tag is added and wraps the selected form element. Although wrapping the form element within the <label> tag may seem like enough, we must, in fact, perform one last step. To create the association between the Label and the form element, we must add the form attribute to the `<label>` tag and apply the form elements name/id as the attribute value, as follows_FIRST:

```
<label for="Microsoft">
```

Now if you save your work and test the page in the browser, you'll notice that the first check box for Microsoft is such that you can directly select the text label and the check box to enable the check box. However, the same isn't true for the other check box items. Go ahead and practice adding the Label to the other options. If you run into any problems, you can always reference the completed `contactus.html` page, included for you in the chapter's downloads.

Summary

This chapter is the beginning of a higher level of web development. Creating forms to interact with an end user starts to show the strengths of the Web and offers endless possibilities.

As you get deeper into this book, you'll start building forms that interact with server-side applications. As you'll see, forms, in conjunction with server-side applications, begin to push the envelope for more engaging experiences for web users.

CHAPTER 8

Using Behaviors

IN THIS CHAPTER

▶ An Introduction to Behaviors

▶ Using the Behaviors Panel

▶ Dreamweaver Behaviors

As we've progressed through the book, we've touched on topics such as client-side web pages and server-side applications. In the previous chapter, for instance, we mentioned that HTML forms are stepping stones to working with server-side applications but still remain an integral part of client-side web page development. What we haven't touched on, however, are the three building blocks that make up client-side web pages or the functionality and look that the end user interacts with.

At the foundation of client-side development lies the first block, HTML/XHTML. Everything we do on the Web, to a certain extent, revolves around markup. Dreamweaver is, by definition, a tool for creating this markup. The second building block, discussed in some detail in Chapters 5, "Page Formatting Using Cascading Style Sheets," and 6, "Page Structuring Using Cascading Style Sheets," is CSS. As we've seen, style sheets control the overall look and appearance of your web pages and, again, are significantly supported by Dreamweaver. The third and final block to client-side web page development, JavaScript, has yet to be discussed.

At its heart, JavaScript exists as a web-based scripting language. Whereas HTML/XHTML defines the structure of our client-side web pages and CSS controls the "look" of our web pages, JavaScript exists to outline the logic that our web pages will have in the form of a full-blown interactive scripting language syntactically similar to, syntactically yet independent of, the object-oriented programming language Java. For instance, you might want to add user interaction to your web page that otherwise wouldn't be available through HTML or CSS—such as creating a pop-up message, a pop-up window, a pop-up menu, or even image-based rollovers for a navigation menu. Even better, you might want to add functionality to the contactus.html page that guarantees that users enter text into all required fields, enter a numeric value where numbers are required, or even enter an email into a text box that requires an email address. Furthermore, you might want to add functionality that forces the browser to check for a specific plugin, such as Flash, and have the browser react accordingly. All this and much more is possible with JavaScript (Behaviors).

As is true with HTML and CSS, you don't need to know JavaScript when working in Dreamweaver, as Dreamweaver writes all the JavaScript to make these actions happen in the form of behaviors. Exposed as canned JavaScript snippets of code and available in the Behaviors panel, the behaviors available in Dreamweaver are ideal for real-world applications where time is of the essence and your JavaScript writing skills are limited.

This chapter prepares you to work with the final building block of client-side web development, behaviors. To begin, you'll need to download the support files online. Like the rest of the chapters in this book, you can work with the examples in this chapter by downloading the files from the book's website. You'll want to replace the files in C:\VectaCorp\ with the files that you download for this chapter.

An Introduction to Behaviors

When you understand how behaviors in Dreamweaver work, you'll grasp the fundamentals of JavaScript. Similar to CSS, JavaScript code is written within the <head> tag of your web page. Unlike CSS, which is written within a <style> declaration block, JavaScript is written within a <script> declaration block complete with the language attribute defining the language to be written in the script. A typical declaration block in a page might look something like this:

```
<html>
<head>
<title>Sample JavaScript</title>
<script language="JavaScript">


</script>
</head>


<body>


</body>
</html>
```

As you can see from the sample, the code declaration block acts as a container for the logic within the web page. However, this code sample is merely a shell of the functionality. To make the page a bit more interactive, we would add three components to this example: an object, an event, and a function that represents the action we want performed. The final product might look something like this:

```
<html>
<head>
<title>Sample JavaScript</title>
<script language="JavaScript">
function showMessage() {
    alert("Hello");
}
</script>
</head>


<body>
<input type="button" value="Click Me" onClick="showMessage();" />
</body>
</html>
```

In this case, a Button object is added as a way for users to initiate the interaction between themselves and the page. Second, the onClick event handler is added as an attribute to the button. Although dozens of event handlers exist for various types of objects, the onClick event handler exists as a way of alerting the browser that when the button is clicked, the click event is raised, the showMessage() function should be called, and the code contained within the function should be executed. Finally, the function showMessage() is added in the code declaration block. This is where JavaScript gets complex because it represents the functionality we want performed when the user clicks the button. In our case, we want to show a pop-up message with the text *Hello*. To do this, we access the alert() function and pass in the literal text "Hello" as a parameter. When all is said and done, the user clicks the button on the page to receive a message similar to Figure 8.1.

FIGURE 8.1   Clicking the button raises the click event, which, in turn, calls the showMessage function. When the function is called, the code is executed and a message appears.

Although this code represents an example of JavaScript in practice, it's important to remember that the example is simple. The more functionality you'll need, the more complex the JavaScript becomes. For those who don't consider themselves JavaScript wizards, behaviors, which are contained within the Behaviors panel, are the perfect alternative to writing JavaScript by hand.

So what was the relevance of the JavaScript example if we'll be using behaviors and the Behaviors panel from here on out? The answer to this question lies in the process we outlined. Within the code declaration block lies the functionality we need, otherwise known as an *action*. To get that action to execute, we need two things: an object (represented by a Button form object) and an event handler (represented by the onClick event set as an attribute within the Button). The beauty of behaviors is that they contain prebuilt actions bundled with a set of events. All you need to do is supply the object in the form of an HTML element, such as a hyperlink, an image, a form object, or even the page as a whole. After you've selected an object to use, you attach the action using the Behaviors panel, pick a supported event, and you're done!

As you can see, behaviors, which are essentially prebuilt sets of actions bundled with various events, are attached to objects by way of the Behaviors panel. To see this process in action, let's turn our attention to the Behaviors panel.

Using the Behaviors Panel

The Behaviors panel, available by selecting the Behaviors option from the Window menu or pressing Shift+F4, is the catalyst for attaching behaviors to objects on your page. Although we'll eventually cover the available behaviors throughout the chapter, for now let's walk through the process of attaching a simple behavior, similar to the one we wrote by hand, using the Behaviors panel. To do this, follow these steps:

1. Create a new HTML page by choosing File, New. When the New Document dialog box appears, select Blank Page, HTML, <none>, and click Create. Immediately save your page as **behaviors.html**.

2. With your cursor in the new blank page, insert a new Button form object by clicking the Button icon from the Forms category of the Insert panel.

3. When the Add Form Tag dialog box appears, click No.

4. With the Button form object selected, change the Action to None so the button doesn't try to submit or reset the nonexistent form when it's clicked. You can also change the button's Value to read anything you'd like. I'll change mine to *Click Me*.

5. If you haven't done so already, open the Behaviors panel by choosing Window, Behaviors. The Tag Inspector panel group will appear with the Attributes and Behaviors panels visible. With the Behaviors panel selected, click the Add (+) icon to expand the Behaviors list and choose the Popup Message Behavior highlighted in Figure 8.2.

6. When the Popup Message dialog box appears, enter some text. I'll enter the text **Hello**. Click OK.

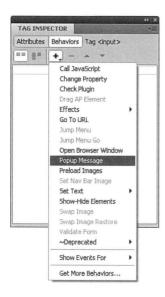

FIGURE 8.2   Select the Popup Message Behavior from the Behaviors panel list.

7. Save your work and test the results in the browser by pressing F12 (Option-F12 on the Mac). Click the button in the browser to see the pop-up message appear as it did in Figure 8.1.

As you can see, attaching behaviors to objects is relatively simple. You select your object and then choose the desired behavior from the list in the Behaviors panel.

Beyond the simplicities of attaching behaviors to objects lies functionality for managing events, event views, and determining browser support. The callouts in Figure 8.3 demonstrate the selectable options outlined within the Behaviors panel.

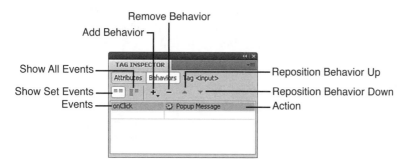

FIGURE 8.3   The Behaviors panel includes functionality for managing behaviors and events associated with behaviors.

The functionality provided within the panel is outlined here:

▶ **Events**—After you've added a behavior, the event associated with the action appears within this column. By default, Dreamweaver lists all events supported by the selected object. Although form objects, hyperlinks, and the page might share similar events, other objects might have different events altogether. To pick a different event for a selected object, click just to the right of the event in the event column and choose the event from the drop-down menu (see Figure 8.4).

FIGURE 8.4   Supported events for a particular object appear in the events drop-down menu.

NOTE

Depending on the selected object, event names may appear in parentheses. In general, these events are reserved for (but don't necessarily have to be used for) links. Selecting an event that appears within parentheses automatically adds a null link (javascript:;) to the hyperlink's href attribute. This prevents the link from trying to refresh the page by calling the JavaScript function.

▶ **Action**—The action associated with the behavior appears in this column. The action cannot be changed, but can be modified by double-clicking it. Doing so opens the original dialog box associated with the behavior. You can also choose the Edit Behavior option from the panel's Options submenu to edit an existing behavior.

▶ **Show Set Events**—Click this icon to display only events that have been attached to a particular object.

▶ **Show All Events**—Click this icon to display all events supported by a particular object, even though they might not be in use. After you've entered this mode, you can associate behaviors with particular events by selecting the event and then clicking the Add (+) icon and selecting a behavior.

▶ **Add (+)**—Use this submenu to pick from the list of Dreamweaver behaviors. This option is covered in more detail later in this section. You can also choose the Add New List Item option from the panel's Options submenu to add a new behavior.

▶ **Remove (–)**—After you've added a behavior, you can remove it by selecting it and clicking the Remove (–) button. You can also choose the Delete Behavior option from the panel's Options submenu to remove a behavior.

▶ **Reposition Behavior**—When you have multiple behaviors associated with a particular object, use the up and down arrows to (re)position particular behaviors within the list. Doing this allows you to set which behaviors are called before or after others.

Dreamweaver Behaviors

For the most part, the functionality outlined in these bullet points is useful only after you've added a behavior. As I've mentioned, you can add a behavior by selecting the object on the page, clicking the Add (+) icon, and then picking one of the following preinstalled behaviors from the list:

▶ Call JavaScript

▶ Change Property

▶ Check Plugin

▶ Drag AP Element

▶ Effects

▶ Go to URL

▶ Jump Menu and Jump Menu Go

▶ Open Browser Window

▶ Popup Message (already discussed)

▶ Preload Images

▶ Set Nav Bar Image

▶ Set Text

▶ Show-Hide Elements

▶ Swap Image and Swap Image Restore

▶ Validate Form

▶ Deprecated Behaviors

▶ Show Events For

Choosing the appropriate behavior is up to you. Unfortunately, trying to figure out what each behavior does can be a daunting task. For this reason, we'll describe each behavior (with the exception of the Popup Message behavior we covered at the beginning of the chapter) throughout the remainder of this chapter. (Before we do however, I want to discuss the last option available from the Add Behavior list first: the Show Events For submenu.

If you notice from the list, the Show Events For submenu contains a list of browser versions, a generic HTML 4.01, and the backward-compliant 4.0 and later browsers options. The browser selection you make from this menu determines which events appear in the Events pop-up menu. Older browsers generally support fewer events than newer browsers, and in most cases, the more general your choice of target browsers, the fewer events are shown. For example, if you select Netscape 4.0 from the Show Events For submenu and then select the events menu for a particular behavior, the events shown within the Events pop-up menu for the Behavior are limited. Alternatively, if you choose the Internet Explorer 6.0 option from the Show Events For submenu, a much longer list is shown within the events list for a particular behavior. Because Internet Explorer 6.0 is a much newer browser, it supports numerous events that aren't supported in older browsers. Netscape 4.0 and Internet Explorer 4.0 browsers are still in use, albeit in very small percentages, so Dreamweaver provides the 4.0 and Later Browsers option for backward-compatability. The needs of your organization will dictate which event set you use. If you're developing for the Web and want to target the greatest number of people, leave the HTML 4.01 option selected.

You've probably noticed that the Events drop-down menu associated with a particular behavior contains event handlers that are easy to understand just by their names and others that are not so easy to understand. Before we begin discussing the different types of event handlers, let's quickly highlight the more popular event handlers that you might decide to use with your behaviors. For the most part, the following event handlers are the ones that you'll use most often:

- **onClick**—Event is fired and action is called when the object is clicked.

- **onDblClick**—Event is fired and action is called when the object is double-clicked.

- **onMouseDown**—Event is fired and action is called while the user's left mouse click is down. This event works well when you need to call an action repeatedly while the user holds the mouse button down—as is done while dragging an object, for instance.

- **onMouseUp**—Event is fired and action is called when the user's left mouse clicks up. The is similar to the onClick event.

- **onMouseOver**—Event is fired and action is called when the user's cursor rolls over an object. This is ideal when working with rollover images.

- **onMouseOut**—Event is fired and action is called when the user's cursor rolls out of an object. This is also used when working with rollover images.

- **onFocus**—Event is fired and action is called when the object is highlighted. For instance, if my cursor is in a text field and I press the Tab key to highlight the next object (possibly another text field), the next object has focus, and the previous text field loses focus.

- **onBlur**—Event is fired and action is called when the object loses its highlight state. For instance, if my cursor is in a text field and I press the Tab key to highlight the next text field, the next text field has focus, and the previous text field loses focus. That loss of focus is considered blurred.

▶ **onLoad**—Event is fired and action is called when the page is loaded. This is ideal to use when you want to open a pop-up window (to display a survey, for instance) when the page loads.

▶ **onUnLoad**—Event is fired and action is called when the browser is closed or a different page is loaded, or the Escape key is pressed during the page download.

Now that you have an idea as to what behaviors are, you're familiar with the Behaviors panel, you understand how behaviors are attached to objects, and you understand the fundamentals of event handlers and how they interact with objects (such as the button), let's move forward and begin outlining each behavior in detail.

Call JavaScript

You can use the Call JavaScript behavior when you want to write inline JavaScript for an object without having to switch to Code view. To demonstrate this behavior, let's add a Close Window button to the page. When the user clicks this button, we'll use one of the built-in JavaScript functions (`close()`), to display a Close Window confirmation dialog box. Because no behavior exists for this action, we'll use the Call JavaScript behavior to write it ourselves. Begin by following these steps:

1. With your cursor in the page, insert a new Button form object by clicking the Button icon from the Forms category of the Insert panel.

2. When the Add Form Tag dialog box appears, click No.

3. With the Button form object selected, change the Action to None so that the button doesn't try to submit or reset the form when it's clicked. You can also change the label to read anything you'd like. I'll change my button's label to say `Close Window`.

4. With the Close Button selected, choose the Call JavaScript behavior from the Add (+) menu in the Behaviors panel. The Call JavaScript dialog will appear.

5. Within the dialog box, enter the code `window.close();`. This is the JavaScript code that you would write to initiate the browser's closing of the browser window.

6. Click OK.

7. If the selected event isn't onClick, change it to the onClick event now.

Save your work and preview the results in the browser by choosing F12 (Option-F12). You'll notice that when you click the Close button in Internet Explorer, a Close dialog box appears, asking whether you want to close the browser window similar to Figure 8.5.

FIGURE 8.5   The Close Window dialog box asks you whether you'd like to close the existing browser window.

As you can see, the Call JavaScript behavior allows you to quickly write inline JavaScript functions that don't already exist as behaviors. As you saw, the Call JavaScript behavior allows us to write code without having to switch to Code view and run through the process of adding the event handler to the object and then having to add the code declaration block complete with the code. While the example was simple, your JavaScript could become complex. The Call JavaScript behavior is always up to the task regardless of complexity.

Change Property

You can use the Change Property behavior as a way of changing the physical characteristics of a particular object that was initially set with CSS. For instance, when a button is clicked, you might want to set the background color of an AP Element, set the text value of a text box, and so on. For our example, we'll use the Change Property behavior to change the background color of a `<div>` when the button is clicked. You can do this by following these steps:

1. With your cursor in the page, insert a new Button form object by clicking the Button icon from the Forms category of the Insert panel.

2. When the Add Form Tag dialog box appears, click Yes.

3. With the Button form object selected, change the Action to None so that the button doesn't try to submit or reset the form when it's clicked. You can also change the Label to read anything you'd like. I'll change mine to say **Set Background Color**.

4. Now add a `<div>` just underneath the button by choosing Insert, Layout Objects, Div Tag. When the Div Tag dialog box appears, enter the name **myDiv** within the ID text box and click OK. The new **`<div>`** element will appear on the page. Change the default text to read: This element will have its background color changed.

5. With the Set Text button selected, choose the Change Property behavior from the Add (+) menu in the Behaviors panel. The Change Property dialog box appears.

6. In the dialog box, select the DIV option from the Type of Element menu; choose the Div "myDiv" option from the Element ID menu; choose the BackgroundColor option from the Select menu in the Property option group; and type the text **Red** into the New Value text box. When you've finished, the results will look similar to Figure 8.6.

FIGURE 8.6   Customize the Change Property dialog box.

7. Click OK.

8. If the selected event handler isn't `onClick`, change it to `onClick` now.

Save your work and preview the results in the browser by choosing F12 (Option-F12). You'll notice that when you click the Set Text button in the browser window, the background color of the text (which is contained within the `<div>`) has its background color changed. (see Figure 8.7).

FIGURE 8.7   Clicking the button causes the background color of the DIV to change.

Although we've covered only the basics related to the Change Property dialog box, you can begin to see the benefits it outlines. Beyond the simplicities of working with `<div>`s, the Change Property dialog box also supports the following options:

▶ **Type of Element**—Select from a list of 13 supported elements. The elements that can have properties set include div, span, paragraph (p), table row (tr), table cell (td), image, form, check box, radio button, text field, text area, password, and list/menu (select).

▶ **Element ID**—After you've selected the type of element for which you want to change the property, the elements—if they exist on the page—appear within this list.

▶ **Property: Select**—Customizable properties for the selected element appear within this list.

▶ **Property: Enter**—Although Dreamweaver includes common customizable properties, other less frequently used properties must be added by hand in this text box.

▶ **New Value**—Enter the new value for the customized property in this text box.

Check Plugin

The Check Browser behavior makes it possible to check whether end users have a specific plugin such as QuickTime, Flash, Shockwave, LiveAudio, or Windows Media Player installed on their systems. If the plugin is detected, you can send the users to a specific page (or keep them on the current page). If it's not found, however, you can direct them to an alternative page (maybe a page that contains text only). To demonstrate this behavior, follow these instructions:

1. With your cursor in the same page we've been working with, insert a new Button form object by clicking the Button icon from the Forms category of the Insert panel.

2. When the Add Form Tag dialog box appears, click No.

3. With the Button form object selected, change the Action to None so that the button doesn't try to submit or reset the nonexistent form when it's clicked. You can also change the Label to read anything you'd like. I'll change mine to say **Check Plugin**.

4. With the Button object selected, choose the Check Plugin behavior from the Add (+) menu in the Behaviors panel. The Check Plugin dialog box appears.

5. As you can see, the dialog box allows you to check for one of the five plugins listed earlier by choosing the specific option from the Plugin: Select menu. If the plugin you need is not listed in the menu, click the Plugin: Enter option button and enter one of your choice in the text box. In the If Found, Go to URL text box, enter the URL to go to if the plugin is found. Alternatively, enter the URL of the page to go to if the plugin is not found in the Otherwise, Go to URL text box. Often, visitors without the plugin are prompted by the browser to download the plugin. If the plugin content is not essential to your page, leave the final Always Go to First URL If Detection Is Not Possible check box option deselected. When you've finished, your dialog might resemble mine (see Figure 8.8).

FIGURE 8.8 Check for the Flash plugin and enter separate pages to go to depending on whether the plugin is detected.

6. Click OK.

7. If the selected event handler isn't onClick, change it to onClick now.

Save your work and test the page in the browser by choosing F12 (Option-F12). If you're using a modern browser that has the Flash plugin already installed, the page should stay on the page you're working with (behaviors.html) right after you click the Check Plugin button. If your browser doesn't have the Flash plugin installed, however, you're immediately redirected to the Adobe website.

To take full advantage of this behavior, the ideal scenario would have you placing this behavior on the main page of your site. Rather than forcing users to click a button to make a determination as to whether they have the plugin, you might even attach the behavior to the load event of the page. This way, the plugin is detected upon the user visiting the main page of your site. Because the detection occurs on the page load, it's out of sight, out of mind.

Drag AP Element

Another interesting and feature-rich behavior is the Drag AP Element behavior. You can use this behavior to create drag-and-drop functionality on your page. Maybe you're developing a children's web-based tutorial where feedback is given when the child drags an object onto or within the space of another object. If that's the case, this behavior is perfect. To give you an idea as to how the Drag AP Element behavior works, follow these steps:

1. Within the behaviors.html file, create a new AP Element (it doesn't matter where, because it will appear above anything on the page anyway) by choosing Insert, Layout Objects, AP Div. The new AP <div> will appear on the page.

2. Find an image (any image will do) from within the Images folder in the Files panel and drag it into the AP <div>. I've dragged the image logo_vconvert.gif into the AP <div>.

3. Deselect the image and AP <div> by placing your cursor anywhere on the page (making sure that nothing on the page is selected). Choose the Drag AP Element behavior from the Add (+) menu in the Behaviors panel. The Drag AP Element dialog appears. Although I'll eventually provide a detailed description of the options in this dialog box, for now click OK.

4. Make sure that the event associated with this behavior is onMouseDown. This event allows the user to drag the image contained in the AP <div> only while the user is holding down the image.

Save your work and test the page in the browser by choosing F12 (Option-F12). You'll notice that if you click, hold, and drag the image, you can position the image anywhere you want on the page.

Although the capability to reposition an AP <div> is core to the Drag AP Element behavior, other options exist in the Drag AP Element dialog box for extending the functionality exposed by the behavior. To review these options, right-click (Ctrl-click) the behavior in the Behaviors panel and choose the Edit Behavior option from the context menu to reopen the Drag AP Element dialog box. (You could also double-click the behavior to edit

8

it or select Edit Behaviors from the Panel Options menu.) When the dialog box opens, you'll notice the following options on the Basic tab:

▶ **AP Element**—Assuming you have multiple AP `<div>`s in the page, select the specific AP `<div>` to drag from this menu.

▶ **Movement**—Select an option from this menu to either constrain or unconstrain the AP Element's movement as it's being dragged. Choose Unconstrained movement when working with online puzzles and other drag-and-drop games. Choose the Constrained option when working with controls such as sliders.

▶ **Drop Target**—The *drop target* is the x,y coordinate of the spot to which you want the visitor to drag the AP `<div>`. Click the Get Current Position button to automatically fill in the Left and Top coordinate values based on the current position of the AP `<div>`.

▶ **Snap if Within**—Assuming you're working with a drop target, enter a pixel value in this text box to have Dreamweaver automatically snap the AP `<div>` and its contents to the drop target when the AP `<div>` is within the specified number of pixels.

Switch to the Advanced tab of the Drag AP Element dialog box to reveal the following options:

▶ **Drag Handle**—By default, Dreamweaver allows you to click, hold, and drag within any part of the AP `<div>` to drag it. If you want to constrain the drag to a specific portion of the AP `<div>`, choose the Area Within Element option and fill in the coordinates for left, top, width, and height. This option is particularly useful when a portion of the AP `<div>` suggests dragging, such as a title bar or even the handle within a slider.

▶ **While Dragging**—Enable this check box to leave the AP `<div>` on top of other AP `<div>`s while it's being dragged. You might also choose the Restore Z-index option if you want to keep the AP `<div>` on top of other AP `<div>`s while it's being dragged but restore it to a lower z-index after it has been dropped. You can also enter JavaScript code within the Call JavaScript text box that will be executed while the AP `<div>` is being dragged.

▶ **When Dropped**—Enter custom JavaScript code within this text box and choose the Only if Snapped check box to execute JavaScript code when the user drops the AP `<div>` on a specific target. This option is particularly useful when you want to provide a pop-up feedback message confirming that the user got the right answer when the user dropped the AP `<div>` in the correct target.

Effects Behaviors

One of the newer set of behaviors is the Effects set of behaviors. Part of the Spry Framework (discussed in more detail in Chapter 24, "Working with the Spry Framework for Ajax"), the Effects set of behaviors enables you to work with various types of special functionality, including the following:

▶ Appear and Fade

▶ Blind

▶ Grow and Shrink

▶ Highlight

▶ Shake

▶ Slide

▶ Squish

So that you understand how this new set of behaviors works, let's discuss each of them.

Appear/Fade

The first behavior outlined within the Effects submenu in the Behaviors list is the Appear/Fade behavior. You can use this behavior with any form object, link, image, <div>, and so on to force an object to either fade away or reappear. To use this behavior, follow these steps:

1. Place your cursor just after the Check Plugin button and press Enter to create some space for your new button. Now insert a new Button form object by clicking the Button icon from the Forms category of the Insert panel.

2. When the Add Form Tag dialog box appears, click No.

3. With the Button form object selected, change the Action to None so that the button doesn't try to submit or reset the nonexistent form when it's clicked. You can also change the Label to read anything you'd like. I'll change mine to read **Fade/Appear**.

4. With the new button selected, choose the Appear/Fade behavior from the Effects submenu, available by choosing the Add (+) button in the Behaviors panel. The Appear/Fade dialog box will appear, similar to Figure 8.9.

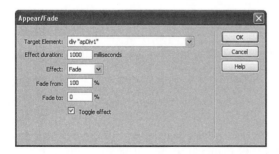

FIGURE 8.9   The Appear/Fade behavior allows you to attach functionality to a form object, link, image, <div>, and so on that forces the element to fade away or reappear.

5. Although we'll eventually cover the functionality outlined within this dialog box, for now, simply choose the `div "apDiv1"` (the AP <div> that we created earlier

which contains the `logo_vconvert.gif` image) option from the Target Element menu. Make sure the Fade option is selected from the Effect menu, enable the Toggle effect check box, and click OK.

6. If the selected event isn't `onClick`, change it to `onClick` now.

Save your work. Immediately a Copy Dependent Files dialog box will appear. As you'll see in Chapter 24, Spry and features surrounding the Spry implementation rely on prebuilt external JavaScript, and in some cases CSS, files to work. In this case, because we're technically using a Spry Effect, Dreamweaver must copy the `SpryEffects.js` JavaScript file into the directory SpryAssets for the Appear/Fade behavior to work. Click OK now to have these files copied over.

Press F12 (Option-F12) now to preview your page in the browser. When the page appears, click the button. As you'll see, the AP `<div>` that contains our `logo_vconvert.gif` image fades away slowly. Now click the button again. You'll notice that the image reappears slowly.

In the previous steps, we selected options from the Target Element and Effect menus to select both the element that we wanted to target with the effect and the effect itself. As you can see from Figure 8.9, other options exist within the dialog box, including the following:

▶ **Target Element**—From this menu, select the object's ID to identify which object to which you want to apply the effect.

▶ **Effect Duration**—Enter a numeric value within this text box to define the time it takes for the effect to occur in milliseconds.

▶ **Effect**—Select the effect you want to apply from this menu. Options include Fade or Appear.

▶ **Fade From**—Enter a numeric value in this text box to define the percentage of opacity you want the effect to have when it appears.

▶ **Fade To**—Enter a numeric value in this text box to define the percentage of opacity you want to fade to.

▶ **Toggle Effect**—Select this check box if you want the effect to be reversible, going from fade to appear and back again with successive clicks.

Blind

You can use the Blind behavior with the `<div>`, `<h1>`, `<h2>`, `<h3>`, `<h4>`, `<h5>`, `<h6>`, `<p>`, and other tags to force an element to disappear or reappear using a masking blind effect. To use this behavior, follow these steps:

1. Place your cursor next to the Fade/Appear button created in the previous section. Insert a new Button form object by clicking the Button icon from the Forms category of the Insert panel.

2. When the Add Form Tag dialog box appears, click No.

3. With the Button form object selected, change the Action to None so that the button doesn't try to submit or reset the nonexistent form when it's clicked. You can also change the Label to read anything you'd like. I'll change mine to read **Blind**.

4. With the new button selected, choose the Blind behavior from the Effects submenu, available by choosing the Add (+) button in the Behaviors panel. The Blind dialog box will appear, similar to Figure 8.10.

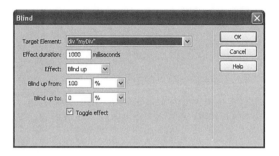

FIGURE 8.10   The Blind behavior can be used to force an element to disappear or reappear using a masking blind effect.

5. While we'll eventually cover the functionality outlined within this dialog box, for now, simply choose the div "myDiv" (the AP <div> that we created earlier that contains the the text) option from the Target Element menu. Make sure the Blind up option is selected from the Effect menu, enable the Toggle effect check box, and click OK.

6. If the selected event handler isn't onClick, change it to onClick now.

Save your work and preview the page in the browser by choosing F12 (Option-F12). When the page appears, click the button. As you'll see, the AP <div> that contains our text disappears slowly, using a masking effect moving from the bottom and going up. Click the button again. As you'll notice, the text reappears slowly using the same style but in reverse.

In these steps, we selected options from the Target Element and Effect menus to select both the element that we wanted to target with the effect and the effect itself. As you can see from Figure 8.10, other options exist within the dialog box:

▶ **Target Element**—From this menu, select the element's ID to which you want to apply the effect.

▶ **Effect Duration**—Enter a numeric value within this text box to define the time you want it to take for the effect to occur, in milliseconds.

▶ **Effect**—Select the effect you want to apply from this menu. Options include Blind up or Blind down.

▶ **Blind up From**—Enter a numeric value in this text box to define the blind-scrolling starting point as a percentage or as a pixel number. These values are calculated from the top of the object.

▸ **Blind up To**—Enter a numeric value in this text box to define the blind-scrolling end point as a percentage or as a pixel number. These values are calculated from the top of the object.

▸ **Toggle Effect**—Select this check box if you want the effect to be reversible, scrolling up and down with successive clicks.

Grow/Shrink

You can use the Grow/Shrink behavior with the <div>, <h1>, <h2>, <h3>, <h4>, <h5>, <h6>, <p>, and other tags to force an element to disappear slowly—as if the element were shrinking into obscurity. Alternatively, you can apply an effect that forces the element to reappear slowly—as if it were growing. To use this behavior, follow these steps:

1. Place your cursor next to the Blind button created in the previous section. Insert a new Button form object by clicking the Button icon from the Forms category of the Insert panel.

2. When the Add Form Tag dialog box appears, click No.

3. With the Button form object selected, change the Action to None so that the button doesn't try to submit or reset the nonexistent form when it's clicked. You can also change the Label to read anything you'd like. I'll change mine to read **Grow/Shrink**.

4. With the new button selected, choose the Grow/Shrink behavior from the Effects submenu, available by choosing the Add (+) button in the Behaviors panel. The Grow/Shrink dialog box will appear, as shown in Figure 8.11.

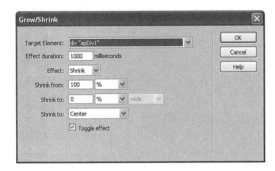

FIGURE 8.11   The Grow/Shrink behavior can be used to force an element to disappear or reappear using a shrinking or growing effect.

5. Although we'll eventually cover the functionality outlined within this dialog box, for now, simply choose the div "apDiv1" (the AP <div> that we created earlier that contains the logo_vconvert.gif image) option from the Target Element menu. Make sure the Shrink option is selected from the Effect menu, enable the Toggle effect check box, and click OK.

6. If the selected event isn't onClick, change it to onClick now.

Save your work and preview the page in the browser by choosing F12 (Option-F12). When the page appears, click the button. As you'll see, the AP <div> that contains our logo_vconvert.gif image shrinks slowly until it is completely gone. Click the button again. You'll notice that the image grows slowly until it reappears at its original size.

In the previous steps, we selected options from the Target Element and Effect menus to select both the element that we wanted to target with the effect and the effect itself. As you can see from Figure 8.11, other options exist within the dialog box:

- ▶ **Target Element**—From this menu, select the object ID of the object to which you want to apply the effect.

- ▶ **Effect Duration**—Enter a numeric value within this text box to define the time it takes for the effect to occur, in milliseconds.

- ▶ **Effect**—Select the effect you want to apply from this menu. Options include Grow or Shrink.

- ▶ **Shrink From**—Enter a numeric value in this text box to define the object's size when the effect starts. This is a percentage of the size or a pixel value.

- ▶ **Shrink To**—Enter a numeric value in this text box to define the object's size when the effect ends. This is a percentage of the size or a pixel value. If you choose pixels for either the Grow/Shrink From or To boxes, the wide/high field becomes visible. Depending on the option you choose, the element will grow or shrink proportionately.

- ▶ **Shrink To (menu)**—Select whether you want the element to grow or shrink to the upper-left corner of the page or into the page's center.

- ▶ **Toggle Effect**—Select this check box if you want the effect to be reversible, growing and shrinking with successive clicks.

Highlight

You can use the Highlight behavior with form objects, links, images, and <div> and other tags, to create a highlighting effect for the particular element. To use this behavior, follow these steps:

1. Place your cursor next to the Grow/Shrink button created in the previous section. Insert a new Button form object by clicking the Button icon from the Forms category of the Insert panel.

2. When the Add Form Tag dialog box appears, click No.

3. With the Button form object selected, change its name to **btnHighlight** (so that we can identify it later) and change the Action to None so that the button doesn't try to submit or reset the nonexistent form when it's clicked. You can also change the Label to read anything you'd like. I'll change mine to read Highlight.

4. With the new button selected, choose the Highlight behavior from the Effects submenu, available by choosing the Add (+) button in the Behaviors panel. The Highlight dialog box will appear, as in Figure 8.12.

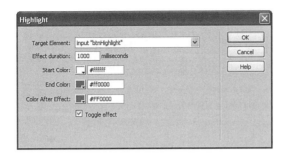

FIGURE 8.12 The Highlight behavior can be used to create a custom-color highlight for an element.

5. Although we'll eventually cover the functionality outlined within this dialog box, for now, choose the `input "btnHighlight"` option from the Target Element menu. Select a red color from both the End Color and Color After Effect menus, enable the Toggle effect check box, and click OK.

6. If the selected event isn't `onClick`, change it to `onClick` now.

Save your work and preview the page in the browser by choosing F12 (Option-F12). When the page appears, click the button. As you'll see, the image highlights red. Click the button again. You'll notice that the image highlight fades away.

In the previous steps, we selected options from the Target Element menu. As you can see from Figure 8.12, other options exist within the dialog box:

▶ **Target Element**—From this menu, select the ID of the object to which you want to apply the effect.

▶ **Effect Duration**—Enter a numeric value within this text box to define the time it takes for the effect to occur, in milliseconds.

▶ **Start Color**—Select the color you want the highlight to start with.

▶ **End Color**—Select the color you want the highlight to end with. This color lasts only as long as the duration you define in the Effect duration text box.

▶ **Color After Effect**—Select the color for the object after the highlight has finished.

▶ **Toggle Effect**—Select this check box if you want the effect to be reversible, cycling through the highlight colors with successive clicks.

Shake

You can use the Shake behavior with form objects, links, images, and <div> and other tags, to force the element to shake from side to side. To use this behavior, follow these steps:

1. Place your cursor next to the Highlight button created in the previous section. Insert a new Button form object by clicking the Button icon from the Forms category of the Insert panel.

2. When the Add Form Tag dialog box appears, click No.

3. With the Button form object selected, change the Action to None so that the button doesn't try to submit or reset the nonexistent form when it's clicked. You can also change the Label to read anything you'd like. I'll change mine to read **Shake**.

4. With the new button selected, choose the Shake behavior from the Effects submenu, available by choosing the Add (+) button in the Behaviors panel. The Shake dialog box will appear (see Figure 8.13).

FIGURE 8.13   The Shake behavior can be used to force an element to shake from side to side.

5. Choose the `div "apDiv1"` option from the Target Element menu and click OK.

6. If the selected event isn't `onClick`, change it to `onClick` now.

Save your work and preview the page in the browser by choosing F12 (Option-F12). When the page appears, click the button. As you'll see, the `logo_vconvert.gif` image contained within our AP `<div>` shakes from side to side.

Slide

You can use the Slide behavior with any form object, link, image, `<div>`, and so on to force an object to disappear as if it were sliding away. Alternatively, you can use this behavior to force an object to reappear as if it were sliding into view. To use this behavior, follow these steps:

1. Place your cursor next to the Shake button created in the previous section and insert a new Button form object by clicking the Button icon from the Forms category of the Insert panel.

2. When the Add Form Tag dialog box appears, click No.

3. With the Button form object selected, change the Action to None so that the button doesn't try to submit or reset the nonexistent form when it's clicked. You can also change the Label to read anything you'd like. I'll change mine to read **Slide**.

4. With the new button selected, choose the Slide behavior from the Effects submenu, available by choosing the Add (+) button in the Behaviors panel. The Slide dialog box will appear as it does in Figure 8.14.

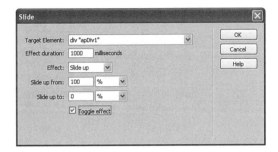

FIGURE 8.14   The Slide behavior allows you to attach functionality to a form object, link, image, <div>, and so on that forces the element to disappear and reappear as if it were sliding away/into view.

5. Although we'll eventually cover the functionality outlined within this dialog box, for now, choose the div "apDiv1" (the AP <div> that we created earlier which contains the logo_vconvert.gif image) option from the Target Element menu, make sure the Slide up option is selected from the Effect menu, enable the Toggle effect check box, and click OK.

6. If the selected event isn't onClick, change it to onClick now.

Save your work and preview the page in the browser by choosing F12 (Option-F12). When the page appears, click the button. As you'll see, the AP <div> that contains our logo_vconvert.gif image slides away until it disappears. Now click it again. You'll notice that the image slides back into view.

In the previous steps, we selected options from the Target Element and Effect menus to select both the element that we wanted to target with the effect and the effect itself. As you can see from Figure 8.14, other options exist within the dialog box:

▶ **Target Element**—From this menu, select the object's ID that you want to apply the effect to.

▶ **Effect Duration**—Enter a numeric value within this text box to define the time it takes for the effect to occur, in milliseconds.

▶ **Effect**—Select the effect you want to apply from this menu. Options include Slide Up or Slide Down.

▶ **Slide Up From**—Enter a numeric value in this text box to define the sliding starting point as a percentage or as a pixel number.

▶ **Slide Up To**—Enter a numeric value in this text box to define the sliding end point as a percentage or as a positive pixel amount.

▶ **Toggle Effect**—Select this check box if you want the effect to be reversible, sliding up and down with successive clicks.

Squish

You can use the Squish behavior with form objects, links, images, and <div> and other tags to force the element to disappear and reappear using an effect that makes the object appear to be squished. To use this behavior, follow these steps:

1. Place your cursor next to the Slide button created in the previous section. Insert a new Button form object by clicking the Button icon from the Forms category of the Insert panel.

2. When the Add Form Tag dialog box appears, click No.

3. With the Button form object selected, change the Action to None so that the button doesn't try to submit or reset the nonexistent form when it's clicked. You can also change the Label to read anything you'd like. I'll change mine to read **Squish**.

4. With the new button selected, choose the Squish behavior from the Effects submenu, available by choosing the Add (+) button in the Behaviors panel. The Squish dialog box will appear (see Figure 8.15).

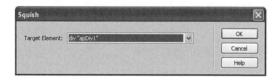

FIGURE 8.15 The Squish behavior can be used to force an element to appear and reappear as if it were being squished.

5. Choose the div "apDiv1" option from the Target Element menu and click OK.

6. If the selected event isn't onClick, change it to onClick now.

Save your work and preview the page in the browser by choosing F12 (Option-F12). When the page appears, click the button. As you'll see, the logo_vconvert.gif image contained within our AP <div> disappears as if it were being squished. Click the button again to force the image to reappear.

Go to URL

Possibly the easiest behavior to use aside from the Popup Message behavior is the Go to URL behavior. You can use this to quickly associate a link with a form object (such as a Button). Because form objects (such as the button) don't support the href attribute (the attribute used when linking text and images), you must create links using JavaScript instead. This JavaScript is automated using the Go to URL behavior.

To attach this behavior to a Button object, follow these steps:

1. With your cursor in the same page we've been working with, insert a new Button form object by clicking the Button icon from the Forms category of the Insert panel.

2. When the Add Form Tag dialog box appears, click No.

3. With the Button form object selected, change the Action to None so that the button doesn't try to submit or reset the nonexistent form when it's clicked. You can also change the Label to read anything you'd like. I'll change mine to read **Visit Vecta Corp**.

4. With the Button object selected, choose the Go to URL behavior from the Add (+) menu in the Behaviors panel. The Go to URL dialog box appears.

5. Initially, the dialog box allows you to choose which window to open the link in. Because we're not working with frames, the only option in this list box is Main Window. Unless you're working with frames, this option is fine. You also can specify the path of the URL to link the Button form object to within the URL text box. I'll enter the full path to the Vecta Corp website, which is **http://www.vectacorp.com**. When you've finished, your dialog box might resemble mine (see Figure 8.16).

FIGURE 8.16   Enter the path to the Vecta Corp website in the URL text box.

6. Click OK.

7. If the selected event isn't onClick, change it to onClick now.

When you've finished, save your work and test the page in the browser by choosing F12 (Option-F12). When the page loads, click the Visit Vecta Corp button. You should immediately be redirected to the website.

NOTE

While the Go To Url behavior is certainly nice, you should stray away from relying on it (and the Jump Menu behavior mentioned in the next section) exclusively, especially for the main navigation of your site. The reason for this is simple, some users might have JavaScript disabled in their browsers. If they were to click on your navigation menu that relied on this behavior, they wouldn't be taken anywhere.

Jump Menu and Jump Menu Go

In the previous chapter, we used the Jump Menu object located in the Forms category of the Insert panel to build a drop-down menu-based navigation system. Remember that we clicked the icon in the Insert panel to launch the Jump Menu dialog box, which allowed us to dynamically add items to a list. When we finished adding items, we clicked OK, and the finished product ended up looking something like Figure 8.17 (also available by opening jumpmenu.html located in the project folder).

FIGURE 8.17   The Jump Menu form object allowed us to build a drop-down, menu-based navigation system.

The problem with the Jump Menu form object is that you can't simply reselect the icon within the Insert panel to relaunch the Jump Menu dialog box if you needed to make edits to an existing Jump Menu. Fortunately, the Jump Menu dialog box is just a front for the Jump Menu and Jump Menu Go behaviors. Notice that selecting the Drop Down Menu or Button form objects displays the Jump Menu and Jump Menu Go behaviors in the Behaviors panel. Even better, if you double-click the action in the Behavior list or right-click (Control-click) the action and select Edit Behavior from the context menu, the Jump Menu dialog box reopens—complete with the original menu items you entered (see Figure 8.18) when selecting this object in the previous chapter.

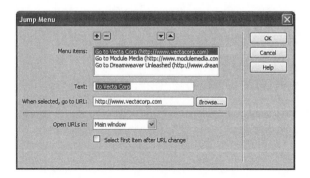

FIGURE 8.18   Double-click the action in the Behavior list to reopen the original Jump Menu dialog box, complete with the menu items you originally entered.

This isn't the behavior's only use. You can use the Jump Menu and Jump Menu Go behaviors to build a Jump Menu complete with a Go button from scratch. To do this, follow these steps:

1. If you haven't done so already, open the jumpmenu.html page.

2. Place your cursor just after the existing menu and press Enter.

3. Insert a new Drop Down Menu form object by clicking the List/Menu icon located in the Forms category of the Insert panel. Name the drop-down menu **JumpMenu2**.

4. Now insert a new Button form object next to the Drop Down Menu by clicking the Button icon in the Forms category of the Insert panel. Give the new Button the text label **Go** and change the Action to None to prevent the form from trying to submit or reset.

5. With the Drop Down Menu selected, choose the Jump Menu behavior from the Add (+) menu in the Behaviors panel. The Jump Menu dialog box appears.

6. Customize the Jump Menu by adding menu items to the list as you did in the previous chapter. When you're finished, click OK.

7. Now select the Go button and choose the Jump Menu Go behavior from the Add (+) menu in the Behaviors panel. The Jump Menu Go dialog box appears similar to Figure 8.19.

FIGURE 8.19   The Jump Menu Go dialog box allows you to select a Drop Down Menu control to associate the Go button with.

8. As you can see, the dialog box allows you to select an existing Drop Down Menu located within a form. Because we named our Drop Down Menu JumpMenu2, select it from the list and click OK.

Save your work and test the page within the browser by choosing F12 (Option-F12). Selecting an item from the list should automatically redirect you to the appropriate page. However, the first item in the list is already selected; selecting it doesn't force the menu to jump to the appropriate page. Click the Go button.

NOTE

It might seem odd that the initially selected item in the menu doesn't jump when selected. If you select the menu within the Document window and look at its event in the Behaviors panel, you'll notice that it uses the onChange event. The drawback to this event is that it doesn't recognize the action of selecting an already selected item as a change in the menu. For this reason, the Go button is an integral part of the functionality of the Jump Menu. Selecting the Go button at any time, even with an initially selected item, forces the Jump Menu to respond.

Open Browser Window

Our next stop is the infamous pop-up window. Otherwise known as the Open Browser Window behavior, you can use this functionality as a way to open internal and external websites in a separate preconfigured window with specific width and height dimensions, among other functionalities. We've all seen them, right? The small secret cameras or travel advertisements that appear when you visit your favorite website are examples of this behavior. Although I would certainly discourage you from using this behavior for purposes such as these, there are, in fact, many less obtrusive uses for this behavior. To demonstrate the use of the Open Browser Window behavior, follow these steps:

1. Reopen the behaviors.html page if it's not already open.

2. Place your cursor just after the previous Visit Vecta Corp button and press Enter.

3. Insert a new Button form object by clicking the Button icon located in the Forms category of the Insert panel. When the Add Form Tag dialog box appears, click No. Give the new Button the text label **Open Vecta Corp** and change the Action to None to prevent the form from trying to Submit or Reset a nonexistent form.

4. With the Button selected, choose the Open Browser Window behavior from the Add (+) menu in the Behaviors panel. The Open Browser Window dialog box appears, as it does in Figure 8.20.

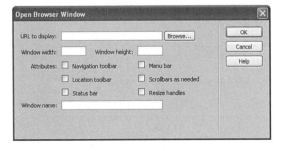

FIGURE 8.20   Use the Open Browser Window dialog box to customize properties for the pop-up window.

5. The Open Browser Window dialog box allows you to customize numerous properties, including the URL to display, the width and height of the window to open the URL in, and a simple name to assign to the pop-up window. You can also customize various attributes including whether scrollbars should be added, whether to allow the user to resize the browser window after it's been opened, and so on. For our purposes, enter the URL **http://www.vectacorp.com** in the URL to Display text box and assign the dimensions **400** for width and **400** for height. When you've finished, click OK.

As expected, the onClick event is assigned to the Button form object. Of course, if we really wanted to annoy our users, we could change that event to onLoad. That alteration would cause the Open Browser Window action to execute when the page is loaded, as opposed to when the user physically clicks the button. In an effort to maintain retention rates among our users, we'll keep the onClick event so that our users have to click for themselves to see the pop-up window.

To preview the finished product, save your work and preview the page in the browser by selecting F12 (Option-F12). As you can see from Figure 8.21, clicking the button opens the Vecta Corp website in a small 400×400 pixel window.

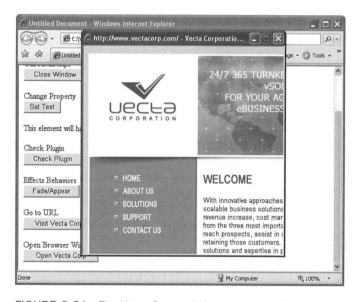

FIGURE 8.21   The Vecta Corp website appears within a small browser window.

Notice that the pop-up window is fairly plain and doesn't allow for much interaction in terms of scrolling to see all the website content, or even resizing the window to make it bigger. If you want this functionality for your pop-up windows, the Open Browser Window dialog box allows you to customize various attributes, including setting check boxes for scrollbars and resize handles. In fact, the Open Browser Window dialog box supports the following functionality (accessible by double-clicking the behavior in the Behaviors panel):

- ▶ **URL to Display**—In this text box, enter the URL of the site you'd like to display within the pop-up window.

- ▶ **Window Width and Height**—Enter the width and height (in pixels) at which you want the pop-up window to initially display in these text boxes.

- ▶ **Attributes**—Use these check boxes to set whether you want to display the navigation toolbar, a location toolbar, a status bar, a menu bar, enable scrollbars, or even provide resize handles. For our example, let's check the Scrollbars as Needed option and the Resize Handles option.

- ▶ **Window Name**—Enter a value in this text box to uniquely name the browser window. This value is optional because Dreamweaver will assign your window a unique name if none is provided.

Save your work and preview the page in the browser by choosing F12 (Option-F12). This time, when the pop-up window opens, you are free to resize and scroll through the pop-up window as needed.

Preload Images

Typically added to image rollovers (covered later in this chapter) or when the page loads for the first time, the Preload Images Behavior can be used as a way of forcing the browser to load certain elements first, before other elements on the page are rendered. This behavior is beneficial when working with image rollovers because they require two images to function correctly. As you'll see, when the page loads, a user sees the first image. As soon as the user's cursor rolls over the image, an event (typically the mouseover event) kicks in and calls necessary JavaScript code that changes the image to a second, usually different-colored image. On slower connections, the second image might appear as a broken image for a split second while it is loading. To avoid showing a broken image icon (even for a short time), use the Preload Images behavior. This behavior forces the browser to load all images that are viewable on the page, and to preload any images that might not be viewable on the page but must be queued for use in an effect such as a rollover. This behavior is automatically added for you when working with rollovers in Dreamweaver. As a matter of completeness, Adobe chooses to continue making this behavior available.

Set Nav Bar Image

Recall that in Chapter 2, "Building a Web Page," we used the Navigation Bar dialog box, available by selecting Insert, Image Objects, Navigation Bar, to build a fully functional navigation bar complete with images that changed color when the user's cursor rolled over them. Remember that the dialog box allows us to add navigation bar elements; give the navigation bar element a unique name; add up, over, and down image states; set alternate text; give the element a link; set the layout of the navigation bar (in terms of using tables for structure); and even set whether the images should preload (covered in the previous section). The beauty of the Navigation Bar dialog box is that it allows us to work with the navigation bar as a whole, rather than adding individual rollover images five different times as we would have had to do with the Rollover Image option, also available in the Image Object submenu within the Insert panel and covered in Chapter 2.

TIP

You can still work with the navigation bar as a whole by reselecting the Navigation Bar option in the Image Objects submenu. Although you can't build another navigation bar on the same page, selecting this option when you have an existing navigation bar reopens the Navigation Bar dialog box with your configured values prepopulated.

But what if we want to work with individual navigation bar elements within the context of the whole navigation bar? Even better, does a behavior exist for changing a second image on the page to something else while I roll over an element within my navigation bar? The answer is yes! This is where the Set Nav Bar Image behavior comes in. The Set Nav Bar Image behavior, aside from allowing you to work with individual navigation bar elements independently of the others, also allows you to set the image state of a second image anywhere on the page dynamically when you roll over an image in the navigation bar. A perfect example of when you'd want to use this type of functionality is when you're working with a navigation bar of employee names. In the example that we'll build, we'll have images that represent the executive team of our fictitious Vecta Corp company. Initially, we'll display Ferris's headshot because he's the founder, but as a user rolls over names in the navigation bar, we'll use the Set Nav Bar Image behavior to dynamically change the headshot of Ferris to the headshot of the person whose name you've rolled over. To do this, follow these steps:

1. Create a new page by choosing File, New. The New Document dialog box appears. Choose Blank Page, HTML, <none>, and click Create. The new page will appear. Immediately save the page as navbar.html within the root of your project (same location as behaviors.html).

2. With your cursor on the page, navigate to the Images folder and drag out the four images titled xferris_up.gif, xagnes_up.gif, xherbert_up.gif, and xpat_up.gif. Give each image a unique name in the Name field in the Property inspector. Also, make sure to add line breaks between the images so that the finished version resembles a vertically structured navigation bar similar to Figure 8.22.

3. Add a few more line breaks and drag the head_ferristhefounder.gif image into the page. This image is located in the Images folder of the project. Name the image **ferrisheadshot** in the ID text box in the Property inspector.

4. Select one of the navigation bar images, such as Agnes's (xagnes_up.gif), and select the Set Nav Bar Image behavior from the Add Behavior list in the Behaviors panel. The Set Nav Bar Image dialog box appears similar to Figure 8.23.

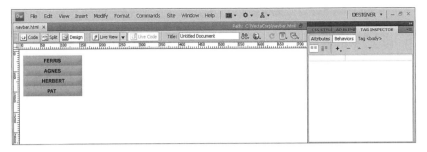

FIGURE 8.22   Add the four nav bar images to the page, creating line breaks between them.

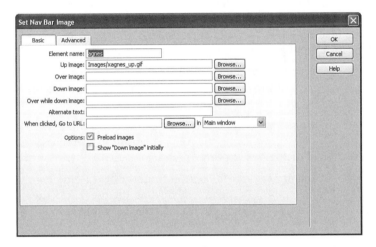

FIGURE 8.23   Attach the Set Nav Bar Image behavior to an image in your nav bar.

5. The Set Nav Bar Image dialog box is split into two tabs. The Basic tab contains the same customizable properties that the Navigation Bar dialog box does. Because you should already be familiar with the options, I won't take the time to explain them again. The only property that we need to set here is the Over image. Select the Browse button and browse to and select the image `xagnes_over.gif`.

6. Switch to the Advanced tab. This is where you can dynamically set the image that should appear in place of the existing headshot when a user rolls over the specific nav bar image. Because we're attaching this behavior to Agnes's nav bar image, select the `ferrisheadshot` option from the Also Set Image list box.

7. Browse to Agnes's headshot (`head_agnestheaccountant.gif`) in the To Image File text box. The image is located in the Images folder of the project.

8. Click OK.

To test the functionality, save your work and preview your page in the browser by choosing F12 (Option-F12). As you'll notice, rolling over Agnes's nav bar image changes Ferris's headshot to Agnes's. Rolling out of her nav bar image causes the headshot to return back to normal (to Ferris's headshot).

To finish off this page, return to Dreamweaver and repeat steps 4–8 for the other three images within the navigation bar.

Set Text

You can use the Set Text group of behaviors to dynamically set text values within a frame, an AP Element, the browser's status bar, and a text field. To give you an idea as to how this behavior works, follow these steps:

1. Reopen or switch back to the behaviors.html page that you've been working with and place your cursor just after the Open Vecta Corp button. Press Enter.

2. Insert a new Button form object by selecting the Button icon located in the Forms category of the Insert panel. When the Add Form Tag dialog box appears, click No. Give the new Button the text label **Set Text** and change the Action to None to prevent the nonexistent form from attempting to submit or reset itself.

3. Insert a new Text Field form object next to the button by selecting the Text Field icon located in the Forms category of the Insert panel. When the Add Form Tag dialog box appears, click No.

4. With the Button selected, choose the Set Text of Text Field behavior from the Set Text submenu of behaviors available by clicking the Add (+) button in the Behaviors panel. The Set Text of Text Field dialog box appears.

5. In this dialog box, choose the input "textfield" option from the Text Field menu and enter the message that should appear in the text field when the user clicks the button in the New Text area. For this example, enter the text **Hello World** and click OK.

6. Ensure that the onClick event is associated with the Button.

Save your work and test the page in the browser by choosing F12 (Option-F12). When the page appears, click the Set Text button. Immediately the text *Hello World* is shown within the text field.

Show-Hide Elements

The Show-Hide AP Elements behavior can be used to show or hide the contents in an AP <div> when an element on the page is selected, unselected, rolled over, rolled out, and so on. To use this behavior, follow these steps:

1. Place your cursor just to the right of the Set Text button (and Text Field) and press Enter.

2. Insert two new Button form objects by selecting the Button icon located in the Forms category of the Insert panel twice. When the Insert Form Tag dialog box appears, click No. Change the Action for both buttons to None.

3. Change one button's text Label to read **Show** and the other button's text label to read **Hide.**

4. Select the Show button and choose the Show-Hide Elements behavior from the Add (+) menu in the Behaviors panel. The Show-Hide Elements dialog box appears.

5. As you can see from the dialog box, the Elements list box displays elements, including AP <div>s on the page. Select the div "apDiv1" option (the AP <div> that contains the logo_vconvert.gif image) and click the Show button. Click OK.

6. Repeat steps 4 and 6 for the Hide button, but this time when you select the div "apDiv1" option within the list, click the Hide button within the dialog box.

Save your work and test the page in the browser by choosing F12 (Option-F12). You'll notice that you can click the Show and Hide buttons to either show or hide the AP <div> on the page.

Swap Image and Swap Image Restore

Similar to the Rollover Image option available from the Image Objects submenu in the Insert menu, the Swap Image behavior allows you to quickly construct a rollover for a specific image. Whereas the Rollover Image dialog box provides an intuitive interface for quickly creating a rollover image, the Swap Image behavior provides the flexibility to manipulate more advanced features (such as the capability to swap multiple images from one triggering action) associated with rollover images. Working with the Swap Image behavior is just as easy as working with the Rollover Image dialog box, but requires a few more steps. To work with the Swap Image behavior, follow these steps:

1. Place your cursor just after the previous Show and Hide buttons and click Enter.

2. Find the image xagnes_up.gif located within the Images folder and drag it into the page.

3. With the image selected, uniquely identify it by typing the name **agnes** into the Image ID text box located in the Property inspector.

4. Select the Swap Image behavior from the Add (+) menu in the Behaviors panel. The Swap Image dialog box appears similar to Figure 8.24.

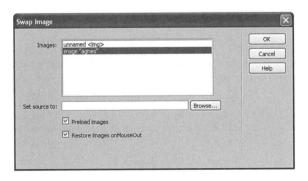

FIGURE 8.24   The Swap Image Behavior dialog box allows you to create a rollover for an image.

As you can see from Figure 8.24, the following functionality is revealed within the dialog box:

▶ **Images**—Use this list box to select the image for which you want to create a rollover. As you can see, our newly dragged-in image Agnes appears within the list. It's important to note that the Swap Image behavior is attached to a single object, in our case the Agnes button. Setting the source to multiple images within this dialog box would cause other images to swap states when I rolled over the Agnes image. If this is not the desired effect, attach a separate Swap Image behavior to each and every element that will have a rollover effect.

▶ **Set Source To**—Browse to the file you want to use as the rollover. For our example, we'll browse to the xagnes_over.gif image located in the Images folder.

▶ **Preload Images**—A few sections ago, we discussed the Preload Images behavior. In that discussion, I mentioned that preloading images, especially when working with rollover images, is important. Preloading images prevents a user with a slow connection from seeing a broken image while the secondary image is trying to load when the mouse rolls over an image. I recommend leaving this option checked at all times.

▶ **Restore Images onMouseOut**—Unchecking this box causes the image to remain in its rollover state. Checking this box ensures that the rollover image returns to its original state when the user's mouse rolls back out of the image.

5. After you've added the Set Source to path, click OK.

6. Before you test the functionality, make sure that the Behaviors panel lists the onMouseOver event for the Swap Image behavior and the onMouseOut event for the Swap Image Restore behavior. If they're not properly associated, do that now by choosing the correct event.

Save your work and test the page in the browser by choosing F12 (Option-F12). As you'll see, rolling over the image causes the secondary image to appear.

Validate Form

One of the last behaviors included in Dreamweaver's Behaviors panel is the Validate Form behavior. You can use this behavior as a way of validating or requiring inputs within form objects. For instance, in our contactus.html page, we outlined various text field form objects. Because these form objects are responsible for collecting vital information about a customer, we'll want to make sure that the user enters values into these fields before submitting the form. Furthermore, we'll want to make sure that the inquiring customer enters a correctly formatted email. This and more is possible with the Validate Form behavior. Using the Validate Form behavior is as simple as selecting the form to which you want to attach the behavior, selecting the behavior, and configuring the fields to be validated in the dialog box. To do this, follow these steps:

1. Open the contactus.html page.

2. Select the Submit button.

3. With the button selected, choose the Validate Form behavior available by clicking the Add (+) button in the Behaviors panel. The Validate Form dialog box appears, as shown in Figure 8.25.

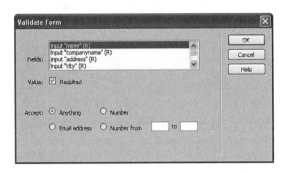

FIGURE 8.25   The Validate Form dialog box allows you to set fields whose content will be verified.

As you can see from the dialog box, the following functionality is revealed:

▶ **Fields**—Select a named text field from this list box to set its validation rules. The naming convention in this list box is such that the type of form object is listed (input) followed by its name in parentheses ("name", "companyname", "address", and so on).

▶ **Value: Required**—Selecting a form object from the Fields list and then checking this box guarantees that the specific form object will be required by the browser. If a user fails to add at least one character value before submitting the form, an error message appears, and the form is not submitted.

▶ **Accept: Anything**—Selecting a form object from the Fields list and then selecting this option button instructs the browser to accept anything within the form object, even if it's left empty. If the Required check box is also selected, any value will be accepted in the form object and the form object must not be left empty.

▶ **Accept: Number**—Selecting a form object from the Fields list and then selecting this option button instructs the browser to accept any numeric value in the form object. However, the form object can be left empty. If the Required check box is also selected, a numeric value *must* be entered into the form object.

▶ **Accept: Email address**—Selecting a form object from the Fields list and then selecting this option button instructs the browser to accept any value within the form object that appears to resemble an email address. However, the form object can be left empty. The formula for determining a valid email address is at least one character, an @ symbol, at least one more character, a . (period) symbol, followed by at least one more character. If the Required check box is selected, a value must be entered into the form object that resembles an email address.

8

▶ **Accept: Number From**—Selecting a form object from the Fields list and then selecting this option button instructs the browser to accept any numeric value within the
form object that falls between a range of values specified within the first and second
text boxes. However, the form object can be left empty. If the Required check box is
selected, a numeric value must be entered into the form object that falls between a
range of values specified within the first and second text boxes.

4. For our demonstration, set all the form objects as required. However, make sure that
the zip field accepts only a number. When you've finished, click OK.

5. Make sure that the event associated with the behavior is onClick. If it's not, select
that event now.

Save your work and test the page in the browser by choosing F12 (Option-F12). As you
can see from Figure 8.26, an alert message is displayed when you try to submit the form
without entering values within the required text fields.

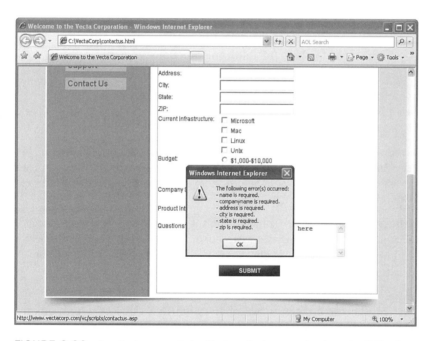

FIGURE 8.26   An alert message is displayed when you try to submit the form without entering
values into fields that are set as required.

NOTE

Although the Validate Form behavior certainly works well, it's important to note that
there are additional methods for validating text-based input. As you'll see in Chapter
24, Adobe has included a rich set of Spry features for a much better user experience
when working with form-based validation such as this.

Deprecated Behaviors

In Dreamweaver CS4, six behaviors that have existed in previous versions of Dreamweaver are marked as deprecated in this current version:

- ▶ Check Browser
- ▶ Control Shockwave or Flash
- ▶ Play Sound
- ▶ Show and Hide Pop-Up Menu
- ▶ Timeline

Although using these behaviors is still possible to a certain extent, don't expect support from Adobe should your website not work correctly as a result of using these behaviors. Additionally, the deprecated status of these behaviors should tip you off to the fact that inclusion of these behaviors in future versions of Dreamweaver isn't likely.

Check Browser

It's considered common practice in web development to create pages suited for the variety of browsers currently available. The reason for this is simple: Users who visit your website using Internet Explorer 7.0 will have a much richer experience than those visiting your website using Netscape 4. To accommodate both users, you might decide to create two different websites—one that includes limited functionality and is mostly text-based, and another much richer design that could potentially include CSS, JavaScript, and perhaps Flash animations. The dilemma is that you'll need some mechanism for detecting the type of browser the user is using to visit your site and then react to that discovery by displaying the appropriate content. The Check Browser behavior does just this. To demonstrate this behavior, follow these instructions:

1. Open the `behaviors.html` file if it's not already open. Place your cursor next to the Agnes button that we used for the Swap Image behavior demonstration and click Enter. Immediately add a Button form object by selecting the Button icon from within the Forms category in the Insert panel.

2. When the Add Form Tag dialog box appears, click No.

3. With the Button form object selected, change the Action to None so that the button doesn't try to submit or reset a nonexistent form when it's clicked. You can also change the Label to read anything you'd like. I'll change mine to say **Check Browser**.

4. With the Button object selected, choose the Check Browser behavior from the Add (+) menu in the Behaviors panel. Remember, the Check Browser behavior is contained within the ~Deprecated submenu of behaviors. The Check Browser dialog box appears.

5. The dialog box allows you to check for Netscape versions before or after 4.0 and for Internet Explorer versions before or after 4.0; you can react accordingly by specifying the URL of the web page you want to use if the browser is 4.0 or later, and an alternative URL if the browser is earlier than version 4.0. A third drop-down menu specifies which URL to redirect to if it's any browser other than Netscape or Internet

Explorer 4.0. To test the functionality, let's add the path `behaviors.html` to the URL text box and `altpage.html` to the Alt URL text box. When you've finished, the results will look similar to Figure 8.27.

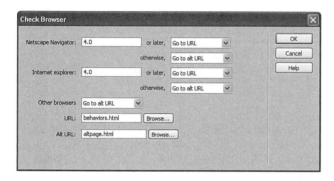

FIGURE 8.27   Customize the Check Browser dialog box so that it goes to `behaviors.html` if the browser version is Netscape or Internet Explorer version 4.0 or later.

6. Click OK.

7. If the selected event isn't `onClick`, change it to `onClick` now.

Based on our additions, when we click the Check Browser button in Internet Explorer or Netscape versions 4.0 or later, the page should refresh itself because we've told it to go to `behaviors.html`. However, if we click the Check Browser button in Netscape or Internet Explorer versions 4.0 and earlier—or any browser other than Netscape or Internet Explorer, such as Firefox—the page is redirected to `altpage.html`. Try it for yourself in all three browsers. You'll notice that when you preview the page in Firefox and click the Check Browser button, the page redirects to `altpage.html`.

The problem within this behavior is immediately noticeable. The dialog box should provide options for all browsers, not just Internet Explorer or Netscape.

Control Shockwave or Flash

As you'll see in Chapter 14, "Integrating with Photoshop, Fireworks, and Flash," you can control the animation of Flash movies using the Control Shockwave or Flash behavior. For instance, you might want to add a button that, when clicked, plays, stops, or goes to a specific point in the movie's timeline. All of this, as you'll see in Chapter 14, is possible with the Control Shockwave or Flash behavior.

Play Sound

The next behavior in the deprecated list of behaviors is the Play Sound behavior. You can use this behavior as a way of playing sound files such as MP3, MIDI, and WAV in the browser window. Although popular browsers such as Internet Explorer, Firefox, and so on can play most sound files directly within the browser, others might require additional software such as QuickTime to play the sound correctly. Netscape might even prompt you with a dialog box giving you the option of choosing the external audio player (QuickTime, Windows Media Player, iTunes, or RealAudio) to use.

Playing audio in the browser is covered in much more detail in Chapter 13, "Incorporating Video and Audio," but for now let's explore this simple behavior. To work with the Play Sound behavior in your web page, follow these steps:

1. Place your cursor just after the Check Browser button and click Enter.

2. Insert a new Button form object by clicking the Button icon in the Forms category of the Insert panel. When the Insert Form Tag dialog box appears, click No. Give the new Button the text label **Play Sound** and change the Action to None to prevent the form from submitting or resetting.

3. With the Button selected, choose the Play Sound behavior from the Add (+) menu in the Behaviors panel. Again, the Sound behavior is located within the ~Deprecated submenu of behaviors. The Play Sound dialog box appears.

4. Browse to select a sound file. I've included a simple MIDI file in the Media folder of your project called `PlaySound.mid`. Choose it.

5. Click OK.

6. Ensure that the `onClick` event is attached to the Button.

Save your work and test the page within the browser by choosing F12 (Option-F12). The sound is played when the button is clicked. Depending on your browser/audio software configuration, the use of third-party software may or may not be needed. In my case, the QuickTime player was loaded within the browser to play the MIDI file.

> **NOTE**
>
> You should be aware that a Stop Sound behavior doesn't exist for the Play Sound behavior. Therefore, the only way to stop the sound file from playing is to close the browser. If your users find your sound file annoying, they might be tempted to close the browser or navigate to a different page in an effort to avoid the sound.

Show Pop-Up Menu and Hide Pop-Up Menu

The Show Pop-Up Menu and Hide Pop-Up Menu behaviors exist to support old Dreamweaver web pages that relied on this behavior. Prior to Dreamweaver CS3, the Show Pop-Up Menu and Hide Pop-Up Menu behaviors could be used to create a CSS-based pop-up menu. In Dreamweaver CS3 and CS4, this menu has been completely replaced by the Spry Menu bar. As you'll see in Chapter 24, and as I'm sure veteran Dreamweaver users can attest to, the Spry Menu bar is a much better and more easily configurable alternative to the deprecated Show Pop-Up Menu Bar behavior.

Timeline

Similar to the Show Pop-Up Menu and Hide Pop-Up Menu behaviors, the Timeline set of behaviors exists only to support old Dreamweaver pages that relied on timelines for web-based animations. Because the code that Timelines and Timeline behaviors created in most cases wasn't standards-compliant, Adobe has made the decision to no longer support Timelines as of Dreamweaver CS4.

Summary

As you've seen throughout the chapter, behaviors, outlined in the Behaviors panel, offer a new level of development possibilities that require little knowledge of JavaScript. By using some of the behaviors described in this chapter, you can offer a broad range of interactivity for your users that requires little or no development time.

Throughout the chapter, I introduced various concepts including JavaScript and how JavaScript code and events are added to the page. This set up a foundation for discussing the Behaviors panel, the catalyst that drives the addition of behaviors. As we progressed through the chapter, we looked at the various behaviors included in the Behaviors list in Dreamweaver, including how to use these behaviors to manipulate the properties of objects, pop-up messages, and open browser windows; apply effects to objects; show and hide objects; apply rollover effects, and more.

As we jump right into the next part of Dreamweaver, we'll begin to move away from static web page development and into the world of team collaboration and task automation. We'll begin to discuss topics related to working within teams, including using check-in/check-out, versioning, Contribute, templates and library items, and much more!

PART III

Team Collaboration and Task Automation

IN THIS PART

Building Dreamweaver Websites Within Teams

Dreamweaver, like most visual editors, allows you to quickly and easily design websites. Through the use of its many panels, windows, inspectors, and bars, Dreamweaver—in conjunction with your creativity—can facilitate this evolution. What makes Dreamweaver unique, however, are the subtle features that help you along as either an individual website developer or a developer working in a collaborative team.

Later, we'll discuss the nuances that make Dreamweaver unique from other web page editors (we've already gone over some), but this chapter focuses on the exclusive functionality available for working in teams. Specifically, we'll discuss Dreamweaver's built-in source control functionality in its file Check In and Check Out system. Using this functionality, you can easily share remote files with other members of your team without worrying about who's working on what or whether you'll be overriding someone else's work if you save a file remotely. Additionally, we'll review Design Notes in great detail. Although you can use Design Notes as an aid in individual development, Design Notes really come in handy when working with offsite collaborative teams. Instead of picking up the phone and manually telling someone about changes or revisions that need to be made to a file, you can simply add a Design Note to a file. The Design Note is also uploaded to the remote server. You can set the properties so that when a member of the team opens the file, the Design Note automatically opens, revealing the changes or revisions that need to be made. We'll also discuss Dreamweaver's handling of site reports. As a manager of a web development team, you might find this functionality particularly useful in that you can generate reports on a file, a group of files, or an entire site regarding issues such as poorly written HTML, invalid HTML, or even who has checked out what and for how long. Finally, we'll review Dreamweaver's integration with third-party source control options such as Microsoft's Visual SourceSafe, the IETF's open standard WebDAV, and Subversion control.

Like the rest of the chapters within this book, you can work with the examples in this chapter by downloading the files from the book's website. You'll want to replace the files in `C:\VectaCorp\` with the files that you download for this chapter. As you'll learn, the downloads for this chapter are separated into two folders: Local (empty) and Remote (this folder contains all of our project files). Because we'll be discussing topics that relate to remote file collaboration, file Check In and Check Out, and dealing with third-party file repositories, we need to simulate a local and remote environment. This is done by creating two folders in your chapter downloads—one for your local files, and one to represent remote files. Keep in mind that you'll also need to update your site reference to point to the Local folder instead of the `C:\VectaCorp` root. We'll do this a bit later.

Using File Check In and Check Out

As I've just mentioned, you can use Dreamweaver's file Check In and Check Out functionality as a way to work with individual files within your collaborative team. The benefit to using file Check In and Check Out is simple and is best explained through the following scenario: Assume for a moment that you're working in a team of two or more developers. Also assume that although you're the primary developer for the project, a second developer decides to help you out and copies a file from the remote server to his local computer to do some work on that file. However, the other developer is unaware that you've already copied the file and have begun working on it. When you've finished working for the day, you copy the file back to the remote server and assume everything is fine. The other developer, thinking he's helping you out, makes changes to the file and also uploads the file to the remote server, essentially overwriting all the work that you just spent the better part of a day on. Situations such as this can easily be prevented by enabling and working with the file Check In and Check Out features built directly into Dreamweaver.

Working with these features, however, requires some initial setup. Up to this point, we've been working specifically with local files, meaning that you downloaded the files from the book's website, extracted them, copied them to a folder on your hard drive, and then defined a site directly in the local files in Dreamweaver. With file Check In and Check Out, this simplistic model wouldn't make sense. Remember, file Check In and Check Out assumes that you're working with *teams*. Members of your team won't be connecting directly to your computer; instead, they'll be connecting to a remote server, possibly even the company's web server. The remote server in this case not only acts as the web server, but also as a central repository for web files. Because this is the case, we'll have to emulate our fictitious company's web architecture model by defining a remote server (the fictitious company's web server) and a local site (your computer). When we're finished, the model will resemble Figure 9.1.

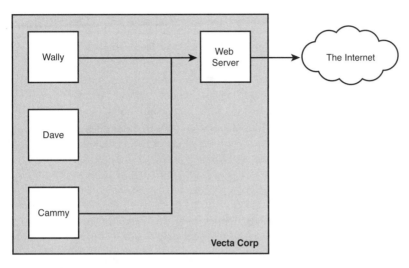

FIGURE 9.1   The ideal scenario has you as a single developer connecting to a remote computer that acts as the company's web server.

Before you scramble to find a web-hosting provider, it's important to understand that the file Check In and Check Out features can easily be integrated with computers that reside within the same network. Your company's web server could be a computer that resides on the company's network. This means that you can work with examples in this chapter using your computer (assuming your computer is the development and web server) or two computers that might share the same network. If you're using your computer as both the development and web server, your web architecture model might resemble Figure 9.2.

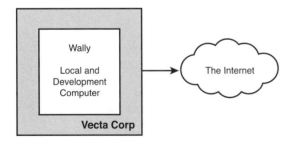

FIGURE 9.2   Realistically, many readers of this book will be developing and testing from the same computer that they use to access the Internet.

Either model you choose to implement is fine. Although the first model is much more flexible for working in teams, the second model will work just fine for the examples in this chapter, and probably resembles your workflow now, anyway.

NOTE

If you've downloaded the files from the website, you'll notice that files contained within the VectaCorp folder are separated into two folders called Local and Remote. I'll make the assumption that most readers of this book don't have a second server running on their home network or don't have the capability to easily connect to a web-hosting provider. Because this is the case, we'll follow along with the second model (shown in Figure 9.2); that is, simulating a remote web hosting environment by separating our project into two folders: Local, which represents our local development computer, and Remote, which represents our fictitious remote web hosting provider.

Enabling Check In and Check Out

Now that you understand the model that the file Check In and Check Out functionality works under, let's set it up. Follow these steps:

1. If you've haven't changed the site definition for Chapter 9 yet (outlined in the beginning of the chapter), it's okay—we'll use this time to do that. With Dreamweaver open, select Site, Manage Sites. The Manage Sites dialog box opens.

2. Select the VectaCorp site within the list and click the Edit button. The Site Definition for Vecta Corp dialog box appears.

3. Within the Local Info category, we'll want to make one change. We'll change the Local root folder to point to C:\VectaCorp\Local\. After you've made that change, the screen will resemble Figure 9.3.

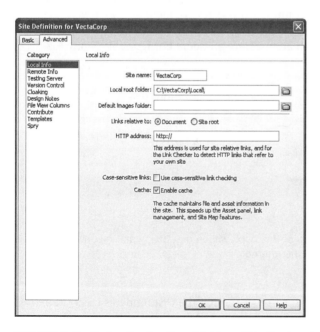

FIGURE 9.3   Define the Local root folder within the Local Info category to point to the location where you want local files to be stored while in development.

TIP

If you're implementing the first model, where your local and remote files are located on two separate machines, your Local root folder would remain the same, or look like `C:\VectaCorp\`.

4. With the Local root folder set, you can switch over to the Remote Info category. Select the Local/Network option from the Access list. More options are now available. Within the Remote folder text box, enter or browse to the path of VectaCorp's fictitious remote web server. In our case, the remote files are located in `C:\VectaCorp\Remote\`.

TIP

If you're implementing the first model, where your local and remote files are located on two separate machines, your Remote folder might point to the organization's web folder on the network using the following model: `\\<servername>\<webfolder>`. This path will work, assuming that your site is shared on the network. If it's not, you'll need to contact your system administrator for further details.

5. Your next step will be to click the Enable File Check In and Check Out check box.
6. With the check box enabled, we can now set other options for identifying the person checking files in and out. Specifically, we can enter the name and email address of the user (you). We can also check the Check Out Files When Opening check box. Doing this guarantees that whenever we open a file that has already been checked in on the local side, the file will automatically be checked out on the remote side. After you've finished setting the final three options, your Remote Info screen should resemble mine, shown in Figure 9.4.
7. Click OK to close the Site Definition for Vecta Corp window.
8. Click Done to close the Manage Sites dialog box.

We're now ready to start checking out files. Before we do, however, we'll want to synchronize the local folder with the files contained in the Remote folder. This will ensure that the files in the Local folder are exact copies of those within the remote. You can synchronize the files by following these steps:

1. Select Site, Synchronize Sitewide.
2. When the Synchronize Files dialog box appears, select the Entire Vecta Corp Site option from the Synchronize menu. Also, choose the Get Newer Files from Remote option from the Direction menu.
3. Click Preview.
4. When the Synchronize preview window appears, click OK to proceed with the synchronization.

Now you can click the Expand/Collapse icon in the Files panel to expand it, if necessary. As you can see from Figure 9.5, the remote files (located in the `C:\VectaCorp\Remote\`

folder) appear in the left pane, and the local files (located in the `C:\VectaCorp\Local\` folder) appear on the right.

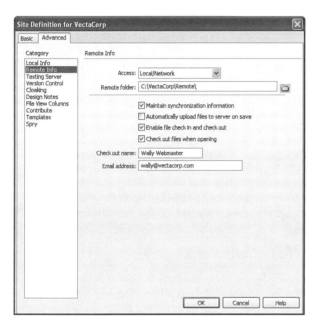

FIGURE 9.4   Set the properties to identify the person checking files in and out.

FIGURE 9.5   Expanding the Files panel reveals the remote files on the left and the local files on the right.

You'll also notice that the local files appear with small lock icons next to them. Because we've enabled Check In and Check Out functionality in the Site Definition process, these files will be locked by default. And because we haven't checked these files out, opening them in their current state would result in Dreamweaver opening these files for viewing purposes in read-only mode. To edit these files, we'll have to check them out. Let's do that now.

Checking Files In and Out

Now that you've enabled the Check In and Check Out feature, you can begin using it for the defined Vecta Corp site. To do so, right-click (Control-click) a file within the Local Files list and choose the Check Out option from the context menu (see Figure 9.6).

FIGURE 9.6   Select the Check Out option from the context menu of the file you want to check out.

Next, Dreamweaver asks if you want to include dependent files when checking out the HTML file. Because we have read-only copies in our Local folder, we'll select No. As you can see from Figure 9.7, the file is checked out to you.

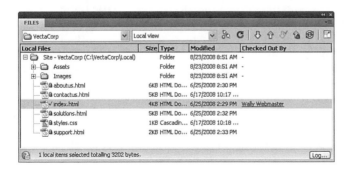

FIGURE 9.7   The file is checked out to you. You can tell by the icon change and the user's name in the Checked Out By file view column.

TIP

When we defined our site in Chapter 3, "Dreamweaver Site Management," we enabled the Check Out Files When Opening check box. Because this is the case, we need only to open the local file (by double-clicking to open it) in Dreamweaver. As soon as we do this, the file is automatically checked out.

You can tell the file is checked out to you because the file's icon changes from a lock icon to a green check mark icon. This means the file is checked out. Furthermore, your name appears in the Checked Out By file view column. As you can see, these properties are set in both the Remote and Local panes. This means that when a member of your collaborative team defines a site to the same Remote folder, your name will appear as the user who has checked out the file. If the other user tries to check out the same file, that user won't be able to do so. The other user will be able only to view the file, not write to it. Now that the file has been checked out to you, you can open it and make any necessary changes. When you've finished, you can check it back in by right-clicking (Control-clicking) the file within the Local Files list and choosing the Check In option. Furthermore, if you check out a file and aren't happy with the changes that you've made, you can also select the Undo Check Out option from the context menu. Doing this replaces the local file with the last version that was checked in from the remote.

Up until now, we simply right-clicked onto the file in the Files panel to check out and check in a file. But that's not the only way. The following list outlines the various methods that you might decide to implement to check a file in, check a file out, undo a checkout, or determine which user has a file checked out:

▶ **Right-clicking in the Files panel to access the context menu**—As you saw in the previous paragraph, the easiest way to check in or check out a file or files, undo a checkout, or see which member of your collaborative team has a file checked out, is to simply right-click the file(s) in the Files panel and choose from one of the four options (Check In, Check Out, Undo Check Out, and Show Checked Out By...) available to you from the context menu.

▶ **Using the toolbar in the Files panel**—The toolbar in the Files panel also outlines two icons that allow you to check in or check out a selected file. To use these options, simply select a file from the Files panel and then choose either the Check Out button to check out the selected file from the remote web server, or the Check In button to check the file into the remote web server. You'll notice that icons don't exist for undoing a checkout or to see which member of your collaborative team has a file checked out.

▶ **Using the Site menu**—Options for checking in a file, checking out a file, undoing a checkout, or seeing which member of your collaborative team has a file checked out are also available directly from the Site menu. Unlike the context menu option on the Files panel, the four options (Check In, Check Out, Undo Check Out, and Show Checked Out By...) are only available to you when a file is open and only work on the open file.

▶ **Using the File menu in the Document toolbar when a file is open**—Options for checking in a file, checking out a file, undoing a checkout, or seeing which member of your collaborative team has a file checked out are also available directly from the File management menu in the Document toolbar when a file is open. Again, unlike the context menu option on the Files panel, the four options (Check In, Check Out, Undo Check Out, and Show Checked Out By...) are only available to you when a file is open, and only work on the open file.

Maintaining Design Notes

One of the most underused features available in Dreamweaver is that of associating Design Notes with web pages. As an individual web developer, you can create Design Notes in an effort to keep tabs on progress and to write general notes to yourself or others about a particular file. When you go to open the file, you can have the Design Note automatically open and remind you of what needs to get done. From a team collaborative standpoint, you can associate Design Notes with your web pages as a way to alert other developers in your team about changes made, changes that might need to be made, or specific items within the file that require attention.

Enabling Design Notes

Enabling Design Notes for your web pages is as simple as opening the site definition for the particular site you're working with and clicking a check box. In our scenario, we'll want to enable Design Notes for the defined Vecta Corp site. To do this, follow these steps:

1. Open the Manage Sites dialog box by choosing Site, Manage Sites. The Manage Sites dialog box appears.

2. Now select the Vecta Corp site and click the Edit button. The Site Definition for Vecta Corp dialog box appears.

3. Select the Design Notes category. The Design Notes screen appears.

4. Within the Design Notes screen you can do three things: The first check box enables Design Notes. Make sure to check this box to enable Design Notes for the Vecta Corp site. The Clean Up button next to this option deletes all existing Design Notes within the site. The third and final option at the bottom of the screen ensures that Design Notes, located within a _notes folder in the defined site, are automatically uploaded to the remote server when you check in a file or upload it manually to the remote server. Make sure this option is enabled so that others in your collaborative

team can see the Design Notes you create and vice versa. After you've finished making the changes, click OK to close the Site Definition dialog box.

TIP

It's important to note that Dreamweaver uses Design Notes for launching and editing features when integrating with Flash and Fireworks. Design Notes are also used to store settings when you're working with Design-Time style sheets and the Live Data view. For this reason, it's generally a good idea to leave these options enabled even if you don't plan to work with Design Notes.

---

5. Click Done to close the Manage Sites dialog box.

Design Notes have now been enabled for your site.

Setting the Status of Files with Design Notes

After you've enabled Design Notes, you're ready to start working with them. One ideal usage for Design Notes would be for writing notes to yourself about a particular file. It's important to realize that Design Notes are associated with particular files within a site, not with the site as a whole. To associate a Design Note with a file, you can do one of two things. First, you can choose the Design Notes option by right-clicking (Control-clicking) on the checked out file in the Local Files list that you want to create a Design Note for. I'll choose index.html. Second, you can open the checked out file (index.html) by double-clicking it in the Local Files list. With the file open, you can choose the Design Notes option from the File menu. Either method opens the Design Notes dialog box, as shown in Figure 9.8.

As you can see from Figure 9.8, the dialog box is separated into two parts: the Basic Info and All Info tabs. We'll discuss the All Info tab in the next section; for now, let's discuss how you can set the status of and write notes about a particular file using the Basic Info tab. As you can see from Figure 9.8, the screen is divided into the following segments:

▶ **File**—This read-only text label displays the name of the file that the Design Note will be associated with.

▶ **Location**—This read-only text label displays the path to the file location on the local computer.

▶ **Status**—Choose an option from this menu to set the status of the file. Options include Draft, Revision1, Revision2, Revision3, Alpha, Beta, Final, and Needs Attention. For our example, choose the Needs Attention option.

▶ **Insert date**—Clicking this icon inserts a date stamp into the Notes text box. Click this button now to insert a date stamp.

▶ **Notes**—Use this multiline text box to enter any notes to yourself or members of your team about the file. The text you enter here is completely up to you, but you'll generally want to associate the note with the status option you select. For our example, add the text: **We still need to update our solution offerings for this month**, preferably just to the right of the date stamp.

▶ **Show When File Is Opened**—Enabling this check box assures that the Design Note appears automatically when the file is opened each time. For our example, check this box.

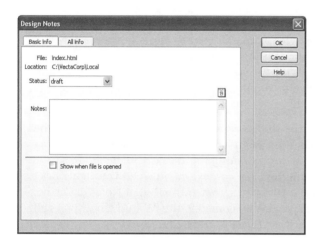

FIGURE 9.8   The Design Notes dialog box allows you to associate Design Notes with a particular file.

Click OK to create the Design Note. Initially, you won't notice any additions to the folder or file structure of the site. However, opening the Local folder (`C:\VectaCorp\Local`) within your computer's file explorer reveals the new _notes folder that Dreamweaver adds for you. Within the _notes folder, you'll see the `index.html.mno` file. This XML-based file represents the Design Note for `index.html`.

> **NOTE**
>
> By default, Dreamweaver creates one MNO file per web page document. That's not to say that multiple users can't create multiple notes for a single MNO file. When new notes are created, they are appended to the MNO file. Furthermore, the MNO file keeps track of which users open the file.

Now that the Design Note has been applied, you can check your file into the remote web server if you want. When you or another member of your collaborative team check this file out for editing, the Design Note will automatically appear, alerting you to the work that needs to be done.

Creating Customized Design Notes

In the previous section, we examined the Basic Info tab of the Design Notes dialog box. For the most part, a large majority of the functionality that you'll need to interact with as it relates to Design Notes can be found within that tab. Other times, however, you'll want to create custom Design Notes that relate to specific aspects of your project. For instance, you might want to define various resources (such as graphic designer, project manager, lead developer) related to a project so that when users open the Design Note, they know who to contact if they have a question. Or you might want to create a custom note that defines how many man hours have been dedicated to a specific file. As you'll see in the next section, you can then associate specific file view columns with a particular Design Note. Even better, you can enable file view column sharing so that everyone in the team can see the custom Design Notes directly from within the Site Management window.

All this begins with the All Info tab of the Design Notes dialog box. To demonstrate the functionality within this screen, reopen the Design Notes dialog box by either choosing the Design Notes option from the File menu (assuming the index.html file is already open) or choose the Design Notes option from the context menu when you right-click (Control-click) the index.html file in the Files panel. When the Design Notes dialog box opens, click the All Info tab. As you can see from Figure 9.9, the All Info tab displays all the information you entered within the Basic Info tab line by line.

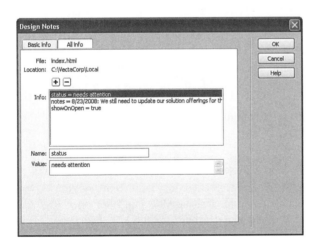

FIGURE 9.9   Initially, the All Info tab displays notes created within the Basic Info tab.

The All Info tab is divided into the following features:

▶ **File**—This read-only text label displays the name of the file that the Design Note will be associated with.

▶ **Location**—This read-only text label displays the path to the file location on the local computer.

▶ **Info**—This list box displays notes defined in the Basic Info tab as well as custom notes you specify in this screen. You can add a new note by clicking the Add (+) icon located just above the Info list box. Do that now.

▶ **Name**—Use this text box to enter the custom name of the new note. Enter the text `ManHours` here.

▶ **Value**—Use this text box to enter the value associated with the name of the new note. Let's assume that we have eight billable hours accrued for `index.html` so far. Because that's the case, enter **8** in this text box.

When you've finished making the necessary additions within the All Info pane, click OK. Again, you won't notice too much of a difference. To see the notes, you either have to reopen this screen (which isn't very intuitive), or you can create custom view columns within the Site Management window. This process is discussed in the next section.

Viewing Design Notes

The easiest way to view Design Notes is to right-click (Control-click) the file within the Files panel and choose the Design Notes option from the contextual menu. Doing this opens the Design Notes dialog box and displays notes for the specific file. This process is great if you're an individual developer and you remember which files have Design Notes and which don't. If you're working in a team, however, this process isn't very intuitive. A better method of viewing Design Notes is by enabling the Notes file view column within the Site Management window. Remember that in Chapter 3 we turned the Notes column off. To view Design Notes for particular files within the Site Management window, we'll need to turn that column back on. To do that, follow these steps:

1. Select Site, Manage Sites.
2. When the Manage Sites dialog box appears, select the VectaCorp site and click Edit.
3. Select the File View Columns category.
4. Within the File View Columns screen, select the Notes column from the list and click the Show check box.
5. Click OK to close the Site Definition dialog box.
6. Click Done in the Manage Sites dialog box.

To view the Design Notes now, click the Expand/Collapse icon within the Files panel to expand it, if necessary. As you can see from Figure 9.10, files that have note associations display a small note icon.

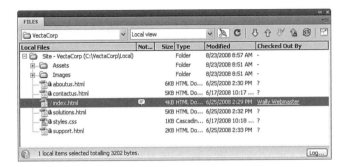

FIGURE 9.10   Files that have Design Notes associated with them display a small note icon.

When you check the file back in, the Design Note will go with it. From a collaborative standpoint, this allows other members of your team to see which files do and don't have notes associated with them. Now, to view the note, double-click the icon. The Design Notes dialog box appears.

Beyond the simplicity of viewing Design Notes within file view columns lies the capability to view custom Design Notes within a custom file view column. For instance, we might want to share with the team how many billable hours have been accrued by people working on the particular file, in which case we'd want to create a custom file view column to display that Design Note (created in the previous section). To do this, follow these steps:

1. Select Site, Manage Sites.
2. When the Manage Sites dialog box appears, select the VectaCorp site and click Edit.
3. Select the File View Columns category.
4. Within the File View Columns screen, click the Add (+) icon to create a new custom file view column. By default, the file view column is initially populated with the name "untitled".
5. With the new file view column selected in the list, change the column name to **ManHours.**
6. Enter the text **ManHours** in the Associate with Design Note text box. After you've made the additions, the screen will resemble Figure 9.11.
7. Click OK.
8. Click Done within the Manage Sites dialog box.

To view the new file view column, click the Expand/Collapse icon within the Files panel, if necessary, to expand it. As you can see from Figure 9.12, the ManHours file view column appears and displays the value 8 (relating to 8 billable man hours) for index.html.

Again, to prove that Dreamweaver uses the _notes folder for more than just Design Notes, open the folder that contains your files and examine the _notes folder. A new file called dwSiteColumnsAll.xml is created and represents any custom file view columns we create.

FIGURE 9.11   Create a new custom file view column and associate it with our custom ManHours Design Note.

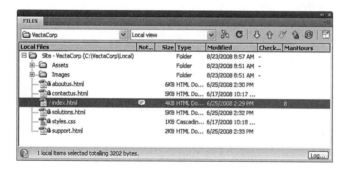

FIGURE 9.12   The custom file view column appears with the numeric value 8 for index.html.

File View Column Sharing

In the previous couple of sections, you saw how easy it was to create custom Design Notes and custom file view columns. You also saw how easy it was to associate the custom file view column with the Design Notes so that the note becomes viewable within the columns in the Files panel. Unfortunately, our current configuration limits the file view column's visibility to only you. This becomes obvious when you open the expanded Files panel. As you'll notice, the ManHours value displays 8 on the local side but not on the remote side.

To share the value of the custom file view column, we must enable file view column sharing. You can do this by following these steps:

1. Select Site, Manage Sites.

2. When the Manage Sites dialog box appears, select the VectaCorp site and click Edit.

3. Select the File View Columns category. As you'll see, the Enable Column Sharing check box is not enabled. Enable it now. This will share all columns with your collaborative team.

4. Although the Enable Column Sharing check box enables you to share columns with a collaborative team, values for custom columns aren't automatically shared. To share them, you must select the custom column and enable the Share with All Users of This Site check box. I'll do that for the ManHours custom column. When you've finished making the adjustment, the File View Columns screen will resemble Figure 9.13.

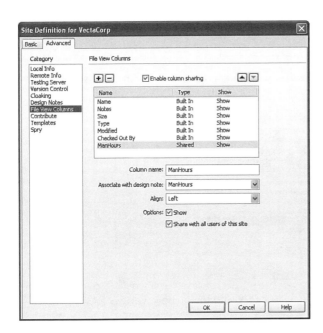

FIGURE 9.13   The Enable Column Sharing check box enables us to share all column names with other users of the team.

5. Click OK to close the Site Definition dialog box.

6. Click Done within the Manage Sites dialog box.

When you click Done, the Local and Remote panes refresh, and the value 8 also appears within the ManHours file view column on the remote side.

Generating Workflow Site Reports

In Chapter 3, we briefly covered site reports. Site reports offer a quick and visual method of generating reports on various aspects of your site, including files that have been recently modified, files that have poorly written HTML, and so on. For the most part, we discussed HTML-based reports and briefly skimmed over workflow reports. Because workflow reports relate specifically to team collaboration in that they allow you to create reports on files that are checked out, files that have Design Notes associations, and files that have been recently modified, we'll take the time to discuss the topic in greater detail here.

To begin using site reports, choose Site, Reports. The Reports dialog box appears, similar to Figure 9.14.

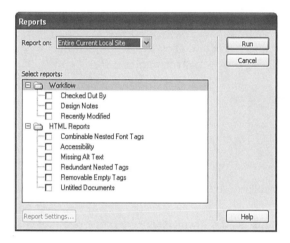

FIGURE 9.14   Use the Workflow options in the Reports dialog box to generate visual reports on files that have been checked out by someone, files that have Design Note associations, and so on.

As you can see, the Reports dialog box is split into two distinct sections: Workflow and HTML Reports. For this chapter, we'll consider the Workflow options. If you want more information on HTML Reports, refer back to Chapter 3. As you can see from Figure 9.14, workflow reports are divided into three options: Checked Out By, Design Notes, and Recently Modified. Let's discuss each in depth.

Checked Out By Reports

As a web manager, you can use the Checked Out By option as a way of generating reports for files that are checked out by a specific user, or anyone in your collaborative team. Although the impact that this option has on small sites is minimal, it can be extremely useful for large collaborative teams that deal with sites containing thousands of folders, nested folders, and files. To generate a Checked Out By report, follow these steps:

1. If you haven't opened the Site Reports dialog box, do that now by choosing Site, Reports.

2. Select the Entire Current Local Site option from the Report On menu.

3. Click the Checked Out By check box.

4. Click Run.

Dreamweaver displays one file (`index.html`) within the Site Reports panel because this is the only file that is currently checked out.

In this scenario, we enabled the Checked Out By option and clicked Run. Doing this gives us a list of all the files checked out by anyone within the defined site. To run a report filtered by a particular user, follow these steps:

1. With the Site Reports panel still open, click the Play icon to relaunch the Reports dialog box.

2. Select the Entire Current Local Site option from the Report On menu.

3. This time, enable the Checked Out By check box and click the Report Settings button to open the Checked Out By dialog box, similar to Figure 9.15.

FIGURE 9.15   The Checked Out By dialog box allows you to filter results by a specific user.

4. With the dialog box open, enter the name **Wally Webmaster** (or a name of a user that you know has a file checked out) and click OK.

5. Click Run.

This time, the Site Reports panel displays the name of the user that matches the filtered query and lists only the files checked out by that user.

Design Notes Reports

Another site report option available to you is that of generating reports on files that have Design Notes associations. You might decide to use this option to filter by files in a site that have their status set to Needs Attention. You might also decide to check on custom Design Notes, for instance, checking files where the ManHours are greater than 8. As a project manager, this would allow you to track development progress and restrict development on files where the development time is getting out of hand. To generate a Design Notes report, follow these steps:

1. With the Reports dialog box open, select the Entire Current Local Site option from the Report On menu.

2. Click the Design Notes check box.

3. Click Run.

As you can see from Figure 9.16, Dreamweaver displays the only file that has Design Notes associated with it (index.html).

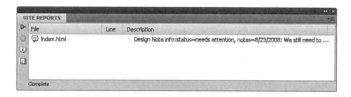

FIGURE 9.16   Files that have Design Notes associations are displayed within the Site Reports tab of the Results panel.

You'll also notice that the Description column displays the attributes of the Design Notes. Unfortunately, the content is too long to fit within our small screen. To view all the information associated with the Design Notes, right-click (Control-click) the specific result and choose More Info from the context menu. Dreamweaver displays the entire description in the Description dialog box. You can click OK to close it.

In this scenario, we checked the Design Notes option and clicked Run. Doing this gives us all files that have Design Notes associations within the defined site. To run a report filtered by a specific property within Design Notes, follow these steps:

1. With the Site Reports panel still open, click the Play (Reports) icon to relaunch the Reports dialog box.

2. Select the Entire Current Local Site option from the Report On menu.

3. This time, enable the Design Notes check box and click the Report Settings button to open the Design Notes dialog box, similar to Figure 9.17.

FIGURE 9.17   The Design Notes dialog box allows you to filter by specific property within Design Notes.

4. With the dialog box open, enter the text **ManHours** into the first text box, choose the Matches Regex option from the menu, and enter the text **>=8** into the last text box. Click OK.

5. Click Run.

Again, the Site Reports tab in the Results panel displays the results of the filtered query. In this case, because man hours (ManHours) are (Matches Regex) greater than or equal to the numeric value of 8 (>=8), the `index.html` file is shown within the Site Reports panel.

Recently Modified Reports

The final workflow report available to you is that of generating reports on files that have been recently modified. To generate this type of report, follow these steps:

1. With the Reports dialog box open, select the Entire Current Local Site option from the Report On menu.
2. Click the Recently Modified check box.
3. Click Run.

The Results panel will display files that have been modified within the past seven days. Notice that a web page containing a list of files that that have been recently modified also appears (see Figure 9.18). The nice part of this page is that it's sortable, allowing you to sort based on files within the page. Even better, you can print this page out and file it for your records.

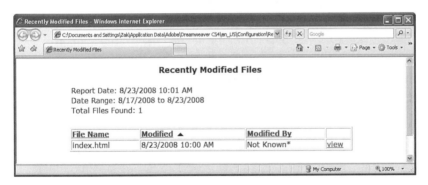

FIGURE 9.18   Files that have been modified within the past seven days are displayed within the Results window and on a new HTML page.

In this scenario, we checked the Recently Modified option and clicked Run. Doing this gives us all files that have been modified within the defined site in the past seven days. To run a report filtered by a different date range, follow these steps:

1. With the Site Reports panel still open, click the Play (Reports) icon to relaunch the Reports dialog box.
2. Select the Entire Current Local Site option from the Report On menu.
3. This time, click the Recently Modified check box and click the Report Settings button to open the Recently Modified dialog box, seen in Figure 9.19.
4. With the Recently Modified dialog box open, select the Files Created or Modified in the Last option and enter **1** into the Days text box. Click OK.

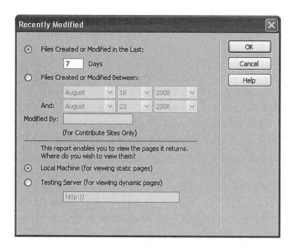

FIGURE 9.19   The Recently Modified dialog box allows you to filter by a specific date range.

5. Click Run.

In this case, the requested report returns no results because nothing was modified in the last day. Other options available in the Recently Modified dialog box include the following:

▸ **Files Created or Modified in the Last**—Enter a number in this text box to report on all files modified within the number of days you specify.

▸ **Files Created or Modified Between**—Select a month, day, and year range to report on all files that have been modified within a specific time frame. As an option, you can also enter a username to limit your search to specific Contribute users who have recently modified files. This text box becomes enabled only when the site has been configured to run with Contribute. We'll discuss Contribute in more detail in the next chapter.

▸ **Report View**—Select one of these option buttons to indicate where you want to view files listed in the report. Options include Local Machine (default) and Testing Server.

Implementing Source Control with Visual SourceSafe

As you saw in the beginning of this chapter, Dreamweaver outlines functionality that allows you to use file Check In and Check Out within its framework. The functionality and implementation is simple; you check out a file within Dreamweaver and then the program automatically locks it by creating a duplicate of the filename with an LCK extension.

This LCK file contains the username and email address of the user who has checked out the file. This way, when someone else defines the same site, the LCK file is read into Dreamweaver, and the user is alerted to the file's checked-out status in the expanded Files panel. Although this process works well if your organization exclusively uses

Dreamweaver, it wouldn't be the ideal solution if you work in large, enterprise-level environments where different departments could potentially be using programs other than Dreamweaver.

For instance, whereas the marketing and web development departments could be using Dreamweaver, the engineering group could be using something different in Microsoft's Visual Studio. Executives and admins could make simple edits to web pages using Microsoft Word, and network administrators might use Microsoft Expression Web to edit web-based network documentation and FAQs. You can begin to see that a train wreck is imminent. A company executive might dislike the wording on his/her bio and instruct the admin to edit the page. With Microsoft Word in hand, the admin could open the page and make edits. Word, not recognizing the LCK file association, would proceed with the modification. Even worse, anyone with access to the web server could easily go into the folder that contains the LCK files and delete them. To avoid a scenario such as this, you and your organization might decide to integrate a more robust, enterprise-level source control and versioning software package, such as Microsoft's Visual SourceSafe.

Available for the relatively low price of $50–$100, SourceSafe is an excellent third-party source control and versioning package that you can easily tie right into Dreamweaver. At its heart, SourceSafe functions much like Dreamweaver in that you can check out, make changes to, and then check in files. Beyond the simplicities of Dreamweaver, however, SourceSafe also integrates versioning so that at any time during development, you can revert back to an older version of the same file, also known as *rolling back*. Furthermore, SourceSafe uses its own proprietary database, effectively preventing prying eyes from viewing and making changes to files. On top of these benefits, SourceSafe includes features for comparing code (line by line) for one version of a file to any older checked-in version of the same file.

With all this said, you still might be a bit foggy as to whether you need source control and versioning software. In general, keep the rules outlined in Table 9.1 in mind when making decisions about purchasing source control and versioning software.

TABLE 9.1   Keep These Rules in Mind When Deciding to Use Source Control in Your Organization

Organization Size	Rule
1 developer	Source control is not immediately necessary.
2–6 developers	Dreamweaver's integrated source control will suffice.
6 or more developers	You might want to think about purchasing/using a product such as Visual SourceSafe, CVS (Mac), or Subversion.

NOTE

The most popular versioning software for OS X is Concurrent Versions System (CVS), which is an open-source (free) alternative to Microsoft's Visual SourceSafe for Mac users. There are many places on the Internet to obtain CVS, but the most convenient method is by installing the Xcode tools located on your OS X Install DVD. Every copy of OS X ships with CVS. Just like SourceSafe, you can roll back to past versions of files you're working on and restore them should you make a modification that you later realize was unwanted. For detailed information on setting up CVS on OS X, with a strong slant toward both static and interpreted web development (HTML, PHP, Perl, and so on), look no further than http://developer.apple.com/internet/opensource/cvsoverview. html. Additionally, if you want a free alternative to Visual SourceSafe and are running Windows, an option might be Subversion control, discussed later in this chapter.

Dreamweaver's integration with SourceSafe is simple. Although you'll still be required to set a Local folder path, the Remote path will be set up to point to your SourceSafe database.

NOTE

This book isn't intended to cover the installation procedure for SourceSafe. Instead, it's assumed that your organization already has SourceSafe installed and that you have read/write access to the organization's main SourceSafe database.

To configure Dreamweaver to work with SourceSafe, let's start by configuring SourceSafe on the server. You can do this by following these steps:

1. Start by logging in to the SourceSafe database. When the Visual SourceSafe Login dialog box appears, enter your credentials and click OK.

2. Right-click the database root ($/) and select the Create Project option, as shown in Figure 9.20 (my Visual SourceSafe installation resides on a PC running Vista).

3. When the Create Project dialog box appears, enter the name **VectaCorp** and click OK. The new VectaCorp project will appear under the root.

4. Open the folder that contains the remote files either for your organization or for Vecta Corp and drag all the files (the Assets folder, Images folder, and root files) into the project within SourceSafe.

5. When the Add File dialog box appears, click OK.

6. When the Add Folder dialog box appears, enable the Recursive check box (see Figure 9.21). This option adds all folders and files within that folder to SourceSafe without your having to add everything one by one.

7. Right-click the Vecta Corp project in SourceSafe and choose the Check Out option. The Check Out VectaCorp dialog box appears. Enable the Recursive check box (Figure 9.22) and click OK.

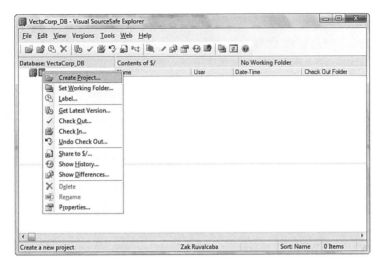

FIGURE 9.20   Create a new project in the database root.

FIGURE 9.21   Add files and folders into the project in SourceSafe.

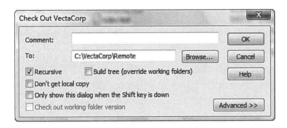

FIGURE 9.22   Check out all the files within SourceSafe.

8. Now that all the files are checked out, we'll check them back in, but we'll remove the local copy from the Remote folder. This will ensure that all file references are contained within SourceSafe exclusively. To do this, right-click the project in SourceSafe and click the Check In option.

9. When the Check In dialog box appears, enable both the Recursive and Remove Local Copy check boxes, as illustrated in Figure 9.23, and click OK.

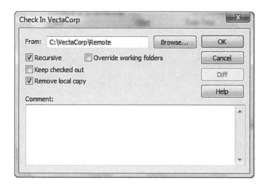

FIGURE 9.23   Check all the files back in using recursion and remove the local copy.

With that done, the files are removed from the file system and are stored exclusively within SourceSafe. We're now ready to move back to the local development machine and start configuring Dreamweaver to use SourceSafe. Before we do, however, make note of the SourceSafe database path. Mine is as follows (but yours will differ): `C:\Program Files\Microsoft Visual SourceSafe\Databases\srcsafe.ini`. This is the path that you will need when defining the site within Dreamweaver.

Now let's configure Dreamweaver. You can do this by following these steps:

1. With Dreamweaver open, select the Manage Sites option from the Site menu. The Manage Sites dialog box appears.

2. Select the VectaCorp site and click Edit. The Site Definition for the VectaCorp dialog box appears.

3. Although your Local info should remain the same, the Remote Info will change to coincide with the SourceSafe configuration. Select the Remote Info category.

4. Select the Microsoft Visual SourceSafe option from the Access drop-down menu.

5. Click the Settings button. The Open Microsoft Visual SourceSafe Database dialog box appears.

6. Within the Database Path text box, enter or browse to the path to the `srcsafe.ini` file on your server. In my case, the path to my INI file on the remote computer is `C:\Program Files\Microsoft Visual SourceSafe\Databases\srcsafe.ini`.

7. Enter the Vecta Corp project name within the Project text box. This text box should read: $/VectaCorp.

NOTE

In SourceSafe, the "$/" signifies the root of the database's folder structure, similar in concept to Window's C:\.

8. Enter the Username and Password (this is the username and password you created when installing SourceSafe; if your network administrator installed SourceSafe, you will need the administrator to provide it for you) to log in to the SourceSafe database. When you've finished, the configured dialog box will resemble Figure 9.24.

FIGURE 9.24   Configure access to the SourceSafe database using the Open Microsoft Visual SourceSafe Database dialog box.

9. Click OK to close the Open Microsoft Visual SourceSafe Database dialog box.

10. Click OK to close the Site Definition for VectaCorp dialog box.

11. Click Done to close the Manage Sites dialog box.

Now expand the Files panel, if necessary, by clicking the Expand/Collapse icon. With the window open, click the Connect icon to open the SourceSafe database in the Remote pane. Now you can right-click files and select the Check Out option to check out files from Visual SourceSafe exclusively to you.

By using SourceSafe, you're relying on a third-party utility to store your files within a database. The obvious benefit in doing this is that you're not relying on Dreamweaver's creation of a LCK file to manage a file's read-only/write state. A third-party source control solution such as Microsoft's Visual SourceSafe offers a more robust alternative to using Dreamweaver's simple file system-based methods.

Using WebDAV

Up until this chapter, we've discussed File Transfer Protocol (FTP) as the primary method for transferring files from the local computer to the remote computer. What many developers don't realize, however, is that FTP has its disadvantages, specifically the following:

▶ Using FTP requires that you open additional ports on your firewall, which can increase the attack surface of your network and make it more susceptible to penetration by attackers.

▶ FTP has no file-locking mechanism, so it's possible for two users to upload different versions of the same file simultaneously, causing one to be overwritten.

▶ The FTP approach means you have to edit your content locally on the client. In other words, to edit a page already on the web server, you must download it to the client, edit it there, and then upload it again to the web server. This is a time-consuming and inefficient approach to managing content.

The solution to these problems is WebDAV, an alternative protocol used for publishing and managing content to web servers. An extension of the HTTP/1.1 protocol, WebDAV overcomes the three issues previously described as follows:

- ▶ WebDAV uses port 80, the same port used by HTTP for web access. Therefore, using WebDAV means you don't have to open any extra ports on your firewall.

- ▶ WebDAV lets only one user modify a file at a time, while allowing multiple users to read it. This approach allows files to be locked while they are being edited, preventing unexpected changes from occurring.

- ▶ WebDAV lets you edit files on the server instead of needing to download them first to the client. Editing files remotely using WebDAV is as easy as if they were locally present, and the whole process is transparent to the content producer.

Aside from these benefits, WebDAV is easy to configure and begin working with. Although we won't cover installation of WebDAV on the remote web server, we will discuss how to connect to, publish, and remotely modify content using WebDAV within Dreamweaver. Before we begin configuring Dreamweaver to use WebDAV, we'll want to do two things on the server. (If you do not have access to the server and your system administrator has already given you the path to the folder that you'll use to publish using WebDAV, skip down to the next section discussing WebDAV and Dreamweaver integration.)

> **NOTE**
>
> WebDAV can be installed and configured on numerous operating systems running a variety of web servers. Because this section isn't meant as an introduction to WebDAV installation on the broad range of web servers, I'll quickly cover the steps using Windows Server 2003/IIS as an example.

First, we'll want to make sure WebDAV is enabled. If you don't have access to the remote WebDAV installation, check with your system administrator. Second, we'll want to create a new virtual directory within your web server so that we can publish files to it using WebDAV. Again, if you don't have access to your remote web server, check with your system administrator. Your system administrator will be able to tell you whether WebDAV is enabled. If it is, the administrator should be able to create a new WebDAV-enabled folder for you by following the process outlined next. Let's walk through this process now:

1. Open the IIS installation on your server and select the Web Server Extensions option (assuming your web server is running on Windows Server 2003).
2. Make sure that the WebDAV option is listed and allowed. If it's prohibited, click the Allow button.
3. Now expand the Web Sites tree node, right-click the Default Web Site node, and choose the Virtual Directory option available from the New submenu.
4. When the Virtual Directory Creation Wizard appears, click Next.
5. Enter the alias name **VectaCorp** and click Next.

6. Browse to the VectaCorp path on the server and click OK. Click Next.

7. Enable the Read, Run, Write, and Browse option and click Next.

The new virtual directory will now be created in IIS. This is the directory (WebDAV enabled) to which we will be publishing.

With the server configured to use WebDAV, you're now ready to configure Dreamweaver. You can configure Dreamweaver to use WebDAV by following these steps:

1. With Dreamweaver open, select the Manage Sites option from the Site menu. The Manage Sites dialog box appears.

2. Select the Vecta Corp site and click Edit. The Site Definition for Vecta Corp dialog box appears.

3. Although your Local Info should remain the same, the Remote Info will change to coincide with the WebDAV configuration. Select the Remote Info category.

4. Select the WebDAV option from the Access drop-down menu.

5. In the URL text box, enter the URL to the virtual directory. In my case, the WebDAV-enabled Vecta Corp virtual directory is located on a remote web server running Windows Server 2003 and is located at the following path:
   `http://zakswebserver/VectaCorp/`, where `zakswebserver` represents the web server's default root and `VectaCorp` represents the WebDAV-enabled virtual directory created within the web server's root in the previous steps.

6. Now enter your login, password, and email into the respective text boxes. When you've finished configuring the dialog box, it will resemble Figure 9.25.

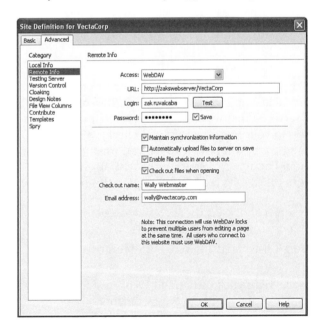

FIGURE 9.25   Configure the WebDAV Connection dialog box.

7. Click OK to close the WebDAV Connection dialog box.

8. Click the OK button to close the Site Definition for Vecta Corp dialog box.

9. Click Done to close the Manage Sites dialog box.

Now expand the Files panel, if necessary, by clicking the Expand/Collapse icon. With the window open, click the Connect icon to open the WebDAV-enabled folder in the Remote pane. Now you can right-click files and select the Check Out option to check out files exclusively to yourself.

Using Subversion Control

Unlike Microsoft's Visual SourceSafe (which costs money), CVS (which works only on a Mac), or WebDAV (which must be supported by the remote web server), Subversion is a third-party source control and versioning product that is gaining steam in terms of popularity and usage among developers. With this latest version of Dreamweaver, Adobe heeded the call that developers have been making for years—that is, full support for a true source control and versioning product that is not operating system-specific, as is the case with CVS (Mac) and Visual SourceSafe (Windows). And while Dreamweaver still maintains its support for these and other products, Subversion is unique in that it can be installed and used on virtually any type of server and environment. Whether you're using Windows, UNIX, Linux, or Mac OS X, Subversion can be easily installed and implemented with Dreamweaver. Additionally, Dreamweaver has full support for Subversion, allowing you to maintain copies of all of your project files, maintain backups of project files, perform comparisons of multiple files, check files in and out, and more. Subversion is also ideal in single-developer scenarios, as it allows you to maintain project histories, separating each version of a project so that you can roll back/recover a previous version of a project with ease.

Setting up Subversion is no easy task. Most of the software uses the command line and is definitely not for the faint of heart. Due to the lengthy procedures for installing and configuring Subversion, I'll instead refer you to the official documentation located at http://subversion.tigris.org/faq.html. If you know you have Subversion installed and ready to go, then follow instructions outlined next to connect Dreamweaver to your Subversion server and begin working:

1. Begin by starting the Subversion server if it's not already started. You can do this by opening a command prompt and typing the following line: `svnserve -d -r "c:\svn_repository"`. Don't close the command prompt; instead simply minimize it.

2. Now switch over to Dreamweaver and choose Site, Manage Sites. Choose the defined VectaCorp site and choose Edit. The Site Definition for VectaCorp dialog box appears.

3. Choose the Version Control category and pick the Subversion option from the Access menu. Choose the SVN option from the Protocol menu. Enter **localhost** in the Server Address text box. Enter /**VectaCorp** in the Repository Path text box. Enter your username and password for logging into the Subversion server in their respective text boxes. The configured dialog box will resemble Figure 9.26.

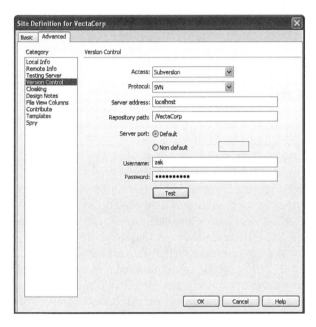

FIGURE 9.26   Configure Dreamweaver's Version Control category to use Subversion control.

4. Click OK to close the Site Definition for VectaCorp dialog box. Immediately Dreamweaver will alert you to the fact that the VectaCorp project directory doesn't exist within the Subversion server. Click the Yes button to create it now.

You're now ready to begin using the source control and versioning features built into Dreamweaver for use with Subversion. However, before we get to those features, notice one unique aspect about the Files panel. Look closely and you'll see that all of the files within your Files panel have the plus (+) icon next to them, similar to Figure 9.27. This is because the project on the Subversion server is new, and the files haven't been checked in yet.

To check your files into Subversion, right-click on the main project folder and choose the Check In option from the context menu that appears. Immediately the CheckIn dialog box appears, similar to Figure 9.28.

Click Commit to add all of the files to Subversion now. Although it might not be immediately noticeable, your files are now committed to and managed by Subversion. To give you an idea of how this works, try double-clicking on a file in the Files panel. A dialog box immediately appears asking if you'd like to open a copy of the file in read-only mode (View), or if you'd like to open a copy of the file so that you can make edits to it (Make Writeable). Choose the Make Writeable option to open the file.

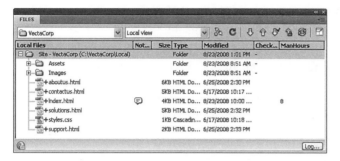

FIGURE 9.27   Your files within the Files panel have a plus (+) icon next to them because they need to be checked into Subversion.

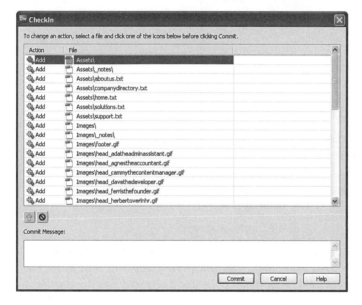

FIGURE 9.28   The CheckIn dialog box allows you to check in files or your entire project into Subversion.

Now that your project is managed by Subversion, let's take this time to outline some of the features built into Dreamweaver for working with Subversion. Specifically, the following options become available to you from within the Version Control subdirectory that becomes available when you right-click the project or file within the Files panel:

▶ **Get Latest Versions**—Gets the latest version of a file from Subversion. You'll want to perform this operation often, usually before working on a file in Dreamweaver.

▶ **Update Status**—Simply refreshes the current status of the file on your system.

▶ **Mark As Resolved**—This option marks your local copy of a file as current if there are conflicts with the versions of a file. Conflicts usually occur when you and someone in your collaborative team make changes to the same file. You must then resolve those conflicts manually using a file comparison program.

▶ **Show Revisions**—As shown in Figure 9.29, you can use the Show Revisions dialog box to examine versions of a file. Additionally, you can use this dialog box to examine any stored version of a file (View), compare a stored version of a file to your current local copy (Compare to Local), compare two versions of the same file using your file comparison program (Compare), or promote a revision to the current working version, which will overwrite your most recent file (Promote to Current).

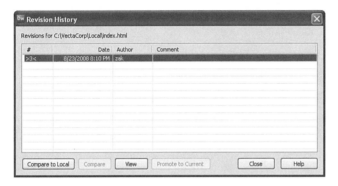

FIGURE 9.29   The Show Revisions dialog box allows you to examine stored versions of a file, compare stored versions of a file with your local copy, and more.

▶ **Lock/Unlock**—Use the Lock and Unlock options to lock or unlock files from modification by other members of your collaborative team.

▶ **Go Offline**—Disconnects you from the Subversion server.

▶ **Clean Up**—When Subversion modifies a working copy of a file, it tries to perform this operation as safely as possible. Before changing anything, it writes its intentions to a log file, executes the commands in the log file, and then removes the log file. If a Subversion operation is interrupted, the log files remain on disk in a virtual state of limbo. The Clean Up operation searches your working copy and runs any leftover logs, removing any locks in the process. This ensures that your current file and revisions of that file in Subversion are always in a consistent state. If Subversion ever tells you that some part of your working copy is "locked," then this is the command that you should run.

Dreamweaver developers have long been waiting for a true source control and versioning platform that is easy to use, and more important, available on multiple operating systems. With Subversion and its integration with Dreamweaver, developers now have that platform. And although the integration with Subversion is still not perfect, it's a giant step in the right direction.

Summary

Dreamweaver supports numerous options for working in collaborative teams. Whether you're simply generating reports, maintaining Design Notes, or implementing built-in and third-party source controls options, it's hard to argue that Dreamweaver's team collaborative integration isn't solid.

Throughout the chapter, we discussed numerous options for working with teams—specifically, using simple file Check In and Check Out, maintaining Design Notes, using site reports, sharing file view columns, and integrating the third-party source control option in Microsoft's Visual SourceSafe, the open source WebDAV, or Subversion. In the next chapter, we'll take our collaborative efforts one step further and discuss Adobe's solution for content management in Contribute.

CHAPTER 10

Managing Website Content Using Contribute

Publishing content for the Web is becoming increasingly easy. In fact, most word processing applications now allow you to save a document as an HTML file. Because most people are quite capable of opening a word processor and selecting the Save As option from the File menu, publishing web-based content will continue to grow exponentially on a year-to-year basis. With so many web development editors and even pseudo editors (Word, WordPad, WordPerfect, Pages, and so on) on the market today, it's nearly impossible to impose any sort of standards-compliant method for creating and distributing content on the Web. Of course, it becomes much easier to require particular methods when working in corporate environments because organizations can set limitations concerning the web-publishing software that a company is allowed to use. Unfortunately, drawbacks still exist. If the software you decide to use is enterprise-level, such as Dreamweaver, the need for training can still pose a major concern. Let's face it: Although Dreamweaver is a powerful tool for performing any web-related task, it's definitely overkill for the administrative assistants who simply want to change a few words in an executive's web-based biography. On the other hand, if the software is easy to use and lightweight, the needs of the company might not get met because the functionality provided by the software might not be enough to fulfill the company's needs. This is where a program such as Adobe's Contribute plays a role.

Contribute is an inexpensive and lightweight, although still powerful, alternative to buying multiple licenses of more expensive enterprise tools such as Dreamweaver for users who might not need something so muscular. Even better, Contribute solves the dilemma outlined in the previous chapter of accidentally overriding a previous user's work. As you'll see throughout this chapter, Contribute solves the content-management needs of organizations by revealing an easy-to-use, efficient, and enterprise-level web publishing alternative.

Like the rest of the chapters within this book, you can work with the examples in this chapter by downloading the files from the book's website. You'll want to replace the files in `C:\VectaCorp\` with the files that you download for this chapter. Like the previous chapter, the files for this chapter are divided into two folders: Local and Remote. Contribute, like the topics we discussed in the previous chapter, relies on local files and remote files.

Content Management Using Contribute

As a slimmed-down version of Dreamweaver, Contribute makes it easy for anyone to connect to a website, make edits to it, and then publish changes, all without having to learn much more. If you know how to type a URL into the address bar of a browser, you can connect to a site using Contribute. If you can type and save text in a word-processing document, you can make changes within Contribute, and if you know how to click a button (I'll assume that you are quite capable of doing that), you can publish edited content within Dreamweaver.

Contribute is the perfect alternative for users in an organization whose primary role isn't to create, edit, and publish web pages. For instance, in our organization, we might want to allow Cammy the Content Manager, Tina the Tech Writer, and Ada the Administrative Assistant, access to specific parts of our website, but only to make simple changes. For the organization, this has two benefits. The first and most obvious one is that we don't have to buy three more licenses of Dreamweaver for users who otherwise might not use its full potential; instead, we can buy three licenses of Contribute at a much lower price. Second, it allows you, the site administrator, to police who has access to which sites, what kind of access they have, and even to ensure that pages you've created won't be accidentally over-written by someone who has limited experience. As an example of how users within our fictitious Vecta Corp company will be publishing content within our site, take a look at the diagram in Figure 10.1.

As you can see from Figure 10.1, Wally the Webmaster, Pat the Programmer, and Dave the Developer can continue to use Dreamweaver to publish content to the company's website. Ada the Administrative Assistant, Cammy the Content Manager, and Tina the Tech Writer, however, can use Contribute because their roles are limited to simple text-based changes and edits. With that said, let's walk through the process of deciding who within our organization needs Contribute and then install the application.

Installing Contribute

For the most part, installing Contribute is just as easy, if not easier, than installing Dreamweaver. The tougher task initially is deciding who within the organization needs it. As a general rule, consider the circumstances outlined in Table 10.1.

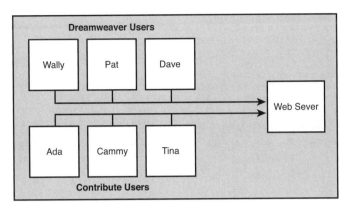

FIGURE 10.1   Developers within our organization can continue to use Dreamweaver, and those with limited web-development experience will use Contribute.

TABLE 10.1   Deciding Who Needs Dreamweaver, Contribute, or Both

User	Role	Application(s)
Wally	Site administrator. Will make changes to all pages within the website and also delegate Contribute roles.	Dreamweaver and Contribute
Pat and Dave	Developer and programmer for the website. They need full access to all pages within the site.	Dreamweaver only
Tina, Cammy, and Ada	On occasion, these people will need to make simple changes to specific pages on the website.	Contribute only

Knowing what we know now about the users of and contributors to our site, we can come to the conclusion that Wally, Tina, Cammy, and Ada will need Contribute installed on their computers. You might be wondering why Wally needs Contribute installed if he'll be using Dreamweaver for making changes on the website. Dreamweaver allows you to administer and delegate users and roles directly from within the Site Definition dialog box, but for this functionality to work, Contribute has to be installed along with Dreamweaver. Next, let's walk through the process of installing Contribute on Tina's, Cammy's, Ada's, and your (Wally's) computers:

1. If you haven't purchased a copy of Contribute and would like to try it out, you can download a 30-day evaluation version from Adobe's website at www.adobe.com/downloads/.

2. Assuming that you've downloaded the trial software, double-click the Zip file to extract the installer.

3. Double-click the installer to begin the installation.

4. When the Welcome screen appears, click Next.

10

5. Accept the user license agreement and click Next.

6. Choose the folder that you want Contribute to be installed into and click Next.

7. Choose options for creating desktop and QuickLaunch shortcuts, set accessibility for either yourself or for any users of your computer, and click Next.

8. In the Confirmation screen, click Install to proceed with the installation.

That's all there is to it! Of course, in our scenario, we'd want to repeat these steps for every Contribute user. Because we're assuming the role of Wally the Webmaster for this chapter, we're set to go.

Administrating Contribute-Enabled Sites in Dreamweaver

Again, because we're assuming the role of Wally the Webmaster, our next step will be to enable Contribute compatibility for our Vecta Corp website. After that's done, we'll want to set roles and delegate permissions for specific users (namely Ada, Cammy, and Tina). To enable Contribute compatibility for the Vecta Corp site, follow these instructions:

1. Assuming Dreamweaver is open, select the Manage Sites option from the Site menu. The Manage Sites dialog box appears.

2. Choose the Vecta Corp site from the list and click Edit. The Site Definition for Vecta Corp dialog box appears.

3. Select the Contribute category and select the Enable Contribute Compatibility check box. Immediately, Dreamweaver displays the Contribute Site Settings dialog box. Within this dialog box, enter your full name and email address. This is the information that Contribute will share with other users on your collaborative team. After you've made those edits, click OK to close the dialog box.

NOTE

For Dreamweaver to accept the check box selection, FTP must be the configured option within the Remote Info category. If you have a different access method specified, you will need to configure this first. Additionally, for Contribute compatibility to work, Design Notes must be enabled. Contribute, like many other features in Dreamweaver, relies on Design Notes for storing critical information about files.

---

4. After your name and email address have been specified, Dreamweaver displays two read-only labels (Rollback and CPS), the Site Root URL text box, and the Administer Site in Contribute button. Enter the name of the URL for your organization's website in the Site Root URL text box. For Vecta Corp, that URL will be **http://www.vecta-corp.com/vc/**. Obviously, your organization's URL will be different.

NOTE

Remember, in our Vecta Corp scenario, the Local computer is represented as each individual developer's personal folder on his or her computer, and the Remote folder is the physical location of the Vecta Corp files on the remote web server. For Contribute purposes, however, we'll need to enter the site root URL or, more specifically, the URL that outside users will use to view the Vecta Corp site (http://www.vectacorp.com/vc/).

5. Click Test to force Dreamweaver to check connectivity. After Dreamweaver connects to the Contribute site, a message similar to the one shown in Figure 10.2 appears. If you're unable to connect, revisit the Remote Info category and make sure that your FTP settings are correct.

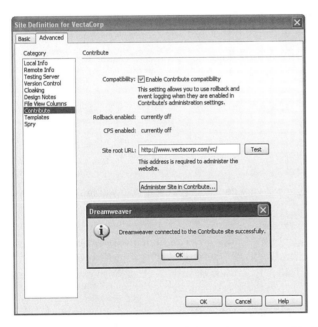

FIGURE 10.2   Test the connection to the site root URL. If Dreamweaver can connect, it will display a message confirming a successful connection.

10

With the Site Root URL in place, we're technically finished, although we've yet to delegate permissions for Contribute users. Before we do that, let's review the location of our files and the architecture we're dealing with here. You can follow along by reviewing the diagram in Figure 10.3.

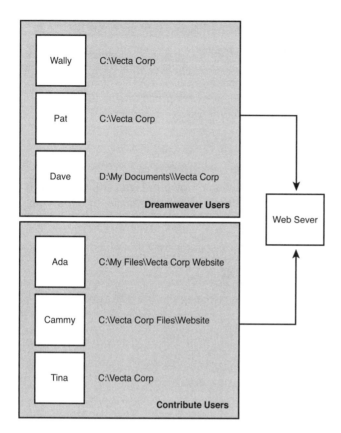

FIGURE 10.3   The Contribute architecture will vary depending on your role within the organization.

As you can see from Figure 10.3, the Local root folder for each Dreamweaver user will differ depending on where the user wants the local files stored. The remote files are located on the web server in the same folder regardless of user, accessible to everyone who has permissions.

We'll now want to delegate roles and permissions for our Contribute users. But first let's review the Contribute administration integration within Dreamweaver. To launch the Contribute Site Administrator, click the Administer Site in Contribute button located just below the Site Root URL text box in the Contribute screen. Immediately, Dreamweaver launches a dialog box similar to the one in Figure 10.4, asking for two things: whether to use standard word processing or Dreamweaver-style editing when making text-based changes within web pages.

First and foremost, the dialog box reveals two option buttons allowing you to determine whether pressing Enter/Return key renders a line break or a paragraph break in Contribute. These options are detailed next:

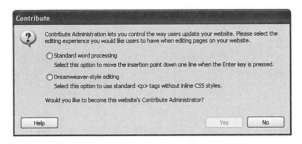

FIGURE 10.4   The Contribute Style and Site Administration Chooser allows you to determine whether the Enter/Return key renders a line break or a paragraph break when pressed. It also allows you to set yourself as the site's administrator.

> **Standard Word Processing**—Select this option if you want to treat the Enter/Return key the way it is in word processors. Whenever a user presses Enter/Return, the cursor is brought down to the next line and an HTML <br /> tag is created.

> **Dreamweaver-Style Editing**—Select this option if you want the Enter/Return key to be treated the same way it would be in Dreamweaver, as a <p> tag addition. Users will have to know to press Shift+Enter/Shift+Return to go to the next line.

Let's assume that our content contributors are total novices. We'll choose the Standard Word Processing option. Dreamweaver then asks whether you want to become the site's Contribute Administrator. Click Yes, and the Administer Website dialog box (Figure 10.5) appears.

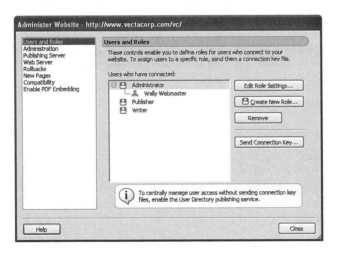

FIGURE 10.5   The Administer Website dialog box allows you to create roles, edit existing roles, and send connection keys.

As you can see from Figure 10.5, the dialog box is broken down into the following categories:

▶ Users and Roles

▶ Administration

▶ Publishing Server

▶ Web Server

▶ Rollbacks

▶ New Pages

▶ Compatibility

▶ Enable PDF Embedding

To gain a firm understanding of each category, let's discuss each in more detail, beginning with creating new users and roles.

Defining Users and Roles

The driving force behind the Site Administration dialog box is the Users and Roles screen, shown in Figure 10.5. Use this screen to create new Contribute roles, edit properties for existing roles, and add new users to a role by sending them a connection key file (discussed later in the chapter). As you can see from Figure 10.5, roles are broken down into the following three categories by default:

▶ **Administrator**—The administrator has unrestricted access to the site within Dreamweaver *and* Contribute. The administrator sets roles, settings for roles, and gives access to Contribute users. The administrator can also edit and publish content freely using both Dreamweaver and Contribute.

> **NOTE**
>
> You are not limited to assigning only a single administrator—you can add as many administrators as you want.

▶ **Publisher**—Users defined as publishers have permission to modify and publish content from within Contribute but cannot set roles and permissions. Administrators can edit settings for the Publisher role so that users with this role can insert only images and edit and publish text, essentially preventing publishers from rearranging the overall look of the site within Contribute.

▶ **Writer**—Users defined as writers have limited access. In fact, writers can modify only text. Rather than publishing the text when they're finished making changes, they send drafts to either administrators or publishers for review. The publisher or administrator can then decide to either publish, reject, or send the file back to the writer for review/changes.

Other features in this screen include the capability to edit settings for an existing role, create a new role, remove existing roles, and send connection keys. Although we can live with the existing roles, let's edit the Publisher role so that publishers can't insert their own images into a web page. We'll assume that the company's design is set in stone and that we do not want to allow anyone to make changes to it. To edit settings for the Publisher role, select the Publisher role from the list and click the Edit Role Settings button. The Edit Publisher Settings for Vecta Corp dialog box will appear as they do in Figure 10.6.

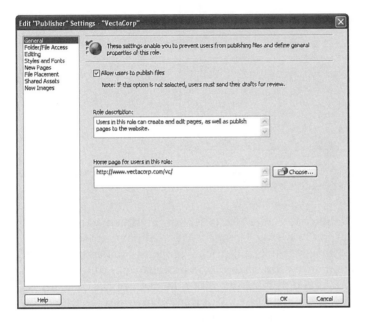

FIGURE 10.6   Use the Edit Role Settings dialog box to configure particular options for an existing role.

As you can see from Figure 10.6, the Edit Role Settings dialog box is divided into the following categories:

► **General**—Use the General screen, shown in Figure 10.6, as a way to enable or disable the selected role's capability to publish content to the live site. You can also create a text-based description of what the role can and can't do and set the default home page (maybe a directory within the main site) for users of that role. For our purposes, we'll leave the options as they are.

► **Folder/File Access**—Use the options shown in Figure 10.7 to set specific folders that users can edit. Because we want users to be able to edit all HTML files, we'll leave the options as they are. By default, Dreamweaver doesn't allow users to delete files even if they have permission to do so. If you want to allow users to delete files, enable the Allow Users to Delete Files They Have Permission to Edit check box.

10

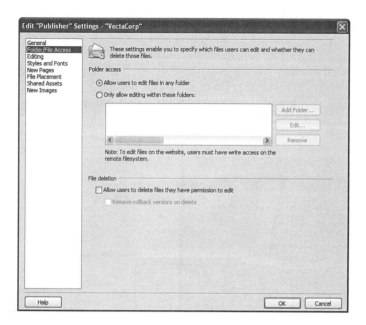

FIGURE 10.7 Use the Folder/File Access screen to enable only specific folders within the site root and allow users permission to delete files.

▶ **Editing**—Use the options shown in Figure 10.8 to set how users interact with the development environment in Contribute. Options include editing restrictions (including the addition of images), paragraph spacing properties similar to the ones set when the Administration screen first opened, and miscellaneous editing options, including accessibility options and third-party options. Remember, our company is strict about the overall look of the website, so we'll want to allow users only within specified roles to make text edits and formats. You can do this by selecting the Only Allow Text Editing and Formatting option button (shown selected in Figure 10.8).

▶ **Styles and Fonts**—You can use options available within this screen as a way of setting what kind of styles users can apply to elements within pages in Contribute. For instance, we can set preferences that restrict the addition of styles to those contained within the styles.css file located within the root of our Vecta Corp directory. To do this, enable the Show Only CSS Styles Included in This CSS File option button and browse to the CSS file located in the root of the Vecta Corp directory. Also, disable the Allow Users to Apply Fonts and Sizes, the Allow Users to Apply Bold, Italic, Underline, Strikethrough, and Fixed Width Styles, and the Allow Users to Apply Font and Background Color check boxes. Setting these properties forces users to implement styles (within the styles.css file) as set by the marketing department and perhaps outlined within a corporate style guide of some sort. The result of the changes made to this screen will resemble those in Figure 10.9.

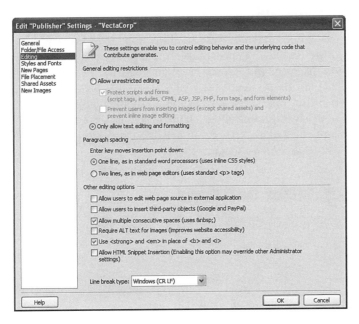

FIGURE 10.8 Use options in the Editing screen to set how users interact with editing features in Contribute.

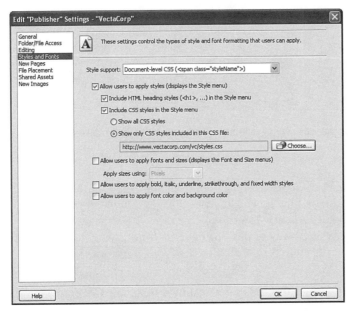

FIGURE 10.9 Use options in the Styles and Fonts screen to set what kind of style properties can be applied to pages within Contribute.

▶ **New Pages**—Use the powerful options in this screen to dictate how users can create new pages. For instance, you may or may not want to allow users to create new pages. If you do, you'll want to disable the check boxes and also decide whether to use Dreamweaver templates (discussed in Chapter 12, "Working with Templates and Library Items"). If you decide not to use templates, make a specific page or set of pages available to users when they open the New Document dialog box. If you want to restrict the creation of new pages, disable all check boxes in this screen. Because our content editors will simply be making changes to existing pages, we'll disable all these options. The result will look similar to Figure 10.10.

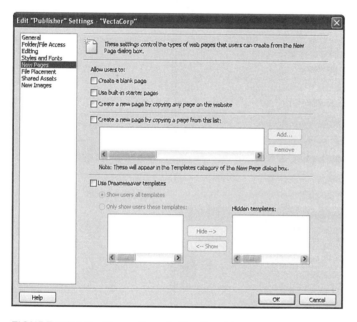

FIGURE 10.10 Use options in the New Pages screen to restrict or allow the creation of new pages within Contribute.

▶ **File Placement**—The File Placement screen (shown in Figure 10.11) outlines properties that allow you to configure how users add styles, images, Microsoft files, PDF files, and so on to existing documents. You can also cap the size of pages that users try to link to. This is an excellent way of preventing users from linking to pages that are inaccessible because of the sheer size of the page. For our purposes, we'll leave this screen as is.

▶ **Shared Assets**—You can use the list in this screen (shown in Figure 10.12) to add, edit existing, and remove shared asset allocations for the site. For instance, your company might make a Flash file available for use on all company web pages. If that's the case, you'll want to add that shared asset to the list in this screen so that users in a particular role can add that asset to their pages. Again, we'll leave this screen as is.

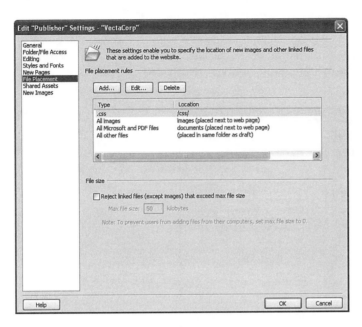

FIGURE 10.11   Use properties in the File Placement screen to limit the types of files added to pages in Contribute. You can also use this screen to cap the size of pages linked from existing pages.

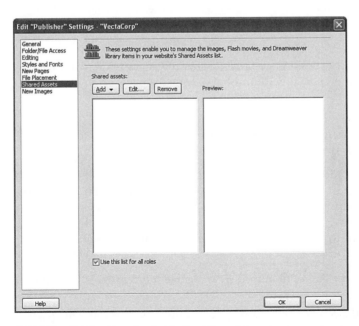

FIGURE 10.12   Use the list in the Shared Assets screen to share assets across roles.

▶ **New Images**—Use the options in the New Images screen (shown in Figure 10.13) to set default options exposed when images are added to pages in the site. You can also set a cap (in KB) on images inserted on pages. Because we've prevented users from adding images to pages in this site, these options are disabled.

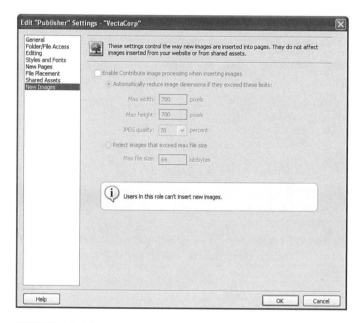

FIGURE 10.13   Use options in the New Images role to set how images are inserted into the page in Contribute.

When you've finished configuring options for the Publisher role, click OK to commit the changes to the role and return back to the Administer Website dialog box.

Administration

You can use options in the Administration screen (shown in Figure 10.14) to set the default email and password for the administrator of the site.

You can also remove administration for the site (for instance, if you no longer need to manage the site in Contribute) by clicking the Remove Administration button. Because we set ourselves as the site administrator (as Wally) when this screen first appeared, our email is carried over from Dreamweaver and added into the Contact Email Address text box in this screen. What we still want to do, however, is set an administrator password. To do that, follow these steps:

1. Click the Set Administrator Password button. The Change Administrator Password dialog box appears.

2. Enter a password into the New Password text box and then re-enter the same password in the Confirm New Password text box.

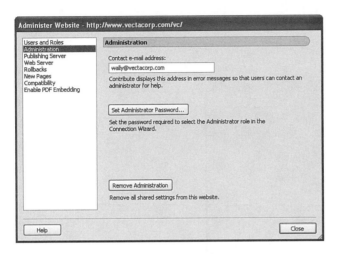

FIGURE 10.14 Use the Administration screen to configure the default email and password of the site administrator.

3. Click OK.

That's it—you've now password-protected the administration screens for this site.

Publishing Server

Out of the box, Contribute relies on the administrator to manually set folder permissions for the site on the server. Although this can easily be done using the operating system's file explorer, it becomes a hassle and is generally inconvenient when setting permissions for hundreds of users. Fortunately, operating systems such as Windows will set the default permission to allow everyone access to a particular folder when it's first created. This is the reason we are allowed to add users freely in the Contribute Administrator dialog box. The downside to this freedom is that it doesn't prevent users from manually entering the folder on the server and moving, deleting, or adding new files. In the real world, allowing everyone access to the company's files on the web server would be unthinkable. Generally, the head of your IT department would lock down the folder on the web server containing all the organization's web files to everyone in the organization except one or two people. In situations such as these, it wouldn't make a lot of sense for the IT administrator to manually set permissions to allow scores of potential users access to a website folder on the server; you'd be at your desk all day just configuring roles and adding users in Contribute—and then you would have to verbally communicate to the IT administrator which people require access to the particular folder on the server.

To solve this dilemma, Contribute has introduced Publishing Services. Part of the Web Publishing System suite, Publishing Services is an administration tool that ties into your company's folder and security administration interface (LDAP or Active Directory). Publishing Services provides a centralized interface, accessible from the screen shown in

10

Figure 10.15, where you can add users to a role and then assign permissions to them for the site folder.

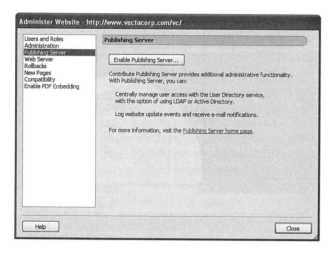

FIGURE 10.15   You can use Publishing Services as a centralized mechanism for setting folder permissions.

It's important to note that Publishing Services is a separate product from Contribute. If you'd like more information on Publishing Services, visit www.adobe.com/products/ contribute/server/. In our examples, we'll keep it simple and just rely on the folder permissions that are already in place.

> **NOTE**
>
> You probably noticed the text label that appeared in the Contribute category in the Site Definition dialog box for the Contribute Publishing Service. This text label displays the status of Contribute Publishing Service if it is on.

Web Server

You can use the options in the Web Server screen (Figure 10.16) to configure Contribute and Contribute users to work with your web server.

For instance, options exist for setting alternative URLs that Contribute users could potentially access. Generally, you will see URLs listed in two ways: by domain name and by IP address. Although both addresses work for connecting to the web server, Contribute uses this list to allow or deny access to the web server if a user types in what appears to be a valid address that is not listed.

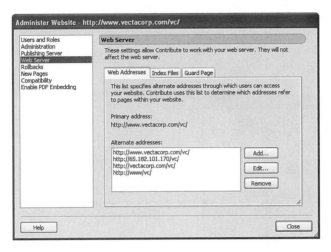

FIGURE 10.16   Use the options in the Web Server screen to configure Contribute and Contribute users to work with your web server.

The second tab on this screen allows you to work with options for setting default pages within the web server. For the most part, the web server uses a traditional list of index files. If your default file is not listed (maybe it's called mypage.html), you must manually add it here.

The final tab in this screen allows you to specify a *guard page*. Use the guard page as a way to prevent users from accessing the _mm folder (automatically added to the site when working with Contribute) directly from Dreamweaver or Contribute. By default, Contribute sets the guard page to the main page in the directory (usually index.html, default.html, home.html, and so on.). For our purposes, there shouldn't be anything we need to modify here.

> **NOTE**
>
> The _mm folder is where Contribute keeps files that are being reviewed or worked on. When a user edits a page in Contribute, a working copy is placed into this folder. Technically, the user is making changes to the file that resides in the _mm folder, not the file that's live on the site. After a file is approved/published, Contribute then copies the files from the _mm folder and overwrites the previous copy on the live server.

10

Rollbacks

Rolling back web pages is the process of going back to a previous version of a web page after it has been published. For instance, assume Cammy the Content Manager makes a few changes to a page in the website and then, using Contribute, publishes her finished work. By default, Contribute stores a copy of the previous version in a _baks folder within the _mm folder root. As an administrator, you decide to review Cammy's work and happen to find glaring errors. Rather than bringing the site down to fix the mistakes, you can right-click (Control-click) the file in the Files panel and choose the Roll Back Page option. Dreamweaver, interfacing with Contribute, digs the old version out of the _baks folder and replaces the live version with the older, accurate version. You can enable rollbacks and specify the number of rollback steps in the screen shown in Figure 10.17.

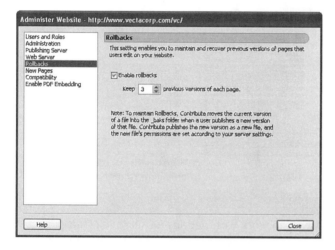

FIGURE 10.17   You can enable rollbacks by simply clicking the check box. You can also set a numeric value indicating the number of times to roll back.

This is a feature I always implement in my sites. It's a handy mechanism to have—especially if you accidentally delete a file or simply want to revert to an older version. To enable this feature, click the check box. Keep the number of rollback steps at 3.

CAUTION

Be mindful of the number you set for rollbacks. Each rollback version consumes storage space on the server. If you're limited on server storage space, you might think about keeping this number as low as possible or even disabling the feature altogether.

NOTE

You probably noticed the text label that appeared within the Contribute category in the Site Definition window for Rollbacks. This text label will display the status of rollbacks when it's enabled or disabled for the Contribute-enabled site.

New Pages

Similar to the document encoding screen within the Page Properties dialog box in Dreamweaver, you can use the New Pages screen, shown in Figure 10.18, as a way to set the document encoding that should be used for your web pages in Contribute.

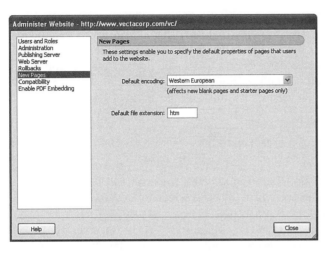

FIGURE 10.18   Set the document encoding type and the default extension of the page when a new page or template is created within Contribute.

You can also set the default file extension to use when creating new pages from a blank page or template in a site. Again, we'll keep this screen as it is.

Compatibility

The Compatibility screen, shown in Figure 10.19, lets you provide editing and publishing access to older versions of Contribute.

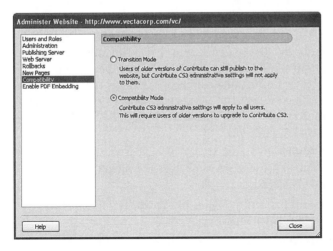

FIGURE 10.19   Set a method of Contribute interoperability in the Compatibility screen. You can decide whether to have newer versions and older versions of Contribute work together.

10

Selecting the Transition Mode option allows you to share features between previous and current releases of Contribute. Be aware, however, that only shared features are interoperable. Choose the Compatibility Mode option when you want to isolate all features exposed by newer versions of Contribute from older versions. Users who use an older version of Contribute will be required to install the most current version. Because in our example we know everyone will be using the same version of Contribute, keep the Compatibility Mode option button selected.

Enable PDF Embedding

The final set of options within the Administration screen is the Enable PDF Embedding option button group. You can use the options within this screen as an Administrator to restrict users from embedding PDF documents as objects in a web page. If users are allowed to insert embedded PDF objects, they can choose to insert the document either as a link or as an embedded PDF. However, if users are not allowed to embed PDF objects, they only have the option to insert the PDF document as a link.

Sending Connection Keys to Contribute Users

Now that you've successfully configured properties for the Publisher role, it's time to delegate access to the three Contribute users (Ada, Cammy, and Tina) within our company. This can be accomplished easily by sending *connection keys*. Taking the form of an STC file accessible from the Users and Roles category, the connection key can either be opened or imported into Contribute by the end user and contains all the necessary configuration information our three users will need to successfully connect to the Vecta Corp website as publishers. To send a connection key, follow these instructions:

1. Within the Administer Website dialog box, switch to the Users and Roles category and click the Send Connection Key button. The Send Connection Key dialog box appears, shown in Figure 10.20.

2. As you can see from Figure 10.20, the first screen within the wizard allows you to set how you will send the connection settings to the individual Contribute users. Options include the capability to send the same connection settings that you use (excluding role information) or to configure the connection settings differently for Contribute users. For our purposes, choose Yes, enable the Include My FTP Username and Password check box, and click Next.

3. The next screen in the wizard (shown in Figure 10.21) allows you to set the type of role that the invited users will have. Because we want to create three Publishers, select the Publisher option and click Next.

4. The third screen within the wizard (shown in Figure 10.22) allows you to set the method for sending the connection key file (STC file).

   Options include sending the STC file as an attachment via email or saving the STC file to your computer. If you select the email option, Contribute creates a nice email template and automatically attaches the encrypted STC file to the body of the email.

This is the option we'll select. Second, you'll want to enter a password that Contribute users will use to decrypt the emailed STC file. After it is decrypted, the STC file becomes usable within Contribute. For security reasons, you'll want to verbally communicate the decryption password to Contribute users. Enter a password now (I'll enter **vectacorp**) and click Next.

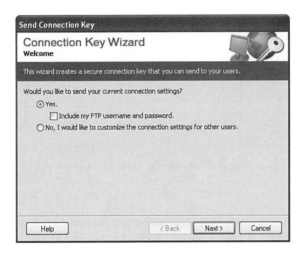

FIGURE 10.20   The Send Connection Key dialog box allows you to create and send connection keys.

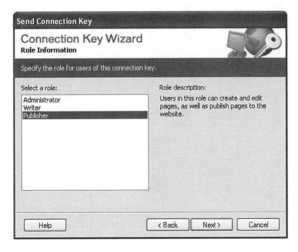

FIGURE 10.21   Set the type of role that invited users will have.

5. The final confirmation screen allows you to perform a final check on the settings to be emailed to the Contribute users. Double-check your settings and click Done.

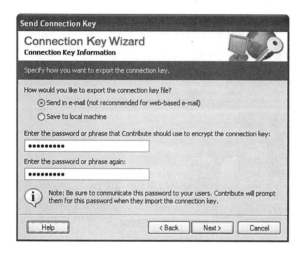

FIGURE 10.22   Choose an option from this screen to either send the connection key in an email or to save it to your computer.

6. As you can see from Figure 10.23, the connection key is attached as an STC file to the Contribute-generated email template. In the To field, enter all the email addresses that this email will be sent to and click Send.

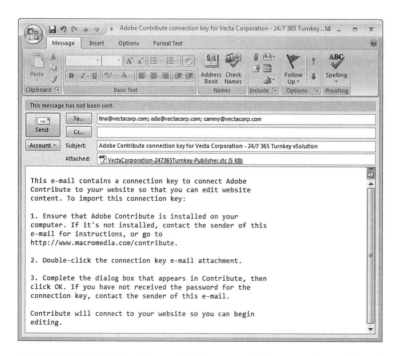

FIGURE 10.23   Enter the email addresses of the users that will receive the connection key and click Send.

That's it! You've effectively sent the connection key to users within your organization. The next step is for the receiving users (Ada, Cammy, and Tina) to check their email and open the connection key within Contribute. After they've done this, they'll be able to make edits to the Vecta Corp site within Contribute.

Using Contribute to Make Basic Edits

Assuming the role of Ada, Cammy, or Tina, we'll now walk through the process of opening the connection key within Contribute. After the key has been imported into Contribute, we'll use the program to make basic edits to the Vecta Corp site and then publish our changes to the web server. To import the connection key into Dreamweaver, you can do one of two things: You can double-click the STC file from the email, or you can open Contribute and click the Import button from the My Connection dialog box (available from the Edit menu in Contribute). To make things easy, we'll use the first option. To open the key in Contribute, follow these steps:

1. To get the full effect of how connection keys work, try using a completely different computer and logging in with the account that has access to the email account that contains the Contribute connection key. If you don't have access to a second computer, that's fine—simply double-click the STC connection key file. Contribute opens and the Import Connection Key dialog box appears, similar to Figure 10.24.

FIGURE 10.24   Double-click the connection key file. Contribute will open and the Import Connection Key dialog box appears.

2. Assume that I'm logged into Ada's computer. Notice the dialog box shown in Figure 10.24; it allows me to enter my name, my email, and the secret decryption key (that I specified as **vectacorp**). Add the unique information for the first user, entering **Ada** for name, **ada@vectacorp.com** for email, and **vectacorp** for the

password and click OK. As you can see from Figure 10.25, the dialog box disappears and the Vecta Corp site opens within Contribute.

FIGURE 10.25   The Import Connection Key dialog box disappears and the Vecta Corp page appears within Contribute.

3. To see the defined connection for the Vecta Corp site, choose the My Connections option from the Edit menu. The My Connections dialog box appears, similar to Figure 10.26. You'll see that the website Name, Address, Role, and Administrator values appear, as they've been defined, in the row.

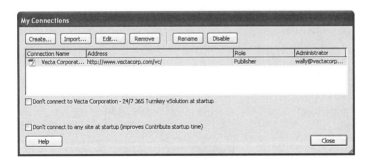

FIGURE 10.26   The defined Contribute site appears within the My Connections dialog box.

4. To close the My Connections dialog box, click Close.

As a content contributor, you're now ready to make changes to the Vecta Corp site using Contribute. To do this, click the Edit Page button at the top-left corner. Immediately, the page opens in Edit Mode, shown in Figure 10.27, with the same structure it had when it was defined in Dreamweaver.

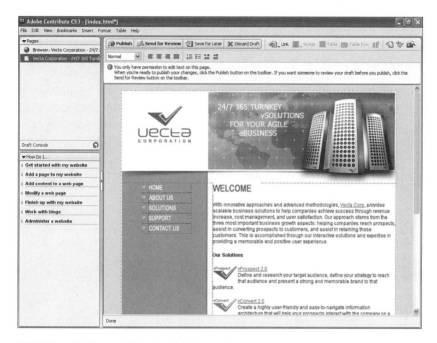

FIGURE 10.27   Clicking the Edit Page button launches the Vecta Corp website in Edit Mode.

Try making changes to the page (remove rows from tables, remove images, and so on). You'll quickly realize that all you're allowed to do as a publisher is edit text. Of course, this is by design. As an administrator, you edited the publisher role to allow only text edits. To demonstrate how easily text edits can be made, I'll highlight the last sentence of text within the opening paragraph and press the Delete key.

With the text now gone, you have two options for saving: You can publish the page to the live server by clicking the Publish button, or you can send the page for review by clicking the Send for Review button, located just to the right of the Publish button. Doing this allows content managers or site administrators to review your changes and then approve or reject them before they go live.

10

NOTE

Had we created users under the writer role, the Publish button wouldn't be available. Instead, the writer would have to send the content for review and allow either a publisher or site administrator to approve or reject the changes.

For our purposes, click the Publish button. Dreamweaver displays a Contribute dialog box informing you that the changes have been published to the live server. Click OK to see the final results within the Browser view.

Rolling Back Pages in Dreamweaver

Assuming the role of the Site Administrator once again, assume for a moment that the change Ada just made is unacceptable. Under these circumstances, you might want to roll back the change to its original version. Because we've enabled the Roll Back Page option in the Rollbacks category in the Administer Website dialog box, this will be possible. Before we walk through the process of rolling back a design, let's reopen the Administer Website dialog box (assuming it's not already open) so that you can see the addition of the new user within the Publishing role. When you open the Administer Website dialog box, shown in Figure 10.28, you'll see the new user (Ada) in the Publisher role.

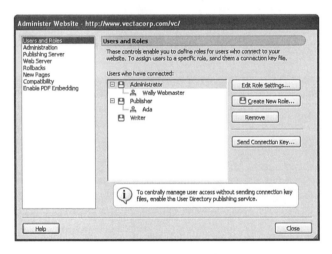

FIGURE 10.28   The new content publisher (Ada) appears within the Publisher role.

To remove this user, you would select the user's name and click the Remove button. Although we're certainly angry with Ada for making unacceptable changes to the site, we don't want to remove her from the publisher list. Instead, we'll roll back her changes. To do this, follow these steps:

1. If you haven't done so already, close the Administer Website dialog box by choosing the Close button. Close the Site Definition dialog box by choosing the OK button.

2. To see the changes Ada has made to the pages on the live server, we must synchronize the files on the remote server with those on our local computer. To do this from within Dreamweaver, select the Synchronize Sitewide option from the Site menu. The Synchronize Files dialog box appears.

3. Select the Entire Vecta Corp Site option from the Synchronize menu. Choose the Get Newer Files from Remote option from the Direction menu and click Preview.

4. When the Preview dialog box appears, make sure the `index.html` file is listed and click OK. The files should now be synchronized.

5. Now open the local copy of `index.html`. You'll notice that the changes Ada sent to the site have indeed been made.

6. To roll back the page, close it from the document window, check it in (right-click/Control-click on the file within the Files panel and choose the Check In option), and then click the Expand/Collapse icon from the Files panel, if necessary, to expand it.

7. Now right-click (Control-click) the `index.html` file in the Remote Site pane to access the context menu and click the Roll Back Page option. The Roll Back Page dialog box appears, similar to Figure 10.29.

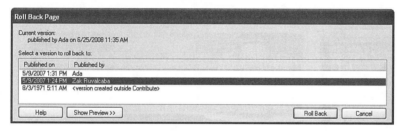

FIGURE 10.29   The Roll Back Page dialog box displays older versions of the design.

8. Select the version you want the page to be rolled back to (by date or name) and click the Roll Back button.

Now view the site in the browser. You'll notice that the original page replaces the one Ada created.

Summary

As you have seen, Contribute is a powerful program that allows organizations to share web-based publishing rights with users who wouldn't ordinarily be given access to the site using Dreamweaver. Contribute allows site administrators to feel comfortable with nontechnical users making changes to the company's online presence because they can ratchet down the number of options available to the user within the Administer Website dialog. Even better, through Contribute's draft review process and Dreamweaver's rollback feature, changes can easily be reverted back to their original state with little or no harm to the company's overall identity.

In the next chapter, we'll begin to move away from the team collaborative aspects of Dreamweaver and begin to review some of the task automation features built into Dreamweaver's framework.

10

CHAPTER 11

Enhancing Workflow

As you've seen, Dreamweaver outlines numerous features for simplifying the development and management of your websites. Features such as the Site Files panel, File Check In and Check Out, CSS integration, the Insert panel, Contribute integration, and so on all make Dreamweaver's support unmatched for designing web pages unassisted or within teams. In this chapter, we'll discuss some of the simple, yet sometimes overlooked, nuances that further improve how you work with your websites in Dreamweaver. As we progress through the chapter, we'll discuss asset management using the Assets panel, simple find and replace using the Find and Replace dialog box, pinpoint reversal of changes using the History panel, and task automation using various commands. The features that we discuss in this chapter should further support the notion that Dreamweaver is unprecedented in its support for creating spectacular websites effortlessly.

Like the rest of the chapters within this book, you can work with the examples in this chapter by downloading the files from the book's website. You'll want to replace the files within C:\VectaCorp\ with the files located in Exercises\ Chapter11\Beginning\.

Working with the Assets Panel

Similar in concept to the Assets folder we defined within the root of our Vecta Corp site, the Assets panel is a central repository for website components. However, unlike the Assets folder contained within our Vecta Corp project, the Assets panel contains items that our website can and will use. Items such as images, Shockwave files, QuickTime files,

Flash files, JavaScript files, and even colors and links are all considered assets and are all managed in the Assets panel by Dreamweaver. By having access to these items in one central location, you're offered the benefit of quick access to any one of these items in Dreamweaver. No more shuffling around, searching for the same content in the local root folder. Furthermore, the Assets panel offers a Favorites feature that allows you to filter out more commonly used assets. Often, websites have thousands of assets—and for the most part you're not going to need immediate access to all of them at the same time. In this situation, the Favorites feature allows you to store more commonly used items, such as a company logo, colors that you've been using throughout the site regularly, or even commonly used hyperlinks that you use most often, into a small subsection of items.

> **NOTE**
>
> Because the Assets panel more or less indexes all your site's content, you must have a local root folder already defined. Dreamweaver then scans the files within your defined site and makes them visible within the appropriate categories in the Assets panel.

To open the Assets panel, choose the Assets option from the Window menu or press F11 (Option-F11 on a Mac); or, if you have the Files panel already open, simply choose the Assets tab located just to the right of the Files tab. As you can see from Figure 11.1, the Assets panel comes into view.

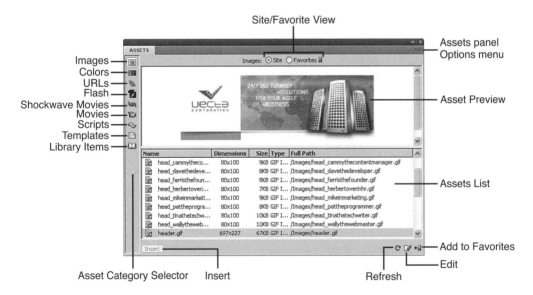

FIGURE 11.1   The Assets panel is a central repository for usable items within your defined site.

11

As you can see from the callouts in Figure 11.1, the Assets panel is divided into separate sections:

▶ **Asset Category Selector**—The Assets panel is a repository for different types of usable items within your site, including images, links, colors, media files, library items, and so on. All these items are divided into categories represented by the vertically listed icons in this menu.

▶ **Assets List**—The lower-middle portion of the panel is a list of all the assets within the site for the particular category.

▶ **Preview**—The top portion offers a preview of the selected asset in the list.

▶ **Site/Favorite View**—Choose an option from this group to either display every asset within your defined site or only those assets that you've manually added to your Favorites list. This option is discussed in more detail later in the chapter.

▶ **Panel Options menu**—Like every other panel in Dreamweaver, the Assets panel Options menu gives you quick access to alternative options. Options listed within this menu include the capability to copy an asset to another defined site, locate an asset within the site, refresh and re-create the site list, and more.

▶ **Insert, Refresh, Edit, Add to Favorites icon group**—Use the icons listed in here to insert a new asset into your document, refresh your site list, edit an asset within the appropriate internal or external editor, and add an asset to the Favorites list.

As you've probably noticed, the Asset Category Selector within the Assets panel lists several types of icons, each representing the different types of assets that are managed within the panel. These options include the following:

▶ **Images**—Any image that is stored within your defined site, such as JPEG, GIF, or PNG, will automatically be added to the images assets list. In our scenario, the Assets panel will read all the images located within our Images folder because that's where all our images happen to be contained.

▶ **Colors**—This category contains all the colors used throughout your site, including background colors, link colors, text colors, and so on.

▶ **Links**—This category lists all the external links used throughout the site, which include absolute paths such as http, https, ftp, and even other URLs used by JavaScript, email (mailto), and local file links.

▶ **Flash**—This section stores all your SWF files. Any SWF file found within your defined site will appear here.

▶ **Shockwave Movies**—Any Shockwave movie (SWD), typically generated by Director, that is found within your local root folder or defined site will be available in this section.

▶ **Movies**—This section stores movie files such as QuickTime, Real Media, Windows Video, MPEGs, and more that are found within your defined site.

▶ **Scripts**—This category will contain external scripts found within your defined site. It's important to note that only *external* script documents appear in the Assets panel. Scripts written within the <head> tag of your HTML pages are not listed here.

▶ **Templates**—Templates can add a great deal of consistency and organization within a site design. You can access all your site templates here. Templates are covered in great detail in the next chapter.

▶ **Library**—In the Library section of the Assets panel, you can create, access, and manage a site's Library items. Library items are similar to templates in terms of their functionality; however Library items are single components that are meant to be used throughout the entire site (such as navigation bars). Library items are also covered with more detail in the next chapter.

NOTE

For the most part, Dreamweaver automatically scans your defined site and picks out the assets it can work with. You can always use the Cloak feature to prevent Dreamweaver from scanning files located within a particular folder. The Assets folder (remember, separate from the Assets panel), for instance, is an excellent candidate for cloaking. For the most part, the Assets folder in our site contains PSD, FLA, TXT, and DOC files that we can't use within our site anyway. Cloaking this folder would prevent Dreamweaver from scanning that folder and importing any unneeded files into the Assets panel.

How the Assets Panel Works

Now that you have a simple understanding of what the Assets panel provides, it's important to understand how the Assets panel works. The Assets panel neither scans the structure of your site every time Dreamweaver is opened, nor does it scan the structure of your site when you open the Assets panel. Instead, the Assets panel, like many of the other features within Dreamweaver, works off of the site's cache. In Chapter 3, "Dreamweaver Site Management," we discussed that the site cache was Dreamweaver's way of taking a digital "snapshot" of the folder and file structure of your site. Many features in Dreamweaver—namely the Check Links feature, the Site Map feature, and more importantly the Assets panel—rely on this snapshot for quick and efficient management of files. Therefore, it's important that this feature is enabled when you're defining or editing a site within Dreamweaver. If your Assets panel isn't listing items, chances are you've disabled the Site Cache check box. To re-enable it, follow these steps:

1. Select the Manage Sites option from the Site menu. This launches the Manage Sites dialog box.

2. Select the Vecta Corp site and click the Edit button. The Site Definition dialog box appears.

3. Be sure the Advanced tab is selected and you're in the Local Info category. Click the Enable Cache check box located toward the bottom of the Local Info screen, as shown in Figure 11.2.

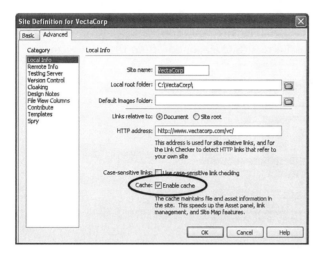

FIGURE 11.2   Enable the site cache in the Site Definition dialog box to ensure that your assets will appear in the Assets panel.

4. Click OK to close the Site Definition dialog box. Immediately Dreamweaver scans the files within your site and closes the Site Definition dialog box.

5. Click Done to close the Manage Sites dialog box.

For the Assets panel to display your site assets, you'll want to refresh the panel. This process is outlined next.

Refreshing the Assets Panel

At some point in the development of your website, you'll find that you'll need to refresh the Assets panel so that the content is being displayed correctly. The Assets panel automatically updates every time you restart the site, but if you're in the middle of a project, that's not the case. That's why there's a Refresh button, located in the bottom portion of the panel, as shown in Figure 11.3.

There are numerous instances when you'd need to update or refresh the Assets panel, such as the following:

▶ If you exported a graphic from Fireworks or Photoshop into the local root folder while Dreamweaver was running. In this scenario, you would need to refresh to make that content viewable in the Assets panel.

▶ If you use the Site Files panel to remove an asset, which would ultimately delete the file from the defined site, you would need to refresh the Assets panel to see the change.

▶ If you deleted an image or asset outside of Dreamweaver, such as in Windows Explorer, you would not only have to refresh the Assets panel for it to reflect the change, but you will also have to re-create the entire site cache. To re-create the entire site cache, you can access the Assets Panel Options menu located in the top-right corner of the Assets panel and choose Recreate Site List, as shown in Figure 11.4, or you can hold down the Ctrl (⌘) key while clicking the Refresh icon within the icon bar located near the bottom of the panel. Finally, you can right-click (Control-click) in the Assets panel and choose the Recreate Site List.option from the context menu.

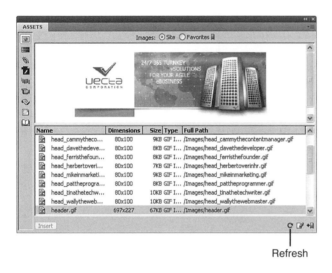

Refresh

FIGURE 11.3   The Assets panel has a Refresh button to ensure that the most up-to-date content is being viewed.

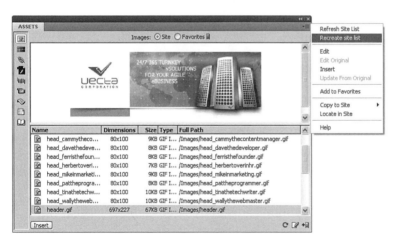

FIGURE 11.4   Use the Options menu in the Assets panel either to refresh the Assets panel or re-create the site list.

▶ If you've deleted some files that contain the only or last instance of a color or link asset, you should refresh the Assets panel to completely remove the color references from the Assets panel.

Inserting Assets into Your Web Pages

A couple of methods exist for inserting assets into your documents. What you want to insert will determine which method you should use. By far the simplest method of inserting an asset is to highlight the asset in the Assets panel and click the Insert button located near the bottom-left of the panel. Doing this inserts the asset at the point at which your cursor was placed.

Alternatively, you could drag an asset out of the Assets panel and drop it into a spot within your document. To try this, follow these steps:

1. Create a new document by choosing File, New. The New Document dialog box appears. Select Blank Page, HTML, <none>, and click Create.

2. Make sure your Assets panel is open. To open the Assets panel, choose the Assets option from the Window menu, press F11 (Option-F11), or select the Assets tab if the Files panel group is open.

3. Now select the Images category within the Assets panel, if it's not already selected. Remember, this is the first icon in the category group along the left side.

4. You can browse through the images, looking at the previews within the Asset panel's preview window. When you find one that you're happy with, select it.

5. With the image selected, click and drag the graphic into the page. After you let go of the mouse button, the image will be added to the page.

Another way to get assets into your page, as I mentioned earlier, is to select the asset and click the Insert button on the Assets panel. This technique is important, especially when applying links to images or colors to text. To apply links to an existing image, follow these steps:

1. Select the image that you've just added within the document.

2. With that image selected in the document, switch to the Link category in the Assets panel (the third icon down in the Category group). As you'll see, you should only have one link asset (the mailto link that exists on the support page).

3. To attach the link to the image, click the Apply button (formerly the Insert button). The link text field of the Property inspector now shows the link you applied to the graphic.

It doesn't stop there. You could also apply colors to elements on the page, apply links to text, drag media files into the page, and so on. The possibilities are limited only by the types of assets in your site.

Customizing the Assets Panel

The Assets panel was incorporated into Dreamweaver to enhance workflow. The Dreamweaver development team knew that for workflow to be enhanced, it was important to allow people to customize features to better suit their work habits. The Assets panel is no exception. One of the more important workflow features within the Assets panel is the

Favorites list. This list can save you a tremendous amount of time shuffling through thousands of images, links, and so on. A section in this chapter titled "Adding Assets to Your Favorites" covers the process in greater detail.

Another option you have for customizing your experience with the Assets panel is changing the listing order of the assets. For example, switch to the Images category in the Assets panel. As you'll notice, the default listing order is alphabetical, from A to Z for the name or value of the asset. If you click the Name title header in the Assets panel, you flip the order from ascending (A to Z) to descending (Z to A). You can click any one of the headers to sort the list by that particular category. For example, if you wanted to sort by the smallest to largest file size, click the Size header; if you wanted to sort by the type of asset, click the Type header, and so on.

You can further customize the appearance of the Assets panel by resizing the columns. To do this, hold your mouse pointer directly over the line dividing the columns. When the mouse pointer changes into a two-way arrow, click and drag the dividers in whichever direction you want to resize the columns. By resizing the columns, you can see additional content, such as the type and possibly the full path of the asset within your computer.

Managing Your Assets

Now that you've been working with assets, let's look at how you can manage them in your own sites and how you can share them with other sites. Often, you'll be working in a site and wishing you could have access to another site's assets. This is not an unreasonable request—it will just take a few steps of preparation. To copy assets from one site to another, follow these steps:

1. Select the assets you want to copy in the Assets panel. To select multiple assets, you can either hold down the Ctrl (⌘) key while clicking the assets of your choice, or hold down the Shift key to select a range of items.

2. Right-click (Control-click) the asset within the list, or you can access the Options menu in the top-right corner of the Assets panel. In the menu, choose Copy to Site, as shown in Figure 11.5.

3. When you choose the Copy to Site option, a submenu appears offering all the possible sites you can copy the assets into. Choose the site that you want the selected assets to be available in. These files will then be copied into the site's corresponding folders. If the site does not contain the same folders for the files to be copied into, the folder will automatically be created to accommodate the assets.

Copying assets to other sites is that simple! Open the site into which you copied the assets to make sure that they appear in the Assets panel on that site; keep in mind that you might have to refresh the panel.

Another concern you might have when working with Assets is where the actual files are located. As you know, you can always see the path on the far right side of the Assets panel. Alternatively, you could use the Locate in Site option as a quick way of forcing the cursor to the file within the File's panel. When you choose the Locate in Site command, Dreamweaver opens the Files panel and highlights the location of the selected files in the Assets panel. As Figure 11.6 illustrates, I have two images selected in the Assets panel as I right-click and choose the Locate in Site command from the context menu.

FIGURE 11.5   With assets highlighted, you can copy them to other sites by choosing the Copy to Site command in the context or Options menu.

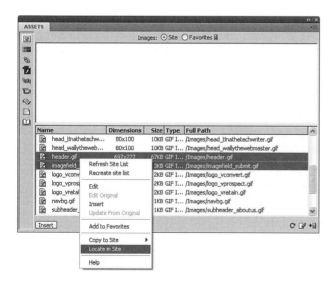

FIGURE 11.6   By right-clicking (Control-clicking) the highlighted asset, I have the option to choose the Locate in Site command to find those files within the Files panel.

As Figure 11.7 shows, the Files panel appears with the selected files highlighted within the list.

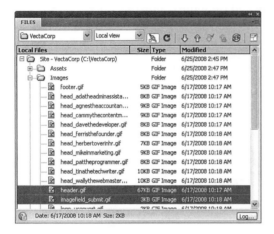

FIGURE 11.7   After I choose the Locate in Site command, the Files panel highlights the location of the selected assets.

Editing Assets

After using an asset, you might decide that you want to edit some of its properties within an external editor. For example, if you need to update an image, you can change or edit that image within the external editor of choice with a simple click of a button. To edit an image asset, do one of the following:

▶ Highlight the image in the Assets panel and click the Edit icon located near the bottom-right corner of the panel in the icon group. This action automatically launches the default editor for that file format.

▶ The second technique is a bit quicker. Double-click the asset icon. Doing this also launches the default editor for that file type.

▶ A third method is to right-click (Control-click) the asset within the Assets panel and choose the Edit option from the Context menu.

Although this process seems simple, it's not that intuitive for unsourced assets, such as links and colors. These assets aren't actually linked to a physical item on your computer; therefore, when you edit them, they'll only be updated in the Assets panel for future use. If you want colors and links to be updated in the same way that images are, you'll need to work with library items, discussed in the next chapter.

To edit assets such as colors and links, they must be contained within the Favorites section of the panel. When you click the Favorites option button, your favorite colors and links will be revealed. To add something to your Favorites list, refer to the following section of this chapter. When you have the color you want selected, click the Edit button and the Color Picker appears below the color name, as shown in Figure 11.8.

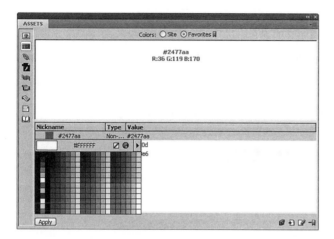

FIGURE 11.8   The Color Picker appears inside the Assets panel when you're editing a color. The color has to be located under the Favorites portion of the panel.

If the Color picker is open, and you decide you no longer want that color, press Esc to close the Color picker without changing to a new color.

Editing a link is very similar: Highlight the link and click the Edit button at the bottom-right corner of the panel. This action opens the Edit URL dialog box, as displayed in Figure 11.9, which allows you to specify a new URL.

FIGURE 11.9   When you edit a link, the Edit URL dialog box is launched.

> **NOTE**
>
> As you've seen, color and URL assets can be edited only when listed under your Favorites. The reason for this is primarily because changes made here are global. If you were to accidentally make a change to a color or URL asset, all elements in the site that use that asset would be affected. To prevent accidental global edits, Dreamweaver requires you to add it to your Favorites (covered next) and then edit the Favorite.

Adding Assets to Your Favorites

By adding assets to your Favorites, you can greatly increase productivity. When you're dealing with the Assets panel for an entire website, the content often can become unwieldy. Many times, while navigating through the Assets panel, you're looking for a specific file that you use frequently. Instead of having to search for these files again and again, you can store them in a Favorites list, offering more direct access.

There are several ways to add assets to a Favorites list. You can use any one of the following techniques:

▶ Highlight the asset or assets you want to add to the Favorites, and in the Assets panel's Options menu, choose Add to Favorites (see Figure 11.10).

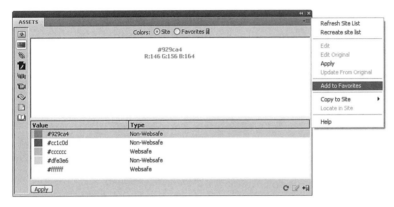

FIGURE 11.10   You can add an item to your Favorites by selecting the asset and choosing Add to Favorites from the Assets panel's Options menu.

▶ Select the asset or assets that you would like to add to the Favorites and right-click (Control-click) in the Assets panel. In the context menu, choose Add to Favorites.

▶ Select the assets you want to add to the Favorites list and click the Add to Favorites icon, located at the bottom-right of the Assets panel in the icon group.

▶ Highlight an asset already placed within a document, right-click (Control-click) the item, and choose Add to Image Favorites from the context menu, as shown in Figure 11.11.

Removing Favorites

You can easily remove an asset from your Favorites list by following these steps:

1. Select the Favorites option button in the Assets panel.

2. Select or highlight the asset you want to remove.

3. Click the Remove from Favorites icon (where the Add to Favorites icon was), located in the icon group near the bottom of the panel. You can also right-click (Control-click) the asset in the panel and choose Remove from Favorites in the context menu. Finally, with the asset selected, you can also press the Delete key on your keyboard.

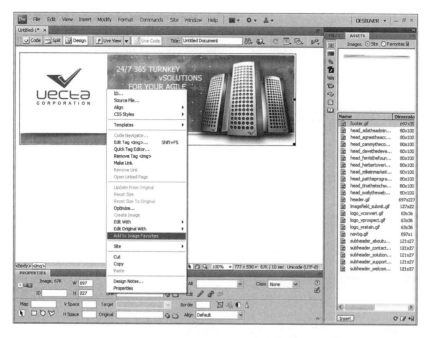

FIGURE 11.11   You can also add an item to the Favorites by right-clicking (Control-clicking) an instance within the document.

NOTE

When deleting favorites, you're not actually deleting the file from your site; rather, you are just removing a text-based reference of that asset from the Favorites list.

Creating Folders to Organize Favorites

Another way to manage your favorite assets is to organize them into separate folders. Doing so affords you the opportunity to organize by attributes other than the categories specified by the Assets panel. For example, in your Images category, you can create several folders for the different types of images. You could create a folder called Headshots, which would contain the different headshot images within your site. You could also set up a folder called Subheaders, which would contain all the subheader images used by the overall design of the site. The possibilities are endless, yet it does offer another way for the Assets panel to increase your productivity for a more efficient workflow. To create a new folder for Favorites, follow these steps:

1. Make sure the Assets panel is open. Highlight all the subheader and headshot images, right-click on them, and choose Add to Favorites from the context menu that appears. The selected images will now be added to your Favorites list.

2. Now select the Favorites radio button to switch to the Favorites view.

3. Click the New Favorites Folder icon located at the bottom-right corner of the panel. You can also create a new folder by right-clicking (Control-clicking) the assets and choosing the New Favorite Folder command from the context menu. Both options are illustrated in Figure 11.12.

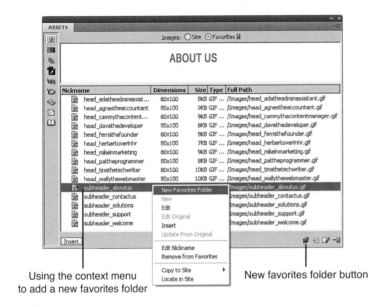

Using the context menu
to add a new favorites folder

New favorites folder button

FIGURE 11.12   Right-click the Favorites list and choose the New Favorites Folder option.

4. Name the folder and drag any asset that you want categorized into that folder, as shown in Figure 11.13.

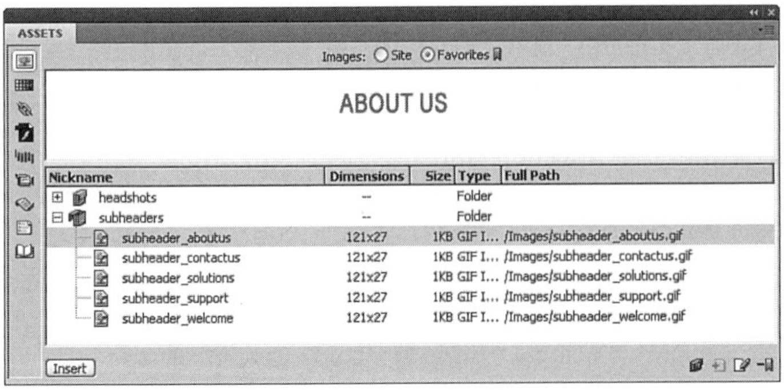

FIGURE 11.13   Drag asset favorites into their new folder.

Creating New URL and Color Assets

You can create new color and URL assets right within the Assets panel. To create new assets for either of these categories, make sure you're within the Favorites section. To create a new color, click the New Color button located toward the bottom of the Assets panel. You can also access that option by choosing the New Color option from the panel's Options menu located in the top-right corner of the panel. When you choose the new color command, a swatch displays allowing you to choose a color, as shown in Figure 11.14.

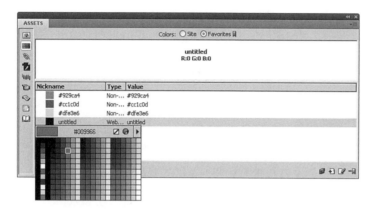

FIGURE 11.14   You can easily create a new color asset from within the Assets panel.

Finally, after choosing a color, you can highlight it in the Assets panel and give it a nickname. Creating a new link is just as easy: Select the URL category and be sure to view the Favorites section. Toward the bottom of the panel, click the New URL button, which launches the Add URL dialog box. Here. you can define the nickname and the URL you want the asset to link to.

Using Find and Replace

One of the most useful Dreamweaver features is the Find and Replace dialog box. Unlike most Find and Replace options included with word processing programs and the like, the Dreamweaver Find and Replace dialog box allows you to search and then replace elements within an entire site, a current document, selected text, open documents, a specific folder, and even selected files within a site. Even better, you can use the Find and Replace dialog box as a way to search for elements within source code, text within the Design or Code views, text within specific tags, or specific tags in general. Furthermore, the Find and Replace dialog box doesn't require you to have a page open to run it; rather, you can open the dialog box at any time while Dreamweaver is open. To open the dialog box, choose Edit, Find and Replace. The Find and Replace dialog box will open similar to Figure 11.15.

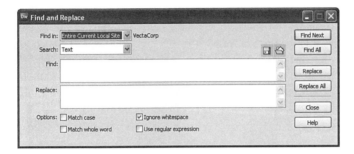

FIGURE 11.15   Use the Find and Replace dialog box as a way to search for various types of elements.

As you can see from Figure 11.15, the basic Find and Replace dialog box displays the following functionality:

▶ **Find in**—Choose an option from this menu to set the location of the search. Options include searching selected text, a current document, open documents, a folder, selected files within a site, or the entire current local site.

▶ **Search**—Choose an option from this menu to set the type of element you want to search for. Options include source code, text, advanced text (text and code combined), and a specific tag. When you select the Text (Advanced) or Specific Tag option, the Find and Replace interface changes to support selections of element types and element values similar to Figure 11.16.

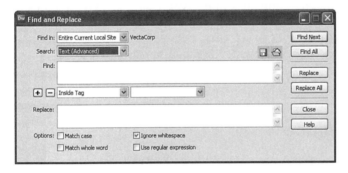

FIGURE 11.16   Selecting the Text (Advanced) and Specific Tag options causes the interface of the dialog box to change in support of the selection of element types and element values.

▶ **Save/Load Query**—After you perform a search (otherwise known as a *query*) that you're happy with, you can easily save it by clicking the Save Query icon. This action launches the Save Query dialog box, which allows you to save the query anywhere on your computer as a DWR file. Alternatively, you can load a saved query by clicking the Load Query icon. Doing this launches the Load Query dialog box, which allows you to open an existing DWR file.

▶ **Find**—Enter the element that you want to search for in this text box. In most cases, the element you enter here will be plain text.

▶ **Replace**—Enter the element that you want to replace the element you are searching for in this text box.

▶ **Options**—Use the check boxes in this group as a way to refine your search so that the element to be searched matches the case of what you type into the Find text box. Other options include matching the whole word to be searched for, ignoring whitespace, or using regular expressions, if you know how to write them.

▶ **Find Next/Find All**—Use the Find Next button as a way to step through the occurrences of the elements you are searching for on a page-by-page basis. Each page is opened individually. Alternatively, you can choose the Find All button. Doing this displays all the results in a list within the Search tab of the Results panel.

▶ **Replace/Replace All**—Use the Replace button as a way to replace the searched value with the value entered in the Replace text box. Alternatively, you can choose the Replace All button. Doing this replaces all instances listed within the Results tab of the Results panel with the value entered into the Replace text box.

To demonstrate the Find and Replace dialog box's functionality, let's perform a couple of searches: one basic and one advanced. To perform the basic search, follow these steps:

1. With the Find and Replace dialog box open, select the Entire Current Local Site option from the Find In menu.

2. Choose the Text option from the Search menu.

3. Enter the text **Vecta Corp** into the Find text box.

4. Disable the Match Case check box.

5. Click the Find All button.

As you can see from Figure 11.17, the results of the search are displayed within the Search panel.

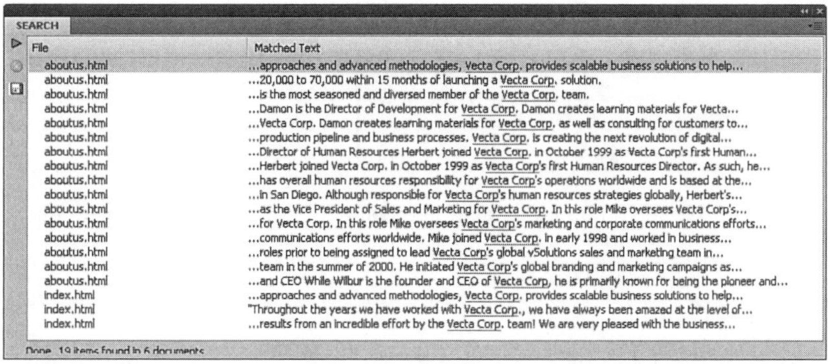

FIGURE 11.17   The results of the search are displayed within the Search panel.

As you can see from Figure 11.17, the Matched Text column displays a short string of text complete with the searched value underlined in red. Remember, we searched for text in the local site. The `index.html` and `aboutus.html` pages happen to be the only pages in our site that have the text *Vecta Corp* within the design. If you wanted to search for the text *Vecta Corp* in source code, you would get much broader results.

To make an edit to that page, you could double-click the row within the Search panel. Doing this opens the page and highlights the matched text within the page. You could also use the Replace and Replace All features to replace this string of text with something different. Because we just want to demonstrate the search functionality, we'll avoid the Replace and Replace All buttons.

Now let's do a more advanced search. In this next example, we'll search for text that is contained within a specific tag using the Text (Advanced) option. To do this, follow these steps:

1. Reopen the Find and Replace dialog box by choosing Edit, Find and Replace, pressing Ctrl+F (⌘-F), or by choosing the small Play icon in the Search panel. Either method reopens the Find and Replace dialog box.

2. Make sure the Entire Current Local Site option is selected from the Find In menu.

3. Choose the Text (Advanced) option from the Search menu. The dialog box's interface will change to accommodate entering text as well as selecting tag searching values.

4. Enter the text **Vecta Corp** into the Find text box.

5. In our scenario, we'll want to search for all instances of the *Vecta Corp* text value that are contained in the `<title>` tag. Knowing this, select the Inside Tag option from the first menu and select the `title` option from the second menu. After you've made your selections, the dialog box will resemble Figure 11.18.

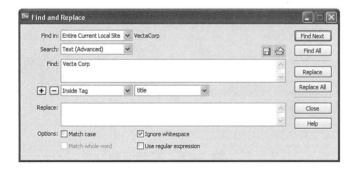

FIGURE 11.18   Customize the search so that you're searching for the text Vecta Corp within the `<title>` tag.

6. Now click the Find All button.

Because we have only five pages, and those five pages contain titles with the text *Welcome to the Vecta Corporation*, the Search tab within the Results window displays five results.

As you can see, the Find and Replace dialog box is powerful. It becomes extremely powerful when searching for specific tags. Assume for a moment that you have a site that contains 1,000 pages. Also assume that each page used different style sheets, which were created by a different department. What if you were asked to replace all style sheet references on every page to match a single style sheet reference called `styles.css`? You'd be working for hours, opening every page, and changing the style reference to point to `styles.css`. Using the Specific Tag option in the Find and Replace dialog box, this effort would be minimal. Figure 11.19 shows what the Find and Replace dialog box might look like to accomplish this task.

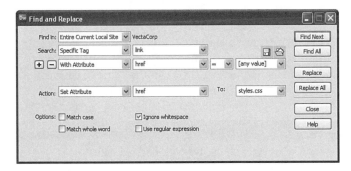

FIGURE 11.19   Using the Specific Tag option, you could easily search for specific tags and attributes and then replace that tag or attribute with a custom value.

As you can see from Figure 11.19, our search would involve locating the `<link>` tag with the attribute `href` with the attribute value set to anything. The query might look like this:

```
<link href="<anyvalue>">
```

That value would be set to `styles.css` or

```
<link href="styles.css">
```

The possibilities are endless. You'll quickly notice that dozens, if not hundreds, of possibilities exist using the many options that are available within the menus.

Using the History Panel

You can use Dreamweaver's History panel as a way to undo multiple steps at once. Although the Undo option within the Edit menu is still the ideal option for going back in time a step at a time, the History panel allows you to see numerous steps and even go back in time any number of steps at once. To open the History panel, choose Window, History. The History panel appears, similar to Figure 11.20.

FIGURE 11.20   The History panel allows you to go back in time by any number of steps at once.

As you can see from Figure 11.20, the History panel features a slider that can be dragged up and down to undo or redo multiple steps at once (limited only by the number you specify within the Maximum Number of History Steps text box in the General category of the Preferences dialog box).

TIP

Out of the box, Dreamweaver supports 50 history steps. Beyond that, old steps are removed to make room for newer steps. Depending on how much memory your computer has, you might want to increase this number. To do this, select Edit, Preferences. When the Preferences dialog box appears, select the General category and increase the Maximum Number of History Steps value accordingly.

Perhaps the most valuable feature outlined in the History panel is the capability to replay steps and record commands. We'll cover this next.

Working with Commands

At the heart of task automation and workflow enhancement lie commands. Commands, located within the Commands menu, are prebuilt as well as user-built pieces of functionality that, when executed, perform various actions on your web pages, such as cleaning up your HTML/XHTML code, applying Dreamweaver's source formatting to your HTML code, creating an automated web photo album, and more. We've already covered a couple of commands in previous chapters (such as the Sort Table and Check Spelling commands), and others will be covered in future chapters, but three commands stand out as workflow enhancement features and will be covered in this chapter. These commands are

- Record commands
- Apply Source Formatting
- Clean Up (X)HTML and Clean Up Word HTML

Recording New Commands

One of the benefits to working with commands in Dreamweaver is that they're not static, meaning that what you get out-of-the box is not all you have to work with. Instead, Dreamweaver allows you to download free commands from the Dreamweaver Exchange (covered in the online Appendix B, "Extending Dreamweaver") or even create your own commands by recording the steps you take within Dreamweaver and then playing them back. Furthermore, you can even highlight a number of steps within the History panel and save the steps as a command for use later in your web pages. Throughout this section we'll explore the different options for working with self-made commands using the recording features in the Commands menu, as well as the Save Selected Steps as a Command option from within the History panel.

Let's begin by exploring the recording features. To record a new command, follow these steps:

1. Create a new blank HTML page by choosing File, New. Choose Blank Page, HTML, <none> and click Create.

2. With the blank page now open, choose Commands, Start Recording.

3. Type the text `Welcome to the Vecta Corp site!`

4. Press the Enter (Return) key.

5. Choose Commands, Stop Recording.

6. To play the newly recorded command, choose Commands, Play Recorded Command.

Alternatively, you can click the Replay button in the History panel while the Run Command step is highlighted in the History list. Doing this allows you to continuously replay the recorded command without having to access the Commands menu each time.

Although the process of recording a command and replaying it numerous times seems like a beneficial alternative to retyping the text each and every time, it does have its limitations. For instance, closing Dreamweaver or flushing the Clipboard will delete the recorded command. What if you wanted to save the command so that you could use it within any site, at any time, even after you've closed and reopened Dreamweaver? To do this, you have to create and save a command. You can do this by following these steps:

1. To save a command, let's first backtrack out of what we've done by moving the slider in the History panel back up to the top of the list. Alternatively, you could choose the Clear History option from within the History panel options menu. Again (without choosing the Start Recording option), enter the text `Welcome to the Vecta Corp Site!` and then click Enter.

2. Now highlight both entries in the History panel and choose the Save As Command button, as shown in Figure 11.21. The Save As Command dialog box appears.

FIGURE 11.21   Highlight the two entries within the History panel and click the Save As Command button.

3. Within the Save As Command dialog box, enter the text **Vecta Corp Welcome** and click OK.

4. You can now access the command at any time by choosing the name from the Commands menu, similar to Figure 11.22.

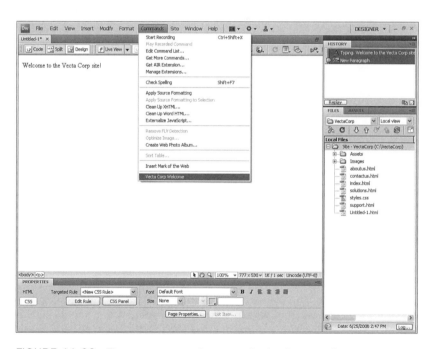

FIGURE 11.22   The new command appears in the Commands menu.

You'll now be able to access this command at any time, even if you close and reopen Dreamweaver. If you find that you're no longer using a command, you can remove it from the list by choosing Commands, Edit Command List. The Edit Command List dialog box will appear, similar to Figure 11.23.

FIGURE 11.23   The Edit Command List allows you to delete commands from Dreamweaver.

As Figure 11.23 indicates, you can rename and remove a command from the list. To remove a command from the list, choose the command and click the Delete button. Dreamweaver will prompt you with a message asking whether you're sure you want to delete the command. Click Yes. The command will be permanently deleted.

Apply Source Formatting

You can use the Apply Source Formatting command as a way to reapply Dreamweaver's default tabs, indents, and so on to the HTML code of your web pages. Alternatively, you can use the Apply Source Formatting to Selection command to reapply Dreamweaver default formatting to a specific selection of code while in Code view. As an example of how the Apply Source Formatting feature works, follow these steps:

1. Open a Vecta Corp page from the Files panel and immediately switch to Code view.

2. Highlight all the code by choosing Edit, Select All or by pressing Ctrl+A (⌘-A).

3. Now select the Outdent Code icon located third from the bottom within the Code toolbar until all your code is lined up with the left edge of the Document window. The code will resemble Figure 11.24.

4. To reapply Dreamweaver's default formatting, choose the Apply Source Formatting command from the Commands menu. As you can see from Figure 11.25, indentations, tabs, and so on are reapplied, resulting in much cleaner and easier-to-decipher code.

Of course, if you wanted to apply Dreamweaver's source formatting to a selection, you could choose the Apply Source Formatting to Selection option from the Commands menu instead.

Clean Up (X)HTML and Clean Up Word HTML

One of the last actions that I perform before I call a web page complete (aside from using the Apply Source Formatting command) is the Clean Up (X)HTML command. Let's face it, although Dreamweaver writes excellent HTML in the background, there will be many times where you'll add code, remove code, add some more code, remove some more code, and so on. Throughout the development life of the page, the code can become unsightly and, thus, will need a little attention. You can use the Clean Up (X)HTML command as a way of cleaning up or fixing problems with your code. For instance, you can use this command to search for and repair empty tags, redundant nested tags, non-Dreamweaver HTML comments, and special markup that Dreamweaver might add, or even specific tags that you want to specify. Furthermore, you can have the Clean Up HTML command combine nested `<font>` tags when possible and even show the results within a log when it's finished.

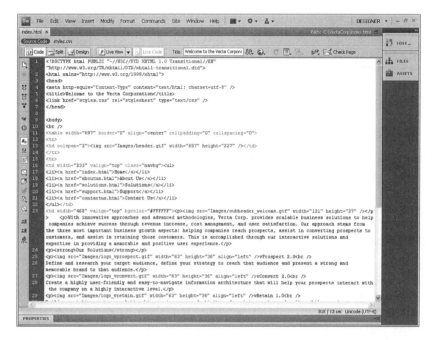

FIGURE 11.24   Remove the existing formatting from the HTML code.

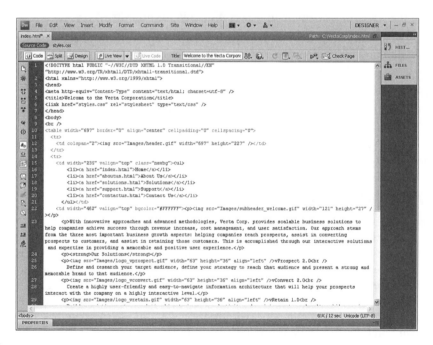

FIGURE 11.25   Reapply Dreamweaver's formatting by choosing Commands, Apply Source Formatting.

> **NOTE**
>
> Depending on the document type definition of your document, this command will change to either a Clean Up HTML or Clean Up XHTML option. Although the functionalities outlined by the two options are similar, they warrant mention.

To demonstrate the Clean Up XHTML command's use, follow these steps:

1. Begin by opening the page `cleanuphtml.html` located in the Assets folder. As you'll see, the page is basic, but contains numerous errors (most of which I purposely included) that we'll need to fix.

2. Choose the Clean Up HTML option from the Commands menu. The Clean Up HTML / XHTML dialog box appears, as shown in Figure 11.26.

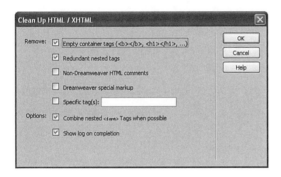

FIGURE 11.26   Run the Clean Up (X)HTML command.

3. You can leave the default options selected because you'll use these most of the time. Click OK.

4. As you'll notice, Dreamweaver shows a log detailing the errors that were found and fixed.

Alternatively, you could also use the Clean Up Word HTML option to fix the code mess for which Microsoft Word's HTML editor is infamous. To demonstrate the use of this command, follow these steps:

1. Open the page `cleanupwordhtml.html` located within the Assets folder.

2. Switch to the Code view to see the 270 or so lines of code that we'll need to clean up.

3. Choose the Clean Up Word HTML option from the Commands menu. The Clean Up Word HTML dialog box appears, as shown in Figure 11.27.

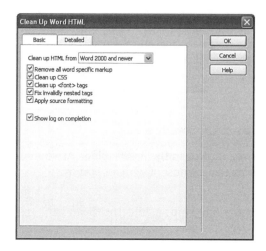

FIGURE 11.27   Run the Clean Up Word HTML command.

4. Again, we'll leave the default options selected because you'll use these most of the time. Click OK.

5. As you'll notice, Dreamweaver shows a log, detailing the numerous errors that were found and fixed.

Now switch to the Code view and see the result. As you might have noticed, Dreamweaver compacted the code down to 30 or so lines!

Summary

As you have seen throughout the chapter, Dreamweaver includes numerous options for enhancing your workflow processes. Throughout the chapter we explored the Assets panel, the History panel, the Find and Replace dialog box, how to record new commands, and how to use the Apply Source Formatting and Clean Up (X)HTML/Clean Up Word HTML commands.

In the next chapter, we'll take workflow enhancement to a new level by introducing templates and library items.

Working with Templates and Library Items

Chances are, if you're reading this book from cover to cover, your interests lie in building large-scale websites that employ intricate navigation structures and contain large amounts of information you want to present in a clean and easy-to-find manner. Furthermore, you're probably looking to build a site that doesn't require a lot of setup time and is easy to maintain after it has been built. This is where Dreamweaver templates and library items come in.

Using templates and library items can be an incredible timesaver for both the setup and maintenance phases of your site. If your goal is to build a site that consists of 100 or more pages, it would be beneficial to design one page and then derive every document within the site from that one master page, or template. Similarly, if your site employs the same navigation menu throughout, it might be advantageous to create the navigation menu as a library item and then allow your website to share the one library item throughout.

Templates and library items provide added benefits from a maintenance perspective. Because the design for every page of your site is prebuilt and contained within a master template, making changes to all 100 or more pages of your site is simply a matter of making the change to the one master template, and that change is instantly propagated down to all *derived pages* (pages in the site based on the template). If you're working with library items, the same philosophy holds true. One version of a navigation menu is created, saved as a library item, and then shared across the site. Changes made to the library item not only affect the library item, but also every page within the site that relies on it.

As you'll learn in this chapter, Dreamweaver outlines numerous features for working with templates and library items. Whether you're building them from scratch, building a template/library item from an existing design, or basing a web page on of a prebuilt template, this chapter unleashes the power that Dreamweaver templates and library items offer.

Like the rest of the chapters within this book, you can work with the examples in this chapter by downloading the files from the book's website. You'll want to replace the files within C:\VectaCorp\ with the files located in Exercises\Chapter12\Beginning\.

Understanding Dreamweaver Templates

Although the concept of templates can seem like a broad term, thinking analogously can aid in understanding the framework behind Dreamweaver templates. Think of professions in the real world as examples. For instance, furniture makers use templates to duplicate furniture based on a master design. To add uniqueness to each furniture piece, they might use different dyes or leather colors. Clothing manufacturers create one pattern and base future clothing pieces from the master pattern. Welders create jigs as a way of precisely duplicating curves when welding metal. The list goes on and on. Templates are a way for individuals to create a master design or pattern and then derive future designs from that master design, effectively ensuring consistency and uniformity across future versions of that design.

The profession of web development is no different. Using the Vecta Corp organization as an example, assume that our organization has numerous departments. Also assume that each department wants to create its own web presence within a Vecta Corp intranet site. Although the overall framework of the site must remain the same, each department is welcome to customize the content that appears on its particular page. This is where templates become useful. As the webmaster, your task is to create one master template file. When that master template file is done, we can base other pages on that master. For instance, we could create the Main page, the About Us page, the Solutions page, the Support page, and the Contact Us page. Even better, we could allow the web developers from each department to derive their own pages from our template for each of their own department sites. The obvious benefit is that this will ensure a consistent look and feel between the corporate Internet and intranet sites. The major benefit goes beyond consistency and uniformity and includes maintainability.

Now assume that we need to add a link to the navigational structure of the site. Traditional methods would have us opening every page in our site and manually adding the new link to the navigation menu. Even worse, we would have to ask all web developers in each department to also make the change in their individual websites. Because every developer works a bit differently, this could result in errors within the structure of the navigation menu. Because we've decided to use a template, however, we simply have to make the change in the master template file, update the site, and instantly all pages derived from the template file are edited appropriately. Figure 12.1 illustrates this point. You can begin to see the benefits that templates provide.

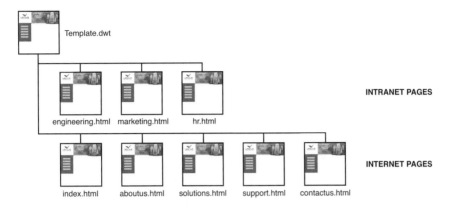

FIGURE 12.1 Numerous pages are based on a master template, including corporate web pages and interdepartment pages residing on the company's intranet.

Dreamweaver templates give you far more flexibility than just creating a design that acts as a master for other future designs. By default, when a new page is derived from a template file, the regions within the page become locked. Locked portions of the page cannot be edited or changed in the derived page. The idea is to create editable regions in the template file so that when new pages are derived from the master template file, developers can make changes only to the editable regions, effectively preserving the overall design and structure of the site from accidental modifications. As it stands, Dreamweaver supports four types of regions within a template:

▶ **Editable regions**—The simplest way of allowing users to make additions to a template-derived page is to add editable regions. Editable regions allow users of a template-derived page to make changes to all parts of the region, including tags and tag attributes within the region.

▶ **Editable attributes**—By default, Dreamweaver locks all tags not within editable regions. You could optionally set editable attributes as a way of allowing users to make changes to specific attributes within a locked tag. For instance, you might want to allow users to change the border size of a table while still maintaining the default cell padding and cell spacing.

▶ **Optional regions**—As a template designer, you could easily add an optional region to a template. This allows users of a template-derived page to add or not add content to that region. If content is not added to that optional region, the area doesn't appear when viewed in the browser.

▶ **Repeating regions**—As a template designer, you might want to add a repeating region to elements such as tables. This allows users of template-derived pages to add content to tables that vary depending on length. In our case, we'll create a company events table within the intranet-based department web pages. These company events tables will actually be tables that include repeating regions.

Figure 12.2 shows how these regions might be applied to our Vecta Corp interdepartmental pages to create an organization-wide intranet template.

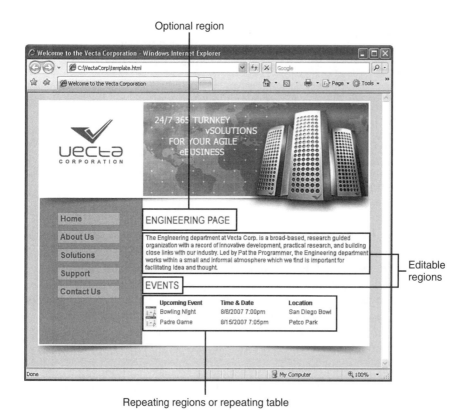

FIGURE 12.2   Editable, optional, and repeating regions can be added to a template for numerous design options.

Now that you have a visual idea as to how our template might look, let's actually build it!

Creating a New Template

Creating a new template in Dreamweaver is simple. For the most part, it's a matter of creating a new blank document and choosing File, Save As Template. Unfortunately, this method won't do us any good because it doesn't contain any graphics that represent the overall design of our Vecta Corp site. In fact, the best method for establishing a template is to simply create your design as you normally would, excluding any content that you feel might change on a page-to-page basis. When you have the design exactly the way you want it, choose File, Save As Template. Dreamweaver converts the document into a DWT (Dreamweaver Template) .dwt file and places it in a Templates folder (created automatically for you by Dreamweaver) in your site.

To get you started, go ahead and open the `template.html` file included with the files for this project.

12

> **NOTE**
>
> I'll assume that you're familiar with creating the structure of the Vecta Corp design. Because of space constraints, rather than walking you through the process of rebuilding the design, I've included it as a prebuilt page called `template.html`. To review the process of creating the page, refer to Chapter 2, "Building a Web Page," Chapter 4, "Web Page Structuring Using Tables," or Chapter 6, "Page Structuring Using Cascading Style Sheets." To keep things relatively simple for now, the page that I've prebuilt for you uses templates.

As you can see in Figure 12.3, the design acts as a shell for the content that will eventually appear on the page.

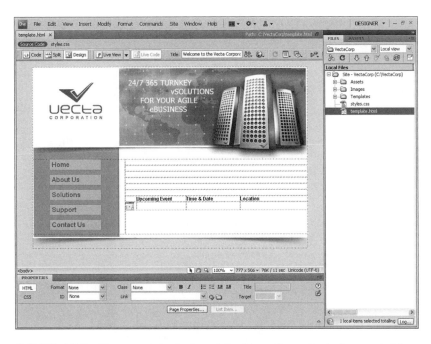

FIGURE 12.3   The complete design of the Vecta Corp site before saving it as a template.

This page will serve as the overall template for the site. Because this is the case, you don't want to add any content yet. Anything added to the page before it's converted to a template will be locked into any template-derived pages. For now, you want to create only the structure. Later, we'll add editable regions that define areas where users (developers in other departments in our organization) can add their own content. Now choose the Save

As Template option from the File menu. The Save As Template dialog box appears (see Figure 12.4).

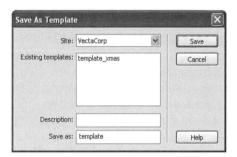

FIGURE 12.4   The Save As Template dialog box allows you to save a template in a defined site.

The Save As Template dialog box allows you to save the page as a template in any defined site. The Save As Template dialog box outlines the following functionalities:

- **Site**—Select the defined site in which you want to save the template. By default, Dreamweaver creates a new Templates folder in the defined site (if the folder doesn't already exist) and places the template file in that folder. For our example, choose the Vecta Corp site.

- **Existing Templates**—This list displays the existing templates in the selected site. This list is merely a reference so that you don't accidentally save a template with the same name as one that already exists. In our case, you'll see one template that I've included for this chapter: template_xmas, which we'll use a bit later on in the chapter.

- **Description**—Provides a brief description about your template in this text box. Information such as under what circumstances the template should be used.

- **Save As**—Enter a value in this text box to uniquely identify your template. This is the name given to the DWT file. For our purposes, name the file **template**. Later, you'll notice the file has been saved as **template.dwt**.

To create the new template, click the Save button. Notice that Dreamweaver launches an Update Links dialog box. Because newly created templates reside in the Templates folder, Dreamweaver must update any links in the page to coincide with the change. For instance, our navigation menu lists five links that point to index.html, aboutus.html, and so on. Because our template file now resides in the Templates folder, the new links will change and should now point to ../index.html, ../aboutus.html, and so on. Rather than forcing you to change the links manually, Dreamweaver scans the site cache and immediately recognizes the change; it then alerts you with the Update Links dialog box, allowing you to let Dreamweaver make the link changes automatically. Click Yes to update all the links in the page.

With the template now created, you'll immediately notice the new template (`template.dwt`) is placed directly in the Templates folder (also shown in Figure 12.5).

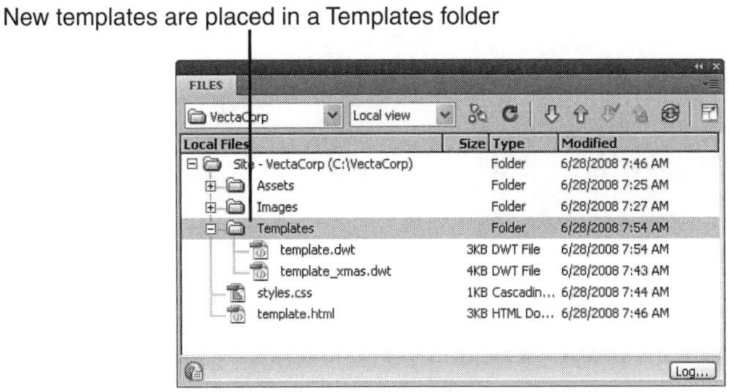

New templates are placed in a Templates folder

FIGURE 12.5   Templates are placed in the Templates folder.

Remember, if this were the first template we were creating for the site, Dreamweaver would have automatically created the Templates folder for us. Because the Templates folder was already available (I created it to store a template for another lesson), Dreamweaver simply uses the one that's already there.

With the new template created, you can now start adding editable regions.

Defining Editable Regions

As the template designer, your main task, aside from designing the structure of the template, is to outline areas of the page to which other developers can add content. You can do this by outlining editable regions. In our case, we'll want to add three editable regions: one for the main subheader image that appears at the top of the page, one for the content that appears below it, and one for the events subheader that department users can customize according to their departments' names. To add an editable region, follow these steps:

1. Place your cursor in the first cell of the Content table and choose Insert, Template Objects, Editable Region (Ctrl+Alt+V/Control+Cmd+V). Alternatively, you could right-click the cell and choose the New Editable Region option from the Templates submenu after the context menu appears. Furthermore, you could choose the Editable Region option from the Templates submenu in the Common category of the Insert panel.

2. Either method you choose to insert a new editable region opens the same New Editable Region dialog box. Enter a somewhat descriptive name in the Name text box so that users understand what is supposed to be added in the editable region. I'll type **Main Subheading** and click OK. By default, Dreamweaver adds the teal visual aid that represents the editable region (see Figure 12.6).

Editable Region visual aid

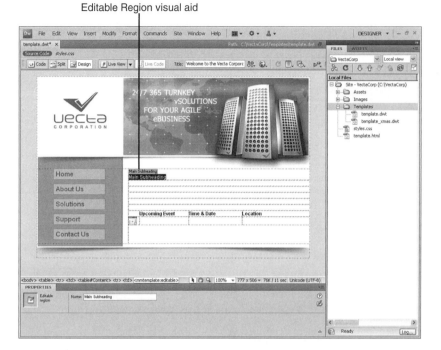

FIGURE 12.6   The teal visual aid represents the editable region in the template.

TIP

By default, editable regions appear in the color teal; however, you can customize these color preferences. If you're working on a teal-colored site and you want to change the color of the editable regions, choose the Highlighting category in the Preferences window and make changes as you see fit from the Editable Regions color picker.

3. Notice that Dreamweaver automatically adds text in the editable region. For the most part, you'll want to make this text descriptive so that developers using the template know what to add in the editable region. Because this editable region is reserved for a subheader image, replace the *Main Subheading* text with an image placeholder to alert developers to use an image that coincides with their department name. To add the image placeholder, remove the text and choose Insert, Image Objects, Image Placeholder. The Image Placeholder dialog box appears.

4. In the dialog box, enter the text `Main_Subheading`, give the image placeholder a width of **229** and a height of **27**, and choose a default color. I'll sample the red from the header image's logo at the top of the page. After you've made the changes, click OK. The new image placeholder is added to the editable region.

5. Now that you have a general idea how editable regions are created, try adding two more on your own. First, create an editable region for the main content that will

appear two cells below the editable region you just added. Second, add one more editable region, complete with a second image placeholder, two cells above the current events table that represents the department events header developers for each department will add. The template, complete with three editable regions, should resemble Figure 12.7.

6. Save your work.

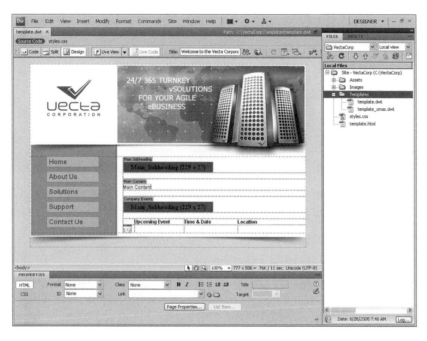

FIGURE 12.7   Add two more editable regions, one for the main content and another for the second subheader image that will appear for the department events.

Deriving a New Page from a Template

With the new template created and editable regions defined, users can now begin using the template by creating a new instance of the template. Playing the role of the department web developer for this section, we'll do just that. To create a new page based on a template, follow these steps:

1. Select File, New. The New Document dialog box appears.

2. Select Page from Template, Vecta Corp. Notice the Vecta Corp site contains the template file within the Template for Site "Vecta Corp" list. Also notice a preview (see Figure 12.8) that displays an image representation of the template file.

FIGURE 12.8   A preview of the template is displayed in the Preview pane of the New Document dialog box.

3. If you want to maintain a connection between the template-derived page and the template itself, keep the Update Page When Template Changes check box enabled.

4. Click Create to open a new instance of the template.

The page opens in the Document window but clearly resembles the original template file. Before you assume that you've done something wrong, notice two distinct changes: First, the page has a distinct yellow border surrounding it with a small flag that describes the page as derived from a template called *template*.

Second, if you hover over areas that weren't designated as editable regions, the locked region cursor appears. You'll quickly realize that only areas marked as editable regions allow users to place their cursors inside and make changes. Let's do that next.

Adding Content to Editable Regions

As a user of a template-derived page, we're at the mercy of the template designer. Dreamweaver locks the design of a template, and only the template designer can delegate which areas in the template, marked by editable regions, can be customized. In our template, we've set aside two editable regions for image subheadings (marked with image placeholders) and one editable region for plain text. These are the only areas in the template that the user of the template file can customize. For the most part, adding content within an editable region is a matter of placing your cursor in the editable region and typing. However, other options exist for adding or modifying content in editable regions:

▶ Select the editable region, in which case the content in the editable region is highlighted. You can then begin typing or edit the existing image placeholder so that it uses an image.

▶ Place your cursor in the editable regions and select the `<mmtinstance:editable>` tab in the Tag Selector.

▶ Choose the region name from the bottom of the Modify, Templates submenu.

Whichever method you choose allows you to make changes in the editable region. Now suppose that we're the web developers for the Engineering department and that we're ready to customize this template-derived page accordingly. To customize the page by adding content to the existing editable regions, follow these steps:

1. Change the source of the image placeholders in both the Main Subheading and Company Events editable regions to point to the `header_engineering.gif` image and the more generic `subheader_events.gif` image, located in the Images folder. You can do this by selecting the image placeholder and then dragging the point-to-file icon into the respective image (see Figure 12.9), or by double-clicking the place-holder image.

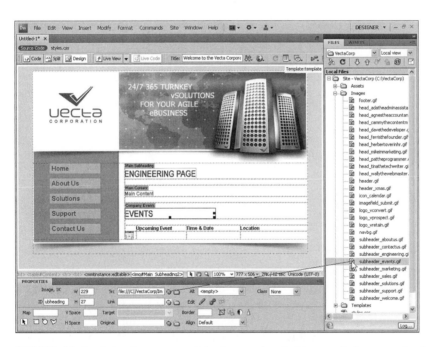

FIGURE 12.9   Point the source of the image placeholders to their respective images in the Images folder by using the point-to-file icon.

2. Remove the existing text from the Main Content editable region.

3. Open the `engineeringcontent.txt` file located in the Assets folder, select all of the content, copy it, and then switch back over to your web page.

4. Paste the copied text into the Main Content editable region. The text appears in the editable region, as shown in Figure 12.10.

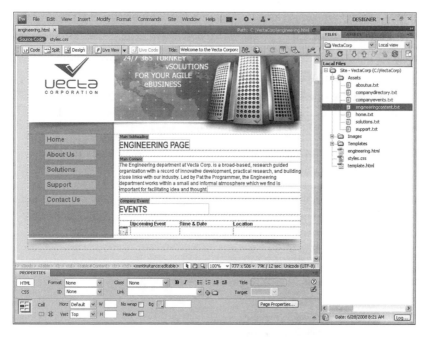

FIGURE 12.10   Add the content in the `engineeringcontent.txt` file to the Main Content editable region.

5. Save the page as **engineering.html.**

That's all there is to it. So far, we've only added content to editable regions. But as you'll see in the coming sections, adding content to other regions, such as optional and repeating regions, is just as easy.

Creating an Editable Tag Attribute

As you've seen thus far, Dreamweaver templates are a viable option when you want to disseminate a consistent look and feel throughout your organization. The downside to using templates, however, is that you're either locking the entire template (in which case nothing is customizable by a template-derived page), or you're outlining editable regions (in which case everything in the editable region is customizable). What if you wanted to allow users to customize the background color of the page (the `bgcolor` attribute of the `<body>` tag)? This doesn't seem like a far-fetched request; you might want to allow the various departments to customize the background color of their respective pages. Unfortunately, because the template locks the `<body>` tag, there's no access to the `bgcolor` attribute of the tag. Think again! Dreamweaver's second method of defining editable content in templates solves this dilemma.

By defining editable tag attributes, Dreamweaver allows the template designer to precisely control which tags and even which attributes within tags a user of a template-derived page can edit. This functionality is key, especially when you want to allow customizations of attributes such as the bgcolor attribute of the <body> tag that would otherwise be locked by the template. The various types of attributes that Dreamweaver allows you to mark as editable include text, numbers, URLs, colors, and even Boolean values such as the readonly and multiple attributes for form elements. Even better, Dreamweaver makes it easy to customize these attributes by providing a centralized Editable Tag Attributes dialog box that makes the attributes of the selected element available from a drop-down menu. Furthermore, Dreamweaver allows you to edit which attribute values that you as the template designer want to expose by the editable attribute. More on this later. For now, let's focus on making an attribute editable. To do this, follow these steps:

1. If you still have the engineering.html page open, close it now and open the template.dwt file (contained within the Templates folder).

2. With the template page open, select the <body> tag from the Tag Selector. The entire page is highlighted.

3. Choose Modify, Templates, Make Attribute Editable. The Editable Tag Attributes dialog box appears, similar to Figure 12.11.

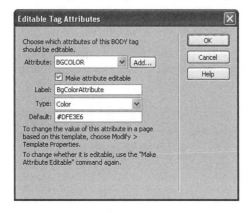

FIGURE 12.11   The Editable Tag Attributes dialog box allows you to customize which attributes of the selected tag you want to allow the user of the template-derived page to customize.

NOTE

By default, the Attribute menu shows the only attribute that's been added to the <body> tag when the template was first created. If an attribute doesn't exist in this menu and you want to add it now, click the Add button. A dialog box appears that allows you to add a supported attribute to the <body> tag on-the-fly. This process works for any tag.

4. Click the Add button. When the dialog box appears, enter the text **bgcolor** and click OK.

5. To ensure that the bgcolor attribute is editable, enable the Make Attribute Editable check box. The Label, Type, and Default text boxes become visible and display the default values associated within those properties.

6. Because the `bgcolor` attribute of the `<body>` tag is a color, choose the Color option from the Type menu. Other selectable options in this menu are the following:

   ▸ **Text**—Select this type for attributes that require text-based values, such as the `<img>` tag's `alt` attribute.

   ▸ **URL**—Select this type for attributes that require URL-based attributes, such as the `<a>` tag's `href` attribute.

   ▸ **Color**—Select this type for attributes that require the color picker to become visible, such as the `bgcolor` attribute for the `<body>` tag.

   ▸ **True/False**—Select this type for attributes that require true or false values, such as the `readonly` or `multiple` attributes for form elements.

   ▸ **Number**—Select this type for attributes that require numeric values, such as the `width` and `height` attributes of the `<img>` tag or the `cellspacing` and `cellpadding` attributes of the `<table>` tag.

7. Enter the name **BgColorAttribute** in the Label text box as well as the #DFE3E6 value in the Default text box. When you've finished making the customization, your dialog box should resemble mine, also shown in Figure 12.11. Click OK.

8. Save the template. Dreamweaver recognizes that other pages in the defined site are using this template and asks you to update the template files by displaying an Update Template Files dialog box.

9. Click Update. Dreamweaver presents a log of files that were updated.

10. Click Close.

You won't notice any changes in Design view right away, but switching to Code view reveals the addition of the editable attribute as follows:

```
<body bgcolor="@@(BgColorAttribute)@@">
```

In this case, Dreamweaver specifies the `bgcolor` attribute as editable by setting its value to a dynamic parameter (specified by the opening @@ and closing @@ symbols) named `BgColorAttribute`. Inspecting the `<head>` tag reveals that that parameter is actually listed in a Dreamweaver comment as follows:

```
<!-- TemplateParam name="BgColorAttribute" type="color" value="#DFE3E6" -->
```

This `TemplateParam` tag is used by Dreamweaver to identify the editable attributes and provide their types with a default value.

Setting Editable Attributes

After you've specified which attributes users implementing template-derived pages can customize, Dreamweaver provides a straightforward interface for customizing the properties. Again, let's switch hats and play the role of the Engineering department's web developer. Assuming this role, let's work with the freedom we've just been given by the template designer and customize the background color of the page to a color that more closely matches the red contained within the Vecta Corp logo. To do this, follow these steps:

1. Close all open documents and reopen the `engineering.html` page. You'll immediately notice that the default color we've specified for the background is applied.

2. With the page open, notice the new menu item located in the Modify menu called Template Properties. Choose it. The Template Properties dialog box appears.

3. In the `BgColorAttribute` text box, enter the hex value **#CC1C0D** and click OK. The engineering page's background color is now customized to match the color in the Vecta Corp logo.

4. Save your work.

Working with Repeating Regions

Editable regions provide some level of flexibility in terms of allowing users working with template-derived pages to add and modify content in areas on the page that you, as the template designer, specify as editable. In our example, we made the assumption that various departments in our organization would need to create an instance of the template and customize certain areas (editable regions) to suit their needs. Up to this point, we've discussed allowing the users to customize the small subheading images by allowing them to replace image placeholders with their own department-specific images. We also added a third editable region that allowed users to add text for the main content of the template-derived page. What we haven't done yet is set aside the Events table as editable.

The challenge with making the Events table editable is that we need to be careful not to make the entire table editable. Technically, we could create one big editable region and then place the Events table in that editable region. The problem with this approach is that users would be able to change the heading that appears in the table as well as the small calendar icon that appears just to the left of each row. Because we want to keep a level of consistency across departments, allowing department users to do this wouldn't be the best idea. Instead, we can keep the locked design of the table but set aside a row in the table as a repeating region. This would allow users to continuously add rows to the table and at the same time will preserve the overall look and feel of the table.

To enable a repeating region for the Events table, follow these steps:

1. Open the `template.dwt` file if isn't already open. Select the first row in the Events table by placing your cursor in one of the cells in the row you want to select and choose the `<tr>` tag from the Tag Selector. The row is selected.

2. Choose Insert, Template Objects, Repeating Region. The New Repeating Region dialog box appears.

3. Enter the name **EventItems** and click OK. A light blue visual aid similar to the editable region appears, surrounding the selected row in the table.

4. Our next step is to define the three cells in the repeating region as editable regions: Place your cursor in each cell and choose Insert, Template Objects, Editable Region.

When the New Editable Region dialog box appears, name your editable regions **UpcomingEvent**, **TimeDate**, and **Location**, respectively. When you finish adding the three editable regions, the table should resemble Figure 12.12.

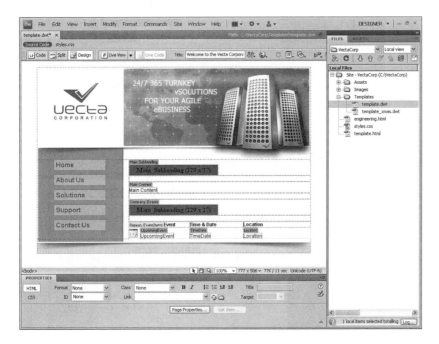

FIGURE 12.12   Add three new editable regions in the repeating region of the Events table.

5. Save your work.

Alternatively, you can create a table with repeating rows by choosing Insert, Template Objects, Repeating Table. Selecting this option reveals the Insert Repeating Table dialog box, similar to Figure 12.13.

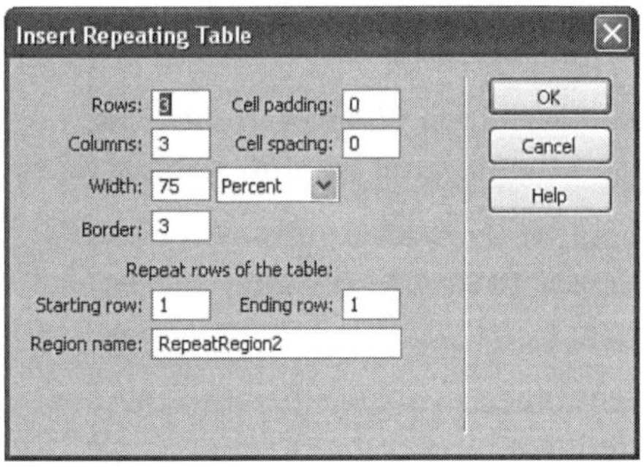

FIGURE 12.13   Use the Repeating Table option to quickly create a table that has repeating rows.

The Insert Repeating Table dialog box allows you to quickly construct a table by customizing Rows, Columns, Width, Border, Cell Padding, and Cell Spacing values. The second half of the dialog box allows you to set the starting and ending rows for the repeating row as well and the name to be associated with the repeating region. Personally, I prefer to construct the table on my own and then designate the repeating and editable regions because this method is much more flexible for creating column headers and graphics that I want to appear next to each row. The method you decide to use is entirely up to you.

Adding Content to Repeating Regions

As we did with the editable regions example, let's switch roles for this section and play the role of a department web developer. Assume that we need to add some department events to our new template-derived page. To do this, follow these steps:

1. Open the engineering.html file if it's not already open. Notice the interface changes to the Events table. This is our repeating row functionality in action.

2. To make customizations to the Events table, start by typing text directly into the editable regions in the first row. When you've finished, your row, complete with customized text, should resemble Figure 12.14.

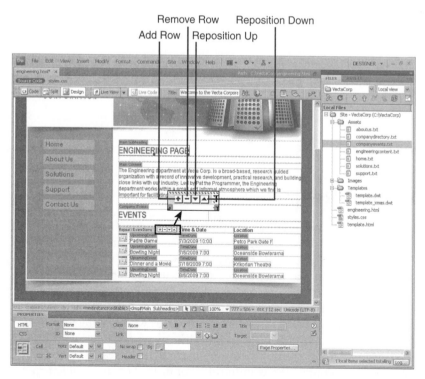

FIGURE 12.14   Add a new custom event to the first row in the Events table.

3. Now let's add a second event. Unfortunately, the table is locked by the template, so using traditional methods of adding rows to the table won't work. Instead, we must use the small buttons that appear in the repeating region. As you can see from the callouts in Figure 12.14, buttons exist for adding, removing, and reordering rows in the Events table.

4. Because we need to add a new row, click the Add Row (+) icon. This action adds a new row to the Events table. We can now add custom text to the new row to complete the addition of the second row to the Events table.

We can also remove and reorder items in the table by clicking other options in the button menu. The downside to using this menu, however, is that it appears only when invisible elements are turned on. If you're like me and prefer not to have invisible elements turned on, adding new rows to the repeating table could pose a challenge. To demonstrate this, turn invisible elements off by disabling the Invisible Elements option located in the Visual Aids menu in the Document bar. Notice that the small button menu for adding, removing, and reordering rows in the Events table no longer exists. To continue to add and reorder rows within the repeating table when invisible elements are turned off, we must turn to the options available from the Modify, Templates submenu:

▶ New Entry Before Selection

▶ New Entry After Selection

▶ New Entry Up

▶ New Entry Down

To cut, copy, or delete rows within a repeating table, choose one of the options available from the Edit, Repeating Entries submenu:

▶ Cut Repeating Entry

▶ Copy Repeating Entry

▶ Delete Repeating Entry

Defining Optional Regions

Optional regions are some of the more powerful customizable regions. Optional regions allow you to list multiple options, such as images, within a region on the template and then allow users of the template-derived page to determine which image they want to use. To further understand how the optional region can be beneficial to a template, think about our Vecta Corp organization. Currently, we specify an image placeholder in the Main subheading's editable region. We automatically assume that the department web developer will browse the company's directory of images (tedious work, by the way) and find the appropriate image to place in that area. Technically, there's nothing preventing the department web developer from selecting a custom image that he created to put into that spot instead. By creating an optional region in this spot instead of an editable region, we get to dictate which images the developers can choose from. For instance, in the

Images folder, we have three versions of the subheader image:
`subheader_engineering.gif`, `subheader_marketing.gif`, and `subheader_sales.gif`. We could easily replace the Main Subheading editable region with three optional regions, effectively forcing the department web developer to pick from one of the three only. To demonstrate how this is done, follow these steps:

1. Save and close any open documents and reopen the `template.dwt` file.

2. Delete the existing Main Subheading editable region by selecting it and pressing Delete.

3. With your cursor still in the cell, choose Insert, Template Objects, Optional Region. The New Optional Region dialog box appears, similar to Figure 12.15.

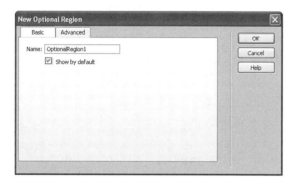

FIGURE 12.15   The New Optional Region dialog box allows you to establish an optional region in the template.

4. The dialog box is split into two tabs: Basic and Advanced. We'll discuss the Advanced tab later, so for now make sure that the Basic tab is selected.

5. On the Basic tab, you have the option of defining the name for the optional region as well as defining whether that region will display by default when the user opens the template-derived page for the first time. Enter the text **Main SubMarketing** into the Name text box and disable the Show by Default check box.

6. Click OK.

7. Replace the text in the optional region with the `subheader_marketing.gif` image located in the Images folder.

8. Place your cursor next to the newly created optional region and perform steps 3 through 7 again for both the engineering and sales images. When the New Optional Region dialog box appears for these two regions, make sure to uncheck the Show by Default check box. When you've finished, the page should resemble Figure 12.16.

FIGURE 12.16   Add two more optional regions and two new images for engineering and sales.

9. Save your work and update the pages that use the template.

NOTE

Because we've removed an editable region (Main Subheading) that the
`engineering.html` page depends on, Dreamweaver launches the Inconsistent Region
Names dialog box. This dialog box is used by Dreamweaver as way to facilitate the
mapping of old editable regions (that might have been deleted or renamed) to new
ones. More information on this dialog box is provided later in the chapter. For now,
choose the Nowhere option from the Move Content to New Region menu and click OK.

Combining Editable and Optional Regions

On occasion, you might find that an optional region has to contain editable text, in
contrast to an image as we've outlined in the previous section. To handle this,
Dreamweaver provides the Editable Optional Region option. Available by choosing Insert,
Template Objects, Editable Optional Region, the Editable Optional Region feature establishes an editable region within the boundaries of an optional region.

TIP

You can also add an editable region to an existing optional region without using the
Editable Optional Region option. To do this, place your cursor in the optional region and
choose Insert, Template Objects, Editable Region.

Setting Optional Region Properties

Like editable attributes, optional regions are inserted into the document as instance parameters. To demonstrate this, switch to Code view and notice the following three lines of code inserted near the top of the page:

```
<!-- InstanceParam name="Main SubMarketing" type="boolean" value="false" -->
<!-- InstanceParam name="Main SubEngineering" type="boolean" value="false" -->
<!-- InstanceParam name="Main SubSales" type="boolean" value="false" -->
```

Like editable attributes, the optional region is an instance parameter that can be set using the Template Properties dialog box by the user of the template-derived page. Unlike editable attributes, however, the parameter attributes in the InstanceParam tag are slightly different. By default, optional regions are set as type Boolean because their visible values are either shown (true) or not shown (false). The Type and Value properties of the InstanceParam tag reflect these properties.

As a user of a template-derived page, you can easily set these parameters on the page using the Template Properties dialog box. Because we've already started working with the engineering.html file, go ahead and reopen that page so that we can set which heading image becomes visible. To do this, follow these steps:

1. Save and close any open documents and open the engineering.html page.

2. Select Modify, Template Properties. The Template Properties dialog box appears, similar to Figure 12.17.

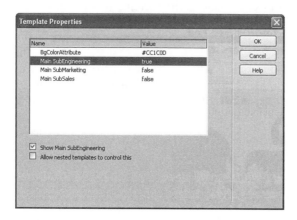

FIGURE 12.17   The Template Properties dialog box reveals the three optional regions as well as the editable attribute.

3. When you open the Template Properties dialog box, the three optional regions become visible in the list. Also notice that their Boolean type is set as a true/false

value. Because we're working with the Engineering page, select the Main SubEngineering option and click the Show Main SubEngineering check box to set the action of the region to `true`.

4. Click OK. The Engineering subheading image becomes visible on the page.

5. Save your work.

Nested Templates

In most cases, templates, combined with the flexibility of editable, optional, and repeating regions, are enough for most web development tasks. In some rare cases, however, single locked regions might be too rigid to be useful. Assume for a moment that Vecta Corp has decided to branch out into three separate companies in support of their three solutions (vProspect, vConvert, and vRetain). Although the Vecta Corp parent company still wholly owns the three subsidiaries, each of the three companies' websites should have a slightly different look and feel than the parent company's. One way of achieving this is to create different templates—one for the parent company site and one for each subsidiary company site that's a slight variation (maybe a different color scheme) of the parent. The downside to this approach is maintainability. If the parent site were to be customized, changes wouldn't trickle down to the four subsidiary sites because they're based on entirely different templates. To fix this problem, we could create a *nested template*. A nested template works much like the name says: It's a template wrapped within the framework of a second template. In the preceding model, we could easily solve the maintenance issue by creating a template for our parent company and then create nested templates for our subsidiary sites. This way, if customizations are made to the parent template, the changes trickle down to all the descendant pages. Because nested template development in Dreamweaver isn't all that intuitive, follow these steps to see how they work:

1. Create a master template as you would normally. That is, create the structure of your site and then choose the Save As Template option from the File menu. In our case, we would create the header and logo that represents the main Vecta Corp site and save that as a template.

2. Insert editable, optional, and repeating regions wherever you want variable content to appear in the template. Save the template when you're ready.

3. Create a new document based on the template file by choosing File, New. Select Page from Template, Vecta Corp, and then choose the template that you created in steps 1 and 2 and click Create.

4. With the template-derived page open, choose Insert, Template Objects, Make Nested Template. The Save As Template dialog box appears.

5. Enter a name for the nested template and click Save. A new nested template is created.

6. In the new nested template, make any changes needed to the editable regions. These changes are locked in any document that's based on this nested template.

7. Add any new editable, optional, or repeating regions to the nested template. Editable, optional, and repeating regions added to nested templates appear as orange rather than the default teal color.

8. Save the file to complete the customization of the nested template.

When you're ready to create template-derived pages from the new template, choose File, New. Select Page from Template, Vecta Corp, and then choose the nested template, and click Create. You'll now be able to customize areas that were set aside as editable within the nested template, not the original parent.

Templates and the Assets Panel

As your site grows, so too will the number of templates it employs. In general, overall management of site templates is handled by the Templates category in the Assets panel, shown in Figure 12.18.

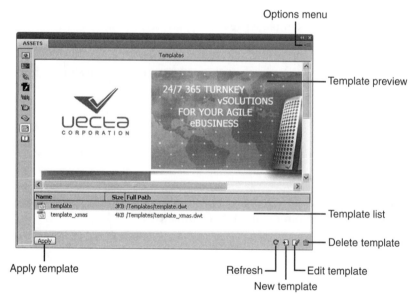

FIGURE 12.18   Use the Templates category in the Assets panel to manage site templates.

The Assets panel is separated into the following areas:

▶ **Template List**—Displays a list of DWT files (templates) in a defined site. The list provides the name of the template, its size in kilobytes, and the path (usually in the Templates folder of the defined site).

▶ **Template Preview**—Displays a preview image of the template.

▶ **Apply**—Applies a selected template to an existing page in the Document window. This button is covered in more detail later in the chapter.

▶ **Refresh Site List**—Refreshes the template category to reflect changes made within the Files panel.

▶ **New Template**—Creates a new DWT file in the Templates folder of your defined site. When this button is clicked, a new template instance appears in the template list.

▶ **Edit**—Launches the selected template from the template list in a new Document window for editing.

▶ **Delete**—Deletes a selected template.

▶ **Options Menu**—Displays advanced options for working with and managing templates. These options are outlined in more detail in the following discussion.

For the most part, general management of site templates can be handled through the small button bar that appears at the bottom of the Template category in the Assets panel. For more advanced options, however, access options located in the panel's Options menu:

▶ **Refresh Site List**—Refreshes all templates in the template list.

▶ **Recreate Site List**—Reloads the template site list into the site cache.

▶ **New Template**—Starts a new blank template.

▶ **Edit**—Opens the selected template in a new Document window instance for editing.

▶ **Apply**—Attaches a template to a page that isn't derived from a template. Dreamweaver asks you to map template regions to areas on the page. More on this later.

▶ **Rename**—Allows you to rename the selected template.

▶ **Delete**—Deletes a selected template.

▶ **Update Current Page**—Applies any changes made in a template to the current page assuming that page is derived from the modified template.

▶ **Update Site**—Applies any changes made in a template to all derived pages in the site list.

▶ **Copy to Site**—Allows you to copy the selected template to another defined site.

▶ **Locate in Site**—Opens the Site list and highlights the selected template.

Managing Templates Using the Assets Panel

As described in the previous section, numerous options exist for managing templates in the Assets panel. We've covered topics such as refreshing the site list, re-creating the site cache, updating the current page, updating the site, copying to the site, and locating in the site as they relate to other aspects of development. In this section, I'll introduce you to alternatives for creating new templates, editing templates, opening a new page based on a template, and deleting templates straight from the Assets panel.

You can create a new blank template by choosing the New Template option from the Assets panel's Options menu. Doing this allows you to establish a new empty template and then edit it when you're ready. To do this, follow these steps:

1. Select the New Template option from the Assets panel's Options menu. A new untitled template is created (see Figure 12.19).

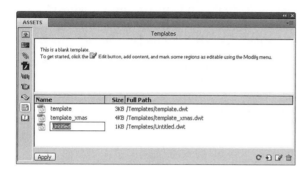

FIGURE 12.19   A new untitled blank template is created in the template list.

2. Enter a name for your new template and press Enter to apply the name.

3. With the new template selected in the list, click the Edit icon (located second from the right in the icon bar). You can also press Enter with the template selected to open the template in Edit mode.

4. Insert page elements and editable regions.

5. Save your work.

You can delete a template by selecting it from the list and either pressing the Delete key on your keyboard or clicking the Trash icon (located first from the right in the button bar). Note that Dreamweaver won't alert you of files that are tied to that template. After you delete a template, ties to that template are broken.

CAUTION

When you delete a template, not only are the ties to that template broken, but also the DWT file is permanently deleted from the site.

Finally, you can create a template-derived page straight from the Assets panel, effectively saving you from the more tedious approach of choosing File, New, locating the template, and clicking Create. To do this, right-click the template in the template list and choose the New From Template option from the context menu. Selecting this option opens an instance of the template in the Document window.

Applying Templates to Existing Pages

Dreamweaver makes it easy for you to apply various template designs to an existing document while maintaining your current content. When would this come in handy? Assume you were building various designs for a client in the hopes that the client would choose one and then build the company website based on that design. Rather than designing numerous templates and then numerous template-derived pages for each of the templates, you could easily create one template with a set of editable regions and then a template-derived page that would represent the client-supplied content to add. If the client didn't like the original template, no problem, you can keep the content you already added to the template-derived page. You'd simply create other templates (with the same editable regions as the original) and apply the template to the existing template-derived page.

Numerous possibilities for this feature exist. A second example is an existing page updated seasonally. You could create four templates that represent the four seasons of the year. When you're ready to apply the appropriate seasonal template, open the template-derived page and choose the Apply Template feature. Let's describe this process in more detail:

1. Start by opening the `engineering.html` page.

2. Switch to the Templates category in the Assets panel.

3. Select the `template_xmas` option from the template list. This is the template that I've included for you in the chapter downloads.

4. Click Apply.

As you can see from Figure 12.20, the Vecta Corp Christmas template is applied to the engineering page.

Because the editable regions in both the template and `template_xmas` pages coincide with those in the `engineering.html` page, the transition is seamless. But we can easily switch back to the regular template when we're ready. To demonstrate the switch back, let's use the Apply Template to Page method from the Modify menu:

1. With the `engineering.html` page still open, choose Modify, Templates, Apply Template to Page. The Select Template dialog box appears.

2. Choose the template you want to apply to the `engineering.html` page from the templates list and click Select.

The original template is now reapplied.

Mapping Template Regions

When Dreamweaver applies a template to a page, it attempts to match the regions on the two pages with one another. If there is a one-to-one correspondence with the regions on the template page and the ones on the normal page, the transition happens smoothly. If the regions do not match, however (maybe you called an editable region in a new template *NewHeading* but that same region is called *MyHeading* in the page), Dreamweaver gives you the opportunity to line up the inconsistent region names using the Inconsistent Region Names dialog box, shown in Figure 12.21.

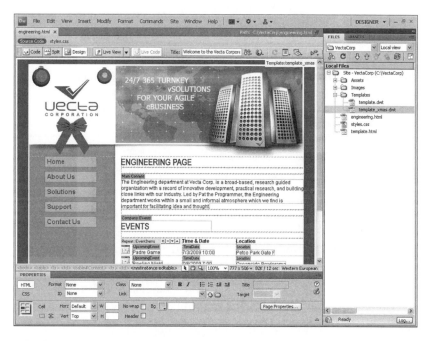

FIGURE 12.20   The Vecta Corp Christmas template is applied to the engineering page.

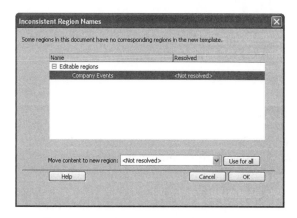

FIGURE 12.21   The Inconsistent Region Names dialog box allows you to remap inconsistent region names between two pages.

The Inconsistent Region Names dialog box appears automatically when Dreamweaver finds regions that don't match between a template and a page for which the template is being applied. Dreamweaver will not let you proceed until all inconsistent regions have been addressed.

> **NOTE**
>
> The Inconsistent Region Names dialog box is a way for Dreamweaver to map editable regions in a template to specific areas in a page. However, more often than not, Dreamweaver cannot map a specific area to a region, especially when that region doesn't exist. Because this is the case, you have the option of ignoring a region; by choosing the Nowhere option from the Move Content to New Region menu, you can instruct Dreamweaver to disregard the mapping of a particular region.

To remap regions using the Inconsistent Region Names dialog box, follow these steps:

1. Open the `template.dwt file` if it's not open already.

2. Select the Company Events editable region and delete it.

3. Save the page. Immediately, the Update Template Files dialog box appears; click Update.

4. Because the `engineering.html` page is dependent on that editable region, the Inconsistent Region Names dialog box will appear, similar to Figure 12.21.

5. Select the Company Events option from the Editable Regions list.

6. Select the Nowhere option from the Move Content to New Region menu and click OK to fix inconsistent regions in the `engineering.html` page.

If there are regions you want to map from one page to the other, those regions appear in the drop-down menu. Rather than choosing the Nowhere option, you could instead select the region name to which you want to remap the inconsistent region.

Removing Template Markup

From time to time, you'll find that you've made mistakes when building a template. Maybe template markup was inserted, and now you want to remove it. Fortunately, Dreamweaver makes removing template markup just as easy as it was to insert it. To accomplish this, a couple of methods for removing template markup exist. First, you can open the template page, switch to Code view, and manually remove the template markup code. Second, and by far the easiest, is to use the Modify, Templates, Remove Template Markup option.

To remove template markup from a page, follow these steps:

1. Open the template page.

2. Place your cursor near the region whose markup you'd like to remove.

3. Choose Modify, Templates, Remove Template Markup.

Notice that the initial text contained in the region remains, but the template markup is completely removed.

Changing the Default Document

Whenever you create a new document using Dreamweaver, a new instance of a prebuilt template located in the C:\Program Files\Adobe\Adobe Dreamweaver CS4\configuration\DocumentTypes\NewDocuments folder is opened for your use. Depending on what type of file you decide to work with, Dreamweaver includes prebuilt HTML so that you don't have to write it from scratch. For instance, the initial markup for a new HTML document resembles the following:

```
<!DOCTYPE HTML PUBLIC "-//W3C//DTD HTML 4.01 Transitional//EN"
"http://www.w3.org/TR/html4/loose.dtd">
<html>
<head>
<meta http-equiv="Content-Type" content="text/html; charset=">
<title>Untitled Document</title>
</head>
<body>
</body>
</html>
```

In keeping with its philosophy of extensibility, Dreamweaver allows you to open these templates, modify them, and then save them for use later. Why would you want to do this? Assume that you are building a template for a client, and the client wanted to include its own meta information in every page. Rather than manually copying this meta information into every page each time a new page is created, you could easily modify the initial template to include the meta information. This way, each time the user selected the new document option, the template information is automatically included with each page that is created. To modify the initial default document, open the appropriate template file (the type is viewable in the Type view column for your operating system's file explorer) located in the C:\Program Files\Adobe\Adobe Dreamweaver CS4\configuration\ DocumentTypes\NewDocuments folder, make the necessary changes, and click Save. To test your changes, choose the New option from the File menu, select the appropriate default document, and click Create.

Working with Library Items

One of the challenges facing web developers is that of repeating content on their websites. Navigation menus, company logos, copyright notices, and so on are all pieces of functionality consistently applied across an entire site. However, until now no central interface existed for globalizing that content to prevent the tedious task of opening every page and making the same change across every page in the site. Enter *library items* and *server-side includes*. Library items provide a way to create the functionality once and then share that functionality across multiple pages on your site. When the time comes to make updates, you make the change once in the central library item file, save your work, update your site, and then changes instantly trickle down to the files in your site that use the library item.

For the rest of this chapter, we'll examine the power and importance of library items in your site. We'll discuss the fundamental differences and similarities between library items and templates and, of course, provide an example as it relates to the Vecta Corp project. In addition, you'll learn to use server-side includes. Server-side includes are another method for globalizing content within your websites and also allow you to display information directly from the server.

Understanding Library Items

Library items, like templates, provide a method for creating a centralized piece of functionality that multiple pages in your site can use. The major differences between templates and library items, however, is that templates generally represent the overall design of a site. You create one master template file, define editable regions, and then establish pages based on that template (also known as a template-derived page). If changes need to be made to the design of the website, you'd open the template (DWT) file, make the change, save the file, and Dreamweaver updates all the pages based on the template file. In general, the model shown in Figure 12.1 accurately depicts the template-based model.

Library items, on the other hand, aren't meant to control the design of the site as a whole but are meant to define pieces of functionality—such as navigation menus, copyright notices, or a company logo—that have the potential of changing throughout the context of the site. For instance, assume you have a navigation menu being used by 100 pages on your site. Also assume that the footer of every page contains a copyright notice complete with a smaller navigation menu that is also being shared by 100 pages on your site. Now imagine that your supervisor decides to change a link within the navigation menu and to customize the copyright notice to include the current year. Traditional methods would call for the tedious process of opening all 100 pages and making the changes manually. Library items remedy this problem by allowing you to componentize navigation menus, copyright notices, company logos, and so on into one file and then include that file into every page on your website. Later, if changes need to be made, you open the one library item, make the changes, save the file, update the site—and instantly, all 100 pages that use the library item are updated automatically. Figure 12.22 outlines the library-item-based model.

Knowing what you know now of library items and templates, there's nothing that would prevent you from using the two together. In fact, templates and library items have the potential for working well together. For instance, assume that your organization uses the same template for both its intranet and Internet sites. In this case, you would have two navigation menus: one for the public site and one for the intranet site. Rather than creating two different templates, you could use the same template and just create two different library items that represent the two navigation menus. The model in Figure 12.23 describes this scenario.

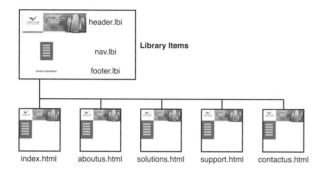

FIGURE 12.22   Library items provide a way to componentize smaller pieces of functionality so that they can easily be shared across the entire site and updated centrally.

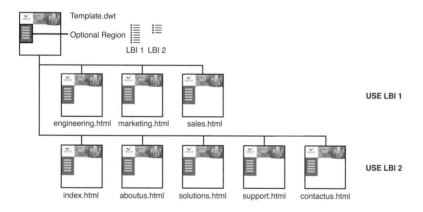

FIGURE 12.23   Library items can work with templates in scenarios where you want to use one template in conjunction with multiple navigation menus.

Mirroring the process of templates, as soon as you create a new library item, Dreamweaver automatically creates a Library folder within your defined site and places the library item (LBI) file in that folder. Also similar to templates, library items are centrally managed from the Assets panel, discussed next.

Using the Assets Panel to Manage Library Items

Similar to templates, library items can be created, edited, and managed from the Library Items category in the Assets panel (see Figure 12.24).

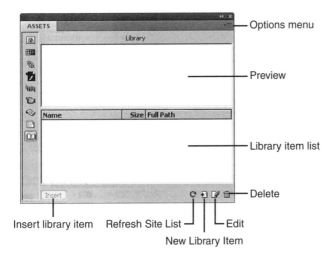

FIGURE 12.24   Use the Library Items category in the Assets panel to manage library items in your defined site.

The Library Items category of the Assets panel is separated into the following areas:

▶ **Library Item list**—Displays a list of LBI files or library items in a defined site. The list provides the name of the library item, its size in kilobytes, and the path (usually within the Library folder of the defined site).

▶ **Preview**—Displays a preview image of the library item.

▶ **Insert library item**—Inserts the selected library item into the page at your cursor's position within the page.

▶ **Refresh Site List**—Refreshes the library item category to reflect changes made within the Files panel.

▶ **New Library Item**—Creates a new LBI file in the Library folder of your defined site. When this button is clicked, a new library item instance also appears in the library item list.

▶ **Edit**—Click this button to launch a selected library item from the library item list in a new Document window for editing.

▶ **Delete**—Deletes a selected library item.

▶ **Options Menu**—Displays advanced options for working with and managing library items.

For the most part, general management of library items can be handled using the small button bar at the bottom of the Library Item category in the Assets panel. For more advanced options, however, access the options in the panel's Options menu.

Options in the Library Items panel's Options menu include the following:

- **Refresh Site List**—Refreshes all library items in the library item list.

- **Recreate Site List**—Reloads Dreamweaver's site cache.

- **New Library Item**—Creates a new, blank library item.

- **Edit**—Opens the selected library item in editing mode. When the library item has been opened, you can make necessary changes, save the document, and then update the site.

- **Insert**—Inserts a library item into an existing page.

- **Rename**—Renames the selected library item.

- **Delete**—Deletes a selected library item.

- **Update Current Page**—Applies any changes made to a library item to the current open page that uses the library item.

- **Update Site**—Applies any changes made to a library item to all pages that use the library item in the current open site.

- **Copy to Site**—Copies the selected library item to another defined site.

- **Locate in Site**—Opens the File panel and highlights the library item in the list.

Creating Library Items

Two methods exist for creating library items in your site. First, you can create a new blank library item in the Assets panel and then add your content to the newly created file. Alternatively, you can highlight an existing element on a page and click the New Library Item icon at the bottom of the Library Items category in the Assets panel to convert that existing element to a library item. For our Vecta Corp example, we'll review both methods. First, we'll examine the process of creating a new library item and then adding the footer content to it. Second, because all the pages in our site use or will use the navigation menu, we'll convert our existing navigation menu into a library item so that all pages in our site can use the library item.

> **TIP**
>
> You can also create a new library item directly from the New Document dialog box. To use this method, choose File, New. Select Blank Page, Library item, and click Create.

Creating a New Blank Library Item

One of the methods of creating library items is to click the New Library Item icon in the Assets panel. Doing this creates a new blank library item that can be opened and edited to your liking. After you've edited the content, save the library item, close it, and then add it to any pages in your site. To create a new library item for your site using this method, follow these steps:

1. Switch to the Library Items category in the Assets panel and click the New Library Item icon. Alternatively, choose the New Library Item option from the Assets panel's Options menu. Either method you choose creates a new untitled library item, similar to Figure 12.25.

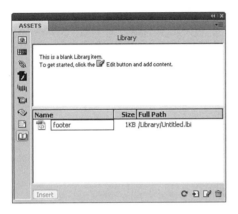

FIGURE 12.25   A new untitled blank library item is created in the Library Item list.

2. Enter a name for your new library item (I'll call mine **footer**) and press Enter to apply it to the item.

3. With the new library item selected in the list, click the Edit icon (located second from the right in the button bar). You can also select the library item and press Enter to open the library item in Edit mode.

4. Switch to the Files panel, open the footer.txt (contained within the Assets folder), select all of the content, copy it, and then paste it into the open library item.

5. Format the content to your liking. I'll center the content on the page and add an email hyperlink to the Questions or Comments? text.

6. Save your work, close the library item, and switch back the Library Items category in the Assets panel. The Library Item preview window shows what the new library item looks like (see Figure 12.26).

NOTE

CSS style classes cannot be added to newly created library items. An alternative method is to create the library item directly within the web page, apply your styles to see how it would look, and then save the element as a library item. This method is described in the next section.

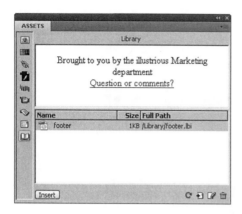

FIGURE 12.26   The new library item appears in the Library Item list. A preview of the library item is also shown.

Converting Existing Elements to Library Items

A second— and quite possibly more flexible—method for creating library items is to convert an existing element on a web page to a library item. This method provides two benefits: First and most important, it allows you to see how the library item looks in the context of the page design. Second, it allows you to apply style classes to the element before actually converting over to a library item. Because you can't apply styles directly to existing library items, this method is generally preferred.

> **TIP**
>
> Although the editing mode for library items doesn't support the capability to apply classes, there is a workaround: If you recall, in Chapter 5, "Page Formatting Using Cascading Style Sheets," we discussed the topic of design-time style sheets. Design-time style sheets are ideal to use with library items because you can apply temporary styles to a library item while you are designing it. When the library item is added to a web page, the Design-time style sheet isn't carried over; the library item takes on the look of the web page it resides in, based on the styles applied within the page.

To demonstrate the process of converting existing elements to library items, follow these steps:

1. Open the main template called `template.dwt` located within the Templates folder.

2. Select the list within the navigation cell. You can do this easily by placing your cursor within the cell and then choosing the `<ul>` tag within the tag selector.

3. Switch to the Library Items category in the Assets panel and click the New Library Item option. Dreamweaver displays a dialog box alerting you that CSS styles won't appear in the library item's Edit mode because the CSS style link isn't copied along with the library item.

4. Click OK to accept the notification. As you can see in Figure 12.27, the navigation bar is highlighted (as a visual aid) and an untitled library item appears in the library items list.

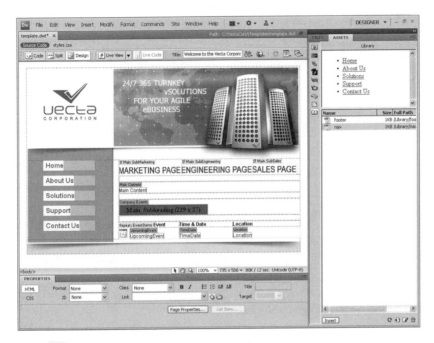

FIGURE 12.27   The new library item appears in the Library Items list.

5. Name your new library item **nav** and press Enter to apply the change.

That's all there is to it. In the next section, we'll explore methods for adding library items to your web pages.

Inserting Library Items into Web Pages

After you've created a library item, adding it to your web pages is as simple as dragging and dropping. In the previous two sections, we created two library items—one for the footer of every page and another for the navigation menu of the website. In a real-world scenario, you'd probably open every page within your existing site, remove the existing navigation menu (assuming that one existed), and then replace it with our new library item. Because we simply converted the existing navigation menu to a library item and that library item exists within a template, there's no need to do anything further. Every template-derived page will take on the new navigation menu. However, the footer has yet to be added to the page. To add it, follow these steps:

1. Open the template.dwt file if it's not already open.

2. Switch to the Library Item category in the Assets panel and select the footer library item.

3. Drag the `footer` library item underneath the table. The footer appears on the page, similar to Figure 12.28.

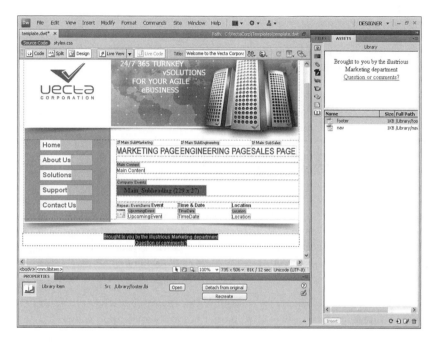

FIGURE 12.28   The footer library item appears at the bottom of the page.

4. Save the template and update any pages that are derived from the template.

Editing Library Items and Updating the Site

The benefit to using library items is that they can be edited centrally using a familiar interface in Dreamweaver's Design mode and then saved across the website. What this means is that, as with templates, changes can be made to one file, saved, and Dreamweaver instantly updates all files in the defined site that use that library item. To demonstrate this, assume that your supervisor has just accused you of being a wise guy for using the word *illustrious* in the footer to describe the Marketing department. To get back on his good side and avoid the wrath of Mike in Marketing, your supervisor asks you to change the word *illustrious* to the more subtle word *distinguished*. Had we not been using library items, we would be required to open every page within the site (or the main template file) to make these modifications. Because we're using library items, however, the change requires us to do little more than open the `footer` library item file, make the change, and save it. To do this, follow these steps:

1. If you haven't already done so, switch to the Library Items category in the Assets panel.

2. Select the `footer` library item and click the Edit icon located second from the right in the button bar. The footer opens.

3. Change the text *illustrious* to **distinguished** and choose the Save option from the File menu. The Update Library Items dialog box appears, similar to Figure 12.29.

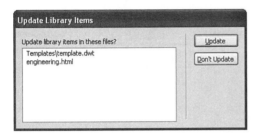

FIGURE 12.29   The Update Library Items dialog box displays a list of files that use the library item being edited.

4. The Update Library Items dialog box displays a list of files in the defined site that use the library item you just edited. Click the Update button. Dreamweaver scans and updates all the footer library items in your site accordingly. A log of completion will display the result of Dreamweaver's site scan and subsequent updates. Click Close to close the log.

Close the footer.lbi file and try opening one of your HTML pages. Notice that the footer on the pages of your defined site now reflect the change made to the library item.

Renaming Library Items

Like every other file in the Site panel, library items can easily be renamed at any time. When you rename a library item, Dreamweaver performs a scan of files and displays the same Update Pages dialog box presented to you in the previous section, allowing you to update all pages that use the selected library item (in this case, updating them to use the new filename). In fact, you can rename library items in the Library folder in the Site panel or directly in the library items list in the Assets panel. To demonstrate how library items can be renamed, follow these steps:

1. Close all open HTML pages and switch to the Library Items category in the Assets panel.

2. Right-click the nav library item and choose the Rename option from the context menu. Alternatively, select the Rename option from the panel's Options menu. Either method you choose allows you to rename the file.

3. Change the item's name to **navigation** and press Enter to apply the change.

4. The Update Files dialog box appears. Click Update. Dreamweaver scans the HTML files and updates all library items within the site accordingly.

You can also rename files directly from the Files panel. To use this method, follow these steps:

1. If you're still in the Assets panel, switch to the Files panel.

2. Expand the Library folder.

3. Right-click the `footer.lbi` file and select the Rename option from the Edit submenu of the context menu. Alternatively, select the file and press the F2 key to rename the file.

4. Change the name back to **nav** and press Enter to apply the change.

5. The Update Files dialog box appears; click Update. Dreamweaver scans the HTML files and updates all library items in the site accordingly.

Moving Library Items to a New Site

The obvious benefit to using library items is that you can create small pieces of functionality that can easily be shared across multiple pages in your site. But the functionality doesn't have to be limited to a single site. Dreamweaver offers the benefit of copying library items from one site to another. This means that you have to create a library item only once; if you ever feel compelled to use that functionality in another site, you can copy the library item to that site directly in Dreamweaver. To copy a library item from the Vecta Corp site to another site, follow these steps:

1. With the Vecta Corp site as the current site, switch to the Library Items category in the Assets panel.

2. Right-click the library item you want to copy. From the Copy to Site submenu of the context menu, choose the site name to which you want to copy the library item.

> **NOTE**
>
> If a Library folder doesn't exist in the site to which you're attempting to copy the library item to, Dreamweaver automatically creates the folder for you.

Although the method you used for copying a library item was simple enough, you can perform the same operation by choosing the Copy to Site option from the Assets panel's Options menu.

Deleting Library Items

As is the case with files in the Files panel, library items can be deleted at will. To delete a library item, select it from the library item list in the Assets panel and click the Delete button located in the bottom-right corner of the Assets panel. Alternatively, select the LBI file in the Library folder in the Files panel and press the Delete key.

When you delete a library item from the library items list, only the library item markup in the file that uses the item is removed. The tie between the library item within the page and the actual file in the Library Items list are said to be broken.

If you do accidentally delete a library item, you can easily re-create it by right-clicking the orphaned library item and choosing the Recreate option from the context menu.

After you've chosen the Recreate option, refresh the site list in the Files panel (by clicking the Refresh Site List button—the first icon in the button bar in the bottom-right corner of the Assets panel) to see the LBI file reappear.

If you decide that you do, in fact, want to remove references to library items from each of your HTML pages, you can right-click the library item in the page and choose the Detach from Original option from the context menu. Dreamweaver removes the reference to the library item completely. After you've deleted the reference to the library item from each web page, the actual item—such as the navigation bar or footer—is still on the page until you physically delete it. You can now safely delete the library item from the Files panel or the Assets panel without worrying about creating an orphaned library item in the web page.

Working with Server-Side Includes

Similar to library items, server-side includes (SSIs) allow you to create pieces of functionality that can be shared among various web pages and be edited and updated centrally. In some ways, you can consider SSIs the predecessor to library items because SSIs have been with us long before the inception of Dreamweaver's library items. The major differences between the two, however, are that library items have a familiar editing interface (they can be directly modified, managed, and updated in Dreamweaver's development environment at design time), whereas the server handles the updating of SSIs at runtime (when the files are actually processed by the server for viewing by the user). Furthermore, SSIs can also include server variables such as the current date and time, the date on which the file was last saved, and even the size of a file as compared to a second file.

> **NOTE**
>
> Because SSIs pose a potential security risk, not all web-hosting providers will support them. Check with your web-hosting company before deciding to use SSIs in your websites.

At its foundation, SSIs are used to include the contents of files within the scope of a second file, much like the way library items work. Typically, the code used to insert SSIs resembles the following:

```
<!-- #include file="ssi/footer.htm" -->
```

As you can see from the code, the standard HTML opening and closing comment tag is used to wrap the SSI directive. In this case, the directive is #include and contains the attribute file that specifies the document-relative file path to include in the web page. To include a file relative to the current site's *root*, the include changes to use the virtual attribute instead of the file attribute, as follows:

```
<!-- #include virtual="/ssi/footer.htm" -->
```

Working with SSIs in Dreamweaver is a snap because Dreamweaver's translator makes SSIs visible during the design process. As long as the Show Contents of Included File check box (located in the Invisible Elements category of the Preferences window) is selected, as shown in Figure 12.30, SSIs display in your pages in Dreamweaver without a problem.

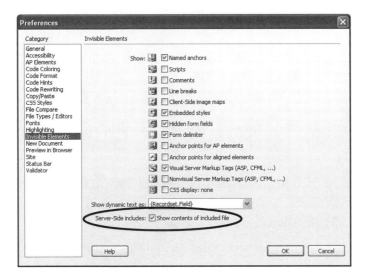

FIGURE 12.30   Make sure that the Show Contents of Included File option is selected in the Preferences window.

One of the major benefits to using SSIs is that information coming in from the server can be included in the web page itself. For instance, the `<!-- #echo -->` tag is used to define custom variables and environment variables that are to be returned when the page is called on the server. *Environment variables* are information available on the server, such as the date a file was last modified or its URL. Table 12.1 displays a list of server tags and a few of their more important attributes.

TABLE 12.1   Server Tags and Their Attributes

Tag	Attribute	Description
`<$I<!-- #config -->;description of><!-- #config -->`	`errmsg`, `timefmt`, or `sizefmt`	The config directive controls various aspects of file parsing, including the customization of error messages, file size, or time and date displays.
`<$I<!-- #include -->;description of><!-- #include -->`	`file` or `virtual`	Use this tag to insert a second document into the document to be parsed.
`<$I<!-- #echo -->;description of><!-- #echo -->`	`var` or environment variables such as `DOCUMENT_NAME`, `DOCUMENT_URI`, `DATE_LOCAL`, `DATE_GMT`, or `LAST_MODIFIED`	Prints the value of one of the include environment variables.

<$l<!-- #fsize -->;description of><!-- #fsize -->	file or virtual	Displays the size of the specified file.
<!-- #flastmod --><$l<!-- #flastmod -->;description of>	file or virtual	Displays the last modification date of the specified file.
<$l<!-- #exec -->;description of><!-- #exec -->	cmd or cgi	Executes a given system (shell) command or CGI script.

Now that you have an idea of the flexibility that server-side tags and includes provide, let's examine how to add a server-side include to a web page. To do this, follow these steps:

1. Open a blank HTML page by choosing File, New. Choose Blank Page, HTML, <none>, and click Create.

2. Select Insert, Server-Side Include. The Select File dialog box appears.

3. Browse to the Library folder of the defined Vecta Corp site and choose the nav.lbi file.

4. Click OK. The navigation menu is included as a server-side include within the page.

5. Switch to the Split Code/Design view and notice that the server-side include tag is added to the code.

6. To edit the SSI, select the SSI and click the Edit button in the Property inspector. Dreamweaver immediately launches a new Document window instance for the LBI file.

TIP

In our scenario, we used an existing LBI file as a server-side include. The beauty of SSIs is that they're not limited to file extension types. For instance, you can use LBI, SSI, HTM, TXT, SHTML, and more as included files.

Summary

As you have seen in this chapter, working with templates in Dreamweaver offers a robust and intuitive method for developing and managing an organization's look and feel. In this chapter, you learned about templates—how to build templates from scratch, how to define editable, repeating, and optional regions, and how to apply templates to existing pages. Reinforced by those basic concepts, you also learned about more advanced features, such as template management using the Assets panel, how to apply templates to existing pages, remapping inconsistent template regions, removing template markup, and changing the default document using Dreamweaver.

Additionally, we introduced library items, discussing the differences between them and templates. We also reviewed how they are created and managed using the Assets panel, how they're edited, updated, renamed, and deleted. At the end of the chapter, we looked at server-side includes, their similarities with library items, and how they differ in that they can communicate with the server by returning important server-side messages, date and time values, and so on.

In the next chapter, we'll begin moving from task automation and workflow enhancement to incorporating multimedia and animation. We'll look at how to incorporate multimedia elements such as audio and video, and then look at Dreamweaver's integration with complementary programs such as Fireworks, Photoshop, and Flash.

12

PART IV

Incorporating Multimedia and Animation

IN THIS PART

Incorporating Video and Audio

It's funny that we live in a world where cinemas and video rental stores are within miles of our homes. We log on to online video rental stores and even subscribe to video-on-demand services for our televisions. Yet with all of this at our fingertips, we're always amazed when we see a small, jerky, and grainy video on the Web.

Why is that? Because of the promise of high-quality digital video being available to us when we want it and whenever we want it. In the past few years, companies such as Microsoft, Apple, Real, Autodesk, Adobe, Sorenson, DivX, and so on have made strides in delivering on that promise. With streaming technologies, better codecs (compression algorithms), and generally higher bandwidth in our homes, the promise of delivering small-sized, high-quality web video is coming to fruition.

Dreamweaver offers unprecedented support for incorporating video and audio files into your web pages. Whether you're working with Windows Media, Real Media, QuickTime, Flash Video, MP3, or MIDI files, Dreamweaver will get you off and running quickly and effortlessly.

As you've done with the rest of the chapters in this book, you can work with the examples in this chapter by downloading the files from the book's website. You'll want to replace the files located at `C:\VectaCorp\` with the files that you download for this chapter at `Exercises\Chapter13\ Beginning`.

Video on the Web

For people not in the computer industry, it's hard to understand why video on the Web isn't as prominent as text, images, and even music. Let's face it—we live in a society that's infatuated with reality television shows, sitcoms, soap operas, sports, sports reality shows—the list goes on and on. When we're done watching our television shows, we make our way to the computer to check our email and download music. Unfortunately, the two mediums remain separate entities: We watch television for video and we move over to the computer for mail, still images, and music. To understand why this is the case, we must first understand the media, its size, and underlying format.

In most cases, the video you see on your television is analog video, whereas computers recognize purely digital formats. Although analog video can easily be converted to a digital format, in reality this is only the beginning of the solution. Televisions recognize standard formats and sizes, while computers vary greatly in detail. Some people have slow computers, some have fast computers, some people have lots of RAM, and others have only a little. Some users have dial-up modems, others have broadband, some users own a PC, others a Mac. When all is said and done, the blame can be assigned to the variations of computer brands, computer configurations, and Internet connection speeds across the multitude of users. With televisions, we don't have to worry about types, connection speeds, or even the size or lack of size of your televisions. Televisions were invented to play video and evolved from one standard delivery format: the radio signal.

All this sounds disheartening, but it gets worse. Not only are we affected by varying computer types, RAM, processor speeds, and connection speeds, but media players have also been adopted to view specific media formats on different computers. Can you imagine turning on your television and tuning to a high-definition channel, only to be rejected because a "high-definition player" wasn't installed on your television when it left the factory?

Although all this might be enough to make you forget web-based video altogether, it's important to understand that times are changing. People are buying faster computers. The number of people who own broadband in their homes is on the rise. Companies such as Microsoft, Apple, and Real have introduced media players that are interoperable with each other's media formats. Add to this programs such as Autodesk's Cleaner, Sorenson's Squeeze, and Adobe's Flash Video that produce smaller, high-quality web-based video, and it's easy to see why you'll want to incorporate video on your websites as well.

Download, Progressive Download, and Streaming

One of the biggest reasons why negative feelings about video on the Web exist is because of the lack of knowledge in terms of accessing the video after it's on the Web. Essentially, there are three methods for accessing video on the Web:

- ▶ Direct download
- ▶ Progressive download
- ▶ Streaming

The simplest method for accessing video on the Web is to allow your users to download the video file. By placing a link on your site, you can allow your users to download the video, store it on their hard drives, and then play it in the appropriate media player whenever they want. Although this method is the most direct, it provides little in terms of protecting your video from being distributed without your permission.

The second method for accessing video on the Web is similar to the first but differs in its approach. *Progressive downloading* is the process of downloading video to your computer in the form of a file that can be saved after the video has been cached to your machine. The video downloads to your computer, playing off your hard drive locally, generally without you knowing that the file has even been downloaded. The result is cleaner, bigger, crisper, higher-quality video. The downside is that it can take longer to view the video because you have to wait for it to download to your machine. However, with a fast Internet connection, you might not notice the difference because when enough of the video has downloaded, the video starts playing, using the playing time as download time for the rest of the video.

A streaming file is different and more complex. The idea behind streaming video is that the user clicks a file, and the file starts a short process (several seconds) called *buffering*. (The computer downloads a sufficient number of kilobytes for the first segment of the clip.) During this process, the screen is blank, and the user must stand by until the buffering process is complete. When the clip starts playing, the user watches the first segment while the rest of the information continues to stream simultaneously to achieve smooth and continuous playing. The obvious advantage of this method is that the user doesn't have to wait until the complete file is downloaded, resulting in faster viewing of the video file. The disadvantages are that the user can't move back and forth on the clip's timeline while the clip is playing. Also, the quality is generally lower. Streaming enables, among other things, control of buffering time (usually 8 to 25 seconds) and whether the viewer is allowed to save the video file to the hard disk. Table 13.1 outlines the three video delivery formats and highlights when they should be used in your projects.

TABLE 13.1   Video Delivery Formats

Factor	Direct	Progressive	Streaming
Clip is under 5 seconds long	X	X	—
Clip is 5 to 30 seconds long	—	X	X
Clip is more than 30 seconds long	—	—	X
Low viewership expected	—	X	—
Medium-to-high viewership expected	—	—	X
Instant start	—	—	X
Intellectual property protection	—	—	X
Live video streams	—	—	X
Variable streaming rates based on visitor's bandwidth	—	—	X

Of course, how you view that video is entirely up to the media type, which ultimately means that you'll need the appropriate media player installed on your computer to view the media type. Media players are discussed in the next section.

Media Players

To view video on the Web, you must have a media player. Regardless of whether you are allowing your users to download, progressively download, or stream media files, users must have a media player that supports the media type you're offering on your web pages. Many sites offer media content in three formats—Windows Media Player, Real Media, and QuickTime—and a fourth, Flash video, is slowly gaining steam and making its mark on the Web.

The world of media players is constantly changing. As of this writing, Apple has announced QuickTime 7.5, Microsoft is shipping Windows Media Player 11, Real is allowing free downloads of its RealPlayer (in Basic or Plus versions), and, as of the release of CS4, Adobe is working on its beta version of Flash Player 10. Today's media players play much more than video. Microsoft's Windows Media Player, Real's RealPlayer, and Apple's iTunes allow direct purchases and subsequent downloads of music and movies directly from their players. Even better, these players are now directly integrating mobile devices such as Apple's iPod, Creative's Nomad series, and even Windows Media Player for Pocket PC. Beyond that, most media players are interoperable for all but proprietary formats, meaning that they'll all play many standardized media types with few to no problems.

> **TIP**
>
> The Windows Media Player for the Mac is outdated and incompatible with most Windows Media content currently on the Web. Mac users who want to view Windows Media content can do so with the help of Flip4Mac WMV components for QuickTime, which are available at http://www.flip4mac.com/wmv_download.htm.

RealMedia

RealNetworks (Real) was the first to offer a streaming server and is considered the pioneer of streaming video. RealPlayer supports video, images, text, Flash movies, and audio.

The three primary software components of RealMedia are listed here:

▶ **RealPlayer**—By far one of the most versatile media players on the market, Real's RealPlayer can play various media types. RealPlayer can be downloaded for free at www.real.com. Additionally, services such as Rhapsody (an online music store), RadioPass (offers online radio station access), and SuperPass (provides video on demand) can be purchased for prices ranging from $9.99/month–$12.99/month, or RadioPass for $49.99/year.

▶ **RealProducer**—You can use this encoding software as a way to convert audio and video (MPEG, QuickTime, Windows Media, and so on) into Real's native RealAudio and RealVideo formats. You can download RealProducer Basic for free or get the full-featured RealProducer Plus for about $200 at www.realnetworks.com/products/producer.

▶ **Helix Server and Helix Proxy**—Whether you are getting started or have been streaming for some time, the Helix Server and Helix Proxy product lines from Real have been designed to help you deliver the highest quality digital media experience to the largest audience at the lowest cost. The Helix product line is the most powerful server software available for streaming media files across an intranet, the Internet, or over a mobile network. More information can be found at www.realnetworks.com/products/media_delivery.html.

Real is undoubtedly the pioneer in streaming video and by far offers the most versatile media player in that its RealPlayer product is supported by more platforms than any other media player on the market today. The RealPlayer is available for Windows, Mac, UNIX, Linux, OS/2, and Palm OS. Beyond compatibility, RealPlayer offers subscription-based plans to view certain content from BBC News, Sporting News Radio, CBS, ABC, NBC, and more than 3,200 radio stations around the globe.

QuickTime

Apple was ahead of its time back in the early 1990s when it introduced an application called QuickTime. QuickTime was the first application that enabled you to play digital video on a computer. Today, QuickTime sets the standard in multimedia playback, offering a clean, brushed-aluminum interface for viewing video on the Web.

Often, people confuse QuickTime with the QuickTime Video format. The QuickTime Player is a separate application dedicated to viewing different content, including QuickTime Video, Flash movies, Windows Media, 3D objects (QuickTime Virtual Reality—QTVR), MP3, MPEG, and much more. Like Real, QuickTime has these main software components:

▶ **QuickTime Player**—Like the RealPlayer, which plays native RM files, the QuickTime Player plays native MOV files and can play many more formats. You can learn more about, and download the QuickTime Player for free, at www.apple.com/quicktime/player.

▶ **QuickTime Player Pro**—For $29.99, you can purchase a key code that unlocks all the content-creation features built into QuickTime. Using the key code turns the QuickTime Player into QuickTime Pro, which essentially allows you to convert media files into QuickTime MOV files, enables video compositing capabilities, and so on. For much more information on the features and benefits of QuickTime Pro, visit www.apple.com/quicktime/pro.

▶ **QuickTime Broadcaster**—QuickTime Broadcaster is a free application designed to allow users to easily broadcast live events, meetings, and more on the Internet. More information on QuickTime Broadcaster can be found at www.apple.com/quicktime/broadcaster.

▶ **QuickTime Streaming Server**—Like Real's Helix Server, the QuickTime Streaming Server allows video to be streamed over the Web. Unlike Real's Helix Server, however, the QuickTime Streaming Server can be downloaded for free at www.apple.com/quicktime/streamingserver/.

QuickTime offers the highest-quality video playback, and because of its support for MPEG-4, QuickTime is quickly becoming a standard for quality-conscious developers. Currently, QuickTime Player is available for Mac OS and Windows. For more information on MPEG-4 and Apple's contributions to the standard, visit Apple's website at www.apple.com/quicktime/technologies/mpeg4.

Windows Media

Enjoying a large share of the market and installed on all Windows operating systems, Windows Media Player has become an extremely viable platform for viewing video both on your desktop and directly through the web browser. Like Real's RealPlayer, the Windows Media Player has the capability to play numerous video formats, such as ASF, ASX, AVI, MPG, MOV, and WMV; it can also play audio formats such as MP3, AIF, and AU. Software involved with Windows Media includes the following:

▶ **Windows Media Player**—As mentioned, Windows Media Player comes preinstalled on all Windows operating systems and is ready to play numerous video and audio formats. For more information and the latest updates for Windows Media, visit the website at www.windowsmedia.com.

▶ **Windows Media Server**—Like Real's Helix Server and QuickTime's Streaming Server, Microsoft provides server software in its Windows Media Server product that allows you to stream live or on-demand content to Windows Media Players both on desktops and wireless devices such as Pocket PCs. More information can be found at the Windows Media Server website at www.microsoft.com/windows/windowsmedia/forpros/server/server.aspx.

Flash Video

As I've already mentioned, the slow evolution of quality video on the Web is caused in large part by the variety of media players, platforms, and user configurations. Flash Video (represented by the FLV extension), aims to fill the need. Supported by Flash Player 7 and later, Flash Video offers technological and creative benefits that allow designers to create immersive, rich experiences that fuse video with data, graphics, sound, and dynamic interactive control.

The benefits to using Flash Video are extensive. First, no additional plugins are required of the user (aside from the Flash plugin). As long as the user has the Flash Player plugin version 7 or later, viewing Flash Video isn't a problem. Second, and possibly more important, Flash Video files load quickly and provide a rich and immersive experience for the end user. Because Flash Player treats Flash Video as just another media type, you can layer, script, and control video just like any other object in a SWF file. As it relates to Dreamweaver, Flash Video can be embedded directly in a web page. This means that the file plays directly in the page, in contrast to launching a pop-up window that can inter-rupt the user experience. As you'll see later in the chapter, creating Flash Video is a snap and generally involves encoding a video file to the Flash Video format using a program that comes with Flash (Flash Video Encoder). After the file has been encoded, the resulting FLV file can be embedded directly into a web page using Dreamweaver.

Working with Video Clips

Unless you're working with streaming media, working with video clips in both Dreamweaver and the browser is extremely easy and generally self-explanatory. For the most part, you add a media file by embedding the file into the web page (discussed later); then save the document and view the page in the desired browser. Depending on the media type you decide to use, the browser recognizes the format, launches the appropriate plugin (if it is installed), and plays the video. If the browser can't play the video (maybe the plugin isn't installed), you have the option of manually providing the location of the media player's plugin.

In general, if you're working with short video clips (10–20 seconds in length), it's okay to embed the video clips into the web page so that when the user clicks the file, a progressive download is forced. A second option is to create links on your web page that users can click to download the media file and play the files on the computer later. When down-loaded and viewed in a media player, a video file typically resembles Figure 13.1, showing the QuickTime Player.

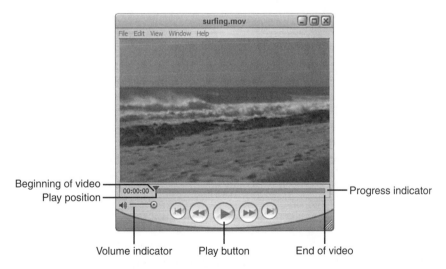

FIGURE 13.1   All media players typically have a beginning, an end, progress indicator, a play position, a volume bar, and a traditional Play button.

Most media players look and function similarly. Many have a beginning, an end, a progress indicator (seek bar), a play position, a volume bar, and traditional Play, Stop, and Pause buttons.

In terms of video formats to use in your web pages, QuickTime movies (MOV), AVI, MPG, Windows Media Video (WMV), RealMedia (RM), and Flash Video (FLV) make good candidates because these are the most widely supported formats by the four media players. With that said, MOV, RM, WMV, and FLV files have been included (within the Media folder) with the files you downloaded for this chapter so that you can follow along with the examples.

Linking Video

One of the simplest methods for allowing users access to your video files is to create links directly from your website. In this scenario, the user clicks the link, the browser figures out which plugin it needs to launch, and the file plays either in the browser or externally in the media player (if the browser didn't find the appropriate browser plugin). To create a link to video in a web page, follow these steps:

1. Open the `linkingvideo.html` page included with the downloaded files for this chapter. You'll notice that three bullet points exist for linking the three types of media files (located in the Media folder).

2. Highlight the first bullet point (*View QuickTime version*) and drag the point-to-file icon into the `surfing.mov` file located in the Media folder.

3. Repeat steps 1 and 2 for the other two bullet points, linking the RealMedia bullet point to the `surfing.rm` file and Windows Media bullet point to the `surfing.wmv` file. When you've finished, you should have three bulleted links, each pointing to a different media type.

4. Save your work.

Preview the page in the browser by pressing F12 (Option-F12). When the page loads in the browser, click the QuickTime link. You'll quickly notice that the QuickTime movie is progressively downloaded and played in a new browser instance.

You can also right-click (Control-click) the link and choose the Save Target As option from the context menu to save the media file to disk for playback later. In this case, you would save the file to your hard drive. When you're ready to view the video, double-click the file; the appropriate media player opens and begins playing the file.

Embedding Video

In the previous section, you explored a possibility for allowing users to access your media files by linking the video files to your web page. The obvious drawback to this method is that when the link was clicked, the media file progressively downloaded and played in a new browser window instance. Essentially, the user was taken away from your site and forced to watch the video in a blank browser page, interrupting the overall user experience of your website. This video-watching experience could be enhanced by allowing your users to watch the video clip directly on the web page through a process known as *embedding*. By embedding video clips into the page, the browser forces the progressive download of the file directly within the context of the overall design. Embedding video gives the web designer control over other options, including sizing, vertical and horizontal spacing, specifying a plugin source, alignments, borders, and more. To embed a video into a web page, follow these steps:

1. Open the `embeddingvideo.html` page included with the downloaded files for this chapter.

2. To embed a video within the page, choose Insert, Media, Plugin. The Select File dialog box appears.

3. Browse to the `surfing.mov` file and click OK. Alternatively, you can embed a media file into a web page by dragging it from the Files panel and into the page. Either method creates a small 32-pixel by 32-pixel icon on the page similar to the one shown in Figure 13.2.

FIGURE 13.2   When media elements are embedded into the page, a small 32-pixel by 32-pixel icon is created by default.

4. You can resize the default icon to match the size of the video it will play. Because the `surfing.mov` video file is 260 pixels by 170 pixels, select the plugin icon and enter the values **260** and **170** into the W and H text boxes in the Property inspector.

5. Save your work.

Preview the page in the browser by pressing F12 (Option-F12). When the page loads in the browser, the movie is downloaded and played within the context of the overall design, similar to Figure 13.3.

FIGURE 13.3   Embedding a video gives you the opportunity to play a video within the context of the overall design.

You probably noticed that other options became available in the Property inspector when you selected the plugin icon. These options include the following:

▶ **Clip Name**—Enter a name in this text box to uniquely identify the media file.

▶ **W and H**—Enter numeric values in these two text boxes to set the width and height (in pixels) of the media file.

▶ **Src**—Displays the full path to the media file.

▶ **Plg URL**—Enter the URL for the company of the specific media type. This way, if users don't have the specific plugin installed, they can visit the URL you attach to download the appropriate plugin.

▶ **Align**—Choose an option from this menu to set the alignment of other elements on your web page in relation to the media file. Options include Default, Baseline, Top, Middle, Bottom, TextTop, Absolute Middle, Absolute Bottom, Left, and Right.

▶ **Play**—Click this button to play the media file directly in Dreamweaver.

▶ **Class**—When working with CSS, apply a custom class to the media file by choosing the class from this menu.

▶ **V and H**—Enter numeric values in these text boxes to set the vertical and horizontal spacing (in pixels) around the media file.

▶ **Border**—Enter a numeric value in this text box to set the border size (in pixels) around the media file.

▶ **Parameters**—QuickTime movie and RealMedia files allow you to specify parameters for the movie to control looping, movie speed, whether to show the menu bar, and so on. Passing parameters into the video file is covered with more detail next.

Passing Parameters into Video Files

In the previous section, we looked at embedding video clips into a web page. You saw that the Property inspector outlines various attributes for the embedded video, including the movie name, the source of the file (Src), the width and height of the clip (W and H), and the website or location of the plugin if it is not found on the user's browser (Plg URL). Although the Property inspector outlines numerous properties supported by the embedded video, it doesn't show them all. A number of other properties can be added to the embedded video to control aspects of the video clips using the Parameters dialog box. QuickTime and RealMedia files can also accept parameters passed to the file from the web page.

Table 13.2 outlines parameters supported by QuickTime video clips.

TABLE 13.2   Supported QuickTime Parameters Continued

QuickTime Parameter	Value
Autoplay	True or False
Bgcolor	Hexadecimal value or valid HTML color
Cache	True or False
Controller	True or False
Dontflattenwhensaving	Added to the tag as an attribute with no values
Endtime	A number
Height	A value in pixels
Hidden	Added to the tag as an attribute with no values
Href	A URL
Kioskmode	True or False

TABLE 13.2   Supported QuickTime Parameters Continued

QuickTime Parameter	Value
Loop	True, False, or palindrome (causes the movie to play alternately forward and backward; useful when working with QuickTime Virtual Reality (QTVR) movies)
Movieid	A number
Moviename	A name
Playeveryframe	True or False
Pluginspage	www.apple.com/quicktime
Qtnextn	A URL
Qtnext	Used to specify the URL of a movie to load and play at the end of the current movie
Qtsrc	A URL
Qtsrcchokespeed	Gives content developers the capability to specify the data rate of a movie being served, regardless of the connection speed an end user has; can be useful when a particular movie is requested from a server by large volumes of users to eliminate congestion in routers
Scale	Tofit, aspect, or a number (default is 1)
Starttime	A number
Target	Name of a valid frame or window (_self, _parent, _top, or _blank)
Targetcache	True or False
Volume	A number from 0 to 100
Width	A value in pixels

TIP

As you can see, numerous parameters and parameter values exist for QuickTime movies. Because all these parameters and their associated values are beyond the scope of this book, refer to www.apple.com/quicktime/tutorials/embed.html for a complete reference.

You can use these parameters for a QuickTime movie by entering the parameter and value pair into the Parameters dialog box. For instance, if you wanted to loop the movie when it ends in the browser, you would use the Loop parameter and set it to true. To add a parameter (like the Loop parameter) to your movie, follow these steps:

1. Open the `embeddingvideo.html` page if it's not open already.

2. With the existing video clip selected, click the Parameters button in the Property inspector. The Parameters dialog box appears.

3. Enter the parameter name **Loop** in the Parameter column and the value `True` in the Value column similar to Figure 13.4.

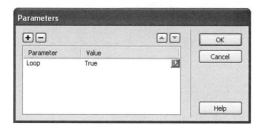

FIGURE 13.4   Enter the `Loop` parameter and set the value to `True`.

4. Click OK.

5. Save your work.

Preview your page in the browser by pressing F12 (Option-F12). This time the movie loops as soon as it reaches the end.

Similar to QuickTime movie files, RealMedia files can also accept parameters. Table 13.3 outlines the parameters supported by RealMedia files.

TABLE 13.3   Supported RealMedia Parameters

RealMedia Parameter	Value
Autostart	True or False
Console	Name, _master, _unique
Controls	All, controlpanel, imagewindow, infovolumepanel, infopanel, playbutton, positionslider, positionfield, statuspanel, statusbar, stopbutton, statusfield, and volumeslider
Nolabels	True or False

By default, RealMedia files have an interface that resembles Figure 13.5 when viewed in the browser. As you can see, the default interface is non-intuitive and doesn't resemble a typical RealMedia player interface.

FIGURE 13.5   The default RealMedia interface isn't very intuitive.

With the addition of a couple parameters, we can customize this interface to look a bit more traditional. To do this, follow these steps:

1. With the `embeddingvideo.html` page open, select the existing QuickTime movie in the Document window and delete it.

2. Choose the Insert, Media, Plugin option. Browse to the `surfing.rm` movie and click OK.

3. When the plugin icon appears on the page, select it and change the width and height properties in the Property inspector to **320** by **240.**

4. Click the Parameters button in the Property inspector to launch the Parameters dialog box.

5. Add the two parameters `Autostart` and `Controls`, setting their values to `True` and `Imagewindow`, respectively. The result resembles Figure 13.6.

6. Click OK.

7. Save your work.

Preview your page in the browser by pressing F12 (Option-F12). This time, the movie starts automatically and doesn't display the control panel as it did in Figure 13.5.

FIGURE 13.6   Enter the `Autostart` and `Controls` parameters for the RealMedia file.

Encoding Flash Video

As mentioned earlier, Flash Video is the newest video format supported by Flash Player 7 and later. Working with Flash Video on the Web is similar in process to the other three video formats except for a couple of minor nuances. First, a standard video file must be encoded using the Flash Video Encoder. Second, the resulting Flash Video file must be imported into the web page in Dreamweaver, as explained in more detail in the next section.

The first and most important step in working with Flash Video in your web pages is to encode a standard video file into the Flash Video format. This can be handled in one of many ways. Out of the box, Flash provides the Flash Video Encoder you can use to encode a standard video file into the Flash Video format. To encode a video file into the Flash Video format, follow these steps:

1. Assuming that you have Flash installed, locate the program directory and choose the Flash Video Encoder program. The application launches and presents an interface similar to Figure 13.7.

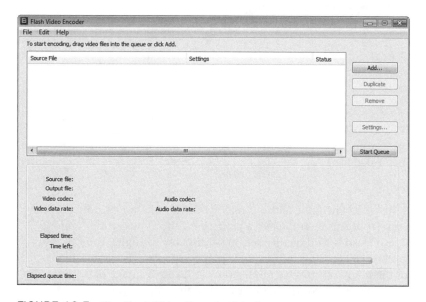

FIGURE 13.7   The Flash Video Encoder interface.

2. As you can see from Figure 13.7, the interface is fairly simple and requires little explanation. To encode a Flash Video file, add a video file to the list; modify the encoding settings as needed; and then begin the queue processing. At this point the Flash Video Encoder encodes your file format to the Flash Video format. Before we get too far ahead of ourselves, however, let's add the movie to the queue. To do this, click the Add button. The Open dialog box appears. Browse to the surfing.wmv or surfing.mov file and click Open. The movie file format appears in the list.

3. By default, video files are encoded using the default Medium Quality setting and are shown in the Settings column after a file has been added to the list. To modify this setting, click the Settings button. The Flash Video Encoding Settings dialog box appears, similar to Figure 13.8.

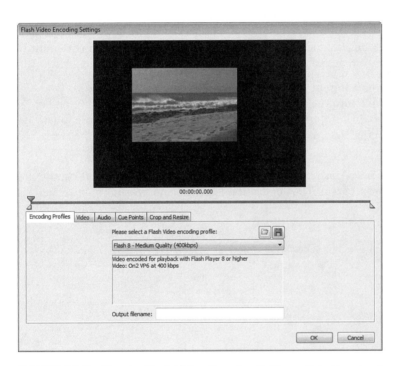

FIGURE 13.8   Use the Flash Video Encoding Settings dialog box to change the default encoding settings for the Flash Video file.

4. Initially, the Flash Video Encoding Settings dialog box displays an encoding profile drop-down menu. From this menu, select a predefined encoding setting (options include Flash 7 and Flash 8, and quality settings from Low to High). You can also click the Show Advanced Settings button to display a complete list of modifiable settings. One of the many settings we might want to take advantage of from this list is Crop and Resize. Switching to this tab reveals cropping sliders you can use to crop the black border out of the video file.

5. Experiment with the many settings available from the Show Advanced Settings menu. For now, limit your video modifications to cropping the black border and click OK.

6. To begin the encoding, click the Start Queue button. The Flash Video Encoding Settings dialog box begins encoding the video file frame by frame. The progress is tracked with the progress indicator similar to Figure 13.9.

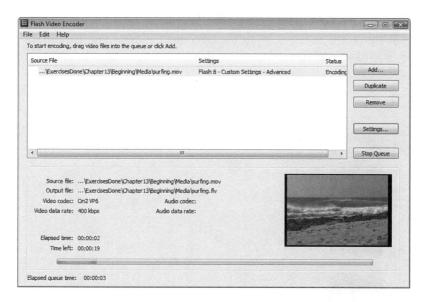

FIGURE 13.9   The progress indicator displays the encoding progress.

7. When the encoding finishes, close the Flash Video Encoding Settings dialog box by clicking the Close button in the top-right corner of the dialog box.

The new surfing.flv file appears in the Media folder of the Vecta Corp project.

Although we used Flash Video Encoder to generate our FLV file, you don't have to use it exclusively. The following programs also support encoding of Flash Video:

▶ Adobe After Effects

▶ Apple Final Cut Express

▶ Apple Final Cut Pro

▶ Apple QuickTime Pro

▶ Avid Media Composer

▶ Avid Xpress DV and Avid Xpress Pro

▶ Sorenson Squeeze

Unless you're using Sorenson Squeeze, you'll need to install the Flash Video Exporter to encode FlashVideo directly from the programs just listed. The Flash Video Exporter can be found at the following URL: www.adobe.com/devnet/flash/articles/flv_exporter.html.

Embedding Flash Video

One of the features introduced in Dreamweaver 8 is the capability to insert and customize various parameters of Flash Video files directly. Formerly a $99 software purchase known as the Flash Video Kit, both Dreamweaver CS3 and CS4 now include the feature for free. To embed a Flash Video file into a web page using Dreamweaver, follow these steps:

1. Open the `embeddingvideo.html` page if it's not open already.

2. Select the current video clip (`surfing.rm`) in the Document window and remove it by pressing the Delete key on your keyboard.

3. To import the FLV file created in the previous section, choose Insert, Media, Flash Video. The Insert Flash Video dialog box appears (see Figure 13.10).

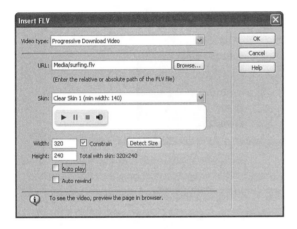

FIGURE 13.10   The Insert Flash Video dialog box facilitates the modification and subsequent insertion of Flash Video files into your web pages.

4. Later in this section, we'll discuss the various properties outlined in this dialog box. For now, click the Browse button and locate the `surfing.flv` file.

5. Enter the values **320** for width and **240** for height and click OK. The Flash Video file is inserted into your web page. Your screen will appear similar to Figure 13.11.

6. Save your work.

To view the Flash Video file in the browser, press F12 (Option-F12). Notice that as long as you have the Flash plugin installed on your browser, the video file appears in your page description. Click the Play button to begin playing the clip.

Aside from simply browsing to and inserting a Flash Video file into the web page, you can also customize the following parameters outlined by the Insert Flash Video dialog box:

▶ **Video type**—Select one of the two options from this menu to have the video file either progressively download or stream to the user.

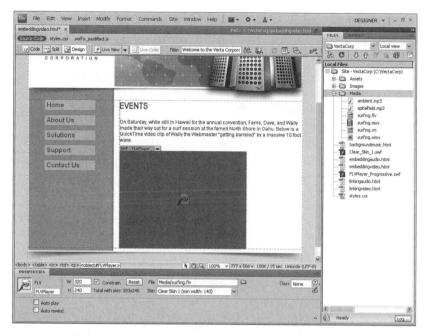

FIGURE 13.11 The Flash Video file is inserted into your web page.

▶ **URL**—Enter the relative or absolute path of the Flash Video file into this text box.

▶ **Skin**—Choose a skin for the video file. The skin you choose here customizes the look of the playback controls as well as the progress indicator.

▶ **Skin preview**—This window displays an image preview of the skin you choose from the Skin drop-down menu.

▶ **Width and Height**—Enter the width and height (in pixels) for the video file.

▶ **Constrain**—Enable this check box to automatically constrain (maintain the aspect ratio of) the width and height of the video file.

▶ **Detect Size**—If you've forgotten the width and height of the video file, click this button to automatically detect these values for the selected video file.

▶ **Auto play**—Enable this check box to have the video file automatically begin playing when the page loads for the first time or when the browser is refreshed.

▶ **Auto rewind**—Similar to loop functionality, enable this check box to have the video file automatically rewind and begin playing if the Auto Play check box is enabled.

Depending on your needs, customize the properties as you see fit. Most of these properties are also available from the Property inspector after a Flash Video file has been inserted.

> **NOTE**
>
> After you've inserted the Flash Video file into your web page, you'll notice a few new files in the Files panel. `Clear_Skin_1.swf`, `FLVPlayer_Progressive.swf`, `Scripts\expressInstall.swf`, and `Scripts\swffix_modified.js` are files that Dreamweaver will copy into your directory by default. The three SWF files are the interface files that the page needs to skin and provide playback controls for the video in the browser. The directory Scripts and associated `swffix_modified.js` are placed in the directory as a way of preventing that annoying Click to Use and Activate This Control tooltip from appearing when you roll your cursor over an embedded video file within Internet Explorer.

Audio on the Web

Audio on the web isn't a new phenomenon. In fact, record labels, bands, and websites such as Napster, Purevolume.com, Real's Rhapsody (formally Listen.com), iTunes, eMusic, and others offer direct downloads and streaming audio directly from their websites at a fraction of the cost of buying the CD from a music store—and have been doing it for years now. With the number of mobile music devices on the market, it's obvious that Internet-based audio, including the distribution of music online, is the most exciting and potentially earth-shaking aspect of the Internet audio scene.

In an effort to keep up with the latest trends, you might be thinking that it's time to begin adding audio to your website. Whether you want to add faint ambient background music or direct downloads of your band's work, adding audio to your web pages in Dreamweaver is simple. The rest of this chapter deals with adding audio to your websites using Dreamweaver. As you'll see, working with audio is similar, if not closely related to, working with video; adding these types of media to your websites is no more complicated than including images and text.

Audio File Formats

Many audio formats are in use today, spanning various platforms and operating systems. Table 13.4 outlines the most common audio formats on the Web. You might already be familiar with some of these.

TABLE 13.4 Common Audio File Formats on the Web

Audio Format	Extension	Description
AIFF	`.aiff`	Developed by Apple, the Audio Interchange File Format can be played in most browsers. However, refrain from using this format in your web pages because the file size is usually large.
Dolby AAC	`.m4a`	www.dolby.com/consumer/technology/aac.html
Flash	`.swf`	Although you might think that Flash's only purpose is to create slick animated movies, think again. Because most browsers support the Flash plugin, think about exporting your audio files as PCM- or MP3-compressed Shockwave Flash movies.
MIDI	`.mid`	Developed in the 1980s by electronic musical instrument manufacturers, the MIDI audio file is an extremely small synthesized audio format. MIDI files were the most common audio format in the 1990s because of their small file size. If you want to hear what your favorite musician sounds like on a keyboard, convert the MP3 to a MIDI file and listen.
MP3	`.mp3`	The most widely known audio format on the Web today is the MPEG Audio Layer 3, or MP3, file format, and for good reason. MP3 files are high-quality (sometimes CD-quality) files that offer excellent compression. MP3 files are also widely supported by nearly every audio and video player, including RealPlayer, QuickTime Player, Windows Media Player, WinAmp, iTunes, and more. Because of bandwidth increases, the MP3 file format has become more popular and has taken over as the *de facto* standard.
QuickTime	`.mov`	A QuickTime movie with audio only.
RealAudio	`.ra`	RealAudio is the audio component of RealMedia. This format has also been widely adopted by a variety of players on the market today and offers good-quality audio at low bit rates. However, the quality is still not as good as MP3.
WAV	`.wav`	Codeveloped by Microsoft and IBM, WAV files are the default audio format for Windows operating systems. Like AIFF on a Mac, WAV files can be played in most browsers, but you should avoid using them on your web pages because of their rather large file size.
Windows Media	`.asx,` `.wma`	When you're working with Microsoft's Windows Media Streaming Server, these audio files are generally available.

13

As you can see, you have numerous options at your fingertips. Depending on your project, you might not have to look any further than MP3. MP3 files are high-quality, highly compressed audio files that can play in nearly all audio players and in nearly all browsers. For the following examples, we'll use the MP3 format because it's the most universal.

Linking to Audio Files

Linking to audio files in your site can be accomplished just as easily as linking video clips. Simply add a link to your web page and point the link source to the MP3 file. When the user clicks the link on the page, the browser loads the appropriate media player and attempts to play the clip. To add a link to your web page that will play an MP3 audio file, follow these steps:

1. Open the `linkingaudio.html` page included with the download files for this chapter. Notice the bullet point for linking the audio file.

2. Highlight the bullet point and drag the point-to-file icon into the `spitalfield.mp3` file located in the Media folder.

3. Save your work.

Preview the page in the browser by choosing F12. When the page loads in the browser, click the link. As you'll see, the MP3 will begin playing using the software that you have configured to work with the browser.

Embedding Audio Files

The upside to linking audio files in the browser is that it gives users a chance to play the audio file when they want to. If you're a musician, linking your audio files to your web pages gives you the opportunity to allow your fans to download your music directly from your website. Of course, the downside to linking audio files from your web pages is also the fact that your fans can download your music directly from your website. Suppose that you don't want users to freely download and distribute your audio files? You can do one of two things: First, you can sample a small portion of the entire clip and post that on your web page. Second, you can embed the clip into the web page. When you embed the clip, you can provide users with the capability to stop, play, set the volume, and use a slider to pan to a specific portion of the audio clip. The obvious benefit is that users can listen to the entire clip but cannot save the clip to disk.

CAUTION

When embedding audio clips into your web pages, it's crucial that you take your user's sensitive ears into consideration. Unsuspecting users who might have accidentally turned the volume up on their speakers could easily browse to your page and be startled when the audio starts. You should always give your visitors a method of stopping any audio that's playing in your pages.

To embed audio in a web page, follow these steps:

1. Open the `embeddingaudio.html` page.

2. Place your cursor just under the paragraph of text and choose Insert, Media, Plugin.

3. Browse to the `spitalfield.mp3` file located in the Media folder and click OK. A new plugin icon appears on the page.

4. The plugin icon's size varies with the audio player you are targeting. For Windows Media player, a good size is 320 pixels wide by 45 pixels high. Change the values for the W and H settings in the Property inspector so that it resembles Figure 13.12.

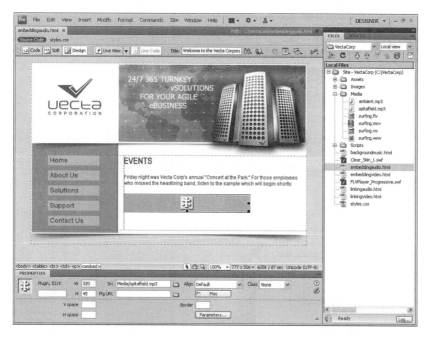

FIGURE 13.12   Resize the plugin icon to coincide with the default Windows Media player size.

5. Save your work.

Preview the page in the browser by pressing F12 (Option-F12). When the page loads in the browser, the audio clip begins playing in an instance of Windows Media player directly within the browser (see Figure 13.13).

NOTE

The MP3 file began playing in Windows Media Player because that's my operating system's default media player. Results vary, depending on which player is configured to run for a specific file type on your system.

FIGURE 13.13   The audio clip begins playing in an instance of Windows Media player directly in the browser.

In this example, we used Windows Media Player to play our MP3 clip. Depending on the file type of the audio clip, the appropriate player is automatically chosen by the browser.

In some rare cases, visitors to your website might not have an audio player installed to handle playing audio files directly in the browser. If this is the case, the user can click the plugin icon. The browser redirects the user to the appropriate page for downloading plugins required to play audio files within the browser.

Playing Background Music

When used tastefully, faint ambient background music can be an added plus to your website. As mentioned in the previous section, however, if you use music inappropriately (adding blaring music that starts without notice), your users will wish they never visited your site and will probably quickly close the page.

To add background music to your web page, follow these steps:

1. Open the `backgroundmusic.html` file.

2. Place your cursor just under the paragraph of text and choose Insert, Media, Plugin.

3. Browse to the `ambient.mp3` file located in the Media folder and click OK. A new plugin icon appears on the page. Keep the plugin icon's default size. (Its size won't matter in this case.)

4. Select the plugin icon and click the Parameters button in the Property inspector. The Parameters dialog box appears.

5. Add the `hidden`, `autostart`, and `loop` parameters and set all their values to `true`.

6. Click OK to close the Parameters dialog box.

7. Save your work.

Preview the page in the browser by pressing F12 (Option-F12). When the page loads in the browser, the audio clip begins playing faintly in the background. Notice that the default audio player is hidden from view and that the clip loops to the beginning to produce continuous sound.

Summary

Adding media such as rich video and audio is a great way to add depth to your site. And both of these mediums can remain optional for the end user. Although both options require plugins in the user's browser, they often add to the uniqueness of your website's existing content.

With web users demanding more from their web experiences, offering digital video and audio on your site might just be the ticket for getting them to return to your site time and time again.

In the next few chapters, we'll stray from the traditional mediums of video and audio and look at Dreamweaver's integration with the complementary programs Fireworks, Photoshop, and Flash.

Integrating with Fireworks, Photoshop, and Flash

Adobe's Fireworks and Photoshop have quickly grown to become two of the premier image-editing programs used by graphics professionals. With features that allow for the quick optimization, cropping, and resizing of images, combined with the power to make colors transparent, change contrast, and color balance, it's clear why they have become the standard for web professionals as well. And while Fireworks has always been primarily geared toward image creation, editing, and optimization for web development, Photoshop has built a reputation for serving more than just the professional print designer.

When was the last time you built a website for a client who thought everything was perfect the first time around? In the real world, this is never the case. Fortunately, Dreamweaver's integration with image editing programs such as Fireworks and Photoshop makes it simple to quickly edit and optimize images directly from Dreamweaver. With a simple click of an icon within the Property inspector in Dreamweaver, you can quickly and effortlessly launch graphics for editing purposes within either Fireworks or Photoshop. After you've made a change to the graphic, you click Done in Fireworks or Save in Photoshop, and the image is instantly updated in Dreamweaver. Gone are the days of fumbling for original images, opening them directly in a dedicated image-editing program, making changes, exporting your work, saving the original, and then reimporting the completed image into Dreamweaver.

In this chapter, we'll harness the web-centric power that Fireworks and Photoshop provide. We'll browse for images, edit and optimize images, create new images, use Fireworks HTML code, and even create a full-featured web photo album with little to no effort. In the second half of the chapter, we'll introduce Dreamweaver's integration with Flash. You'll learn how to embed Flash movies in your web pages, pass parameters into those movies, control Flash movies using behaviors, and work with round-trip Flash editing.

To take advantage of these integration features, it's important to have these programs installed on your computer. If you don't have access to full versions of Fireworks, Photoshop, or Flash, you can download the trial versions from Adobe's website at www.adobe.com/products/fireworks/, www.adobe.com/products/photoshop/, and www.adobe.com/products/flash/.

> **NOTE**
>
> This chapter assumes that you've purchased a standalone version of Dreamweaver. If that's the case, Fireworks and Photoshop won't be installed by default. You'll either have to purchase the software separately or download the trial versions for use as you complete the exercises in this chapter. Additionally, you might have purchased one of the creative suites that may or may not have these programs already installed. For more information on Adobe's suite of products, visit www.adobe.com/products/creativesuite/.

As you've done with the rest of the chapters in this book, you can work with the examples in this chapter by downloading the files from the book's website. You'll want to replace the files in C:\VectaCorp\ with the files included in Exercises\Chapter14\Beginning\.

Specifying External Editors

Depending on the order in which you installed Dreamweaver and Fireworks/Photoshop/Flash, you might have to make changes to the File Types/Editors category in the Preferences dialog box. Options within the File Types/Editors category in the Preferences dialog box exist to allow Dreamweaver to establish communication with and easily send files to its sibling programs Fireworks, Photoshop, and Flash.

> **NOTE**
>
> The File Types/Editors category is covered with much more detail in Appendix C, "Defining Preferences."

In a nutshell, the File Types/Editors category in the Preferences window, shown in Figure 14.1, allows you to specify which external applications you want to handle image editing for specific file types. Another option that you might notice right away is a text box for defining the path to Fireworks. Dreamweaver uses this path when sending image files (such as GIF, JPG, and PNG) specifically to Fireworks during round-trip editing scenarios. We'll discuss this in more detail later.

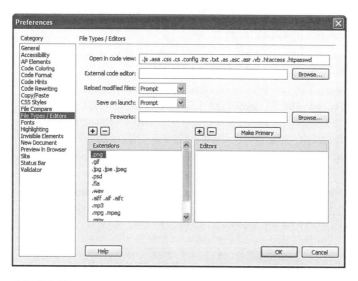

FIGURE 14.1 In the Preferences dialog box, under the File Types/Editors category, you can specify which application you want to use to edit a particular file type. Additionally, when working with round-trip editing, you might want to specify the path to Fireworks on your computer.

For the most part, common image types such as GIF and JPG are already associated with either Photoshop or Fireworks in this screen. Similarly, FLA/MOV file types are usually associated with Flash (assuming it's already installed). In some cases, they might not be, and you'll need to walk through the configuration process manually. To demonstrate the process, we'll walk through the steps one at a time using a file in the infrequently used (in relation to GIF and JPG) PNG file type. Because PNG files are native to Fireworks and have the potential for use on the Web, we'll use this opportunity to associate the PNG file format with Fireworks (assuming that it isn't already associated).

NOTE

It's not uncommon to see new installations of Dreamweaver that don't have the PNG and JPG file types associated with an external image editor by default. In some cases, I've even seen the GIF file format associated with Internet Explorer. If you look closely in Figure 14.1, I don't currently have an editor associated with the PNG file type, and I have fresh installation of Dreamweaver. In scenarios such as these, the steps we cover in the following section will help guide you through the process of (re)associating these file types with either an editor or the correct type of editor.

To set the application association, follow these steps:

1. Open the Preferences dialog box by choosing Edit, Preferences (Dreamweaver, Preferences).

2. In the Preferences dialog box, choose the File Types/Editors category.

3. In the File Extension list, choose the file extension you want to (re)associate with an application. For now, select the PNG file format.

4. Click the Add (+) button just above the Editors option box to launch the Select External Editor dialog box.

5. With the Select External Editor dialog box open, navigate to `C:\Program Files\Adobe\Adobe Fireworks CS4\fireworks10.exe` (`/Applications/Adobe Fireworks CS4/Adobe Fireworks 10.app`) and click Open. Notice that the new editor is added to the Editors list, associating itself with the PNG file format.

6. If you have more than one application associated with a particular file type and prefer to use the application you just selected as the default, highlight it in the Editors list and click the Make Primary button. Notice that to the right of the application name, it reads (`Primary`). This application acts as the default editor when you ask Dreamweaver to edit that particular file type.

NOTE

Associating PNG files with Fireworks is a step in the right direction. Because PNG files are native to Fireworks, it makes sense to make this association. Depending on the graphics editor you prefer, you might also want to set Fireworks as the primary editor for GIF and JPG files. Of course, Fireworks isn't the only program you might decide to use with the PNG, GIF, and JPG file formats. Adobe Photoshop is also an excellent alternative. If you'd rather use Photoshop as the default editor, run through the same steps that you went through previously, adding Photoshop from the following path: `C:\Program Files\Adobe\Adobe Photoshop CS4\Photoshop.exe` (`/Applications/Adobe Photoshop CS4/Adobe Photoshop CS4.app`).

Setting the File Types in the Preferences dialog box is a necessary step to ensure integration with Fireworks and Photoshop. With these programs now set, you can easily launch images directly within one of these programs (covered next) by either selecting the image and then choosing the specific program's icon from the Property inspector. Or you might even decide to right-click (Control-click) on an image and choose the Edit with Fireworks/Edit with Photoshop options from the context menu. Doing this would launch your image directly within the specific program for editing.

Editing Images in Dreamweaver with Fireworks or Photoshop

Imagine building a website for a client who wasn't satisfied with the images you added to the client's web pages. Making changes to the images could be a tedious, multistep process that involves opening the original image within Fireworks or Photoshop, making the necessary changes, exporting the original image as a web-safe GIF, JPG, or PNG file, and then switching back to Dreamweaver to reimport or reset the image. Doing this over and over would be enough to make you pull your hair out in frustration. Fortunately,

Dreamweaver's integration with its sibling programs makes image editing directly from Dreamweaver virtually effortless. To edit an image directly within Fireworks/Photoshop, follow these steps:

1. Open the `companyevents_surfpics.html` file included with the chapter downloads.

2. Insert the `SurfingOahu.gif` image located in the Images folder of your defined site by selecting it and dragging it into the newly created page, preferably under the paragraph of text. As you'll see, the 400 by 250 pixel image is inserted.

3. As I'm sure you've noticed, the image is a bit too big for our design. We'll use this opportunity to edit the image in an effort to reduce its dimensions. To edit this image using Photoshop or Fireworks, select the image. The Property inspector changes, revealing the Edit button shown in Figure 14.2. Figure 14.2 shows a Fireworks icon, but if Photoshop is set up as your default editor for GIF images, your icon will be a Photoshop icon instead.

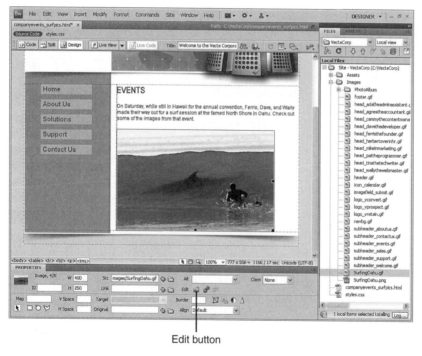

Edit button

FIGURE 14.2   The Property inspector offers the option to edit the selected image.

4. Click the Edit button to automatically launch Photoshop or Fireworks and open the image for editing within the program. In Photoshop, the selected image is opened for editing, no questions asked. If you're using Fireworks, it immediately displays a

dialog box asking you if you want to open a Fireworks PNG file as the source of the graphic, or if you want to continue opening the original file, as shown in Figure 14.3.

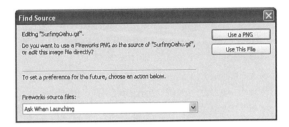

FIGURE 14.3   A dialog box appears as Fireworks launches, asking you to determine the source of the image you want to edit.

In Chapter 2, "Building a Web Page," we briefly discussed the process of *round-trip editing*. Round-trip editing is the process of opening an original file to make changes and then exporting it back to the original program all in one shot. With Dreamweaver and Fireworks, true round-trip editing works best with Fireworks-native PNG source files. For this reason, I've included the original PNG file for the SurfingOahu.gif image in the Images folder (SurfingOahu.png). If you're using Fireworks for this process, select the Always Use Source PNG option from the Fireworks source files menu and click the Use a PNG button. The Open dialog box appears.

Browse to the SurfingOahu.png image located in the Images folder and click Open. The original version appears in Fireworks, similar to Figure 14.4. As you can see, the original image is even larger than the GIF image that currently resides on our page in Dreamweaver.

5. Whether you're using Fireworks or Photoshop, the image is now ready for editing. In our case, we want to resizé it. To do this, choose Modify, Canvas, Image Size (for Fireworks) or Image, Image Size (for Photoshop). The Image Size dialog box will appear for the specific program (both are shown in Figure 14.5).

6. Regardless of which program you're using, enter **300** within the Width text box. The Height text box's value should automatically change to 188 (because the Constrain Proportions check box is selected). Click OK. The image is now resized.

7. If you're using Fireworks, you can finalize the image and return to Dreamweaver by simply clicking the Done button. This action brings you back into Dreamweaver with the new, updated image, dropped back into place (see Figure 14.6).

   If you're using Photoshop, choose File, Save. Close Photoshop, return to Dreamweaver, right-click (Control-click) the image, and choose Reset Size from the context menu. This operation refreshes the image to reflect the newer, edited size.

8. Save your work.

As you can see, the process of resizing an image directly from Dreamweaver is a snap. We selected the image; clicked the Edit icon within the Property inspector, which opened the image in either Photoshop or Fireworks; made our edits; clicked Done or File, Save; and instantly Dreamweaver was updated to reflect the changes we made. If you've decided to use Photoshop, you'll need to click the Reset size icon in the Property inspector (or right-click the image and choose Reset Size from the context menu) to update the dimensions.

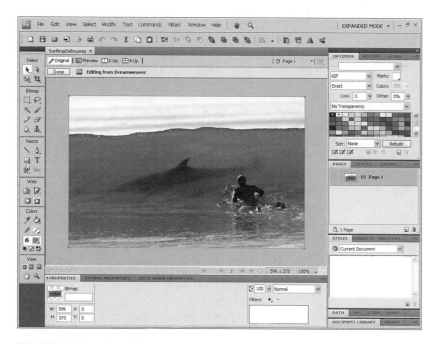

FIGURE 14.4   The original image appears in Fireworks for editing.

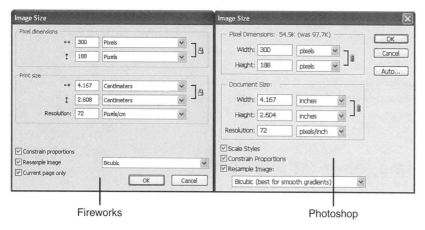

Fireworks   Photoshop

FIGURE 14.5   The Image Size dialog boxes in Fireworks and Photoshop allow you to resize an image.

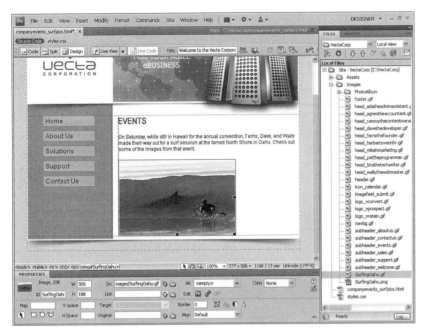

FIGURE 14.6   Clicking the Done button returns you to Dreamweaver with the newly updated image visible.

NOTE

As you might have noticed, the advantage to using Fireworks over Photoshop for direct image editing from Dreamweaver is that of round-trip editing. With Photoshop, the selected image is launched within Photoshop. Making changes to this image changes the original. The user still has to click File, Save, close Photoshop, return back to Dreamweaver, and manually reset the image's size to reflect the changes. With Fireworks, the user clicks Edit and Fireworks is launched—in which case you're given the opportunity to select an image's source. You have the option of making changes to the original or the copy and then clicking a Done button. Doing this automatically saves the image (or a copy), minimizes Fireworks, and then resets the size of the image for you within Dreamweaver.

Browsing Images in Adobe Bridge

One of Dreamweaver's newest integration features, Adobe Bridge, is an easy-to-use asset manager geared toward the visual user. Ever wish you could preview an image before selecting it for insertion into your web pages? Are you frustrated when you have to rely on the operating system's file explorer for visual representations (via icons) of media elements on your computer, or do you just need more information than it can show (such as image ISO settings or color profile data)? Do you have so many images in your project that even

Dreamweaver's Assets panel is slow to load your images? Have you ever wished Dreamweaver would allow you to associate keywords with your assets so that you could easily find every file, images, text, HTML file, and so on related to Vecta Corp (or any other client)? Adobe Bridge aims to solve these issues by allowing you to easily and visually organize, browse, locate, and view creative assets for your projects directly from Dreamweaver through Adobe Bridge.

So that you understand how Adobe Bridge works, let's browse through the images in our currently defined site from Dreamweaver using Adobe Bridge. To do this, follow these steps:

1. Select File, Browse in Bridge. Adobe Bridge appears with your files (including the Assets and Images folders), HTML files, and CSS style sheet available for selection in the Content panel.

2. Double-click the Images folder within the Content panel. Immediately, all your images are shown as thumbnails within the Content panel.

3. Select a thumbnail to display a larger version of the image within the Preview window, similar to Figure 14.7.

FIGURE 14.7   Adobe Bridge allows you to browse, locate, and view creative assets within your projects directly from Dreamweaver.

4. After you've located the creative asset you want to use within your project (assuming you're not browsing within the defined site), you can copy the asset to your defined site by right-clicking (Control-clicking) the image thumbnail within the Content panel and choosing Move To/Copy To, and then choosing the defined site or folder.

5. When you're done browsing in Bridge and want to go back to Dreamweaver, choose File, Return to Adobe Dreamweaver—or close Adobe Bridge.

Aside from simply browsing to, locating, and previewing images, Adobe Bridge provides the following functionality:

▶ Browse, locate, and preview images from your computer as well as Adobe's Stock Photos website.

▶ Highlight multiple thumbnails within the Content panel and then choose Stacks, Group as Stack to organize groups of images in a stack as if they were a deck of cards.

▶ Create labels and ratings for favorite images.

▶ Rename large amounts of creative assets using a batch rename tool.

▶ Add metadata to your creative assets for cataloging and for faster, more refined searching from Bridge and other Bridge-integrated programs such as Photoshop, Illustrator, and InDesign.

▶ Create an InDesign or Photoshop contact sheet from your images.

▶ Create a slideshow or web photo gallery from your images.

▶ Plug your digital camera into your computer (via USB or FireWire, for example) and browse the images on it directly from Adobe Bridge by choosing File, Get Photos from Camera.

Although we've merely scratched the surface as to the functionality Adobe Bridge can provide, you have, at the very least, gotten a preview of what this small yet powerful application gives you. For more information on Adobe Bridge, visit the Adobe website at www.adobe.com/products/creativesuite/bridge/.

Replacing Image Placeholders

As discussed in Chapter 2, you can use image placeholders as a way of creating temporary empty frames for your images. Doing this allows you to design the site first and add the graphics later. Image placeholders allow you to facilitate a smooth interaction between the web developer and the graphics department; they allow you to experiment with images to see which sizes and/or orientations look best in relation to the rest of the page layout. When you're satisfied with the positioning and size of the placeholders in relation to the rest of the design, you can easily launch Fireworks (currently the only supported program for direct editing of image placeholders). When launched from Dreamweaver, a new document window opens in Fireworks, sized to the dimensions of the image placeholder within Dreamweaver. To see this in action, follow these steps:

1. Create a new HTML page by choosing File, New. Choose Blank Page, HTML, <none>, and click Create.

2. Insert a new image placeholder by choosing Insert, Image Objects, Image Placeholder. The Image Placeholder dialog box appears.

3. Give your new image placeholder the name **SurfingOahu** (this is used merely for reference and is the text that appears on the placeholder in Dreamweaver), a width of **300**, and a height of **188**. Click OK. The new image placeholder appears on the page.

4. Select the image placeholder. Doing this reveals the Create button in the Property inspector. Click the Create button to launch Fireworks. Alternatively, you could right-click (Option-click) the image and choose Create Image from the context menu that appears. After Fireworks opens, a new document is created with the width of 300 pixels and a height of 188 pixels (the size of the image placeholder).

5. Playing the role of the graphics department, choose the Import option from the File menu. The Import dialog box appears, allowing you to browse for and select an image to import into Fireworks. Locate the SurfingOahu.gif image in the Images folder of the project and click Open.

6. The dialog box closes and your cursor changes, indicating that you need to place the image into the workspace. Position your cursor on the top-left edge of the workspace and click the left mouse button. The image is placed into the workspace.

7. Click Done. Dreamweaver asks you to save the original file, providing the name you originally gave the image placeholder. Keep the default name SurfingOahu.png, browse to the Images folder, and click Save.

8. Dreamweaver asks you to export the GIF image. Again, keep the default name, browse to the Images folder, and click Save. The image placeholder is updated with the newly created image.

This process was meant as a simple image placement example demonstrating the use of Fireworks to replace image placeholders. It's important to understand the role and power of image placeholders. In conjunction with "Lorem Ipsum" text, image placeholders can be used to design Dreamweaver-based prototypes that you can show to your clients for their approval. After the approval is given, you can begin designing the final artwork based on the dimensions outlined by the placeholders.

> **NOTE**
>
> Direct editing of image placeholders from Dreamweaver is currently supported only in Fireworks. If you don't have Fireworks, you can still use Photoshop; however, it's more of a hands-on process. You'll have to manually open Photoshop, create a new document with the sizes of your image placeholder, create your artwork, save the image, and then use the point-to-file icon visible in the Property inspector in Dreamweaver when the placeholder is selected to replace the image placeholder with your newly saved image.

Optimizing Images

As I'm sure you've noticed, working with images on the Web opens a new door of possibilities. In fact, some of the most compelling websites on the Internet use images as a way of making their websites stand out from others. The quality of web designers isn't measured merely by their knowledge of HTML, CSS, and Dreamweaver; they're also measured by how well they can work with image-editing programs such as Fireworks and Photoshop to create engaging graphics for their sites. The problem is that you can create the most compelling graphics on the Web, but if the image is so large that it takes too long to download on slow connections, you'll force most of your users to navigate away from your site, essentially invalidating the purpose of creating the compelling graphic to begin with. This is where image optimization comes in.

Image optimization is the process of getting an image to the smallest possible file size while maintaining an acceptable level of quality. Generally, image optimization involves removing color from an image to reduce the file size. Rather than downloading or purchasing programs that perform optimization on images, you can use a command built right into Dreamweaver, called Optimize Image. To use this command, follow these steps:

1. Open the document you were working with in the previous section.

2. Highlight the image in the document and choose Commands, Optimize Image. The Find Source dialog box appears (assuming Fireworks is your default editor).

3. Much like the previous examples, the Find Source dialog box allows you to make a decision on whether to optimize from the original PNG file or to use the image you're currently working with, be it a GIF, JPG, or PNG, in Dreamweaver. For this example, click the Use This File button.

4. This time, rather than Fireworks or Photoshop fully launching, the Image Preview dialog box launches.

The Image Preview dialog box is split into two tabs: the Options tab and the File tab. Let's discuss each briefly.

The Options Tab

Features outlined in the Options tab allow you to set the actual compression algorithm for the image. For instance, the Format menu contains compression options such as GIF, JPG, and PNG. Selecting these options changes the color palette that is applied to the image. Because the option you select from this menu ultimately guides the options available to you in the dialog box, let's break them down:

▶ **GIF**—This option allows you to save the document as a GIF. As you saw earlier in the book, GIFs are best used for graphics with fewer colors and for color without much tonal range. When saving a GIF image, you save a color look-up table with it. The lower the number of colors stored in the palette, the smaller the file size. You can also adjust the loss of the GIF image to effectively eliminate redundant or unnecessary information from the file, removing pixels from the image and reducing the file size. Finally, when you optimize an image as a GIF, you can add transparency by removing a specified color from the image.

▶ **JPEG**—This file format is best for saving images with many colors or for colors with tonal range (typically, photographs fit this description). Notice that when you select this option, a quality slider becomes available. JPEG compression works by removing pixels from the graphic, which reduces the file size. The lower the quality percentage you set in the slider, the more pixels it removes, providing a smaller file size. Be aware that there is no standard quality setting. Each image is different. Therefore, you'll have to find the balance for the graphic you're working with at that particular moment in time.

There is also an option for smoothing, which blurs the pixels a bit. Smoothing can be beneficial if you have to really squeeze the file size down and take the image to the edge where some artifacting (random pixelation) is visible. If you do see compression artifacting, sometimes a small amount of smoothing can help camouflage the image quality deterioration.

▶ **PNG 8/24/32**—PNG files are most closely related to the GIF file format and work in much the same way. You can preserve and create transparency; however, with PNG 24 and PNG 32, more colors are available to you. The PNG file format was—and I guess still is—supposed to wipe out the GIF file format, but the complications between the browser wars left the PNG file format fighting for compatibility. Depending on the browser usage of your target audience, PNG files may or may not be a good choice for you because versions of Internet Explorer prior to version 7 will display PNG files but will not show their transparency automatically. For much more detailed information on PNG files, see www.libpng.org/pub/png/.

For our example, choose the GIF option from the Format menu. One of the more important options revealed when you select the GIF option from the Format menu is the Color menu, shown in Figure 14.8.

From the Color menu, you can choose how much color the image should have. For instance, normal GIF images (without further compression) have a 256-color palette associated with them. Selecting 128 from this menu cuts the amount of color the image has in half, dramatically lowering the file size. (Note that you can see the file size in the Preview bar just above the image.) Additionally, you can remove individual colors by right-clicking (Control-clicking) a color cube and selecting the Delete Color option from the context menu.

Finally, you can allow the Image Preview to remove unused colors automatically by enabling the Remove Unused Colors check box.

NOTE

The process of optimizing images is extensive, so much so that entire books are devoted to the topic. Unfortunately, we just can't discuss each and every feature as it relates to the topic here. If you'd like more information on image optimization, visit the Sams website and research the books available for the topic. If you'd like to see what some of the these features do and you're not an expert in image optimization, click the 2 Up option and experiment by modifying some of the image optimization properties for the second image.

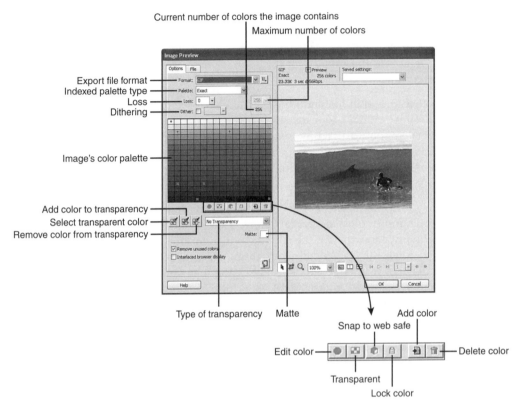

FIGURE 14.8   Numerous options are revealed to you when you select the GIF option from the Format menu.

The File Tab

The File tab interface of the Image Preview dialog box, shown in Figure 14.9, offers basic options for working with the file size. Options such as image scaling in percent and pixels as well as specific areas of the image to export back to Dreamweaver are available within this tab:

▶ **Scale**—Use the options on the Scale pane to change the physical dimensions of the image. For instance, you can use the Percentage slider to change the image size based on a specific percentage. You can use the W and H text boxes to change the width and height of the image in pixels. Finally, you can check the Constrain check box to resize the image proportionally.

▶ **Export Area**—This area is more or less a place to specify how you want the image cropped. If you select the Export Area check box, you get a bounding box around the image. You can drag any of the handles of the bounding box, in which case the corresponding x, y, w, and h values automatically update.

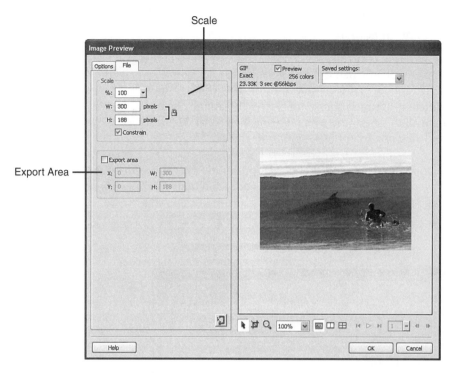

FIGURE 14.9   The File tab offers different options for changing the dimensions of the image.

Additional Options in the Image Preview Dialog Box

Aside from the more obvious options we've covered thus far, the Image Preview dialog box also provides access to features for interacting with the image, such as the Pointer, Crop, and Zoom tools, and more. Shown by the callouts in Figure 14.10, these tools allow you to easily work with the image in the Image Preview dialog box's environment.

▶ **Optimize Site Wizard**—Even if you're a pro at optimizing graphics, you'll find this wizard quick and convenient. When you click this button, a small dialog box opens, allowing you to enter a desired file size. Fireworks then reduces the image down to meet the file-size requirement. If the image quality is too poor, you'll have to accept a higher file size for that image.

▶ **Pointer tool**—The pointer tool is the black arrow, which allows you to select the image. If you cannot see the entire image in the dialog box, click the image with the Pointer tool (it automatically turns into the Hand tool) and drag to reposition the image.

▶ **Crop tool**—If you need to crop the image, use this tool. Simply position the bounding box around the image to determine how you want it cropped.

▶ **Zoom tools**—These tools enable you to zoom into the image by placing your cursor over it and clicking. You can zoom out of the image by holding down the Alt key while clicking with the Zoom tool. You can also use the drop-down menu to choose the level of magnification.

▶ **Preview window controls**—Here you can determine whether you want two or four preview panes open when optimizing an image. Click the 2 Up or the 4 Up buttons, depending on how many views you want. This can be beneficial because you can apply different optimization settings to each pane in the dialog box and then compare them all to determine which setting is optimal. Figure 14.11 shows the Image Preview dialog box with the 4 Up button clicked.

When you're done tinkering with the image optimization settings, click the OK button. The Image Preview dialog box closes, and the image is updated in Dreamweaver with the newly optimized image.

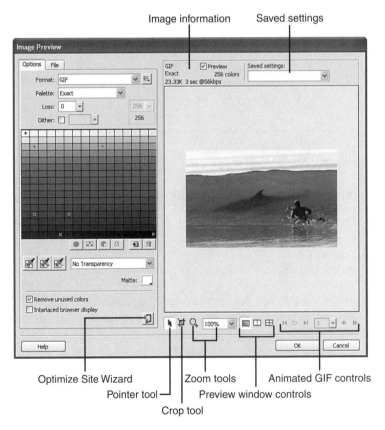

FIGURE 14.10   The Image Preview dialog box offers several tools for optimizing graphics.

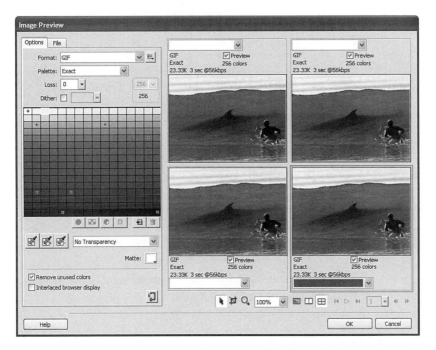

FIGURE 14.11   The Image Preview dialog box, shown with four panes open, previews different compression settings at the same time for you to compare.

NOTE

Whether the original PNG image is optimized along with the GIF image depends on which option you select from the Original Source File menu. If you choose the Always Use Source PNG option, the original PNG image is optimized along with the exported GIF file. Of course, this assumes that you have Fireworks installed, and that it's set as the default editor.

Ultimately, how you optimize the image depends on your target audience. If you're working on an intranet site where everyone in your organization has high-speed connections and the web server resides on the same network, image optimization might not be your number-one priority. However, if you know that a certain percentage of your target audience visits your site using dial-up connections, image optimization can become much more important.

Creating Rollover Buttons in Fireworks

One of the most common tasks in any web development endeavor is to create a menu that features rollover buttons. In Chapter 2 we used prebuilt rollover images available from the Insert, Image Objects, Rollover Image command. In Chapter 8, "Using Behaviors," we looked at the Swap Image and Swap Image Restore behaviors as alternatives for incorporating rollover images in your web pages. What we didn't do, however, is examine exactly how those images were created. Using Fireworks in conjunction with Dreamweaver, we'll do that now. To create a rollover image using Fireworks, follow these steps:

1. Open Fireworks. Create a new document by choosing File, New. This launches the New Document dialog box. Specify a width of 150 pixels, a height of 25 pixels, a resolution of 72 pixels/inch (the default for web images), and click OK.

2. From the Tools panel, choose the Rectangle tool, a fill color, and a stroke color. Next, draw a box on the document that spans the entire height and width of the document (150×25).

3. With the rectangle selected, press F8 to bring up the Convert to Symbol dialog box. In the Name text box, type a unique name for your new symbol and choose the Button Type, as shown in Figure 14.12, and click OK.

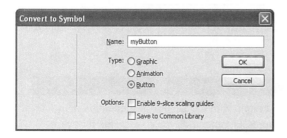

FIGURE 14.12   Give your new symbol a name and change the Type option to Button.

4. Use the Text tool to add some text to your graphic. I'll add the text **Click Me.**

5. Select the Pointer tool from the Tools panel and double-click the symbol to open the Symbol Property inspector (see Figure 14.13).

FIGURE 14.13   Double-click the new symbol to open the Symbol Property inspector.

6. Select the Over option from the State drop-down menu. Clicking the Copy Up Graphic button, near the bottom-right corner of the workspace, allows you to carry over any attributes, including the graphic as a whole, from the Up state. Do this now.

7. After you click the Copy Up Graphic button, the Up state is copied to the Over state. Notice that all the tools are still available to you. Highlight the selection and choose a different fill color from the Tool's panel. This is the color the button will change to when the user hovers the mouse over the button.

8. Now choose the Down option from the State drop-down menu. In the Down state, click the Copy Over Graphic button. The Down state now has the same attributes as the Over state. Select the symbol and change the color again. This is how the button will appear when the end user actually clicks the button.

9. Finally, choose the Active Area option from the State drop-down menu. This is the same concept as a *hot spot* in an image map. The active area defines what area activates the button. For best results, make sure that the active area covers the area of the entire rectangle of your button. Click the small, blue back arrow that appears in the upper-right corner of Fireworks when you're finished making all changes.

10. Click the Preview tab at the top of the document window to see how your button will behave.

In our case, we're simply demonstrating how the process is performed using one image. If you were creating a complete navigation menu, you'd repeat these steps for the other images in your navigation menu.

Now that you have a button made, you're ready to export it from Fireworks. For a rollover graphic to work, JavaScript is written to a new HTML page. Our goal is to take the HTML page and the resulting button images that Fireworks creates and import them into Dreamweaver. To do this, follow these steps:

1. In Fireworks, select File, Export. The Export dialog box opens.

2. Browse to the root folder in the defined site.

3. Give the new HTML file a name such as **rollover.html.**

4. Select the HTML and Images option from the Export list.

5. Enable the Put Images in Subfolder check box and browse to find the Images folder in the local root folder of the site you are working with in Dreamweaver.

6. Click Save.

7. Return to Dreamweaver and open the `rollover.html` file. Switching to Code view reveals the JavaScript code (and HTML) that Fireworks created (see Figure 14.14). The browser reads this code and displays the appropriate images to the user depending on user/mouse rollover states.

When you get over the initial awe of this streamlined functionality, you'll begin to wonder how to use the rollover image—including the JavaScript code—in the context of your web design. This is discussed in the next section.

Inserting Fireworks HTML

Sure, the `rollover.html` file is nice, but who wants to redevelop a new design to fit around the rollover image? This is where the Insert Fireworks HTML features comes in. The Insert Fireworks HTML feature allows you to take the existing page (rollover.html), including the Fireworks-generated JavaScript, and directly insert it into a predesigned web page, companyevents_surfpics.html for example, in Dreamweaver. Like most other features in Dreamweaver, the process is quite simple. To insert Fireworks HTML, follow these steps:

1. Open the companyevents_surfpics.html page and place your cursor anywhere in the document to act as the insertion point for the Fireworks HTML.

2. Choose Insert, Image Objects, Fireworks HTML. The Insert Fireworks HTML dialog box appears.

3. Browse for the HTML file that was generated by Fireworks (rollover.html). After you've selected it, click OK to return to the Insert Fireworks HTML dialog box. If you prefer, click the Delete File After Insertion check box to completely remove the rollover.html file after Dreamweaver finishes importing it into the document. This saves you from having to go back later and manually remove the file, but the downside is that you no longer have the file around should you make a mistake. I recommend deleting it manually until you are comfortable using this feature. When you're ready to finish importing, click OK.

4. The button now appears inside your Dreamweaver document.

5. Save your work.

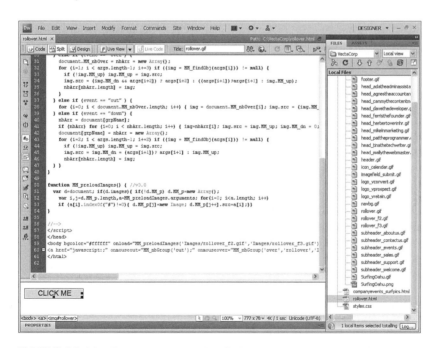

FIGURE 14.14   Fireworks-created JavaScript is written to the new file.

Preview your work in a browser by pressing F12 (Option-F12. As you'll notice, the rollover works perfectly. Even better, all the JavaScript code required for the rollover to work is automatically copied out of `rollover.html` and placed into the appropriate section of the page (in code) for `companyevents_surfpics.html`.

Creating a Web Photo Album

If you're a web designer and use images on your website, you've probably visited online stock image websites such as Corbis, iStockPhoto, Photodisc/Getty Images, and the like. If you've visited those sites and performed searches for images, you've seen their catalogs of image thumbnails. If you haven't visited these sites, you've no doubt seen functionality such as this. When you click the image thumbnail, a higher-resolution, usually larger image appears; the display usually includes more information about the image. Although the functionality might seem complex, the reality is that Dreamweaver has a utility that generates catalogs of thumbnail images that, when clicked, open to a much larger version of the image. You might have other uses for this same functionality (perhaps to create a web photo album for your family that functions the same way as this example does).

The Create Web Photo Album command, available from the Commands menu, outlines a unique interface, tied directly into Fireworks, that allows you to generate a web photo album in your web pages. Even better, the Create Web Photo Album command works with a folder of images in any of the following formats: GIF, JPG, TIF, PSD, PICT, BMP, and PNG. The images can be resized for thumbnails anywhere from 36×36 pixels to 200×200 pixels. Traditionally, creating functionality such as this was an extremely tedious task because the web developer would have to open the many images to use within the site, resize them, resave them, and then import them into some structure in a web page. The Create Web Photo Album command streamlines this functionality into one simple-to-use interface.

In this section, we'll examine the Create Web Photo Album command and create a web photo album for the surfing images located in the Assets folder. To create the web photo album, open Dreamweaver and follow these steps:

1. Create a new page by choosing File, New. Choose Blank Page, HTML, <none>, and click Create.

2. In the new page, select Commands, Create Web Photo Album. The Create Web Photo Album dialog box appears, similar to Figure 14.15.

3. The first and most obvious option in this dialog box is to give your album a title. Enter the text **Surfing Album** in the Photo Album Title text box.

4. If you want to enter a subheading for the photo album, enter that text in the Subheading Info text box. For simplicity, I'll leave mine blank.

5. If you want more detailed information about the photo album, enter text in the Other Info text box. Again, I'll leave mine blank.

6. Choose the source folder for the original images. Click the Browse button in the Source Images Folder File field and browse to the PhotoAlbum folder (contained within the Images folder) in the defined Vecta Corp site.

14

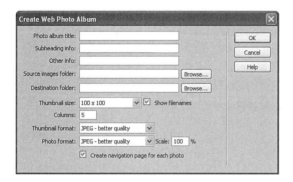

FIGURE 14.15 The Create Web Photo Album dialog box is packed with several options to get your images organized in an easy-to-navigate page.

7. Choose the destination folder for the thumbnail images (the folder that will contain the minimized thumbnail images Fireworks will create for you). Because all our images are contained in the Images folder, browse to it in the Destination Folder File field.

8. Choose the size at which you want the thumbnails to be created. Because we have limited space on the page, I'll choose the 72×72 option from the Thumbnail size menu. Also, we don't care about displaying the image's filename under the image, so disable the Show Filenames check box.

9. Change the number of columns you want your thumbnails to appear in on the page. Again, because we have limited space, reduce the default number from 5 to 3.

10. Choose a thumbnail format for your images. The menu offers four options: GIF WebSnap 128, GIF WebSnap 256, JPEG—Better Quality, and JPEG—Smaller File. Choose the appropriate option based on your target audience's connection speed. I'll leave it set to the default (JPEG—Better Quality).

11. You also have the option of choosing the file type for the larger version of the image. Again, I'll leave mine at the default (JPEG—Better Quality).

12. Enable the last option, Create Navigation Page for Each Photo, if you want to generate a navigation widget at the top of each page that contains the larger image. I'll leave this option checked. When you've finished configuring the dialog box, click OK.

13. Fireworks launches and processes the images (as you can see by the progress bar in the Batch Process dialog box that Fireworks displays).

14. After the process is complete, a dialog box alerting you that the album has been created appears. Choose OK.

Dreamweaver closes the dialog box and generates a layout of pictures in a web photo album.

As you'll see, Dreamweaver automatically generates folders (images, pages, and thumbnails) within your existing Images folder; these new folders represent the various components of the photo album. The index.html page that's generated as the contact sheet is stored in the root of the Images folder. Preview this page in a browser by pressing F12

(Option-F12). In the browser, click any of the thumbnail graphics; you are linked to a page with a larger version of the image. Figure 14.16 shows that Dreamweaver includes a navigation bar in the top-left corner.

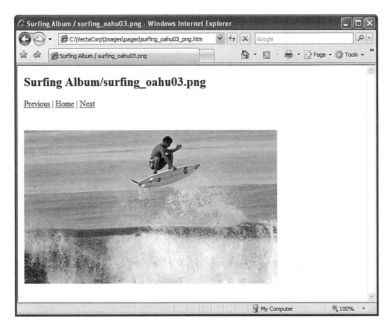

FIGURE 14.16   After clicking any thumbnail, you're taken to a page with the full-sized image. You can also navigate through the other pages with full-sized images from these pages.

You'll notice that the interface that is created automatically by Dreamweaver isn't all that aesthetically pleasing. If you decide instead that you want this slideshow elsewhere in your site (maybe within a page that you've created based on a template), you could select all of the content on the page by choosing Edit, Select All, choose Edit, Copy, and then paste the copied content within the page of your choice. If you do copy and paste the contact sheet into another page, you'll have to run the link checker (choose Site, Check Links Sitewide) to fix the resulting broken references to the thumbnail files and the link between the thumbnail and the larger image's page.

Integrating with Flash

Some of the most feature-rich and interactive websites on the Internet today use Flash technology. Did you ever visit a website that loaded a vector-based game, invited you to play, and then loaded a travel website when you started to play the game? How many sidebar "mini games" have you seen that invite you to "shoot the paparazzi," "kill the ninja," "punch the monkey," or "shoot the duck"? Flash is by far the most widely distributed and widely used platform for delivering rich media over the Web. Whether you're

using Flash for movies, games, marketing purposes, or simply to create stunning animations for your personal or company website, Flash offers designers and developers total
freedom from restrictive HTML standards and provides a great alternative to static web
page development.

In this section, you'll discover how to work with Flash movies in Dreamweaver. You'll
learn how to embed Flash movies in your web pages, pass parameters into those movies,
control Flash movies using behaviors, and work with round-trip Flash editing.

Inserting Flash Movies into Dreamweaver Documents

In keeping with consistency and intuitiveness, inserting Flash movies into a web page is
similar to, if not the same as, inserting images, video, and audio. To insert a Flash movie
into a web page, follow these steps:

1. Start by removing the existing `index.html` file. If you recall, this file was used in
   conjunction with Fireworks when building out our rollover. The content that the file
   contains is no longer needed, but the name of the file is. Now make a copy of the
   `companyevents_surfpics.html` page by selecting it within the Files panel, choosing
   Edit, Copy, and then selecting Edit, Paste. A copy of the file will be created. Now
   rename that file by highlighting it within the Files panel and press F2. Rename the
   file **`index.html`**.

2. Open the file by double-clicking it within the Files panel. Highlight the content that
   we've been working on up to this point and delete it. You should be left simply with
   the subheader image for events. If you'd like, go ahead and replace that image with
   the `subheader_welcome.gif` image located in the Images folder of the site.

3. Now place your cursor next to the subheader image and press Enter (Return) to
   create a new paragraph. With your cursor underneath the subheader image, choose
   Insert, Media, SWF. The Select File dialog box appears.

4. In the Select File dialog box, browse to the Media folder and select the `movie.swf`
   file. Click OK (Choose).

NOTE

Flash movies are typically saved as FLA files in Windows and as MOV files on a Mac.
To use a Flash file in a web page, the FLA/MOV file must be exported from Flash as a
Shockwave Flash file (SWF).

The new movie appears in the web page, similar to Figure 14.17.

Save your work and test the page in the browser by pressing F12 (Option-F12). As long as
the Flash plugin is installed for the particular browser that you've chosen to preview the
page within, the movie plays without fault in the web page.

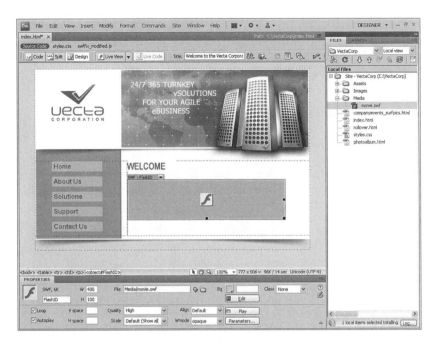

FIGURE 14.17   The Flash movie, represented by the plugin icon, appears in the web page.

TIP

Using the Insert, Media submenu isn't the only way to insert Flash movies into a web page. Other options include the Media submenu within the Common category of the Insert panel. You can also drag and drop the file located in the Flash Movie category of the Assets panel or drag it from the Files panel.

A Flash movie appears in the Document window as a gray box, as do other audio and video elements. Unlike audio and video elements, however, a Flash movie is easily recognizable in the Document window by the Flash logo centered in the gray box. Additionally, you might have noticed the small eye icon located just to the right of the visual aid. You can click this icon to switch between two views. The first view is the one you're seeing now—the Flash movie represented by the Flash logo in the gray box. The second view shows you the view that users will see if they don't have the Flash plugin installed on their browsers. Of course, you're free to customize this view in any way you'd like to make it more visually appealing or to blend into your site's color scheme.

Similar to audio and video elements, Flash movie properties can be controlled using the Flash Property inspector, shown in detail in Figure 14.18.

FIGURE 14.18   Flash movie properties can be controlled using the Property inspector.

The Flash Property inspector outlines the following properties:

▶ **Movie ID**—Enter a value in this text box to uniquely identify the Flash movie. Just above the text box, a label appears, indicating the type of element selected, as well as the file size.

▶ **W and H (Width and Height)**—Enter numeric values within these text boxes to set the width and height of the Flash movie in pixels. Remember that unlike images, Flash movies are inherently vector-based. This means that you can override the default width and height settings in the movie and expect the same quality.

▶ **File**—Displays the path to the Flash movie within the defined site.

▶ **Bg (Background Color)**—Choose a color from the color picker to set the background color of the Flash movie from within Dreamweaver.

▶ **Edit**—Used in round-trip Flash editing, this button launches the original Flash (FLA/MOV) movie in Flash.

▶ **Class**—When working with CSS, apply a custom class to the Flash movie by choosing the class from this menu.

▶ **Loop**—Check this box to force the Flash movie to return to the beginning and start over when it reaches the end.

▶ **Autoplay**—Check this box to force the browser to begin playing the Flash movie as soon as the page loads.

▶ **V Space and H Space**—Enter numeric values in these text boxes to set the vertical and horizontal spacing in pixels around the Flash movie.

▶ **Quality**—Choose an option from this menu to set the quality of antialiasing during playback in the browser. Options include High, Low, Auto High, and Auto Low:

    ▶ **High**—Antialiasing is turned on. This slows down playback considerably on slower computers.

    ▶ **Low**—No antialiasing is used in the movie. Choose this option when quick playback is essential.

    ▶ **Auto High**—Animation begins in High quality mode but switches to Low if playback is too slow.

    ▶ **Auto Low**—Animation begins in Low quality mode but switches to High if the user's computer is fast enough.

- ▶ **Scale**—Choose an option from this menu to determine how the movie should fit within the constraints of the width and height specified by the W and H text boxes. Options include Default (shows the entire movie), No Border, and Exact Fit.

- ▶ **Align**—Choose an option from this menu to set the alignment of elements surrounding the Flash movie.

- ▶ **Wmode (Window Mode)**—Choose an option from this menu to set the transparency of the window that the Flash movie will play within. In previous versions of Dreamweaver, modifying this property required working with parameters, a slightly less intuitive method. In Dreamweaver CS4, the Flash movie's window can easily be set to either opaque or transparent by simply selecting an option from this new menu.

- ▶ **Play**—Click this button to play the Flash movie in Dreamweaver. After the movie begins playing, the Play button becomes a Stop button, allowing you to stop the playback of the animation and return the movie to its default "gray box" state.

- ▶ **Parameters**—Clicking this button launches the Parameters dialog box. You can use the Parameters dialog box, discussed in the next section, as a way to dynamically control elements of a Flash movie.

Although most of these options are similar to other audio and video properties, they differ in certain respects. Experiment with the options to see how each can work best for your particular situation.

> **NOTE**
>
> Another Adobe media type that we haven't discussed is Shockwave Director. Represented by the SWD file extension, Shockwave Director files are similar to Flash movies in that they're inherently vector-based—but they use a slightly different plugin. To insert a Director media file, choose Insert, Media, Shockwave. All the properties in the Property inspector outlined in this section also apply to SWD files.

Additional Flash Parameters

For most users, the properties outlined within the Property inspector will suffice. In rare instances, however, you might decide to modify additional parameters not listed in the Property inspector. In cases such as these, select the Flash file and click the Parameters button in the Property inspector to launch the Parameters dialog box, shown in Figure 14.19.

> **NOTE**
>
> As you can see from Figure 14.19, two parameters are already specified for you. The swf version parameter instructs the browser to load a minimum plugin version when attempting to play the Flash movie. The express install parameter points to a Flash movie (in a Scripts directory created for you in your site) used to install the Flash player on your visitor's browser if it's not present.

14

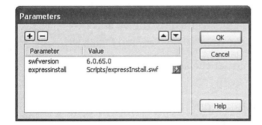

FIGURE 14.19   Additional Flash movie properties can be controlled using the Parameters dialog box.

As you did with video and audio parameters in the previous chapter, you can add Flash parameters to the Parameters list by clicking the Add (+) button. Then enter the name of the parameter in the Parameter column, followed by the value in the Value column. When you finish adding the new parameter, click OK to close the Parameters dialog box and commit the additions. Following are the possible parameters for Flash movies:

▶ **salign**—L (Left), R (Right), T (Top), or B (Bottom)—Determines how the movie will align itself to the surrounding frame when the Scale attribute is set to Show All. Furthermore, you can use this parameter to determine which portion of the image is cut off when the Scale attribute is set to No Border. Possible values include L, R, T, and B. You can also use these values together; for instance, you might decide that the left and top of the movie should be cut off. In this case, you would specify LT for the value.

▶ **swliveconnect**—true or false—Use this parameter when working with FSCommands or JavaScript in your Flash movies. Because Netscape initializes Java when it is opened, the Flash movie will attempt to use Java to work with FSCommands or JavaScript to communicate with the plugin interface LiveConnect. Because not all movies use FSCommands or JavaScript (indeed, Adobe is discouraging Flash developers from using FSCommands in their Flash movies for security reasons), setting this parameter to false prevents the Flash movie from trying to communicate with the LiveConnect plugin interface.

Controlling Flash Movies with Dreamweaver Behaviors

Chapter 8 introduced many of the behaviors built into Dreamweaver; you learned about several other behaviors in subsequent chapters. The final behavior we've yet to cover is the Control Shockwave, or SWF behavior. Using this behavior, you can easily create HTML-based navigation options that can play, stop, or rewind the Flash movie in your web page.

To use the Control Shockwave or SWF behavior with a Flash movie, follow these steps:

1. Create a new page by choosing File, New. Select Blank Page, HTML, <none>, and click Create. Immediately save your page as **flashbehaviors.html.**

2. Insert the `movie.swf` file into the page, this time by finding it within the Media folder of your defined site and dragging it out onto the page.

3. Select the Flash movie on the page and enter a unique name for it in the Name text box in the Property inspector. I'll call my Flash movie **theMovie.**

4. Disable both the Loop and Autoplay options in the Property inspector.

5. Insert three form object buttons onto the page. When the Add Form Tag dialog box appears, choose No. Change the Action property for each button to None, and label them **Play**, **Stop**, and **Rewind**, respectively. The result will resemble Figure 14.20.

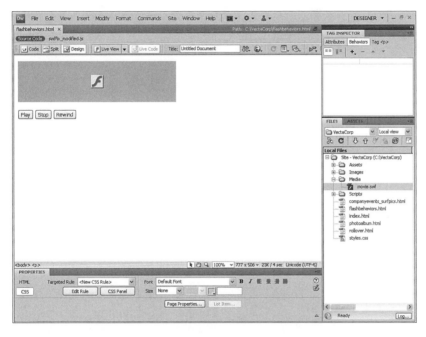

FIGURE 14.20   Insert three form buttons onto the page, change their Actions to None, and label them Play, Stop, and Rewind, respectively.

6. Open the Behaviors panel by choosing Window, Behaviors or by pressing Shift+F4.

7. Select the Play button on the page and choose the Control Shockwave or SWF behavior, available by clicking the Add (+) button in the Behaviors panel and choosing the behavior from the ~Deprecated submenu. The Control Shockwave or SWF dialog box appears, similar to Figure 14.21.

8. From the Control Shockwave or SWF dialog box, select the movie you want to control from the Movie menu. Because we're working with only one movie on this page, select the Movie "theMovie" option.

9. Enable the Play option button and click OK. Make sure that the `onClick` event is associated within the behavior in the Behaviors panel.

FIGURE 14.21   The Control Shockwave or Flash dialog box allows you to set Play, Stop, or Rewind actions for buttons on the page.

NOTE

In addition to playing, stopping, and rewinding, you can take the user to a specific frame number within the Flash movie. To do this, choose the Go to Frame option and type a numeric value in the provided text box.

10. Repeat steps 7–9, attaching Stop and Rewind actions to the Stop and Rewind buttons, respectively.

11. Save your work.

You can test the results in the browser by pressing F12 (Option-F12). The Flash movie appears in the browser window. Click the Play button to begin playing the movie. Click the Stop and Rewind buttons to test their functionality, as well.

Round-Trip Flash Editing

Earlier in the chapter, you learned that the Property inspector integrates an Edit button when you're working with certain file types, such as images. When the image is selected, you can click the Edit button to launch either Fireworks or Photoshop and open the original version of the image, allowing you to make edits. When you finish making the edits, you can click Done to see the results within Dreamweaver. This process, known as round-trip editing, is also available for Flash movies. As was the case with Fireworks, this feature relies on having Flash installed on your computer, and the original FLA/MOV file must be present.

To work with round-trip Flash editing, follow these steps:

1. Select the movie.swf Flash movie and click the Edit button in the Property inspector.

2. Dreamweaver opens Flash and attempts to automatically open the selected movie's source FLA/MOV file. If it can't open the original file automatically, it prompts you for the location of the original file.

3. After the original movie opens in Flash, the Flash Document window indicates that you're editing a movie from Dreamweaver. Make your changes to the movie.

4. When you finish making your edits, click the Done button. Flash saves your changes to the source FLA/MOV file, updates the SWF file, minimizes Flash, and then changes focus back to Dreamweaver.

Summary

You can see the power and workflow advantages of using Dreamweaver with complementary applications such as Fireworks. As you have seen, Adobe has done an outstanding job of tightly integrating Fireworks with Dreamweaver. With features that enable you to edit and optimize images, create images, rollovers, web photo albums, and more, it's hard for a web designer to disagree that the marriage between Dreamweaver and Fireworks is a development advantage. And, although the tight integration between Dreamweaver and Fireworks is obvious, Adobe is no doubt making strides to guarantee that future versions of Dreamweaver will also include similar features for Photoshop integration.

In the latter half of the chapter, you also saw the interaction between Dreamweaver and Flash. You saw how easy it was to insert Flash-based media into a web page in Dreamweaver. Toward the end of the chapter, you learned how behaviors can control the playing, stopping, and rewinding of a Flash movie directly from your web page.

This chapter officially concludes the "static" portions of web page development. From this point forward, we'll turn our attention to creating web applications using "dynamic" web technologies such as ASP, PHP, and ColdFusion.

14

PART V

Dynamic Web Page Development

IN THIS PART

CHAPTER 15

Introduction to Web Applications

What is a web application? That's the question I'll try to answer in this chapter. Anyone who has spent any amount of time with web applications might tell you that they consist of many pieces all working harmoniously together to facilitate interaction between an end user and a web server. You might have a website that consists of HTML, CSS, and JavaScript. Additionally, you might have a web server with an installed server-side technology such as ASP, ASP.NET, ColdFusion, or PHP that responds to requests or interactions between the website and the web server. Furthermore, you might employ some sort of data-storage mechanism that takes the form of a database, XML file, or other data source.

The simple fact is that web applications encompass many technologies, languages, platforms, and needs. For this reason, there's no simple definition for the term *web application*. Some say that web applications are like computer-based applications in that they allow you to store, query, and interact with data in and from a database. That is the traditional and basic definition of a web application; the truth is, web applications extend well beyond that.

In this introductory chapter, we'll demystify the term *web application*, discussing terms such as *client-side development*, *static web page creation*, *server-side development*, *databases*, and much more. By the end of the chapter, you should have a firm grasp on what web applications are, what purpose they serve, how they're implemented within the scope of Dreamweaver, and more importantly, how we'll use web applications to build a dynamic Vecta Corp application. Toward the end of the chapter, we'll introduce the dynamic portions of the Vecta Corp site, including pages that we'll build for the site, such as an employee store, a dynamic company directory, and a set of administrative pages.

Client-Side Versus Server-Side Web Development

In the introduction to this chapter, I teased you about what a web application is but stopped short of actually defining it. Simply put, a web application is a website that contains static and dynamic pages working together to facilitate interaction between a user and a web server. That clears it all up, right? To sum up this rather lame attempt at defining web applications, think of what we've done so far. Up to this point, we've built simple web pages (static ones), pressed F12, and magically the page appeared in the browser window as it was intended. Nothing special was required from us, we didn't have to install anything on the computer to get it to work (aside from Dreamweaver), and best of all, we didn't have to manually write any code in the Code view of the web page. If we were to diagram the process involved for a user browsing to your static web page (assuming that it was hosted by a web hosting provider rather than by your computer), the process might resemble what's shown in Figure 15.1.

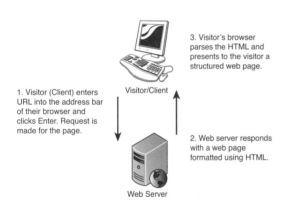

3. Visitor's browser parses the HTML and presents to the visitor a structured web page.

1. Visitor (Client) enters URL into the address bar of their browser and clicks Enter. Request is made for the page.

Visitor/Client

2. Web server responds with a web page formatted using HTML.

Web Server

FIGURE 15.1   Static web pages follow a simple flow: The user requests the page and the web server displays it.

Two major components make up static web pages: the client and the web server. The client makes a request by typing the URL of your website into the address bar of the browser and pressing Enter. At this point, a request is made to the web server. The web server, recognizing this request, sends HTML back to the client, whose browser parses the content out of the HTML tags and displays the text, images, and media (what the original developer of the page intended to be seen) to the user. This process is often referred to as *client-side development* because you're using simple client-side technologies such as HTML, CSS, or JavaScript—technologies meant to be processed by the client browser that require very little, if anything, from the actual web server.

Dynamic pages, on the other hand, work differently and to a certain extent are a bit more complex in their implementation. Dynamic pages contain instructions in the form of a scripting language—or, in some cases, a full-blown object-oriented programming language that gets processed on the web server. Sometimes the instructions or code is self-contained, and sometimes it's mixed in with HTML code, but ultimately that code is processed and executed by a web server. If we were to diagram the process involved for a user browsing to your dynamic web page (assuming that it was hosted by a web-hosting provider rather than by your computer), it might resemble the process shown in Figure 15.2.

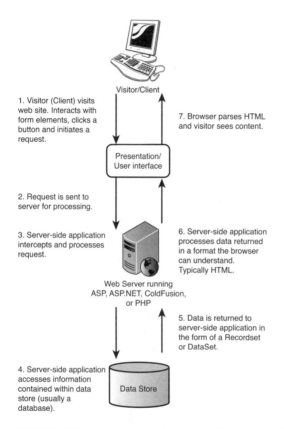

1. Visitor (Client) visits web site. Interacts with form elements, clicks a button and initiates a request.

Visitor/Client

7. Browser parses HTML and visitor sees content.

Presentation/ User interface

2. Request is sent to server for processing.

3. Server-side application intercepts and processes request.

6. Server-side application processes data returned in a format the browser can understand. Typically HTML.

Web Server running ASP, ASP.NET, ColdFusion, or PHP

5. Data is returned to server-side application in the form of a Recordset or DataSet.

4. Server-side application accesses information contained within data store (usually a database).

Data Store

FIGURE 15.2   Dynamic web pages follow a complex flow: The user interacts with the page and sends a request to the server; the server processes the request and finally sends a response back to the client.

Dynamic websites, like static websites, rely on the two client and server components. The fundamental difference, however, is that the server has much more to do for dynamic web pages than it did for static web pages. Although the user still makes a request for the initial page, dynamic web pages rely on user interaction (typically through form elements) for further requests to be made to the server. With static websites, a single request is made to the page. Unless the user hyperlinks to another page, the information sits there, waiting to be read by the user. Dynamic websites facilitate interaction. Ultimately, there could be dozens, possibly hundreds, of requests made to the server by way of form objects, hyperlinks, and so on. The process is actually simple: The user interacts with form objects (maybe by typing a username and password into a series of text boxes), clicks a button, and the request is sent to the server. The server recognizes that a request being made uses a server-side technology (ASP, ColdFusion, or PHP) to process that request (maybe by comparing the values of the text boxes with a username and password stored in a database) and then sends a response back to the client. The response could be a page redirection to the main page after the user has logged in, or it could be a friendly message indicating that the username and password combination typed in are invalid.

That's the point with dynamic web pages: You write the code in a page that figures out how to handle requests coming from the client. The pages are said to be *dynamic* because they're not just sitting on the client's browser waiting to be read or clicked. Rather, the information is dynamic; it facilitates user interaction and responds accordingly. Better yet, dynamic pages can use conditional logic and mathematical equations, send emails, write to the file system, and—most importantly—interact with file storage mechanisms such as databases and XML files.

Web Applications

In the previous section, we outlined the differences between static client-side and dynamic server-side web pages. We said that dynamic server-side web pages welcome interaction from the end user by outlining a series of carefully crafted form objects. When the user submits the form (containing the form objects) to the web server for processing, the dynamic portions of the page kick in and process the incoming request. The result of the processing is ultimately piped back to the user in a friendly format (such as HTML).

Dynamic web pages, however, are merely cogs within a grander system; they are individual pages that make up a part of the whole. In the web development world, dynamic web pages are parts of a web application. Ultimately, a web application consists of many dynamic web pages that perform numerous operations, depending on various factors built in to the pages. Figure 15.3 illustrates this example with more detail.

A web application could consist of numerous dynamic web pages, each performing its own unique task. In our Vecta Corp example, we might initially expose a simple login page. If the user logs in correctly, we take the user to the main page. If the login attempt fails, however, the user is redirected back to the login page and receives an error message. From the main page, a user can visit various other dynamic web pages such as the company directory (which pulls employee information from a database), the employee store (which pulls product information from a database), and perhaps an admin page reserved specifically for administrators. If the user is an admin, the user can modify employee information, create new employees, and even delete existing employees. As you can see, all these dynamic pages working together make up a well-oiled web application.

As we've mentioned, web applications are made up of different components, otherwise known as *tiers*. These tiers make up the web architecture of your site. Ever heard of the term *3-tiered web application*? In this scenario, the term *tiered* refers to the components or tiers that make up the web application as a whole. At the very least, you'll almost always have a 2-tiered web application: The first tier is that your users/clients will want to visit your site. The second tier is the web server on which the web application is hosted. The third tier could be the data tier, or where your data storage mechanism (database) resides. For the most part, the following tiers represent a traditional 3-tiered web application's architecture:

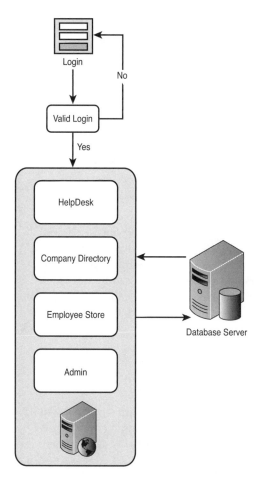

FIGURE 15.3   Web applications consist of numerous dynamic web pages that together make up the unique functionality of the application.

- ▶ **Presentation**—The presentation tier is everything that your clients/users will see. Everything from the user interface, images, media, JavaScript (client-side logic), and CSS composes the presentation tier. The previous 14 chapters have gotten you up to speed as it relates to the presentation tier.

- ▶ **Application**—The application is the code running on the server that contains processing instructions utilizing technologies such as Microsoft's ASP or ASP.NET, Adobe's ColdFusion, or the open source PHP. We'll be discussing these technologies and how they can be used within Dreamweaver throughout the next several chapters.

▶ **Data**—The data tier should and will be the lifeblood of your organization. Represented by a database—or in some cases, a flat file (XML)—the data tier contains all the user information, product information, usernames, and passwords for your web application. We'll discuss this option in Chapter 17, "A Database Primer."

All in all, web applications serve a valuable purpose in web development. Many web developers find it more convenient to use web applications in place of static pages. Although the time-to-market is slower for web applications than for static pages, maintenance and return on investment (ROI) far outweigh the time it takes to develop the application. After the web application has been developed, updating content within a database that ultimately appears within the browser is a snap. Furthermore, the look and feel (design) of the site can easily be separated from the content, essentially disconnecting the designer and the developer and ultimately making each portion of the web application autonomous.

In the previous chapters, we've been discussing the many facets of Dreamweaver that facilitate client-side development. As you've seen, working with web pages in the Dreamweaver Document window is simple. Flanked by the numerous panels in Dreamweaver's development environment, it's hard to disagree that working with static web pages is a breeze. Making the switch to dynamic web development is not easy. For this reason, an introduction to the different tiers of a web application and an in-depth discussion of the various parts is necessary before we make the giant leap to dynamic web development. In the next few sections, we'll dissect each of these tiers, discussing the detailed components that make up each tier.

Client-Side Technologies

The presentation tier—or more specifically, what your users interact with—is composed of many client-side web technologies, all serving a specific purpose depending on the developer's intentions. As you've seen throughout the book thus far, client-side development can (and usually will) include the following technologies:

▶ **HTML**—Generally considered the foundation for all that is the Web, HTML serves as the structural markup for client-side web pages. HTML is hard to ignore when working with websites. Because the browser can parse only HTML markup, even if you're working with server-side applications, HTML is what is ultimately sent back to the client from the server.

▶ **CSS**—As you've seen throughout the book, Cascading Style Sheets (CSS) provide the look or design of the client-side web page. Using CSS, designers can control the look of text, links, form objects, the page, and more.

▶ **JavaScript**—Often referred to as *client-side logic* (as opposed to the topic of this and subsequent chapters, server-side logic), JavaScript—written within a `<script>` tag nested within the `<head>` tag of the HTML document—outlines unique properties for working with conditional logic, calculations, validation, and more in a web page.

▶ **Media Elements**—Embedded into the web page using the `<embed>` or `<object>` HTML tags, media elements such as Flash, Director, video, audio, and more enhance the user experience by incorporating a unique multimedia experience that can be engaging and stunning.

At the risk of rehashing technologies and languages we've covered in previous chapters, suffice it to say that client-side elements are still extremely important when you're working with server-side technologies. Server-side technologies are merely responsible for processing requests from the client. What the client sees in the response is ultimately going to be formatted using the client-side technologies we've already covered in the book.

Server-Side Technologies

Server-side technologies are software components that handle most, if not all, of the business logic in a web application. When a user submits data from a form (run on the client), that data is sent to the web server for processing. The web server, using a server-side technology, processes the form (maybe inserts data into a database), and then sends a response back to the client. The process is fairly straightforward and, save for a few minute details, the process is the same regardless of which server-side technology is being used to process the request.

Over the past 15 years, as the Web has matured, dozens of server-side technologies have appeared. Most server-side technologies have a lot in common. For example, most of them interact with relational databases; they can process complex requests from web browsers and can write files to and read files from a file system. So which option is the best for you? Most are pretty much the same, so choosing an option isn't just a case of features, it's a matter of personal preference, as well as cost and skillsets available. Web developers soon discover that the most important criteria for selecting a server-side technology is its flexibility, ease-of-use, maintainability, and then its feature set. Will the option you choose allow you to easily access a database? Build objects to keep redundant code to a minimum? Process multiple simultaneous users quickly? It's a lot like buying a pair of jeans: Go with what looks good and fits right. The three major technologies that we'll discuss throughout the book include (ordered alphabetically, not by preference):

▶ ASP

▶ ColdFusion

▶ PHP

Although Chapter 16, "Working with Server-Side Technologies," certainly goes into more detail, the following sections outline the three fully supported server-side technologies in Dreamweaver, their nuances, and the positives and negatives for using each. My hope is that by the time you begin reading Chapter 16, you'll have picked the server-side technology to use with the Vecta Corp project.

> **NOTE**
>
> It's important to note that in reality there are many more server-side technologies than just the three that are supported by Dreamweaver. ASP, which is fully supported in Dreamweaver, is considered outdated and has been replaced with ASP.NET. Although Dreamweaver supports up to ASP.NET 1.1, it could not compete with free Microsoft products already on the market that handle ASP.NET 2.0 and ASP.NET 3.5. Accordingly, the decision was made to no longer support future versions of ASP.NET in Dreamweaver. This also holds true for Sun Microsystem's Java-based JSP. With that said, we'll discuss the three fully supported technologies: "classic" ASP, ColdFusion, and PHP.

ASP

ASP, or Active Server Pages, is a Microsoft-developed web-scripting language that took the web development world by storm when it was introduced in the mid-1990s. Like many other server-side technologies, ASP enables you to embed special instructions in HTML pages that can do a variety of tasks, such as connect to a database, perform looping instructions, conditionally test for certain values, send emails, and read from and write to the file system. ASP runs natively on Microsoft's IIS web server. This means that if you have Windows XP Pro, Windows Server 2000, Windows Server 2003, or Vista, ASP is already installed and ready to go.

Although ASP pages are generally written using VBScript (a derivative of Visual Basic), ASP also supports JavaScript. Furthermore, ASP supports ActiveX Data Objects (ADO) for connecting to databases, Collaboration Data Objects (CDO) for sending emails, and more.

- ▶ **Positives**—Adobe claims that ASP is used by roughly 60% or more of Dreamweaver users. This means that support is high and extensions are plentiful. Although the trend is slowly moving to other server-side technologies, such as ColdFusion and PHP, ASP is still the number one server-side technology used by Dreamweaver.

- ▶ **Negatives**—ASP, like PHP, is *interpreted*. This means that every time a page is sent to the server for processing, a DLL intercepts and interprets the ASP code line by line. This usually results in a much slower response than is the case with compiled technologies, such as ColdFusion (and ASP.NET, JSP and CGI of years past). Furthermore, support for "traditional ASP" is slowly fading. Microsoft has tried weaning developers over to the next generation technology—ASP.NET—for quite some time.

ColdFusion

In early 2001, Macromedia (which has since been acquired by Adobe Systems, Inc.) acquired a company by the name of Allaire, along with a key server-side technology component named ColdFusion and the tool used to develop ColdFusion pages, ColdFusion Studio. Described as a rapid server-side scripting technology for creating web applications, ColdFusion uses a language called ColdFusion Markup Language (CFML) to interact with databases and dynamically created pages. CFML tags are embedded directly into HTML, and each command has a start tag and an end tag similar to HTML. Here's a simple CFML tag:

```
<cfmytag>Content goes here</cfmytag>
```

Each ColdFusion application is a set of pages with CFML commands in them. Developers can use the built-in functions, create their own, integrate COM (Microsoft's Component Object Model), C++, or Java components into their code, and even build their own components using ColdFusion Components (CFCs).

Now an essential technology in the Adobe web development line, ColdFusion relies on the ColdFusion Application Server. After it's installed, the application server functions similar to the .NET Framework (for ASP.NET) in that it closely monitors and manages ColdFusion web applications. Furthermore, you can use the ColdFusion Administrator, available as a stand-alone web application, to manage everything from data sources, memory usage, mail server properties, caching, error logs, and more.

15

▶ **Positives**—Well supported and documented by Adobe. Extremely stable in most cases. Dreamweaver includes numerous features for developing ColdFusion applications. Furthermore, free downloadable extensions are plentiful.

▶ **Negatives**—Although the developer edition of ColdFusion is free, the standard and enterprise versions of ColdFusion are expensive—$1,299 for the Standard Edition and $5,999 for the Enterprise Edition. Support is also expensive. Expect to pay a going rate of $500 for a support phone call. Because ColdFusion remains the only server-side technology on the market that costs money, its cost alone has traditionally been the major deterrent to its use.

PHP

It's hard to argue that PHP has taken the web development world by storm. PHP is a lightweight, easy-to-learn, and quickly deployed open-source scripting language with a number of convenient features. The language's lineage is Perl and C, so many developers familiar with those languages will find making the switch to PHP very easy.

PHP works well with many database solutions, but it is almost always mentioned in the same breath as the open source MySQL database (discussed in the next section). PHP can run on Windows, UNIX, and Mac servers; it supports IIS, Apache, and other web servers. As for functionality, PHP has limited support for object-oriented programming, nesting of modules, and custom functions. It has a rich set of built-in tools that let you access XML files, mail servers, database archives, Java APIs and objects, the server's file system, and a lot more.

PHP commands (called *directives*) are embedded into HTML pages between special tags (<? and ?>). These directives are handed off to the PHP engine by the web server, which then processes the directive and hands output back to the web server for display in the web browser.

▶ **Positives**—PHP is extremely trendy and widely used. Numerous start-up kits make learning PHP easy and intuitive. Realizing PHP's growing potential, Adobe has included rich features within Dreamweaver for working with PHP development. Lastly, PHP coexists with other open source movements such as Linux, Apache, and MySQL, making the overall development experience from OS to web server to database to server-side web technology totally free!

▶ **Negatives**—Like traditional ASP, PHP is interpreted code, which makes the processing of PHP pages slower than compiled options such as ColdFusion. Furthermore, because PHP is an open source technology, support is limited to forums, blogs, and documentation provided by the PHP community.

Database Options

Not too long ago, databases were the realm of specialized people. If a database was too slow, that was okay because it sat on a mainframe and processed inventory and payroll checks. Now databases are everywhere, and they're hooked into seemingly every single web application. Today's databases need to be fast, reliable, and scalable. If a database goes down (or slows down), a company's revenue might suffer because its only sales channel might be an online catalog with a shopping cart connected to the database.

As you will see in Chapter 17, a database is a collection of information stored in logical containers called *tables*. Each table normally contains related information, such as user information, personal statistics, product data, inventory information, and much, much more. Depending on the database you use, extended features for working with databases exist, such as stored procedures, triggers, views/queries, and security options.

Numerous databases are available to you. In fact, more databases exist than do server-side web technologies. Like server-side technologies, the database you choose is ultimately up to you because most are interoperable with the various server-side web technologies on the market today. Factors for choosing a database include reliability, support for the server-side technology you plan to use, *scalability* (whether the database can handle the growing amount of work in a graceful manner), cost, and *extensibility* (how easy is it to back up information, restore it in case of failure, merge data in and out, and automate processes).

As with server-side technologies, dozens of databases are available, but I'll outline only the ones used in the scope of this book. Each database has its own strengths and drawbacks. Some are free and some cost thousands of dollars to license. The database options we'll discuss include (listed in alphabetical order, not personal preference):

▶ Access

▶ SQL Server

▶ MySQL

NOTE

It's important to note that other database options exist. Oracle, IBM's DB2, Sybase, dBase, FileMaker Pro, and others are all viable alternatives. Because of page limitations, this book covers only the three databases mentioned in the previous bullet points.

Access

Access is Microsoft's database solution for developers and small companies wanting to build or house data within a small, yet reliable store. Because Microsoft Access is inexpensive and easy to acquire, it's usually the perfect choice for discussion and is used often in books such as this one. Although we won't be covering data access until Chapter 17, you might want to start thinking about the scope of your needs and choose a database accordingly. If you work at a small company and are looking for something inexpensive, reliable, and easy to use, Access might be for you. You can find more information on Access from Microsoft's website at http://www.microsoft.com/office/access. Here you can find the latest updates, news, and purchase information for Microsoft Access.

TIP

If you plan on purchasing Access, consider purchasing the Microsoft Office bundle (Access, Word, Outlook, PowerPoint, and Excel for the price of about $500, versus Access alone for about $200).

Because of its widespread availability and portability, I'll use Access as the database for a lot of the examples in this book. Of course, when there are features in Dreamweaver that differ with a particular database, I'll highlight those features and processes as well.

SQL Server

SQL Server 2005 is Microsoft's database solution for medium-to-large companies and enterprises. It's quite a bit more expensive than Access, it generally requires its own "database server" (the third tier we looked at), and at times it requires the hiring of a certified database administrator (DBA) to maintain. However, SQL Server 2005 offers a robust and scalable solution for larger web applications due, in part, to its unique core of features, including online transaction processing (OLTP), indexing, data transformation services, profiling, a query analyzer, and a robust and intuitive database management system (DBMS) in SQL Server Management Studio. If you'd like more information regarding SQL Server 2005, visit the following Microsoft website: www.microsoft.com/sql.

I will assume that if you're reading this book, you probably don't want to invest in something as massive as SQL Server 2005 and that your needs are better suited to something free, but just as powerful for testing and development purposes. If this is the case, Microsoft's SQL Server 2005 Express Edition is perfect for you. Simply put, SQL Server 2005 Express Edition is Microsoft's free enterprise-level database alternative to SQL Server 2005. It functions and stores data exactly as SQL Server 2005 does, but is meant for smaller organizations looking to get their feet wet with Microsoft database technologies before migrating to the enterprise version of SQL Server 2005. In general, most of the features found in SQL Server 2005 exist in Express Edition. The minor differences are as follows:

▶ Lack of support for enterprise features

▶ Limited to one CPU

▶ 1GB memory limit for the buffer pool

▶ Databases have a 4GB maximum size

Although some other minor features aren't supported in the Express Edition that are supported in the full version, for the most part the two products are identical and are ideal for use within the scope of this book. For more information on SQL Server 2005 Express Edition, including links to download the database and information on how to install it, visit Microsoft's website at www.microsoft.com/sql/editions/express/.

TIP

One of the pluses to using SQL Server 2005 and SQL Server 2005 Express Edition is the Management Studio and Management Studio Express database management system (DBMS). Its simplicity and navigation structure make working with SQL Server 2005 enjoyable and easy. If you plan to install and work with SQL Server 2005 or SQL Server 2005 Express Edition, you might think about downloading and installing this powerful application as well. Whereas Management Studio comes with SQL Server 2005, SQL Server 2005 Express Edition requires Management Studio Express. You can download this free application from the following website: www.microsoft.com/downloads/details.aspx?FamilyId=C243A5AE-4BD1-4E3D-94B8-5A0F62BF7796.

MySQL

Although MySQL works well with many server-side technologies, it is usually mentioned in the same breath as PHP. MySQL is a free, open-source relational database system. Its popularity on the database side matches PHP's popularity on the web-development side.

MySQL allows for blazing-fast selection of data and comparable performance for data inserts and updates. The native command-line interface supports Linux, Windows, and Mac OS X environments. If you don't like the thought of messing around with a command-line interface, don't despair; MySQL also offers numerous GUI-based tools for administering a MySQL database, including permissions, backups, restores, and queries.

> **NOTE**
>
> Don't let the words *open source* scare you away. Although MySQL was once used primarily by geeky hackers, MySQL has evolved into a full-functioning and respected database capable of any commercial operation. In fact, the entire Google search engine is built using MySQL technology.

Although MySQL doesn't support the same myriad of features that other enterprise databases such as SQL Server 2005 and Oracle do, its developers are making improvements all the time. At the time of this writing, MySQL 6.0 is available for preview (MySQL 5.1 is the current stable version) and includes features that other databases have implemented for years, including views, stored procedures, and more.

For more information on MySQL, visit the website at dev.mysql.com.

Structured Query Language

Information contained within a database is useless unless you have the means of extracting it. The Structured Query Language (SQL) is the language that does just that. SQL allows for quick, but sophisticated, access to the database data through the use of queries. Queries pose questions and return the results to your web application. But don't think of SQL as simply a way of extracting information. SQL can accomplish a variety of tasks, allowing you to not only extract information from a database, but to add, modify, and delete information as well.

SQL has its origins in a language developed by IBM in the 1970s called SEQUEL (for Structured English Query Language) and is still often referred to today as "sequel." It's a powerful way of interacting with current database technologies and their associated tables. SQL has roughly 30 keywords and is the language of choice for simple and complex database operations alike. The statements you'll construct with these keywords range from the simple to complex strings of subqueries and table joins.

> **NOTE**
>
> Although all databases support basic SQL (the SQL we'll be using throughout the book), others go well beyond the basics and incorporate their own proprietary syntax to support structured data, variables, error handling, flow control statements, loops, conditionals, transactions, and more. For instance, Microsoft's implementation of SQL is known as Transact-SQL or T-SQL. Oracle's implementation of SQL is known as Procedural Language SQL or PL/SQL. The list goes on and on.

15

Working with Data Source Names

To understand data source names is to understand how applications connect to database data through the web server's operating system. At this foundation lies Open DataBase Connectivity (ODBC), a standard database access method developed by the SQL Access group in 1992. The goal of ODBC is to make it possible to access any data from any application, regardless of which database management system is handling the data. ODBC manages this feat by inserting a middle layer, called a *database driver*, between an application and the database. The purpose of this layer is to translate the application's data queries into commands that the database understands. For this to work, both the application and the database must be ODBC-compliant; that is, the application must be capable of issuing ODBC commands and the database must be capable of responding to them.

Data Source Names (DSNs), provide Dreamweaver with connectivity to a database through an ODBC driver. The DSN contains a database name, directory, database driver, UserID, password, and other information. After you create a DSN for a particular database, you can use the DSN in an application to call information from the database.

In general, there are three types of DSNs:

▶ **System DSN**—Can be used by anyone who has access to the machine. DSN info is stored in the Registry on Windows and in the Preferences on a Mac.

▶ **User DSN**—Created for a specific user. Also stored in the Registry on Windows and in the Preferences on a Mac.

▶ **File DSN**—DSN info is stored in a text file with the DSN extension, usually in the root of the web application's directory on Windows and in the Preferences on a Mac.

One of the benefits of using Dreamweaver is that you don't have to create DSNs manually. Dreamweaver allows you to connect and create DSNs directly from its development environment. We'll get into this in more detail in Chapter 19, "Working with Dynamic Data."

> **NOTE**
>
> There is also what is known as a "DSN-less connection." Instead of using a DSN to connect to a database, the developer specifies the necessary information right in the application. With a DSN-less connection, the developer is free to use connection standards other than ODBC, such as Microsoft's OLE DB or Apple/IBM's OpenDoc (a standard meant to replace ODBC).

The Dynamic Vecta Corp Intranet Application

Up to this point, we've used various web pages in the Vecta Corp site as examples of how to work with basic page formatting techniques, tables, CSS, forms and form objects, behaviors, AP elements, and more. Up until now, the process has been simple: We create a new page, add some images and text to the page, format it with tables or divs, and then save it for viewing in the browser. In a real-world scenario, however, our workflow process would be inadequate and inefficient. Imagine having 500 pages within a site and trying to perform day-to-day web-maintenance operations. As it relates to our Vecta Corp example, the process might resemble the following scenario:

▶ **Company Events**—As a web developer, your job is to manually add and remove company events as they're announced. After the company event is on the main page, you must also create a dedicated page for the company event that includes pictures, directions, times, and perhaps a reservation system that, you guessed it, would be manually updated by you based on email reservations sent to you.

▶ **HelpDesk**—The HelpDesk functions as a repository for employee hardware, software, and general office maintenance problems. In a traditional scenario, you are responsible for fielding emails from employees with problems and then manually posting information to the website so that the IT department can view the problems and respond accordingly. Even worse, after the IT department responds and fixes the problem, they would send you an email so that you could manually remove the ticket from the site.

▶ **Company Directory**—As the web developer, your job is to continuously add, modify, and remove employees from the employee directory page. Given today's volatile marketplace, this in itself could become a daunting task!

▶ **Employee Store**—As the web developer, your job also involves manually adding, modifying, and removing products from the company's employee store. But wait, there's more. You are also responsible for fielding emails from employees who are interested in a product, collecting cash, giving the employee the product, and then manually updating a spreadsheet of inventory information.

After reviewing this process, you've probably come to one conclusion: job security! As you can see, these tasks are enough to keep you busy all day, leaving little time for your talents and skills elsewhere on the website. Rather than taking a design or development role as it relates to the website, you might be stuck in maintenance mode, constantly adding, updating, and removing data from the website.

This is where dynamic web pages and web applications come into play. Using a web application containing numerous dynamic web pages, you could easily streamline your workflow so that it begins to model the following workflow process:

▶ **Company Events**—Rather than manually adding, removing, and deleting company events, you tie the main page of the site to a database. A table within the database could contain the company events that are, in turn, fed to an HTML table within the main page. Even better, you can create a second page that allows Herbert in HR to add, update, and remove company events from the database using a simple administrative web page.

15

▶ **HelpDesk**—Instead of fielding emails from employees who have problems, why not create a two-page HelpDesk system in which employees can create new HelpDesk tickets? These tickets can be stored in a table in the database. A second administrative page, accessible by the IT staff, provides a list of employees with problems (fed in from the database). When the problem has been fixed, the IT staff member selects from a drop-down menu that changes the status of the HelpDesk ticket from Open to Closed.

▶ **Company Directory**—Rather than manually adding, modifying, and removing employees from the company directory, you can easily create functionality within an administrative page that allows you to centrally add, modify, and delete employees from a database table. This approach effectively eliminates the need for manually connecting to the site, opening the HTML page, making changes, and then re-uploading the site.

▶ **Employee Store**—By far the most complex part of the Vecta Corp site is the employee store. Manually trying to add, modify, and remove products as well as collect cash, distribute products, and update inventories can be an extremely time-consuming process. Instead, add the products to a database and display those products within a dynamic page. Add shopping cart functionality to the page that allows users to add and update a shopping cart on their own. When it comes time to check out, you can easily integrate payment system functionality such as PayPal to automate the process of collecting money from the employee.

▶ **Admin**—As the web developer/administrator, you'll want a centralized interface for adding, modifying, and deleting employees. Additionally, you'll want to centrally add, modify, and remove product information from your site. This is where the administrative page comes in. By creating a digital dashboard of sorts, you can easily fulfill these tasks without ever having to connect to your site within Dreamweaver.

After reviewing this process, you're probably starting to wonder about that job security. The downside to using dynamic web pages and databases is that you're effectively taken out of some of the processes you've become accustomed to dealing with. The upside is that you can now focus on building more applications for your organization. Even better, you can now focus on designing and developing the fun stuff! And though the initial setup and development time is greater for our web application than for the equivalent static pages, the benefits down the line far outweigh the time it would take to develop the application. Keep in mind that Dreamweaver cuts your development time in half. Because you're working with an intuitive visual editor and not coding by hand, the time needed to create the dynamic Vecta Corp web application in Dreamweaver will be short.

The next nine chapters of the book involve building the dynamic pages for the Vecta Corp employee store. As you've seen from the bullet points describing the pages above, our web application has the potential of becoming a massive undertaking, so we'll focus on the employee store page. I'll outline how to work with databases in Dreamweaver by establishing a connection to a database, how to create bindings to the database, and how to work with the many server behaviors in Dreamweaver to build view catalog page, login functionality, search functionality, and more. By the book's end, you should be able to take the concepts learned in the next nine chapters and build out the rest of the pages outlined in the previous bullet points.

Summary

Understanding what a web application is—and how different it is from a static website—is only the first step in creating one. Making decisions about server-side technologies and databases all comes down to one thing: What tools are easily available?

If your company has Oracle installed and there are plenty of PHP developers available to build and support your web application, that's likely the way you'll go. However, if you are running a small company and cost is an issue, PHP/MySQL, ASP/Access, or ColdFusion/Access might be more prudent.

In the next chapter, you'll take the foundation-level concepts from this chapter to the next level. You'll actually pick a server-side technology to use, learn how to install it, and then configure it to work with Dreamweaver and the Vecta Corp application.

15

Working with Server-Side Technologies

Now that you've been formally introduced to the terminology of server-side web development—including dynamic web pages, web applications, databases, SQL, and DSNs—you're ready to move forward into the realm of the installation, set up, and configuration for the actual server-side technology you plan to use.

By now you should have some sort of idea about the architecture of your organization. Do you have Windows XP Home, a Windows server-based operating system such as Windows XP Pro, Windows Server 2000 or 2003, or are you running Mac OS X? Are your plans to develop web applications using a development machine and then upload the finished product to a web hosting provider when you're finished? Do you want to minimize installation and configuration? Are you merely a novice who is interested in tinkering with dynamic web page development? The answers to these questions can help you quickly determine what server-side technology and ultimately what web server you'll need to use with Dreamweaver. It's important to note that Dreamweaver's functionality for creating dynamic web pages is nearly identical regardless of server-side technology. And because you won't be interacting with the code all that much, picking a server-side technology shouldn't be all that difficult; they all have the same bells and whistles built into Dreamweaver. After you get past the installation and configuration routines covered in this chapter, the rest of the examples in the book apply regardless of the platform you use.

If you haven't made a decision on the server-side technology you want to use, don't worry. In this chapter, I'll demystify each of your options. I'll provide an overview of the web server we'll be using for the examples in this book, as well as alternatives you might decide to use on your own. We'll also detail the nuances, installation procedures, and configuration routines (if any) for the three server-side technologies that we'll cover throughout the rest of the book. By the end of the chapter, you'll have a web server up and running, a server-side technology installed and configured, and a simple dynamic page working!

Picking a Web Server

In the previous chapter, I made reference to the fact that users interact with web applications through a series of carefully crafted form objects exposed to the user in the browser window. The user interacts with the form objects and then typically clicks a button, expecting to see results. What we haven't discussed, however, is how those results are returned to the user.

In general, servers rely on a piece of software that is crucial in the HTTP request/response process. This piece of software, the *web server*, is primarily responsible for managing various websites, FTP sites, a mail client, and more on our server. Working in conjunction with the server-side technology, the web server is also responsible for facilitating the handoff between the client's request, the server-side technology used to handle the request, the collection of the response from the server-side technology, and the subsequent handoff of the response back to the client browser.

In a nutshell, without a web server, a server-side technology can't function. And if a server-side technology can't function, dynamic web page development is useless. If you're reading this book, chances are you're looking to build web applications and then transfer them to your web hosting provider upon completion.

> **NOTE**
>
> You don't have to be reliant on a web hosting provider to host your web applications. Depending on your skill set and what your Internet service provider allows, you might decide to build your own web server and host your own web applications. Of course, this is beyond the scope of this book, but it's something to consider as your skills increase.

With that said, choosing a web server is simply a matter of answering a few simple questions. First, are you on a Mac, or are you on a PC running Windows? And, if you're running Windows, are you using Windows XP Home or Windows XP Pro, Vista, or a Windows server-based operating system such as 2000 Server or 2003 Server? Next, is the web hosting provider that you'll ultimately be transferring your files to running Linux or Windows as the operating system that hosts the web server? Answering these questions will help you pick a web server and more importantly, pick a server-side technology, that works in conjunction with that operating system and web server software. For the most part, the majority of web hosting providers support either Linux or Windows. With that being said, the web servers running on those operating systems will either be Apache or Internet Information Services (IIS), respectively.

NOTE

Obviously, Apache and IIS aren't the only web servers on the market. Other web servers exist and are viable solutions in most cases—including Sun's iPlanet, IBM's WebSphere, and more. These web servers can run just as well on Mac and UNIX/Linux environments as they can on Windows machines.

Knowing which operating system and web server your web hosting provider operates under will help you choose from which software to configure your computer locally. For the most part, the following three will serve all readers of this book enough to follow along with the examples:

▶ **Internet Information Services (IIS)**—Internet Information Services is Microsoft's enterprise-level web server that comes preinstalled on most Windows server-based operating systems, including Windows XP Pro, Windows Server 2000, Windows Server 2003, and all Vista editions. If you and your web hosting provider's operating system is on this list, chances are this is the route you'll want to take.

▶ **XAMPP**—Short for *Cross-Platform (X), Apache, MySQL, PHP, and Perl*, XAMPP is slowly making a name for itself as an easy-to-install and easy-to-use software solution that mirrors remote installations of the Apache web server, the MySQL database, and the server-side technology PHP. If you desire a simple installation with almost zero setup time, XAMPP might be for you. Because XAMPP is a small, lightweight development web server that generally supports only Apache, MySQL, and PHP, you'll want to make sure that your web hosting provider supports these technologies before opting for this. If you're running Windows XP Home Edition and your web hosting provider supports PHP development, this will be your only choice for completing the examples in this book, as Windows XP Home doesn't support IIS.

▶ **MAMP**—Short for *Macintosh, Apache, MySQL, and PHP*, MAMP, like XAMPP, is an easy-to-use and easy-to-configure software solution that you can use on your Mac OS X to mirror remote web server installations of the Apache web server, the MySQL database, and the server-side technology PHP. If you're running on a Mac OS X, this is the option for you. Later in the chapter, we'll walk through getting MAMP installed and configured so that you can follow along with the examples in this book.

As you can see, we've excluded no one. Whether you're running Windows XP Home, Pro, Windows Server, Vista, or Mac OS X, a solution exists to get you working with the examples throughout the rest of the book. With that said, let's begin to discuss the three with much more detail, including getting them set up and running so that you can begin working with the examples moving forward.

Working with Internet Information Services (IIS)

Internet Information Services is Microsoft's enterprise-level web server solution and is in use by roughly 50% of the public web hosting providers as of the time of this writing. IIS comes bundled with most Microsoft server-based operating systems, including Windows 2000 Pro, Server and Advanced Server, Window 2003 Server, Windows XP Pro, Windows Vista Home Premium, Vista Business, Vista Ultimate, and Vista Enterprise.

Depending on the Windows version you have, IIS installs when the OS is installed, but in other cases, you must manually walk through the process of setting it up on your own. More on this later.

Table 16.1 outlines the major Windows operating systems and shows whether the web server comes preinstalled with the specific operating system.

TABLE 16.1   Major Windows Systems and IIS Support

OS	Web Server	Pre-Enabled?	Technologies Supported
Win 95, 98, ME, XP Home	None	N/A	N/A
Win XP Pro	IIS 5	No	All
Win 2000 Pro	IIS 5	No	All
Win 2000 Server	IIS 5	Yes	All
Win 2003	IIS 6	Yes	All
Win Vista Home Premium	IIS 7	Yes	All
Win Vista Business	IIS 7	Yes	All
Win Vista Ultimate	IIS 7	Yes	All
Win Vista Enterprise	IIS 7	Yes	All

Although IIS comes preinstalled on all of the operating systems mentioned in Table 16.1, it doesn't come pre-enabled on all of them. If you're not sure whether IIS is pre-enabled and the operating system that you're running is in the table, you can use one of these three methods to find out:

▶ Check for a folder called Inetpub located in the root of your system (typically the C:\) drive. If you have that folder—as well as the wwwroot folder within it—chances are you're fine.

▶ Select Start, Settings, Control Panel, Administrative Tools. If you have a menu item for Internet Services Manager, IIS is indeed installed.

▶ Navigate to http://localhost in a browser. If you see the IIS Welcome screen, IIS is installed and running.

If IIS is there, you've got the web server installed and you're ready to begin working with the examples in this book. If not, follow the steps in the next section to get it installed.

Installing IIS

One of the questions in application development is whether IIS has to be installed even if you are not hosting your own web applications. The answer is *yes*. Even if you are uploading your web applications using FTP to your web host provider, it's always a good idea to mirror the configuration of the remote web hosting provider for two reasons. First, Dreamweaver won't let you build web applications without web server software installed. Second, mirroring the configuration of your remote web hosting provider will guarantee that the applications you build locally will transfer over without failure when you're ready to upload them.

NOTE

As you've seen, Dreamweaver allows you to define a testing server when you define a site. The site that you define within IIS (covered later) will become the site you specify in the testing server category in the Site Definition dialog box.

IIS comes with most versions of server-based Windows operating systems, but it's not installed automatically in all versions, which is why it might not be present on your computer. If you've come to the conclusion that IIS isn't installed on your computer and you have a compatible operating system listed in Table 16.1, follow these steps to install it:

1. Access the Control Panel by choosing Start, Settings, Control Panel.

2. In the Control Panel, select Add or Remove Programs. In Vista, the menu item is titled Programs and Features.

3. Choose Add/Remove Windows Components. In Vista, the menu item is titled Turn Windows Features On or Off. The list of components becomes visible within a few seconds.

4. In the list of components, enable the Internet Information Services (IIS) option. If you're using Vista, you might take the time to expand the Internet Information Services node, expand the World Wide Web Services node, expand the Application Development Features node, and then enable ASP. This will guarantee that traditional ASP will work with Vista.

5. Click Next (Windows may or may not prompt you to insert the original Windows software CD) to install IIS.

6. After IIS is installed, close the Add or Remove Programs (Programs and Features) dialog box.

You can now check to see whether IIS installed correctly by performing one or all three checkpoints highlighted in the previous section.

You are now ready to begin hosting web applications. Although we won't cover how to configure IIS for external use, I will show you how to configure IIS to support local development of ASP, ColdFusion, and PHP applications so that you can upload them later to your external web host provider.

Configuring IIS

Although little configuration needs to be done to begin working with IIS, I will use this section to introduce some basic features and functionality within IIS. Reading this section will help you better troubleshoot problems that might arise later in development. This section explains the following topics:

▶ Where to keep files on the web server

▶ Using Localhost

Now that you have IIS up and running, let's take a closer look at where the files for your web applications are kept on the computer. Up to this point, we've been saving our projects in the `C:\VectaCorp\` directory. This works fine for static web pages because we're merely testing the functionality of the pages in the browser. IIS works a bit differently, however. By default, IIS reads and processes the code in the file from the `C:\Inetpub\` `wwwroot\` folder. If you open this folder and compare it to the folder tree in IIS, you'll notice some similarities. Although it is not a requirement to keep applications in this folder, it is generally considered a good repository for storing and managing your server-side applications.

> **NOTE**
>
> Technically, your files don't have to be in `C:\Inetpub\wwwroot\`. You can also create what's called a *virtual directory*. A virtual directory is essentially an alias within IIS that points to a folder somewhere else on your computer. To make things easier, however, we'll work with `C:\Inetpub\wwwroot\` for the rest of the book.

So that we can test how our web server works, let's create a new folder within `C:\Inetpub\wwwroot` and add a simple HTML page to the new folder. You can do this on your own by following these steps:

1. Open Windows Explorer and navigate to the root of `C:\Inetpub\wwwroot`.

2. Within wwwroot, create a new folder called **VectaCorp**.

3. Open the VectaCorp folder.

4. Right-click an empty area in the folder and choose New, Text Document from the context menu.

5. After you select the New Text Document option, you can rename the file. Change the name, including its extension, to **index.html**. This action converts the text document to an HTML file.

6. Right-click the file and choose Open With, Notepad from the context menu. The file will open in Notepad.

7. In the document, add the following basic HTML:

```
<html>
<head>
<title>Sample HTML Page</title>
</head>


<body>
<h1>Hello World</h1>
</body>
   </html>
```

8. Save the page and close Notepad.

That's it! You've just created your first basic page within the context of the web server. In the next section, we'll browse to the page using the default name of the web server.

Now that you have a new file in `C:\Inetpub\wwwroot\VectaCorp`, your web server has access to it. If you've been developing static HTML web pages for a long time, habit might drive you to open files directly in your browser. Dynamic pages can't be opened directly from the browser because your web server needs to have a crack at the file before it is sent to your browser for display. If the application server doesn't get the chance to interpret the request coded into a dynamic page, the code behind the dynamic page is never converted into HTML that your browser can understand.

To repeat: Dynamic pages can't be opened directly from the browser. Instead, you'll have to open the browser and navigate to the web directory using the local web address for your computer, also known as http://localhost (or by the IP address http://127.0.0.1). More specifically, because the VectaCorp folder is located in `C:\Inetpub\wwwroot\VectaCorp` on your computer, you can access it directly from the browser by typing in the URL **http://localhost/VectaCorp**. Try it now to see the result. You'll quickly notice that a page containing the text *Hello World* is displayed.

In this case, the process was simple. Because our default page is essentially an HTML file, nothing is really required of the web server. Most of the work in this case is handled by the browser. The browser parses the literal text out of the HTML tags and presents the text *Hello World* to the user. Because our page contained only HTML, we could have just as easily opened the page directly in the browser, displaying the same results. Remember though, that the web server (IIS) is the only piece of software that can access your server-side code (such as ASP, ColdFusion, or PHP) directly. For this reason, it's a good idea to get into the habit of accessing your dynamic pages directly from http://localhost/VectaCorp/. This is how it will be done throughout the rest of the book, both manually and via Dreamweaver.

16

Working with XAMPP

XAMPP is a cross-platform initiative aimed at delivering the web server Apache, the database MySQL, the server-side technology PHP, and the programming language Perl to developers regardless of operating system. Although other software solutions such as MAMP (which is meant to work only with Mac OS X) or IIS (which works only with Windows server-based operating systems) are meant to work with specific platforms, XAMPP, as the name implies (X meaning cross-platform), can be installed and configured to work with Windows, Linux, Solaris, and Mac OS X, making it much more flexible and preferable to those who are unsure where their applications will end up.

If you're using Windows XP Home Edition, XAMPP might be the direction you choose to go. You'll be limited to Apache, MySQL, and PHP, and you'll need to make sure your web hosting provider supports these technologies, but at least you'll be able to follow along with all of the examples in this book.

Installing XAMPP

Installing XAMPP is a simple matter of browsing to a website, downloading an executable, and following a simple-to-use wizard. Whereas IIS really took some time to explain and get going, XAMPP is somewhat straightforward and relatively easy to configure. To install XAMPP, follow these steps:

1. Open a browser window and navigate to www.apachefriends.org/en/xampp.html.

2. Scroll halfway down the page until you find the link titled XAMPP for Windows. Click it to be redirected to a download page.

3. As of the time of this writing, XAMPP 1.6.7 is generally available. Click the Installer link to begin downloading the xampp-win32-1.6.7-installer.exe installer.

4. With the installer downloaded, double-click it now to begin the installation.

5. Accept all the defaults until you come to a screen that has a subsection titled SERVICE SECTION. Make sure to check all three check boxes for Install Apache as Service, Install MySQL as Service, and Install Filezilla As Service.

6. Click Install to begin the installation. At some point, a command-line utility will execute during the installation of Apache, and Windows will ask you whether to keep blocking the Apache HTTP Server. Make sure to click the Unblock button.

You're done! Even if you're using Windows XP Home, which doesn't support IIS, you'll now be able to follow along with the examples in this book. The next section will help you better understand where files are generally located and how they can be referenced via a web browser when using XAMPP.

Configuring XAMPP

Although little configuration needs to be done to begin working with XAMPP, I will use this section to introduce some basic features and functionality within XAMPP. Reading this section will help you better troubleshoot problems that might arise later in development. This section explains the following topics:

▶ Where to keep files on the web server

▶ Using Localhost

Now that you have XAMPP up and running, let's take a closer look at where the files for your web applications are kept on the computer. Up to this point, we've been saving our projects in the C:\VectaCorp\ directory. This works fine for static web pages because we're merely testing the functionality of the pages in the browser. XAMPP (which uses the Apache web server) works a bit differently, however. By default, XAMPP reads and processes the code in the file from the C:\xampp\htdocs\ folder.

So that we can test how our web server works, let's create a new folder within C:\xampp\ htdocs\ and add a simple HTML page to the new folder. You can do this on your own by following these steps:

1. Open Windows Explorer and navigate to the root of C:\xampp\htdocs\.

2. Within htdocs, create a new folder called **VectaCorp**.

3. Open the VectaCorp folder.

4. Right-click an empty area in the folder and choose New, Text Document from the context menu.

5. After you select the New Text Document option, you can rename the file. Change the name, including its extension, to **index.html**. This action converts the text document to an HTML file.

6. Right-click the file and choose Open With, Notepad from the context menu. The file will open in Notepad.

7. In the document, add the following basic HTML:

```
<html>
<head>
<title>Sample HTML Page</title>
</head>


<body>
<h1>Hello World</h1>
</body>
   </html>
```

8. Save the page and close Notepad.

That's it! You've just created your first basic page within the context of the Apache web server.

Now that you have a new file in C:\xampp\htdocs\VectaCorp\, your web server has access to it. If you've been developing static HTML web pages for a long time, habit might drive you to open files directly in your browser. Dynamic pages can't be opened directly from the browser because your web server needs to have a crack at the file before it is sent to

16

your browser for display. If the application server doesn't get the chance to interpret the request coded into a dynamic page, the code behind the dynamic page is never converted into HTML that your browser can understand.

To repeat: Dynamic pages can't be opened directly from the browser. Instead, you'll have to open the browser and navigate to the web directory using the local web address for your computer, also known as http://localhost (or by the IP address http://127.0.0.1). More specifically, because the VectaCorp folder is located in C:\xampp\htdocs\VectaCorp\ on your computer, you can access it directly from the browser by typing in the URL **http://localhost/VectaCorp**. Figure 16.1 shows what the page looks like in the browser so that you can visualize the point I'm trying to make with the URL.

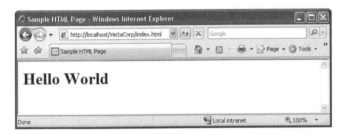

FIGURE 16.1   http://localhost/VectaCorp is the URL that points to the folder C:\xampp\htdocs\VectaCorp\.

In this case, the process was simple. Because our default page is essentially an HTML file, nothing is really required of the web server. Most of the work in this case is handled by the browser. The browser parses the literal text out of the HTML tags and presents the text *Hello World* to the user. Because our page contained only HTML, we could have just as easily opened the page directly in the browser, displaying the same results. Remember though, that the web server (Apache) is the only piece of software that can access your server-side code (PHP in XAMPP's case) directly. For this reason, it's a good idea that you get into the habit of accessing your dynamic pages directly from http://localhost/VectaCorp/. This is how it will be done throughout the rest of the book, both manually and via Dreamweaver.

Working with MAMP

Another option for working with the examples in this book on Mac OS X is MAMP. *MAMP*, which is the acronym given to *Macintosh, Apache, MySQL, and PHP*, is a software package that you can download and install onto your Mac OS X. One simple installation procedure installs the Apache web server, the MySQL database, and the server-side technology PHP onto your computer. No fumbling with configuration files, no installing numerous software packages—everything is conveniently installed in one handy installation routine.

> **TIP**
>
> In this book, we use MAMP as the all-in-one web server, database server, server-side technology solution on Mac OS X. However, it's not the only one. XAMPP, which we used to configure Windows XP Home, also has a download available for Mac OS X. Based on my experience with both products, I have to say that MAMP is a cleaner and much easier-to-use solution for Mac OS X. If MAMP existed for Windows XP Home, I'd probably use it instead of XAMPP.

Installing MAMP

Installing MAMP is a simple matter of browsing to the MAMP website, downloading an image file, mounting the image, and then simply copying over the necessary files into your Applications folder. To install MAMP, follow these steps:

1. Open a browser window and navigate to www.mamp.info/en/download.html.

2. Click the MAMP & MAMP Pro 1.7.1 link to begin downloading the 127MB DMG file.

3. As soon as the DMG file finishes downloading, the image will automatically mount for installation, and a screen similar to the one shown in Figure 16.2 will appear.

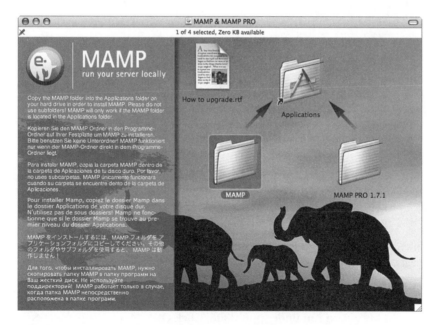

FIGURE 16.2   The MAMP DMG file will automatically mount for installation, and a window will automatically appear with a shortcut to your Applications folder.

4. Drag the MAMP folder into your Applications folder to begin copying the files over. After the files finish copying, you can unmount/eject the image by dragging the drive icon into the trash.

You're done! You'll now be able to follow along with the examples in this book even if you're using a Mac. The next section will help you better understand where files are generally located and how they can be referenced via a web browser when using MAMP.

Configuring MAMP

For the most part, configuring MAMP is a simple, painless process that involves nothing more than opening the MAMP application, starting the web and database servers, and then changing the default port numbers for the applications to coincide with the examples that we'll be using throughout the book. To configure MAMP, follow these steps:

1. Navigate to the MAMP folder, which should be located within your Applications folder. Once there, double-click on the MAMP application to launch the administrative screen, shown in Figure 16.3.

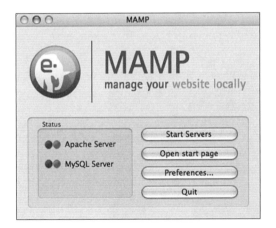

FIGURE 16.3   The MAMP administrative screen allows you to start and stop the web and database servers, customize port numbers, and more.

2. Click the Preferences button to launch the Preferences window. After the Preferences window appears, choose the Ports category.

3. Click the Set to Default Apache and MySQL Ports button. MAMP immediately configures Apache to run under port 80 (the default port for the Internet, regardless of web server) and MySQL to run under port 3306. Click OK.

4. Click the Start Servers button. The Apache and MySQL Server icons should now be green (instead of the red that is the default when the servers are turned off), indicating that the servers have been started.

5. To keep MAMP running in the background, simply minimize it. Closing it will stop the servers and prevent you from continuing with the examples in the book.

Although little configuration needs to be done beyond what we've just accomplished, I will use the rest of this section to introduce some basic features that will help you navigate MAMP from a web browser. This will help you better troubleshoot problems that might arise later in development and, more importantly, will help you better understand setup processes for PHP within Dreamweaver later. Specifically we'll address the following:

▶ Where to keep files on the web server

▶ Using Localhost

Now that you have MAMP up and running, let's take a closer look at where the files for your web applications are kept on the computer. Up to this point, we've been saving our projects in the /Applications/VectaCorp/ directory (on Mac). This works fine for static web pages because we're merely testing the functionality of the pages in the browser. MAMP (which uses the Apache web server) works a bit differently, however. By default, MAMP reads and processes the code in the file from the /Applications/MAMP/htdocs/ folder.

So that we can test how our web server works, let's create a new folder within /Applications/MAMP/htdocs/ and add a simple HTML page to the new folder. You can do this on your own by following these steps:

1. Navigate to /Applications/MAMP/htdocs/.

2. Within the htdocs folder, create a new folder called **VectaCorp**.

3. Open a text editor such as TextEdit.

4. In the document, add the following basic HTML:

```
<html>
<head>
<title>Sample HTML Page</title>
</head>


<body>
<h1>Hello World</h1>
</body>
   </html>
```

5. Select Format, Make Plain Text.

6. Immediately save the file as index.html and place it within the newly created VectaCorp folder located within the htdocs folder.

7. Save the page and close TextEdit.

That's it! You've just created your first basic page within the context of the Apache web server (which is bundled with MAMP).

Now that you have a new file in /Applications/MAMP/htdocs/VectaCorp/, your web server has access to it. If you've been developing static HTML web pages for a long time, habit might drive you to open files directly in your browser. Dynamic pages can't be opened directly from the browser because your web server needs to have a crack at the file before it is sent to your browser for display. If the application server doesn't get the chance to interpret the request coded into a dynamic page, the code behind the dynamic page is never converted into HTML that your browser can understand.

To repeat: Dynamic pages can't be opened directly from the browser. Instead, you'll have to open the browser and navigate to the web directory using the local web address for your computer, also known as http://localhost (or by the IP address http://127.0.0.1). More specifically, because the VectaCorp folder is located in /Applications/MAMP/htdocs/VectaCorp/ on your computer, you can access it directly from the browser by typing in the URL **http://localhost/VectaCorp**. Figure 16.4 shows what the page looks like in Safari so that you can visualize the point I'm trying to make with the URL.

FIGURE 16.4   http://localhost/VectaCorp is the URL that points to the folder /Applications/MAMP/htdocs/VectaCorp/.

In this case, the process was simple. Because our default page is essentially an HTML file, nothing is really required of the web server. Most of the work in this case is handled by the browser. The browser parses the literal text out of the HTML tags and presents the text *Hello World* to the user. Because our page contained only HTML, we could have just as easily opened the page directly in the browser, displaying the same results. Remember though, that the web server (Apache) is the only piece of software that can access your server-side code (PHP) directly. For this reason, it's a good idea that you get into the habit of accessing your dynamic pages directly from http://localhost/VectaCorp/. This is how it will be done throughout the rest of the book, both manually and via Dreamweaver.

Working with ASP

Quite possibly the simplest technology to use in conjunction with Dreamweaver dynamic web page development is ASP. ASP, or Active Server Pages, is a Microsoft-developed web scripting language that took the web development world by storm when it was introduced in the mid-1990s. ASP is easy to understand and easy to use—and setup is a breeze because the required files are preinstalled on virtually all Windows servers.

Like many other server-side technologies, ASP enables you to embed special instructions in HTML pages that can do a variety of tasks, such as connect to a database, perform looping instructions, conditionally test for certain values, send emails, read from and write to the file system, and more. Because ASP runs natively on Microsoft's IIS web server, installing ASP generally means installing IIS. If IIS is up and running, chances are, so is

ASP. It's no wonder that the majority of users who create dynamic web pages in Dreamweaver still use traditional ASP as their server-side technology of choice; if you have IIS installed, there's little or no setup and nothing to install.

Creating a Simple ASP Page

Let's walk through the process of creating a simple ASP page. Not only will this process help familiarize you with the technology, but you'll also get a decent understanding of how IIS handles the processing of a dynamic ASP page. To create a simple ASP page, follow these steps:

1. Create a new folder in `C:\Inetpub\wwwroot\` called **VectaCorpASP**.

2. Open Notepad (we'll get to Dreamweaver later).

3. In the document, add the following code:

```
<html>
<head>
<title>Sample ASP Page</title>
</head>


<body>
<h1>This is plain text</h1>
<h1><%= "This is ASP writing text to the browser dynamically" %></h1>
</body>
   </html>
```

4. Save your work as **sample.asp** in the new folder named C:\Inetpub\wwwroot\VectaCorpASP\.

TIP

If you plan to try out numerous server-side technologies (which you can do in IIS), it's beneficial to create the folder with the VectaCorp name followed by the three-letter server-side technology you plan to use. This convention prevents you from continuously having to redefine the site for every server-side technology.

To test your work, open the browser and type the URL http://localhost/VectaCorpASP/ sample.asp into the address bar. Two lines of text appear in the browser. Although the result might not seem all that awe inspiring, think again: You've just created your first dynamic web page using ASP. Look at the code again and see whether you can pick apart the dynamic portions of the page. For the most part, 8 of the 9 lines of code on the page are plain old HTML that IIS does nothing with. It simply lets the browser parse the HTML tags and presents the text inside them to the user. Line 7, however, works a bit differently:

```
<h1><%= "This is ASP writing text to the browser dynamically" %></h1>
```

16

In this case, we use what's called a *code render block* to dynamically display the text *This is ASP writing text to the browser dynamically* within a <h1> HTML tag. IIS, recognizing that this code render block exists, intercepts the request and calls for help from the asp.dll located in the C:\Windows\system32\inetsrv\ folder. The asp.dll processes the request and takes the code render block to mean "Print out the text *This is ASP writing text to the browser dynamically*" on the page. This response is sent back to IIS and ultimately back to the browser, formatted using the <h1> tag. Although the process might seem complex, it happens so fast that a user rarely knows that a dynamic page is even being used.

See how easy that was? In this example, we manually wrote ASP code. The beauty in using Dreamweaver is that you don't have to. Dreamweaver writes all the necessary code for you. More on this later. For now, let's focus on getting our project configured so that we can use ASP to create dynamic Vecta Corp pages.

Configuring Vecta Corp to Run Under ASP

Up to this point, we've been working primarily from C:\VectaCorp\. From now on, we'll work from C:\Inetpub\wwwroot\VectaCorpASP\ (assuming that you're using ASP). Because this is the case, we need to reconfigure the site definition to point to the new folder we've created. Furthermore, we need to configure the Testing Server category in the Site Definition window to provide Dreamweaver with information specific to the technology you plan to use for the defined site. To configure our Vecta Corp application to run under ASP, follow these steps:

1. If you haven't downloaded the files for this chapter, do so now. Open the folder for Exercises\Chapter16\Beginning\VectaCorpASP\, copy the contents of the folder, and paste them into the newly created VectaCorpASP folder in C:\Inetpub\wwwroot\VectaCorpASP\. Now you have all the images, a template, and an index.asp page to get you started. Specifically, after you've copied the files over, you should have Images, a Template folder that includes the main template for the site, a CSS file, an index.asp page, and the sample.asp page that you built in the previous section.

2. Open Dreamweaver if you haven't already done so and choose the Manage Sites option from the Site menu.

3. Select the existing Vecta Corp site from the list and click Edit. The Site Definition for the VectaCorp dialog box appears.

4. In the Site Name text box, rename the site from VectaCorp to **VectaCorpASP**.

5. Browse to the C:\Inetpub\wwwroot\VectaCorpASP\ folder within the Local Root Folder field. Leave everything else as is. The result is shown in Figure 16.5.

6. Switch to the Testing Server category.

7. Select the ASP VBScript option from the Server model menu.

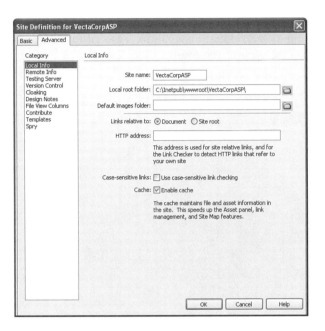

FIGURE 16.5   Rename the site definition and set the local root folder to point to the
C:\Inetpub\wwwroot\VectaCorpASP\ folder.

8. Choose the Local/Network option from the Access menu. New properties become
   available that allow you to configure the location of the remote folder as well as the
   URL prefix for the remote folder.

9. Browse to the same C:\Inetpub\wwwroot\VectaCorpASP\ path in the Remote Folder
   text box. In most cases, this value is prepopulated when you select the
   Local/Network option from the Access menu.

> **NOTE**
>
> When working with web applications, the ideal scenario is that you'll have a develop-
> ment machine, a production machine (server), and a testing server. Realistically, not
> everyone can afford another server just for testing purposes. Most of us will rely on the
> development machine to function as a testing server as well. For this reason, we'll
> leave the testing server path as is. If you do have a dedicated testing server, you'd
> probably still choose the Local/Network option from the Access tab; however, rather
> than finding the machine locally, you'd browse to it on the network.

10. Now enter the URL to our Vecta Corp site in the URL Prefix text box. This value
    should read http://localhost/vectacorpasp/. Remember that localhost, like every
    other domain name (yahoo.com, google.com, and so on) is a URL that is accessible
    from a browser. Rather than accessing the site from a server miles away, the browser

knows that localhost (and the IP address 127.0.0.1 associated with it) is the URL for the local instance of IIS (your computer). It doesn't have to look too far for your files. When you finish configuring this screen, the result will look similar to Figure 16.6.

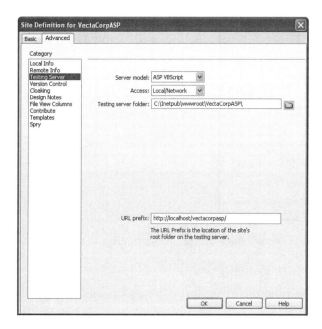

FIGURE 16.6   Configure the Testing Server category.

11. Click OK to close the Site Definition for VectaCorpASP window.

12. Click Done to close the Manage Sites dialog box.

You're now ready to begin building dynamic Vecta Corp pages using Dreamweaver and ASP!

Using ASP in Dreamweaver

Depending on the server technology you decide to use, features (as they relate to the specific server technology) within the Dreamweaver interface will change. For the most part, however, you can bank on the fact that the following features will always be available in Dreamweaver when you're working with any server-side technology:

▶ **The Insert panel**—A visual representation of objects available in the Insert menu, the Data category in the Insert panel (shown in Figure 16.7), allows you to visually insert various types of dynamic objects onto your page. Furthermore, when working with ASP, an ASP category also becomes available, which allows you to choose from ASP-specific options.

FIGURE 16.7   Use the Insert panel as a visual tool for inserting dynamic objects on your page.

▶ **The Insert menu**—Use the Data Objects and ASP Objects submenus in the Insert menu to insert both generic data objects as well as ASP-specific objects.

▶ **The Application panel**—Split into four tabs—Databases, Bindings, Server Behaviors, and Components—the Application panel provides the means for connecting to and accessing database data, binding that data to elements on the page, and accessing the various application objects that were also available from the Insert menu. When working with dynamic pages in Dreamweaver, you should always have this panel open. The Server Behaviors tab of the Application panel is shown with more detail in Figure 16.8.

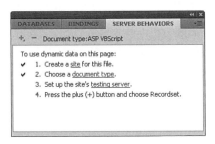

FIGURE 16.8   Use the Application panel when working with databases, binding database data to your dynamic pages, and working with various application objects.

▶ **The Tag Chooser**—If you want to make fine-tuned changes in your ASP code, you can always choose specific tags from the Tag Chooser, shown in Figure 16.9. When you choose an option from the Tag Chooser (available by choosing Insert, Tag), the Properties dialog box for the particular tag opens, allowing you to further customize attributes of the tag.

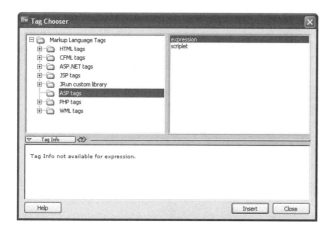

FIGURE 16.9   Use the Tag Chooser to manually insert specific tags relating to the particular server-side technology.

▶ **The Reference panel**—If you ever need help regarding the various ASP objects, Data objects, or tags, you can always reference them in the Reference panel, available by choosing the Reference option from the Window menu.

Earlier I mentioned that most of the dynamic functionality built into Dreamweaver is the same regardless of the server-side technology you decide to use. This becomes obvious with the Insert, Data Objects submenu and the Data category in the Insert panel. The objects listed in these menus outline generic functionality that remains consistent regardless of server-side technology. What does change is the option below the Data Objects option in the Insert menu. This option (varies from ASP Objects, ColdFusion Objects, and PHP Objects, depending on which server-side technology you decide to use), displays specific content accordingly.

Working with ColdFusion

In early 2001, Macromedia (which was itself acquired by Adobe in 2005) acquired a company by the name of Allaire. With the acquisition, the company also acquired a key server-side technology component named ColdFusion and the tool used to develop ColdFusion pages, ColdFusion Studio (now directly integrated into Dreamweaver). Described as a rapid server-side scripting technology for creating web applications, ColdFusion uses a language called ColdFusion Markup Language (CFML) to interact with databases and dynamically created pages. CFML tags are embedded directly into HTML, and each command has a start tag and an end tag similar to HTML. Each ColdFusion application is a set of pages with CFML commands in them. Developers can use the built-in functions, create their own, or integrate COM, C++, or Java components into their code.

Now an essential technology in the Adobe web development line, ColdFusion relies on the ColdFusion Application Server. After it's installed, the application server closely monitors and manages ColdFusion web applications, insuring consistency and reliability with the operating system it's running on. Furthermore, you can use the ColdFusion Administrator, available as a standalone web application, to manage everything from data sources, memory usage, mail server properties, caching, error logs, and more.

Installing ColdFusion

Although ColdFusion isn't as straightforward an installation as ASP is (ASP is already installed when IIS is enabled), it's still fairly simple. To get started, you'll need to download either the developer edition (recommended) or the 30-day trial edition available from the Adobe website at www.adobe.com/products/coldfusion/.

> **NOTE**
>
> For development and testing purposes, the ColdFusion Developer Edition will work just fine. It's a single-user license, which means it will work only on your local development machine where the IP address is 127.0.0.1. This is fine for our purposes.

> **NOTE**
>
> One of the cool features of ColdFusion is that it allows you to run ColdFusion in conjunction with IIS or through its stand-alone built-in development web server. To minimize problems (and the time it takes to troubleshoot them if they arise), we'll simply run ColdFusion using the stand-alone web server. What this means is that regardless of the operating system, if ColdFusion is the route you want to take with the examples in this book, you won't be excluded.

The following steps assume that you're installing the product from the downloaded installer executable on a Windows machine:

1. Double-click the downloaded executable installer file. ColdFusion prepares the installer.

2. After a few seconds, a ColdFusion dialog box will appear, asking you to select the language version for the installer. Select your language and click OK.

3. A welcome screen appears. Click Next.

4. You are asked to accept the terms of the License Agreement. If you do, enable the Accept check box and click Next.

5. You are asked to enter your ColdFusion serial number. Because you're installing the Developer Edition, enable the Developer Edition check box and click Next.

6. Choose the Server Configuration option button and click Next to proceed to the Sub-component Installation screen. For simplicity's sake, uncheck the .NET Integration Services and Adobe LiveCycle Data Services ES check boxes and click Next.

16

7. Choose the location where you want to install the ColdFusion files. By default, the installer tries to install to the C:\ColdFusion8 (/Applications/ColdFusion8 on a Mac) folder. Accept this option by clicking Next.

8. Choose the Built-in Web Server (Development Use Only) option and click Next.

9. Specify a password for the ColdFusion Administrator (covered in the next section) and click Next.

CAUTION

Do not forget the administrator password. The password you enter in step 9 is the password you will use to log in to the ColdFusion Administrator. If you forget your password, you will have to uninstall and then reinstall ColdFusion. So that we're on the same page, go ahead and make the password `vecta`.

---

10. Enable the RDS check box, and enter the password **vecta** within the Password and Confirm Password text boxes. Click Next.

TIP

Remote Development Services (RDS) lets you access a remote ColdFusion application server using HTTP. Using RDS, Dreamweaver users can securely access remote files and data sources, build SQL queries from these data sources, and debug CFML code. It's generally a good idea to configure RDS on development machines and to disable it on production machines.

---

11. Click Install to begin the installation.

12. When the installation ends, click Done.

13. The installer will automatically open a browser window and redirect you to the ColdFusion Administrator. Log in using the **vecta** password. ColdFusion Administrator will then perform the final configurations needed on your computer. When the configuration wizard completes, click OK and then close the browser.

That's it! You now have the ColdFusion server installed and are ready to begin building dynamic Vecta Corp pages using ColdFusion and Dreamweaver. For the most part, you've done everything you need to do to get working with the examples moving forward. What we'll do next is introduce the ColdFusion Administrator, create a simple ColdFusion page within the context of the built-in web server, and then discuss Dreamweaver's integration with ColdFusion.

The ColdFusion Administrator

After you've installed ColdFusion, you can set properties for the application server by using the ColdFusion Administrator. The ColdFusion Administrator allows you to perform administrative tasks for the application server, such as adding and configuring a data source, scheduling application page execution, configuring an RDS password, setting security settings, and more.

You can access the ColdFusion Administrator by entering the URL http://127.0.0.1:8500/CFIDE/administrator/login.cfm.

NOTE

Notice the port number 8500 appended to the 127.0.0.1 within the URL. Because we're working with the development web server, ColdFusion uses a port number other than the standard port 80 for security purposes (and to avoid conflict with the standard port number should you run IIS in conjunction with the built-in web server). Take note of this port number, as you'll need to configure Dreamweaver later when you define your site to use it.

To log in to the Administrator, type the password (vecta) you entered during the ColdFusion installation process (step 9 in the previous section). When you are logged in, you will see a myriad of modifiable settings similar to Figure 16.10.

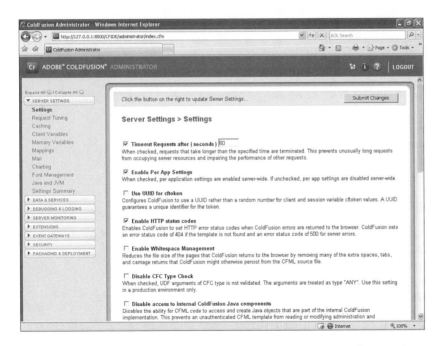

FIGURE 16.10   The ColdFusion Administrator allows you to configure various aspects of the ColdFusion Application Server.

The ColdFusion Administrator allows you to configure numerous aspects of the application server, including the following notable categories:

▶ **Server Settings**—Set various generic properties of the application server including caching, client variables, memory variables, the default mail server, dynamic charting, and more.

▶ **Data & Services**—Access options in this category to configure data sources, web services, and more.

▶ **Debugging & Logging**—Choose options in this category to set various debugging options for your code. Furthermore, you can set how and where ColdFusion logs errors, and more.

▶ **Extensions**—Use options in this category to set how ColdFusion interacts with Java applets, CORBA connectors, and more.

▶ **Security**—Set various security-related settings by accessing options in this category. Options include setting the administrator password and the RDS password, as well as specifying security information for individual data sources, ColdFusion tags, ColdFusion functions, files and directories, and servers/ports.

Creating a Simple ColdFusion Page

Now that you've had an introduction to ColdFusion and the ColdFusion Administrator, let's walk through the process of creating a simple ColdFusion page. Not only will this process help familiarize you with the technology, but it also gives you a basic understanding of how the built-in web server works in conjunction with ColdFusion to process ColdFusion markup pages. To create a simple ColdFusion page, follow these steps:

1. Create a new folder within `C:\ColdFusion8\wwwroot\` called VectaCorpCFM.

2. Open Notepad. (We'll get to Dreamweaver in a few sections.)

3. In the document, add the following code:

```
<html>
<head>
<title>Sample ColdFusion Page</title>
</head>


<body>
<h1>This is plain text</h1>
<h1>Hello it is: <cfoutput>#DateFormat(Now(), "MM/DD/YY")#</cfoutput></h1>
</body>
   </html>
```

4. Save your work as **sample.cfm** in the new folder named C:\ColdFusion8\wwwroot\ VectaCorpCFM\.

To test your work, open the browser and type the URL **http://localhost:8500/VectaCorpCFM/sample.cfm** into the address bar. As you can see from Figure 16.11, two lines of text appear on the page.

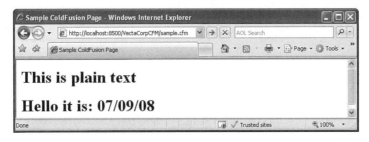

FIGURE 16.11   Two lines of text appear on the page. Some of this text is plain text parsed from <h1> tags in the browser. The date, however, is dynamically generated.

Although this result might not seem all that awe-inspiring, think again: You've just created your first dynamic web page using ColdFusion. Look at the code again and see whether you can pick apart the dynamic portions of the page. For the most part, 8 of the 9 lines of code on the page are plain old HTML that the application server does nothing with. It simply lets the browser parse the HTML tags and present the user with the text inside them. Line 7, however, works a bit differently:

```
<h1>Hello it is: <cfoutput>#DateFormat(Now(), "MM/DD/YY")#</cfoutput></h1>
```

In this case, we use a <cfoutput> tag to dynamically display the text *Hello it is* in a <h1> HTML tag. The web server, recognizing that this code render block exists, intercepts the request and calls for help from the application server. The ColdFusion application server processes the request and interprets the <cfoutput> tag to mean "Output today's date using the standard MM/DD/YY format" onto the page. This response is sent back to the application server, and ultimately back to the browser, formatted using the <h1> tag. Although the process might seem complex, it happens so quickly that a user rarely knows that a dynamic page is even being used.

See how easy that was? In this example, we manually coded ColdFusion markup. The beauty in using Dreamweaver is that you don't have to code at all. Dreamweaver writes all the necessary markup for you. More on this later. For now, let's focus on getting our project configured so that we can use ColdFusion to create dynamic Vecta Corp pages.

16

Configuring Vecta Corp to Run Under ColdFusion

Up to this point, we've been working primarily from C:\VectaCorp\. From now on, we'll work from C:\ColdFusion8\wwwroot\VectaCorpCFM (assuming that you're using ColdFusion). Because this is the case, we need to reconfigure the site definition to point to the new folder we've created. Furthermore, we need to configure the Testing Server category in the Site Definition window to provide Dreamweaver with information specific to the technology you plan to use for the defined site. To configure our Vecta Corp application to run under ColdFusion, follow these steps:

1. If you haven't downloaded the files for this chapter, do so now. Open the folder Exercises\Chapter16\Beginning\VectaCorpCFM\, copy the contents of the folder, and paste them into the newly created VectaCorpCFM folder in C:\ColdFusion8\ wwwroot. Now you have all the images, a template, and an index.cfm page to get you started. Specifically, after you've copied the files over, you should have Images, a Template folder that includes the main template for the site, a CSS file, an index.cfm page, and the sample.cfm page that you built in the previous section.

2. Open Dreamweaver if you haven't already done so and choose the Manage Sites option from the Site menu.

3. Select the existing Vecta Corp site from the list and click Edit. The Site Definition for VectaCorp dialog box appears.

4. In the Site Name text box, rename the site from VectaCorp to VectaCorpCFM.

5. Now browse to the C:\ColdFusion8\wwwroot\VectaCorpCFM\ folder in the Local Root folder category. Leave everything else as is.

6. Now switch to the Testing Server category.

7. Select the ColdFusion option from the Server model menu.

8. Choose the Local/Network option from the Access menu. New properties become available that allow you to configure the location of the remote folder as well as the URL prefix for the remote folder.

9. Browse to the same C:\ColdFusion8\wwwroot\VectaCorpCFM\ path in the Remote Folder text box. In most cases, this value is prepopulated when you select the Local/Network option from the Access menu.

> **NOTE**
>
> When you're working with web applications, the ideal scenario is that you'll have a development machine, a production machine (server), and a testing server. Realistically, not everyone can afford another server just for testing purposes. Most of us will rely on the development machine to function as a testing server as well. For this reason, we'll define our testing server as the local development machine. If you do have a dedicated testing server, you'd use the RDS option instead as it would make it a lot easier to transfer files to and from the testing environment.

10. Enter the URL to our Vecta Corp site. This value should read http://localhost:8500/vectacorpcfm/. Remember that localhost, like every other domain name (such as yahoo.com and google.com) is a URL accessible from a browser. Rather than accessing the site from a server miles away, the browser knows that localhost (and the IP address 127.0.0.1 associated with it) is the URL for the local instance of IIS (your computer). Because this is the case, it doesn't have to look too far for your files.

TIP

You'll notice that in step 10, we associated a port number (8500) with the domain name localhost. The ColdFusion development installation, unlike IIS, XAMPP, and MAMP which default to the industry standard port 80, uses 8500 so as to not interfere with a possible separate web server installation. For more information on port numbers, visit the following web site: http://searchnetworking.techtarget.com/sDefinition/0,,sid7_gci212811,00.html/

---

11. Click OK to close the Site Definition for VectaCorpCFM window.

12. Click Done to close the Manage Sites dialog box.

You're now ready to begin building dynamic Vecta Corp pages using Dreamweaver and ColdFusion!

Using ColdFusion in Dreamweaver

Depending on the server technology you decide to use, features outlined within Dreamweaver's interface change. For the most part, however, you can bank on the fact that the following features are always available when working with any server-side technology, including ColdFusion:

▶ **The Insert panel**—A visual representation of objects available in the Insert menu, the Data category in the Insert panel allows you to visually insert various types of dynamic objects onto your page. Furthermore, if you are going to be using ColdFusion, you'll also have two additionally categories titled CFForm and CFML. Like ASP, the CFML category outlines ColdFusion-specific objects, and the CFForm category outlines ColdFusion form objects. More on these later in the book.

▶ **The Insert menu**—Use the Data Objects and ColdFusion Objects submenus in the Insert menu to insert both generic Data objects as well as ColdFusion-specific objects.

▶ **The Application panel**—Divided into three tabs (Databases, Bindings, and Server Behaviors), the Application panel provides the means for connecting to and accessing database data, binding that data to elements on the page, and accessing various application objects. Additionally, a fourth panel is available by choosing Windows, Components. You can use this panel to facilitate the consumption of web services or work with ColdFusion Components (CFC). More on this later in the book.

▶ **The Tag Chooser**—If you want to make fine-tuned changes in your ColdFusion markup, choose specific elements from the Tag Chooser. Available by choosing Insert, Tag, you can choose an option from the Tag Chooser to open the Properties dialog for the particular tag, allowing you to further customize attributes of the tag.

▶ **The Reference panel**—If you ever need help regarding the various ColdFusion objects, Data objects, or tags, you can reference them from the Reference panel by choosing the Reference option from the Window menu.

Earlier, I mentioned that most of the dynamic functionality built into Dreamweaver is the same regardless of the server-side technology you decide to use. This becomes obvious with the Data Objects submenu in the Insert menu and the Data category in the Insert panel. The objects listed in these menus outline generic functionality that remains consistent regardless of server-side technology. What does change is the option below the Data Objects option in the Insert menu. This option (which varies among ASP Objects, ColdFusion Objects, and PHP Objects, depending on which server-side technology you decide to use), displays specific content accordingly.

Working with PHP

It's hard to argue that PHP Hypertext Preprocessor (PHP) has taken the web development world by storm. PHP is a lightweight, easy-to-learn, and quickly deployed open source scripting language with a number of convenient features. The language's lineage is Perl, C, and Java, so many developers familiar with those languages will find making the switch very easy.

PHP works very well with many database solutions, but it is almost always mentioned in the same breath as the open source MySQL database (discussed with greater detail in the next chapter). PHP can run on Windows, UNIX, and Mac servers; it supports IIS, Apache, and other web servers. As for functionality, PHP has limited support for object-oriented programming, nesting of modules, and custom functions. It has a rich set of built-in tools that let you access XML files, mail servers, database archives, Java APIs and objects, the server's file system, and a lot more.

In this section, you'll get a grasp on PHP. You'll learn how to install it and how to create a simple page using PHP; you'll understand how IIS and PHP work together and how to configure a site for use with PHP. Finally, you'll learn about the many features that Dreamweaver exposes for working with PHP, as well as configuring Dreamweaver to work with PHP and MySQL together.

> **NOTE**
>
> If you're using XAMPP on Windows or MAMP on Mac OS X, you can skip the installation section as you'll already have it installed and ready to go. The next section pertains only to those running the IIS web server.

Installing PHP

Installing PHP to work with IIS is a simple matter of visiting the PHP website, downloading an installer, and running it. Configuring PHP to work in conjunction with Dreamweaver and MySQL is a bit more involved, but that's a process we'll get to later in the book. For now, let's walk through the process of installing PHP to work with IIS using the installer so that we can create and process a simple PHP page in the next section. To install PHP, follow these steps:

> **NOTE**
>
> As of the time of this writing, the current PHP installer does not manually configure script mappings in IIS 6 or IIS 7 (installed by default in all Vista editions). If you plan to install PHP on Vista, you'll need to consult the PHP installation documentation, available at www.php.net/manual/en/.

1. Open a browser and navigate to the site www.php.net/downloads.

2. On the Downloads page, click the PHP 5.2.6 installer link located in the Windows Binaries category. You are redirected to a site mirror to begin your download.

> **NOTE**
>
> As of this writing, PHP's current version is 5.2.6, with a release date of May 6, 2008. Don't worry if your version is different; as long as the major version is 5, everything should function smoothly.

3. Click any of the country-based links to begin your download. When the download completes, proceed to the next step.

4. Locate the `php-5.2.6-win32-installer.msi` file and double-click it to begin the PHP installation.

5. When the Welcome screen appears, click Next.

6. Agree to the license agreement by enabling the check box and then clicking Next.

7. Choose the default folder to install PHP to. By default, PHP attempts to install to `C:\Program Files\PHP\`. This directory is as good as any, so click Next.

8. Choose the web server type to which you'll be installing PHP. For our purposes, choose IIS CGI and then click Next.

9. You'll be directed to the Programs to Install screen. Leave all the options as they are and then click Next one last time to proceed to the final screen.

10. Click Install to begin the installation procedure.

After PHP finishes installing, click Finish to complete the installation routine. That's it! PHP is now installed and ready to go with IIS. In summation, the installer automatically configures IIS (except for Windows Vista) so that files with the .php extension are processed using the php-cgi.exe executable located in the C:\Program Files\PHP folder (/Application/MAMP/bin/php5/bin/php-cgi/ on Mac OS X using MAMP). Similar to the way asp.dll processes ASP pages, php-cgi.exe is the executable used to process PHP pages.

Again, if you're using XAMPP on Windows or MAMP on Mac OS X, you're ready to go. There's no additional installation or configuration required.

Creating a Simple PHP Page

Now that you've had an introduction to PHP, let's walk through the process of creating a simple PHP page. Not only will this process help familiarize you with the technology, you'll also get an understanding of how the web server handles the processing of dynamic PHP pages in conjunction with the php-cgi.exe executable. To create a simple PHP page, follow these steps:

1. Create a new folder in C:\Inetpub\wwwroot\ (C:\XAMPP\htdocs\ when using XAMPP and /Applications/MAMP/htdocs/ when using MAMP) called VectaCorpPHP.

2. Open Notepad (TextEdit on Mac).

3. In the Notepad (TextEdit) document, add the following code:

```
<html>
<head>
<title>Sample PHP Page</title>
</head>


<body>
<h1>This is plain text</h1>
<h1><? echo "This is PHP writing text to the browser dynamically" ?></h1>
</body>
   </html>
```

4. Save your work as **sample.php** in the new folder named VectaCorpPHP.

TIP

If you plan on trying out numerous server-side technologies, it's beneficial to create the folder with the VectaCorp name followed by the three-letter server-side technology you plan to use. This convention prevents you from continuously having to redefine the site for every server-side technology.

To test your work, open the browser and type the URL **http://localhost/VectaCorpPHP/ sample.php** into the address bar. As you can see from Figure 16.12 (shown in Safari on a Mac), two lines of text appear in the browser.

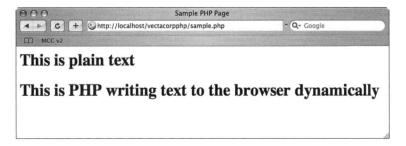

FIGURE 16.12   Two lines of text appear in the browser (shown in Safari on a Mac).

Although this result might not seem all that awe-inspiring, think again: You've just created your first dynamic web page using PHP. Look at the code again and see whether you can pick apart the dynamic portions of the page. For the most part, 8 of the 9 lines of code in the page are plain old HTML that the web server does nothing with. It simply lets the browser parse the HTML tags and presents to the user the text inside them. Line 7, however, works a bit differently:

```
<h1><? echo "This is PHP writing text to the browser dynamically" ?></h1>
```

In this case, we use what's called a *code render block* to dynamically display the text *This is PHP writing text to the browser dynamically* within a <h1> HTML tag. The web server, recognizing that this code render block exists, intercepts the request and calls for help from the php-cgi application. The php-cgi application processes the request and interprets the code render block to mean "echo, or print out, the text *This is PHP writing text to the browser dynamically*" on the page. This response is sent back to the web server and ultimately back to the browser, formatted using the <h1> tag. Although the process might seem complex, it happens so fast that a user rarely even knows that a dynamic page is being used.

See how easy that was? In this example, we manually wrote PHP code. The beauty in using Dreamweaver is that you don't have to write code at all. Dreamweaver writes all the necessary code for you. More on this later in the book. For now, let's focus on getting our project configured so that we can use PHP to create dynamic Vecta Corp pages.

Configuring Vecta Corp to Run Under PHP

Up to this point, we've been working primarily from C:\VectaCorp\ (/Applications/ VectaCorp/ on a Mac). From now on, we'll work from C:\Inetpub\wwwroot\VectaCorpPHP (C:\XAMPP\htdocs\ if you're using XAMPP or /Applications/MAMP/htdocs/ if you're running MAMP on a Mac). Because this is the case, we need to reconfigure the site definition to point to the new folder we've created. Furthermore, we need to configure the Testing Server category in the Site Definition window to provide Dreamweaver with information specific to the technology you plan to use for the defined site. To configure the Vecta Corp site to run under PHP, follow these steps:

1. If you haven't downloaded the files for this chapter, do so now. Open the folder for Exercises\Chapter16\Beginning\VectaCorpPHP\, copy the contents of the folder, and paste them into the newly created VectaCorpPHP folder. Now you have all the

images, a template, and an `index.php` page to get you started. Specifically, after you've copied the files over, you should have Images, a Template folder which includes the main template for the site, a CSS file, an `index.php` page, and the `sample.php` page that you built in the previous section.

2. Open Dreamweaver if you haven't already done so and choose the Manage Sites option from the Site menu.

3. Select the existing Vecta Corp site from the list and click Edit. The Site Definition for the VectaCorp dialog box appears.

4. In the Site Name text box, rename the site from VectaCorp to **VectaCorpPHP**.

5. Browse to `C:\Inetpub\wwwroot\VectaCorpPHP\` (`C:\XAMPP\htdocs\VectaCorpPHP` if you're using XAMPP or `/Applications/MAMP/htdocs/VectaCorpPHP/` if you're running MAMP on a Mac). in the Local Root folder category. Leave everything else as is.

6. Switch to the Testing Server category.

7. Select the PHP MySQL option from the Server Model menu.

8. Choose the Local/Network option from the Access menu. New properties become available that allow you to configure the location of the remote folder as well as the URL prefix for the remote folder.

9. Browse to the same `C:\Inetpub\wwwroot\VectaCorpPHP\` path in the Remote Folder text box (`C:\XAMPP\htdocs\VectaCorpPHP` if you're using XAMPP or `/Applications/MAMP/htdocs/VectaCorpPHP/` if you're running MAMP on a Mac). In most cases, this value is prepopulated when you select the Local/Network option from the Access menu.

> **NOTE**
>
> When working with web applications, the ideal scenario is that you'll have a development machine, a production machine (server), and a testing server. Realistically, not everyone can afford another server just for testing purposes. Most of us will rely on the development machine to function as a testing server as well. For this reason, we'll configure our testing server with the same information as our development machine. If you do have a dedicated testing server, you'd probably still choose the Local/Network option from the Access tab; however, rather than finding the machine locally, you'd browse to it on the network.

10. Enter the URL to the Vecta Corp site in the URL Prefix text box. This value should read http://localhost/vectacorpphp/. Remember that localhost, like every other domain name (such as yahoo.com and google.com) is a URL accessible from a browser. Rather than accessing the site from a server miles away, the browser knows that localhost (and the IP address 127.0.0.1 associated with it) is the URL for the

local instance of IIS (your computer). Because this is the case, it doesn't have to look too far for your files.

11. Click OK to close the Site Definition for VectaCorpPHP window.

12. Click Done to close the Manage Sites dialog box.

You're now ready to begin building dynamic Vecta Corp pages using Dreamweaver and PHP.

Using PHP in Dreamweaver

Depending on the server technology you decide to use, features exposed in Dreamweaver's interface will change. For the most part, however, you can bank on the fact that the following features are always available when working with any server-side technology:

▶ **The Insert panel**—A visual representation of objects available in the Insert menu, the Data category in the Insert panel allows you to visually insert various types of dynamic objects onto your page. If you're working with PHP, an additional category titled PHP outlines PHP-specific options that you might decide to use within your pages.

▶ **The Insert menu**—Use the Data Objects and PHP Objects submenus in the Insert menu to insert both generic Data objects as well as PHP-specific objects.

▶ **The Application panel**—Divided into three tabs (Databases, Bindings, and Server Behaviors), the Application panel provides the means for connecting to and accessing database data, binding that data to elements on the page, and accessing the various Data objects that were also available from the Insert menu. When working with dynamic pages in Dreamweaver, you should always have this panel open.

▶ **The Tag Chooser**—If you want to make fine-tuned changes to your PHP code, you can choose specific tags from the Tag Chooser. Available by choosing the Tag option from the Insert menu, you can choose an option from the Tag Chooser to open the Properties dialog box for the particular tag, allowing you to further customize attributes of the tag.

▶ **The Reference panel**—If you ever need help regarding the various PHP objects, application objects, or tags, you can reference them from the Reference panel, available by choosing the Reference option from the Window menu or by pressing Shift+F1.

Earlier, I mentioned that most of the dynamic functionality built into Dreamweaver is the same, regardless of the server-side technology you decide to use. This becomes obvious with the Data Objects submenu in the Insert menu and the Data category in the Insert panel. The objects listed in these menus outline generic functionality that remains consistent regardless of server-side technology. What does change is the option below the Data Objects option in the Insert menu. This option (which varies from ASP Objects, ColdFusion Objects, and PHP Objects, depending on which server-side technology you decide to use) changes and displays specific content accordingly.

Summary

This chapter covered a lot of ground. We've provided a brief introduction to setting up the IIS web server, outlined alternatives (XAMPP/MAMP) in case you're following along on Windows XP Home or Mac OS X, and also walked through each server-side technology (ASP, ColdFusion, and PHP) and learned how to install it, configure it for Dreamweaver, and even create a sample page using each individual server-side technology.

In the next chapter, we'll briefly move away from server-side technologies and into the realm of databases, database design, and database development. We'll introduce the three databases supported in this book: Access, SQL Server 2008 Express, and MySQL. We'll discuss installation, configuration, and how to build the Vecta Corp Employee Store database using the database of your choice.

CHAPTER **17**

A Database Primer

As you begin to build dynamic web applications using Dreamweaver, it will become increasingly obvious that you'll need to store data in some sort of storage mechanism and allow access to it through your web application. Whether you are building a small, company-wide intranet store with access limited to employees or a feature-rich Internet web store that millions will visit, you will need some system for storing all the order, customer, cost, and product information. You might not want to stop there. You might also want to include some way of tracking how many of a certain item you have left in your inventory. You might even need to determine how many items are selling during a particular week of the month. If that's the case, you will need some way of determining sales transactions. Like a filing cabinet that stores files and, subsequently, data within those files, you will need some mechanism of storing all your data for easy access and quick retrieval. That mechanism is the database.

In this chapter, we'll demystify databases. We'll cover basic database concepts such as tables, columns, and rows, as well as advanced concepts such as stored procedures, views and queries, security, relationships, and keys. Then we'll talk about the three databases covered in this book: Access, Server 2008 Express, and MySQL. We'll dissect their installation and configuration and provide an overview of the database management systems utilized by each. Finally, we'll provide a high-level overview of the Vecta Corp database and its tables.

As you've done for the rest of the chapters in this book, you can work with the examples in this chapter by downloading the files from the book's website. As you'll see throughout the chapter, the downloadable files include complete versions of the databases used throughout the book.

Anatomy of a Database

In 1970, E. F. Codd, an IBM employee, proposed his idea for what would become the first relational database design model. His model, which proposed new methods for storing and retrieving data in large applications, far surpassed any idea or system that was in place at that time. His idea of "relational" stemmed from the fact that data and the relationships between them were organized in "relations," or what we know today as tables. Even though Codd's terminology of what we refer to as tables, columns, and rows was different, the premise behind the relational model has remained consistent. Although the model has undergone revisions and changes since he presented it, the idea of storing and retrieving information in large applications has not changed, solidifying the need for the relational database model.

The best way to think of a database is in terms of a filing cabinet. The filing cabinet contains drawers, the drawers contain folders, and the folders contain documents that have information on them. A database is similar in concept. A *database* (the filing cabinet) contains drawers, otherwise known as *tables*; those tables contain folders, or *columns*, which in turn contain rows of information pertaining to the particular column that they're in.

For a moment, let's take the web store example (crudely outlined in Chapter 15, "Introduction to Web Applications") and break it down to see exactly what kind of information we would need and just how we could organize it to make it manageable with a database.

- ▶ **Customers**—We need some way of keeping track of all our registered customers, along with shipping/billing addresses, credit card information, and so forth.

- ▶ **Products**—We need some way of differentiating among all our products, including sizes, colors, prices, quantities left in stock, and other characteristics that relate to a specific item.

- ▶ **Orders**—Whenever a product is purchased from the online store, that order should be stored somewhere in a queue of sorts so that the shipping and receiving department can process the order.

- ▶ **Transactions**—We need to include a history of all transactions and a way of knowing which customers are ordering what products so that we can recommend products to people dynamically in the future.

Traditionally, we could take all these elements and create a text document or perhaps a spreadsheet and physically write on these documents whenever someone orders a product. We could take these documents and store them in folders alphabetically and even store all the folders within one central filing cabinet. Although this is a traditional example of how business can work, it closely resembles how the modern database operates in relation. The filing cabinet—the drawers, folders, and even the documents within them—all represent the basic components of a modern database structure:

- ▶ Database management system

- ▶ Database

- ▶ Tables

- ▶ Columns

- ▶ Rows

Let's discuss each component in more detail.

The Database Management System (DBMS)

The *database management system (DBMS)* represents the framework from which you design, store, and manage all the databases that you create. Figure 17.1 shows SQL Server 2008's Management Studio Basic. Management Studio is a centralized location for managing and interacting with all your SQL Server databases.

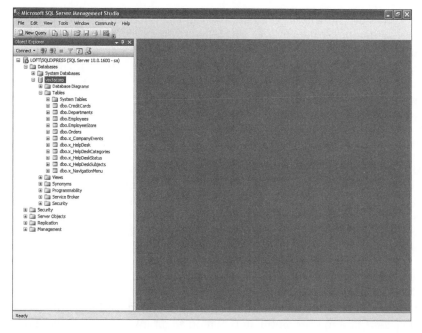

FIGURE 17.1   Management Studio is an example of a database management system (DBMS) used with SQL Server 2008.

Although smaller databases such as Access do not have what is traditionally known as a DBMS, Access does provide a way of interacting with and managing a single database file. Figure 17.2 shows how you can open a database through Access.

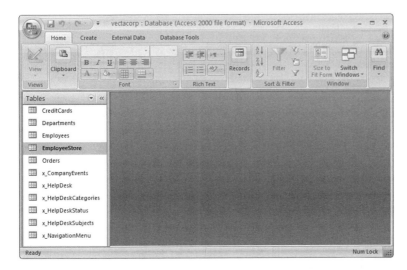

FIGURE 17.2   Access does not provide a typical DBMS, but it does allow for access to any single database file.

If you look at the Vecta Corp store example again, you can begin to imagine how the DBMS looks much like the filing cabinet discussed earlier. Unlike a filing cabinet, however, which typically contains two to four drawers, a DBMS can manage hundreds, possibly thousands of databases (which can contain hundreds and thousands of tables)—all of which are immediately at your fingertips. Later in this chapter, we'll look at the various database management systems that exist on the market today for interacting with SQL Server 2008 Express and MySQL, including the File Manager for Access.

The Database

Inside your DBMS, you have the potential for storing hundreds, if not thousands, of databases. Although for most projects you would never need more than one database, you might in the future realize that your project has grown far beyond the scope of a single database—that because of security or maintenance reasons, you require more. Figure 17.3 shows MySQL Administrator with a list of three catalogs (otherwise known as databases) housed within its framework.

Tables

After a database has been created, you might want to begin storing information relevant to a specific part of the store. As mentioned earlier, tables are very similar to file cabinet drawers. It would be a mistake to store all the information about inventory, product information, customers, and even transactions in one drawer; instead, you'll break out these categories of information and create different drawers or tables to store all this information.

Figure 17.4 shows the Vecta Corp store database in MySQL Administrator. By selecting the Vecta Corp store database from the view in the left column, you can begin to see all the tables that reside within the store.

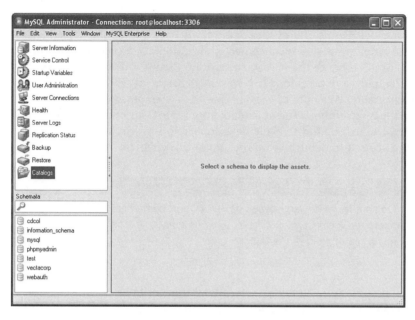

FIGURE 17.3   MySQL Administrator and a list of the databases it contains.

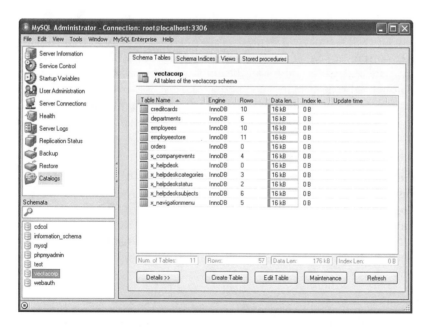

FIGURE 17.4   Selecting the vectacorp database reveals all the tables associated with the project.

Notice that there are more tables than just the four outlined in the beginning of the chapter. Breaking data up into separate, easily managed tables is consider good database design, and it's generally a good idea to conserve space and reduce redundancy (that is, data in tables that already exists in other tables or duplicate data in the same table). For instance, as far as the Employees table is concerned, you could have a customer that has multiple credit cards on file—hence the need for a separate CreditCards table. You will also have customers/employees who belong to a specific department—hence the need for a separate Departments table. We could even go beyond this example and create a separate table for CreditCardTypes, assuming a customer could use more than one credit card. This process of organizing data in an effort to avoid data duplication within tables is known as *normalization* and is discussed in depth toward the end of this chapter.

> **NOTE**
>
> In this example, customers represent employees of Vecta Corp. Remember, we're build-ing an internal web store for Vecta Corp employees. For this reason, the database table has been named Employees instead of Customers.

Before you begin any project, you will typically sketch all this out in an effort to reduce data duplication in your tables. Again, how you branch out your information and create tables depends on the scope of your project.

Columns

After you outline all your tables, your next step is to decide what information to include within those tables. For instance, you might want to include first name, last name, phone number, address, city, state, ZIP, and so on for all the employees in your company in the Employees table. You might also need to include product names, descriptions, and some sort of unique identification in your EmployeeStore table. You might even want to combine certain aspects of certain tables and place them into the Orders table—for example, you might end up with information from the Employees table as well as from the EmployeeStore table to come up with a final order requisition.

Theoretically, columns represent bits of information or more detailed descriptions of the table in which they are contained. For instance, if you have an Employees table, chances are high that you'll have names and physical addresses of those employees represented by columns within the database. Furthermore, if you had an EmployeeStore table, chancs are that you'll probably have columns for names and descriptions of the items that the store carries. Figure 17.5 shows what the Employees table might look like after columns have been outlined.

Rows

Think back to the example I mentioned earlier regarding the documents within the folders and the folders within the drawers contained within the filing cabinet. Rows repre-sent the actual data in those documents. Similar to the columns within the tables, rows represent the actual data within the columns. When employees/customers begin purchas-ing items, the rows in the Orders table begin to expand and fill up with information, similar to Figure 17.6.

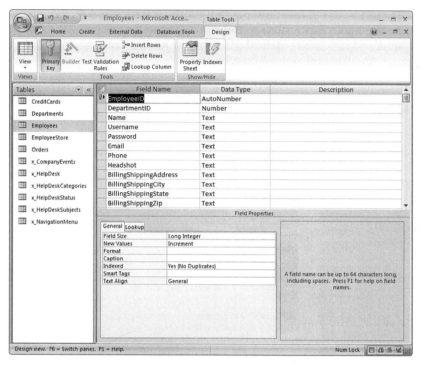

FIGURE 17.5   The Employees table displays all the columns associated with it.

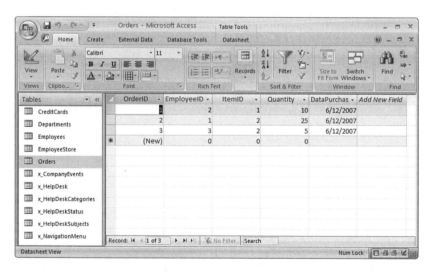

FIGURE 17.6   The Orders table with multiple rows of information.

Database tables have the potential for containing millions of rows. Technically, this is your data. The many rows of information contained in your database tables are what you'll ultimately display in your web applications. Whether you're displaying product information for employees to select, order information for the shipping and receiving department to review, or employee information for administrators to configure, the rows in your databases tables and the data contained within those rows are what you'll ultimately be interacting with inside the web application.

Beyond the Basics

Now that we've gotten the basic structure of a database out of the way, let's begin thinking about what really drives the database. Aside from the data in the tables, other characteristics and functions of the database can improve performance, reduce network traffic, increase security, decrease development time, and dramatically decrease maintenance efforts. Some of these functions and characteristics are listed here:

- ▶ Stored procedures
- ▶ Triggers
- ▶ Views and queries
- ▶ Security
- ▶ Relationship management
- ▶ Keys
- ▶ Normalization

It's important to understand that these concepts are not relevant to all databases. For instance, concepts such as stored procedures, triggers, and views are all relevant to SQL Server. Access, being the proverbial little brother of SQL Server, refers to views as queries. Security management is handled at the file level rather than per database or by database operation, as it is in SQL Server. MySQL, being relatively new on the scene (in contrast to the other two databases) doesn't support a lot of the features that SQL Server does. In some cases, terms that you'll find in SQL Server are named differently in MySQL.

Stored Procedures

Stored procedures are a way of actually storing code that you use to work with your database in the database itself. They are a way of modularizing repetitive code so that you never have to write the same line of code in your applications more than once. You create a stored procedure within your database and call it through your application, passing in parameters as necessary. In return, the stored procedure executes complex tasks and can return information back to the application that is calling it.

Let's use the Vecta Corp store as an example. In our application, we might want to create two ways of updating registered users within our database. From a user's standpoint, the customer might want to edit existing passwords, personal information, or perhaps shipping information. From an administrative standpoint, the admin might also want the capability to update a given user's information. Although the front-end user interface will look completely different for the users and administrator, the code that accesses the database and performs the actual data modification can be the same. This concept is outlined visually in Figure 17.7.

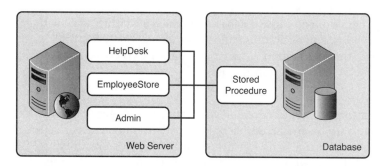

FIGURE 17.7   Stored procedures allow you to consolidate repetitive functionality by modularizing it into a single function residing on the database server rather than the web server.

By creating a stored procedure, we would essentially eliminate the arduous task of writing repetitive code for both user and administrator instances. We write it once as a stored procedure and allow the user and administrator to access the stored procedure the same way.

Triggers

Triggers, which are similar to stored procedures, can be set up to run with your database data. *Triggers* are predefined events that run automatically whenever a specified action (preferably the Insert, Delete, or Update commands) is performed on a physical file. Although it might sound a bit confusing as to what triggers actually are and what they can do, think of triggers as a way of enforcing business rules you might have described within your database. Triggers enforce stability and integrity within your tables.

For example, in the Vecta Corp database, you'll have a table for employee orders, called Orders. If the employee ended a relationship with the Vecta Corp store, you would have the potential for orders in the Orders table that are not associated with any employee. Triggers would enforce business rules by making sure that if an employee ended a relationship with Vecta Corp (maybe they quit or were fired), not only is their information in the Employees table deleted, but the data in the Orders table (which had a direct relationship with data in the Employees table) would be deleted as well.

Views and Queries

Views (SQL Server/MySQL) and *queries* (Access) are awkward to think about at first because their names are deceiving. Views and queries aren't actually what their names imply; rather, they are virtual tables whose contents are defined by a query. Much like a real table with rows and columns, views and queries exist as stored sets of data values. Rows and columns of data come from the tables that are referenced and are produced dynamically by the database when the view or query is called from the application.

For example, you could have multiple databases set up throughout your company—one for sales, one for marketing, and possibly one for operations. You could use views and queries to combine similar data from all those databases to produce a virtual table with sales numbers, marketing reports, and even information from operations. After the query/view has been created, the information is easily accessible by your web application. We'll cover views and queries at a basic level in the next chapter.

Security

Security is always important to any facet of development, not just web development. Ensuring that your database is secure and accessible only by certain individuals or departments is crucial. Many database management systems provide a way to set security options for users and groups of users who are allowed to access the database either individually or within their own web applications. Figure 17.8 shows how you could modify permissions (select the User Information category and specify details for a new user account) for specific users using MySQL Administrator.

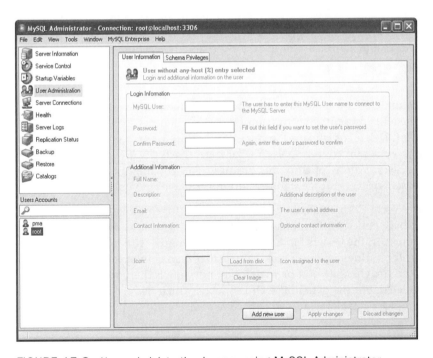

FIGURE 17.8   User administration is easy using MySQL Administrator.

Access, on the other hand, enables you to modify security settings by right-clicking the database file, selecting Properties, and choosing the Security tab, as shown in Figure 17.9.

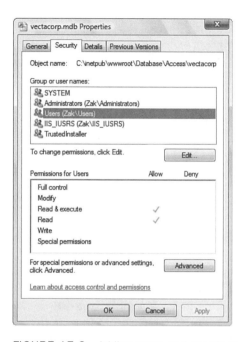

FIGURE 17.9   Adding users and permissions to an Access database file.

Access itself allows you to control permissions for a particular database file. You can modify permissions for a database file by first opening the database file. Next, select Tools, Security, and User and Group Permissions. The User and Group Permissions dialog box allows you to specify which users get Read and Modify permissions or no permissions at all. You can even modify or set permissions for specific tables, queries, forms, and reports.

Relationship Management

When you create new tables in your database, an important aspect to consider is that of relationships. We have already touched on what relationships are and how they relate to your tables. For example, you could create a separate table for credit cards and assign that table a relationship with the Employees table. The reason for doing this is simple: It allows you to store more than one credit card for a particular employee. In this scenario, we'd create a separate table for credit cards and assign each row in that column a unique identifier, usually an automatically generated number. The relationship would exist between the unique identifier in the Employees table (CustomerID) and that identifier in the CreditCards table. Figure 17.10 shows a relationship between the Employees table and the CreditCards table using Access's relationship modeler.

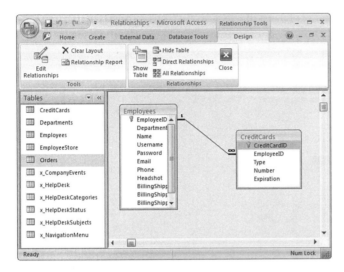

FIGURE 17.10   Relationships are added to avoid data duplication in tables.

In general, when you work with relationship modeling, three types of relationships exist:

▶ **One-to-one**—A one-to-one relationship means that for each record that exists in one table, only one other related record can exist in another table. One-to-one relationships are rarely used, and when they are, it's usually because of a limitation with the database that requires data to be stored separately—usually because of the database's size.

▶ **One-to-many**—A one-to-many relationship is by far the most common of relationship types. A one-to-many relationship means that for each record in one table, multiple records can exist in a second table. These records are usually related based on a unique number (a primary key). In the employees/credit cards example I mentioned earlier, a one-to-many relationship created a relationship between one customer and the many possible credit card numbers that could be stored in a second (credit cards) table.

▶ **Many-to-many**—A many-to-many relationship exists when many records in one table are related to many records in a second table. Many-to-many relationships are difficult to illustrate in a typical relational database model and are not often used in practice.

Keys
Many of the records in your database will contain information that is very similar in nature. You might have a thousand customers in your Employees table, and a hundred of those customers might be from San Diego. If you extracted all those records from the database, how would you be able to differentiate among all the records? Obviously you could differentiate by name, but what if you had three records in the database with the name John Smith from San Diego? A way to differentiate is through the use of unique keys.

Think about why uniqueness is so important. If you had more than one record in the database that was the same, what would be the sense in storing multiple copies? It would be a waste of space. Also, if you tried to update or delete a record from a database that matched a second record, the database would not be able to match the record you were trying to work with, and you might end up deleting the wrong record, throwing an error, or corrupting the data in your tables. Records can be identified through the use of three kinds of keys:

▶ **Candidate keys**—A candidate key is a set of columns that are unique across the board. Take the following example:

ZIP	Area
92069	San Marcos
92115	San Diego
92105	San Diego
92128	San Diego

In this example, the ZIP column could be considered a candidate key because the values never repeat. Although the Area names do repeat, together with the ZIP value, they become unique and can make up a candidate key. Because the Area column contains repetitive information, it cannot be considered for a candidate key and could never be unique.

▶ **Primary keys**—Whereas candidate keys can be made up of several columns, a primary key (PK) is usually made up of a single column that designates a row in the table as unique. For the most part, primary keys can exist even though they have no relationship to the data being stored. Database developers often create primary keys with an automatically generated number, guaranteeing that the row always increments by one and remains unique from any other records. Primary keys are the most useful when referenced from a second table through the use of foreign keys. The table that follows illustrates a simple table within a database that contains information about a user's area. Because the primary key is different, the records remain completely unique even though data within the Area column repeats.

AreaPK	Area
1	San Marcos
2	San Diego
3	San Diego
4	San Diego

17

Foreign keys—A foreign key (FK) is a column that contains values found in the primary key of another table. A foreign key can be null and almost always is not unique. Consider the following example:

ZipPK	ZipCode
1	92069
2	92115
3	92105
4	92128

AreaPK	AreaName	ZipFK
1	San Diego	3
2	San Diego	2
3	Tijuana	—
4	San Marcos	1
5	San Marcos	1
6	San Diego	4
7	San Diego	4

The ZipFK column in the second table is a foreign key to the ZipPK primary key in the first table. Notice that the ZipPK values are unique and not null, but the ZipFK values might be null and often repeat. A *null* foreign key means that row does not participate in the relationship. In a one-to-many relationship, the primary key has the "one" value, and the foreign key has the "many" values.

Normalization

As discussed earlier in the chapter, normalization is the process of organizing data in an effort to avoid duplication. Often this process involves separating data into discrete related tables. Advantages to normalization usually include space, performance, and easier maintenance.

Typically, normalization involves the process of identifying all the data objects that should be in your database, all their relationships, and defining the tables required and the columns within each table. Consider how the EmployeeStore table would look if we did not normalize the data into separate tables:

Customer	Order	Price
Zak	Shirt	$12
Zayden	Shirt	$12
Zak	Pants	$35
Makenzie	Shoes	$75
Jessica	Blouse	$20
Zaven	Shoes	$75
Jessica	Blouse	$20

If the preceding table was used specifically to keep track of the price of items and you wanted to delete a price, you would end up deleting an employee as well. Instead, you could separate the employees into their own table and the products along with their prices into a second table. If a specific employee orders a product, the product and its price are placed into a third Orders table along with the corresponding customer data referenced by a one-to-many relationship.

For the most part, normalization isn't a feature of the database; rather, it's a practice you should follow. On that point, there are roughly four normalization forms that define how data is laid out within a database:

- ▶ **The first normal form**—The first normal form states that all rows in a table must contain different data. No duplicate rows are permitted. It also states that all entries in a specific column must be of the same type—for instance, a column named Customer must contain only names of customers.

- ▶ **The second normal form**—The second normal form states that no field can be inherited from another field. For example, if you store the full name of a customer in the Employees table, you cannot create a second field to store only the last name of a customer, because the data would be redundant.

- ▶ **The third normal form**—The third normal form states that duplicate information is not allowed in the database. This is the model you achieved in the foreign key example. Instead of storing the credit cards of a customer within the Customers table, you separate that information out into a second table, allowing for multiple credit cards to be entered.

- ▶ **Domain/key normal form**—A domain/key normal form states that a key uniquely identifies each row in a table. By enforcing key restrictions, the database is freed of modification irregularities. Domain/key normal form is the normalization form that most database developers try to achieve.

17

Installing a Database

Now that you have a general idea as to what a database is and you understand some of the concepts that drive database functionality, it's time to actually choose and install one. Just like the server-side technology that you picked, the database you choose should coincide with your business practices, budget, scalability needs, desired features, and more. Dreamweaver supports any ODBC-compliant database; unfortunately, we can't cover them all in this book, so for development purposes, the decision has been made to support the following three databases:

▶ **Access**—Access is Microsoft's database solution for developers and small companies who desire to build and/or house data within a small, yet reliable, store. Access supports queries (called views in other databases), keys, security, and relationship management but falls short of supporting important database features such as stored procedures. If you elect to go the route of IIS using ASP, ColdFusion, or PHP as the server-side technology, this might be the database you would use.

▶ **SQL Server 2008 Express**—SQL Server 2008 is the enterprise alternative for databases such as Access. It supports important database functionality such as stored procedures, views, keys, security, relationship management via diagrams, and more. The downside is that SQL Server 2008 is an enterprise-level database, and as such, costs a lot of money. If your organization plans to buy SQL Server 2008 at some point in time, you can always develop using the free development version of SQL Server 2008 in SQL Server 2008 Express. SQL Server 2008 Express is a free alternative for SQL Server 2008 developers who want to harness the power and flexibility of SQL Server 2008 now but plan to upgrade to the enterprise alternative later. Again, if you select IIS using ASP, ColdFusion, or PHP as the server-side technology, this will be a viable option as well.

▶ **MySQL**—The free, open source database known as MySQL has been gaining a lot of steam over the years. MySQL provides a free, robust alternative to costly databases options such as SQL Server 2008. It's important to note that the PHP model in Dreamweaver supports only MySQL. As it relates to this book, if you choose XAMPP (Windows) or MAMP (Mac OS X), then you're tied to PHP, and you must use MySQL. But don't think of this as negative. Remember, PHP and MySQL are already pre-installed and preconfigured with XAMPP and MAMP. What this means for you is that half of the content that we'll cover in this chapter (as it relates to MySQL) is already done for you!

Of course, there's nothing stopping you from installing all three options. Access is file-based, which makes it no different from having Word, Excel, or even Dreamweaver open. SQL Server 2008 Express and MySQL run as independent Windows services, which means that they'll never overlap, and data is always guaranteed to be stored independently of the other storage mechanism.

> **NOTE**
>
> Examples in this book use MySQL. Although references are always made to other database products, the core functionality of the Vecta Corp project is added under the assumption that you're using MySQL. For the most part, database integration in Dreamweaver is handled the same, regardless of which database you use. Therefore, after you've defined the database in Dreamweaver (covered in Chapter 19, "Working with Dynamic Data") working with database data is the same, regardless of the database you choose.

Installing Access

Access is Microsoft's database solution for developers and small companies alike who desire to build and/or house data in a small, yet reliable store. Because Microsoft Access is inexpensive and easily to get (either from Microsoft's website or as an installation option with Microsoft Office), it's usually the perfect choice for discussion and use in books such as this one.

For the most part, Microsoft Office includes Access. If you've already installed Microsoft Office on your computer, but didn't install Access at the same time, you'll need to add it to your installation. The following assumes that you have Microsoft Office 2000, XP, 2003, or 2007 handy and that you will be installing from that CD:

1. Navigate to the Add or Remove Programs menu located within the Control Panel. This is called Programs and Features in Vista.

2. Select your Microsoft Office installation from the Programs menu and select Change.

3. When the Microsoft Office Setup dialog box appears, select Add/Remove Features and click Next.

4. From the Access program menu, select Run from My Computer.

5. Click Update. You are prompted to insert your Microsoft Office CD, so make sure that it is handy. Access is now installed.

That's all there is to it. You are now ready to begin working with Access.

17

> **TIP**
>
> Of course, if you don't have Microsoft Office 2000, XP, 2003, or 2007, you're not completely out of luck. You can download and install a 45-day free trial from Microsoft's website at office.microsoft.com/en-us/access/. Also on the website, you can find the latest updates, news, and purchase information for Microsoft Access.

Deploying the Access Database

As you might have noticed by now, I've included sample Access (MDB), SQL Server 2008 (MDF and LDF), and MySQL (SQL) database files for you to use. Rather than forcing you to create the database from scratch including all the tables, columns, and necessary rows of data, I've taken it upon myself to do the dirty work for you. What you will have to do, however, is take the database file that I've provided and deploy it to your project folder so that it can be accessed centrally from Dreamweaver. You can do this now by creating a new folder within C:\VectaCorp<*servermodel*>\ called **Database**. Now find the vectacorp.mdb file included with this chapter's downloads and copy it into that folder.

That's it! The Access database needed for the examples throughout the rest of this book is now deployed.

The Access File Manager

Although Access doesn't work within the framework of what is considered a DBMS, its built-in file manager does offer some similarities. Remember that Access databases are self-contained MDB files that, when double-clicked, open within the Microsoft Access program.

Using the file manager, you can create tables, columns, data types for columns, and even add rows with data to the tables. Furthermore, you can perform standard database operations such as create queries, manage security restrictions, back up a database, and more.

If you'd like to explore the Vecta Corp Access database, browse to the Database folder within C:\VectaCorp<servermodel>\ and double-click the vectacorp.mdb file. We'll explore the structure of the database in more detail later in the chapter.

Installing SQL Server 2008 Express

SQL Server 2008 is Microsoft's database solution for medium-to-large companies and enterprises. It is quite a bit more expensive than Access, it generally requires its own dedicated "database server," and at times it requires the hiring of a certified database administrator (DBA) to maintain. However, it also offers a robust and scalable solution for larger web applications, which is the major reason why you'd want to invest your time in it.

I will assume that if you're reading this book, you probably don't want to invest in something as massive as SQL Server 2008 and that your needs are better suited to something free, but just as powerful, for testing and development purposes. If this is the case, SQL Server 2008 Express is perfect for you. SQL Server 2008 Express is Microsoft's free database alternative to SQL Server 2008. It functions and stores data exactly as SQL Server 2008 does, but is meant for smaller-scale operations. After you get your feet wet with SQL Server 2008 Express, or if the needs of your organization warrant scaling up, you might like to think about upgrading to a more robust database in SQL Server 2008.

To download and install SQL Server 2008 Express, follow these steps:

1. Browse to the SQL Server 2008 Express website located at www.microsoft.com/express/sql/download/default.aspx. From this page, browse to the SQL Server 2008 Express with Tools link and click it. Immediately you'll be redirected to a Microsoft

page that contains the download link. Find the download button for the filename SQLEXPRWT_x86_ENU.exe and click it to download the installer.

2. When the executable has been downloaded to your computer, double-click the file to begin the installation. The installer will unpack the necessary files and then launch the Installation Center dialog box. Select the Installation link from the category selector on the left and then choose the New SQL Server stand-alone installation or add features to an existing installation option.

3. You then advance to the System Configuration Check screen. The installation performs a configuration check on your computer to determine whether you have the necessary requirements to proceed. If you don't, the Status and Message columns will alert you of the issue. You must resolve any issues before proceeding with the installation. If the configuration check returns successfully for all actions being checked, click Next to proceed.

4. The first screen that appears in the Installation wizard is the Product Key. Since we're installing the Express version, click Next.

5. The next screen that you come to is the License Terms screen. Accept the terms by enabling the check box and then click Next to proceed.

6. The Installation wizard will then proceed to the Setup Support Files screen. Click Install to begin the installation of these files which are necessary for SQL Server 2008 Express to function.

7. Again you will come to a Setup Support Files screen. The Installation wizard will again perform a series of checks that must be met before continuing. If any of these checks fails, you will need to address the issue before continuing. Assuming all of the checks passed, click Next to proceed.

8. Within the Features Selection screen, check the Database Engine Services and Management Tools - Basic check boxes and click to proceed.

9. Click Next and proceed through the Instance Configuration and Disk Space Requirements screens.

10. In the Server Configuration screen, choose the NT AUTHORITY\NETWORK SERVICE option from the Account Name menu and leave the Password field blank. Click Next to proceed.

17

11. Within the Database Engine Configuration screen, choose the Mixed Mode option button. The Enter and Confirm Password text boxes are enabled. Enter the password **vecta** in both text boxes. This is the password that you will use to log in to the database from Dreamweaver. The default username will be sa. In order to proceed however, you'll need to add a system administrator. This can be done easily by clicking the Add Current User button. Click Next.

12. In the Error and Usage Report Settings screen, click Next without enabling either of the two check boxes.

13. The installer will perform one more compatability scan. Assuming everything pans out, click Next to proceed to the Ready to Install screen.

14. The Ready to Install screen will provide a summary of the options that you've selected up to this point. Click Install to begin the installation of SQL Server 2008 Express. The Installation wizard proceeds with the installation and displays a confirmation screen when finished. Click Finish to close the Installation wizard.

That's it! You now have SQL Server 2008 Express and Management Studio Basic installed on your computer.

Deploying the SQL Server 2008 Express Database

As you might have noticed by now, I've included sample Access (MDB), SQL Server 2008 (MDF and LDF), and MySQL (SQL) database files for you to use. Rather than forcing you to create the database from scratch, including all the tables, columns, and necessary rows of data, I've taken it upon myself to do the dirty work for you. What you will have to do, however, is take the database file that I've provided and deploy it to your project so that it can be accessed centrally from both Management Studio Basic and Dreamweaver. You can do this now by creating a new folder within C:\VectaCorp<*servermodel*>\ called Database. Now find the vectacorp.mdf and vectacorp.ldf (MDF is the file type associated with SQL Server 2008 database files) files included with this chapter's downloads and copy them into that folder.

That's it! The SQL Server 2008 database needed for the examples throughout the rest of this book is now deployed. Let's next attach, connect to, and browse through the structure of the database so that you're prepared for the database structure walk-through located near the end of the chapter.

SQL Server Management Studio Basic

To use SQL Server 2008 Express effectively, you'll need to work with SQL Server Management Studio Basic (Management Studio). Management Studio is a free DBMS provided by Microsoft that allows you to manage your instance of SQL Server 2008 Express locally. What's nice about Management Studio, aside from the fact that it's free, is that it lets you manage databases, tables, columns, column types, stored procedures, and more— all the tasks that we'll want in an effort to manage our databases before we attempt to access the data via Dreamweaver. The good news is, unlike previous versions of SQL Server Express, SQL Server 2008 Express installs Management Studio for you. What this means is that the tools you need to get up and running with the Vecta Corp database are already installed and ready to use. With that said, let's open Management Studio now and get the Vecta Corp database configured to run within the context of SQL Server 2008 Express.

The first step is to open Management Studio. You can do that by selecting Start, Programs, Microsoft SQL Server 2008, SQL Server Management Studio. Immediately the program launches and presents you with a login screen similar to Figure 17.11.

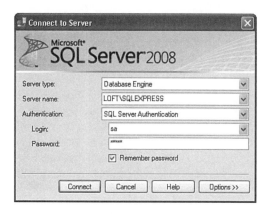

FIGURE 17.11   Log in to Management Studio by first entering your credentials.

Start by selecting the SQL Server Authentication option from the Authentication menu. Type **sa** into the Login text box and type **vecta** into the Password text box. Click Connect to login and connect to SQL Server 2008 Express.

Now that you're logged into Management Studio, the next step is to attach the prebuilt Vecta Corp database to your SQL Server 2008 Express instance.

> **NOTE**
>
> I've provided the completed database model for you. Rather than forcing you to build the database and build each and every table (and associated columns for every table), and then build rows within the tables, I've simply included the databases for you to use. What you will have to do is manually attach the database instance to the database server using Management Studio.

The attach process can be handled directly from Management Studio. To attach the prebuilt Vecta Corp database to the database server, follow these steps:

1. Right-click the Databases node within the Object Explorer panel and choose the Attach option. The Attach Databases dialog box appears.

17

2. Click the Add button. The Locate Database Files dialog box appears. Browse to Database folder located within C:\VectaCorp<servermodel>\, select the vectacorp.mdf file, and click OK.

3. Click OK to close the Attach Databases dialog box. The vectacorp database will now appear in the Object Explorer panel, as shown in Figure 17.12.

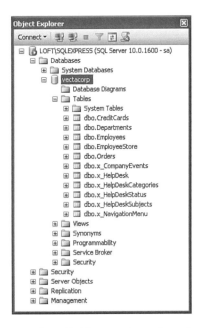

FIGURE 17.12   The Vecta Corp database is now attached to your instance of SQL Server 2008 Express.

If you find some time, explore the features of Management Studio. Practice creating databases, tables, columns, and so on. Doing so will help you get acquainted with Management Studio's interface and its functionality.

Installing MySQL

As mentioned previously, MySQL is both free and open source, but don't let the *free* or *open source* references fool you. MySQL has proven over the years to be as robust, secure, and scalable as any enterprise alternative, including Microsoft's SQL Server, Oracle, or IBM's DB2.

If your goal in reading this book is to side with the open source movement and you're running XAMPP for Windows/MAMP for Mac OS X, MySQL is your best bet and is available as a free download from www.mysql.com.

> **NOTE**
>
> If you're using XAMPP or MAMP, there's no installation or configuration required past what we've already done in the previous chapter. If this is the case, go ahead and skip down to the MySQL Administrator section to learn how to install useful tools for managing the Vecta Corp database. If you're relying on MySQL being installed along with IIS, read on.

To download and install MySQL, follow these steps:

1. Browse to dev.mysql.com/ and click the GA 5.0.51 link located under the MySQL Server Community Edition category on the left navigation menu. You are redirected to a page that allows you to select between the free community server edition or the alternative enterprise edition. Click the Download button located within the MySQL Community Server box.

2. Now choose your operating system from the Operating System Link menu that appears. The following steps assume you are using Windows.

3. On the download selection page within the Windows downloads, click the Pick a Mirror link in the Windows Essentials (x86) section. You are redirected to the registration page.

4. If you choose to register, go ahead and do so now. Otherwise, click the No Thanks, Just Take Me to the Downloads! link. You are redirected to the mirror selection page.

5. Click a desired mirror and begin downloading the `mysql-essential-5.0.51b-win32.msi` file.

6. After you've downloaded the installer, double-click the `mysql-essential-5.0.51b-win32.msi` file to begin the installation.

7. Click Next to proceed from the Welcome screen.

8. Select the Typical Installation option and click Next.

9. Click Install to begin the installation.

10. When the files have been installed, proceed through the final few screens until you reach the Configure the MySQL Server now screen. Click Finish.

The database is now installed. The next series of steps involves configuring the database server on your machine. To proceed through the configuration process, follow the steps outlined here:

1. Click Next.

2. Choose the Detailed Configuration option and click Next.

3. Choose the Developer Machine option and click Next.

4. Choose the Multifunctional Database option and click Next.

5. Choose the default installation directory and click Next.

6. Choose the Decision Support (DSS)/OLAP option and click Next.

7. Accept both enabled options in the networking screen and click Next.

8. Choose the Standard Character Set option and click Next.

9. Choose the Install as Windows Service option and click Next.

10. Enter the password **vecta** within both the New Root Password and Confirm text boxes. Click Next.

11. Click Execute to begin the configuration process.

12. Click Finish to complete the Configuration wizard.

That's it! You've successfully installed and configured MySQL on your computer. To ensure that the installation was successful and that the database server is running, click Start, Settings, Control Panel, Administrative Tools, and Services. In the Services window, scroll down and find the MySQL option. If the status reads *started*, the database server is indeed started, and the installation was successful. If it's listed but not started, right-click the option and choose the Start option from the context menu.

You're now ready to begin developing web applications with IIS that use MySQL as the database. Before you begin, however, you'll want to install the free MySQL DBMS: MySQL Administrator. Let's discuss that next.

Deploying the MySQL Database

As you might have noticed by now, I've included sample Access (MDB), SQL Server 2008 (MDF and LDF), and MySQL (SQL) database files for you to use. Rather than forcing you to create the database from scratch, including all the tables, columns, and necessary rows of data, I've taken it upon myself to do the dirty work for you. What you will have to do, however, is take the database file that I've provided and deploy it to your project so that it can be accessed centrally from both MySQL Administrator and Dreamweaver. You can do this now by creating a new folder within C:\VectaCorp<*servermodel*>\ called **Database**. Now find the vectacorp.sql file included with this chapter's downloads and copy it into that folder.

That's it! The MySQL database needed for the examples throughout the rest of this book is now deployed. Let's next restore, connect to, and browse through the structure of the database so that you're prepared for the database structure walkthrough located near the end of the chapter.

MySQL Administrator

To use MySQL effectively, you'll need to download and install MySQL Administrator. MySQL Administrator is a free DBMS that allows you to manage your instance of MySQL using a slick and easy-to-use interface. What's nice about MySQL Administrator, aside from the fact that it's free, is that it lets you manage databases, tables, columns, column types, security, and more.

> **NOTE**
>
> If you've downloaded XAMPP or MAMP, you have software built into those programs that will allow you to manage your instance of MySQL. Personally I don't prefer these utilities as they're counterintuitive and not at all user-friendly. The free MySQL Administrator, which is available from the MySQL website, is a much better software package and preferable to what's built into XAMPP and MAMP.

To download and install MySQL Administrator, follow these steps:

1. Navigate to dev.mysql.com/downloads/gui-tools/5.0.html.

2. Under your operating system's downloads section, choose the Pick a Mirror link. For Windows, choose the Windows (x86) option. You are redirected to a mirror selection page.

3. If you choose to register, go ahead and do so now. Otherwise, click the No Thanks, Just Take Me to the Downloads! link. You are redirected to the mirror selection page.

4. Choose a mirror to begin downloading the installer.

5. When you've downloaded the installer file, double-click the file to begin the installation for the GUI tools and MySQL Administrator.

6. The installation is fairly straightforward. Enable the default options as you proceed through the screens and click Finish when the installation completes.

After you've installed MySQL Administrator, select Start, Programs, MySQL, MySQL Administrator (/Applications/MySQL/MySQL Administrator) to open the MySQL Administrator. The login screen will appear similar to Figure 17.13.

Enter **localhost** into the Server Host text box, enter **root** into the Username text box, and type **vecta** into the Password text box. If you're using XAMPP, we haven't configured a database password, so go ahead and leave that blank. Click OK to login and open MySQL Administrator.

Now that you're logged into MySQL Administrator, the next step is to import (MySQL uses the term *restore*) the prebuilt Vecta Corp database into MySQL. The restore process can be handled directly from MySQL Administrator. To restore the prebuilt Vecta Corp database, follow these steps:

1. In MySQL Administrator, click the Restore category located in the navigation menu on the left. The General tab of the Restore pane appears by default.

2. Click the Open Backup File button located at the bottom of the screen. The Open dialog box appears.

17

FIGURE 17.13   MySQL Administrator requires you to provide the username, password, and server instance.

3. Locate the vectacorp.sql file located in the Database folder within your web folder and click Open. Fields that were previously disabled in the Open dialog box are now enabled.

4. Keep all the default settings on the General tab and click the Start Restore button.

5. MySQL begins the restore process. Click Close when the restore process finishes.

To see the imported database, click the Catalogs link located in the navigation menu on the left side. As you can see from Figure 17.14, the Vecta Corp database is now contained within our MySQL instance.

If you have some time, explore the features of MySQL Administrator. Practice creating databases, tables, columns, and so on. Doing so will help you get acquainted with MySQL Administrator's interface and its functionality.

For the most part, you've downloaded and installed everything you need to get started with PHP and MySQL without the use of Dreamweaver. However, because we plan on using Dreamweaver to build PHP pages that tie into a MySQL database, you'll need to perform some minor tweaks on the php.ini file as well as download some additional files to get Dreamweaver to work correctly with PHP and MySQL.

NOTE

Again, you will only need to perform additional steps if you're working with MySQL and PHP in conjunction with IIS. If you're using XAMPP or MAMP, you're ready to go, and you can safely skip the next section.

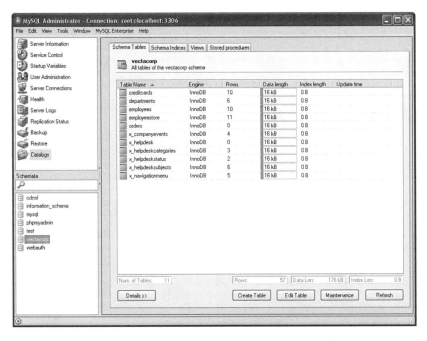

FIGURE 17.14   The Vecta Corp database is now restored into our instance of MySQL.

Configuring PHP to Work with Dreamweaver

Although it might seem that you've done everything you need to do to get PHP and MySQL working with Dreamweaver, think again. There are still a couple of minor adjustments that need to be made for Dreamweaver to recognize your MySQL database under the PHP server model:

▶ Download and unpack the PHP 5.2.3 zip package. This contains a new "ext" folder that contains the php_mysql.dll file. Dreamweaver needs this .DLL to communicate with your MySQL database through PHP.

▶ Configure the php.ini file to read the "ext" folder as well as the php_mysql.dll file.

Let's now walk through the steps. First, you want to download and unpack the PHP 5.2.3 zip package. You can do this by following these steps:

1. Navigate to www.php.net/downloads.php in your browser.

2. On the page, select the PHP 5.2.3 zip package. You are redirected to a mirror selection page.

3. Select a mirror and begin downloading the zip package.

17

4. After it is downloaded, open the zip package and extract the files to the C:\PHP folder, overwriting any files along the way.

5. After you've successfully unpacked and replaced the files in the C:\PHP directory, your directory structure will resemble a much more extensive one similar to Figure 17.15.

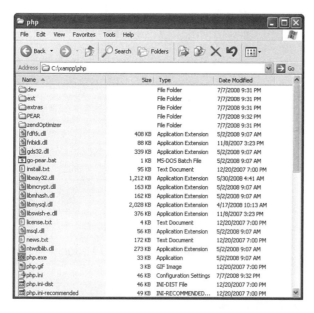

FIGURE 17.15   Unpack the files in the PHP 5.2.3 zip package into C:\PHP, overwriting the necessary files along the way.

Look in the C:\PHP\ext folder. Halfway down the list, you'll have a php_mysql.dll file. This is the file that Dreamweaver needs to communicate with MySQL through its interface. Before that communication can be established, however, you'll want to configure the php.ini file. The php.ini file is a configuration file tapped by Dreamweaver before actually communicating with the php_mysql.dll file. If the php.ini file doesn't make reference to that DLL (or if the reference is commented within the INI file), communication won't be established. To configure the php.ini file now, follow these steps:

1. Open the php.ini file located in C:\PHP. By default, the file should open in Notepad. To use line numbering, try opening the file in Dreamweaver.

2. Scroll down to line number 524 and change the line extension_dir = "./" to read extension_dir = "c:\PHP\ext".

3. Scroll down to line number 666 and uncomment the ;extension=php_mysql.dll line by removing the leading semicolon.

4. Save the php.ini file and close it.

5. When you modify php.ini, you must reset IIS: Restart IIS by choosing Start, Run, and typing the **iisreset** command. Click OK to restart IIS.

That's it! You're now ready to begin using the MySQL database under the PHP server model in Dreamweaver. More on that in a couple of chapters.

An Overview of the Vecta Corp Database

Now that you've become familiar with the inner workings of a database and you've effectively imported/restored the Vecta Corp database into your database of choice, open the DBMS you plan to use so that we can walk through the various tables contained in the Vecta Corp database.

> **NOTE**
>
> For the sake of simplicity, we'll walk through the next examples using Access. However, if you've imported/restored the database on your DBMS of choice, the overall structure for the Vecta Corp database should appear in your DBMS similar to the way it does in Access. At the very least, you can follow along and understand the inner pinnings and various tables contained in the Vecta Corp database using your DBMS of choice.

As you can see from Figure 17.16 (which is a more detailed view of Figure 17.2), numerous tables exist, all of which will make up the Vecta Corp application.

FIGURE 17.16   The Vecta Corp database contains numerous tables that will eventually help make up the dynamic Vecta Corp application.

The rest of the chapter discusses the various tables contained within the Vecta Corp database. The idea is that you become familiar with the various tables and the information within those tables that we'll expose within our Vecta Corp web application. Specifically, we'll discuss the following tables:

- ▶ The Employees table

- ▶ The Departments table

- ▶ The CreditCards table

- ▶ The EmployeeStore table

- ▶ The Orders table

- ▶ Other tables

Remember, we cannot possibly cover every aspect of the Vecta Corp web application. Instead, the rest of the book focuses on the Employee Store segment of the web application. As you'll see in the section "Other Tables," I've included numerous other tables so that you can practice the concepts presented in the rest of the book on your own. Let's get started!

The Employees Table

The Employees table is reserved for all users accessing and purchasing items from our Vecta Corp intranet store. The idea is that most tables in the database reference an employee to a certain extent. As you'll see later, other tables such as Orders, CreditCards, Departments, and HelpDesk have a relationship of some kind with an employee in the Employees table. For instance, an employee belongs to a department, an employee can have and ultimately store numerous credit cards, an employee can have multiple orders on file within the employee store, and last, an employee can have numerous help desk tickets submitted.

Opening the database reveals the underlying design behind the Employees table (see Figure 17.17).

Field Name	Data Type	Description
EmployeeID	AutoNumber	
DepartmentID	Number	
Name	Text	
Username	Text	
Password	Text	
Email	Text	
Phone	Text	
Headshot	Text	
BillingShippingAddress	Text	
BillingShippingCity	Text	
BillingShippingState	Text	
BillingShippingZip	Text	

FIGURE 17.17   The Employees table contains numerous fields regarding employees' personal information.

The Employees table includes such data as name, address, email, username, password, and phone number. Specifically, the data is outlined as follows:

Field Name	Data Type	Key
EmployeeID	AutoNumber	PK
DepartmentID	Number	FK
Name	Text	
Username	Text	
Password	Text	
Email	Text	
Phone	Text	
Headshot	Text	
BillingShippingAddress	Text	
BillingShippingCity	Text	
BillingShippingState	Text	
BillingShippingZip	Text	

As you can see, the table's structure is fairly self-explanatory. The only fields that probably need a bit of explaining are the EmployeeID and DepartmentID fields. Earlier in this chapter, we discussed the concept of relationships and, more specifically, keys. We said that one-to-many relationships rely on primary and foreign keys. In this case, the EmployeeID field is the primary key for this table and is identified as such by the small key icon that appears just to the left of the field.

Any relationship that exists between the Employees table and another table is governed by the primary key field. In this case, there's a catch. We also have a foreign key, the DepartmentID field. Although it's hard to tell that this field is considered a foreign key (there's no icon identifying the field as such), we know that for every department that exists in our company, we'll have numerous employees that work in the department. To outline this conceptually in a database, we set aside the DepartmentID field in the Departments table as the primary key and then create a similar DepartmentID field in the Employees table as the foreign key. This way, we need only reference the department by its unique identifier (its primary key) in the Employees table. To visualize this concept, look at the diagram in Figure 17.18.

As you can see from the diagram (available by choosing the Relationships option from the Tools menu), a one-to-many relationship exists between the DepartmentID primary key in the Departments table and the DepartmentID foreign key in the Employees table.

17

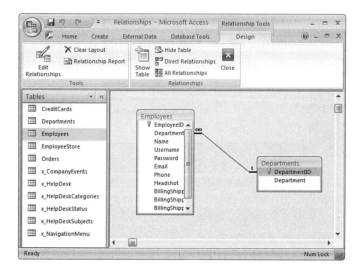

FIGURE 17.18   A one-to-many relationship exists between the Departments table and
Employees table.

Now let's open the Employees table in a Datasheet view. As you can see from Figure 17.19,
all the employees that will be listed in the companydirectory.html page are listed in the
Employees table.

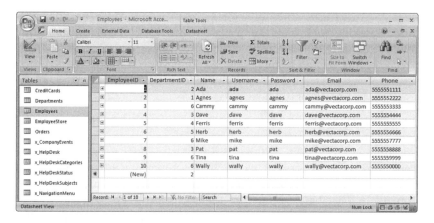

FIGURE 17.19   All Vecta Corp employees are listed, complete with their personal information,
in the Employees table.

After you grasp the concept of relationships and keys, creating relational database structures is a piece of cake. If you haven't totally grasped it yet, don't worry, there are more
tables that we'll be outlining that employ the same concepts. Let's move forward.

The Departments Table

Considered a "lookup" table, the Departments table will rarely grow in size and will almost never be modified. Lookup tables, such as the Departments table, serve one purpose, namely to separate potentially redundant data out of one table into a separate, easier-to-manage table. For a moment, assume that we don't have a Departments table and that instead, that information is located in the Employees table similar to the following:

Name	Department	...
Ada	Administration	...
Agnes	Administration	...
Cammy	Administration	...
Dave	Engineering	...
Ferris	Executive	...
Herb	Human Resources	...

As you can see from the table, the Department *Administration* appears three times. You can imagine if we had thousands of users in the Employees table how inefficient this would become. Instead, we can separate potentially redundant information out of the Employees table and create a new table—in this case, Departments. The Departments table contains single instances of the departments, which are referenced from tables, like the Employees table, through a foreign key.

Looking at the structure of the Departments table reveals the following fields:

Field Name	Data Type	Key
DepartmentID	AutoNumber	PK
Department	Text	

As you can see from the table and as we mentioned in the previous section, the DepartmentID field is the primary key for the Departments table. To establish a relationship with other tables, we reference the DepartmentID primary key via a foreign key in the table from which we want to establish a relationship. In our case, the Employees table will have a relationship with the Departments table. The second field, Department, is merely the text field that will contain the rows of department names.

Looking at the Datasheet view for the Departments table reveals the six departments within Vecta Corp (see Figure 17.20).

Because we have six departments listed and because a relationship has been established between the Employees and Departments tables, a user *must* belong to one of these departments. Maintaining integrity of this relationship is known as *referential integrity*.

17

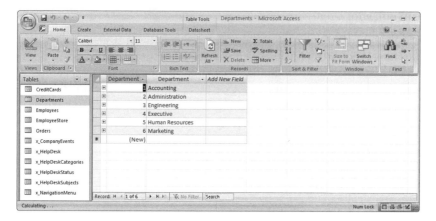

FIGURE 17.20   The Departments table contains six entries that represent the six Vecta Corp departments.

Referential integrity dictates that data contained in a field of a table that has a relationship established must be able to be linked to its primary table. In our case, if we entered the number 7 in the DepartmentID field of the Employees table, our database would return an error because the DepartmentID 7 doesn't exist in the Departments table.

The CreditCards Table

The next table to consider is the CreditCards table. Like the Departments table, redundant information would appear in the Employees table if we had to list the employee multiple times simply because the employee wanted to store more than one credit card. Instead of listing the employee twice, we create a separate table for credit cards. The relationship exists between the EmployeeID primary key in the Employees table and the EmployeeID foreign key in the CreditCards table. The CreditCards table exposes the following structure:

Field Name	Data Type	Key
CreditCardID	AutoNumber	PK
EmployeeID	Number	FK
Type	Text	
Number	Text	
Expiration	Date/Time	

If you open the CreditCards table in the Datasheet view, you can clearly see that eight of the nine employees are storing one credit card on file. This point is illustrated in Figure 17.21.

The employee with the EmployeeID of 9 however, is storing both a Visa and a MasterCard. This validates the one-to-many relationship. One employee could potentially have many credit cards on file.

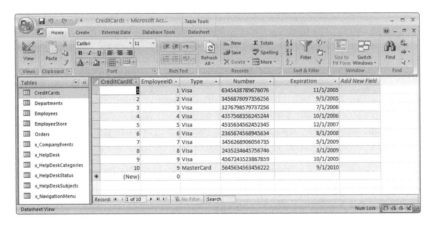

FIGURE 17.21   Eight employees have one credit card on file. One employee has two credit cards on file.

NOTE

Of course, we could normalize the CreditCards table even more. For instance, if we know that Vecta Corp accepts only Visa, MasterCard, American Express, and Discover, we could easily create a new table called CreditCardTypes. That table, like the Departments table, would have two fields: CreditCardTypeID and CreditCardType. We could then create a one-to-many relationship between the CreditCardTypes table and the CreditCards table. There does come a point where you can overnormalize your database. In this case, however, it would make perfect sense.

The EmployeeStore Table

The next, and possibly most important, table for us is the EmployeeStore table. We'll use the EmployeeStore table as a way to store all the items we'll be selling in the Vecta Corp employee store. If you've opened the EmployeeStore table in Design view, you'll notice that it has the following structure:

Field Name	Data Type	Key
ItemID	AutoNumber	PK
ItemName	Text	
ItemDescription	Memo	
ImageURL	Text	
Cost	Currency	
Quantity	Number	

In this case, the ItemID serves as the primary key within the table. However, a relationship will be made between this table and the Orders table (mentioned in the next section). Because an employee could have many orders, a relationship is established between the EmployeeStore table and the Orders table so that we know which item is on order.

Also notice one unique field in the EmployeeStore table: the ImageURL. In this case, we are storing the path to the image on the computer. This keeps our database lightweight because we use the file system to store images while our database merely acts as a reference to those images.

Looking at the Datasheet view reveals all of the items that the Vecta Corp store will carry. As you can see in Figure 17.22, the Vecta Corp store will carry items ranging from T-shirts to stickers to golf balls.

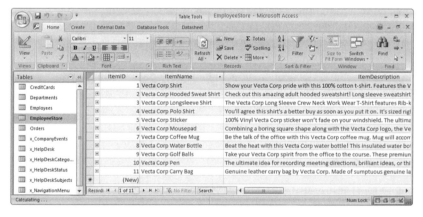

FIGURE 17.22   The Vecta Corp employee store carries numerous items ranging from shirts to golf balls.

If you take a look at the relationship diagram shown in Figure 17.23, you'll see the one-to-many relationship between the EmployeeStore table and the Orders table.

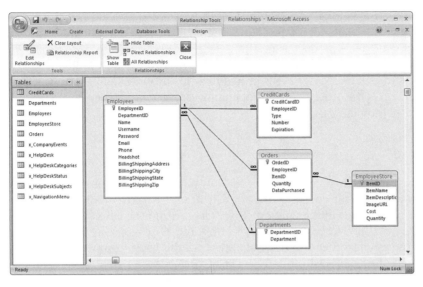

FIGURE 17.23   One item could have many orders.

Remember that every item in the EmployeeStore table could potentially have many orders, thus the reason behind the one-to-many relationship.

The Orders Table

The Orders table will be used as a temporary repository to house items that customers are planning to purchase. This allows us to keep track of who's ordering what and also allows the shipping and receiving departments to process the order. Looking at the Design view of the table reveals the following structure:

Field Name	Data Type	Key
OrderID	AutoNumber	PK
EmployeeID	Number	FK
ItemID	Number	FK
Quantity	Number	
DatePurchased	Date/Time	

You'll notice that this table's structure is a bit different from the ones mentioned thus far. In this case, not only do we have a primary key, but we also have two foreign keys. The reason for this is simple. The Orders table will have a relationship with two tables rather than to just one. Each employee could potentially have an order. Thus, we'd need

17

a relationship between the EmployeeID primary key in the Employees table and the EmployeeID foreign key in the Orders table. Furthermore, as we stated in the previous section, each order will have a product association. Because this is the case, we'd need a relationship between the ItemID primary key in the EmployeeStore table and ItemID foreign key in the Orders table. The OrderID primary key in the Orders table simply acts as a unique identifier and is the order number that employees reference if they have questions about a particular order.

Other Tables

As mentioned earlier in the chapter, we cannot possibly cover all aspects of the Vecta Corp web application throughout the course of this book. Instead, we'll cover basic functionality such as showing all records in the EmployeeStore table within the employee store web page. Furthermore, we'll allow users to select items from the employee store and add them to their cart. Because it'll be difficult to cover all aspects of the Vecta Corp web application, I have outlined other tables within the Vecta Corp database so that after you grasp the basic concepts of selecting, inserting, modifying, and deleting, you can take those concepts and integrate the rest of the Vecta Corp functionality on your own. The tables I've outlined for you to work with on your own are the following:

▶ **CompanyEvents**—Rather than having to manually open the main page and make modifications to the company events section, you could just as easily integrate functionality that allows extraction from this database table.

▶ **HelpDesk**—One of the web pages in our Vecta Corp intranet site provides the capability for users to submit help desk tickets. The HelpDesk table acts as a central repository for employee problems to which the IT department can react.

▶ **HelpDeskCategories**—A simple lookup table, this table filters such problems as Hardware, Software, or Workstation-related ones.

▶ **HelpDeskStatus**—A second lookup table, this table allows the status of a help desk ticket to change to either Open or Closed.

> **NOTE**
>
> Although it might seem more trouble than it's worth to implement the HelpDeskStatus table for only two options (Open and Closed), by including this table in the database, we make the database expandable. If the Vecta Corp help desk needs more sophisticated tracking mechanisms, for example, the HelpDeskStatus table can expand to include OnHold, NeedsAttention, and NeedsOtherResources status markers.

▶ **HelpDeskSubjects**—A third lookup table, this table contains descriptions for the help desk category, or more specifically, it contains detailed information about the specific problem.

▶ **NavigationMenu**—One of the problems you'll quickly notice in our web application is that the navigation menu is static. If we needed to add a new navigation menu item, we would have to open the main template and make the change. Storing the navigation menu in a database table allows us to dynamically create navigation menu items, which, in turn, are displayed on the web page.

If you look in the database, you'll notice that these tables are preceded with the letter *x*. The *x* stands for *Xtra*, and also serves as a way of keeping these tables grouped separately and out of the way from tables that we do plan to use.

Summary

This chapter has introduced you to some simple, yet important, concepts—mainly data storage. You learned about the skeleton of a database, which is composed of tables, columns, and rows, and about crucial concepts that can aid in performance, maintenance, and efficiency.

More importantly, you looked at the various databases supported in this book. You learned about Access, SQL Server 2008 Express Edition, and MySQL as well as the DBMSs that work in conjunction with them. You saw how to obtain and install the necessary software, how to create tables, columns, and rows, and how to attach/restore the Vecta Corp database so that you can work with dynamic Vecta Corp data in your database of choice from Dreamweaver. As the chapter progressed, we also looked at the many tables contained within the Vecta Corp database. You looked at the Employees, Departments, CreditCards, EmployeeStore, and Orders tables as well as the other tables left open so that you can continue to work with the Vecta Corp web application on your own.

The next chapter begins to put everything that we've learned up to this point into practice. Let's start building the dynamic Vecta Corp web pages!

17

CHAPTER **18**

A SQL Primer

At this point, you are familiar with just how easy it is to create a database using Access, SQL Server 2005 Express, or MySQL. In the coming chapters, you'll learn just how easy Dreamweaver makes it to extract from, insert into, update within, and delete information from your database. Although Dreamweaver provides a simple process for the extraction of data from your database, you might quickly find your application growing far beyond the scope of simple data extraction. The kind of applications you eventually build will have a direct impact on how complex your use of a data-access language will be. Dreamweaver provides a simple and easy-to-use process for commonly used data extraction and filtering tasks, but if you truly want to get the most out of Dreamweaver and ultimately your applications, you should become familiar with the topics discussed in this chapter.

The Structured Query Language

This chapter focuses on the language of today's database. The *Structured Query Language*, or *SQL* (pronounced "sequel"), was established in the 1970s as a way of interacting with the tables of the current database technologies of the time. With dozens of clauses, keywords, and operators, SQL quickly became the language standard for simple and complex database operations. The keywords that you construct, also known as *statements*, range from a simple few to a complex string of subqueries and joins. Although this chapter cannot begin to cover all there is to know on the subject, it can provide you with an introduction to beginning and advanced SQL statements, clauses, joins, subqueries, and action queries. The concepts you learn in this chapter will help you interact with data in your database on a more advanced level using Dreamweaver.

Basic SQL

Just as your savings account would be useless without a valid ID or bank card to get to that money, information contained within a database is useless data unless you have the means of extracting it. SQL is the language that does just that; it allows for quick and complex access to the data contained in your database through the use of queries. *Queries* pose the questions and return the results to your application, usually in the form of a *recordset*.

> **CAUTION**
>
> Don't think of SQL as simply a way of extracting information. The SQL language can be complex, allowing not only queries from a database, but it can add, modify, and delete information from a database, as well.

Consider trying to extract information from the EmployeeStore table of the Vecta Corp database. Recall that the EmployeeStore table resembles the table that follows (although this table does not show the ItemDescription and Headshot columns):

Field Name	Date Type
ItemID	AutoNumber
ItemName	Text
Quantity	Currency
Cost	Number

You can then list products in rows that would look like the following:

ItemID	ItemName	Cost	Quantity
1	Vecta Corp Shirt	$12.99	100
2	Vecta Corp Hooded	$29.99	100
3	Vecta Corp Longsleeve	$19.99	100
4	Vecta Corp Polo	$23.99	100
5	Vecta Corp Sticker	$1.99	100
6	Vecta Corp Mousepad	$4.99	100

ItemID	ItemName	Cost	Quantity
7	Vecta Corp Coffee Mug	$6.99	100
8	Vecta Corp Water Bottle	$9.99	100

Consider some important aspects about the previous table and the columns and data contained in the eight rows. The EmployeeStore table contains four columns: an ItemID with an AutoNumber that increments a value whenever an item is added; an ItemName that contains a Text data type allowing for a simple title of the product to be added; a column for Cost with a Currency data type that allows us to store price information for each specific item; and a Quantity column with a Number data type that allows us to store a numeric value indicating how many of a specific item we have left in our inventory. The last thing to consider is the data contained in the table. We are storing a list of Vecta Corp employee store items that are to be sold from the Web Store application.

Now what? You have the table created, columns and data types have been outlined, and you have rows of data in the table. Our next step is to get to our data somehow. The next few sections outline how to use SQL to extract data from your tables.

The SELECT Statement

The foundation to all SQL queries is the SELECT statement. Made up of two keywords, the SELECT statement provides a means for retrieving the data from the database. In its simplest form, the SELECT statement is written using the following elements:

- ▶ **SELECT**—The SELECT keyword is used to identify the statement or action you are attempting to perform on the database. Other keywords include INSERT, DELETE, and UPDATE. More on these later.

- ▶ *** or field names**—The asterisk or names of the fields tell the statement which columns you want to extract data from. In this case, the asterisk means "all fields."

- ▶ **FROM**—The FROM keyword identifies which table to extract the data from. The FROM keyword is required with all SELECT statements.

- ▶ **Table name(s)**—The table name from which you want to extract the data.

The following example extracts all records from your EmployeeStore table:

```
SELECT * FROM EmployeeStore
```

The preceding statement uses two keywords—the SELECT keyword and the FROM keyword—to extract all records from the EmployeeStore table. The previous statement would produce the following results (some fields have been excluded in order to fit on the page):

18

ItemID	ItemName	Cost	Quantity
1	Vecta Corp Shirt	$12.99	100
2	Vecta Corp Hooded	$29.99	100
3	Vecta Corp Longsleeve	$19.99	100
4	Vecta Corp Polo	$23.99	100
5	Vecta Corp Sticker	$1.99	100
6	Vecta Corp Mousepad	$1.99	100
7	Vecta Corp Coffee Mug	$1.99	100
8	Vecta Corp Water Bottle	$9.99	100

Selecting Certain Fields

If you did not want to select all the fields in the database table, you could modify the field names to include only the fields that you wanted:

```
SELECT ItemID, ItemName, Cost
FROM EmployeeStore
```

Notice that the preceding statement retrieves the data only from the ItemID, ItemName, and Cost fields. The preceding query produces the following results:

ItemID	ItemName	Cost
1	Vecta Corp Shirt	$12.99
2	Vecta Corp Hooded	$29.99
3	Vecta Corp Longsleeve	$19.99
4	Vecta Corp Polo	$23.99
5	Vecta Corp Sticker	$1.99
6	Vecta Corp Mousepad	$1.99
7	Vecta Corp Coffee Mug	$1.99
8	Vecta Corp Water Bottle	$9.99

Notice that in this case, the ItemDescription and Quantity columns are excluded. You could also modify the statement in an effort to retrieve the same information in a different order. For example, we could switch the field names by placing ItemName in front of ItemID, like this:

```
SELECT ItemName, ItemID, Cost
FROM EmployeeStore
```

This code would give the following result:

ItemName	ItemID	Cost
Vecta Corp Shirt	1	$12.99
Vecta Corp Hooded	2	$29.99
Vecta Corp Longsleeve	3	$19.99
Vecta Corp Polo	4	$23.99
Vecta Corp Sticker	5	$1.99
Vecta Corp Mousepad	6	$1.99
Vecta Corp Coffee Mug	7	$1.99
Vecta Corp Water Bottle	8	$9.99

Selecting Unique Data

The information in the EmployeeStore table contains duplicate values. As you can see, we have three items in our table that are priced at $1.99. If someone wanted to know about the unique variety of prices in our database, we would have to modify the statement to produce distinct results. The DISTINCT keyword can be used before the Cost field in this case to extract from the table only unique instances of data contained in that field.

```
SELECT DISTINCT Cost
FROM EmployeeStore
```

The preceding statement would produce the following result:

As you can see, in this case all cost information is displayed, but the results are limited to unique price instances. $1.99 is listed only once rather than three times.

Cost
$12.99
$29.99
$19.99
$23.99
$1.99
$9.99

18

Clauses

Clauses are portions of SQL that allow for further refinement of the query or additional work that must be accomplished by the SQL statement. The following clauses are covered in this section:

▶ The WHERE clause

▶ The ORDER BY clause

▶ The GROUP BY clause

The WHERE Clause

The WHERE clause is used in conjunction with the SELECT statement to deliver a more refined search based on individual field criteria. This example could be used to extract a specific employee based on a name:

```
SELECT *
FROM Employees
WHERE Name = 'Ada'
```

Notice that the selection is made only when a certain criteria is true. If a record with the name of Ada did not exist, it wouldn't return anything. But what if we had more than one Ada in the database? You could refine your search even further by using the AND operator:

```
SELECT *
FROM Employees
WHERE Name = 'Ada' AND Phone = '5555551111'
```

In this case, even if two Adas were listed in our database, we can assume that they don't have the same phone number. In this situation, the query returns one result (assuming, of course, that the two Adas aren't roommates).

The ORDER BY Clause

The ORDER BY clause provides you with a quick way of sorting the results of your query in either ascending or descending order. Consider the following table of information:

EmployeeID	Name	Email
1	Cammy	cammy@vectacorp.com
2	Ferris	ferris@vectacorp.com
3	Ada	ada@vectacorp.com
4	Dave	dave@vectacorp.com
5	Agnes	agnes@vectacorp.com

If you selected all the records by using a SELECT all statement (SELECT *), it would return all the results, ordering them based on the value in the EmployeeID field: 1 through 5.

Using the SELECT statement with an ORDER BY clause allows you to sort based on a different field name:

```
SELECT *
FROM Employees
ORDER BY Name
```

The preceding statement would return results in the following order:

EmployeeID	Name	Email
3	Ada	ada@vectacorp.com
5	Agnes	agnes@vectacorp.com
1	Cammy	cammy@vectacorp.com
4	Dave	dave@vectacorp.com
2	Ferris	ferris@vectacorp.com

You can also order by multiple columns by adding a comma after the field name and entering a second field name:

```
SELECT *
FROM Employees
ORDER BY Name, Phone
```

In this case, all records with identical Name fields are sorted by phone.

TIP

You might decide to sort the results of your query in either ascending or descending order. When this is the case, you can use the ASC and DESC keywords preceding the field names as follows:

```
SELECT *
FROM Employees
ORDER BY Name, Phone DESC
```

The GROUP BY Clause

When a query statement includes a GROUP BY clause, the SELECT statement for that query can list functions while operating on groups of data values in other columns. For example, data within the Orders table could look similar to the following table:

OrderID	EmployeeID	ItemID	Quantity
1	1	2	2
2	1	4	4

18

OrderID	EmployeeID	ItemID	Quantity
3	3	8	4
4	4	7	2
5	5	2	2
6	5	7	1

If you wanted to retrieve the total number of orders that were received, you could run the following query:

```
SELECT COUNT(Quantity) AS NumberOfOrders
FROM Orders
```

The result would return the following:

NumberOfOrders
6

In this case, we're exploring two unique concepts. First, we're selecting a count, using the built-in COUNT function to return a total number of orders for the Quantity column. Second, we're using the AS keyword to create a virtual field called NumberOfOrders. This gives us a total count of orders and stores that number (6) temporarily within a virtual field called NumberOfOrders.

You could use the GROUP BY clause in this instance to group the orders by EmployeeID as follows:

```
SELECT EmployeeID, COUNT(Quantity) AS NumberOfOrders
FROM Orders
GROUP BY EmployeeID
```

The result would be as follows:

EmployeeID	NumberOfOrders
1	2
3	1
4	1
5	2

The result is based on the fact that employees 1 and 5 made two orders each, while employees 3 and 4 made one order each.

The INSERT Statement

Collecting information from your users is not uncommon and, in most cases, it is a necessity. When you collect information such as registration information, you're not querying data, but rather you're inserting data into the database. In our Vecta Corp example, for instance, we'll create an Admin page that allows administrators to insert new employees into the database. To illustrate this point, consider the Employees table and some of the fields that make it up:

Field Name	Date Type
EmployeeID	AutoNumber
DepartmentID	Number
Name	Text
Username	Text
Password	Text
Email	Text
Phone	Text
Headshot	Text
BillingShippingAddress	Text
BillingShippingCity	Text
BillingShippingState	Text
BillingShippingZip	Text

You could easily insert a new record into the Employees table using the following INSERT statement:

```
INSERT INTO Employees
    (DepartmentID, Name, Username, Password, Email,
     Phone, Headshot, BillingShippingAddress, BillingShippingCity,
     BillingShippingState, BillingShippingZip)
VALUES
    (1, 'Zak', 'zak', 'zak', 'zak@modulemedia.com', '5555555555',
     'Images\head_zak.gif', '555   Sample St.', 'San Diego', 'Ca', '92115')
```

The preceding statement inserts all the values you specified into the proper columns within the Employees table. The INSERT keyword generally uses the following elements:

▶ **INSERT**—The INSERT keyword is used to identify the statement or action you are attempting to perform on the database.

18

▶ **INTO**—The INTO keyword specifies that you are inserting something into a specific table.

▶ **Table name**—The name of the table into which you want to insert the values.

▶ **VALUES**—The actual values to be inserted.

You could also use the SELECT statement within the INSERT statement to literally copy information from one table to the other:

```
INSERT INTO Transactions (EmployeeID, Name, Email)
SELECT EmployeeID, Name, Email
FROM Employees WHERE EmployeeID = 1
```

The preceding statement assumes that we have a Transactions table. At any rate, this statement effectively copies from the Employees table the EmployeeID, Name, and Email whose EmployeeID is equal to 1 and copies this data into the Transactions table.

The UPDATE Statement

The UPDATE statement is used to define changes within your database tables. As you're probably aware, database information is not static, but is instead constantly changing depending on user feedback or input. As an example, assume that an administrator wanted to change specific data (maybe a username and password) for a particular employee within the Employees table. To make these changes to an existing record in the table, an UPDATE statement would have to be used.

The UPDATE statement requires certain keywords, operators, and usually a WHERE clause to modify the specific record; for instance:

```
UPDATE Employees
SET Name = 'Cammi'
WHERE EmployeeID = 3
```

This statement effectively changes Cammy's name to "'Cammi" because she matches the EmployeeID of 3.

> **NOTE**
>
> *Operators* enable you to connect certain portions of your statement, whereas *clauses* allow for more refined queries and searches. Both are discussed later in the chapter.

You don't have to use the EmployeeID field with the WHERE clause. Instead, you could use Cammy's name as follows:

```
UPDATE Employees
SET Name = 'Cammi'
WHERE Name = 'Cammy'
```

In this case, all instances of "Cammy" are replaced with "Cammi" in the database.

The DELETE Statement

The DELETE statement can be used to remove unneeded records from the database. For instance, if you wanted to remove all employees from the Employees table, we might write a DELETE statement as follows:

```
DELETE
FROM Employees
```

The preceding statement effectively removes all the employees from the Employees table. Of course, this doesn't make much sense! You wouldn't want to just go and remove all employees from your database. Instead, you might want to delete a specific employee—for instance, if an employee quits or is fired. If this were the case, you could append a WHERE clause to your statement to remove one record:

```
DELETE
FROM Employees
WHERE EmployeeID = 2
```

This statement removes only the record where the EmployeeID is equal to 2. As was the case with the UPDATE example, you could also delete a user by name:

```
DELETE
FROM Employees
WHERE Name = 'Agnes'
```

This statement removes all records from the Employees table whose Name field matches "Agnes."

Expressions

If you are the least bit familiar with programming languages, you know that *expressions* are anything that, when calculated, result in a value. For instance, 1 + 1 = 2 is an example of an expression. Expressions in SQL work similarly. Consider the following data that could appear in the Employees table:

EmployeeID	FirstName	LastName
1	Ada	Spada
2	Agnes	Senga
3	Cammy	Franklin
4	Dave	Terry
5	Ferris	Wheel

You could use a simple SELECT statement to display the information exactly as it appears in the preceding table, or you could write an expression that appends the FirstName and LastName fields together. The query would look like this:

```
SELECT EmployeeID, FirstName & LastName AS Name
FROM Employees
```

Notice the & operator. The & operator is used to concatenate, or join, two fields into one virtual field using the AS keyword. The results would display as follows:

EmployeeID	Name
1	AdaSpada
2	AgnesSenga
3	CammyFranklin
4	DaveTerry
5	FerrisWheel

Notice that there is no space between the first and last names. To add a space, you need to add a literal string value as follows:

```
SELECT EmployeeID, FirstName & ' ' & LastName AS Name
FROM Employees
```

> **NOTE**
>
> Depending on the database you use, the & operator might not work as a way of concatenating values. Some databases, such as SQL Server 2005, use the + operator to concatenate values.

> **NOTE**
>
> You might have noticed that we've been using single quotes in every SQL statement. The reason for this is simple: When you construct your SQL statements in Dreamweaver, the server-side language encloses the entire statement in double quotes. For the statement to be valid, strings within a SQL statement must be enclosed within single quotes.

Adding the space results in a gap between the first and last names as follows:

EmployeeID	Name
1	Ada Spada
2	Agnes Senga
3	Cammy Franklin

EmployeeID	Name
4	Dave Terry
5	Ferris Wheel

Operators

In the previous section, you were introduced to the use of the & operator. *Operators* are used in programming languages to aid in the evaluation of expressions. The following table lists operators with which you should become familiar:

Operator	Description
*	The multiplication operator is used when multiplying fields or values.
/	The divide operator is used when dividing fields or values.
–	The minus operator is used when subtracting fields or values.
>	The greater-than operator is used in WHERE clauses to determine whether a first value is greater than the second, such as this:

```
SELECT *
FROM Employees
WHERE EmployeeID > 10
```

The result returns all the EmployeeIDs after 10.

<	The less-than operator is used in WHERE clauses to determine whether a first value is less than the second, such as this:

```
SELECT *
FROM Employees
WHERE EmployeeID < 10
```

The result returns EmployeeIDs 1–9.

>=	The greater-than-or-equal-to operator is used in WHERE clauses to determine whether a first value is greater than or equal to the second, such as this:

```
SELECT *
FROM Employees
WHERE EmployeeID >= 10
```

The result returns EmployeeIDs of 10 and greater.

18

Operator	Description
<=	The less-than-or-equal-to operator is used in WHERE clauses to determine whether a first value is less than or equal to the second, such as this: ``` SELECT * FROM Employees WHERE EmployeeID <= 10 ``` The result returns all the EmployeeIDs between 1 and 10.
<>, !=	When comparing values, use these keywords to check and make sure that one value is not equal to a second value.
AND	Typically used with the WHERE clause in the SELECT statement. The AND operator returns a second value, such as this: ``` SELECT * FROM Employees WHERE EmployeeID = 1 AND EmployeeID = 2 ```
OR	Typically used with the WHERE clause in the SELECT statement. The OR operator can be used when a certain condition needs to be met or when you can settle for a second, such as this: ``` SELECT * FROM Employees WHERE EmployeeID = 1 OR EmployeeID = 2 ```
LIKE	The LIKE operator is generally used with WHERE clauses when a wildcard needs to be performed, such as this: ``` SELECT * FROM Employees WHERE Name LIKE 'A%' ``` This result returns all employees whose names start with A. Our result returns Ada and Agnes because both their names begin with the letter A.
NOT	Typically used in conjunction with the LIKE operator, the NOT operator is used when a value is *not* going to be LIKE the value of a second, such as this: ``` SELECT * FROM Employees WHERE Name NOT LIKE 'A%' ``` In this case, all names other than Ada and Agnes are returned.

Operator	Description
	The underscore operator is used with WHERE clauses and is performed when you do not know the second value, such as this:
| | ```
SELECT *
FROM Employees
WHERE BillingShippingState LIKE 'A_'
``` |
| | The result, in this case, returns all states that begin with the letter A, such as AK, AL, AR, and AZ. |
| % | The multiple-character operator is similar to the underscore operator except that it allows for multiple characters, whereas the underscore operator allows for only two. This operator is used in more situations than the underscore operator. |

Functions

Aside from using operators to manually construct expressions, SQL provides built-in *functions* (small blocks of code that can perform operations and return a value) you can use.

> **NOTE**
>
> One function that we've already discussed is the commonly used COUNT function. If you can recall, the COUNT function simply returns a numeric count for a field based on a pre-specified condition.

Functions are available simply by making a call to them and passing the value and/or values on which you want the function to operate.

> **NOTE**
>
> The functions outlined in the next sections represent a generic list of SQL functions. It's important to realize that not all databases support the same functions. Although in most cases all databases support similar functions, the way the function is written can differ syntactically from database to database. In the next sections, I'll provide you with a broad list of these functions. However, it's up to you to consult your database documentation for the appropriate syntax variation for the function.

Date and Time Functions

Date and time functions allow for manipulations using dates and times that are stored within your database. For instance, if you wanted to return all items from the Orders table that were purchased on October 30, 2007, you might write the following code:

18
```

```
SELECT *
FROM Orders
WHERE DatePurchased LIKE '10/30/2007'
```

This code would produce the following results:

OrderID	EmployeeID	ItemID	Quantity	DatePurchased
24	3	2	1	10/30/07

If you wanted to find all the orders from the previous month, you could use the DATEADD() function:

```
SELECT *
FROM Orders
WHERE DatePurchased > DATEADD(m, -1, Date())
```

Assuming that the current date was 6/30/05, the results would be as follows:

OrderID	EmployeeID	ItemID	Quantity	DatePurchased
24	3	2	1	6/15/05
2	2	2	1	6/11/05
11	6	3	1	6/14/05

TIP

In the preceding example, we included three values within the parentheses of the DATEADD function. These values are known as *parameters*. Parameters are values that you pass into the function so that it knows what to do or how to return the value.

Also notice that the DATEADD() function accepts parameters. These parameters include the following:

▶ This parameter specifies which part of the date/time object you want to work with. Typically, you would want to use one of a few values: m for month, w for week, d for day, h for hour, n for minute, s for second, and so forth.

▶ How much time to add or subtract—in the preceding example, I subtracted one month.

▶ The date you want to use—In the preceding example, I called another function, the system date, as the date I wanted to use. When you use the DATE() function, you are effectively reading the date and time from the computer and passing it in as a value.

There are many other date and time functions. Too many, in fact, to cover in this small section. Date and time functions are among the most widely used functions in SQL and are worth the research.

The COUNT() Function

One of the most commonly used functions (and one that we've already discussed) is the COUNT() function. The COUNT() function is used when you want to perform a count of records. Consider the following data from the Orders table:

OrderID	EmployeeID	ItemID	Quantity	DatePurchased
24	3	2	1	6/30/05
2	2	2	2	6/30/05
11	6	3	2	6/30/05

You could use the following code to count the number of orders you have taken in a day from the Orders table:

```
SELECT COUNT(Quantity) AS NumberOfOrders
FROM Orders
```

The statement would result in the following:

NumberOfOrders
3

Notice that you pass in the field name as a parameter in the COUNT() function. The parameter is evaluated, and a value is returned into a virtual field named NumberOfOrders.

The SUM() Function

Unlike the COUNT() function that returns a value from a calculation on the number of fields, the SUM() function performs a calculation on data within those fields. If, for instance, you needed to know the total number of items you sold, you could modify the preceding statement to read as follows:

```
SELECT SUM(Quantity) AS Total
FROM Orders
```

The statement would produce the following results:

Total
5

Rather than simply doing a count on the records, the sum is calculated based on the values within the specified field. Because a total of five items were ordered, this value is shown.

18

The AVG() Function

The AVG() function returns the average of values in specific fields. Consider the following orders in the Orders table:

OrderID	EmployeeID	ItemID	Quantity	DatePurchased
24	3	2	1	6/30/05
2	2	2	3	6/30/05
11	6	3	5	6/30/05

To get the total average of items being ordered, we might write a statement that resembles the following:

```
SELECT AVG(Quantity) AS Average
FROM Orders
```

The statement would produce the following result:

Average
3

Of course, this is because the average of the numbers 1, 3, and 5 is 3.

The MIN() and MAX() Functions

The MIN() and MAX() functions enable you to find the smallest and largest values of a specific record. To get the minimum quantity ordered, you could write a statement such as this one:

```
SELECT MIN(Quantity) AS Minimum
FROM Orders
```

Based on the Orders table data from the previous section, the preceding statement produces this result (because the minimum value in the Quantity field is 1):

Minimum
1

To receive the maximum value of a record in the database, try this statement:

```
SELECT MAX(Quantity) AS Maximum
FROM Orders
```

Based on the Orders table data from the previous section, the preceding statement produces this result (because the maximum value in the Quantity field is 5):

Maximum
5

Arithmetic Functions

Aside from using SUM(), MIN(), MAX(), and AVG(), a few other arithmetic functions can help you when calculating fields in your database. They are as follows:

Function	Description
ABS()	Returns the absolute value
CEIL()	Returns the largest integer value not greater than the value
FLOOR()	Returns the smallest integer value not greater than the value
COS()	Returns the cosine of the value where the value is provided in radians
COSH()	Returns the hyperbolic cosine of the value where the value is provided in radians
SIN()	Returns the sine of the value where the value is provided in radians
SINH()	Returns the hyperbolic sine of the value where the value is provided in radians
TAN()	Returns the tangent of the value where the value is provided in radians
TANH()	Returns the hyperbolic tangent of the value where the value is provided in radians
EXP()	Returns the mathematical constant e raised to the provided exponential value
MOD()	Returns the remainder of a value divided by a second value
SIGN()	Returns the sign of the argument as –1, 0, or 1, depending on whether the value is negative, zero, or positive
SQRT()	Returns the non-negative square root of a value
POWER()	Returns the result of a value raised to the power of a second value
LN()	Returns the natural logarithm of a value
LOG()	Returns the logarithm of a value in the base of a second value

18

String Functions

String functions are similar to other functions except that they work with literal text values rather than numerical values. The following string functions are the most common.

Function	Description
CHR()	Converts an ASCII value to its string equivalent.
CONCAT()	Concatenates (merges) two strings into one.
INITCAP()	Capitalizes the first letter of each word in provided string.
UPPER()	Returns the provided string in all uppercase.
LOWER()	Returns the provided string in all lowercase.
LPAD()	Returns a value padded on the left based on the numerical value you specify.
RPAD()	Returns a value padded on the right based on the numerical value you specify.
LTRIM()	Trims a specified amount of space or characters from the left side of a string.
RTRIM()	Trims a specified amount of space or characters from the right side of a string.
REPLACE()	Changes a portion of the string with a value that you specify. REPLACE() accepts three parameters: string, target, and replacement string.
SUBSTR()	Returns the substring of a value that begins at a positive value and is certain number of characters long. SUBSTR() accepts three parameters: string, position, and length.
LENGTH()	Returns the string length in number of characters.

Joins

Up to this point, you have focused primarily on extracting data from a single table. Depending on how advanced your database becomes, at times you might want to extract data from multiple tables at once. If that is the case, you will need to use *joins*. Although there are several types of joins, two types will be covered here:

▶ Inner joins

▶ Outer joins

Inner Joins

Of the different types of joins, inner joins are by far the most popular. Inner joins enable you to see all the records of two tables that have a relationship established. Remember that the Employees and the CreditCards tables have an established one-to-many relationship. The two tables in the Vecta Corp database resemble the following:

EmployeeID	Name
1	Ada
2	Agnes
3	Cammy
4	Dave
...	...

EmployeeID	Type	Number
1	Visa	6345438789678076
2	Visa	3456878097356256
3	Visa	3276798579737256
4	Visa	4357568356245244
...	...	...

Assume that you wanted to extract the information from the Employees table for EmployeeID 2. If not for inner joins, you would have to use two SELECT statements as follows:

```
SELECT *
FROM Employees
WHERE EmployeeID = 2
```

and

```
SELECT *
FROM CreditCards
WHERE EmployeeID = 2
```

You can begin to see how tedious this could get, not to mention that it is completely inefficient. To solve this problem, an INNER JOIN could be used as follows:

```
SELECT
Employees.EmployeeID, Employees.Name,
CreditCards.Type, CreditCards.Number
FROM Employees
INNER JOIN CreditCards
ON Employees.EmployeeID = CreditCards.EmployeeID
```

18

The join effectively produces one virtual table with the following results:

EmployeeID	Name	Type	Number
1	Ada	Visa	6345438789678076
2	Agnes	Visa	3456878097356256
3	Cammy	Visa	3276798579737256
4	Dave	Visa	4357568356245244
...	...	...	...

Notice that the preceding table now becomes more efficient and manageable. Also notice that, rather than referencing the names of the tables, you used the TableName.Field notation. This is crucial when using joins; otherwise, you would end up with two EmployeeIDs without a direct reference to its corresponding table.

> **NOTE**
>
> Note the use of the ON operator in the preceding SQL INNER JOIN statement. The ON operator instructs the SQL statement to join two tables on a specific primary and foreign key pairing.

Outer Joins

Outer joins enable rows to be returned from a join in which one of the tables does not contain matching rows for the other table. Suppose that you have two tables that contain the following information:

EmployeeID	Name	AddressID
2	Ada	45634
4	Agnes	34754
5	Cammy	
10	Dave	97895
...	...	...

AddressID	Address
45634	555 Sample St., San Diego
34754	343 Chestnut Rd., San Diego
97895	523 Main St., San Diego
...	...

Consider the following INNER JOIN statement, issued on the preceding tables:

```
SELECT
Employees.Name, Employees.AddressID,
Address.AddressID, Address.Address
FROM Employees
INNER JOIN Address
ON Employees.AddressID = Address.AddressID
```

It returns the following results:

Name	AddressID	Address
Ada	45634	555 Sample St., San Diego
Agnes	34754	343 Chestnut Rd., San Diego
Dave	97895	523 Main St., San Diego

Notice that the record that did not contain an AddressID was excluded. Now consider the following OUTER JOIN statement:

```
SELECT
Employees.Name, Employees.AddressID,
Address.AddressID, Address.Address
FROM Employees
OUTER JOIN Address ON Employees.AddressID = Address.AddressID
```

The results of this statement are slightly different:

FirstName	AddressID	Address
Ada	45634	555 Sample St., San Diego
Agnes	34754	343 Chestnut Rd., San Diego
Dave	97895	523 Main St., San Diego
Cammy		

As you can see, in the case of the OUTER JOIN, all data is returned, even if no address is present for Cammy.

Subqueries

Sometimes it may not be possible to retrieve the results you need using a simple SELECT statement. At times, you might need to create a SELECT statement and compare the results to that of another statement. In that case, you would want to use subqueries. A *subquery* is a query nested inside another query. There are two types of subqueries you can use:

▶ The IN operator

▶ The embedded SELECT statement

The IN Operator

The IN operator is used in a SELECT statement primarily to specify a list of values to be used with a primary query. A classic example is if you wanted to find all your employees who lived in California and its border states such as Arizona, Nevada, and Oregon. You could write a SELECT statement using the IN operator to accomplish that:

```
SELECT *
FROM Employees
WHERE BillingShippingState IN ('CA', 'AZ', 'NV', 'OR')
```

This statement effectively returns all the employees who live in the states of California, Arizona, Nevada, and Oregon.

The Embedded SELECT Statement

An embedded SELECT statement is used when you want to perform a secondary query within the WHERE clause of a primary query. Suppose that you wanted to see a list of employees who have completed orders for the week. If that were the case, your query might look like this:

```
SELECT *
FROM Employees
WHERE EmployeeID IN
     (SELECT DISTINCT EmployeeID
        FROM Orders)
```

Generating Queries Visually

Queries lay the foundation for data extraction from databases. You have seen how to create simple and complex queries by hand, and you now have a grasp of how they are constructed with clauses, operators, conditions, and expressions. Unfortunately, like most programming and authoring languages, perfection takes time and practice. Fortunately, there is an easier way.

Rather than manually writing all your SQL statements, you can rely on features built in to your DBMS to create them for you. If you've been experimenting with Access on your own, for instance, you've noticed the Queries tab on the left column. Queries can be constructed and saved for reuse in the future by using the Query Designer (see Figure 18.1).

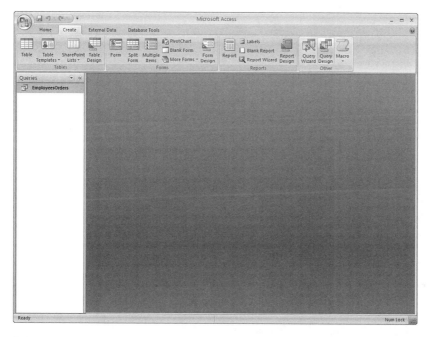

FIGURE 18.1   The Query Designer streamlines the way queries are created in Access.

> **NOTE**
>
> If you're using SQL Server 2005 Express Edition, you can still follow along with the instructions provided. Open Management Studio Express, expand your database, right-click on the Views folder, and choose New View. If you're using MySQL as your database of choice, you can follow along by using MySQL Query Browser. Available by selecting Start, Programs, MySQL, MySQL Query Browser, MySQL Query Browser allows you to visually work with queries just as Access does with queries or Management Studio Express does with Views. The instructions provided should translate over to your database without any problems.

Generating Queries Using Access Query Designer

The easiest and quickest way to generate queries in Access is by creating them in Design view. To create a simple SELECT query, follow these steps:

1. Assuming you're using Access 2007, choose the Create option from the menu.
2. Now click the Query Design button highlighted in Figure 18.1.

3. Select the tables you want to include in your query from the Show Table dialog box, as shown in Figure 18.2. For this example, select the Employees table and click Add.

FIGURE 18.2   The Show Table dialog box enables you to select the tables you want to include in your query.

4. Click Close to close the Show Table dialog box.

5. After your table is added to the designer, you are free to select the fields to include in the statement, the table those fields reside in, how to sort the records, and various criteria to include. For this example, select Employees.* from the Field drop-down list, as shown in Figure 18.3.

NOTE

If you want to limit your query to two fields rather than the whole table, you can select one field from the Field drop-down list, move over to the right column, and select a different field.

6. After your query has been established, select SQL View from the View menu.

That's it! Figure 18.4 shows the resulting query in the SQL View window.

You're now free to save your query for later use. Save your query with a name that is relevant to what it performs by choosing File, Save As.

TIP

So far, you've learned how to write queries on your own. But how does Dreamweaver use those queries to extract data from the database? For the most part, you can construct your queries in Access, copy the SQL code, and then paste it into the Recordset dialog (covered in the next chapter). Even better, Dreamweaver allows you to use saved queries directly from Dreamweaver. For instance, if you wanted to create a complex join, you could create the statement in Access, save the query, and then use the query from Dreamweaver. More on this in the next few chapters.

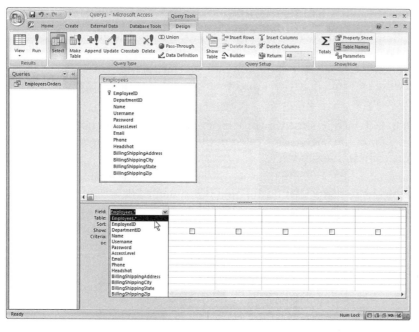

FIGURE 18.3   You can select which fields to include in your query. For our purposes, we want all employees, so we choose Employees.*.

FIGURE 18.4   SQL View presents the SQL code you can copy and paste into your application code.

Generating Queries with Relationships

In the previous section, we used the Query Editor to construct a simple query. Obviously, the resulting SQL code would have been just as easy to write by hand. The true power of the Query Editor is that it can generate those complex statements with relationships that everyone hates to write by hand. To create a slightly more complex query that uses a relationship, follow these steps:

1. If you're still in SQL View, choose Design View from the View menu now. Right-click in the Design view of the query you created in the preceding section. Select Show Table from the context menu.

2. From the Show Table dialog box that opens, select the CreditCards table and click Add. Notice the one-to-many relationship that is maintained between the two tables.

3. In the second column, select CreditCards.*. Figure 18.5 shows the view you should be seeing.

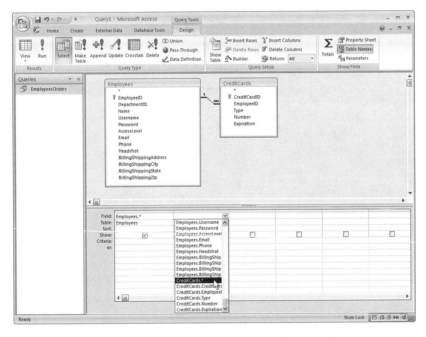

FIGURE 18.5   Select CreditCards.* to show all credit card fields.

4. Select View, SQL View. Figure 18.6 shows the query that is generated, complete with the INNER JOIN.

Figure 18.7 shows the datasheet view available from the View menu. Notice that the query includes all fields from both the Employees and the CreditCards tables.

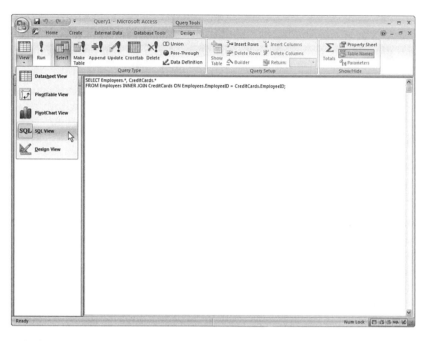

FIGURE 18.6   Access displays the complex **INNER JOIN** in its SQL View.

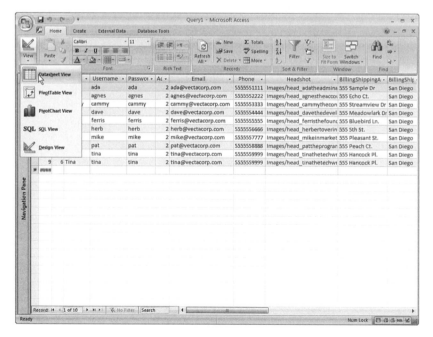

FIGURE 18.7   Access displays the results of joining two tables.

This is just the tip of the iceberg! We've used Access's Query Designer to create simple `SELECT` and `INNER JOIN` statements that would require very little effort to build by hand. As your applications grow in size and complexity, the Query Designer will prove invaluable as it will allow you to build much more complex statements with very little effort.

Remember, Access's Query Designer isn't the only tool available for creating queries visually. Views, which are SQL Server's version of queries, can be handled visually within Management Studio Express. Furthermore, if you're using MySQL, MySQL Query Browser allows you to visually create queries using a similar approach to Access's Query Designer.

Summary

Data access is a crucial component to any application, and SQL provides the bridge and communication to that data. As you have seen, SQL not only returns simple results from individual tables, but it also can produce complex data queries complete with filtering, sorting, expressions, and even nested statements. In the next chapter, you'll begin putting the knowledge you've gained about databases and the language that connects those databases together into a web application.

CHAPTER 19

Working with Dynamic Data

IN THIS CHAPTER

▶ Connecting to a Data Source

▶ Building the Vecta Corp Employee Store

Throughout the book you've learned about numerous important introductory-level concepts as they relate to web application development. First, you learned about dynamic web pages and web applications. Next, you learned how to define a site and set up necessary testing server parameters so that you can use technologies such as ASP, ColdFusion, and PHP in Dreamweaver. Then you saw how databases such as Access, SQL Server 2005 Express Edition, and MySQL can serve as a backbone for data in your organization. You learned about the various databases, what tables, columns, and rows are, and how to take existing databases and attach/restore them in your database management system for use within Dreamweaver. What you haven't learned to this point is how to take all those foundation-level concepts and bring them together using Dreamweaver to create a truly dynamic database-driven page. That's where this chapter comes in.

In this chapter, we'll take all the concepts you've learned up to this point and put them into practice. You'll see how to connect Dreamweaver to your specific database using DSN and DSN-less connections. Next you'll learn about extracting data from the database to create the View Catalog page for the Vecta Corp employee store. As we progress, you'll learn about the many features exposed in the Application panel group to help you interact with your dynamic web pages easily in Dreamweaver. Starting to get excited? Good! This is where the previous 18 chapters begin to come together to form web applications.

As you've done with the rest of the chapters in this book, you can work with the examples in this chapter by downloading the files from the book's website. Remember, you'll

want to save the files for Chapter 19 (not the folder) in the
`C:\Inetpub\wwwroot\VectaCorp<technology>` (IIS), `C:\xampp\htdocs\VectaCorpPHP`
(XAMPP), `/Applications/MAMP/htdocs/VectaCorpPHP` (MAMP), or
`C:\ColdFusion8\wwwroot\VectaCorpCFM` (ColdFusion) directories.

Connecting to a Data Source

The first step in working with dynamic data in Dreamweaver is to properly define a
website. This important step establishes a connection between Dreamweaver and the files
on your computer. Aside from that, however, it also allows you to tell Dreamweaver what
server-side technology you plan to use for the defined site. This process is important
because Dreamweaver must configure its interface according to the server-side technology
you pick.

The second step in working with dynamic data is to establish a connection between
Dreamweaver and your data source. Numerous methods exist for connecting your web
applications to your data sources (in Dreamweaver), including the following:

▶ DSN Connection (supports Access, SQL Server 2005 Express Edition, and MySQL via
   ASP)

▶ DSN Connection via RDS (specifically for ColdFusion)

▶ Custom Connection String/DSN-less Connection

▶ OLE DB Connection (specifically for ASP.NET, which is no longer supported in
   Dreamweaver but can be used by other server models such as ASP, as well)

▶ MySQL Connection (specifically for PHP)

As you can see, numerous methods exist for connecting your web applications to your
data sources. The server-side technology you plan to implement in conjunction with the
data source you plan to employ will guide the method you'll use to connect with. In
general, there's no preferred method. The method that works best for you is the route you
should ultimately take. To help you make the decision, I've outlined each connection
method in the next few sections.

Connecting to a Data Source Using a DSN

As mentioned in Chapter 15, "Introduction to Web Applications," to communicate with
database data, a bridge of communication must be established between the web application in Dreamweaver and the actual data source. This bridge of communication is handled
through a Data Source Name (DSN).

To understand the concept of DSN is to understand how applications connect to database
data using the web server's operating system. As you learned in Chapter 15, at this foundation level is Open DataBase Connectivity (ODBC), a standard database access method
developed by the SQL Access group in 1992. The goal of ODBC is to make it possible to
access any data from any application, regardless of which database management system is
handling the data. ODBC manages this by inserting a middle layer, called a *database driver*,

between an application and the database. This layer translates the application's data queries into commands that the database understands. For this to work, both the application and the database must be ODBC-compliant; that is, the application must be capable of issuing ODBC commands, and the database must be capable of responding to them.

DSNs provide connectivity to a database through the ODBC driver. The DSN contains a database name, directory, database driver, UserID, password, and other information. After you create a DSN for a particular database, you can use the DSN in an application to call information from the database.

NOTE

For the most part, ODBC drivers that connect web applications to Access and SQL Server come preinstalled with the operating system, so there's nothing to download. However, if you plan to use MySQL, you'll need to download the latest ODBC 5.1 driver. The driver, titled Connector/ODBC 5.1, can be found along with the other MySQL downloads at dev.mysql.com/downloads/index.html. Of course, if you're using XAMPP or MAMP, these drivers come preinstalled, and there's nothing further that you'll need to download.

A disadvantage to using DSNs is that they're generally less efficient than other standards when connecting to data sources. However, they are probably more than adequate for low-to-moderate production servers. If you're developing a more robust application, you might want to consider some of the other methods discussed later in this chapter. If you plan to develop a web application with PHP, for instance, note that these technologies do not directly support DSNs; you must use an alternative connection standard (such as OLE DB), also discussed later in this chapter.

DSNs, however, are great to use, especially in the development phase of the application. On a Windows machine, DSNs are managed though the ODBC Data Source Administrator and support the creation of DSNs for Access and SQL Server 2005 Express Edition databases as well as MySQL databases (after the driver has been installed). In the next three sections, you'll learn how to create a DSN for the three supported databases in this book. Let's begin.

NOTE

On a Mac, DSNs are managed through the ODBC Administrator, available by choosing Go, Utilities, ODBC Administrator. Although we won't be walking through the process of defining a DSN on a Mac in this chapter, the functionality exposed by the Windows-based ODBC Data Source Administrator and the Mac-based ODBC Administrator is relatively similar. Concepts discussed for one apply to the other.

Defining a DSN to an Access Database

To create a DSN that connects to an Access database, follow these steps:

1. Choose Start, Settings, Control Panel.

19

2. Inside the Control Panel folder, double-click the Administrative Tools folder to open it.

3. Inside the Administrative Tools folder, double-click the Data Sources (ODBC) icon to launch the ODBC Data Source Administrator dialog box.

4. In the ODBC Data Source Administrator dialog box, click the System DSN tab. The System DSN tab lists all DSNs previously configured on your system.

5. Click the Add button on the System DSN tab to open the Create New Data Source dialog box, as shown in Figure 19.1.

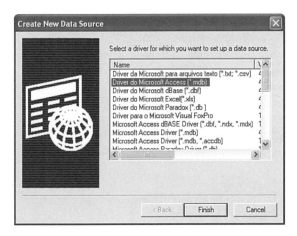

FIGURE 19.1   The Create New Data Source dialog box provides the options for choosing the appropriate driver for the database to which the data source will point.

NOTE

File, System, and User DSNs all contain the same information about the connection. The major difference between the three is that File DSNs store the information in a file on disk. Although System and User DSNs store the information in the Registry, System DSNs are available to all users on that system box and User DSNs are available only to the user who created them.

---

6. In the Create New Data Source dialog box, choose from the list of drivers that match the database with which you are working. Because we're working with Access in this section, choose the Driver do Microsoft Access [*.mdb] driver. Then click the Finish button to exit the Create New Data Source dialog box and launch the ODBC Microsoft Access Setup dialog box.

7. Specify the name **VectaCorpAccessDSN** as the name for the data source in the Data Source Name text box. Enter a description for the data source, if you want one, in the Description text box.

8. You'll have to point the DSN to the path of your database. Assuming that you're working with ASP, click the Select button on the Database pane. The Select Database

dialog box appears. Browse to the drive and folder that contains the Access database (for our project, it's in `C:\Inetpub\wwwroot\VectaCorpASP\Database`), select the `VectaCorp.mdb` file, and click OK.

9. Now that the database has been selected, you can optionally provide a username and password to access the database by clicking the Advanced button. Doing so launches the Set Advanced Options dialog box. In an effort to keep our example simple, I won't set a username and password at this time. However, when your application goes live, usernames and passwords are parameters you'll no doubt want to configure. The configured ODBC Microsoft Access Setup dialog box will resemble Figure 19.2.

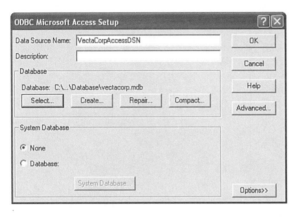

FIGURE 19.2   In the ODBC setup dialog box, you have the option to provide a name, description, and path to the data source.

10. When you finish the ODBC Microsoft Access setup, click OK to exit and return to the ODBC Data Source Administrator dialog box. The new DSN, VectaCorpAccessDSN, appears in the list.

Congratulations! You now have established a connection to an Access database. The next step is to connect to the newly created DSN through Dreamweaver. Before we get ahead of ourselves, however, let's review some of the other methods of establishing connections to databases.

Defining a DSN to a SQL Server 2005 Express Edition Database

To create a DSN that connects to a SQL Server 2005 Express Edition database, follow these steps:

1. Choose Start, Settings, Control Panel. The Control Panel appears.

2. Inside the Control Panel folder, double-click the Administrative Tools folder to open it.

3. Inside the Administrative Tools folder, double-click the Data Sources (ODBC) icon to launch the ODBC Data Source Administrator dialog box.

4. In the ODBC Data Source Administrator dialog box, click the System DSN tab.

5. Click the Add button on the System DSN tab to open the Create New Data Source dialog box.

6. In the Create New Data Source dialog box, choose from the list of drivers that match the database with which you are working. Because we're working with a SQL Server 2005 Express Edition database in this section, choose the SQL Server driver located at the bottom of the list. Then click the Finish button to exit the Create New Data Source dialog box and launch the Create a New Data Source to SQL Server dialog box, as shown in Figure 19.3.

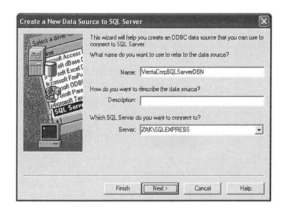

FIGURE 19.3   The Create a New Data Source to SQL Server dialog box allows you to define properties that establish a DSN connection to a SQL server.

7. Specify the name **VectaCorpSQLServerDSN** as the name for the data source in the Name text box. Enter a description for the data source, if you want, in the Description text box.

8. Point the DSN to the path of the SQL Server 2005 Express Edition instance. If the instance doesn't appear in the list, enter the path to the server (mine is ZAK\SQLEXPRESS, but yours will differ depending on the name of your computer) and click Next.

9. Now that the SQL Server 2005 Express Edition server has been defined, you'll need to specify the credentials you use to connect to the database. To do this, select the With SQL Server Authentication Using a Login ID and Password Entered by the User option button and enter the login ID (**sa**) and password (**vecta**) in the Login ID and Password text boxes, respectively. Click Next.

10. The next screen allows you to define which database this DSN should default to. Because we're working with the Vectacorp database, enable the Change the Default Database To check box and select the Vectacorp option from the drop-down menu. Click Next.

11. Click Finish to exit the Create a New Data Source to SQL Server dialog box. Before you exit, the ODBC Microsoft SQL Server Setup dialog appears with a breakdown of selected options. Click the Test Data Source button to test the connection to the database. When

you've finished, click OK to close the dialog box and return to the System DSN tab of the ODBC Data Source Administrator dialog box. The new DSN, VectaCorpSQLServerDSN, appears in the list.

Congratulations! You have successfully established a connection to a SQL Server 2005 Express Edition database. The next step is to connect to the newly created DSN through Dreamweaver. Before we get ahead of ourselves, however, let's review the final method for connecting to a data source using a DSN.

Defining a DSN to a MySQL Database (IIS Users Only)

To create a DSN that connects to a MySQL database, you will need to first install the appropriate ODBC driver, available from the MySQL website. To download the driver, browse to dev.mysql.com/downloads/index.html. Select the Connector/ODBC 5.1 link located under the Drivers and Connectors section and just under the Connector/ODBC subheading. Click the Windows link. Select the Download link to begin the download. After the MSI package has been downloaded, double-click it to install. Accept all the defaults as you progress through the installation wizard until the installation finishes.

> **NOTE**
>
> Remember, if you're using XAMPP or MAMP, you don't have to do any of this. You won't be relying on ODBC to connect to your MySQL database. Instead, you'll be relying on the more flexible OLE DB, which is automatically configured for you when you install XAMPP and MAMP.

After the ODBC driver has been installed, you can follow these steps to establish a DSN that connects to a MySQL database:

1. Choose Start, Settings, Control Panel. The Control Panel appears.

2. Inside the Control Panel folder, double-click the Administrative Tools folder to open it.

3. Inside the Administrative Tools folder, double-click the Data Sources (ODBC) icon to launch the ODBC Data Source Administrator dialog box.

4. In the ODBC Data Source Administrator dialog box, click the System DSN tab.

5. Click the Add button on the System DSN tab to open the Create New Data Source dialog box.

6. In the Create New Data Source dialog box, choose from the list of drivers that match the database with which you are working. Because we're working with a MySQL database in this section, choose the MySQL ODBC 5.1 Driver located near the bottom of the list. Then click the Finish button to exit the Create New Data Source dialog box and launch the Connector/ODBC Data Source Configuration dialog box.

7. Specify the name **VectaCorpMySQLDSN** as the name for the data source in the Data Source Name text box. Enter a description for the data source, if you want one, in the Description text box.

8. Point the DSN to the path of the MySQL instance. You can do this by entering **localhost** in the Server text box.

9. Now that the MySQL server has been defined, you'll need to specify the credentials you use to connect to the database. Type **root** into the User text box.

10. Select the Vectacorp option from the Database drop-down menu. The fully configured dialog box will resemble Figure 19.4.

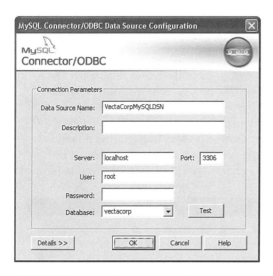

FIGURE 19.4   The Connector/ODBC dialog box allows you to create a DSN for a MySQL database.

11. If you'd like, click the Test button to test the connection between the DSN and the database. If everything is successful, click the OK button to exit the Connector/ODBC dialog and return to the ODBC Data Source Administrator dialog box, where you'll see the new data source name VectaCorpMySQLDSN appear in the list.

Congratulations! You have successfully established a connection to a MySQL database. The next step is to connect to the newly created DSN through Dreamweaver. Before you make the switch to Dreamweaver, however, close the ODBC Data Source Administrator dialog box by clicking OK.

Connecting an ASP Web Application to a DSN

One of the most feature-rich and flexible server-side technologies that Dreamweaver supports is ASP. Although the technology is in its waning days in terms of industry use and support, the integration between the technology and Dreamweaver has never been stronger. This section guides you through connecting a site defined using the ASP server model to either an Access, SQL Server 2005 Express Edition, or MySQL database using a DSN. By following these steps, you can establish a connection with the DSN:

1. If you haven't done so already, open Dreamweaver and choose the VectaCorpASP defined site from the Site list in the Files panel.

2. Open the employeestore.asp page by double-clicking it in the Files list.

3. With Dreamweaver open, open the Application panel group by choosing Window, Databases (see Figure 19.5).

FIGURE 19.5   The Databases panel enables you to configure the connection between Dreamweaver and the DSN.

4. In the Databases panel, click the Add (+) button to access the drop-down menu and choose Data Source Name (DSN) to launch the Data Source Name dialog box.

5. First, determine whether you're using the DSN on the testing server or on your local machine (as specified by the option buttons at the bottom of the dialog box). If you're using the DSN on the testing server, choose the Dreamweaver Should Connect Using DSN On Testing Server option. Because we know that our local machine is acting as the testing server, choose the Using Local DSN option.

6. Enter a name for the connection. We'll name ours **connVectaCorp**, prefixing the VectaCorp name with conn. This prefix provides a decent identification for the Vecta Corp connection; we always know that this name represents the connection string and not the database name or site definition.

7. From the Data Source Name (DSN) drop-down menu, choose the DSN VectaCorpAccessDSN.

TIP

Notice the Define button that appears next to the Data Source Name (DSN) menu. Click this button to launch the ODBC Data Source Administrator directly from Dreamweaver. This allows you to quickly create and manage DSNs without having to manually browse to the Administrator through the operating system.

TIP

If you were using SQL Server 2005 Express Edition or MySQL in conjunction with ASP, you'd select the appropriate DSN from the list. For simplicity's sake, we'll limit our selection to the VectaCorpAccessDSN.

8. If the database you choose (such as SQL Server 2005 Express Edition or MySQL) requires username or password authentication, enter those values into their respective text boxes. The configured dialog box will resemble Figure 19.6.

19

FIGURE 19.6   The Data Source Name dialog box offers the option to configure the connection to the DSN.

NOTE

As you saw within the DSN Administrator, SQL Server 2005 Express Edition and MySQL allow you to define the default schema/catalog that the web application will use. In our case, we defined the vectacorp database as the default schema/catalog to use within the DSN setup. If you prefer to define that in the connection string, click the Advanced button and enter the necessary schema/catalog into the respective text boxes.

---

9. To make sure that your connection is established properly, click the Test button. This action launches an alert message specifying that the connection was made successfully. If the connection was not made successfully, double-check the naming convention of the DSN and be sure that the database file wasn't moved to a different directory (if using Access) or that the database server is running (if using SQL Server 2005 Express Edition or MySQL). You might also receive an error if your login credentials are invalid (SQL Server 2005/MySQL).

10. After you've made a successful connection, click the OK button to close the Data Source Name (DSN) dialog box. The new connection will be available in the Databases panel.

As you can see, establishing communication between the DSN and Dreamweaver is pretty straightforward. In the Databases panel, you can expand the Tables node in the connVectaCorp tree to see a visual representation of the database tables in Dreamweaver. As we progress through the chapter, I'll show you how you can use information made available in this panel group to create dynamic sites.

NOTE

After you've established a successful connection to your DSN, Dreamweaver creates a file within a Connections folder in your defined site. The file, named after the connection name, contains valid ASP code for connecting to your DSN. *Do not remove this file* as it will be included in every dynamic page in your defined site.

Custom Connection Strings with ASP

When developing web applications with DSNs, one of the biggest hassles can be getting the system administrator of the web server to configure the DSN if you don't have access to that area of the server. If you can't get your DSN configured, your application is crippled and useless.

Often, developers like to bypass such ordeals by creating a DSN-less connection. With a DSN-less connection, not only are you freed from the hassles of relying on a system administrator, but you're also free to customize the connection string further than what you can do with the basics provided by DSNs.

A DSN-less connection uses the same drivers as its DSN counterpart; however, the DSN-less connection does not rely on a defined Data Source Name within the ODBC Data Source Administrator dialog box. Instead, you physically write the connection string that your dynamic web pages will use to connect to the database directly. Essentially, you're dropping the DSN "middle man" from the loop.

The syntax for configuring a DSN-less connection varies a bit from database to database, but all have the same five essential parts:

- ▶ **Driver**—The proper name for the driver can be found at the manufacturer's website or locally in your machine's ODBC Administrator dialog box.

- ▶ **Path to Data Source**—Depending on the database you are using, you usually will specify the entire path to the database. However, some databases provide an exception, such as SQL Server and Oracle. The parameter for these databases appears in two parts: an area for both the server address and the database or catalog name.

- ▶ **Username**—If a username is required by the data source, you must provide it in the string.

- ▶ **Password**—If a password is required by the data source, you must provide it in the string.

- ▶ **Provider**—This is an optional entry, but it refers to the mechanics of the ODBC/OLE DB driver. (The provider for ODBC is always MSDASQL.) Because these two elements go hand in hand, if you omit the provider, the connection string will still work.

Because we are working with an Access database called `vectacorp.mdb`, you can easily make a DSN-less connection using a custom string that resembles the following:

```
"Driver={Microsoft Access Driver (*.mdb)};
Dbq=C:\Inetpub\wwwroot\VectaCorpASP\Database\vectacorp.mdb;"
```

As you can see from the connection string, the Provider sets the driver to use the `Dbq` parameter and specifies the path to the database file. If we were making use of a username and password, we would add and set those parameters as well. The benefit to writing the connection string becomes obvious. Not only is it simple and direct, but if we ever needed to modify the connection string (to use SQL Server 2005 Express Edition instead of Access, for example), we simply change a few parameters rather than opening the ODBC

Administrator dialog box and making the change through a long and drawn out wizard. To create a DSN-less connection in Dreamweaver, follow these steps:

1. Be sure that the Databases panel is open by choosing Window, Databases.

2. In the Databases panel, click the Remove (–) button to remove the existing connVectaCorp DSN reference.

3. Click the Add (+) button and choose the Custom Connection String option from the menu. This action launches the Custom Connection String dialog box.

4. Enter the name **connVectaCorp** in the Connection name text box.

5. Type the previously outlined connection (**Driver={Microsoft Access Driver (*.mdb)}; Dbq=C:\Inetpub\wwwroot\VectaCorpASP\Database\vectacorp.mdb;**) into the Connection String text box.

6. Select the Using Driver on This Machine option button. The configured dialog box will resemble Figure 19.7.

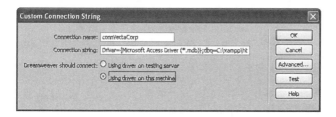

FIGURE 19.7   The Custom Connection String dialog box offers options for defining a custom connection string.

7. To make sure your connection was set up properly, click the Test button. This action should return an alert message saying that the connection was made successfully.

8. Click OK to exit the Custom Connection String dialog box.

Notice that the connection is now available in the Databases panel. If you expand the connVectaCorp reference, the Tables are outlined as they were when a DSN was used.

Again, the method you decide to use is up to you. Many advanced users prefer the custom connection string approach because it provides much more flexibility in the parameters outlined in the connection string. For more information on connection strings—including syntax for Access, SQL Server 2005, MySQL, and more—visit www.connectionstrings.com.

Connecting a ColdFusion Web Application to a DSN Using RDS

Heavily integrated into the Dreamweaver framework is functionality that allows you to connect to a DSN with ColdFusion. Rather than outlining a simple Data Source Name (DSN) dialog box as the ASP model does, Dreamweaver, under the ColdFusion model, allows direct integration with the ColdFusion Administrator. You can establish a connection with the DSN by following these steps:

1. If you haven't done so already, open Dreamweaver and choose the VectaCorpCFM defined site from the Site list in the Files panel.

2. Open the `employeestore.cfm` page by double-clicking it in the Files list.

3. With Dreamweaver open, open the Application panel by choosing Window, Databases.

4. Notice that the Add (+) button doesn't appear in the Databases panel. Instead, Dreamweaver relies on the RDS login to directly log in and retrieve available Data Source Names from the ColdFusion Administrator. Because we haven't defined any Data Source Names in the ColdFusion Administrator yet, you'll see a five-step list allowing you to modify parameters required for setting up the testing server, establishing an RDS password, and modifying Data Source Names, similar to Figure 19.8.

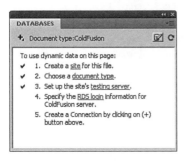

FIGURE 19.8   Because we haven't defined any data sources yet, Dreamweaver outlines a five-step list allowing us to modify parameters required for connecting to Data Source Names in the ColdFusion Administrator.

5. In Chapter 16, "Working with Server-Side Technologies," we established the RDS password to use for connecting Dreamweaver to the ColdFusion Administrator. This is where that password will come in handy. By simply clicking the RDS Login link for step 4, you can have Dreamweaver automatically connect to the ColdFusion Administrator, which in turn is responsible for managing DSNs. Go ahead and click the link for step 4 now. The login dialog box for the ColdFusion Administrator appears. Enter your password (**vecta**) and click Login. You'll immediately be shown a list of built-in sample databases that are included with the ColdFusion development installation.

6. To create a DSN within ColdFusion Administrator (and have it appear within this panel), click the Modify Data Sources Icon, located second from the right in the upper-right corner of the Databases panel. The login web page appears. Again, enter your password (**vecta**) and click the Login button to be redirected to the Data Sources page.

7. To set up a DSN, begin by entering the name **connVectaCorp** in the Data Source Name text box.

8. Select the database driver that you plan to connect the DSN to by selecting the appropriate option from the Driver drop-down menu. For simplicity's sake, choose the Microsoft Access with Unicode option. You should choose the Microsoft SQL Server option if you're working with SQL Server 2005 Express Edition or the MySQL (3)/MySQL 4/5) option if you're working with it. Click the Add button. You'll immediately be redirected to the Data Source configuration page.

8. Enter the path `C:\ColdFusion8\wwwroot\VectaCorpCFM\Database\vectacorp.mdb` into the Database File text box. Click Submit to create the new DSN. Notice that the new connVectaCorp DSN appears in the Connected Data Sources list, similar to Figure 19.9.

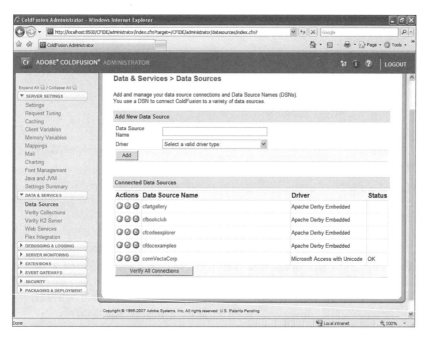

FIGURE 19.9   The new connVectaCorp DSN appears in the Connected Data Sources list.

9. To verify the connection between the DSN and the database, click the Verify All Connections button. If the connection is successful, the word *OK* appears in the Status column.

10. After you've made a successful connection, close the ColdFusion Administrator.

11. In Dreamweaver, click the Refresh button (first icon from the right in the Databases panel). Immediately, Dreamweaver recognizes the new DSN and lists it in the Databases panel, as shown in Figure 19.10.

FIGURE 19.10   The connVectaCorp DSN appears in the Databases list. Expand the tree to see the list of tables within the database.

As you can see, establishing communication between the DSN and Dreamweaver is pretty straightforward. You can expand the Tables node in the connVectaCorp tree to see a visual representation of the database tables in Dreamweaver. As we progress through the chapter, I'll show you how you can use information made available in this panel group to create dynamic sites.

Connecting a PHP Web Application to a MySQL Database

Although the ASP and ColdFusion server models support multiple methods for connecting to data sources, the PHP server model supports only one: a MySQL connection. To create a connection with a MySQL database in Dreamweaver, follow these steps:

1. If you haven't done so already, switch to the defined VectaCorpPHP site and immediately open the `employeestore.php` file.
2. Make sure that the Databases panel is open by choosing Window, Databases.
3. Click the Add (+) button in the Databases panel and choose the MySQL Connection option. The MySQL Connection dialog box appears, similar to Figure 19.11.

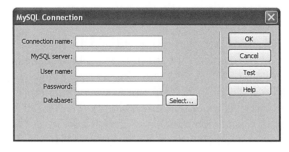

FIGURE 19.11   Complete the requested information in the MySQL Connection dialog box to establish a connection with a MySQL database.

19

4. Enter the name **connVectaCorp** into the Connection Name text box.

5. Enter the IP address or hostname of your MySQL server into the MySQL server text box. In most cases, this value is **localhost**.

6. Specify the database username in the Username text field. If you went with the default installation, the value will be **root**.

7. Specify the database password (**vecta**) in the Password text field. For XAMPP users, leave this value blank.

8. Click the Select button located to the right of the Database text box. This action launches the Select Database dialog box, similar to Figure 19.12; the dialog box is prepopulated with a list of databases housed within your MySQL database instance.

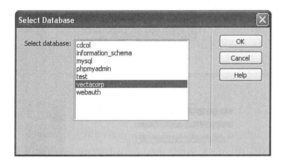

FIGURE 19.12   Select the Vecta Corp database from the Select Database dialog box.

9. Select the Vectacorp database and click OK.

10. To make sure that the connection was properly configured, click the Test button. Dreamweaver opens an alert dialog box indicating whether the connection was made successfully. If you're using XAMPP and you didn't configure a password (we didn't cover it), you'll receive a message alerting you that it is not a good idea to publish a database-driven site to a production server without a password. Simply click OK to bypass the dialog box.

11. Click OK to exit the MySQL Connection dialog box. When you return to the Databases panel, notice that the new connection is available in the list in the Databases panel.

Note that you can expand the Tables node in the connVectaCorp tree to see a visual representation of the database tables in Dreamweaver. As we progress through the chapter, I'll show you how you can use information made available in this panel group to create dynamic sites.

After you've established a successful connection to your MySQL database, Dreamweaver creates a file in a Connections folder in your defined site. The file, named after the connection name and with the PHP extension, contains valid PHP code for connecting to your MySQL database. *Do not remove this file* because it will be included in every dynamic page in your defined site.

Building the Vecta Corp Employee Store

Chances are you're wondering why we're not covering the creation of the Vecta Corp Employee Store in different sections, one for each server model: ASP, ColdFusion, and PHP. The answer to this question is simple; Dreamweaver's core functionality is so similar across the three server models that individual sections for each server-side technology aren't warranted. Instead, we'll build our dynamic web pages using the ASP server model, pointing out the small differences and additions for the other two server models along the way.

In the coming sections, you'll learn to build the dynamic employee store web page using ASP, ColdFusion, or PHP. As the chapter unfolds, you'll learn about the various Dreamweaver features that make working with database data a snap. Specifically, you'll learn about the following concepts:

▶ Recordsets

▶ Paging

▶ Dynamic text

▶ Region repeaters

▶ Showing specific regions (conditionals)

By the end of this chapter, you'll have a fully functional employee store web page that pulls product information directly from a database and displays it for users to purchase. Let's get started.

Creating the EmployeeStore Page

The EmployeeStore page of the Vecta Corp intranet site is the heart of the Vecta Corp web application. After all, this is where Vecta Corp employees come to buy flair and tchotchkes (marketing lingo for lame and unusable stuff) to show off their Vecta Corp pride to co-workers, friends, and family. The idea is that employees will visit the page, and the page will pull information from the EmployeeStore table contained in the vectacorp database and present items to the users for purchase. The users can then click an item, add it to their carts, and complete their purchase using a convenient checkout button. All this functionality will be outlined in time. For now, let's review the basic structure of our vectacorp database—specifically, the EmployeeStore table. As Figure 19.13 indicates, we can expand the EmployeeStore table directly from the Databases panel (by clicking the small (+) icon) to reveal the field names and the data types associated with each field.

FIGURE 19.13   The EmployeeStore table is the central source of data for the EmployeeStore web page.

Table 19.1 outlines the fields in the database table, including the data types used by Dreamweaver.

TABLE 19.1   Fields in the EmployeeStore Database Table

Field Name	Data Type	Description
ItemID	Numeric	The unique identifier for each item in the EmployeeStore table. Whenever we make updates, modifications, or remove items from the EmployeeStore table, this value serves as a base point.
ItemName	WChar	A generic name for each item in the table.
ItemDescription	WChar	A marketing description about the item for sale.
ImageURL	WChar	A path to the image in the Images directory of our defined site. Rather than physically storing the image in the database, we store the image on the file system and reference that image by storing the path in the database. This effectively reduces database file size at the expense of disk space.

TABLE 19.1   Fields in the EmployeeStore Database Table

Field Name	Data Type	Description
Cost	Numeric	A currency value that represents the cost of the item for sale.
Quantity	Integer	A numeric value indicating how many of a specific item are left in stock.

Now that you've seen the database structure, you are ready to begin extracting data from it. Let's build that functionality now.

Creating a Recordset

By now you might be curious about how data in your database can be extracted into your application. Sure, you've learned a lot about SQL and are familiar with the commands to retrieve the information, but now what? SQL alone does not provide enough flexibility to read from the database and write that data to the application; there's still a piece of the puzzle missing. That piece is the recordset.

Recordsets act as an intermediary virtual table between the database and the application. After you write SQL commands to ask questions of the database (known as a *query*), the information retrieved is then stored in a recordset. The programming logic iterates through the recordset and ultimately presents the data to the browser in a structured way. Figure 19.14 illustrates this point.

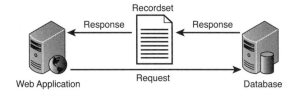

FIGURE 19.14   The application makes a call to the database, which then returns data in the form of a recordset.

Remember that the questions asked of the database are made in the form of queries, and queries are a process that usually involve SQL to structure how the question will be asked. After the question (query) has been asked, the data is returned into a virtual table or recordset. The recordset is then browsed through by the application logic and presented to the user in a structured HTML document.

To demonstrate this point, you can use Dreamweaver to create a simple recordset that will query the EmployeeStore table. To create a recordset, follow these steps:

1. With the Application panel group open, switch to the Bindings tab and click the Add (+) button. Select Recordset (Query) from the list that appears when you click the Add (+) button. The Recordset dialog box appears.

2. In the Name text box, type the name **rsEmployeeStore**.

3. Select the connVectaCorp option from the Connection drop-down menu. If the name of your connection does not appear in the drop-down menu, it means that you haven't yet defined the connection. Review the first part of this chapter for information on creating a connection. Selecting the connection option from the list reveals a set of tables in the Table drop-down list. These are the database tables that exist in the vectacorp database to which you've just connected.

NOTE

If you're using ColdFusion, make note of the User Name and Password text boxes. If your DSN requires authentication before connecting to the data source, enter those credentials here.

---

4. Pick the table in the Table menu for which you want to create a recordset. In our case, choose the EmployeeStore option.

5. You'll have the opportunity to choose all or selected fields from the database table. For the sake of demonstration, keep the All option button selected.

6. Optionally, you can filter and sort the data based on specific values. More on this later. For now, the configured Recordset dialog box should resemble Figure 19.15.

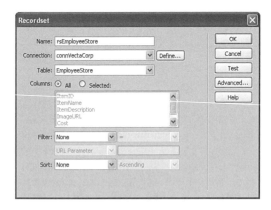

FIGURE 19.15   Fill out all the information in the Recordset dialog box.

7. Click the Test button to see a sample of the results that will be returned. Figure 19.16 shows the returned recordset with all the data from the EmployeeStore table. Now that you know that the recordset works, click OK.

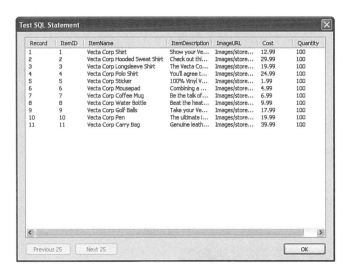

FIGURE 19.16   The test results show the recordset with populated data.

NOTE

The ColdFusion model optionally supports connections using ColdFusion Components (CFCs). Although we will discuss CFCs in Chapter 23, "Working with Web Services and ColdFusion Components," for now just be aware that the option for connecting to a DSN using a CFC is made available by clicking the CFC Query button.

8. Click OK to close the Recordset dialog box. As you'll see, the new Recordset is listed in the Bindings panel.

Note that by selecting the Bindings tab and then expanding the recordset, you can view the field names contained within the recordset (more on this later).

Creating an Advanced Recordset

Simple recordsets can serve your needs well if you are performing simple queries of all or certain fields in a single database table. But what if you wanted to merge two or more tables into one recordset? Unfortunately, the simple method (covered in the previous section) wouldn't do. Although creating advanced recordsets can become very complex, the trade-off is flexibility, scalability, and power.

Rather than creating multiple recordsets in which you store each and every table, you can join two or more tables into one recordset based on a common value. Take the EmployeeStore and Orders tables as examples. Suppose that you were working in the Shipping and Receiving department and your job was to print out a list of all orders for a

19

specific day. You would need to create a recordset that merged the EmployeeStore and Orders tables into one virtual table. Furthermore, you'd also need to include the Employees table because all orders are related not only by products in the EmployeeStore table, but also by the employee from the Employees table. This complex recordset can't be constructed using the Simple recordset view (the basic Recordset dialog). Instead, you'd have to use the Advanced view.

To create a recordset using the Advanced view, follow these steps:

1. In the Bindings panel, choose the Recordset (Query) option from the Add (+) menu. The Recordset dialog box opens.

2. Click the Advanced button. Figure 19.17 shows that the dialog box is relatively similar in design to the Simple view, except that you can enter a SQL query manually rather than allowing Dreamweaver to create it for you.

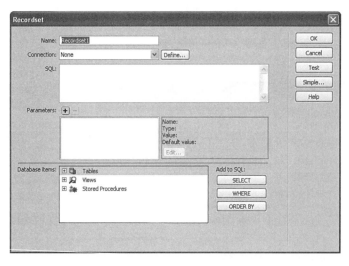

FIGURE 19.17   The Advanced Recordset dialog box enables you to manually type the SQL code, allowing for greater flexibility.

TIP

The Advanced Recordset dialog box also provides limited visual control over the fields you want to include in your query. The Database Items list contains the same tree node that the Databases panel outlines. From this list, you can choose specific tables and then click the SELECT, WHERE, or ORDER BY buttons to include the specific fields in the SQL statement in the SQL multiline text box.

3. If you remember the lengthy code structure for creating SQL joins, begin typing. If you're like me and like to rely on programs to do the work for you, you're in luck.

Access comes installed with a built-in Query Editor. Alternatively, if you're relying on a SQL Server database, open Management Studio and begin a new View. If you're relying on a MySQL database, open MySQL Query Browser and begin a new query. Because we're using Access, go ahead and open the `vectacorp.mdb` file now to launch Access. Assuming you're using Office 2007, choose Create, Query Design to open the Query Editor in Access.

4. Immediately the Show Tables dialog box appears, enabling you to select the tables to include within your query. Select the Employees, Orders, and EmployeeStore tables by holding down the Ctrl key and selecting each table one by one. Click the Add button to close the Show Table dialog box and have your tables added to the Query Editor, as shown in Figure 19.18.

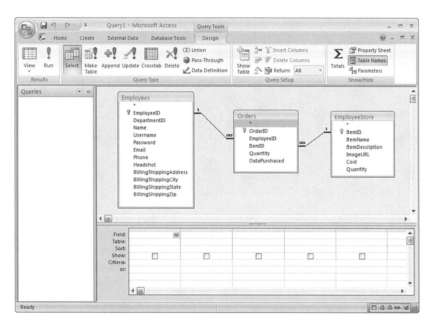

FIGURE 19.18   Add the Employees, Orders, and EmployeeStore tables to the Query Editor in Access.

5. From the drop-down menus that appear next the Field column in the grid, select the `Employees.Name`, `Employees.BillingShippingAddress`, `Employees.BillingShippingCity`, `Employees.BillingShippingState`, `Employees.BillingShippingZip`, `Orders.Quantity`, `Orders.DatePurchased`, `EmployeeStore.ItemName`, and `EmployeeStore.Cost` fields. Remember, we don't always need to extract everything from the database tables. In this case, we want to pull only the data from the three tables that is relevant to the Shipping and Receiving department. Figure 19.19 shows the complete design.

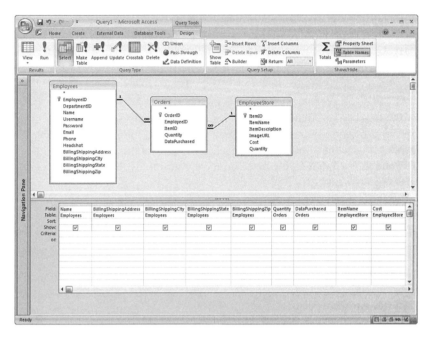

FIGURE 19.19 Select the fields from the tables that you want to include in your query.

6. To use the SQL code that was generated, select SQL View from the View menu. Figure 19.20 shows the SQL code that is generated.

FIGURE 19.20 View the SQL code that Access generated by selecting View, SQL View.

7. Copy the SQL code, save the query as **EmployeesOrders**, and close Access. *Don't forget to save the query.* This step is crucial for the next section.

8. You are now free to paste the code into the SQL box in the Advanced Recordset dialog box in Dreamweaver.

9. Type the name **rsOrders** into the Name text box.

10. Select the connVectaCorp option from the Connection drop-down menu. Figure 19.21 shows the result of the additions.

11. Click the Test button to test the results. As Figure 19.22 demonstrates, a Test grid is presented with a few prepopulated orders. You'll also notice that all the fields are combined into one virtual table resulting from the three original tables.

12. Click OK to close Text SQL Statement window.

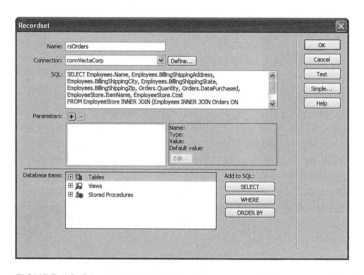

FIGURE 19.21 Paste the SQL code you created in Access into the SQL text box of the Advanced Recordset dialog box.

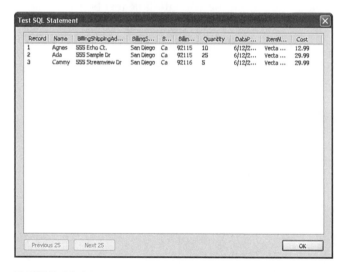

FIGURE 19.22 Combine the contents of three tables into one recordset by using joins.

13. Click OK to close the Recordset dialog box. You'll quickly notice that the new recordset is listed in the Bindings panel.

As you can see, creating a recordset that joins numerous tables together is relatively simple to create, especially when you're relying on complementary programs/tools such as Access's Query Editor, SQL Server Management Studio's View Editor, or MySQL Query Browser, to do the heavy lifting. As you saw, we didn't have to write the SQL by hand to join the tables together, but instead relied on these programs to create an advanced recordset that we can then draw fields from (and ultimately the data contained within those fields) within the Bindings panel. More on this later.

Creating a Recordset from a View

In the preceding sections, you saw how to create both simple and advanced recordsets. The Simple Recordset dialog box allowed you to select a single table and work with the fields in that table in your recordset. The Advanced Recordset dialog box allowed you to paste in SQL statements created in Access's Query Designer (Views in SQL Server's Management Studio, or MySQL Query Browser) to join two or more tables and work with the data from multiple tables in your recordset. Recall that you saved the query you created in Access as EmployeesOrders. Rather than opening Access every time we need to use that query and then copying the SQL statement and pasting it into the Advanced Recordset dialog box, we can use that saved query in Dreamweaver as is. To use the saved query in Dreamweaver, follow these steps:

1. Open the Advanced Recordset dialog box by double-clicking the rsOrders recordset in the Bindings panel. This action launches the Recordset dialog box in the Advanced view.

2. Select the entire SQL query and delete it from the SQL multiline text box.

3. From the Database Items list box, expand the Views selection tree. Notice that the EmployeesOrders view (the query you saved in Access) is shown.

4. Choose the EmployeesOrders view and click the Select button. The SQL statement should resemble the one in Figure 19.23.

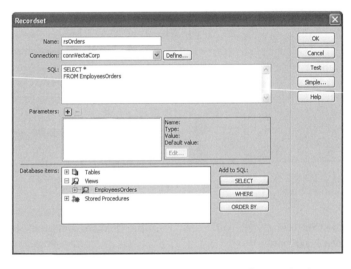

FIGURE 19.23   Choose the query from the Views selection tree.

> **NOTE**
>
> The terms *view* and *query* are essentially the same. Although Access and MySQL call them *queries*, the standard and universal term is *view*. SQL Server 2005 Express Edition and Dreamweaver refer to them as *views*.

5. Click the Test button to see the result of querying the view/query. Click OK to close the Test SQL Statement dialog box. Click OK to close the Recordset dialog box and save the new recordset.

Whether you are creating simple or advanced recordsets in Dreamweaver or using a saved query to create your recordsets, be assured that the process remains relatively simple. As you have seen, even complex SQL statements that join multiple tables can be achieved with ease. The next sections introduce you to methods of extracting the data from the recordset into your application.

Working with Dynamic Elements

Now that you've been able to extract data from your data source, your next step is to structure it within your web page somehow. Dreamweaver's Server Behaviors and Bindings panels provide the capabilities you need to get started producing dynamic elements centralized within the database but revealed by the page.

Dynamic Text

The first step in creating dynamic applications is to try to make all your text as dynamic as possible. That is, allow all your company's valuable information to reside in the database and then pull it out, displaying it in dynamic pages as needed. To start creating dynamic text, begin by creating a table that will serve as the means of organizing the data output. You can accomplish this by following these steps:

1. Replace the text *Content Goes Here* on the EmployeeStore page with a new table by choosing Insert, Table. The Table dialog box appears. This table should have **1** row, **2** columns, a width of **460**, and **0** for border thickness, cell padding, and cell spacing. Click OK after you enter the values. The new table will appear on the page. Assign a width of **160 pixels** to the cell on the left and then **300 pixels** to the cell on the right. Make sure to vertically align both cells.

2. Insert a nested table in the cell on the right. Give this table **3** rows, **1** column, a width of **300**, and **0** for border thickness, cell padding, and cell spacing.

3. Add the text **Name**, **Description**, and **Cost** in the three rows for the table you just created. You might decide to make the text bold so that it stands out to the user. The table resembles the one in Figure 19.24.

19

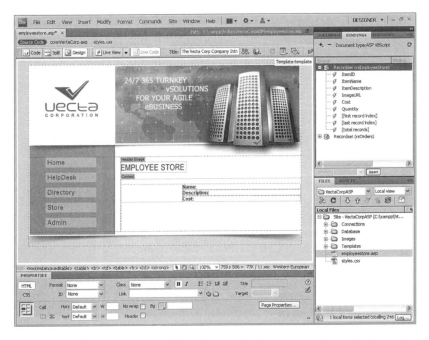

FIGURE 19.24   Insert the table we'll use to structure our dynamic elements.

4. Expand the `rsEmployeeStore` recordset in the Bindings panel to reveal all the fields.

5. Manually click, hold, and drag the ItemName field from the `rsEmployeeStore` recordset in the Bindings panel into the cell for the table you just created, making sure that you drop the field just next to the Name caption.

6. Repeat step 5 for the ItemDescription and Cost, dragging those fields into their proper cells next to their respective captions. The result will resemble Figure 19.25.

7. Save the page and display it in the browser by pressing F12 (Option-F12). As you'll see, the first item in our EmployeeStore database is shown on the page.

Congratulations! You've just taken your first step to working with dynamic web pages. As the chapter unfolds, you'll learn to add dynamic images, repeating regions, pagination functionality, and more. This is just the tip of the iceberg.

Dynamic Images

Now that you've created dynamic text within your application, you're ready to begin adding dynamic images. The images we'll add here are not the typical static images you have used throughout the book; instead, they will be dynamic. Remember, we added the path to the image of each item in the EmployeeStore table. What we want to do now is dynamically show the image, based on the path provided within the ImageURL field, on our dynamic EmployeeStore web page. To do this, follow these steps:

1. Place your cursor in the leftmost cell. (We'll use this cell to place the product's image dynamically.)

FIGURE 19.25   Drag the remaining fields into their respective locations in the table.

2. Select Insert, Image. The Select Image Source dialog box appears.

3. Near the top of the Select Image Source dialog box are options for selecting the image from the File System (static) or from Data Sources (dynamic). Select the Data Sources option. The Select Image Source dialog box's interface changes to allow you to select an image path from the recordset. Select the ImageURL field, as shown on Figure 19.26.

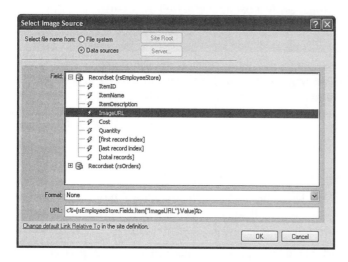

FIGURE 19.26   Select the ImageURL field from the recordset.

4. Click OK. The dynamic image placeholder appears within the cell.

Save your work and test the results in the browser by pressing F12 (Option-F12). The image for the Vecta Corp T-Shirt will now appear next to the item name, description, and cost.

Recordset Paging

Now that you've seen how easy it is to place dynamic content on a page, you'll probably want to begin adding features that allow your users to interact with the content on your pages. Paging, for example, enables your users to page through items in the recordset until they find the item they are looking for. For every press of a button, your users can advance to the next record or, conversely, return to a previous record. Developers gain certain benefits from pagination, including the following:

▶ **Load time**—Rather than the page having to process multiple records at once, it processes only a predefined set of records at a time. Records are loaded only as users advance forward to another record.

▶ **Size constraints**—By paging through a recordset, screen real estate is gained. The records are loaded in a certain area of the page rather than all records showing continuously down the page.

Dreamweaver's pagination behaviors are located in the Add (+) menu in the Server Behaviors panel and include the following behaviors:

▶ **Move to First Record**—Returns the user to the first set of records in the recordset

▶ **Move to Previous Record**—Returns the user back one set of records

▶ **Move to Next Record**—Advances the user one set of records forward

▶ **Move to Last Record**—Advances the user to the last set of records in the recordset

▶ **Move to Specific Record (ASP only)**—Advances or returns the user to a set of records specified by the developer or by a parameter passed by the user

> **NOTE**
>
> In ColdFusion, the pagination behaviors are named a bit differently. For example, ColdFusion uses Move to First Page, Move to Previous Page, Move to Next Page, and Move to Last Page. Additionally, if you plan on adding pagination behaviors using ColdFusion or PHP, a Repeat Region server behavior will have to be added first. This will be covered later.

To begin adding pagination features to your site, follow these steps:

1. Place your cursor just below the table that includes the dynamic data.

2. From the Recordset Paging submenu, available by clicking the Add (+) button in the Server Behaviors panel, select Move to Previous Record.

3. The Move to Previous Record dialog box appears, similar to Figure 19.27. Select the Create New Link: "Previous" option from the Link menu and make sure that the rsEmployeeStore recordset is selected from the Recordset menu. Click OK. A new dynamic Previous hyperlink is created.

FIGURE 19.27   Confirm the settings in the Move to Previous Record dialog box.

> **NOTE**
>
> In the ColdFusion model, a Pass Existing URL Parameters check box appears in this dialog box. Enabling this check box ensures that existing URL parameters are preserved when the user clicks the Next and Previous hyperlinks. Furthermore, ColdFusion and PHP don't support direct paging of records without the use of the Repeating Region Server behavior first. Although the Repeat Region server behavior will be covered later, for now to follow along you'll need to select the containing table that you just added a few sections ago (see Figure 19.24) and choose the Repeat Region behavior from the Server Behaviors menu. Change The Show <number of records> Records at a Time text box's value to **1** and click OK to wrap the table with the new behavior.

4. Add a space after the Previous hyperlink and repeat steps 2 and 3, this time selecting the Move to Next Record option from the Recordset Paging submenu. When you've finished adding both paging widgets, two hyperlinks (one identified as Previous and one as Next) appear under the table, similar to Figure 19.28.

Save your work and test the result in the browser by pressing F12 (Option-F12). You should be able to navigate from the first record in the EmployeeStore database to the next record and back.

In this section, we discussed the Move to Previous Record and Move to Next Record Server behaviors. You should feel free to experiment with the other paging server behaviors at your leisure. Dreamweaver provides behaviors for moving to the last record and to the first record. If you're using the ASP model, you can also include a text box that allows a user to enter the specific record to jump to.

Showing Specific Regions

Now that you have added the capability to cycle through the recordset, consider the following problem: A user clicks Next until he gets to the last record and then is abruptly stopped. He keeps clicking Next but nothing happens. The problem is that the user has reached the end of the recordset and cannot go any further. However, the user has no way of knowing that. To fix this, Dreamweaver provides functionality in the form of a group of Show Region behaviors. For example, we can create a region that contains text alerting the user that he's reached the end of the recordset. When the user reaches the recordset's end, the region is displayed. The complete list of Show Region behaviors is given next:

▶ **Show Region if Recordset Is Empty**—This behavior can be useful to alert a user that an empty result was returned from the database.

▶ **Show Region if Recordset Is Not Empty**—Use this behavior when you want to populate a table of data from results returned from a recordset if it isn't empty.

▶ **Show Region if First Record**—If users are on the first set of records, you can alert them to this fact.

▶ **Show Region if Not First Record**—If users are on anything *except* the first set of records, you can alert them to this fact.

▶ **Show Region if Last Record**—If users are on the last set of records, you can alert them to this fact.

▶ **Show Region if Not Last Record**—As the user cycles through the records, you can provide a message. When the user is on the last set of records, a message can be displayed.

> **NOTE**
>
> Although the functionality is the same across server models, the names of these server behaviors vary slightly under the ColdFusion and PHP server models.

FIGURE 19.28   Dynamic Previous and Next hyperlinks appear under the table that contains the dynamic image and text.

> **NOTE**
>
> In ColdFusion, the conditional behaviors are named a bit differently. For example, ColdFusion uses Show Region if First Page, Show Region if Not First Page, Show Region if Last Page, and Show Region if Not Last Page.

To add a Show Region behavior to your page, follow these steps:

1. Type the text **No more items to view** just below (or to the right of) the Previous and Next paging widgets. This is the "region" that shows when the condition (the current record is the last record in the recordset) is true.

2. With the text highlighted, select the server behavior Show Region if Last Record (Show Region if Last Page in ColdFusion and PHP) from the Show Region submenu. The Show Region if Last Record dialog box appears.

3. Make sure that the `rsEmployeeStore` recordset is selected, and click OK.

Notice that a gray visual aid surrounds the text. This guarantees that the text contained within this region appears only when the user reaches the last record/page in the recordset.

Save your work and run it in the browser by pressing F12 (Option-F12). Click the Next hyperlink until you reach the last record. The message will appear when you reach the end of the recordset.

Again, this is only one example of the server behaviors outlined in the Show Region set of server behaviors. Now that you have a general idea about what the Show Region server behaviors do, feel free to experiment with the others.

Using Repeat Region

Although recordset paging is the ideal model to strive for, at times you might want to display all the records (or a certain number of records) in the database at once. The Repeat Region behavior enables you to create a pattern that repeats within the web page. For instance, in the EmployeeStore page, a table was created to display the content for the image, name, description, and cost. Using the Repeat Region server behavior, you can maintain that structure and repeat the contents for every record (or a certain number of records) in the database. To create a repeatable region on our page, follow these steps:

1. Select the table for which you want the content to repeat. Your selection should resemble Figure 19.29.

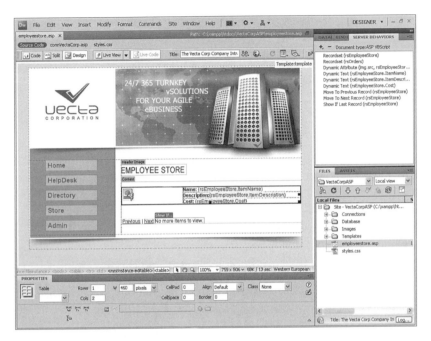

FIGURE 19.29   Select the table for which you want to create the repeatable region.

2. Select the Repeat Region option by clicking the Add (+) button in the Server Behaviors panel. The Repeat Region dialog box appears, similar to Figure 19.30.

FIGURE 19.30   Configure the Repeat Region dialog box to show five records at a time from the `rsEmployeeStore` recordset.

3. The Repeat Region dialog box enables you to enter choices regarding which recordset to create the repeat region for as well as how you want to display the results. Make sure that the `rsEmployeeStore` option is selected from within the Recordset menu. Additionally, make sure that the 5 Records at a Time option is selected. Click OK to apply the server behavior to the selected table.

Save your work and test the results in the browser by pressing F12 (Option-F12). Figure 19.31 shows records grouped in sets of five.

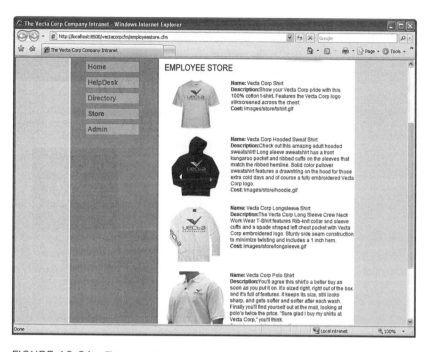

FIGURE 19.31   Five records at a time can be shown when you use the Repeat Region server behavior.

As you can see, you can scroll down the page to view five Vecta Corp items at a time. When you want to view the next five items in the recordset, click the Next hyperlink that we added in the previous section.

> **NOTE**
>
> If you're working with the ColdFusion or PHP server models, the Repeat Region behavior has already been added. To configure it to show five records at a time instead of one, simply double-click the behavior within the Server Behaviors panel and change the Show <number of records> Records at a Time value from **1** to **5**.

19

Summary

Producing dynamic content is the goal of every web page developer. The capability of producing "placeholders" in which text and images seem to magically appear always seems more significant from a development perspective than producing typical static websites. In the past, developers were required to know multiple languages and technologies to accomplish something as simple as a dynamic drop-down list. Dreamweaver provides the capability to produce dynamic content while maintaining its visual editing functionality. Gone are the days of developers having to know everything about ASP, PHP, ColdFusion, ADO, SQL, HTML, JavaScript, CSS, and so on. Although a bit of knowledge is still advantageous, as you have seen throughout this chapter, creating dynamic content in Dreamweaver is largely a matter of dragging and dropping.

With the capability to select database data and present it within a web page now under our belts, we're ready to move forward into the world of data modification—that is, inserting, updating, and deleting data in the database directly from a web page.

Adding and Modifying Data

One of the primary purposes for developing a dynamic web application is not only to be able to view live data from your database, but also to modify, add, or delete the data within it. The last chapter exposed you to a key component of web application development: dynamic data. Unfortunately, that knowledge can take you only as far as being able to physically modify the database when changes need to be made. To truly appreciate the power behind a fully dynamic application, you need to develop that application so that content constantly changes based on user or administrator input. This chapter focuses on creating forms in Dreamweaver that modify, add, or delete items in the database.

Like the rest of the chapters in this book, you can work with the examples in this chapter by downloading the files from the book's website. Remember, you'll want to save the files for Chapter 20 (contained within Exercises\Chapter20\Beginning) in the `C:\Inetpub\wwwroot\VectaCorp<technology> (IIS)`, `C:\xampp\htdocs\VectaCorpPHP` (XAMPP), `/Applications/MAMP/htdocs/VectaCorpPHP` (MAMP), or `C:\ColdFusion8\wwwroot\VectaCorpCFM` (ColdFusion) directories.

Building the Web Store New User Registration Page

Like most web applications, a traditional web store requires a page that allows visitors to register as new users and, ultimately based on certain permissions, to navigate the site, view items, and purchase items from the site based on those permissions or credentials. Our Vecta Corp employee store will function similarly.

A quick overview of the Vecta Corp database reveals that, to create a new employee, you need to collect three major pieces of information. Initially you need to collect all the employee's personal information and store it in the Employees table. Second, you'd probably want to collect credit card information and store it in the CreditCards table. Finally, you must assign the new employee a department to work in. Remember that the Departments table is directly related to the Employees table. Because this is the case, a value must be entered for the DepartmentID field in the Employees table if we are to maintain referential integrity. Realistically, we don't want employees to assign themselves a department. For this reason, we'll assign new users a default DepartmentID of 2, which represents Administration. Later, we'll allow the administrator to go in (by way of an admin page) and assign a department for a specific user.

Before we begin constructing the new user registration web page, let's review the structure of the tables with which we'll interact in this chapter. Recall that the tables that make up employees' information are the Employees, CreditCards, and Departments tables.

On further inspection of these tables, you'll notice that the following fields are necessary for new employees to be created in the Employees table:

Field Name	Data Type	Key
EmployeeID	AutoNumber	PK
DepartmentID	Number	FK
Name	Text	N/A
Username	Text	N/A
Password (Pass in Access)	Text	N/A
Email	Text	N/A

Field Name	Data Type	Key
Phone	Text	N/A
Headshot	Text	N/A
BillingShippingAddress	Text	N/A
BillingShippingCity	Text	N/A
BillingShippingState	Text	N/A
BillingShippingZip	Text	N/A

The following information (which we won't get into in this chapter) must be collected to associate a credit card with a particular employee:

Field Name	Data Type	Key
CreditCardID	AutoNumber	PK
EmployeeID	Number	FK
Type	Text	N/A
Number	Text	N/A
Expiration	Data/Time	N/A

And finally, the Departments table, which represents a specific department in which employees can work, resembles the following:

Field Name	Data Type	Key
DepartmentID	AutoNumber	PK
Department	Text	N/A

Now that you've reviewed the structure of the tables we'll cover in this chapter, let's begin creating the New User Registration form to accommodate the data collection.

NOTE

As was the case in the previous chapter, most of the steps we'll perform in the next few sections can be performed using any server model. When nuances appear across technologies, I will point them out.

20

Creating the New User Registration Form

Most applications, if not all, simulate the fields within a database with HTML form objects. Because form objects allow the user to interact with the web application, they are the perfect channel for collecting information and subsequently inserting that information into the database. Before you can begin creating the New User Registration form, however, you must first create a table to serve as the primary means for structuring the form objects in a cohesive and usable fashion. Begin creating the table by following these steps:

1. Begin creating the New User Registration form by creating a new page from a template. Choose File, New. When the New Document dialog box appears, choose the Page from Template category, select VectaCorpASP (or VectaCorpCFM or VectaCorpPHP, depending on the model you're using in this chapter), choose the template named `template`, and then click Create.

2. Place your cursor in the editable region titled Content, remove the text that exists in the region, and insert a new form by selecting Insert, Form, Form.

3. Let's add our table. First, decide how many rows your table will contain. A quick count of all the necessary fields in the Employees table reveals that you need about 10 rows. However, you might want to include a few more to account for a header, a spacer, and a button element. A safer number would be 14. Knowing that, select Insert, Table. The Insert Table dialog box appears. In the dialog box, create a table that has **14** rows, **2** columns, a width of **450** pixels, and border, cell padding, and cell spacing of **0** pixels. Click OK to insert the new table within the form on the page.

4. Add all appropriate content for personal information, including billing/shipping information and so on, to the table. You can merge cells along the way to create the header. The result is shown in Figure 20.1.

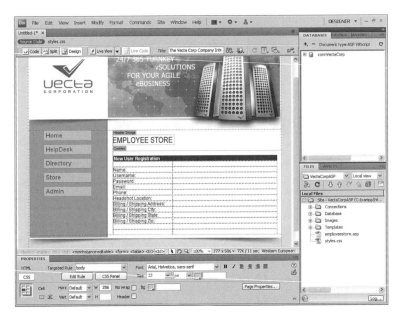

FIGURE 20.1   Add all appropriate content to the new table.

> **TIP**
>
> You can format the table and content in the table as you see fit. Feel free to create styles so that your table and the content within it becomes more attractive. As you'll see from Figure 20.1, I added a header to the table, set the background of the header, added some header text, made it white, and bolded it to make it stand out.

5. You are now ready to begin adding all the form objects for the New User Registration form. The following matrix shows the fields, the appropriate form objects to be inserted, and the unique names to be given to each of the form objects.

Field Name	Form Object	Name
DepartmentID	Hidden Field	departmentid
Name	Text Field	name
Username	Text Field	username
Password	Text Field	password
Email	Text Field	email
Phone	Text Field	phonenumber
Headshot Location	Text Field	headshotloc
BillingShippingAddress	Text Field	billshipaddress
BillingShippingCity	Text Field	billshipcity
BillingShippingState	Text Field	billshipstate
BillingShippingZip	Text Field	billshipzip
	Submit Button	Submit

The result of inserting all these form objects is shown in Figure 20.2.

6. Select the hidden field (departmentid) and assign it a default value of 2 in the Property inspector. Remember that we'll assume that all users inserted into the Employees table will belong to the Administration department when they're first created. It will be the administrator's responsibility to go back in and change the employee's corresponding department later.

Save the page as `register.asp`, `register.cfm`, or `register.php` (depending on the server model you're using) and run it within the browser. The result will look similar to Figure 20.3 (shown using ColdFusion).

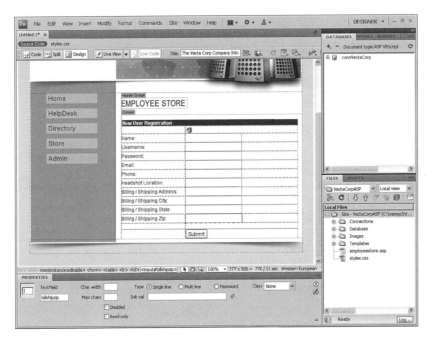

FIGURE 20.2   Insert all the form objects for the New User Registration page.

FIGURE 20.3   The New User Registration page allows the employee to register for the Vecta Corp employee store.

Creating the Recordset

Now that you have the New User Registration form created, you are ready to add the insert functionality. Before you can begin adding any server behaviors, however, you'll need to create a new recordset that represents the Employees table. To create the recordset, follow these steps:

1. Select the Recordset option from the Bindings panel's Add (+) menu. The Recordset dialog box appears.

2. Give the new recordset the name **rsNewEmployee**.

3. Choose the connVectaCorp option from the Connection menu.

4. Choose the Employees option from the Table menu. The completely formatted Recordset dialog box should resemble Figure 20.4.

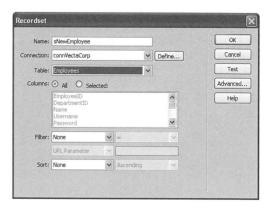

FIGURE 20.4   Format the Recordset dialog box accordingly.

5. Click OK. The Bindings panel now shows the fields contained in the recordset, also shown in Figure 20.5.

Validating the Form

Now that you have the recordset created, you are ready to begin inserting the data into the database. But before you begin, you'll want to add functionality that guarantees that the data going into the database is valid. Because the database tables explicitly define data types for each field, you'll want to make sure that the data the user enters is the same as what is going to be accepted by the database table; otherwise, errors will occur. The Validate Form behavior can be used to trap any errors on the client before a request is sent to the server-side application. To insert the behavior, follow these steps:

1. Open the Behaviors panel by choosing Window, Behaviors. Choose the Submit button form object on the page and select the Validate Form behavior from the Behaviors panel.

2. The Validate Form dialog box appears. Select each of the fields within the Fields list and click the Required check box. Additionally, select the email field from the Field list and choose the Email Address option button. The result is shown in Figure 20.6.

FIGURE 20.5   The Bindings panel lists the fields in the recordset box.

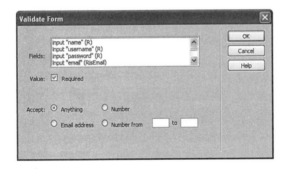

FIGURE 20.6   Select the appropriate options from the Validate Form dialog box.

3. Click OK.

Save your work and test the results in the browser by pressing F12 (Option-F12). Typing incorrect data (specifically in the Email text box) or forgetting to type data in all the fields results in an error message similar to the one shown in Figure 20.7.

Inserting a New User into the Employees Table

Now that you can verify that the data being sent to the database is, in fact, legitimate, you can build the functionality for adding the data to the Employees table. To facilitate this process, Dreamweaver provides an Insert Record server behavior that allows for quick and intuitive insertions into the database table of your choice. To insert a new employee into the Employees table, follow these steps:

1. Place your cursor in the form and select Insert Record from the Add (+) menu of the Server Behaviors panel. The Insert Record dialog box appears.

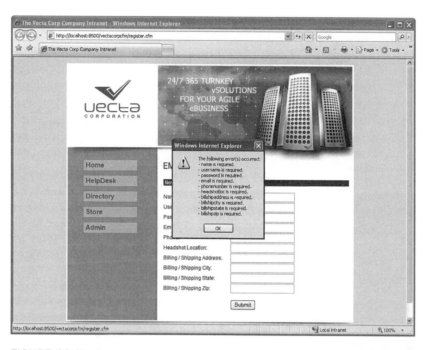

FIGURE 20.7   An error message is displayed if data is missing or is inconsistent.

2. Select connVectaCorp from the Connection menu.

NOTE

Depending on the server model you decide to use, the Insert Record dialog box looks slightly different. Don't worry about the differences, because all the functionality is equally represented across server models. It's merely the ordering of the features that's different.

---

3. Choose the Employees table from the Insert Into Table menu.

4. Leave the After Inserting, Go To text box blank for now. The value you enter here will be used as a redirection page after the new user has successfully registered. We'll define this in the next section.

5. Make sure that the form1 option is selected from the Get Values From menu.

6. The form elements selection box enables you to match up a form object with the corresponding field in the database. In most cases, Dreamweaver figures out the match between the text field name on the form and the database table's field name. If some do not match, however, the value <Ignore> appears. If this is the case, select the appropriate match from the column drop-down list. Refer to the following chart for a reference on which form elements correspond to which field values.

20

Form Element	Column	Submit As
departmentid	DepartmentID	Numeric
name	Name	Text
username	Username	Text
password	Password (Pass in Access)	Text
email	Email	Text
phonenumber	Phone	Text
headshotloc	Headshot	Text
billshipaddress	BillingShippingAddress	Text
billshipcity	BillingShippingCity	Text
billshipstate	BillingShippingState	Text
billshipzip	BillingShippingZip	Text

The completely formatted Insert Record dialog box should resemble Figure 20.8.

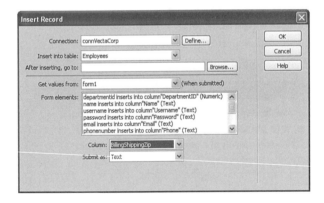

FIGURE 20.8   Format the appropriate values in the Insert Record dialog box.

7. Click OK. The Insert Record server behavior appears in the Server Behaviors panel, and your form is highlighted in blue (because the Insert Record functionality is technically considered an invisible element).

Save your work and test the result in the browser by pressing F12 (Option-F12). Enter values into the text fields and click Submit. If everything functions smoothly, the page refreshes itself. Remember that the refreshing of the page happens because we didn't identify a page to redirect to after the data from the form is inserted into the database. We'll do that in the next section.

To verify that the data was, in fact, inserted into the Employees table, open your respective database and look in the Employees table. A new user has been created.

> **NOTE**
>
> One of the most common problems I have found when working in Dreamweaver is that of inserting records into the database. Generally this problem is isolated to the ASP server model using Access. This is one of the areas where errors in the browser occur quite often. In most cases, this issue isn't a problem with Dreamweaver; instead it has more to do with the fact that write permissions have to be enabled for the database. If you receive HTTP 500 errors, connection errors, and so on, refer to the companion website at www.dreamweaverunleashed.com for troubleshooting tips.

Creating the Redirection Page

The final step we'll want to perform before we can call the New User Registration page complete is to add the functionality that will redirect users to a thank-you page of some sort after they've registered. You can create this functionality by following these steps:

1. While still in the New User Registration page, double-click the Insert Record server behavior. The Insert Record dialog box reappears.

2. Enter the value **x_newusercreated.asp** in the After Inserting, Go To text box. If you're working with ColdFusion, enter **x_newusercreated.cfm**, and if you're working with PHP, enter **x_newusercreated.php**. The Insert Record dialog box should resemble Figure 20.9.

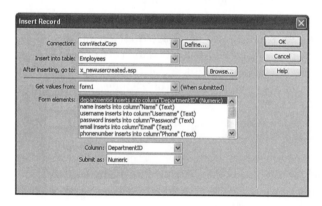

FIGURE 20.9   Add the redirection page as a value in the After Inserting, Go To text box.

3. Click OK. Save your work.

4. Now we'll need to create a new page that represents that redirection page that you just referenced from the Insert Record dialog box. To do this, choose File, New. When the New Document dialog box appears, choose the Page from Template category, select VectaCorpASP (or VectaCorpCFM or VectaCorpPHP, depending on the model you're using in this chapter), choose the template titled `template`, and click Create.

5. In the new page, replace the text *Content Goes Here* in the Content editable region with the text **Thank you for registering as a new user.**

6. Save your page as **x_newusercreated.asp**, **x_newusercreated.cfm**, or **x_newusercreated.php**, depending on the server model you're working with.

That's it! After new users complete the registration process on the site, they are redirected to this page.

Creating the My Account Page

Now that you've added the functionality for employees to register on the site, you'll want to add more functionality to allow them to modify the information they've provided. Suppose that an employee moved to a new location and you shipped a product to the employee's old address. You can imagine the confusion. Fortunately, Dreamweaver provides the Update Record server behavior, which enables you to develop a page for user administrative purposes such as these.

Using dynamic form objects in conjunction with the Update Record server behavior, employees can see the information that resides in the database in editable form objects. After employees edit the appropriate information, they need only submit the form to update the information in the database.

Creating the My Account Form

Because all the information is placed into form objects, the My Account form will be constructed much the same way that the New User Registration form was. To create the My Account form, follow these steps:

1. Begin creating the My Account form by creating a new page from a template. To do this, choose File, New. When the New Document dialog box appears, choose the Page from Template category, select VectaCorpASP (or VectaCorpCFM or VectaCorpPHP, depending on the model you're using in this chapter), choose the template titled `template`, and click Create.

2. Remove the *Content Goes Here* text from the editable region. With your cursor still in the region, insert a new form by selecting Insert, Form, Form.

3. Let's add a table similar to the one we created in the New User Registration form. Choose Insert, Table; the Insert Table dialog box appears. In the dialog box, create a table that has **14** rows, **2** columns, a width of **450** pixels, and border, cell padding, and cell spacing of **0** pixels. Click OK to create the table.

4. Add all the appropriate content for personal information, including billing/shipping information and so on, within the table. You can merge cells along the way to create the header. The result will closely resemble Figure 20.10.

5. You are now ready to begin adding all the form objects for the My Account form. The following matrix shows the fields, the appropriate form objects to be inserted, and the unique names to be given to each of the form objects.

Field Name	Form Object	Name
EmployeeID	Hidden Field	employeeid
Name	Text Field	name
Username	Text Field	username
Password	Text Field	password
Email	Text Field	email
Phone	Text Field	phonenumber
Headshot	Text Field	headshotloc
BillingShippingAddress	Text Field	billshipaddress
BillingShippingCity	Text Field	billshipcity
BillingShippingState	Text Field	billshipstate
BillingShippingZip	Text Field	billshipzip
	Submit Button	Submit

The result of inserting all the form objects is shown in Figure 20.10.

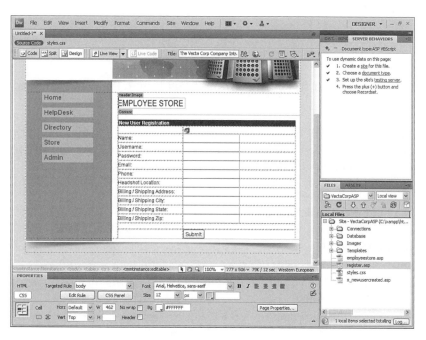

FIGURE 20.10   Insert all the form objects for the My Account page.

Recall that when we created the New User Registration page, we had a Hidden Field for DepartmentID. Because users won't be able to modify the department they belong to, we won't make that value available in this form. (The administrator is responsible for changing this value.) We have, however, replaced the DepartmentID Hidden Field with an EmployeeID Hidden Field. When updates are made to a database, you as the developer must specify which field will be updated. In Chapter 18, "A SQL Primer," we discussed the WHERE clause. The value, typically a numeric primary key, is appended to the WHERE clause so that application logic knows exactly which record in the database table to update. This numeric key is the EmployeeID.

Save the page as **myaccount.asp**, **myaccount.cfm**, or **myaccount.php** (depending on the server model you're using).

Working with Dynamic Form Elements

Now that you have the My Account form created, you'll want to make all those form objects dynamic, meaning that when the page is loaded, corresponding fields from the Employees table automatically appear in the form objects.

In the previous chapter, you learned how to create dynamic text by dragging an item from the recordset onto the page. Dynamic form objects are constructed much the same way in that you can drag an item from the recordset (in the Bindings panel) directly onto the form object to which you want to bind that field. Dynamic form objects can be created using one of three methods:

▶ Dragging a field from the recordset (within the Bindings panel) onto the form object.

▶ Using the Dynamic Form Elements server behaviors set.

▶ Selecting the form object and clicking the lightning bolt icon in the Property inspector to create a binding.

Any one of these three methods will do the job. Dragging an item from the recordset into the form object is probably the easiest and quickest way to accomplish the task, but for the sake of learning all the methods, try binding at least a few of the form objects using the following process:

1. Before you can bind text to a form object, you'll have to create a new recordset. To do that, select the Recordset option from the Bindings panel's Add (+) menu. The Recordset dialog box appears.

2. Enter the name **rsUpdateEmployee**, select the connVectaCorp option from the Connection menu, choose the Employees option from the Table menu, and click OK. The new recordset is created.

3. Select the Dynamic Text Field option from the Dynamic Form Elements submenu by clicking the Add (+) button from the Server Behaviors panel.

4. The Dynamic Text Field dialog box appears, similar to Figure 20.11, allowing you to select the form object you want to make dynamic. Select the "name" in form "form1" option from the Text Field menu.

FIGURE 20.11   The Dynamic Text Field dialog box allows you to create a binding from the recordset to the form object.

5. Click the binding icon (the lightning bolt) to set the binding for the name text field. The Dynamic Data dialog box appears, similar to Figure 20.12.

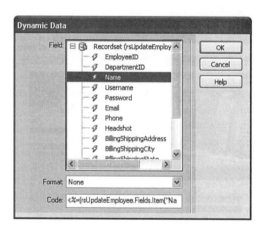

FIGURE 20.12   Click the binding icon to set the value of the dynamic form element.

6. From the Dynamic Data dialog box, select the field from the recordset to which you want to bind the object (for our example, choose Name). You have the option to change the data type as well as the capability to modify the code if necessary.

7. Click OK.

8. Notice that the Set Value To text box in the Dynamic Text Field dialog box now has the value set with the appropriate code. Click OK to complete the binding. Figure 20.13 shows the Name text box with the Name field bound to it. Also notice that the Property inspector shows the bind in the Init Val field.

20

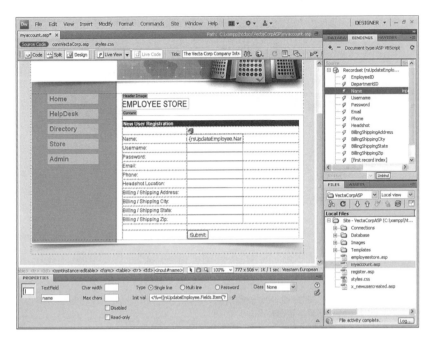

FIGURE 20.13   The field should now be bound to the appropriate form object.

9. Up to this point, you used the Dynamic Form Elements submenu in the Server Behaviors panel to create the binding. As mentioned earlier, there's an easier and much more intuitive way: dragging and dropping from the Bindings panel. To use this method, switch to the Bindings panel and expand the Recordset.

10. Drag the Username field into the Username text box. The binding is instantly created for the username field.

11. Repeat the process for the remaining text fields in the My Account page. Don't forget the EmployeeId Hidden Field; this is by far the most important binding!

Save your work and test the results in the browser by pressing F12 (Option-F12). The result should look similar to Figure 20.14.

Notice that the first record (Ada's information) is displayed in the My Account page. This is because the application doesn't know who we are or what field is representative of us in the Employees table. In Chapter 22, "Security and User Authentication," we'll add functionality that allows the My Account page to identify our login with a specific row in the Employees table. Ultimately, the login functionality we will add will display the appropriate data in the My Account page.

Updating a User in the Employees Table

Now that you have the form created and all the objects are bound to the appropriate data fields, you are ready to add the functionality that enables users to modify their particular information. Remember the EmployeeID Hidden Field you added into the form? This number is eventually used in the WHERE clause of the update to track which employee we should modify information for. If it weren't for this field, the Update Record server behavior wouldn't function properly. To add the Update Record functionality, follow these steps:

1. Place your cursor in the form and select Update Record from the Add (+) menu in the Server Behaviors panel. The Update Record dialog box appears.

2. The Update Record dialog box functions similarly to the Insert Record dialog box, except that you are required to specify the unique key column. For starters, select connVectaCorp from the Connection menu.

FIGURE 20.14   The first record in the Employees table is displayed in the My Account page.

NOTE

As was the case with the Insert Record server behavior, the Update Record server behavior functions the same across the board for the ASP, ColdFusion, and PHP server models. There are slight differences, however; the Update Record dialog box for the ASP server model features a Unique Key column menu. From this menu, you would select the EmployeeID value and set the status of the form element in the Form Elements list to <ignore>. In the ColdFusion and PHP server models, however, this menu doesn't exist. For these server models, you must pass the EmployeeID value. Next to the Submit As menu, enable the check box labeled Primary Key. Making sure that check box is selected ensures that the form updates without failure.

20

3. Now choose the Employees table from the Table to Update menu.

4. Make sure that the rsUpdateEmployee recordset is selected from the Select Record From menu.

5. To append the EmployeeID to the WHERE clause of the UPDATE statement that the Update Record server behavior will eventually generate, select the EmployeeID option from the Unique Key column menu.

6. Enter the value **x_userupdated.asp, x_userupdated.cfm** or **x_userupdated.php** (depending on the server model you are using). As was the case with the New User Registration form, this is the page users will be redirected to after they've made their update.

7. Make sure that the form1 option is selected from the Get Values From menu.

8. Like the Insert Record dialog box, the Update Record dialog box allows you to match up the form elements in the form with the appropriate fields in the database table. For the most part, all the form elements should be matched up for you. Remember that you must select <ignore> for the EmployeeID form element. You'll end up receiving an error if you try to update this field, because it is an automatically generated number in the database and cannot be updated. Figure 20.15 shows the Update Record dialog box with all the necessary values set.

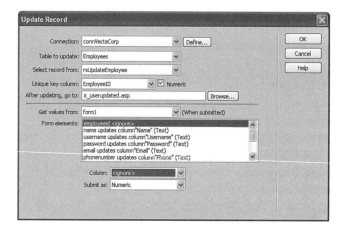

FIGURE 20.15   Complete the modifications to the Update Record dialog box.

9. Click OK. The new Update Record server behavior appears in the Server Behaviors panel, and the form is highlighted in blue (because it is an invisible element).

10. To complete the My Account page, create a new page from the site's Template and call the new page **x_userupdated.asp, x_userupdated.cfm,** or **x_userupdated.php,** depending on the server model you're working with. On the page, enter the text **Your information has been modified.**

Switch back to the My Account page, save your work, and test the result in the browser. After the form appears, change a value in the form (I'll modify Ada's name) and click Submit. After you've done that, open the database table and check to see the result of the modification that was made from the web page.

Using Data Objects to Create an Admin Page

Aimed at giving you quick access to sophisticated interactivity without having to rely on the various panels that encompass all the objects, *data objects* are basically predesigned web components you can use within your application. Data objects are easy to use; in fact, you've already used a lot of them and might not have even known it. Some of the data objects we'll be using are outlined in the following chart:

Object	Supported Technologies	Description
Recordset	All	Launches the Recordset dialog box you normally see when selecting the Recordset server behavior from the Bindings panel.
Command	ASP	Choose this option, also available from the Bindings panel's Add (+) menu, to launch the Command dialog box. From this dialog box, you have the option of creating a reusable command that accepts varying parameters based on the page that is using it. From the Command dialog box, you have the option of connecting to a stored procedure or working with inserts, updates, or deletes.
Stored Procedure	ColdFusion	Choose this option, also available from the Bindings panel's Add (+) menu, to launch the Stored Procedure dialog box. Stored procedures are prebuilt SQL functions that perform a variety of tasks, including insert, update, and delete operations in a database. The beauty in stored procedures is that they accept parameters. Based on these parameters, SQL code on the database, and ultimately the database table itself, can vary in its functionality.

20

Object	Supported Technologies	Description
Dynamic Data (Dynamic Text, Table, Text Field, Checkbox, Radio Group, and Select Field)	All	Enables you to quickly create and format a table complete with bound data from your recordset on-the-fly.
Repeated Region	All	Similar to the functionality outlined in the previous chapter, the Repeated Region object creates a repeated region for a dynamic table.
Show Region	All	Use this set of conditional objects to show or not show specific regions on the dynamic page based on the record count of a recordset or DataSet, or the position within it.
Recordset Paging	All	Includes the Recordset Navigation bar, as well as Move to First, Last, Previous, and Next pagination server behaviors, complete with the Show Region behavior attached. As you've seen in the previous chapter, this set of objects is great for creating sets of dynamic content that can be paged from one set of data to the next based on the user's interaction with a Next and Previous hyperlink/button.
Go To	ASP	Uses the Go To set of objects, also available from the Server Behaviors panel's Add (+) menu, to work with functionality in conjunction with the Master Detail Page Set. You can use the Go to Detail Page or Go to Related Page to automatically redirect the user to a specific page based on dynamic form, URL, or other parameters.
Display Record Count	All	Includes the Recordset Navigation Status objects as well as objects for displaying the starting record number, ending record number, total number of records, and the current page index. The Recordset Navigation Status object includes all this functionality in one object instance.

Object	Supported Technologies	Description
Master Detail Page Set	All	Allows a developer to create a low-detail page that links to a second, more detailed page for a particular record.
Insert, Updated, Delete Record	All	Opens the Insert, Update, or Delete Record dialog box. These dialog boxes facilitate the insertion, update, and deletion of data in the database.
User Authentication	All	Use this set of objects/behaviors, also available from the Server Behaviors panel's Add (+) menu, to create user authentication services for your web application. Functionality includes the capability to log a user in or out or restrict user access to specific pages. More information on this set of objects can be found in Chapter 22.
XSL Transformation	All	Selecting this object launches the XSL Transformation dialog box. From this dialog box, you can provide an XSLT and XML file to dynamically produce a stylized file that is viewable within the browser.

You might have noticed that roughly half the objects listed in the preceding chart have been covered in either this chapter or the previous chapter. For the most part, data objects are global server behaviors used by more than one server model, and except for a few minor details, the functionality exposed by these objects is the same regardless of whether you're using ASP, ColdFusion, or PHP.

In the coming sections, we'll discuss the data objects/server behaviors we haven't gone over yet to create dynamic tables, a navigation bar, and a master detail page set. Combine that with the capability to delete records, and we'll have a fully functioning administration console for employees of our fictitious Vecta Corp company.

Dynamic Tables

You can begin building an administration page for the Vecta Corp website using some of the data objects that come prebundled with Dreamweaver—specifically using dynamic tables. As you'll see, dynamic tables are an excellent choice when you must present large amounts of data in a tablelike database structure.

If you've never used an admin console before, it's is a good way to modify and delete unnecessary products you might not want in the employee store, modify or delete employees that have left the company, and more. Generally, the administrator's page is

20

the heart of the web application because most organizationwide modifications are made from this page. You can begin building the admin page by following these steps:

1. Create a new page by selecting File, New. The New Document dialog box appears. Select the Page from Template category, pick the VectaCorp*<technology>* site, where *<technology>* represents the server model you're working with (ASP, ColdFusion, or PHP), choose the template option, and click Create.

2. The next step is to construct the new recordset. Because we'll try to use the Data Objects submenu as much as possible, select Insert, Data Objects, Recordset. The Recordset dialog box appears.

3. Enter the value **rsProducts** into the Name text box.

4. Choose the connVectaCorp option from the Connection menu.

5. Select the EmployeeStore option from the Table menu.

6. Make sure that the Selected option button is selected from the Columns option button group. The Columns list becomes enabled. Hold down the Ctrl key on your keyboard (⌘ on the Mac) and choose all the fields *except for* the ItemDescription and ImageURL fields. The formatted Recordset dialog box should resemble Figure 20.16.

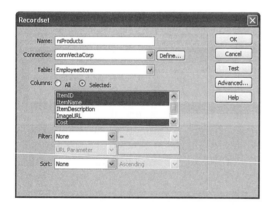

FIGURE 20.16   Format the Recordset dialog box accordingly.

7. Click OK. Dreamweaver alerts you that a new recordset has been created and that you should use the Bindings panel to interact with it. Remember that Data Objects are global server behaviors made available to more than one server-side technology. Even though you're using Data Objects, after they've been added to the page, they're modified by the Bindings or Server Behaviors panels. Again, click OK to close the alert dialog box.

8. Select the *Content Goes Here* text contained within the Content editable region and delete it. In the editable region, insert a new form by selecting Insert, Form, Form.

9. Select Insert, Data Objects, Dynamic Data, Dynamic Table. The Dynamic Table dialog box appears.

10. Choose the rsProducts option from the Recordset menu, enter the value **5** into the Show: Records at a Time text box, and format the border, cell padding, and cell spacing as you see fit. Figure 20.17 shows all the values the table in the admin page should contain.

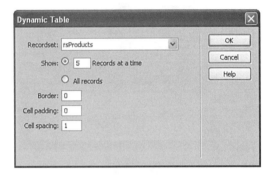

FIGURE 20.17   The Dynamic Table dialog box enables you to configure values for constructing a dynamic table.

11. Click OK. The table is inserted into the workspace, as shown in Figure 20.18. Make any necessary aesthetic adjustments.

Save your work as **admin.asp**, **admin.cfm**, or **admin.php**, depending on the server model you are working with. Now test the results in the browser by pressing F12 (Option-F12). The result looks similar to Figure 20.19.

The Recordset Navigation Bar

Now that you have a dynamic table with data, you can use the Recordset Navigation Bar data object to include pagination features, much like the way we did in the previous chapter. Rather than inserting four separate Paging server behaviors along with four separate Show Region server behaviors, as was done in the previous chapter, however, you can use the Recordset Navigation Bar data object to accomplish the task in a few simple clicks. To insert a Recordset Navigation Bar, follow these steps:

1. Place your cursor just below the dynamic table you created in the preceding section and select Insert, Data Objects, Recordset Paging, Recordset Navigation Bar. The Recordset Navigation Bar dialog box appears.

2. Make sure that the rsProducts option is selected from the Recordset menu.

3. Choose the Text option button from the Display Using option button group.

4. Click OK. The navigation bar appears on the page, similar to Figure 20.20. Notice how all four navigational items are present. The Show Region server behaviors that are attached to this data object cause these items to shift from being visible to invisible, depending on where you are in the recordset.

20

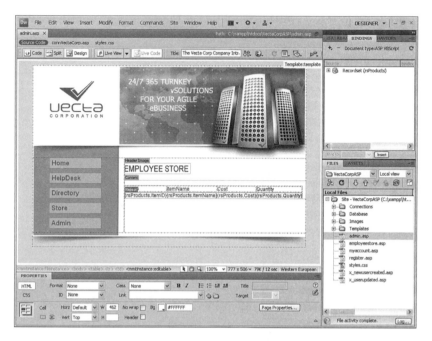

FIGURE 20.18   The table shows the dynamic text in formatted table cells.

FIGURE 20.19   Five records are shown in the dynamic table.

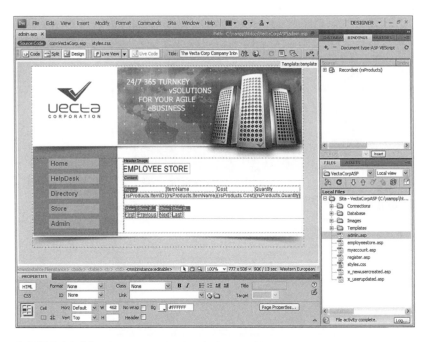

FIGURE 20.20   The navigation bar is inserted into your page.

Save your work and test the results in the browser. The result looks similar to
Figure 20.21. Notice that you can page through five records at a time.

Deleting Records

Up to this point, we've provided a mechanism for displaying and paging through the data
contained in the EmployeeStore table. We've merely provided an alternative method
(using data objects) for functionality that was outlined in the previous chapter. This
section is where the functionality begins to change. In this section, we'll manually create a
new column in the dynamic table, outlining functionality that will allow an administrator
to delete certain products from the EmployeeStore table. To add this functionality, follow
these steps:

1. Add a new column to the dynamic table by right-clicking the ItemID column and
   selecting Insert Column from the Table submenu. A new column appears to the left
   of the ItemID column.

2. Place your cursor in the first cell of the second row and choose Insert, Form, Button.
   A new button is inserted in the cell.

3. Select the button and change the value to Delete in the Property inspector. Also,
   select the None option button from the Action option button group.

20

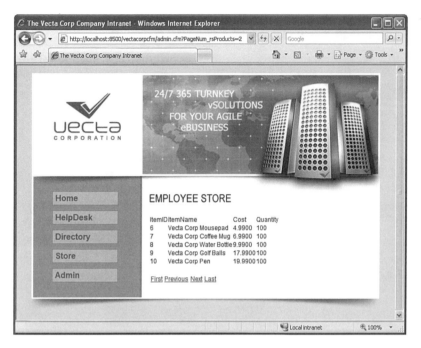

FIGURE 20.21   You can now page through five records at a time.

4. With the button selected, choose Insert, Data Objects, Delete Record. The Delete Record dialog box appears.

5. Choose the connVectaCorp option from the Connection menu.

6. Choose the EmployeeStore option from the Delete from Table menu.

7. Choose the rsProducts option from the Select Record From menu.

8. Select the ItemID option from the Unique Key Column menu.

9. Make sure that the form1 option is selected in the Delete by Submitting menu. The formatted Delete Record dialog box resembles Figure 20.22.

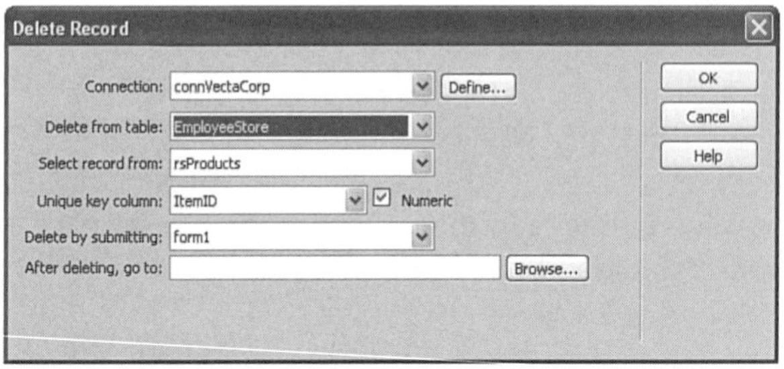

FIGURE 20.22   Format the Delete Record dialog box.

Save your work and test the admin page in the browser by pressing F12 (Option-F12). Navigate a few records and click the Delete button. The page refreshes itself and the selected row disappears. Check the EmployeeStore table to confirm the deletion.

Master Detail Page Set

The Master Detail Page Set data object is one of the most powerful objects built into Dreamweaver. It enables you to create a single page with as many fields from the recordset as you like. You can then make one of the items linkable so that it hyperlinks to a detailed page, revealing more detailed information about the linked item. In our example, we'll use the Master Detail Page Set to link the ItemName field to a second page that provides more information about the selected item. How much more information can we provide? Remember that we excluded the Description and ImageURL fields when we created the Recordset earlier in the chapter. Because these fields are relevant to the item, we'll make these visible in a detailed page to which we'll link from the master page. You can work with the Master Detail Page Set by following these steps:

1. Create a new page by selecting File, New. The New Document dialog box appears. Select the Page from Template category, pick the VectaCorp<*technology*> site, where <*technology*> represents the server model you're working with (ASP, ColdFusion, or PHP), choose the template option, and click Create.

2. Immediately save your page as **admin_master.asp**, **admin_master.cfm**, or **admin_master.php**, depending on the server model you're using.

3. Create a new recordset. To do this, select Insert, Data Objects, Recordset. The Recordset dialog box appears. Enter the name **rsProducts**, select the connVectaCorp connection, choose the EmployeeStore table, and select all the fields from the Columns list. Click OK to create the new recordset.

4. Select the *Content Goes Here* text in the Content editable region and delete it. With your cursor still in the Content editable region, choose Insert, Data Objects, Master Detail Page Set. The Insert Master-Detail Page Set dialog box appears.

5. Make sure that the rsProducts option is selected from the Recordset menu.

6. Select both the ItemDescription and ImageURL fields from the Master Page Fields list and click the Remove (–) button.

7. Select the ItemName field from the Link to Detail From menu.

8. Choose the ItemID option from the Pass Unique Key menu.

9. Choose the All Records option button from the Show option button group.

10. Enter the value **admin_detail.asp**, **admin_detail.cfm**, or **admin_detail.php** (depending on the server model you are using) in the Detail Page Name text box.

11. Leave the Detail Page Fields list box the way it is. The formatted Insert Master-Detail Page Set dialog box should resemble Figure 20.23.

FIGURE 20.23   Configure the Insert Master-Detail Page Set dialog box accordingly.

12. Click OK. You are immediately taken to the detail page (`admin_detail` is automatically created for you because that's the name you supplied in the Master Detail-Page Set dialog box), as shown in Figure 20.24. Save the page.

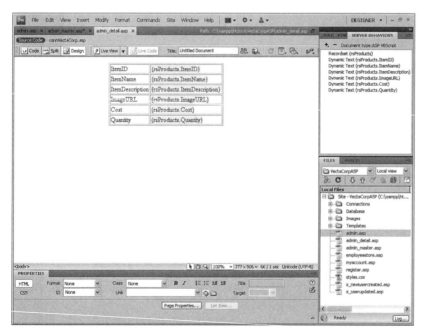

FIGURE 20.24   The detail page shows all the fields you specified.

13. Switch back to the `admin_master.asp`, `admin_master.cfm`, or `admin_master.php` page. Notice that a dynamic table along with a navigation bar and status are inserted for you, similar to the one that we created in the previous sections.

Save your work and test it in the browser. Selecting the ItemName links you to the detail page for that item, revealing more detailed information about the item you selected.

Summary

As you have progressed through the previous two chapters, you have seen the amazing capabilities that Dreamweaver contains as far as reusable components that not only simplify development but also make it much more enjoyable and fun. But it doesn't stop there. As you'll see in the coming chapters, the possibilities are virtually limitless: We'll explore creating search functionality, working with a shopping cart, security and user authentication, and more.

Integrating Search Functionality

As you have seen, a database exists for the sole purpose of storing data. Tables exist to separate that data into well-structured and meaningful blocks of information that can be accessed at any time in an ordered manner. Most successful websites exist because the information in those sites is relatively easy to access. When you search for a book on Amazon.com, for example, you expect to find it within seconds of being on the site. You type a book name, click Search, and the results appear in a well-structured and elegant manner. If you visit eBay's website in an effort to find that treasure someone might be auctioning off, you type the name of the item you are looking for and select a form object, usually a Submit button, to perform the search. It's safe to say that in today's application service provider business model, most companies employ some mechanism for allowing their users quick access to the data that powers the company.

It's true that the Web took off with the inception of the modern search engine. Companies such as Yahoo! and Google, for instance, fueled the medium we know as the World Wide Web by making accessible the information contained within billions of websites on the Internet. Employing basic, filtered, and advanced methods of searching, those companies and others powered the Internet into what we know it as today. But integrating search functionality shouldn't be limited to large corporations or giant search engines that crawl the entire Web. You, too, can implement this same type of functionality on your site, big or small. This chapter focuses on integrating search methods into your web application, specifically providing your users with the ability to search for information that they need in your site.

Like the rest of the chapters in this book, you can work with the examples in this chapter by downloading the files from the book's website. Remember, you'll want to save the files for Chapter 21 (contained within `Exercises\Chapter21\Beginning`) in the `C:\Inetpub\wwwroot\VectaCorp<technology>` (IIS), `C:\xampp\htdocs\VectaCorpPHP` (XAMPP), `/Applications/MAMP/htdocs/VectaCorpPHP` (MAMP), or `C:\ColdFusion8\wwwroot\VectaCorpCFM` (ColdFusion) directories.

Integrating a SQL Search

Finding information in your database can be a simple or a complex process. Depending on the search criteria that you decide to implement, you can give your users the capability to narrow their searches as fine as necessary. Suppose that you wanted to find all employees in your database who have the name *John Smith*; you can create a simple query that selects all the records in the Employees table where the name is equivalent to the name *John Smith*. If you were to write the SQL to handle this, it might look something like this:

```
SELECT Name FROM Employees WHERE Name = 'John Smith'
```

As you learned in Chapter 18, "A SQL Primer," the result of the preceding SQL statement returns all the matching records where the name in the Employees table is equal to the name we're providing, "John Smith." Of course, this is a simple example that uses the most basic of SQL methods to search for a particular item. What if we want to search for users whose names contained the word "Smith"? Or perhaps we want to search for orders that were made in a specific date range. Indeed, the Vecta Corp database is filled with information that users might want access to, including the following:

▶ **Employees**—As an admin, you can perform a search on your Employees table to extract employee-specific information, including name, address, city, state, and so on.

▶ **CreditCards**—Again as an admin, you can perform a search on the CreditCards table to extract all the users' credit card numbers.

▶ **EmployeeStore**—Probably the most important container of information, the EmployeeStore table can be searched by an employee to narrow down an employee's search for a specific product.

▶ **Orders**—As an admin, you can perform a search to determine how many items you sold on a specific day, week, or month. You could also return a statistical analysis of those results to better understand the employees' ordering habits and possibly suggest future products. Furthermore, the shipping and receiving department might want to perform a search for all orders that need to be shipped on a specific day or that need to arrive at their destinations by a certain day. This information can help you determine what kind of shipping services to add to the parcel.

As you can see, just within the Vecta Corp database, there is plenty available to search on. Whether you are approaching the problem as an admin or an employee, the database ultimately is a warehouse of information. How you access that information within Dreamweaver is covered next.

Creating a Search Page

In Chapter 17, "A Database Primer," you learned how to display dynamic data to the user. Recall that we provided a low-level overview of how to quickly create a query using Access. We then saved that query as a view and by using a recordset, we tapped into that query to pull the information out of the database. The problem with that approach is that it's hard-coded, meaning that the data the user ends up seeing always remains the same. What if your users don't want to see what you are choosing to present to them via the view? No doubt your users will want to control what information is presented to them via a search feature. Fortunately for you, you can allow your users to perform a search in your site based on criteria they specify through the use of form objects, recordsets, and parameters. Before we jump ahead, let's dissect a common approach to creating search functionality. Figure 21.1 shows the Amazon website and the search form you would use to search for a book.

FIGURE 21.1   Most large websites employ some way of allowing their users to search for information.

Suppose that you have a database with a list of book titles. The user of the website types a book name; the value of that text box is dynamically appended to a WHERE or a LIKE clause in a SQL statement. The database is then queried, and the results are presented to the user in a well-structured manner. This kind of intuitive functionality isn't limited to large companies such as Amazon and eBay. You, too, can create functionality such as this using

Dreamweaver. To create your own basic SQL-based search page, regardless of server model, follow these steps:

1. Create a new page by selecting File, New. The New Document dialog appears. Select the Page from Template category, select your defined site, choose the template called `template`, and click Create. A new page is created from the template.

2. Immediately save the page as **`search.asp`**, **`search.cfm`**, or **`search.php`**, depending on the server model you're using.

3. Select the *Content Goes Here* text in the Content editable region and delete it.

4. With your cursor still in the editable region, choose Insert, Form, Form. With the form selected, change the value of the Action text box in the Property inspector to read **`search_results.asp`**, **`search_results.cfm`**, or **`search_results.php`**, depending on the server model you're using. Make sure that the GET value is selected from the Method menu. This configuration causes the value the user enters in the text field to be passed along with the URL in the address bar and ultimately allows users to bookmark their search results.

5. Insert a text field form object by selecting Insert, Form, Text Field. With the text field selected, enter the value **`txtSearch`** into the Name text box in the Property inspector.

6. Place your cursor next to the text field and insert a Submit Button form object into the form by choosing Insert, Form, Button. Change the Value text field in the Properties Inspector to read **`Search`**. The result is shown in Figure 21.2.

Save your work and test the results in the browser. Enter a value and click the Search button. As Figure 21.3 shows, the value you enter into the text field is passed along with the URL in the address bar (shown using PHP).

Figure 21.3 shows the value being searched on displayed in the address bar as a parameter appended to the URL string. This is typical for search pages. By passing the search term along the address bar with the URL, you can allow your users to bookmark the results page and return to their searched results at any time. Try this on your own in Amazon to get an idea of how this works. Browse to Amazon's site, search for an item, bookmark the result page, close your browser, reopen it, and then select the bookmarked item. You'll notice that you're instantly returned to the results page, showing the term that you originally search for. This is possible because of the GET method being set on the form within the search page. As soon as the user clicks the Search button, the page is redirected to the results page, but more importantly, the value is taken from the text box and appended to the URL string in the address bar. What we need to do next is capture this parameter being passed along the address bar and re-query the database based on the value.

FIGURE 21.2   Create a new search page by adding the necessary Text Field and Submit Button form objects.

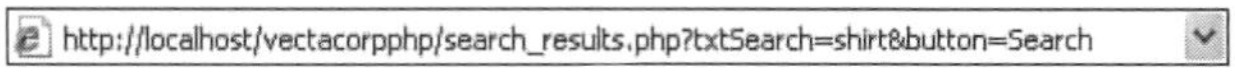

http://localhost/vectacorpphp/search_results.php?txtSearch=shirt&button=Search

FIGURE 21.3   Enter a value in the search text box and click Search. The value is passed along with the URL in the address bar (shown using PHP).

Creating the Search Results Page

Now that the search page has been created, you'll want some way of collecting the value of the user's input and processing the result of the search. The search results page is where all the work is done. The search results page must contain the following components for the search to be processed correctly:

▶ The recordset that represents the table being searched.

▶ The proper filters to capture the user's input from the search page and limit the data being searched based on those filters.

▶ Dynamic text to display the result of the search to the user.

Remember that a recordset is always used to capture the results of the table information. To create a new recordset for the search results page, follow these steps:

1. Create a new page by selecting File, New. The New Document dialog box appears. Select the Page from Template category, select your defined site, choose the template called `template`, and click Create. A new page is created from the template.

2. Immediately save the page as **search_results.asp**, **search_results.cfm**, or **search_results.php**, depending on the server model you're using.

3. Select the recordset option from the Bindings panel's Add (+) menu. The Recordset dialog box appears.

4. Name the recordset **rsSearch**.

5. Select the connVectaCorp option from the Connection menu.

6. Select the EmployeeStore option from the Table menu. We'll assume that users will want to search for items within our store.

7. Choose the All option from the Columns radio button list.

Up to this point, the recordset is configured similar to how we've been configuring it in the previous chapters. What we'll change for this chapter specifically is the Filter set of options. As you can see, the Filter set of options allows you to limit the data being returned from the query and into the recordset by numerous factors. Specifically, the options are as follows:

▶ **Column Filter**—Choose a column from the table to be searched on. This list will display the same columns that the Column list does. However, this list isn't used to select specific columns; it's used to filter data based on a specific column. In our case, we'll assume that users will attempt to find items within the employee store. With that said, choose the ItemName option from this menu now.

▶ **Conditional Expression**—Choose an option from this menu to set the conditional expression to use when performing the filter. Options include Equal (=), Greater Than (>), Less Than (<), Greater Than Or Equal To (>=), Less Than Or Equal To (<=), Not Equal To (<>), Begins With, End With, or Contains. Because we're creating a search based on a keyword, choose the Contains option now.

▶ **Parameter Persistence Method**—When we discuss persistence, we're generally referring to the situation in which a parameter is being carried from one page to the next. This menu displays a list of persistence methods for your parameter. Options include URL Parameter, Form Variable, Cookie, Session Variable, Application Variable, or Entered Value (used primarily for testing the query). Because we're passing our parameter along the URL string, choose URL Parameter.

▶ **Value**—Use this text box to enter the name of the parameter that will supply the parameter value in the URL string. Usually this will be the name of the text field that the user used for supplying the keyword initially. Because our text box was called **txtSearch**, enter that value here. The completely formatted Recordset dialog box will resemble Figure 21.4.

Now that the recordset has been configured, it's probably a good idea to test your work before calling the recordset complete. To test the filter, click the Test button now. The Test Value dialog box appears. Because we know that there are quite a few shirts in our EmployeeStore table, go ahead and enter the keyword **Shirt** now. The result of the query is displayed within the Test SQL Statement window, similar to Figure 21.5.

Click OK to close the Recordset dialog box. Now that the recordset has been created, you'll want to finish off the search results page. To do this, add all the dynamic text elements to the page, dragging the fields from the recordset into their respective positions on the page.

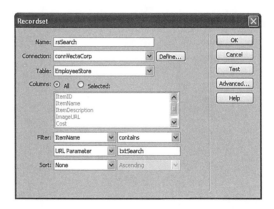

FIGURE 21.4   Use the Filter set of options to limit the data being returned from the query and into the recordset.

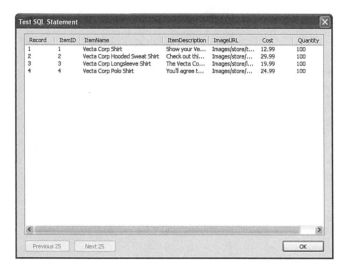

FIGURE 21.5   The result of the search for the keyword Shirt is shown in the Test SQL Statement window.

You might also want to add captions for the field names. In addition, drag the Total Records field into the header so that users are aware of how many records the search produced. (Note that the total record count isn't directly available in the PHP server model, so if you want to display a total record count in the PHP model, choose the Add (+) button in the Server Behaviors panel and choose the Display Total Records option from the Display Record Count submenu.) Figure 21.6 shows the result of the dynamic text and total field additions.

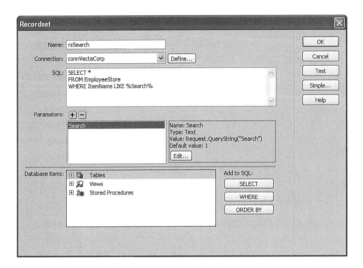

FIGURE 21.6   Add the fields from the recordset as dynamic text. Under the ASP server model, you can also add the total number of records the search produced.

Save your work and test the results in the browser by pressing F12 (Option-F12). Make sure you have the search page open. Type the value **Vecta Corp Shirt** and click Submit. As you'll see, the search produces a filtered result (one record) based on the value entered in the search text box. The results are made possible because of the Filter set of options that we configured.

For the most part, we're done. If you don't care about the more advanced method for working with searches in the recordset, skip past the next two sections. If however, you consider yourself an expert when it comes to writing SQL statements and prefer to write SQL by hand rather than relying on a program to write it for you, read the next section for an alternative method to working with filtered queries in the Recordset dialog box.

Working with Parameters in ASP and PHP

In the previous section, we looked at the basic set of options available within the Recordset dialog box for filtering search results. For the most part, this set of options is all you need. In some cases however, you might want finer control over the filtering, such as having more advanced control over the SQL statements that are being written. This is where the Advanced Recordset dialog box comes in. To use the advanced set of options within the Recordset dialog box, either click the Advanced button now (assuming you still have the Recordset dialog box open from the previous section) or create a new recordset following these steps:

1. Select the Recordset option from the Bindings panel's Add (+) menu. The Recordset dialog box appears.

2. Name the recordset **rsSearch.**

3. Choose the connVectaCorp option from the Connection menu.

4. Click the Advanced button to switch over to the Advanced Recordset dialog box. The dialog box has similar features to the one outlined in the basic view, but with the advanced view you're free to manually write the SQL used in the query. For our purposes, enter the following SQL statement:

```
SELECT *
FROM EmployeeStore
   WHERE ItemName LIKE '%shirt%'
```

5. Click the Test button. The results appear in the Test SQL Statement window, similarly to the way they were shown in the previous section. The difference here obviously is that you were responsible for writing the SQL statement by hand, rather than allowing Dreamweaver to write it for you.

Although the example functions well, it's by no means dynamic. Look closely—as you can see from the SQL statement, we're hardcoding the "shirt" keyword into the SQL statement. If the user wanted to search for "coffee mug" for instance, the search would still return shirts. What we need to do is vary the search based on parameters being passed in. This is where parameters (ASP and ColdFusion) and variables (PHP) come in.

> **NOTE**
>
> Although they're named slightly differently in ASP/ColdFusion and PHP, we'll simply refer to them as parameters from here on out.

Parameters in Dreamweaver's Recordset dialog box allow you to capture user information from sessions, form requests, cookies, and application variables, much like the way that the Filter set of options did in the Simple Recordset dialog box. Parameters let you work dynamically by passing values from one page to another. If you take the search page as an example, a user submits the input in a form object to the search results page. In the search results page, a piece of functionality must be added to capture that input so that it can be automatically appended to the SQL statement's WHERE clause. Enter parameters.

Parameters in Dreamweaver enable you to capture the data being sent from a previous page, store it, and then use it at any time in the current page. If you look closely at the Advanced Recordset dialog box, you'll notice that the middle third of the dialog box is entirely devoted to working with parameters. Facilitated by the Add (+) button, when created parameters contain four properties:

▶ **Name**—The physical name of the parameter.

▶ **Type**—The data type associated with the type of data being stored in the database table.

▶ **Default Value**—A default value to be assigned to the parameter so that its value is never empty at runtime.

▶ **Runtime Value**—The value to assign the parameter.

After the parameter has been created, it functions similarly to how the Filter set of options functions when working in the Simple Recordset view. The difference here however, is that you have slightly more control over what's being written in the SQL statement. Let's set up a parameter now to make the SQL statement we entered in step 4 a bit more dynamic.

> **NOTE**
>
> Parameters are created differently in ASP/PHP than in ColdFusion. The next section is devoted to ColdFusion; here we'll discuss ASP/PHP.

You can set up a parameter to capture the user's input from the search page by following these steps:

1. With the Recordset dialog box still open in Advanced mode, add a parameter to the parameters list by selecting the Add (+) button. The Add Parameter dialog box appears. The parameter should contain the following properties based on the server technology you are using (ASP or PHP):

Model	Name	Type	Default Value	Runtime Value
ASP	Search	Text	abc	Request.QueryString("txtSearch")
PHP	Search	Text	abc	#txtSearch#

> **NOTE**
>
> Notice that we entered the value *abc* as the default value. Because this is a required value, the text *abc* guarantees that at least a value is sent across at runtime.

2. To capture requests made from a form via POST in ASP, you use the Form collection of the Request object, or Request.Form followed by the name of the text box name within quotes. To capture requests made from a form via GET, you use the QueryString collection of the Request object or Request.QueryString followed by the name of the parameter that will be coming across the browser's address bar within quotes. In PHP, it's simply a matter of enclosing the name of the form object with the # symbol. Click OK to close the Add Parameter dialog box.

3. Modify the SQL statement as follows:

```
SELECT * FROM EmployeeStore

    WHERE ItemName LIKE '%Search%'
```

4. As you can see, you want to use the keyword LIKE followed by the name of the variable you just created (Search). Also, we use the % operator as a way of retrieving all the values beginning and ending with the value we're passing in as a parameter. The result of the completely formatted Recordset dialog box should resemble Figure 21.7.

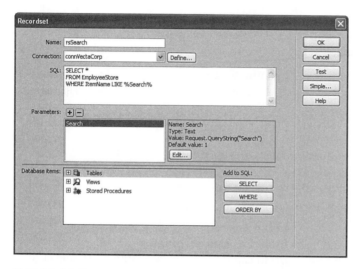

FIGURE 21.7   Format the SQL statement in the Recordset dialog box to accept the Search keyword as a parameter.

5. Click OK. The new recordset appears in the Bindings panel.

Now that the recordset has been created, you'll want to finish off the search results page. To do this, add all the dynamic text elements to the page, dragging the fields from the recordset into their respective positions on the page. You might also want to add captions for the field names. In addition, drag the Total Records field into the header so that users are aware of how many records the search produced. (Note that the total record count isn't directly available in the PHP server model; if you want to display a total record count in the PHP model, choose the Add (+) button in the Server Behaviors panel and choose the Display Total Records option from the Display Record Count submenu.) Figure 21.6 shows the result of the dynamic text and total field additions.

Save your work and test the results in the browser by pressing F12 (Option-F12). Make sure you have the search page open in the browser. Type the value **Vecta Corp Shirt** and click Submit. The search produces a filtered result (one record) based on the value entered in the search text box. The results are made possible because of the parameter we set up, which captured the results of the request sent by the form's submission. The parameter was then appended to the SQL statement, which caused the dynamic search for the object's value.

Working with Parameters in ColdFusion

As with the ASP and PHP server models, search functionality for our Vecta Corp site can easily be created using the ColdFusion server model. The difference between ColdFusion and the other server models lies in how we store and use the value that's coming across, appended to the URL in the address bar. As you saw in the previous two sections, variables and parameters were used for collecting, storing, and then subsequently reusing the value coming across. In the ColdFusion server model, however, variables and parameters are not necessary. Instead we can dynamically append to the WHERE clause of the SQL statement the value of the form name as a parameter, enclosed with # symbols. To demonstrate this, let's build the search functionality in ColdFusion:

1. With the Recordset dialog box still open in Advanced mode, modify the SQL statement to accept the form object's name enclosed with # symbols in the WHERE clause:

```
SELECT * FROM EmployeeStore
    WHERE ItemName LIKE '#txtSearch#'
```

In this case, the txtSearch form name is appended to the WHERE clause as a parameter. ColdFusion is smart enough to check either the HTTP headers or the address bar for a form object that matches the parameter called txtSearch.

2. Click OK. The recordset appears in the Bindings panel.

3. Add all the dynamic text elements to the page (similarly to how we did it in the previous sections), dragging the fields from the recordset into their respective positions on the page. You might also want to add captions for the field names. Figure 21.6 shows the result of the dynamic text additions.

Save your work and test the results in the browser by pressing F12 (Option-F12). Make sure you have the search page open. Type the value **Vecta Corp Shirt** into the text box and click Submit. As you can see, the search produced a filtered result (one record) based on the value we entered in the search text box.

Repeating Regions

Now that your application has search capabilities, you might want to allow the user to see more than one item returned from the search at a time. For now, our search works fine as is because we're performing a search (Vecta Corp Shirt) that returns only one result from the EmployeeStore table. But what if the user performed a search on just the word *shirt*? In this case, our search would return multiple results because numerous items in the EmployeeStore table contain the word *shirt*. But would it really return multiple results? Let's try it! Type the word **shirt** into the search page and click Search. The results page returns just the first item in our EmployeeStore table.

The problem doesn't lie in the functionality we've added; rather, it lies in the functionality we *haven't* added. Our recordset is returning multiple results. The problem is that we haven't added functionality for repeating all the values contained in the recordset within the search results page. To fix this problem, we need only add a repeating region. (Repeating regions were discussed at length in Chapter 19, "Working with Dynamic Data.") To add a repeating region to your results page, follow these steps:

1. Add a line break after the product cost field on the results page and highlight the section of text, including all the dynamic data.

2. Select the Repeat Region server behavior by clicking the Add (+) button within the Server Behaviors panel. The Repeat Region Server Behavior dialog box appears.

3. Select the rsSearch option from the Recordset menu and select the Show All Records option button.

4. Click OK. The Repeat Region invisible element wraps your captions and dynamic text.

Save your work and test the search page in the browser by pressing F12 (Option-F12). Now type a value such as **shirt** into the text box and click Search. Figure 21.8 shows the four records that are displayed in the results page (shown using ColdFusion).

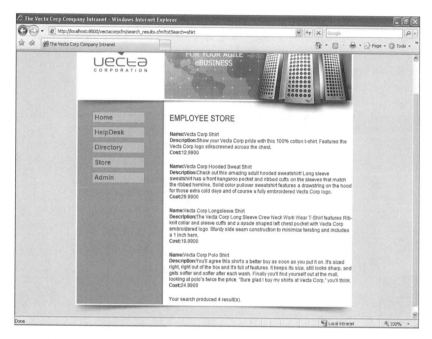

FIGURE 21.8   The Repeat Region server behavior opens the door for your users by allowing them to search for data in the database that might have more than one result.

Displaying Alternative Text

Currently, as users search for data in the database, they are presented with results in a structured format. But suppose that users enter a value to search by and the recordset cannot return a match (the page returns blank)? You can imagine how confused a user might get.

Using the Show Region server behavior set, you can present users with an alternative text message, alerting them of the failed search result and allowing them to link back to the search page to try their search again. To insert the alternative text into your search result page, follow these steps:

1. Open search_results.asp, search_results.cfm, or search_results.php (depending on the server model you're using) and place your cursor just after the last dynamic element that exists on the page. Add a line break.

2. Insert the text **Sorry, your search did not produce a result.** and create a link for the text **Try Again**. Make the Try Again text link back to the search.asp, search.cfm, or search.php page, depending on the server model you're using.

3. Highlight the Sorry text and the Try Again link and select the Show Region If Recordset Is Empty server behavior from the Show Region submenu in the Server Behaviors panel. The Show Region If Recordset Is Empty dialog box appears.

4. Choose the rsSearch option from the Recordset menu and click OK. The Show If Invisible element wraps the text and the link.

Save your work and test the result in the browser by pressing F12 (Option-F12). In the search page, type something you know the search will not produce a result for, such as **Vecta Corp Paperclip** and click Search. Your Sorry message will appear, along with the Try Again link that allows you to link back to the search page, as shown in Figure 21.9 (shown in ColdFusion).

FIGURE 21.9   If the recordset comes up empty, you are presented with the custom message along with a link that allows you to link back to the search page.

Globalizing the Search Functionality

Now that most of the search functionality has been added, you're ready to make it available from every page in the Vecta Corp site. This can be done simply by adding a new link to the navigation menu within the `template` file. To add a new navigation item to the search page, follow these steps:

1. Open the template file that currently resides in the Templates folder for your defined site.

2. Place your cursor to the right of the last Admin link within the navigation menu and press Enter/Return.

3. Enter the text **Search**.

4. Highlight the text and establish a link to the search.asp, search.cfm, search.php page, depending on the server model you're using. The design should resemble Figure 21.10.

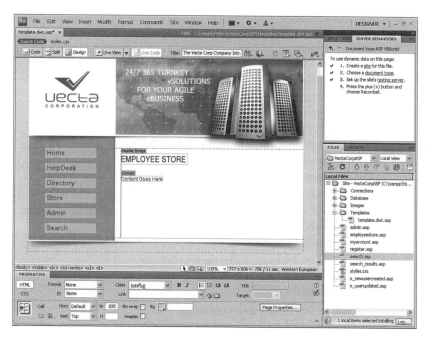

FIGURE 21.10   Add a search link to the navigation menu in the template.

5. Save the page. You will be asked to update all the pages that use the template. Click Yes.

6. The Update Pages dialog box appears, alerting you of the files that Dreamweaver updated.

7. Click Close.

Summary

By now you should have a solid understanding of querying databases, inserting information into databases, and modifying and deleting information within databases. Although it seems as though we've accomplished a lot thus far, in the next few chapters, we'll explore shopping cart functionality, implementing security, defining how your users will access your site, and more.

CHAPTER 22

Security and User Authentication

One of the hottest topics today is security. So much so, in fact, that hundreds of websites, articles, ads, and books exist devoted to the subject. Many companies, consultants, and organizations are dedicated to helping protect you and your company's vital asset—data. It's not a downside by any stretch of the imagination; in fact, major online news sites, portals, and even government agencies have been invaded in one form or another, while employing some measure of security. Although this chapter cannot begin to cover all there is to know regarding the subject, it can help you better understand the basic framework to securing your web applications using a login page, restricting access to specific parts of your site, and more.

Like the rest of the chapters in this book, you can work with the examples in this chapter by downloading the files from the book's website. Remember, you'll want to save the files for Chapter 22 (contained within Exercises\Chapter22\Beginning) in the `C:\Inetpub\wwwroot\VectaCorp<technology>` (IIS), `C:\xampp\htdocs\VectaCorpPHP` (XAMPP), `/Applications/MAMP/htdocs/VectaCorpPHP` (MAMP), or `C:\ColdFusion8\wwwroot\VectaCorpCFM` (ColdFusion) directories.

The security umbrella encompasses many facets of information technology, including web development. This means making sure that users can go where they need to go and see what they're allowed to see in your application. Some steps you could take include ensuring that all visitors to your site log in before they can view any pages, and if they're not logged in, making sure that they can't just accidentally type in the URL to a section of the application specifically meant for an administrator. Although different solutions exist for various applications that you can create—for instance, your web server could provide certain pages to users who have been authenticated by user groups in an intranet environment—this chapter focuses on simple form-based and script-based authentication.

If you're working in the ASP, ColdFusion, or PHP server models, Dreamweaver has a solution for securing the Vecta Corp site in its User Authentication suite of server behaviors. In combination with some simple coding techniques, this chapter enables you to accomplish the following tasks using these server behaviors:

▶ Log in users

▶ Restrict users based on username, password, and access level

▶ Log out users

▶ Create custom error messages

▶ Check for duplicate usernames

Creating a Login Page

The first step to securing any web application is to create a login page for your users. There'd be no point in creating an admin page, for instance, if anyone could use it. Ideally what you want is an application that allows your users to register and navigate through the site based on access rights that you specify. What benefit does this provide? Assume that you want to allow visitors to your site and purchase items without the tedious task of becoming a registered user. The question is then whether your users are repeat customers. If they are and they don't register, they might have to input their personal information more than once, essentially ending up doing more work than it was to simply register the first time. Another benefit of registering your users is that you can store all your users' shipping/billing information, giving them a streamlined experience as they purchase items. As a developer, you might want to generate emails to your registered users, alerting them of specials and bargains. There are many benefits and reasons for maintaining a list of registered users. For the most part, the process is relatively straightforward. Users register on your site. After they are registered, you will want them to access the site through a secure location, typically through a login page.

You've seen login pages before; eBay, for instance, asks you to log in to its site before you can bid on an item. You can see the correlation if you wanted to actually purchase something. How would the application know which shopping cart to place the item into? A login page enables you not only to maintain a list of registered users, but also to create sessions (briefly highlighted in the previous chapter and discussed with more detail later in this chapter) for the users' experience while they're on your site. That way, if a customer wants to purchase something, that item is stored within the logged-in user's cart. You can create a login page for the Vecta Corp site by following these steps:

1. Create a new page by selecting File, New. Choose the Page from Template option, select your defined site, select the template titled login (this is included for you in the chapter downloads) from the defined site, and click Create.

> **NOTE**
>
> Throughout the book, we've been working with the template named `template`. The problem with using this template is that it contains the navigation menu. Users logging in for the first time shouldn't be able to see that menu until they've logged in. Because the login template has the navigation menu completely removed, it's the perfect alternative for the Login page.

2. Select the text *Content Goes Here* from the content editable region and delete it.

3. With your cursor still in the editable region, create a new form by choosing Insert, Form, Form.

4. With your cursor in the form, create a new table by choosing Insert, Table. The Table dialog appears. Assign the table **4** rows, **2** columns, a width of **300** pixels, and a border, cell padding, and cell spacing of **0** pixels. Click OK to create the table within the form.

5. Below the new table, add a link to the New User Registration page. You can do this by placing your cursor next to the table and pressing Enter. Now choose Insert, Hyperlink. The Hyperlink dialog box appears. Enter the text `New User?` into the Text text box and enter the path to `register.asp`, `register.cfm`, or `register.php` (depending on the server model you're using) in the Link text box. Click OK when you're finished. The new link is created below the table.

6. Place your cursor in the first cell of the first column of the new table and add the text `Username:`. Move your cursor to the second cell of the first column of the same table and add the text `Password:`.

7. Place your cursor in the first cell of the second column and add a new text field form object by choosing Insert, Form, Text Field. Name the field `username` in the Property inspector.

8. Place your cursor in the second cell of the second column and add a new text field form object by choosing Insert, Form, Text Field. Name the field `password` in the Property inspector. Also, change the Type value to Password in the Property inspector because this field will accommodate password entries.

9. Place your cursor in the fourth cell of the second column and add a Submit button form object by choosing Insert, Form, Button. Immediately change the label to read `Log In` in the Property inspector. The result is shown in Figure 22.1.

10. Save your work as `login.asp`, `login.cfm`, or `login.php`, depending on the server model you're working with.

Now test the results within the browser by pressing F12 (Option-F12). As you'll notice, the page in the browser resembles a typical login page.

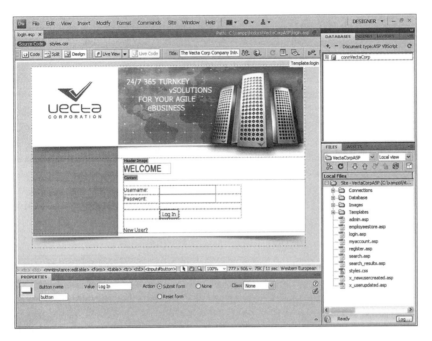

FIGURE 22.1   Add the Log In button form object to the page.

Logging In the User

Now that the basic structure of the login page has been created, you're ready to add the server behavior that facilitates the user login. To add this functionality, follow these steps:

1. With the login page still open, select the Log In User behavior from the User Authentication submenu by clicking the Add (+) button in the Server Behaviors panel. The Log In User dialog box appears.

2. Select the form1 option from the Get Input from Form menu.

3. Choose the username option from the Username Field menu. Also choose the password option from the Password Field menu. These are the fields within the form (form1) that the server behavior will compare when validation is performed.

4. Choose the connVectaCorp option from the Validate Using Connection menu.

5. Select the Employees option from the Table menu.

6. Choose the Username option from the Username Column menu. Also, choose the Password (or Pass) option from the Password Column menu. These are the fields in the database table that the form values (specified in step 3) will be compared against.

7. Type the value **index.asp**, **index.cfm**, or **index.php** (depending on the server model you are using) into the If Login Succeeds, Go To text box. Also type the value **login.asp**, **login.cfm**, or **login.php** into the If Login Fails, Go To text box. Later, you'll see how to customize this value to create custom error messages for the user.

8. Make sure that the Username and Password option button is selected in the Restrict Access Based On option button group. The result of the completely formatted Log In User dialog box resembles Figure 22.2.

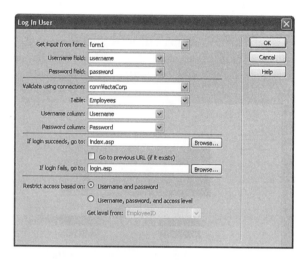

FIGURE 22.2   Format the Log In User dialog box accordingly.

9. Click OK. The new Log In User server behavior appears in the Server Behaviors list, and the form on the page highlights in blue (because it is an invisible element).

TIP

If you have not done so already, you can configure your web server to accept `login.asp`, `login.cfm`, or `login.php` as the default page. You'd want to perform this step so that when your users type in your website address, they're automatically redirected to the login page, instead of a page they're not supposed to see until they log in. To set the login page as the default document within IIS, for instance, start by right-clicking the website in IIS, selecting Properties, and choosing the Documents tab. In the Default Documents list, add the page `login.asp`, `login.cfm`, or `login.php` (depending on the server model you're using).

Save your work. Before you test the login page, you'll need to perform two more steps. First, check the Employees table in the database to make sure that you have a valid username and password to test against. This way, when you log in, you'll be prepared with a set of valid login credentials. Second, create the `index.asp`, `index.cfm`, or `index.php` page so that you'll redirect to a valid document after a successful login. I'll assume that by now, you're armed with enough knowledge from previous chapters in the book to be able to create that page on your own if it's not created already.

After those two steps are complete, you're ready to test the functionality. To do this, press F12 (Option-F12). When the Login page appears, enter the username and password into the appropriate fields and click the Log In button. If you entered the username and password correctly, you are redirected to `index.asp`, `index.cfm`, or `index.php`, depending on the server model you're working with. If you entered the login information incorrectly, however, the Login page simply appears to refresh itself (we'll address this later).

You now have a working Login page. But what exactly is going on? How are the user's credentials tracked, and better yet, how can we use those credentials on other pages in the site to prevent users from trying to access pages without first logging in? The great thing about the Log In User server behavior is that a session variable (covered next) is automatically created for the user, as follows:

```
Session("MM_Username")
```

This session variable can be used in other pages (as you'll see in the next section) using server behaviors, code, or a combination of both to determine whether the user is logged in.

> **NOTE**
>
> The measure of activity that a user spends on a website during a specified period of time is known as a *user session*. The user session begins when the user accesses the application and ends when the user quits the application (by either logging out or closing the browser). Because the user session is typically stored in a browser cookie, developers can take advantage of sessions in an effort to store and persist specific data about the user. The Login User server behavior, for instance, uses user sessions to store a *key* authorizing the user to browse through a site that is protected by a user authentication system like the one we're creating here.

Restricting Access Based on Username, Password, and Access Level

The next step in securing your web application is to restrict those users who do not meet your specified criteria. You can specify this criteria by setting an access level that will eventually be used to track users as they navigate through your site. The reason for establishing access criteria is simple—you want to make sure that your users do not accidentally navigate to a page they are not supposed to see, such as the admin page. The last thing you want is for ordinary users to delete products from the EmployeeStore table via the admin page. You can create access levels for your users by following these steps:

1. Open the database management system for the type of database you are using. The following examples and subsequent screenshots assume that you are using Access. However, you can follow all these examples using Management Studio Express (for SQL Server 2005 Express) or MySQL Administrator (MySQL) as well.

2. With the database open, open the Employees table in Design view. The Employees table appears in Design view, similar to Figure 22.3.

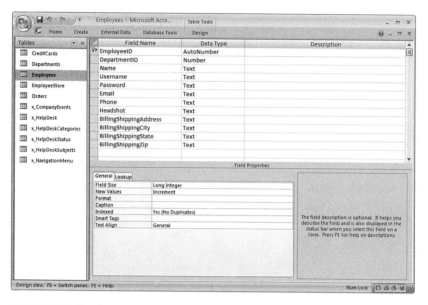

FIGURE 22.3   Open the Employees table in Design view.

3. Right-click the Email field and select Insert Rows, as shown in Figure 22.4.

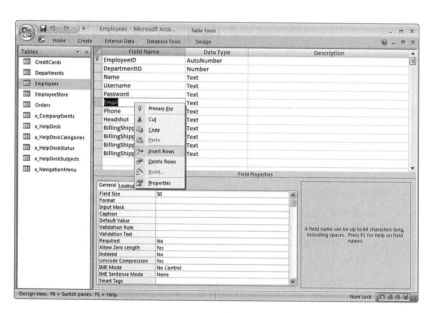

FIGURE 22.4   Insert a new row for the access level field.

4. Call the new field `AccessLevel` and give it a numeric (Number) data type.

5. Save the table by choosing File, Save. Switch to the Datasheet view by clicking the View icon just below the File menu.

6. In the AccessLevel column, assign a value of **2** to all the users except for Wally the Webmaster. Assign him a value of **1**. The result is shown in Figure 22.5.

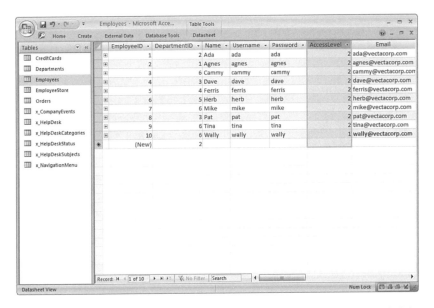

FIGURE 22.5   Give Wally an access level of 1. This makes Wally the administrator of the site.

The following table describes the levels of users and how they will be tracked within the application:

Level	Type	Description
1	Admin	Rights to the entire site
2	User	Rights to all pages, excluding the admin page

7. You're done making changes to the database. Save your work and close out of your database.

8. Switch back to the `login.asp`, `login.cfm`, or `login.php` page in Dreamweaver and reopen the Log In User server behavior by double-clicking it in the Server Behaviors panel. The Log In User dialog box opens.

9. At the bottom of the dialog box, you'll see the Restrict Access Based On option button group. This time, select the Username, Password, and Access Level option button. Choose the AccessLevel option from the Get Level From menu that becomes enabled, as shown in Figure 22.6.

10. Click OK.

11. Save your work.

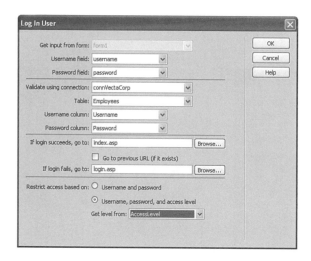

FIGURE 22.6   Change the login criteria to Username, Password, and Access Level.

Although you will not see any changes when you log in, rest assured that a session variable has been set for the access level, named

```
Session("MM_UserAuthorization")
```

As was the case with the session variable `MM_Username` that was created in the previous section, the session variable `MM_UserAuthorization` can also be checked against the Login User server behavior dialog box to check whether a user has the appropriate access level to access a particular page.

Custom Error Messages

Although you can present many error messages to the user, one that must be taken care of right away is the failed login error message. Currently, if a user logs in with an inappropriate username and password, the browser redirects to the same login page and does nothing. Ideally, what you want is a custom error message that alerts the user of a failed login attempt. Knowing this, the user can try to log in again. You can create a simple error message by following these steps:

1. Open the login page if it is not currently open. Add two new rows to the login table just below the button form object that you created previously.

2. Add the text **That is not a valid login.** in the second row. Change the font to a red color so that it appears as if it is an error message.

3. The next step is to somehow capture an error response from the login failure. You can accomplish this by setting a URL parameter in the Log In User dialog box. Open the Log In User server behavior by double-clicking it in the Server Behaviors panel.

When the dialog box opens, add the string **?valid=false** just after login.asp in the If Login Fails, Go To text box, as shown in Figure 22.7.

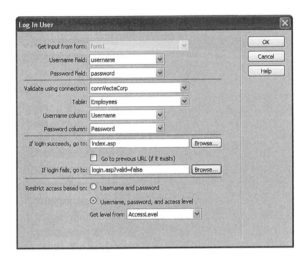

FIGURE 22.7   Add a parameter to the URL string for the failure response.

4. Click OK to close the Log In User dialog box.

5. You'll now want to write some code to capture that parameter if it exists and display the message accordingly. To do this, highlight the error message you created in step 2 and switch to Code view. Replace your selection with the following code (shown in ASP):

```
<% If (Request.QueryString("valid") = "false") Then %>
<span style="color:Red">
That is not a valid login.
</span>
    <% End If %>
```

If you're using ColdFusion, replace it with the following code:

```
<CFIF ISDEFINED("URL.valid")>
    <CFIF URL.valid IS "false">
    <span style="color:Red">
    That is not a valid login.
    </span>
    </CFIF>
</CFIF>
```

If you're using PHP, replace it with the following code:

```php
<?php
if (isset($_GET['valid'])=="false") {
echo "<span style=color:Red>That is not a valid login.</span>";
}
?>
```

As you can probably make out from the code snippet you just added, the idea is to check whether a parameter is being sent across the query string named valid. If there is, and that parameter has a value of false, it will display the message *That is not a valid login*.

Save your work and test the result in the browser by pressing F12 (Option-F12). Enter some bogus information into the username and password text boxes and click Login. This time, you should be presented with the error message.

Checking to See Whether the User Is Logged In

Although you might think your application is completely secure, it is, in fact, still completely vulnerable. What's to stop a user from typing in the URL to your application plus index.asp, index.cfm, or index.php, completely bypassing your login page? You should never expect your users to use the login page simply because it's there. Most browsers even try to guess the URL you are typing by autofilling the complete URL. If users accidentally select the index page, they can easily bypass the login page and jump directly into the site, thus failing to create a session for the user and ultimately causing errors. You can avoid this problem by detecting whether the user's session exists. Because the user session is created at login, if the user tries to bypass the login screen, the application can detect this and redirect the user back to the login page automatically. To add this functionality to your site, follow these steps:

1. Open the admin.asp, admin.cfm, or admin.php page, depending on the server model you're using. We're opening this page because this is one of the only pages in the site to which we want to restrict user access.

2. Select the Restrict Access to Page server behavior from the User Authentication submenu by clicking the Add (+) button in the Server Behaviors panel. The Restrict Access to Page dialog box appears.

3. The Restrict Access to Page dialog box enables you to set user levels that are allowed to enter this page, as well as a redirect URL for the failure. Select the Username, Password, Access Level option button.

4. Click the Define button. The Define Access Levels dialog box appears.

5. From this dialog box, you can customize and configure access levels that are allowed to view your page. Click the Add (+) button and add the value 1 (administrator's access level), as shown in Figure 22.8.

FIGURE 22.8   The Define Access Levels dialog box enables you to set access restrictions for a particular page.

6. Click OK to close the Define Access Levels dialog box.

7. Back in the Restrict Access to Page dialog box, make sure that you select the access level 1 option from the Select Level(s) list box.

8. Type the following value into the If Access Denied, Go To text box:

```
login.asp?login=false
```

Obviously, if you're using ColdFusion, the extension for the login file is .cfm, and if you're using PHP, the extension is .php. Similarly to how we defined the custom error message for the failed login attempt, we'll create a custom error message that displays an error to users, alerting them that they'll need to log in before proceeding to any of the pages in the site. The completely formatted dialog box is shown in Figure 22.9.

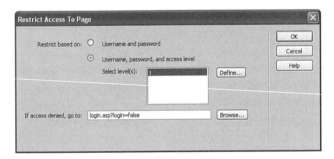

FIGURE 22.9   Add a parameter to the end of the URL so that you can eventually create a custom error message on the login page.

TIP

If you're using ColdFusion, there's one other modification you need to make in the code. In the login.cfm page, switch to Code view and change the scope="Session" attribute and value to scope="Server". This line usually appears as the first line of code in the page.

9. Reopen the login page if it's not open already. Place your cursor below the existing error message and type the text **You must be logged in.**

10. Again switch to Code view and type the following code (shown in ASP), just under the code you entered in step 5 of the previous section:

```
<% If (Request.QueryString("login") = "false") Then %>
<span style="color:Red">
You must be logged in.
</span>

    <% End If %>
```

If you're using ColdFusion, type the following code:

```
<CFIF ISDEFINED("URL.login")>
    <CFIF URL.login IS "false">
    <span style="color:Red">
    You must be logged in.
    </span>
    </CFIF>

    </CFIF>
```

If you're using PHP, type the following code:

```
<?php
if (isset($_GET['login'])=="false") {
echo "<span style=color:Red>You must be logged in.</span>";
}

    ?>
```

As you can probably make out from the code snippet you just added, the plan is to check whether a parameter is being sent across the query string named login. If there is, and that parameter has a value of false, the browser displays the message You must be logged in.

Save your work. This time, make sure that all the browsers are closed. This action effectively terminates all sessions. Reopen the browser and try to go straight to the admin.asp, admin.cfm, or admin.php page without logging in first. You are automatically redirected back to the login page, and the custom error message is displayed.

Now that you know how to add it to the admin page, you'll want to add this functionality to all the pages in the Vecta Corp application that you want to restrict user access to. I'll leave that decision to you.

Logging Out Users

Just as you require your users to log in, you will want them to log out as well. Logging out guarantees that the users' session variables are instantly terminated, forcing them to log in again whenever they return to the site. For the most part, users will simply close the browser, terminating the session, but if users continue to browse online, it might be a good idea to alert them to log out first. Session variables by default remain active for 20 minutes, so if users fail to log out, their sessions will remain active even though they're navigating another website. To create the logout functionality for the Vecta Corp site, follow these steps:

1. Open the Vecta Corp template for the site you're working with. The `template.dwt.asp`, `template.dwt.cfm`, and `template.dwt.php` files are located in the Templates folder in the Site Files panel regardless of the server model you're using.

2. Add a new navigation menu item by placing your cursor just after the Search menu item and press Enter (Return).

3. Type the text **Log Out.**

4. With the text highlighted, select the Log Out User server behavior in the User Authentication submenu by clicking the Add (+) button in the Server Behaviors panel. The Log Out User dialog box appears.

5. The Log Out User dialog box enables you to specify criteria for the logout, including whether the logout will take place when the user clicks a button, a link, or when the page loads. You can also specify a page to redirect the user to after the log out button/link has been clicked. For our project, select the Selection: "Log Out" option from the Link Clicked menu and enter the value **../login.asp**, **../login.cfm**, or **../login.php** (depending on the server technology you're using) in the When Done, Go To text box.

6. Click OK to close the Log Out User dialog box.

7. Save the page and update all pages that share the template.

Test the result in the browser by opening the `login.asp`, `login.cfm`, or `login.php` page and pressing F12 (Option-F12). Log in and navigate through the site. Try clicking the Log Out link. You are immediately redirected to the login page. Try typing **admin.asp**, **admin.cfm**, or **admin.php** (essentially a page that restricts access based on the session) into the address bar, and you should be redirected back to the login page with the error message displayed. The reason for this redirection is simple: Your session doesn't exist anymore. Clicking the Log Out button does two important things: It completely removes the session variables MM_Username and MM_UserAuthorization, and it redirects you to the login page. The important thing to remember is that the two session variables are removed. And because they don't exist, the application treats you as if you've never logged in before.

Revamping the New User Registration Page

Now that most of the site has some sort of security integration, the last order of business is to make the New User Registration Page available only to new users. If a user has already registered, that user won't visit the page, but for users who have never been to the site, the New User Registration page must be made available and easy to find. You've added a link from the login page that jumps directly to the New User Registration page; the problem is that you still have buttons to the left of that page that link to the other Vecta

Corp pages. A new user should not be given the opportunity to navigate to any portions of the site. You can change this by following these steps:

1. Open the `register.asp`, `register.cfm`, or `register.php` page.

2. Select Modify, Templates, Detach from Template.

3. Select the navigation menu to the left of the page and completely remove it.

4. Save your work.

5. Open the `x_newusercreated.asp`, `x_newusercreated.cfm`, or `x_newusercreated.php` page. Select Modify, Templates, Detach from Template. Select the navigation menu and remove it as well.

6. Place your cursor after the text *Thank you for registering as a new user* and press Enter.

7. Choose Insert, Hyperlink. The Hyperlink dialog box appears. Type the text **Log In**. Enter the link **login.asp**, **login.cfm**, or **login.php** (depending on the server model you're using). Click OK to close the Hyperlink dialog box and create the new link.

When a new user registers, the user is taken to the `x_newusercreated.asp`, `x_newusercreated.cfm`, or `x_newusercreated.php` page. This time, however, the user will have the opportunity to click the Log In link to be redirected to the Log In page.

Avoiding Duplicate Usernames

The last order of business is the Check New Username server behavior. The Check New Username server behavior enables you to check the username of the person who is registering on your site to make sure that a duplicate does not exist within the database. This is done to avoid confusion when people register within your site. Have you ever tried obtaining a username with Google, Yahoo!, Hotmail, or AOL? It's almost impossible because most of the usernames are taken. Companies such as these employ these same methods to avoid conflicts between users. You can check for duplicate usernames within your site by following these steps:

1. Open `register.asp`, `register.cfm`, or `register.php`, depending on the server model you're using.

2. With the page open, select the Check New Username server behavior available from the User Authentication submenu by clicking the Add (+) button in the Server Behaviors panel. The Check New Username dialog box appears.

3. The Check New Username dialog box allows you to specify the field in the database to compare the value to. Select the Username option from this menu.

4. The dialog box also enables you to specify a page to redirect to if a duplicate username exists. Enter the following value into this text box:

```
register.asp?username=exists
```

If you're using ColdFusion, the extension for the `register` file is `.cfm`, and if you're using PHP, the extension is `.php`. Figure 22.10 shows the formatted Check New Username dialog box.

FIGURE 22.10   Specify the Username field in the database as well as a parameter so that you can create a custom error message to the user if the proposed username happens to be a duplicate.

5. Click OK to close the Check New Username dialog box. The new server behavior appears in the Server Behaviors panel.

6. You'll now want to add the custom error message that the user will see should there be a duplicate username. To add this message, place your cursor next to the username text field and type the text **Username already exists.**

7. You'll want to capture the parameter that will be sent across if a duplicate username exists. Remember that the parameter is username and the value is exists. To handle this, select the *Username already exists* text, switch to Code view, and wrap the text you wrote with the following code (shown here in ASP):

```
<% If (Request.QueryString("username") = "exists") Then %>
<span style="color:Red">
Username already exists.
</span>
    <% End If %>
```

If you're using ColdFusion, type the following code:

```
<CFIF ISDEFINED("URL.username")>
    <CFIF URL.username IS "exists">
    <span style="color:Red">
    Username already exists
    </span>
    </CFIF>
</CFIF>
```

If you're using PHP, type the following code:

```
<?php
if (isset($_GET['username'])=="exists") {
echo "<span style=color:Red>Username already exists.</span>";
}
    ?>
```

Save your work and test the result in the browser by pressing F12 (Option-F12). Try entering a username that you know already exists, such as **ada** or **wally**, into the Username text field. When you click the Submit button, the error message is shown.

Setting Access Levels

Now that you are checking access levels on pages within the Vecta Corp site, you'll probably want to add some functionality that sets the access level when the new user registers. There are two ways to accomplish this task: First, you could modify the default value property for the field in the database to always be 2 when a new user is created. Second, you could add a hidden field in the New User Registration page and set it equal to a certain number, in this case 2, and have that automatically insert the value into the AccessLevel field in the Employees table along with the rest of the new user information. Because this second approach is the simplest method to demonstrate, let's do that now:

1. Open the `register.asp`, `register.cfm`, or `register.php` page if it's not open already.

2. Somewhere on the page, insert a new hidden field by selecting Insert, Form, Hidden Field. The yellow hidden field invisible element appears. Select it.

3. Name the hidden field **accesslevel** and give it a default value of **2** (because 2 represents an ordinary user). The result of the modifications in the Property inspector resemble Figure 22.11.

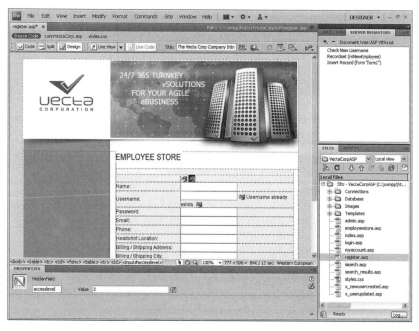

FIGURE 22.11   Add a hidden field, name it **accesslevel**, and assign it a default value of **2**.

4. Modify the Insert Record server behavior so that it inserts this value into the Employees table. To do this, double-click the Insert Record server behavior in the Server Behaviors panel. The Insert Record dialog box appears.

5. Find the access level form object in the Form Elements selection box, select it, and then choose the AccessLevel option from the Column menu similar to Figure 22.12.

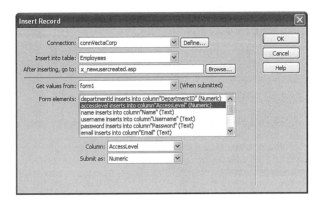

FIGURE 22.12   Associate the access level hidden field with the AccessLevel field in the Employees table.

Click OK to close the Insert Record dialog box. Save your work and test the results in the browser by pressing F12 (Option-F12). Create a new user. When you are finished, check the database to make sure that all the appropriate information was added, including the default access level of 2.

Summary

In this chapter, you examined ways of securing your web applications. You learned about all the behaviors available in Dreamweaver to completely secure your ASP, ColdFusion, and PHP applications. You learned how to build a login form, how to authenticate users against a database, restrict access to specific pages in your site based on access level, create and process error messages, check for existing usernames, and log out users by modifying a central template.

In the next chapter, we'll discuss a topic that is taking the web development world by storm: web services. Additionally, we'll look at another topic that's heavily integrated into Dreamweaver and the ColdFusion server model: ColdFusion Components, or CFCs.

Working with Web Services and ColdFusion Components

Looking back over the past few years, it's hard to imagine networked computers without the Web. The Web allows for networked communication with hundreds of services provided by hundreds of companies and organizations. From a user standpoint, if you can type, you can access these services. From an application service provider standpoint, if you can set up a website, communication is opened up to other services. The problem doesn't lie in the access of those services, but in the communication between the users and the services. The web service movement aims to solve this problem by facilitating the communication between users and services and even between services.

By "services," I don't mean the typical online shopping or auction application, such as Amazon or eBay. Services can range from something as simple as a process that checks the weather or validates a credit card to something as complex as an airline flight reservation service that automatically deducts money from a centralized account that you specify, updates a global calendar that you maintain, and even reserves a hotel and rental car based on the destination that you desire. Seem far off? Think again.

An Introduction to Web Services

Web services are new types of web applications. They are self-contained, modular programs that can be published, found, and called over the Web. They perform functions that can range from something as simple as validating a credit card to updating hotel reservations. After a web service is deployed, users, applications, and other web services can invoke functions (called *web methods*) that you build within the web service. Still seem like it's too good to be true? Think again. Web services are currently being used across a multitude of web initiatives. From Microsoft to Amazon and Orbitz to PayPal, web services are currently being developed, exposed, and consumed across a wide array of industry segments.

So what makes up a web service? The basic framework of a web service lies within its platform. Platform, you ask? Web services, unlike their predecessors (RPC, CORBA, and DCOM), rely on open standards, outlined here:

▶ **XML**—The Extensible Markup Language (XML) is the meta language used to write specialized languages to articulate interactions between clients and services. Web services use XML and XML schema to define the data used within web services.

▶ **SOAP**—The Simple Object Access Protocol (SOAP) is a protocol specification that defines a uniform way of passing XML data between networks. Think of SOAP in terms of HTTP. With HTTP, a user requests a page (usually by typing in the HTTP address), and a response is returned in the form of a website. The protocol that the website was delivered with was HTTP. SOAP, on the other hand, is the protocol used to define how objects are accessed and transferred across networks, typically packaged using XML within a SOAP envelope "wrapper." A user or service makes a SOAP request and a response is returned, as is the case with HTTP.

▶ **HTTP**—The Hypertext Transfer Protocol (HTTP) drives how we access information on the Web. Web services use SOAP in conjunction with HTTP. Because HTTP is the protocol for accessing information on the Web, SOAP can use HTTP to deliver the "wrapped" XML messages in a universal, operating system-independent and server technology-agnostic format.

▶ **WSDL**—The Web Services Definition Language (WSDL) provides a way for web service providers to describe how and what their web services do, where they reside, and how to invoke them. You will use WSDL in more detail later in this chapter.

▶ **UDDI**—The Universal Description, Discovery, and Integration service (UDDI) provides a mechanism for clients to dynamically find other web services. Using a UDDI interface, applications can locate and use other web services. You can think of UDDI as a DNS, or "yellow pages," for business applications or web services.

As you can see, the foundation for web services lies in open standards such as XML, SOAP, HTTP, WSDL, and UDDI. But how do these components make up the web services architecture? Figure 23.1 sheds some more light on the subject.

The building blocks of web services are solidly rooted in open source standards such as XML, SOAP, HTTP, WSDL, and UDDI. But how do you use these standards to create your own web services? For the most part, the development of web services is up to you. More specifically, web services are created by your language of choice in VB .NET, C#, ColdFusion, Java, and more. How you expose, consume, and discover the web service after it's created is ultimately up to the standards mentioned in Figure 23.1.

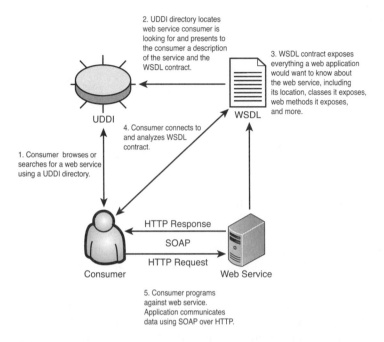

2. UDDI directory locates
web service consumer is
looking for and presents to
the consumer a description
of the service and the
WSDL contract.

3. WSDL contract exposes
everything a web application
would want to know about
the web service, including
its location, classes it exposes,
web methods it exposes,
and more.

UDDI

4. Consumer connects to
and analyzes WSDL
contract.

WSDL

1. Consumer browses or
searches for a web service
using a UDDI directory.

HTTP Response

SOAP

HTTP Request

Consumer

Web Service

5. Consumer programs
against web service.
Application communicates
data using SOAP over HTTP.

FIGURE 23.1   XML, SOAP, HTTP, WSDL, and UDDI are all key components in the web services architecture.

Dreamweaver and Web Services Integration

XML web services are meant to revolutionize the way we do business now and in the future. Many companies have realized this and have begun implementing ways of working with and interacting with web services in their products. Adobe, via Dreamweaver, is no different.

> **NOTE**
>
> Although current and future versions of ASP.NET are no longer supported in Dreamweaver CS4, web services can still be created and consumed by previously supported versions. For this reason, web services will be discussed in this chapter using both ASP.NET and the fully supported ColdFusion server model. Also, even though ASP and PHP support web service development, web service development is not supported out-of-the-box by Dreamweaver and, therefore, is not discussed in this chapter.

Remember the Components panel that was part of the Application panel group? Up to this point, we have only briefly mentioned it; now it's time to go over it in greater detail. You can find the Components panel by selecting the Components tab from the Application panel group, also shown in Figure 23.2.

FIGURE 23.2   The Components panel enables you to work with web services.

The Components panel consists of the following features:

- ▶ **Component Type**—Enables you to specify the type of component you'll be working with. Under the ASP.NET server model, Web Services is the only option. Under the ColdFusion server model, both the ColdFusion Components and Web Services options appear in this menu.

- ▶ **Add Component**—Adds a new component to the development environment. Under the ASP.NET server model, you have the opportunity to add a component using WSDL or by simply browsing to a precompiled class (DLL). Under the ColdFusion server model, you're limited to only WSDL.

- ▶ **Remove Component**—Removes a specific component from the list.

- ▶ **Refresh**—Refreshes references to web services and ColdFusion components.

- ▶ **Component window**—Provides you with a treelike view of your web service, including the name of the service, the class within that service, and all the web methods and properties outlined by the web service.

The most important feature in the Components panel by far is the Add Component option. As you will see in this chapter, adding the web service to your applications can be accomplished in one of two ways (one if you're working in ColdFusion): Add Using WSDL and Add Using Proxy Classes. Because of the relative similarities between the two options, we'll use the Add Using WSDL option for both ASP.NET and ColdFusion examples.

Building a Simple Calculator Web Service

Now that you have a basic understanding of web services, what they do, what they are composed of, and how to implement them using Dreamweaver, let's build a web service that performs a simple calculation of two numbers. After we've created the simple web service, we'll review how to consume it using both the ASP.NET and ColdFusion server models.

You can begin creating your web service by following these steps:

1. Assuming that you're relying on IIS as your web server, begin by creating a new folder in C:\Inetpub\wwwroot called **CalculateService**.

2. In Dreamweaver, create a new document by choosing File, New. Choose the Blank Page category, pick the ASP.NET VB option, choose <none> from the Layout type, and then click Create.

3. Immediately save your file as **calculate.asmx**, saving it to the newly created folder C:\Inetpub\wwwroot\CalculateService. (Note that ASMX is the extension given to Microsoft ASP.NET web services.) Again, ignore the fact that we're creating the web service using Microsoft technologies. The point here is to outline how web services are platform-agnostic and language-independent; not to sell a particular technology over another.

4. Switch to Code view, remove all existing code, and add the following code to the page in its place:

```
<%@ Webservice class="CalculateService" %>
Imports System.Web.Services
Public Class CalculateService
Inherits System.Web.Services.WebService
<WebMethod()> Public Function Calculate(x As Integer, y As Integer) As String
    Return x + y
End Function

  End Class
```

The code should include the Webservice directive, the System.Web.Services namespace import, and the CalculateService class that defines the Calculate function. Notice that the function is distinguished as a web method by the special <WebMethod()> identifier. The function accepts two parameters (x and y) as integers and performs a simple addition on them, returning the value as a string. Save your work.

That's it! You've just created your first web service using Microsoft's ASP.NET technology and the VB .NET language. With the web service now created, you can launch the browser to test its functionality. Testing the web service in a browser is important because it lets us make any necessary tweaks before we consume the web service using either ASP.NET or ColdFusion. To test the web service, open a browser and type the URL **http://localhost/CalculateService/calculate.asmx**. This is the URL to the web service that we just created. Assuming that the .NET Framework is installed on your computer, a service screen appears, showing you a list of all available web methods. Figure 23.3 displays the only method in your web service: Calculate.

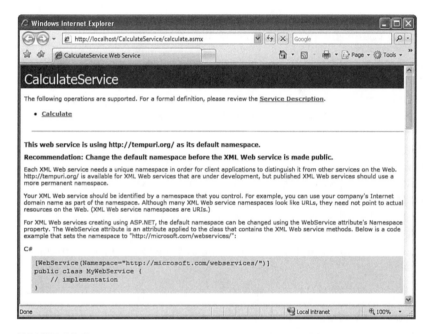

FIGURE 23.3   The service contains just one method—Calculate.

NOTE

Obviously, you never wrote code that resembles what you are seeing. This screen is a service of the .NET Framework and is available with its installation for use in testing web services. The utility allows you to see all the information related to the web service, including the class name, web methods exposed by the service, the WSDL contract, and more.

Now let's test the functionality of the Calculate web service. To do this, select the Calculate link that appears. Immediately, you are redirected to a new screen that enables you to input the x and y values that the function will accept as parameters. Enter numeric values into both the x and y text boxes and then click the Invoke button that appears similar to Figure 23.4.

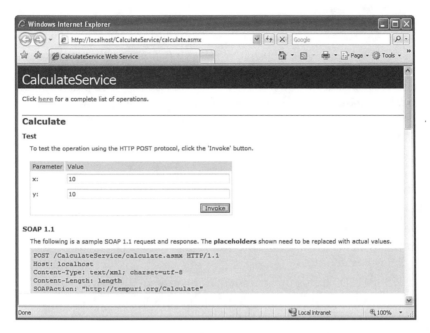

FIGURE 23.4   Click the Invoke button to invoke the function.

A new browser window opens, displaying the result of the calculation in XML format, similar to Figure 23.5.

FIGURE 23.5   The result of the calculation is shown in XML format.

But why is the result shown in XML format? Recall that XML is a universally adopted format for describing data. For this reason, a web service can be created using any language. As long as the output is in XML, any server-side technology consuming that web service can read the result.

Now that the web service is built, we need only to consume the web service using a web application that we are responsible for building. In the next section, we'll build an application and consume the web service using ColdFusion.

Consuming the Calculator Web Service in ColdFusion

Now that our web service is built, we can move forward with consuming the web service using a completely different technology and language in ColdFusion/CFML. This will truly demonstrate the interoperable nature of web services. In a nutshell, we'll be programming against the functionality exposed in the web service using ColdFusion. Our ColdFusion application will dynamically pass x and y values from the ColdFusion application into the web service, collect a result, and process the information accordingly. To create a ColdFusion application that consumes the web service, follow these steps:

1. Open the currently defined VectaCorpCFM site and immediately create a new document by choosing File, New. Select the ColdFusion option from the Blank Page category, choose the <none> option from the Layout type list, and click Create.

2. Save the page as **calculatesample.cfm**.

3. Switch to the Components tab and click the Add Component (+) icon. The Add Using WSDL dialog box appears.

4. With the Add Using WSDL dialog box open, enter the path to the web service's WSDL contract. You can do this by entering the path to the `calculate.asmx` file followed by the **?WSDL** parameter (in this case, type **http://localhost/CalculateService/calculate.asmx?WSDL**) because that is the location of our ASP.NET web service on our IIS web server.

5. Click OK. The web service is listed in the Components panel. Try expanding the nodes of the web service to reveal the class, method, and parameters outlined by the web service, similar to Figure 23.6.

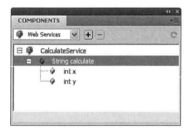

FIGURE 23.6   Expand the nodes of the web service to view the class, method, and parameters exposed by the service.

6. It's time to create the application that will eventually invoke the method exposed by the web service. To do this, start by inserting a new form into the blank page you created in step 1 by choosing Insert, Form, Form. With the form selected, keep the Method at POST and change the Action to `calculatesample.cfm`. In this case, the page will POST to itself.

7. Add two Text Field form objects and a Button form object, naming them **txtX**, **txtY**, and **Submit**, respectively. The result of what you should have thus far is shown in Figure 23.7.

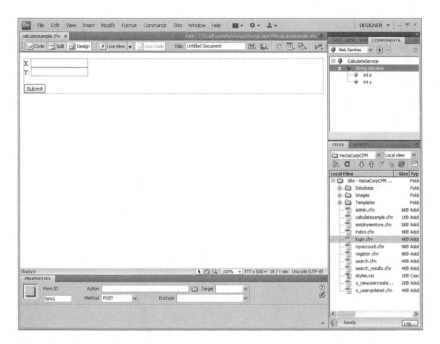

FIGURE 23.7   Add two text fields and a button form object to the form.

8. Switch to Code view. In the <head> tag of the document, enter the following code:

```
<CFOBJECT
    WEBSERVICE="http://localhost/CalculateService/calculate.asmx?WSDL"
    NAME="cs">
<CFIF ISDEFINED("FORM.txtX") AND ISDEFINED("FORM.txtY")>
    <CFSET strVal = cs.calculate(FORM.txtX, FORM.txtY)>
<CFELSE>
    <CFSET strVal = "">
  </CFIF>
```

In this case, the <CFOBJECT> tag is used to make reference to the web service. Using the Webservice attribute, we need only add the location to the WSDL contract as a value. The second attribute, Name, allows us to uniquely name the web service reference so that we can invoke the method later in code. As a value, I entered **cs**, which is short for CalculateService. Next, and more importantly, we use a CFIF tag to determine whether a value has been returned from the txtX and txtY text fields. If not, we set a variable named strVal to nothing. If a value has been returned by the form (the user clicked the Invoke button), we set the same strVal variable equal to the result of calling the Calculate() method and passing in the values of the txtX and txtY form objects as parameters.

9. With the strVal parameter set, we can now output its value under our Invoke form button. You can do this by adding the following code directly beneath the existing Button form object:

```
<CFOUTPUT>#strVal#</CFOUTPUT>
```

As you can see (below the code for the Submit button), the <CFOUTPUT> tag is used to display the value returned by the web service. The result of the code additions resembles Figure 23.8.

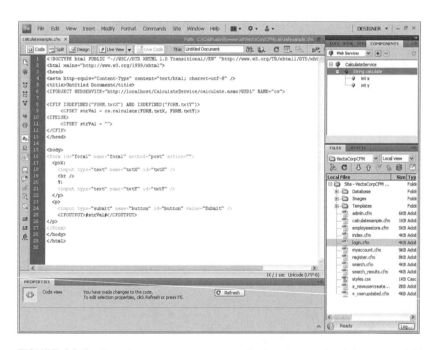

FIGURE 23.8   Use the <CFOUTPUT> tag to display the result of the set variable.

Save your work and test the results in the browser by pressing F12 (Option-F12). Enter a value into the txtX text field and a value into the txtY text field and click the Submit button. The calculation is performed by the ASP.NET-based web service and returns a result to the ColdFusion-based web application, similar to Figure 23.9.

FIGURE 23.9   The ColdFusion application calls the web service, passing in the value of the X and Y text fields. The ASP.NET web service processes the request and sends the result back to the ColdFusion application.

Web Services and Database Interaction

So far, you've learned to use web services to return simple calculations as strings. This section goes beyond the traditional web services paradigm and teaches you how to programmatically access database data through web services. The beauty in this task lies in the fact that you can eliminate the arduous task of repeatedly making database calls through your various dynamic pages by allowing the web service to do all the work.

In this section, we'll build a web service that pulls data from the x_CompanyEvents table contained in the Vecta Corp database. You'll create a ColdFusion Component that pulls data from the x_CompanyEvents table, exposes it as a web service, and then consumes the data using a ColdFusion web application.

Building the Company Events Web Service Using ColdFusion and Components

As you have seen, creating web services in ASP.NET is fairly simple. The only downside to the ASP.NET server model is that you have to code the functionality by hand. Fortunately for you, there's a better way. Because Adobe heavily promotes ColdFusion, creating web services using the ColdFusion server model is slightly more intuitive and can be accomplished using the panels that appear in the Application panel group.

Creating a ColdFusion web service begins with ColdFusion Components (CFCs). The benefit to using CFCs is that they can be created as either standalone components or as publicly accessible web services. To explore this model further, follow these steps:

1. Start by creating a new folder in C:\Inetpub\wwwroot\VectaCorpCFM called cfc.

2. Open the index.cfm file.

3. Open the Components panel by choosing the Components option from the Window menu.

4. In the Components panel, select the CF Components option from the Components Type menu.

5. Click the Add Component (+) button. The Create Component dialog box appears.

6. In the Name text box in the Component section, enter the value **CompanyEvents.** Browse to the C:\ColdFusion8\wwwroot\VectaCorpCFM\cfc folder in the Component Directory File field. The result appears similar to Figure 23.10.

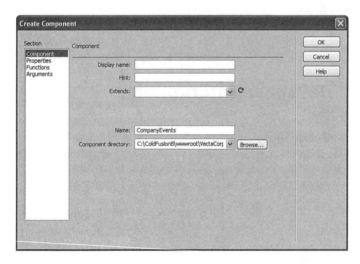

FIGURE 23.10   Give your component a name and a directory to save to.

7. Switch to the Functions section. Click the Add Function (+) button to create a new function. Assign the value **getCompanyEvents** in the Name text box, select the remote option from the Access menu, and choose the query option from the Return Type menu. The results appear similar to Figure 23.11.

8. Click OK. The dialog box closes and the VectaCorpCFM.cfc file opens, complete with the necessary code to get you started (see Figure 23.12).

9. Switch to the Bindings panel and select the Recordset option from the Add (+) menu. The Recordset dialog box appears.

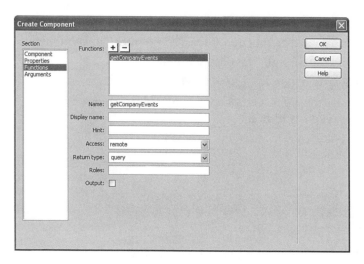

FIGURE 23.11   Give your function a name, an access type, and a return type.

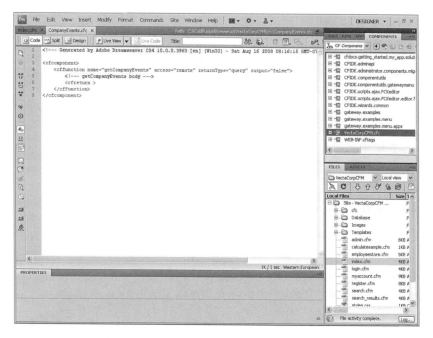

FIGURE 23.12   The new `VectaCorpCFM.cfc` file opens, complete with the necessary code to get you started.

10. Enter the name **rsCE** in the Name text box.

11. Make sure that the getCompanyEvents function is selected from the Function menu.

12. Choose the connVectaCorp option from the Data Source menu.

13. Choose the x_CompanyEvents option from the Table menu.

14. Click the Selected option button from the Columns option button group and highlight only the Event, Date, and Location fields.

15. Click OK. Again, the necessary code is added to the VectaCorpCFM.cfc file, similar to Figure 23.13. Save your work.

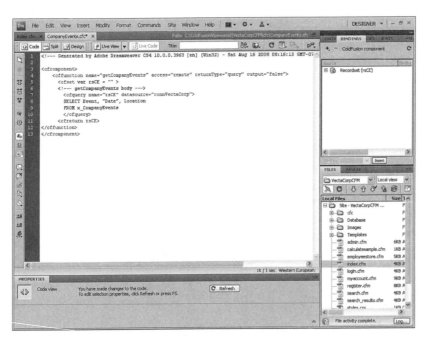

FIGURE 23.13   The appropriate code is added to the VectaCorpCFM.cfc file.

You're done! You've successfully created a ColdFusion web service. In the next section, we'll review the process of consuming the web service using a ColdFusion web application.

Consuming the Company Events Web Service in ColdFusion

With the web service created, you're now ready to add the code to the web application that will consume the data the web service exposes. To add this functionality, follow these steps:

1. Open the `index.cfm` page if it's not already open.

2. Place your cursor after the introductory text and press Enter/Return to give yourself some spacing between the introductory paragraph and the code for the table you're about to add.

3. Switch to Code view and add the following code:

```
<table width="100%" border="0" cellspacing="0" cellpadding="2">
    <tr>
        <td>Event</td>
        <td>Date</td>
        <td>Location</td>
    </tr>
    <cfoutput query="aQuery">
    <tr>
        <td>#Event#</td>
        <td>#Date#</td>
        <td>#Location#</td>
    </tr>
    </cfoutput>

</table>
```

4. Scroll to the top of the page and place your cursor at the top-leftmost position on the page. From the Components panel, expand the `VectaCorpCFM.cfc` node, expand the nested `CompanyEvents` node, and then click, hold, and drag out the query `getCompanyEvents()` function, placing it into the position where your cursor was. The web service call is added as the first few lines of code on the page as follows:

```
<cfinvoke
    component="VectaCorpCFM.cfc.CompanyEvents"
    method="getCompanyEvents"
    returnvariable="getCompanyEventsRet">
</cfinvoke>
```

5. Save your work.

To test the functionality in the browser, press F12 (Option-F12). As you'll see, the company events data is queried from the database by the web service. The web service then presents the data to the web page, which ultimately displays the data within the HTML table.

23

Summary

This chapter introduced you to some introductory concepts as they relate to web services. You learned how to create a simple web service using ASP.NET that we then consumed using the supported ColdFusion server model. You also learned how to create complex web services that interact with databases that return values to the consuming applications using the ColdFusion web services/components model. As you can see, web services provide a lot of programming flexibility and code reuse. When used appropriately, web services in your applications can cut development time and allow you to share vital portions of your applications with the outside world.

Working with the Spry Framework for Ajax

Remember the first time you visited the Flickr website? How about Google Maps? If you're anything like me, you probably right-clicked (Control-clicked) the page, expecting to see a menu of Flash-based options. Were you just as surprised as I was to see that these sites weren't built in Flash? The idea behind Google Maps, Flickr, and many other sites on the Internet today is that they don't use frameworks such as Flash that require years to master and that won't operate unless you have plugins installed on your browser. Instead, these sites and many others use a relatively new technology known as Ajax. *Ajax*, which stands for *Asynchronous JavaScript and XML*, combines advanced JavaScript coding techniques, the manipulation of the Document Object Model (DOM), and XML data to provide an engaging, fast-loading page to your users without the need for annoying page refreshes or third-party plugins.

No doubt you've heard the Ajax buzzword recently. It's hard to go into bookstores or browse technical websites and not see books and articles devoted to the topic. Because it's being touted as a key component of the next-generation Internet, also known as Web 2.0, resources are abundant and the buzz is plentiful. So much so, in fact, that it might seem difficult to sort through all the hype in an effort to understand the true meaning and implementation of this powerful new technology. That's where this chapter comes into play. This chapter aims at demystifying the key component of the next-generation Internet in Ajax and Adobe's implementation of Ajax in Spry. As you'll see throughout the chapter, you'll learn how to integrate XML data within Spry datasets to display in your web pages. You'll learn how to create interactive page regions that update instantly without requiring a full page refresh, and work with Spry widgets to incorporate form validation and advanced page layout options. Let's get started!

Introduction to XML, Ajax, and Spry

As you browse through Dreamweaver's interface and documentation, it might not seem all that obvious that Spry is Adobe's implementation of Ajax. But what exactly does this implementation entail? More specifically, why do we need this implementation? To answer this question, think of the vehicle that you get into every day to drive yourself to work: a car. Sure, we all know what a car is, but let's face it—we don't go to a generic dealership to buy a generic car. Instead, we go to buy a specific automaker's implementation of a car. We pick our car based on brand loyalty, appearance, functionality, and more. This same analogy holds true of Ajax. Ajax is the name given to the overall concept of limited page refreshes, and Spry is Adobe's implementation of Ajax.

The next few sections provide a brief overview of Ajax and Adobe's implementation of Ajax—Spry. We'll begin with a brief overview of the technology used behind the scenes when you're working with Ajax—XML. Next we'll provide a generic overview of Ajax, followed by an in-depth overview of Spry.

> **NOTE**
>
> For more information on the Spry framework for Ajax, you can visit Adobe's Spry website at labs.adobe.com/technologies/spry/home.html.

What Is XML?

HTML, as you know, is short for Hypertext Markup Language. The *markup* refers to the library of tags that describes how data should be organized or structured on the page. The browser then parses the information out of those tags and presents it to the user in a friendly and legible fashion. What HTML doesn't do, however, is give any information about what the data means, which is called *metadata*. Without metadata, search engines and other data-filtering techniques have to rely on keyword searches or content searches to retrieve information for the user.

XML is about metadata, and the fact that different people have different needs for how they categorize and organize data. Like HTML, XML is a set of tags and declarations. Rather than being concerned with how the data is structured and subsequently parsed by the browser, XML provides information on what the data means and how it relates to other data.

In the near term, XML provides an immediate opportunity for intranet database-driven site development. As could be the case with our fictitious Vecta Corp company, departments (including yours) can use the same database in different ways. Accounting needs payable and receivable information. Sales wants to monitor information by salesperson to figure out commission structures, and Marketing wants data organized by product and industry segment to figure out future release strategies. Using XML, you can customize the presentation of the queried data in a fashion most useful to the person making the query.

As is true for HTML, XML's purpose is to describe the content of a document. Unlike HTML, XML does not describe *how* that content should be displayed; instead, it describes what that content *is*. Using XML, the web developer can mark up the contents of a document, describing that content in terms of its relevance as data. Take a look at the following HTML element:

```
<p>Cammy the Content Manager</p>
```

This example describes the contents within the tags as a paragraph. This is fine if all we are concerned with is displaying the words `Cammy the Content Manager` on a web page. But what if we want to access those words as data? Using XML, we can mark up the words `Cammy the Content Manager` in a way that better reflects their significance as data:

```
<employee>Cammy the Content Manager</employee>
```

Notice the `<employee>` tag. Surely an `<employee>` tag doesn't exist in any markup language, does it? The beauty of XML is that it does not limit you to a set library of tags as HTML does. When marking up documents in XML, you can choose the tag name that best describes the contents of the element. For instance, in the preceding example, you might want to differentiate between the employee's name/title and her employee ID. You can do this by using an attribute to describe the employee ID. Because XML allows you to place attributes on elements, you could identify Cammy the Content Manager with the employee ID of `1001` as follows:

```
<employee id="1001">Cammy the Content Manager</employee>
```

As a second example, take a look at the following document, which describes employees working at Vecta Corp:

```
<h1>Vecta Corp Employees</h1>
<table>
    <tr>
        <td>Ada the Admin Assistant</td>
        <td>Cammy the Content Manager</td>
        <td>Damon the Developer</td>
    </tr>
</table>
```

This document provides us with information, but that information isn't too clear. Do these employees have unique employee IDs? Do they belong to a department? As it relates to describing data, the following code might be better suited for the preceding example:

```
<employees>
    <company>Vecta Corp</company>
    <employee>
```

```
        <name id="1001" department="Administration">Ada</name>
        <name id="1002" department="Marketing">Cammy</name>
        <name id="1003" department="Engineering">Damon</name>
    </employee>
</employees>
```

Because XML is concerned with how data should be defined, it does not make a good presentational language. If you created an XML document from the preceding example and tried to view it in the browser, you would get little more than a simple collapsible tree. The problem is that XML is not a presentational language; instead it is used to define data. Presenting XML data so that it can be viewed in the browser can be accomplished by using the Extensible Stylesheet Language (XSL). XSL allows you to apply HTML-like features to an XML document so that it can be presented in a friendly format to the user in a browser window. Consider the following data, which represents information about an employee (Cammy) within the fictitious Vecta Corp company:

```
<?xml version="1.0" ?>
<?xml-stylesheet type="text/xsl" href="employeesTransform.xsl"?>
<employees>
    <employee id="1001">
        <name>Cammy</name>
        <title>Content Manager</title>
        <department>Marketing</department>
        <email>cammy@vectacorp.com</email>
    </employee>
</employees>
```

Although this an example of a simple XML file, you could potentially have hundreds, perhaps thousands, of employees in your Vecta Corp XML file. Therefore, you might need a way of presenting that data in a browser-friendly format. You could apply the following style sheet in this situation:

```
<xsl:stylesheet version="1.0"
xmlns:xsl="http://www.w3.org/1999/XSL/Transform">
<xsl:template match="/">
<html>
<body>
<h2>Vecta Corp Employees</h2>
<table border="1">
    <tr bgcolor="Silver">
        <th align="left">Name</th>
        <th align="left">Title</th>
        <th align="left">Department</th>
        <th align="left">Phone</th>
    </tr>
    <xsl:for-each select="catalog/cd">
    <tr>
```

```
        <td><xsl:value-of select="name" /></td>
        <td><xsl:value-of select="title" /></td>
        <td><xsl:value-of select="department" /></td>
        <td><xsl:value-of select="phone" /></td>
    </tr>
    </xsl:for-each>
</table>
</body>
</html>
</xsl:template>
</xsl:stylesheet>
```

Displaying the file in the browser in this case would result in the employee's data shown in a cleanly formatted HTML table.

XML is about defining what data means (not unlike a database that is used for storage purposes). Unlike HTML, which deals with structuring data, XML deals with defining it. This seems to fall right in line with the concept behind Ajax. The idea is that data is now stored in a flat file (XML), rather than a database that requires a lot of resources from the server, memory on the server, and the browser. Because data can now be stored in a quick and convenient XML file, an intermediary technology such as Ajax can use the data contained within the XML file in an effort to present it within a web page with very little effort. Because our organization's data is stored in an XML file (rather than a database, which would be the traditional storage method), web pages transition more smoothly and load much faster.

What Is Ajax?

As you've read, Ajax is the key component to the next-generation Internet, also known as Web 2.0. Ajax is a technology that came about to solve the dilemma of data presentation and, more specifically, what is required to present data in a usable format in the user's browser. To elaborate on this point, think of the current process of making a page request. It almost always involves the following steps:

1. The user browses to a web page.
2. The user's browser loads the web page.
3. The user interacts with objects on the page to initiate a request to the host computer (web server).
4. The host computer processes the request (maybe extracts data from a database, maybe links to another page) and then sends the response back to the user's browser (client) in a format that the user's browser understands: HTML.
5. The browser displays the result to the user.

You're probably wondering what is wrong with that process. After all, it's the process we've been using for years. It's considered the backbone for client-server (request/response) applications built by application service providers such as eBay.com, AutoTrader.com, e*trade.com, and the like.

Although this process has served us well over the years, it does have some drawbacks. Specifically, in order for new, updated content to appear on the page, a *full page refresh* is required. Even for something as simple as an updated price, a full page refresh is required, which ultimately translates to wait times for your end users. This is where Ajax comes in. The key benefit to Ajax is the capability to use *partial page refreshes*. Because Ajax acts as an intermediary between the host computer and the client, Ajax has the potential to intercept page requests from the client and request only the data from the host computer that must be updated on the client. The preceding steps would change to resemble the following:

1. The user browses to a web page.
2. The user's browser loads the web page and associated XML data.
3. The user interacts with objects on the page to initiate a request to the host computer (web server).
4. The Ajax engine intercepts the request and sends the response back to the client's browser.
5. The browser displays the result to the user.

As you can see from the steps, the host computer (web server) is essentially taken out of the loop. All the data is preloaded into the Ajax engine and ready for delivery. Because of this streamlined process, page updates are much faster and server load is reduced, all of which results in a much more pleasant user experience.

What Is Spry?

Ajax is "what's now" when it comes to web development. So much so, in fact, that such companies as Google, Facebook, Apple, Microsoft, Yahoo!, and many others have invested heavily in the promise of enhanced user experiences through faster loading pages. In 2006, Adobe jumped on the trend by releasing Spry as a publicly available download from the Adobe Labs website. Officially known as the Spry Framework for Ajax, Spry is a collection of JavaScript libraries combined with methods for applying JavaScript functions on standard web pages.

Like most other technologies that Dreamweaver adopts, the majority of the Spry implementation is visual, eliminating the need for learning new technologies. Let's review what Dreamweaver adds under the hood before proceeding with the visual aspects of the Spry framework within Dreamweaver.

When you're working with Spry, two key files, xpath.js and SpryData.js, are required and are generally included for you in your project. Dreamweaver automatically copies these files from the Dreamweaver configuration folder and places them within a SpryAssets folder that it creates at your site root. Dreamweaver next adds the necessary links to these files within your web pages. This code resembles the following:

```
<script src="SpryAssets/xpath.js" type="text/javascript"></script>
<script src="SpryAssets/SpryData.js" type="text/javascript"></script>
```

Depending on what Spry functionality you're working with (Spry widgets or Spry effects), other JavaScript files will be required and are also automatically copied over to the SpryAssets folder for you.

Another unique aspect of the Spry framework is that it's tag-based. Unlike other Ajax frameworks that require embedded JavaScript function calls, Spry uses tag attributes to indicate Ajax functionality. For instance, the following code creates a Spry unordered list:

```
<div spry:region="ds1">
    <ul spry:repeatchildren="ds1">
        <li>{name}</li>
    </ul>
</div>
```

In this case, a standard HTML <div> tag is used to indicate a container of data. That data, which is fed in from a Spry Dataset called ds1, is included using the spry:region attribute. Within the <div>, you'll notice a standard HTML <ul> tag, which is used to indicate an unordered list. The Spry attribute in this case is spry:repeatchildren, which is used to include a child tag contained within the Spry Dataset called ds1. This child tag, name, is included in the list item tag <li> within a pair of braces.

The previous example demonstrates how to use a Spry Dataset (which is essentially created from an XML file) and display that data within an HTML list. But there's more to Spry than just Datasets and lists. In general, Spry focuses on three key areas of web page development:

- ▶ **Data**—Combines XML data with HTML pages. This combination facilitates partial page refreshes, which ultimately enhances the user experience.

- ▶ **Widgets**—Incorporates complex JavaScript and CSS to enable stunning interactive page layouts and form validation.

- ▶ **Effects**—As you saw in Chapter 8, "Using Behaviors," the Effects set of behaviors provides complex movements and interactions for elements within your web pages.

The next few sections explore these Spry areas in much more detail.

Integrating XML Data with Spry

As you've read up to this point, one of the most compelling uses of Spry is to incorporate XML data within a web page. A typical example might include a master/detail scenario, in which a user clicks an item in an effort to see further detailed information about a particular item. To demonstrate this concept, take a look at the RSS Reader Demo, provided on the Adobe Labs website or by following this URL: labs.adobe.com/technologies/spry/demos/rssreader/index.html. As you can see from Figure 24.1, there are four distinct areas: Feeds, Subject, Published Date, and a content area.

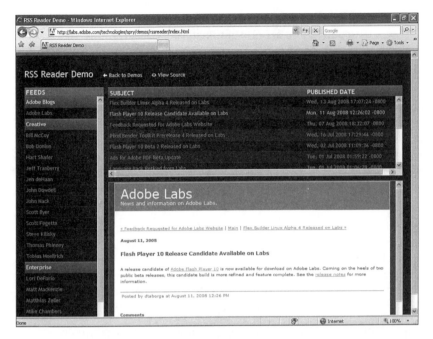

FIGURE 24.1   The RSS Reader Demo on the Adobe Labs website is an ideal example of the use of Spry and partial page refreshes.

The idea is that feeds are alphabetically listed within a container in the left pane. When a user selects a feed by name, in this case Adobe staff member names, numerous subjects of the articles they've written are listed within the Subject pane. The user can then select a subject to display its associated topic within the content area. Try experimenting with the functionality. As you'll quickly notice, when you select a name from the feed list on the left, a brief preloader is shown in the Subject pane because the Subject pane is loading specific content for the feed you've selected. This is partial page refresh at its best—and it's all possible because of Ajax, and more important, Spry. The beauty in this approach is that unlike traditional client/server architecture approaches, an entire page refresh isn't needed. Because only the Subject list is being updated, only that pane is refreshed!

These kinds of applications and more are all possible with Spry, and in general require little effort to accomplish. Over the next few sections, we'll explore the following Spry functionality:

- ▶ Connecting to XML data
- ▶ Defining Spry regions
- ▶ Binding data to the page
- ▶ Repeating Spry regions
- ▶ Working with Spry tables

All of this functionality begins with our data storage mechanism: XML. Let's walk through the process of connecting to our XML file next.

Connecting to XML Data

The backbone of Ajax lies in XML. All of the data you want presented in your web pages will be contained within XML files much like the one outlined here:

```
<employees>
     <employee>
          <name>Ada</name>
          <title>Admin Assistant</title>
          <department>Administration</department>
          <email>ada@vectacorp.com</email>
     </employee>
     <employee>
          <name>Agnes</name>
          <title>Accountant</title>
          <department>Accounting</department>
          <email>agnes@vectacorp.com</email>
     </employee>
<employees>
```

As you can see from the XML snippet (taken from the employees.xml file located in the project downloads for this chapter), the file contains several nodes. The <employees> tag is the node that defines what kind of content will be appearing within the file. The <employee> node is the actual node that repeats. Within each <employee> node we outline several other nodes, including <name>, <title>, <department>, and <email>. All these nodes describe and ultimately store data for use within web pages in our Vecta Corp site.

After the XML file has been created (here I've created it for you), Dreamweaver allows you to establish a connection to that XML file by way of a *Dataset*. All connections to XML data in Dreamweaver (regardless of whether you're working with Spry) are referred to as Datasets. When you're working with Spry, Datasets are created by way of a Spry Dataset. When you're working with Spry, creating a Dataset is crucial because the presentational and data objects that we'll end up working with throughout the chapter rely on a Spry Dataset being created first. So that you understand how to connect to an XML file via a Spry Dataset, follow these steps:

1. Launch Dreamweaver, if necessary, and open the included companydirectory.html file, which is included with the chapter downloads.

2. Choose Insert, Spry, Spry Data Set. Additionally, you could choose the Spry or Data category in the Insert panel and choose the Spry Data Set icon. A third option would be to choose the Spry Data Set option located within the Add (+) menu in the

Bindings panel. Regardless of which method you choose, you get the same result—the Spry Data Set dialog box opens.

3. With the dialog box open, your first task is to give your Dataset a name. Enter the name **dsEmployees** into the Data Set Name text box.

4. The Spry Data Set dialog box allows you to create two types of Datasets: HTML and XML. For now, choose the XML option from the Select Data Type menu.

5. Now click the Browse button and navigate to and select the employees.xml file. Click OK to select it. The employees.xml file appears in the Specify Data File text box and the Row Element box is populated with the nodes in your XML file, as shown in Figure 24.2. If you're working with a web application that dynamically generates XML files, choose the Design Time Feed link and then browse to the path on your testing server that contains the XML file.

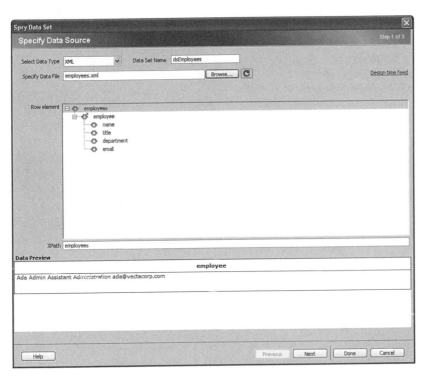

FIGURE 24.2   The Row Element list is populated with the nodes contained in your XML file.

6. In the Row Element list, choose the node you want to work with. In most cases, this should be the node that repeats in the XML file. In our case, this node is the employee node. Select it now. Dreamweaver immediately inserts the appropriate syntax in the XPath text box, and a preview of what your data will look like appears in the Data Preview pane, similar to Figure 24.3. Click Next.

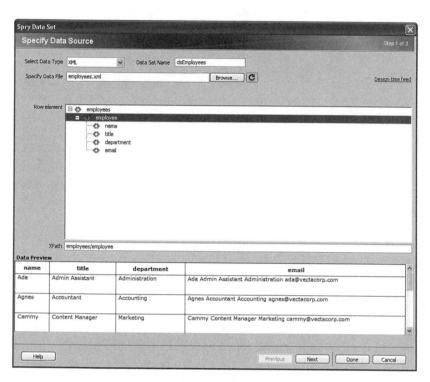

FIGURE 24.3   Preview what your data will look like after it's bound to a repeating Spry element, such as a Repeating Table.

7. In the second window of the Spry Data Set dialog box, you can modify the data type for a particular element within the Dataset. To do this, select the element from the Column Name list and then change the data type from the Type menu. Dreamweaver supports String (the default), Number, Date, and HTML.

8. If you'd like to initially sort the data, choose the specific column from the Sort Column menu. Additionally, choose the direction (ascending or descending) that you'd like to associate with the sort.

9. To avoid duplicate columns, choose the Filter Out Duplicate Rows check box.

10. To have the data updated automatically, select the Turn Data Caching Off and Auto Refresh Data check boxes and then enter a number in milliseconds. Some XML files, such as the one used for the names in the feeds list (shown in the example in Figure 24.1) require few if any updates, whereas others, such as the XML files that drive the topics list, might require frequent updates. If the Auto Refresh Data check box is not enabled, the XML data is loaded just once, when the page is first requested. For our purposes, leave this check box unchecked. Click Next to proceed to the design screen in the Spry Data Set dialog box.

11. The design screen allows you to bind the Spry Data Set to a predefined HTML design. Options include Table, Master/Detail Layout, Stacked Containers, and Stacked Containers with Spotlight Area:

  ▶ **Insert Table**—Choose this option to have Dreamweaver automatically build an HTML table and then include content areas within cells of the table that your XML data will appear within.

  ▶ **Insert Master/Detail Layout**—Choose this option to create a layout not unlike the RSS Reader Demo presented earlier. Initial data is shown within a container (`<div>` tag). Secondary, more detailed information relating to the selected item is then shown within a second (and even third) container somewhere (usually to the right of the master container) on the page. For a visual idea of what the master/detail layout can look like, visit the RSS Reader Demo again at labs. adobe.com/technologies/spry/demos/rssreader/index.html.

  ▶ **Insert Stacked Containers**—Choose this option to have Dreamweaver automatically build container elements (`<div>` tags) on top of each other and then include content areas within those `<div>` containers that your XML data will appear within.

  ▶ **Insert Stacked Containers with Spotlight Area**—Choose this option to have Dreamweaver automatically build container elements (`<div>` tags) on top of each other, similar to the Insert Stacked Containers option. The difference with this option and the previous option is that you have an additional container element that will appear just to the left of the stacked container. This is a perfect place to put an image—for instance, one that you can use to describe the content within the container. An employee directory complete with head-shots is a perfect example for this application, and it's one that we'll explore later in the chapter.

  ▶ **Do Not Insert HTML**—Check this option (the default) if you want full control over the HTML that will be created on the page. You will be responsible for drag-ging out the nodes from the Bindings panel into content areas on the web page.

  Although we'll certainly cover these options with more detail later, for now choose the Do Not Insert HTML radio button and click Done to close the Spry Data Set dialog box.

12. Save your page. Dreamweaver informs you that supporting files (`SpryData.js` and `xpath.js`) will be copied over to your defined site. Both are copied over to the SpryAssets folder mentioned earlier in the chapter. Click OK to proceed with the copy.

With the Spry Data Set now created, you'll immediately notice that Dreamweaver opens the Bindings panel (see Figure 24.4).

As you can see from Figure 24.4, the Dataset, complete with specific columns that are meant to replicate the structure of the XML file, is listed. If you switch to Code view, the following code is added:

```
<script src="SpryAssets/xpath.js" type="text/javascript"></script>
<script src="SpryAssets/SpryData.js" type="text/javascript"></script>

<script type="text/javascript">
<!--
var dsEmployees = new Spry.Data.XMLDataSet("employees.xml", "employees/employee");
//-->
</script>
```

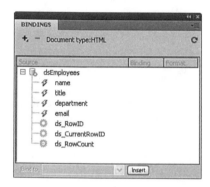

FIGURE 24.4   The Dataset is visible and displays all the nodes in the XML file as columns in the Bindings panel.

The first two lines merely link in the xpath.js and SpryData.js JavaScript files. Again, these files were copied over automatically for you and placed in the SpryAssets folder. The second chunk of (JavaScript) code creates a new instance of the Spry Dataset, passing in the name of the XML file to use and the XPath syntax to use as the repeating region.

With the Dataset now complete, we can turn our attention to more specific functionality, such as defining Spry regions and binding our Dataset data within these regions.

Defining Spry Regions

Now that you've established the data source (the dataset created in the previous section), the next step is to define a Spry region within the page. As the name implies, Spry regions are areas on the page that outline content from the Dataset. In general, Dreamweaver allows you to add Spry regions on the page using either the <div> or the <span> tag. The only difference between Spry and standard HTML is that Dreamweaver adds the proprietary spry:region attribute to define the Dataset that should be used in conjunction with the Spry region. As an example, a typical Spry region might resemble the following code:

```
<div spry:region="dsEmployees"></div>
```

In this example, the HTML <div> tag is used as the actual container for content. The spry:region attribute defines the Dataset name that should be used to populate the <div> tag (container) with data. As you can see, the attribute value is set to dsEmployees, the Dataset created in the previous section.

TIP

In this section we discuss Spry regions. In reality, there are two types of Spry regions: master and detail. Whereas the master Spry region uses the `spry:region` attribute (covered throughout this section), the detail Spry region uses the `spry:detailregion` attribute. This is highlighted visually in the Spry Data Set dialog box. The two can be used simultaneously in instances where detailed information from a selected option should be shown. The RSS Reader Demo (mentioned earlier in the chapter) is a perfect example. When the user selects a feed (master), detailed information (blog postings) appears within the subject list (detail).

However, Dreamweaver doesn't force you to remember code to work with Spry regions. To create a Spry region visually, follow these steps:

1. Place your cursor on the page where you'd like the Spry region to appear (preferably under the Company Directory subheader) and choose Insert, Spry, Spry Region. The Insert Spry Region dialog box appears.

2. Select the tag that you'd like to use as the container (either <div> or <span>) from the Container option button list. For our purposes, select the DIV option.

3. Now choose the type of region that you'd like—either master (Region) or detail (Detail Region). For our purposes, choose the Region option from the Type option button list.

4. Next select the dsEmployees Dataset from the Spry Data Set menu.

5. If you have an element already selected on the page when inserting a Spry region, Dreamweaver gives you the opportunity to either wrap the selection with the Spry region or completely replace the element. Because we're working with a new blank page and there isn't an element already selected, the Insert option button list is disabled. The formatted dialog box should look like the one shown in Figure 24.5.

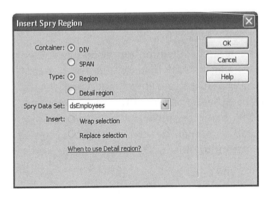

FIGURE 24.5   Format the Insert Spry Region dialog box.

6. Click OK to close the Insert Spry Region dialog box.

After you've closed the Insert Spry Region dialog box, the new Spry region is added to the page, as shown in Figure 24.6.

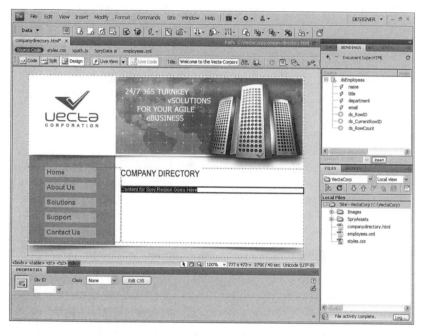

FIGURE 24.6   The Spry region (<div>) is added to the page.

You'll notice that after you insert the Spry region, the dashed box that outlines the default *Content for Spry Region Goes Here* resembles what all <div> tags look like when they're inserted within Dreamweaver. The only differentiating factor between a normal <div> tag and a Spry <div> tag (also known as a Spry region) is that the <div> tag's background color in the Tag Selector is orange.

With the Spry region now on the page, our next step is to bind content. Remember, the Spry region outlines an area on the page in which content will appear. Our next step is to specify which content from our Dataset will appear in the region.

Binding Data to the Page

With a Dataset created and a Spry region now defined, the next logical step is to add data in the region. Dreamweaver provides numerous mechanisms for adding data to your web pages: repeating regions, lists, tables, and even more complex visual components such as the menu bar, tabbed panels, accordion panels, and collapsible panels. All these choices offer visual dialog boxes for customizing how your data should appear within the Spry region. The next sections discuss these topics with greater detail, but for now, let's focus in on the basics of getting content contained in our Dataset onto the web page.

Content contained in your Dataset is added to the page within Spry regions. Specifically, when you add content to the Spry region (`<div>` tag), the element is added using the following syntax:

```
{dataset::element}
```

The braces define the area in which dynamic data will appear. Inside the braces we add the Dataset name, followed by the element within the Dataset that you want dynamically bound to the page. The code can be modified to work for us as follows:

```
{dsEmployees::name}
```

In this example, the first item within the name element in the `dsEmployees` Dataset is dynamically bound to the page. Again, the benefit to using Dreamweaver is that you don't have to remember how Spry elements are bound to the page using code. Instead, you can take a much more visual approach. In general, Dreamweaver supports three methods for binding data to a web page:

▶ Drag and drop the column from the Dataset in the Bindings panel into the Spry region.

▶ Place your cursor within the Spry region, select the column from the Dataset in the Bindings panel that you want included within the region, and click the Insert button.

▶ Switch to Code view, place your cursor within the Spry region (`<div>` tag), and add the code outlined previously.

The binding of elements contained within your Dataset to the page is similar, if not closely related, to working with recordsets in ASP, ColdFusion, and/or PHP. The only significant difference here, however, is that the data is contained entirely within an XML file rather than in a database.

The methods covered in this section will allow you to bind only a single element to a web page. If you'd prefer to show all the data contained within your Dataset, you'll need to use a repeating region.

Repeating Spry Regions

For your Spry regions to have any practical use, you're going to want to include all the data from a particular node in the Dataset. To accomplish this, you'll need to use a repeating region rather than a standard region. Repeating regions, unlike the standard regions that you used in the previous section, allow you to bind all the data contained within a particular node to either a numbered list, an ordered list, a definition list, or a drop-down menu. To accomplish this, Dreamweaver provides the `spry:repeat` and `spry:repeatchildren` attributes. For example, if you wanted to create a Spry repeating region rather than a standard Spry region, your code might resemble the following:

```
<div spry:repeat="dsEmployees"></div>
```

As you can see, the code looks identical to the Spry region except that we use a `spry:repeat` attribute instead of a `spry:region` attribute. The next step would be to add an element that naturally repeats (such as a list or table) to display the contents within the Dataset. More on that later. For now, let's review the process of visually inserting a Spry repeat region:

1. Place your cursor on the page where you'd like the Spry repeat region to appear and choose Insert, Spry, Spry Repeat. The Insert Spry Repeat dialog box appears.
2. Choose the DIV option from the Container option button list.
3. Now select the Repeat option from the Type option button list. You'll also notice the Repeat Children option. For the most part, the two options are identical. The only major difference is that the Repeat Children option is much more flexible and is ideal in scenarios where you want content filtered or conditionally displayed.
4. Select the dsEmployees option from the Spry Data Set menu. The formatted dialog box is shown in Figure 24.7.

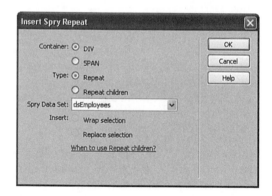

FIGURE 24.7   Format the Insert Spry Repeat dialog box.

5. Click OK to close the Insert Spry Repeat dialog box. The new repeating region is added to the page and closely resembles a standard Spry region.

Like the Spry region, the Spry repeat region contains placeholder text that you'll want to delete before inserting Spry data or HTML tags in the region. After the text has been removed, you can add Spry data or HTML tags containing Spry data that you want to repeat.

The Spry repeat isn't all that useful unless you plan to get your hands dirty and work with Spry in Code view. If you prefer the visual route, adding a repeating list is more up your alley. To insert a repeating list, follow these steps:

1. Remove the previously inserted Spry repeat region. Place your cursor on the page where you'd like the Spry Repeat List to appear and choose Insert, Spry, Spry Repeat List. The Insert Spry Repeat List dialog box appears, similar to Figure 24.8.

FIGURE 24.8   The Insert Spry Repeat List dialog box allows you to add a repeating Spry ordered, unordered, definition, or drop-down list.

2. The Container tag allows you to choose from four supported tags. You can choose the <ul> tag (unordered list), <ol> tag (ordered list), <dl> tag (definition list), and <select> tag (drop-down list). For our example, choose the UL (Unordered List) option.

3. Choose the dsEmployees option from the Spry Data Set menu.

4. Choose the column that you want to appear within the list from the Display Column menu. For our example, I'll choose name.

5. Click OK to close the Insert Spry Repeat List dialog box. If you don't already have a Spry region on the page, Dreamweaver displays a dialog box asking whether you'd like Dreamweaver to include one for you. Choose Yes. You'll immediately notice that the name column (appearing within braces) is shown next to a bullet.

Save your work and preview the results in the browser by pressing F12 (Option-F12). As you'll see, every name within the XML file is displayed on the web page within a bulleted list. Of course, you're not limited to a bulleted list. As you saw in step 2, you can also decide to repeat your data using an ordered list, a definition list, or a drop-down list.

Working with Spry Tables

Although the Spry repeating lists are certainly nice to use, quite possibly the easiest method for incorporating large amounts of data contained within a Dataset is to use Spry tables. Like the Dynamic table (ASP, ColdFusion, PHP), the Spry table allows you to bind large amounts of XML data so that the data is presented in a clean and aesthetically pleasing manner. Also like the Dynamic table, the Spry table takes data contained within an XML file and displays it in a tabular fashion using HTML table tags. Beyond that, the Spry table also outlines functionality that allows you to make the columns in the table sortable. You can even apply custom CSS classes to alternating even or odd rows, selected rows, and rows that your cursor will hover over, all in an effort to make your tables look attractive and eye-catching to your end users. To give you an idea as to how the Spry table works, let's add one now. To add a Spry table, follow these steps:

1. Place your cursor on the page where you'd like the Spry table to appear and then double-click the Spry Data Set within the Bindings panel. The Spry Data Set dialog box appears. Click Next twice to proceed to the Insert Options dialog box, choose the Insert Table radio button, and then click the Set Up button to launch the Insert Table dialog box, similar to Figure 24.9.

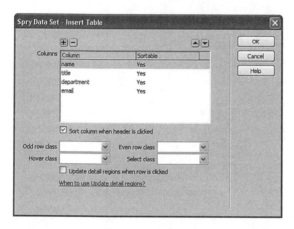

FIGURE 24.9   The Spry Data Set - Insert Table dialog box.

2. As you can see, the Column list contains the name, title, department, and email nodes from the dataset. If you'd like to add or remove columns, click the corresponding (+) and (–) buttons. You can also reposition columns within the table by selecting a column from the list and choosing the reposition buttons located at the top right of the Columns list.

3. If you'd like to make a column sortable (the user may select a column's header, in which case the data in that column sorts in ascending/descending order), click the Sort Column When Header Is Clicked check box.

4. You can also freely select custom CSS classes for alternating odd and even rows in the table, selected rows in the table, and rows in the table that users mouse over from the Odd row class, Even row class, Hover class, and Select class menus. For our purposes, we'll leave these empty.

5. If you're working with master/detail regions, you can force a detailed regions data to refresh when a selection is made from the Spry table by selecting the Update Detail Regions When Row Is Clicked check box. For our purposes, we'll leave it unchecked.

6. Click OK to close the Insert Table dialog box.

7. Click Done to close the Spry Data Set dialog box. The new Spry table appears on the page.

Save your work and preview the page in your browser by pressing F12 (Option-F12). As you can see from Figure 24.10, all the data contained within the XML file is displayed in a clean, organized, tabular structure within the browser.

FIGURE 24.10   All the data contained within the XML file is displayed in a clean, organized, tabular structure within the browser.

Working with Spry Widgets

Just when you thought that Spry lists and tables were the way to go for data presentation, Dreamweaver introduces other flexible and powerful design components called *widgets*. Widgets, which combine HTML, CSS, and JavaScript, provide another option when you're designing interactive, fast-loading layouts and working with form validation. Widgets included with this release of Dreamweaver include the following:

- ▶ Spry Validation Text Field, Textarea, Checkbox, Select, Password, Confirm, and Radio Group
- ▶ Spry Menu Bar
- ▶ Spry Tabbed Panels
- ▶ Spry Accordion
- ▶ Spry Collapsible Panel
- ▶ Spry Tooltip

Although we'll cover some of these controls in depth, in the meantime you can get an idea as to how the validation widgets work by visiting the following URL: labs.adobe.com/ technologies/spry/demos/formsvalidation/index.html. Additionally, you can get a sneak peek at the Spry Accordion in action by visiting the following URL: labs.adobe.com/tech-nologies/spry/demos/products/index.html.

The widgets share common characteristics. They're extremely user-friendly, engaging, and more important, they enhance the aesthetic appeal of your sites. From a development standpoint, widgets are easy to use. Typically they're simple to include because they're just dragged and dropped onto the page. On the page, their properties can be manipulated via the Property inspector, and their appearance can be customized through associated CSS rules, making them easy to integrate into any CSS-based site.

Validating Form Fields

In Chapter 8, you looked at a powerful behavior called Validate Form. This behavior allows you to add functionality to a web page that instructs the browser to prevent submission of a form if a user fails to enter a value into a form field. Additionally, you can check for numeric inputs, numeric ranges, and email address inputs. I made mention of the fact that despite its obvious benefit, the behavior was severely limited in the features that it allows you to validate. For instance, the Validate Form behavior doesn't allow you to check for dates, credit card numbers, ZIP Codes, phone numbers, and the like. Most of those items are common when working with forms in your web pages. Although the Validate Form behavior offers some relief, its lack of functionality becomes clear, leaving many developers with the arduous task of writing a lot of the validation by hand, anyway. That's where Spry Validation comes in handy. The following are seven Spry validation form objects:

- ▶ Spry Validation Text Field
- ▶ Spry Validation Select
- ▶ Spry Validation Textarea
- ▶ Spry Validation Checkbox
- ▶ Spry Validation Password
- ▶ Spry Validation Confirm
- ▶ Spry Validation Radio Group

These seven form fields provide developers with the flexibility of validation that they've been clamoring for over the years. The capability to require input and check for numeric values, email addresses, dates, times, credit card formatting, ZIP Codes, phone numbers, Social Security numbers, currency, and URLs are all available through the Spry validation form fields. Even better, customization of these form fields is a snap because each Spry validation form field exposes a Property inspector that makes customizing properties effortless. So that you understand how these form fields function, let's begin with the Spry Validation Text Field.

Spry Validation Text Field

By far the most flexible Spry validation form field is the Spry Validation Text Field. The Spry Validation Text Field, as its name implies, is a simple HTML text field that has complex JavaScript associated with it. The JavaScript, like other Spry widgets, is contained within an external .js file that resides within the SpryAssets folder. Aside from controlling validation conditions, the JavaScript code is also responsible for guaranteeing the input of data within the text field. When you include a Spry Validation Text Field on the page, you have the capability to check for the following data inputs:

- No input (none)
- Integer
- Email Address
- Date
- Time
- Credit Card
- ZIP Code
- Phone Number
- Social Security Number
- Currency
- Real Number/Scientific Notation
- IP Address
- URL
- Custom inputs

Some of the validation types, such as Date, Time, Credit Card, ZIP Code, Phone Number, Currency, and IP Address, include a range of formats to choose from, making them more flexible for your validation needs.

To insert and configure a Spry Validation Text Field, start by opening the included contactus.html file and then place your cursor in the second cell of the first column (next to the Name text label). Now choose Insert, Spry, Spry Validation Text Field. The Spry Validation Text Field is added to the page. The interesting part about the Spry Validation Text Field is that if you select the text field, the Property inspector is essentially the generic Text Field Property inspector that you saw in Chapter 7, "HTML Forms."

When you select the blue visual aid that surrounds the Spry Validation Text Field, however, the Property inspector comes to life. As you can see from Figure 24.11, selecting the blue visual aid that surrounds the Spry Validation Text Field exposes a collection of new modifiable properties within the Property inspector.

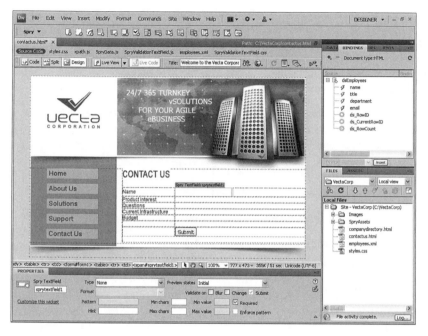

FIGURE 24.11   Select the blue visual aid that surrounds the Spry Validation Text Field to reveal the unique Property inspector options for this element.

The Property inspector reveals the following set of customizable properties:

▶ **ID**—Enter a value here to uniquely name the text field. The default that Dreamweaver inserts is `sprytextfield1`, then `sprytextfield2`, and so on.

▶ **Type**—Set the type of validation that the text field will perform by selecting from one of 14 values from this list.

▶ **Format**—Some of the validation types, such as Date, Time, Credit Card, ZIP Code, Phone Number, Currency, and IP Address, include a range of formats to choose from. For instance, if you choose the Zip Code option from the Type menu, the Format menu provides options to display US-5, US-9, UK, Canada, and Custom Pattern postal codes. You can choose an option from this list to make the validation more dynamic based on the format of the ZIP Code that you want to validate.

▶ **Preview States**—Set the format of the text field and the error message that you want displayed when a user enters invalid formatting, forgets to enter a value, or enters a correct value. Options include Initial (default), Required (highlights the text field in red and shows the message A value is required.), Invalid Format (highlights the text field in red and shows the message Invalid format), and Valid (highlights the text field in green).

▶ **Validate On**—Set the event that triggers the validation. Options include Blue, Change, and Submit. By default, text fields always validate when the form is submitted. Because this is the case, the Property inspector sets the Submit option as checked and disables it so you can't change it. If you'd also like the text field to be validated as soon as the user tabs out of the text field, check the Blur check box as well.

▶ **Pattern**—Enter a custom pattern for validation within this text box. This text box will become enabled only when the Custom option is selected from the Type menu. After the text field is enabled, enter one of the following custom validation patterns:

> ▶ **0**—Represents a digit between 0 and 9

> ▶ **A or a**—Represents case-sensitive alphabetic characters

> ▶ **B or b**—Represents non-case-sensitive alphabetic characters

> ▶ **X or x**—Represents case-sensitive alphanumeric characters

> ▶ **Y or y**—Represents non-case-sensitive alphanumeric characters

> ▶ **?**—Represents any character

▶ **Hint**—Enter the text within this text box that should display to the user as a hint if an error is displayed.

▶ **Min/Max Chars**—Set the minimum and maximum number of characters that should be allowed within the text field in these two text boxes.

▶ **Min/Max Value**—When you're working with numeric types such as Integer, the Min and Max value text boxes become enabled. You can specify minimum and maximum values that the user can enter here. These are ideal when validating ranges.

▶ **Required**—Checked by default, this property guarantees that the text field requires an input by the user.

▶ **Enforce Pattern**—Click this check box to enforce the pattern that you specify within the Pattern text box.

Save your work. Dreamweaver attempts to place SpryValidationTextField.css and SpryValidationTextField.js within the SpryAssets folder. Again, these files are required for controlling the look and functionality of the text field. Click OK. Preview your page in the browser by pressing F12 (Option-F12). When the page appears in the browser, click the Submit button. The text field highlights in red and the error message A value is required. displays on the page. Again, this is a simple example of the power that the text field reveals. We haven't even customized the type of input the text field should validate, but with some simple customizations in the Property inspector, you can ensure that your

Spry Validation Text Field works the way you want it to work, and that it validates the type of data that you need it to validate.

Spry Validation Select

Another Spry validation form field that you might decide to take advantage of is the Spry Validation Select. The Spry Validation Select is nothing more than an HTML-based drop-down menu that has complex JavaScript associated with it to guarantee that a selection has been made before the form is submitted. To insert and configure a Spry Validation Select, follow these steps:

1. Place your cursor in the second cell of the second row (next to the Current Infrastructure text label).

2. Choose Insert, Spry, Spry Validation Select. The drop-down menu is added to the table.

3. Select the drop-down menu (not the Spry visual aid that surrounds it) and choose the List Values button from within the Property inspector. The List Values dialog box appears.

4. Type **SELECT ONE** into the Item Label field, press Tab, and give it a value of **0**; press Tab and type **Windows** into the Item Label field and press Tab again to give it a value of **1**. Pressing Tab to continue to move through the fields, type **Mac** and give it a value of **2**; finally, type **Linux**, give it a value of **3**, and click OK. Notice that SELECT ONE is the default selection in the drop-down menu. Although we want this option to appear, the user should be forced to select something other than this option from the list before submitting the form. This is where the Spry validation comes in.

5. Select the blue visual aid that surrounds the Spry Validation Select. Immediately the Property inspector changes to show the associated properties. For the most part, the Property inspector is simple to use and displays similar properties to the Spry Validation Text Field. To configure the drop-down menu for our purposes, uncheck the Blank Value check box. This assures us that the user must select an option from the list.

6. Now click the Invalid Value check box and enter the value **0** (the value associated with the SELECT ONE option in the drop-down menu) within the provided text box.

Again, the other options are similar, if not the same as the Spry Validation Text Field. For this reason, I'll encourage you to cross reference the properties outlined in the previous section for more information on how these work. For our purposes, simply save your work. Dreamweaver notifies you that it needs to place SpryValidationSelect.css and SpryValidationSelect.js in the SpryAssets folder. Again, these files are required for controlling the look and functionality of the drop-down menu. Click OK. Preview your page in the browser by pressing F12 (Option-F12). Enter a value into the text box and click Submit. Figure 24.12 illustrates the result. The drop-down menu highlights in red and the text Please select a valid item. appears. Also notice that the text box will highlight in green. This is because that option is correct. Only the form fields that require attention will highlight in red.

FIGURE 24.12   An error message appears next to the drop-down menu because we didn't select a valid option from the list.

Spry Validation Textarea

The Spry Validation Textarea, like the text field, is used to collect text from the user. The biggest difference between the text area and the text field, however, is that users can enter one line to several paragraphs of text. Because of this flexibility, there's no mechanism for validating formats in the textarea—a user may enter just about anything within the field. It's not uncommon, however, to validate minimum, maximum, or both values. The Spry Validation Textarea supports this type of validation but takes it one step further. If a user attempts to enter too much text, an error message appears, and the user is prevented from entering any more values within the textarea. To add and configure the Spry Validation Textarea, follow these steps:

1. Place your cursor in the second cell of the third row (just to the right of the Questions text label).

2. Choose Insert, Spry, Spry Validation Textarea. The textarea is added to the table.

3. Select the blue visual aid that surrounds the Spry Validation Textarea. Immediately the Property inspector changes to show the associated properties. Again, for the most part, the properties here are similar to those of the Spry Validation Text Field. The only real difference is the ordering of the properties and the addition of the Min

Chars, Max Chars, Counter, and Block Extra Characters check boxes, which I'll briefly outline. For now, enter the value **100** within the Max Chars text box. This will prevent the user from entering more than 100 characters of text.

4. Make sure that the Block Extra Characters check box is checked. This prevents the user from entering any more characters after reaching the 100-character limit.

5. Now select an option from the Counter option button list. Choose None when you don't want a counter displayed. Choose Chars Count to have a counter incrementally display as the user enters values in the text area. Choose Chars Remaining to have a counter display the number of available characters as the user enters values in the text area. For our purposes, choose the Chars Remaining option.

Save your work. Dreamweaver notifies you that it needs to place `SpryValidationTextarea.css` and `SpryValidationTextarea.js` within the SpryAssets folder. Again, these files are required for controlling the look and functionality of the textarea. Click OK. Preview your page in the browser by pressing F12 (Option-F12). Begin typing into the text area. You'll immediately notice that the counter gets lower and lower as you type. When you reach the limit, you're no longer able to type—and more important, the text highlights in red.

Spry Validation Checkbox

You can use the Spry Validation Checkbox either individually or within groups to check for specific values or enforce a range of selections. Typically, individual check boxes are used in instances where you want to force the user to select a check box, usually because of a legal agreement or terms of use that you are requiring them to agree to. In groups, you can use the check box to allow the user to select an option or several options from the group. The check box, like the other validation form fields, is easy to implement. To insert and configure a Spry Validation Checkbox, follow these steps:

1. Place your cursor in the second cell of the fourth row (next to the Product Interest text label).

2. Choose Insert, Spry, Spry Validation Checkbox. A check box is added to the table.

3. Enter the text **vProspect 2.0** just to the right of the check box.

4. Repeat steps 2 and 3 twice more, adding a Spry Validation Checkbox and then adding the text **vConvert 2.0** and **vRetain 1.0**.

5. Select the blue visual aid that surrounds the first Spry Validation Checkbox. You might have to mouse over the check box to see it. Again, the properties outlined by the Property inspector are similar to that of the Text Field. The difference here is the inclusion of the Required and Enforce Range radio buttons. You would choose Required if it were a single check box that you wanted to validate a selection for, like the Agree To Terms scenario mentioned in the opening paragraph of this section. You would choose the Enforce range radio button when you have a group of check boxes and you want to enforce a minimum and maximum amount of selections, as we do. With that said, choose the Enforce Range (Multiple) radio button and enter the values **1** (meaning the user must be interested in at least one product) into the Mix # of Selection text box and **3** (meaning the user can't be interested in more than

three products) into the Max # of Selections text box. Repeat this process for the other two check boxes.

Save your work. Dreamweaver notifies you that it needs to place `SpryValidationCheckbox.css` and `SpryValidationCheckbox.js` within the SpryAssets folder. Again, these files are required for controlling the look and functionality of the textarea. Click OK. Preview your page in the browser by pressing F12 (Option-F12). Click the Submit button. Dreamweaver displays all the error messages, including the `Please make a selection.` error message next to each check box.

Spry Validation Radio Group

You can use Spry Validation Radio Group to build a group of radio buttons that you'd like to perform validation on. Recall from Chapter 7 that the Radio Group option, available by choosing Insert, Form, Radio Group, allows you to build a group of radio buttons using a handy and simple-to-follow interface, but it won't have Spry validation associated with it. To use the Radio Group so that it does have validation associated with it, we must use Spry Validation Radio Group instead. To use this control, follow these steps:

1. Place your cursor in the second cell of the fifth row (next to the Budget text label).

2. Choose Insert, Spry, Spry Validation Radio Group. The Spry Validation Radio Group appears and at first glance looks and functions exactly the same as the normal Radio Group dialog box we used in Chapter 7. Using the skills that you learned in that chapter, enter the following Labels/Values: **<$1,000, $1,000-$10,000, and >$10,000**. Click OK to insert the Radio Group into the table.

3. Select the visual aid for the Spry Validation Radio Group. You'll notice that there's not much to customize. The Property inspector really allows you to set only whether a value is required, which value should appear as empty, and which value should be interpreted as invalid. For our purposes, you don't need to make any changes.

Save your work. Dreamweaver notifies you that it needs to place `SpryValidationRadio.css` and `SpryValidationRadio.js` within the SpryAssets folder. Again, these files are required for controlling the look and functionality of the textarea. Click OK. Preview your page in the browser by pressing F12 (Option-F12). Click the Submit button. Dreamweaver displays all the error messages, including the `Please make a selection.` error message next to the radio group.

Spry Validation Password and Confirm

Two of the newest additions to the Spry Validation set of controls are Spry Validation Password and Spry Validation Confirm. In a nutshell, Spry Validation Password allows you to insert a text field with the Password action set. As you know by now, this guarantees that when a user enters text into the text field, asterisks (or dots, depending on the browser) will appear. What Spry Validation Password provides that the normal text field does not is the capability to require input in the control, specify a minimum and maximum amount of characters that the text field will accept, and the minimum and maximum amount of text-based characters, numbers, uppercase, and special characters that the text field will accept to create a "strong" password.

You can add Spry Validation Confirm to the page, associate the Confirm text field with a normal Spry Validation Password text field (choosing it from the Validate Against menu) and you instantly get a text field that requires the same input as the previous text field, guaranteeing that the two values must match before the data is submitted for processing.

Extending Layout Options

It's no secret that the Web 2.0 trend is heavily geared toward CSS. Not only is the formatting of sites controlled by CSS, but also to a large extent, so is the structure. To compete with this latest CSS-based structuring trend, Adobe has introduced a collection of page structuring/layout widgets in the form of the Spry Menu Bar, Spry Tabbed Panels, Spry Accordion, Spry Collapsible Panels, and Spry Tooltip widgets, which improve the visual aspects and general aesthetics of your website. To give you an idea as to how these layout widgets can be used, let's add the Spry Tabbed Panels widget now:

1. Create a new page by choosing File, New. Choose the HTML option from the Blank Page category, choose the <none> option from the Layout list, and click Create. A new document window instance appears. Save the page as `sprywidgets.html`.

2. Immediately place your cursor on the page where you want the Spry Tabbed Panels widget to appear and choose Insert, Spry, Spry Tabbed Panels. The Spry Tabbed Panels widget is inserted onto the page, similar to Figure 24.13.

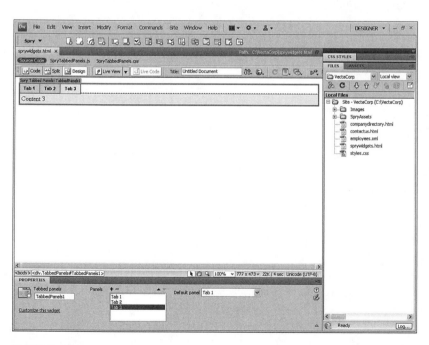

FIGURE 24.13   The Spry Tabbed Panels widget is inserted onto the page.

3. Select the blue visual aid that surrounds the Spry Tabbed Panels widget. The Property inspector changes to accommodate property modifications for the widget.

4. As you can see from Figure 24.13, the Property inspector enables you to do three things. First, you can uniquely identify your Spry Tabbed Panels widget by manipulating its ID. Second, you can add new tabs/panels via the Panels list. Finally, you can choose which panel will display by default by selecting the panel name from the Default panel menu. For example, click the Add (+) panel button to add a new panel to the widget. As you can see, the new tab is added as Tab 3.

Save your work. Immediately, Dreamweaver notifies you that it needs to place `SpryTabbedPanels.css` and `SpryTabbedPanels.js` within the SpryAssets folder. Again, these files are required for controlling the look and functionality of the Spry Tabbed Panels widget. Click OK. Preview your page in the browser by pressing F12 (Option-F12). You'll notice that three tabs appear, each containing its own panel of content. Select each tab to navigate through the panels.

Although the Property inspector allows you to add, remove, reposition, and set the default panel that should appear, customization for the panel can be handled by modifying the tabs/panels within the Document window. For instance, if you'd like to change the tab name, highlight the text within the tab and begin typing. Furthermore, if you'd like to modify the content within the panel, highlight the default placeholder text and begin typing. Customizing the CSS is a bit trickier, but still possible. As Figure 24.14 shows, selecting the Spry Tabbed Panels widget displays a list of all of the classes that are used by the widget within the CSS Styles panel.

FIGURE 24.14 All the CSS for the Spry Tabbed Panels widget (and all other widgets) are displayed within the CSS Styles panel.

To modify a particular class, either select the class and modify the properties from within the Properties pane or double-click the class to open the CSS Style Definition dialog box for easier and more visual customizations.

Working with the other three widgets is similar to, if not easier than, working with the Spry Tabbed Panels widget. To work with the Spry Accordion, Spry Menu Bar, Spry Collapsible Panel, or the Spry Tooltip widgets, insert them as you did the Spry Tabbed Panels widget. Customizing the CSS and modifying the properties for the panel can be done via the CSS Styles panel or the Property inspector, respectively. Figure 24.15 shows all five widgets (inserted with minimal customizations) on a web page.

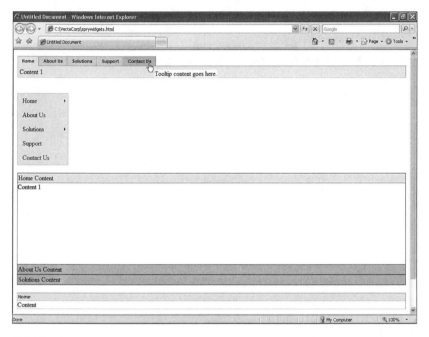

FIGURE 24.15   The Spry Tabbed Panels, Spry Menu Bar, Spry Accordion, Spry Collapsible Panel, and Spry Tooltip widgets together on one page.

Working with RSS Feeds

Quite possibly one of the hottest trends, aside from web services, is that of RSS. Originally developed by Netscape, *Really Simple Syndication (RSS)* is an XML format for syndicating web content. A website that wants to allow other sites to publish some of its content creates an RSS document and registers the document with an RSS publisher. A user that can read RSS-distributed content can then use the content on a different site. Syndicated content includes such data as news feeds, events listings, news stories, headlines, project updates, excerpts from discussion forums, and even corporate information. Although numerous websites are devoted to the topic of helping you publish and distribute RSS feeds, you need look no further than Dreamweaver. With Dreamweaver's built-in

XML/XSL transformation integration, using RSS feeds in your website is a snap. To work with RSS feeds in Dreamweaver using a Spry Dataset, follow these steps:

1. Locate an RSS feed. One of my favorite websites (and a website that I know provides an RSS feed) is www.slickdeals.net. Browse to that website now.

2. In the left corner, below the navigation menu, you'll see a small orange button titled RSS. Click it. You'll be redirected to a second page. Click the link titled "View Feed XML." You're immediately presented with the RSS feed (and the path to the feed in the address bar) in the browser window, similar to Figure 24.16.

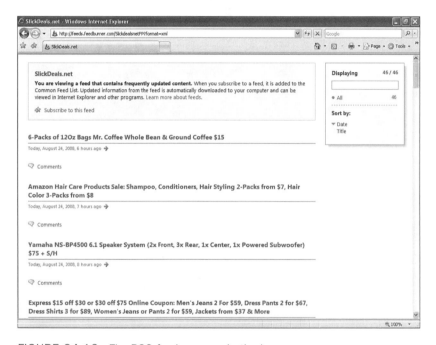

FIGURE 24.16   The RSS feed appears in the browser.

3. Note the path to the feed is feeds.feedburner.com/SlickdealsnetFP?format=xml. Select it and choose Edit, Copy. You can now close the browser.

4. Shift your attention back to Dreamweaver. Create a new page by choosing File, New. Choose the HTML option from the Blank Page category, choose the <none> option from the Layout list, and click Create. A new document window instance appears. Save the page as `rssfeed.html`.

5. Select the XML option from the Select Data Type menu. Enter **dsSlickDeals** into the Data Set Name text box. Finally, paste the URL into the Specify Data File text box. Immediately the Row Element list is populated with the nodes from the Slick Deals XML feed.

6. Select the item node. The Specify Data Source dialog box will resemble Figure 24.17.

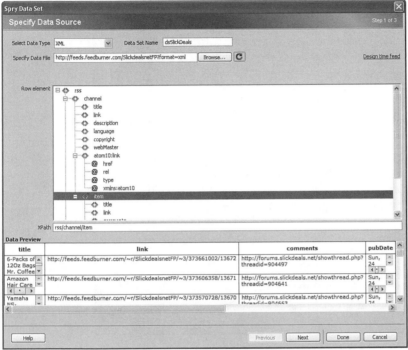

FIGURE 24.17   The Row Element list displays all the nodes from the Slick Deals XML feed.

7. Click Next twice until you arrive at the Choose Insert Options dialog box. This time around, choose the Insert Stacked Containers option and click the Set Up button. The Insert Stacked Containers dialog box appears.

8. For our RSS Reader, we need only the title and link nodes. Select all the nodes except for these two and choose the Remove (-) icon until only the Title and Link nodes remain. Click OK to close the dialog box.

9. Click Done to close the Spry Data Set dialog box. Immediately a set of grayed-out <div>s appears with our XML bindings squarely placed within them.

Immediately Dreamweaver asks you to save SpryStackedContainers.css into the SpryAssets folder. Click OK. Press F12 (Option-F12) to preview your new RSS feed reader in the browser. Immediately Slick Deals' feeds are presented to you within the browser, similar to Figure 24.18.

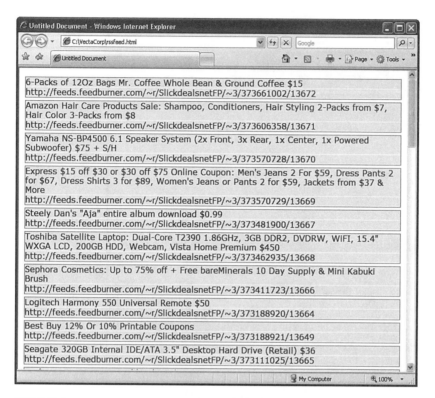

FIGURE 24.18   Slick Deals news feeds are shown in the browser.

Your design doesn't have to stop here. As you'll notice, the hyperlinks aren't automatically associated with their titles, but instead appear as a separate row underneath the title. With some simple configurations, we could just as easily link the titles so that the user can simply click the title to automatically redirect the user to the appropriate page on the Slick Deals site. To do this, follow these steps:

1. Select the {link} binding and remove it from its `<div>`.

2. Now select the {title} binding, switch to the HTML Property inspector, and choose the folder icon located just to the right of the Link text box to create a link for our title. The Select File dialog box appears.

3. Click the Data Sources radio button and then choose the link node from the Field menu, also shown in Figure 24.19.

4. Click OK. Immediately, the binding on the web page becomes a link.

Again, save your work and preview the page in the browser by pressing F12 (Option-F12). As you can see from Figure 24.20, this time each item is displayed with a link automatically associated with the title. If you click on the title, you are automatically redirected to the appropriate page on the Slick Deals website.

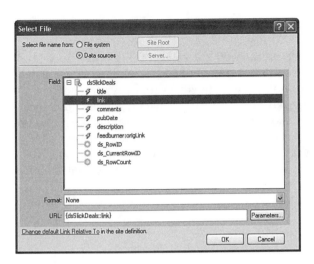

FIGURE 24.19   Select the link node from the Field menu.

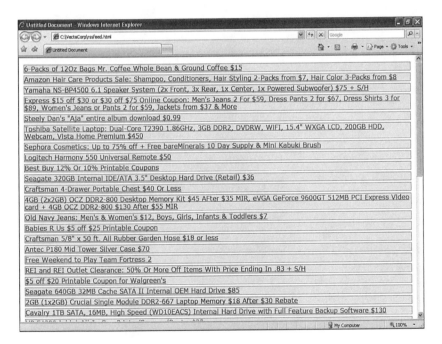

FIGURE 24.20   All SlickDeals feeds are displayed on the page.

Summary

As you have seen, Adobe has made strides in the Web 2.0 realm with its newest Spry framework for Ajax. Although Dreamweaver's integration of Spry is certainly in its infancy, the technology shows definite promise and continues to grow with each release of Dreamweaver. With the capability to quickly and effortlessly generate Datasets and bind the data contained within those Datasets to regions within the page, Spry makes working with Ajax exciting and fun. Combine this with the capability to work with tables and numerous visual enhancements, such as form validation, accordions, tabbed layouts, menu bars, and more, and you can see why the development community is excited about this newest platform.

PART VI

Appendixes (Online)

IN THIS PART

How can we make this index more useful? Email us at indexes@samspublishing.com

assigning

paths to links, 92

targets to links, 93

assistive technologies, Web:805

associating labels with form element, 287-288

Attach External Style Sheet dialog box, 223

Attach Style Sheet dialog box, 54

attaching

behaviors to objects, 293

CSS file, 54, 223-225

attributes

accessibility

accesskey, Web:813

alt, Web:818

label, Web:813

longdesc, Web:813

scope, Web:814

summary, Web:814

tabindex, Web:813

title, Web:813

editable attributes, 421, 432-433

frames

adjusting, Web:901

border, Web:905

margin, Web:905

name, Web:903-Web:904

page, Web:902-Web:903

scroll, Web:904

framesets

adjusting, Web:906

border, Web:907

size, Web:907-Web:908

audio

background music, 488-489

converting into RealAudio format, 468

embedding audio files, 486-488

linking audio files, 486

audio formats

AIFF, 485

Dolby AAC, 485

Flash, 485

MP3, 485

QuickTime Movie, 485

RealAudio, 485

WAV, 485

Windows Media, 485

authentication

access levels, setting, 745-746

custom error messages, creating, 737, 739

duplicate usernames, preventing, 743-744

logging out, 741-742

login pages, 730-731

New User Registration page, 742-743

session variables, 734

unauthenticated users, identifying, 739-741

user access, restricting, 734, 736-737

Autostretch tables, 177

AVG( ) function, 634

AVI video format, 472

B

b tag, Web:857

background color

AP Elements, 242

cells (table), 171-174

tables, setting, 173

background image

AP Elements, 241

applying, 59, 61

background music, 488-489

behaviorFunction( ) function, Web:831

behaviors

actions, 294

adding, 294

applyBehavior( ) function, Web:832

attaching to objects, 293

behaviorFunction( ) function, Web:831

built-in server behaviors, Web:844

Call JavaScript, 297-298

canAcceptBehavior( ) function, Web:837-Web:838

Change Property, 298-299

Check New Username, 743-744

Check Plugin, 300-301

C

framesets

    alternative methods for creating, Web:899-Web:901

    attributes, adjusting, Web:906

    border properties, Web:907

    creating, Web:899-Web:901

    defined, Web:894

    frames, removing, Web:901

    prebuilt, 54, Web:898-Web:899

    saving, Web:911, Web:913

    size properties, Web:907-Web:908

freezing JavaScript, 17

FTP client, 107

full page refreshes, 768

functions

    ABS( ), 635

    arithmetic functions, 635

    AVG( ), 634

    CEIL( ), 635

    CHR( ), 636

    CONCAT( ), 636

    COS( ), 635

    COSH( ), 635

    COUNT( ), 631, 633

    date and time, 631-632

    DATE( ), 632

    DATEADD( ), 632

    EXP( ), 635

    FLOOR( ), 635

    INITCAP( ), 636

    LENGTH( ), 636

    LN( ), 635

    LOG( ), 635

    LOWER( ), 636

    LPAD( ), 636

    LTRIM( ), 636

    MAX( ), 634-635

    MIN( ), 634-635

    MOD( ), 635

    parameters, 632

    POWER( ), 635

    REPLACE( ), 636

    RPAD( ), 636

    RTRIM( ), 636

    SIGN( ), 635

    SIN( ), 635

    SINH( ), 635

    SORT( ), 635

    string functions, 636

    SUBSTR( ), 636

    SUM( ), 633

    TAN( ), 635

    TANH( ), 635

    UPPER( ), 636

G

general preferences, Web:855-Web:857

GET method, 265-266

getting files, 107, 132

GIFs, 82

globalizing search functionality, 726-727

Go To ASP data object, 702

Go to URL behavior, 311

Google Maps, 763

> (greater-than) operator, 629

>= (greater-than-or-equal-to) operator, 629

GROUP BY clause, 623-624

Grow/Shrink behavior, 306-307

guard pages, 381

H

H space, 87

<h1> to <h6> tags, Web:857

header.gif image, adding to header frame, Web:909, Web:911

headers for tables, 151

headings, applying to text, 68

height of images, 86

Helix Proxy, 469

Helix Server, 469

Help, 50, 54

Hidden Field form object, 282-283

hidden panels, 45

I

nesting
 AP Elements, 245-246
 tables, 151, 175-176
 templates, 440-441
Netscape, Web:893
New CSS Rule dialog box, 201
New Document dialog box, 52-54
new features, 8-9, 12-13
New Pages screen (Site Administration dialog), 382
New User Registration page (Web Store application) 686-689, 693-694, 742-743
NFC (Normalization Form Canonical Composition, 60
NFD (Normalization Form Canonical Decomposition), 60
NFKD (Normalization Form Compatibility Decomposition), 60
<noframes*> tag, Web:917
non-breaking space
 allowing multiple consecutive spaces, Web:857
 inserting, 78
normalization
 defined, 590-591
 Domain/Key Normal Form, 591
 First Normal Form, 591
 Second Normal Form, 591
 Third Normal Form, 591
NOT operator, 630

O

objects
 application objects, 701
 Configuration folder, Web:826
 defined, Web:825
 elements of, Web:826-Web:827
 HTML file, Web:826
 image file, Web:826
 inserting, Web:856
 JavaScript file, Web:826
 location of, Web:826

 Objects folder, Web:826
 objectTag( ) function, Web:827
 page titles, Web:827
 predeveloped objects, Web:826
 structure of, Web:826
 sup, Web:827, Web:829
 user interface, Web:827
Objects folder, Web:826
objectTag( ) function, Web:827
ODBC Data Source Administrator, 655
ODBC drivers, 538, 648-649
Office, 535
offscreen rendering, Web:858
onBlur behavior, 296
onClick behavior, 296
onDblClick behavior, 296
one-to-many relationship, 588
one-to-one relationship, 588
onFocus behavior, 296
onLoad behavior, 297
onMouseDown behavior, 296
onMouseOut behavior, 296
onMouseOver behavior, 296
onMouseUp behavior, 296
onUnLoad behavior, 297
Open Browser Window behavior, 315-317
Open Database Connectivity (ODBC), 538
opening
 Assets panel, 394
 Bridge, 25
 Code Navigator, 226
 documents, 25, 52
 documents in tabs, Web:855
 Dreamweaver, 10
 files, 12
Operating system Widget Library (OWL), 9
operators
 & (ampersand), 628
 AND, 630
 defined, 629
 / (divide), 629
 > (greater-than), 629
 >= (greater-than-or-equal-to), 629

How can we make this index more useful? Email us at indexes@samspublishing.com

How can we make this index more useful? Email us at indexes@samspublishing.com

Q

R

recordsets

    creating, 665-670, 672-673, 689

    defined, 618, 701

    views, 672-673

redefining HTML tags as CSS styles, 217

redirection pages, 693-694

redo, 412

references and link validation, 129-130

referential integrity, 609

refreshing

    Assets panel, 395, 397-398

    Components panel, 750

regions

    colors, 426

    combining editable and optional, 438

    editable attributes, 421, 432-433

    editable regions

        adding, 425-427

        combining with optional, 438

        content, 428-430

        defined, 421

    mapping, 444-446

    optional regions

        combining with editable, 438

        defined, 421

        properties, 439-440

    Repeat Region behavior, 679, 681

    repeating regions

        adding, 433-438

        content, 435-436

        defined, 421

    showing specific regions, 677, 679

regions (Spry)

    binding data to, 777-778

    creating, 776-777

    defining, 775

    repeating, 778-780

registration for users, 683-684, 686-687

Related Files Bar, 8, 12-13

relational databases

    history of, 578

    managing, 587-588

    many-to-many relationship, 588

    one-to-many relationship, 588

    one-to-one relationship, 588

    queries, 644, 646

    server-side development, 531

Remote Development Services (RDS), 564

Remote Info, 118-120

Remove Component option (Components panel), 750

removing

    behaviors, 294

    frames from within framesets, Web:901

    template markup, 446-447

renaming

    library items, 456-457

    links, 140

rendering offscreen, Web:858

reopening documents on startup, Web:856

Repeat Region behavior, 679, 681

repeating regions

    adding, 433-438

    content, 435-436

    defined, 421

    dynamic tables, 702

    search results page, 724-725

repeating Spry regions, 778-780

REPLACE( ) function, 636

replacing image placeholders, 500-501

replaying commands, 413

reports

    accessibility, Web:814-Web:816

    workflow

        Checked Out By reports, 347-348

        Design Notes reports, 348-350

        generating, 347

        Recently Modified reports, 350-351

        workflow statistics, 107

Reports command (Site menu), 142

repositioning behaviors, 295

resize handles (AP Elements), 237

resizer behavior, Web:832-Web:836

resizing

    AP Elements, 237

    cells, 165-167

S

How can we make this index more useful? Email us at indexes@samspublishing.com

How can we make this index more useful? Email us at indexes@samspublishing.com

X–Z

FREE Online Edition

Your purchase of **Adobe Dreamweaver CS4 Unleashed** includes access to a free online edition for 45 days through the Safari Books Online subscription service. Nearly every Sams book is available online through Safari Books Online, along with more than 5,000 other technical books and videos from publishers such as Addison-Wesley Professional, Cisco Press, Exam Cram, IBM Press, O'Reilly, Prentice Hall, and Que.

SAFARI BOOKS ONLINE allows you to search for a specific answer, cut and paste code, download chapters, and stay current with emerging technologies.

Activate your FREE Online Edition at www.informit.com/safarifree

> **STEP 1:** Enter the coupon code: FFDUHXA.

> **STEP 2:** New Safari users, complete the brief registration form.
> Safari subscribers, just log in.

If you have difficulty registering on Safari or accessing the online edition, please e-mail customer-service@safaribooksonline.com